R Blakemore

Coventry

October 1985

PERSONNEL MANAGEMENT

£12.95

1/87

698220

PERSONNEL MANAGEMENT
Second Edition

Derek Torrington
J.P., M.Phil., C.I.P.M., F.R.S.A.
(University of Manchester Institute of Science and Technology)

John Chapman
B.Sc., A.M.C.S.T., C. Eng., M.I.Mech. E., F.R.S.H.
(University of Aston Management Centre)

Series Editor

Cary L. Cooper
(Professor of Management Educational Methods,
University of Manchester Institute of Science and Technology)

Prentice/Hall  International

Englewood Cliffs, New Jersey · London · New Delhi
Rio de Janeiro · Singapore · Sydney · Tokyo · Toronto · Wellington

This book is dedicated to

Barbara	Jenny
Mark	Geoff
Helen	Andy
Ian	
Sally	

British Library Cataloguing in Publication Data

Torrington, Derek Peter

Personnel management.—2nd ed.
1 Personnel management
I. Title II. Chapman, John B *1939—*
658.3 HF5549

ISBN 0-13-658328-8

ISBN 0-13-658328 8

Prentice-Hall International, Inc., *London*
Prentice-Hall of Australia Pty. Ltd., *Sydney*
Prentice-Hall of Canada, Ltd., *Toronto*
Prentice-Hall of India Private Limited, *New Delhi*
Prentice-Hall of Japan, Inc., *Tokyo*
Prentice-Hall of Southeast Asia Pte., Ltd., *Singapore*
Prentice-Hall, Inc., *Englewood Cliffs, New Jersey*
Prentice-Hall do Brasil, Ltdx., *Rio de Janeiro*
Whitehall Books Limited, *Wellington, New Zealand*

85 86 87 5 4 3

Typesetting by MHL Typesetting Ltd, Coventry
Printed and bound in Great Britain by
A. Wheaton & Co. Ltd, Exeter

Contents

Preface
TO THE SECOND EDITION

The four years since the first edition of this book have seen some changes in legislation, some new management ideas and a marked decline in the profession of personnel management. Any sustained economic recession finds the personnel specialist vulnerable as the number of people to be employed, trained, appraised and paid dwindles. Unemployment has an even more drastic effect on trade unions, so the industrial relations aspects of personnel work have also moved into a lower gear.

Although we have seen a change of emphasis, with fewer personnel specialists and very few openings for personnel students, we find very little change in the nature of personnel work, which now seems to be reasonably well defined and understood. We have not found any need to change our model of the employment relationship and have not removed or added any chapter. For the first edition we prepared material on the operation of labour markets, pension arrangements and instruction, but eventually discarded them through pressure on space. They remain important subjects which could well have been included in this volume, but there is again no space for them.

We have had many comments on the text which confirm the advice of our publisher to change as little as possible for this edition. We have therefore revised all the legal content up to the end of 1982, up-dated the material in other chapters and undertaken some re-drafting where readers have suggested a change of presentation.

We would again welcome any comments that anyone would be kind enough to send to us.

November 1982

Derek Torrington
John Chapman

Preface
TO THE FIRST EDITION

The work of personnel specialists has become so diverse that a single author finds it difficult to encompass the whole within the scope of his own experience and scholarship. Academic research in the field of personnel management is now so varied and multi-disciplinary that few people can adequately comprehend the significance and the limitations of the conclusions produced by researchers working within a particular discipline. How then can an intergrated work on personnel management be produced?

A possible solution to this problem is to use a collection of specialists, each dealing with a matter on which he claims expertise. The drawback of this approach is that there is no true cohesion of the material.

The solution used in this book is to deploy the understanding and insights of two people, who have both dissimilarity of background and similarity of view. One approaches management problems from an industrial relations perspective; the other from the organisational behaviour point of view. One is both an organisational psychologist and a professional engineer; the other is a professional personnel manager.

We have tried to produce a framework to understand the work of personnel specialists and to integrate their manifold activities in a coherent whole. Within that framework we seek to explain the activities as well as suggesting how they may be carried out.

The book should provide a satisfactory basis for a full course in personnel management or manpower administration, whether the course be undergraduate, post-graduate or professional, as the material is presented in a way that tutors could handle in a variety of ways, according to the educational needs of the students. It could be used as a straightforward account of personnel work. Alternatively the arguments in different chapters could be used as a basis for seminar discussion. A third possibility would be for a student to use a particular chapter as a summary of an area before taking the chapter references as the basis for personal research and development.

For practising managers our aim is to satisfy two needs. We hope, first, that they may be able to freshen up their view of their own work by the framework, commentary and analysis we offer; and, second, that they may use the book as a handy reference volume in the office.

Overseas readers should find the book most useful as an overview of personnel management in the British situation, providing a basis of comparison with their own context.

The discussion of British legal provisions summarises the position at the time of writing.

There are many who have contributed to the preparation of this book and whose assistance we acknowledge. Cary Cooper, and Henry Hirschberg at Prentice-Hall International, got the project going in the first place; Giles Wright and Ron Decent have been instrumental in shaping the book after the initial stage. Ideas and material have come from Will Armour of North Thames Regional Health Authority, Pat Carpenter at Ferranti, Les Cookson and Phil Wilson of Manchester Polytechnic, John Davies of Seddon Atkinson, Christina Deegan of H.R. Howard, John Ithell of the BBC, Martin Price of Mather & Platt, Bill Tyson of CEGB, Mike Whitlock of Sketchley, Betty Wright of United Biscuits and Susan Zentar of Makro.

We are grateful for the permissions we have received to reproduce Figure 17.2 from Macmillan Publishing Co., Figure 17.3 from Harvard Business Review, and Figure 17.8 from the University of Pittsburgh Press.

The authors would appreciate any comments from readers.

April 1979   *Derek Torrington* (University of Manchester
                                                 Institute of Science and Technology)
                                                 John Chapman (University of Aston
                                                 Management Centre)

Section A
THE SETTING OF THE CONTRACTS

1

The Personnel Contract

The objective of this book is to interpret the area of work known as personnel management. To do this we will advance a *philosophy* as well as a *framework* for analysis. Prescriptions for action will be derived from these.

The word 'philosophy' is an unusual one to find in management literature, as it smacks of the abstract and the theoretical, but we see the need for a philosophy as twofold. First, it is axiomatic that actions flow from beliefs. The way we see the world determines the actions we take in our everyday lives, and personnel specialists will act in ways consistent with their explanation of their mission and the way they understand their role. Secondly, we advance a philosophy because personnel work is an area where there has traditionally been uncertainty about role. Legge and Exley[1] provide one of the many analyses of how personnel management has a history of ambiguity. If 'the role represents an entire institutional nexus of conduct'[2] it is important to articulate a philosophy.

A framework for analysis is provided as a means of relating to each other the various elements of personnel work and enabling a degree of integration between them. One of the milestones in the development of personnel management is the work by Northcott, in which he describes his subject as:

> . . . a body of related duties which fit in so well with each other that they can suitably and effectively be made the responsibility of one executive and can be thought of structurally as a department of the business.[3]

Northcott was writing in the aftermath of World War II, before the growth in behavioural science, before the extension of employment legislation and before the development of unionisation. Such coherence as he was able to see has been lessened by a proliferation of theoretical explanations of various phenomena. Psychologists have informed aspects of personnel work for fifty years, but sociological analysis is more recent and usually offers a different explanation. Also we have acquired the new academic disciplines of industrial relations and organisational behaviour. Employment legislation has extended to provide employees with rights that were previously only available as dispensations from a benevolent management. Trade union growth and 'establishment' has altered the power structure within the organisation to an extent that Northcott did not envisage.

It has therefore become difficult for the personnel practitioner to integrate the

3

apparently disparate activities that conventionally make up the specialist function, leading sometimes to a version of the so-called 'trash-can hypothesis', whereby personnel management is viewed as a repository for odds and ends of managerial work that do not find a logical place elsewhere.

This is understandably not the view of those who class themselves as personnel specialists. The Institute of Personnel Management offer the following definition:

> Personnel management is that part of management concerned with people at work and their relationships within an enterprise. Its aim is to bring together and develop into an effective organisation the men and women who make up an enterprise and, having regard for the well-being of the individual and of working groups, to enable them to make their best contribution to its success.[4]

A PHILOSOPHY FOR PERSONNEL MANAGEMENT

Our philosophy is based on the assertion that personnel work has three elements:

   (i) Determining the expectations that employees have of their organisations, and the expectations organisations have of their employees.
  (ii) Setting up a series of contracts or agreements between organisation and employee(s) that describe the mutual expectations.
 (iii) Servicing the contracts to ensure that the expectations are fulfilled.

Justification for this position we derive from several sources. In her work on job satisfaction, for instance, Enid Mumford has developed a particular notion of the employment contract:

> A more realistic approach to job satisfaction may be to look at the individual's needs in work and the extent to which these are being met but also to examine the pressures and constraints, internal and external to the firm, which influence the demands it makes of its employees and hinder its ability to provide maximum job satisfaction. The company, as well as the employee, has needs and these needs must be met if it is to survive and flourish. This approach leads us to consider job satisfaction in two ways. First, in terms of the fit between what an organisation requires of its employees and what the employees are seeking of the firm, and second, in terms of the fit between what the employee is seeking from the firm and what he is receiving.[5]

One element of this view is that the attachments of man the worker to his employment are varied and not as simple as has long been believed. At the end of a long process of investigation into empirical studies that had been conducted in various countries over many years, Dubin and his colleagues expressed the view:

> We no longer believe that there is an economic man, or a psychological man, or a sociological man who does the work of the world and who is to be reached through his pocketbook or his psyche, or his social relations, in order to motivate his work effort. We think the working man is a whole man — he is simultaneously an economic, psychological and sociological person. It is only when the whole man is taken seriously that we can perceive that there are multiple attachments to work.[6]

Another feature that is important is that man will not be coerced.

The employee, unlike the slave, can leave and as the market becomes more highly developed, his opportunity for expressing choice between employers may increase. His opportunity for taking protective action with his fellows also increases. As his tasks become more specialised, or more skilled, or, simply, more interdependent, so the employer's dependence upon his co-operation appears to increase.[7]

McCarthy and Ellis propound an approach to industrial relations which they call 'management by agreement'. They argue that the managements of organisations are subject to increasing challenges both from below and outside the organisation itself and that these challenges can only be turned from destructive to constructive influences if the running of the business is seen as a process of reaching agreement between the management and the employees in all areas of decision-making. Managers do not have a monopoly of wisdom, despite their professional expertise, and negotiated agreement will produce a greater degree of commitment to implementation of decisions:

> First, management by agreement provides the only means of responding to the complex nature of pressures that come from below. Second, it offers the best prospect of gaining agreement for the introduction and application of necessary change within the enterprise. Third, it provides a way of more effectively utilising the potentialities of the work-force itself. Fourth, it is only through the development of new forms of collective bargaining based on the notion of management by agreement that there is any hope of bringing home to workers the reality of the pressures that face the enterprise from outside.[8]

This proposition came before the vogue for participation and industrial democracy, which is another pointer to the logic of the contract approach.

Another reason for putting forward the philosophy we do is the changing nature of the labour force. In our chapter 'The Contract for Work and the Recruitment Overture' (Chapter 5) we show the change from a predominantly manual work force to a predominantly white-collar one. White-collar workers have more varied expectations of the employing organisation than do manual workers.

Batstone and his colleagues[9] demonstrate the differing types of attitude as well as the increasing interest of manual workers in such features of work as effort, management behaviour, fairness and sociability.

In our third chapter we review the knowledge area of industrial relations, and many academics in the industrial relations field have used conflict as a focal point for their analysis. Although this might seem at variance with our thesis, it is obvious that some form of agreement or other form of *modus vivendi* has to be found to accommodate the conflict even if its causes are such that the conflict itself cannot be resolved.

> ... where activities within an organisation require the co-operation of individuals and groups with divergent attitudes and interests, there is a natural tendency for understandings, agreements and rules to emerge from processes of formal and informal negotiation.[10]

A further contribution to our thinking is the work of Schein,[11] the well-known American organisational psychologist, who has coined the term 'the psychological contract'. This is now widely used to cover the non-formal obligations and expectations of both parties to an employment contract. Although our development is wider-ranging, our thinking has been much influenced by his work.

SOME POTENTIAL CRITICISMS OF OUR APPROACH

Our approach is susceptible to criticism, mainly from those identified with views towards the extremes of the radical—conservative spectrum of political opinion. We can mention some of the disagreements.

1. Unilateral decisions

How about the many decisions that are taken by personnel managers that are unilateral and not susceptible to negotiation or participation, so that the agreement-broking approach is irrelevant? Examples from collective bargaining may support the idea, but personnel work is also concerned with activities like selection and dismissal, where decisions are made by members of the managerial elite about people: not with them.

Our argument is that there is a clear trend away from unilateral decision-making in *all* aspects of the employment of people; not simply in collective bargaining. Managers, however, are frequently reluctant to acknowledge the developing reality as they see areas of management prerogative slipping away, and this is why we regard as so important the setting up of a viable and acceptable philosophy of personnel management that does not depend on an assumption of inalienable prerogative.

In selection the orthodox view has been of a management representative scrutinising the submissions of those wishing to join the organisation before allowing in those who were found worthy and turning away those who were found wanting. The underlying assumption is of a queue of appropriate applicants all more anxious to join than the organisation is to admit. This has been supported by some academic analysis and prescription. Personnel specialists have received a plethora of advice on how to assess candidates, how to interact with them to distinguish between truth and falsehood, how to test them psychologically and so on. When the queue has dwindled the orthodox reaction has been to conjure it up again by advertising blandishment. Fordham[12] charts the growth of display advertising as employers have competed with each other. At times of relatively full employment the shortcomings of this approach are obvious, but even when there is high unemployment and more people in the labour market than there are jobs for them to do, the employer still needs to satisfy the employee expectations and make sure that he offers work and conditions that are attractive to those with the specialised skills and interests he needs. From a management point of view high unemployment does not only mean large numbers of people seeking jobs, it can also mean large numbers of people unable to leave the jobs they are in. Dissatisfied employees are a burden on the employing organisation which is unable to offer them the scope they want.

We suggest that the traditional management question about candidates, 'Will this candidate suit me?' or ('. . . suit the job?'), is insufficient and needs to be supplemented by the question 'Will this job suit the applicant?' with all the other questions that flow from it about why certain jobs are hard to fill, what can be done to alter them so as to make them easier to fill, what sort of training applicants will seek, how much money and so forth.

At the other end of the employment history, it is difficult to argue that dismissals are necessarily or ideally agreements, but there is considerable scope for agreement in matters surrounding dismissal. What are the rules of the workplace, breach of which can cause dismissal? Some of these may be the subject of management decree, but most will be overtly negotiated and agreed or tacitly agreed by being accepted. One form of dismissal is redundancy, where there is not only a need for agreement on the procedures to be followed about choosing the redundant but also a statutory obligation to consult before implementation. If one broadens the issue of dismissal to include discipline generally we find clear indications of trends away from unilateralism:

> insofar as it is possible to discern a management philosophy towards discipline, there has been a process of transition from the old coercive/authoritarian approach to a more corrective/democratic approach.[13]

2. Custom and practice

What account do we take of a very important type of employment rule: that stemming from custom and practice? We obviously accept the importance of custom and practice as a determinant of what happens in the place of work, and we also accept that this type of rule is not negotiated, although we would agree with Kingsley Laffer that it is part of an implicit bargain, reached long ago. However, we are concerned here with propounding a philosophy for personnel management, which is an *activity* of certain people, whereas custom and practice is an aspect of the situation in which the activity is carried out.

3. Pluralism and compromise

A further potential criticism is from those who are simply not satisfied with the degree of compromise that this approach acknowledges. On one side are those who see this as an acceptance of the pluralism that was enunciated by Flanders,[14] Clegg[15] and the early writing of Fox.[16]

Some now question pluralism and believe that the problems of industrial relations lie not in negotiated order and formalising the informal but by bringing about a fundamental shift of power and privilege in society.[17,18] This type of analysis may be right or wrong, but it presents an insuperable problem for the type of analysis we are presenting here, in that it removes the debate from the place of work and offers no prescription for employment relationships. Personnel management is not necessarily concerned in *preserving* the prevailing structure of employment and social order, but it is unquestionably concerned in *administering* employment relationships within that structure.

On the other hand there are those like George Ward[19] in the United Kingdom and many analysts in the United States who are concerned with unitary control. The prevalence of this view in the American literature is important to an appreciation of our argument because it is in the literature of personnel management. Jucius,[20] Megginson,[21] and Glueck[22] all describe personnel work in unitary terms, seeing management as leadership, direction and control. Our difference with them may be merely a difference of emphasis, but nevertheless an important difference. We see the United States' attitude to work and the employing organisation as being different from that found in the United Kingdom, with managerial authority more readily accepted and with a different tradition of collective bargaining.

4. Reification

Can we sensibly talk of a contract between an individual and an *organisation*, which is not a thinking creature, but a thing? Are we attributing human characteristics, like needs, to something which is inanimate? Should we not speak of the management of the organisation or the dominant coalition within it, rather than simply — the organisation? Although it is difficult to refute the logic in that argument, we speak of the employing organisation because that is the most common view of those at work: they do not see themselves as employed by individuals, but by an organisation, and they will honour a sense of obligation to the organisation more readily than to an individual within it. Our accounts in the rest of the book will frequently use the terms 'management' or 'manager' virtually synonymously with 'organisation' because we are concerned principally with personnel as an *activity* of managers, but they are representing organisational 'interests', making demands on — and having need of — employees.

A FRAMEWORK FOR ANALYSIS

The outline philosophy advanced in the last few pages will be worked out further in later chapters of the book. We now move to propound a framework for analysis of personnel management. How can the philosophy be used as a basis for a conceptual model that will satisfactorily integrate and relate to each other the various elements that go to make up personnel management activity?

The framework set out in Figure 1.1 assumes three categories of personnel work in the context of four areas of knowledge. The letters A—F refer to the six sections of this book:

A.   The Setting of the Contracts (areas of knowledge)
B & D. The Contract for Work and the Contract for Individual Control (first category of personnel work)
C & E. The Contract for Collective Consent and the Contract for Payment (second category of personnel work)
F.   The Small Print of the Contracts (third category of personnel work)

The first category or grouping is of those activities which relate principally to the individual member of the organisation, as the approach to them is concerned with the employment of a single person and the reaction of that individual to organisational initiatives. Secondly we have grouped together those activities where the emphasis is more collective than individual, and thirdly we have that category of personnel work that consists of administrative methods and techniques that can be applied in a number of different areas.

This is seen as the extent of personnel work as well as the logical grouping of activities. This represents some departure from convention as it does not follow the most common features of professional specialisation — industrial relations, training and development, and general personnel work.

SECTION A. THE SETTING OF THE CONTRACTS

People are employed in organisations, but the people and the organisations are part of a wider society, and personnel work has to be set in a context of general understanding of matters having a bearing on the work, before the work itself can be understood and performed. The areas of knowledge in which understanding is necessary are many. Economics, politics, sociology, psychology, social history,

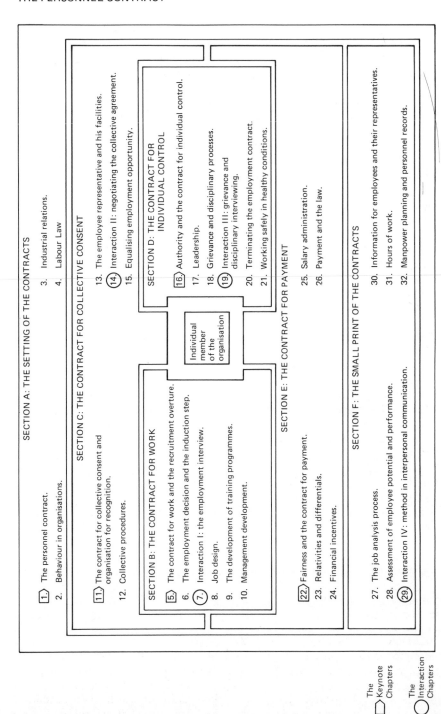

Figure 1.1. A framework for the analysis of personnel management

financial accounting are a few of those which are appropriate. We have identified three which seem especially relevant to the work of the personnel specialist. *Organisational behaviour* is an area of study seeking to understand the behaviour of people in organisations of which those people are an integral part. *Industrial relations* is not exclusively about strikes, nor even about collective bargaining; it seeks to explain the processes of job regulation. These explanations are formulated not only in an organisational context, but taking account of employer and employee collectives, stage agencies and a range of other elements not usually investigated by the organisational behaviourist. *Labour law* is that area of statute and precedent which seeks to provide a framework of legislation for the relationship between the individual and his employing organisation.

SECTION B. THE CONTRACT FOR WORK

Members of organisations are employed to work and they take employment in order to work. However important trade union organisation may be, and however vital the pay bargain is, the basic contract between employee and organisation is for *work* and there are a sequence of personnel activities concerned with the processes of first matching the employee's search for work and the organisation's need for employees, and then developing the capacity of the employee both to perform and achieve.

SECTION C. THE CONTRACT FOR COLLECTIVE CONSENT

The contract for employment that is made between man and the organisation is individual but is reached within a framework for collective consent. There will be one or more collective agreements reached between representatives of the employees and representatives of the organisation. These agreements give consent to a general framework of rules and guidelines for the employment contract.

SECTION D. THE CONTRACT FOR INDIVIDUAL CONTROL

A feature of organisational life is mutual control, with the degree and nature of the controls varying. A traditional view of control is that managers in organisations tell others what to do and then monitor their performance to make sure it is done properly; that is, to the satisfaction of the managers. At the same time, however, individuals are seeking to control the demands which the organisation makes upon them by extending the degree of their autonomy in the work place. Examples here range from the 'manufacturing' of overtime to the extraordinary determination of office workers in destroying the objectives of office landscapers by gradually reorganising the position of filing cabinets and rubber plants to create quasi offices in an open-plan environment. These moves towards mutual control have a core of informal understanding rather than overt agreement, but formality has been introduced by legislation defining employee rights, conferring the inalienable right of a grievance procedure and defining the scope for managers to punish the recalcitrant.

SECTION E. THE CONTRACT FOR PAYMENT

A major dimension of the contract between man and the organisation is for payment. However important it may be to the individual the elements of this contract are collective. Few negotiate individual terms. Most receive 'the agreed rate for the job' and the scope for individual adjustment is at most peripheral. Not only is there likely to be an initiative from the organisation to ensure consistency of treatment between individuals doing the same work, but there will also be trade union negotiation and governmental intervention.

SECTION F. THE 'SMALL PRINT' OF THE CONTRACTS

Just as there are important areas of *general knowledge,* so there are areas of *general skill and method* that may be deployed in various types of agreement broking or as necessary preliminaries to such agreement. We take these out into a separate category so that they are not inflexibly linked with specific events. The most striking example is job analysis, which is an admirable technique but which frequently has its potential value underestimated because in one organisational setting it is used as a part of recruitment and selection and geared exclusively to that application, while in another it will be used only for job evaluation or management by objectives. By disconnecting it from specific functions it can take on enhanced value. The skills and methods may be regarded as a tool kit for general application.

THE FRAMEWORK FOR ANALYSIS AND THE READER OF THIS BOOK

Having differentiated the separate categories of personnel work, we then need to integrate, and the structure of this book has four such integrative features.

(a) INTERACTION

Personnel work involves interacting with people in face-to-face encounters. We identify four types of such encounter, locating them in different sections of the book with a general chapter on interactive method in the closing section. This provides a 'book within a book' and a recurrent, integrative theme.

(b) KEYNOTE CHAPTERS

A second recurring theme is to be found in the opening chapters of sections B, C, D and E. Those four chapters may be read with this one to provide a discussion of the main issues involved in each of the contractual areas.

(c) CROSS-REFERENCING

To some extent the reader may be able to set up his own theme by using the cross-referencing that is provided. With each of the contractual areas there are references back to the most relevant parts of general knowledge and forward to the appropriate skills and method. We naturally hope that this method of reading will only be used *after* the first reading. The text is designed first and foremost to be read as a coherent whole, but it may have later value as a work of reference for use as described in this paragraph.

(d) PROCESS DIAGRAMS

The final means towards integration is the use of a common form of diagrammatic representation for concepts and their inter-relationship. Figure 1.1 encompasses the whole work. Later figures show more detailed breakdowns.

SUMMARY PROPOSITIONS

For one presentation idea we are indebited to Glueck.[22] Periodically we shall present the reader with summary propositions. It is of doubtful value to propound principles, as they imply a guarantee of reliability that the understanding of human behaviour cannot yet provide. Our *propositions* will summarise in standard form certain working hypotheses, which will have been justified in the preceding discussion, even though they are not susceptible to proof. Our first proposition is:

Proposition 1. Personnel management is a series of activities enabling working man and his employing organisation to reach agreement about the nature and objectives of the employment relationship between them, and then to fulfil those agreements.

REFERENCES

1. Legge K. and Exley M., 'Authority, Ambiguity and Adaptation: the Personnel Specialist's Dilemma' in *Industrial Relations Journal,* Autumn 1975.
2. Berger P.L. and Luckman T., *The Social Construction of Reality* (Penguin Press) 1967, p. 92.
3. Northcott C.H., *Personnel Management* (Pitman) 1955, p. 19.
4. Institute of Personnel Management, *The Institute of Personnel Management*, (IPM) 1979.
5. Mumford E., 'Job Satisfaction: A Method of Analysis' in *Personnel Review,* Summer 1972.
6. Dubin R., Hedley A. and Taveggia T.C., 'Attachment to Work', chapter in Dubin, R. (ed) *Handbook of Work, Organisation and Society* (Rand McNally) 1976, p. 324.
7. Anthony P.D., *The Ideology of Work* (Tavistock) 1977, p. 302.
8. McCarthy W.E.J. and Ellis N.D., *Management by Agreement* (Hutchinson) 1973, p. 98.
9. Batstone E., Boraston I. and Frenkel S., *Shop Stewards in Action* (Basil Blackwell) 1977, pp. 122–130.
10. Hyman R. and Brough I., *Social Values and Industrial Relations* (Basil Blackwell) 1975, p. 66.
11. Schein E.H., *Organisational Psychology,* 2nd ed. (Prentice-Hall) 1970, pp. 12–15, 76–79.
12. Fordham K.G., 'Job Advertising', chapter in *Recruitment Handbook,* 2nd ed. (B. Ungerson ed.) (Gower) 1975, p. 60.
13. Department of Employment, *In Working Order – A Study of Industrial Discipline,* Manpower Paper No. 6 (HMSO) 1973, p. 7.
14. Flanders A., *Industrial Relations: What is Wrong with the System?* (Faber & Faber) 1965.
15. Clegg H.A. 'Pluralism in Industrial Relations' in *British Journal of Industrial Relations,* November 1975.
16. Fox A., 'Industrial Sociology and Industrial Relations', Research Paper 3, *Royal Commission on Trade Unions and Employers' Associations* (HMSO) 1966.
17. Goldthorpe J.H., 'Social Inequality and Social Integration in Modern Britain' in *Advancement of Science* 26, 1969, pp. 190–202.
18. Fox A., *Beyond Contract: Work, Power and Trust Relations* (Faber & Faber) 1974.
19. Ward, G., *Fort Grunwick* (M.T. Smith) 1977.
20. Jucius M.J., *Personnel Management,* 7th ed. (Irwin) 1974.
21. Megginson L.C., *Personnel: A Behavioural Approach to Administration,* (Irwin) 1972.
22. Glueck, W.F., *Personnel: A Diagnostic Approach* (Business Publications) 1974.

2

Behaviour in Organisations

The work of the personnel specialist is primarily concerned with the people of organisations and their behaviour within an organisational context. Many practitioners argue, with some justification, that personnel management is an applied behavioural science.

The origins of personnel practice were significantly informed by the science of psychology, and more specifically by the application of this science to organisational problems within the emergent sub-discipline of industrial psychology. As personnel practice developed as a distinct management function, encompassing a wider range of activities, specific theory and research in the fields of sociology and social psychology became important. Increasing managerial concern for problems of human organisation led to further applications for theories, research and techniques from the behavioural sciences. Moves towards greater integration of knowledge and methods logically led many American business schools to establish departments of organisational behaviour (O.B.) to develop an inter-disciplinary understanding of organisational problems. This practice quickly spread to British and other European centres for academic training of managers, so that most have established similar departments today.

Current professional training of personnel specialists has a strong emphasis upon knowledge appropriately selected from the various behavioural sciences, either as separate subject areas or as training within the emerging and inter-disciplinary academic discipline of organisational behaviour. Since 1980 the Institute of Personnel Management membership regulations have focused upon the applications of O.B. to personnel problems, rather than training in the separate subjects of the behavioural sciences. Our discussion in this chapter provides a broad outline of this important knowledge area, together with reference to more detailed sources of information.

1. The Nature of Organisations

Most definitions of the term 'organisation' emphasise a systematic relationship between component parts, each performing some function of the whole, but use the term to describe both method (of organisation) and an entity (the organisation). A problem with organisations as entities arises from the differences in reason for, and nature of, the organisation. It may arise for *technical* reasons, implying a planned inter-relationship of physical or machine components, or alternatively the co-operative work of people to achieve tasks beyond the capacity of individuals acting independently. A human being may be viewed as a *biological* organisation, with chemical, physiological and psychological components, whilst the family as a unit can be considered as an organisation having biological reasons for its existence. Groups, crowds and communities may be viewed as organisations having different *social* reasons for their existence. Other organisations are developed for *industrial* reasons, such as economies of scale and full utilisation of available resources.

These different understandings of the nature of organisation show why research and theory have been developed relatively independently within a number of different academic disciplines. The emergence of O.B. as a distinct discipline arises from the current recognition that each separate discipline or sub-discipline is producing only partial explanations, so that integration is necessary for improved understanding.

This integration has a primary emphasis in the context of business and service organisations, which are deliberately created for technical and industrial reasons. The earlier focus of sociology and organisational theory was on the structural properties of such organisations, to identify general principles of organisational design to aid management to achieve the technical, industrial and other organisational objectives. Technical disciplines similarly emphasised the design and planning of physical and technical resources. Specialist management techniques have developed with a focus on effective decision-making and resource utilisation. Other disciplines, such as industrial psychology and work study, focused on the interaction of people with their working tasks.

The different modes of analysis developed their own view of organisations in terms of the phenomena studied and different theoretical assumptions, but all shared a common assumption that the behaviour of people (individually or collectively) could be analysed as analogous to machine systems; the problem being to develop knowledge and principles for more effective planning, direction and control of human activities. This emphasis on the *formal organisation,* with behaviour planned to achieve organisational goals, was complicated by the increasing recognition of the emergence of the *informal organisation* which people developed for practical or social reasons to satisfy the needs and goals of employees. Further complexity was added by the increasing recognition that, whilst external factors may influence human behaviour, individuals remain able to exercise self-determination of their behaviour and do so to produce activities not planned by management.

As organisations were recognised to be more complex, earlier simplistic formulations were questioned and replaced. A useful analysis by Leavitt[1] introduces a general model, reproduced as Figure 2.1, illustrating a now widely adopted view of the general classes of variable which interact within complex organisations. *Task*

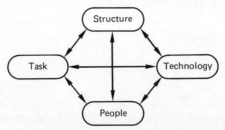

Figure 2.1. Leavitt's general model of organisational variables

variables are concerned with the production of goods or services, all with a specific purpose, resulting in a variety of tasks and operations to be allocated to people. *Technology variables* refer to the problem-solving methods, techniques, tools and machinery used by people in performing their tasks. *Structural variables* refer to the relatively permanent arrangements for organising the technology and tasks, particularly the human tasks involving communication, authority, and decision-making as commonly represented in organisational charts. *People variables* refer to the knowledge, ideas and activities of the human members of the organisation. A major feature of this analysis is the observation that academics, specialists and managers tend to have a narrow focus upon particular variables and relationships, hence a need for multi-disciplinary approaches to understanding human behaviour in organisations and for planning changes, a theme developed further by Leavitt *et al*[2] in an O.B. text.

In studying planned change within organisations and producing a general typology, Chapman[3] considered a modification of Leavitt's analysis useful in clarifying different approaches and perspectives, as illustrated in Figure 2.2 below. The view of *structural* and *task variables* is unchanged, but more clear distinction is made for other classes of variable. *Technology variables* focus upon products, equipment, tools and the other technical/physical artifacts utilised, whilst *technique variables* identify working methods, problem solving techniques, and other programmable activities of people. The *people variables* focus upon individual membership and their specific characteristics (knowledge, experience, skills & abilities, attitudes, etc.), with *process variables* referring to the formal or informal social interaction processes arising from human membership and activities.

Within different specialisms and academic disciplines more specific variables and relationships have been identified and examined, frequently focusing upon similar phenomena from different viewpoints and with different assumptions about influences and causality. As each knowledge area developed there has been increasing overlap of interests and recognition of partial explanations, leading to the development of O.B. as an inter-disciplinary behavioural science concerned with human behaviour within organisations. Most O.B. practitioners recognise the multi-variate and multiple interaction nature of organisational components and subsystems as illustrated in the diagrams. The result is that simple prescriptions for organisational planning or change have limited value, as a change affecting one class of variable will have some effects which may be predictable, but is also likely to affect other variables in a less predictable or totally unexpected manner. This is a further

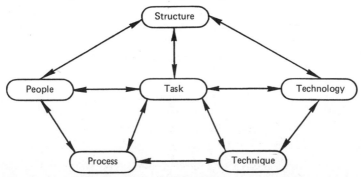

Figure 2.2. A general systems view of organisation — six subsystems of interacting and interdependent variables

justification for our emphasis upon the need for collaborative planning by all relevant parties, as the value of specialist knowledge needs to be tempered by integration of diverse viewpoints and inter-disciplinary exchange of knowledge.

When we return to problems of defining the nature of organisations, it is clear that definitions in terms of structure, task and technology alone are inadequate. These focus upon relatively permanent or static features of organisations, whereas the dynamic properties depend upon the behaviour of people in the formation, operation and development of organisations. A useful review of behavioural definitions is provided by Porter *et al*,[4] which suggests some areas of common agreement. We suggest a general definition, largely behavioural in emphasis, which would be generally acceptable to most practitioners concerned with the study of organisations:

> An organisation comprises individuals and groups of people interacting on a relatively continuous basis and utilising relevant technology, whose activities are differentiated, integrated and directed towards the achievement of common goals and objectives.

Further elaboration distinguishes between specific forms of organisation. A formal organisation is specifically planned or designed to achieve particular goals of the designers, whilst an informal organisation develops more spontaneously to achieve the objectives of members. A social organisation may be formal (e.g. trade union or professional society) or informal (e.g. association for sporting or social activities) but, assuming membership is voluntary, will be closely related to the needs and objectives of members. Industrial, commercial and service organisations are normally formal, being distinguished by the overall goals which are emphasised; the important point is that, being comprised of people, such formal organisations provide a framework within which other informal or social organisations may develop to achieve quite different goals.

2. Objectives of O.B.

O.B. practitioners have a variety of objectives and methods which influence their research and practice, but certain general objectives can be recognised:

(i) *Scientific Research.* Valid knowledge is developed using scientific methods of research, implying systematic data collection about the phenomena studied to aid the process of developing assumptions and hypotheses, which are then tested by carefully designed investigations. A useful discussion by Duncan[5] describes specific problems and methods of O.B. which differentiate it from the physical sciences, though there is the same emphasis on scientific enquiry, measurement and empirical analysis. For more detailed discussion of behavioural science research methodology the texts by Labovitz and Hagedorn,[6] Blalock,[7] Kuhn[8] and Kerlingel[9] make useful starting points.

(ii) *Understanding Past Behaviour.* Research and theory are directed towards understanding of previous behaviour of people, individually and/or collectively, and the factors influencing such behaviour.

(iii) *Explaining Present Behaviour.* This provides a basis for explaining present behaviour by diagnosis based on conceptual frameworks and knowledge of the variables and relationships involved.

(iv) *Predicting Future Behaviour.* The development of any theory is only of value if it has predictive capability, as indicated by Gergen,[10] Bobbitt *et al*[11] and many others. Theories provide the basis for identifying key variables and enable the probable outcome of any changes in these variables to be estimated. Although the 'pure' scientist views theory as an end objective, the 'applied' scientists or practitioner views it as a means to other practical ends, but they share a common concern for the predictive value of their theories.

It would be naive to suggest that the behavioural sciences have moved so far towards achieving these objectives as the physical sciences, but the progress has been rapid, during the past 75 years, in developing knowledge for understanding and explaining behaviour. Predictive capability and theory development has been variable and, with the exception of task-related behaviour as studied by industrial psychologists, predictions tend to improve when collections of people are the object of study. However, as shown by Handy,[12] the achievement of predictive certainty for behavioural phenomena in organisations is likely to prove impossible for at least two reasons:

(i) The multiplicity of variables which influence organisational behaviour, and their multiple interactions, make precise predictions of outcomes unlikely.

(ii) The human ability to override many of the external influences on behaviour, through exercise of independent self-determination.

Whilst predictive certainty is unlikely, probability estimates falling short of certainty but significantly improving upon uncertainty, are already possible in many areas of human behaviour. Behavioural science knowledge and techniques are now widely applied to understanding and influencing human behaviour in many areas.

The successful development of the behavioural sciences is leading to a concern about the ethical and moral problems of influencing human behaviour. Tannenbaum and Davies[13] have produced a summary of the common values shared by most O.B. practitioners, and Benne[14] has discussed the ethical problems to be recognised when acting as a consultant or advisor. Similarly Kelman[15] points to the dilemma between a fundamental value, the freedom of the individual to exercise choice, and the fact that any attempt to influence behaviour change implies some degree of manipulation and external control which violates this value. A subsequent paper by Warwick and Kelman[16] provides a comprehensive analysis of the ethical issues, arising from conflicting values and different methods of manipulation and influence involved in general policies for behaviour change.

These problems are peculiar to the behavioural sciences and to O.B. practitioners in particular, because of the implications of influencing, manipulating or controlling human behaviour. As the potential for influence and prediction improves, such issues need to be recognised more clearly and discussed more openly. At present exploitation is limited only by the personal values, decisions and activities of individual scientists or practitioners. Kelman expresses the view:

> Researchers in this area also have a special responsibility to be actively concerned with the ways in which the knowledge they produce is used by various agencies in their society. Eternal vigilance to the possibilities of manipulation is, of course, the duty of every citizen. But, as producers of knowledge about manipulation, social scientists are in a position similar to that of many nuclear physicists who feel a *special* sense of responsibility for the ways in which their knowledge is used.[17]

This is true for the behavioural science researcher, both 'pure' and 'applied', for the O.B. practitioner or consultant, and for any manager applying behavioural science knowledge and techniques. In the organisational context we consider that any people who are potentially affected by such proposed activities to promote change of behaviour should, as an absolute minimum, be fully informed of their nature and purpose. Our discussions of training (Chapter 9) and management development (Chapter 10) emphasise the need for training to satisfy the objectives of the individual as well as of the organisation.

3. The Development of O.B. Understanding

A comprehensive examination of the development of O.B. understanding requires a detailed analysis of contributions from several behavioural sciences, which would be inappropriate to this text. However we do consider that the historical developments are important to an appreciation of the current knowledge and theory, in addition to enabling a useful re-interpretation of previous research findings, so the interested reader must be referred to other sources.

Perrow[18] provides a detailed overview of organisational theory developments, later adapted as a summary paper and reprinted in Wexley and Yukl[19] together with a complementary review by Lichtman and Hunt.[20] Hicks and Gullett[21] provide a detailed analysis of contributions to major areas of theory and approaches to study of O.B., as do most of our O.B. text references. Pugh *et al*[22] provide a brief summary of the work of important researchers and theorists, as does Pollard,[23] whilst Pugh[24] provides excerpts from the work of important writers.

Another detailed overview is provided, from an organisational sociology perspective, by Silverman.[25] Howell[26] provides a useful summary of relevant theories, in addition to discussion of more specific research in the area of industrial psychology. From an organisational psychology viewpoint, Schein[27] provides a useful summary of relevant industrial and social psychology research and theory. This includes an analysis of changing assumptions about the nature of man, which informs our discussion in Chapter 8.

The dominant framework for the analysis of organisational behaviour at the present time is *systems theory*, providing a framework within which multi-disciplinary research and theory can be integrated. Whilst proposed earlier, the basic concepts were introduced by Weiner[28] in 1948 and developed in several disciplines as indicated by Emery.[29,30] By the early 1960s many behavioural science researchers were emphasising *contingency approaches* in their various explanations of the determinants of behaviour, essentially suggesting that general principles of behaviour cannot be formulated as behaviour is contingent upon the interaction of specific variables in particular situations. The conceptual framework of systems theory fitted well with contingency explanations and, additionally, provided a basis for integrating diverse research findings. This was shown by Katz and Kahn[31] in their analysis of organisation in terms of systems theory, providing also a summary of the key characteristics and concepts of such analysis. Most current O.B. texts use this conceptual framework to analyse behaviour in terms of multiple interactions between interrelated and interdependent variables at different levels of analysis.

4. Organisations as the Context for Behaviour

Most earlier explanations of human behaviour were formulated in simple cause and effect relationships, following the example set by Newtonian physics in the physical sciences. Such explanations of human behaviour were inadequate due to the individual capacity for self-determination and the ability to learn to adapt to changes in the external environment. The modern systems approach views an organisation as a system in interaction with its environment, with basic elements as indicated in Figure 2.3.

The organisation is viewed as a dynamic process involving component parts which are in interaction with each other and the environment of which it is part. It takes inputs of resources and energy from the environment, converting these to outputs towards the environment. In addition information inputs are obtained, together with feedback of results to control the operation of the processes. When the environment has unanticipated influences upon inputs or outputs, the information inputs and feedback enable the process to be controlled or adapted to these influences. The whole world is viewed in terms of such systems, with any particular system interconnected and interdependent with other systems.

Thus the human being is seen as a biological organisational system in interaction with his environment, including the groups or forms of social organisation of which he is part. A group may similarly be viewed as a system, with people as component parts, interacting with its environment including other groups and individuals in

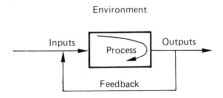

Figure 2.3. Elements of an adaptive open system

the organisational system of which they are components. This approach to organisational analysis has been developed to include technical systems or any forms of organisation which involve connected parts and flows of energy or resources (physical or informational). A comprehensive treatment of organisational analysis, in terms of systems theory, is provided by Burack,[32] who also shows the potential for integrating previous O.B. research within this analytical framework.

Taking this approach we can represent the business, commercial, industrial or service organisations as an overall system to produce the conceptual model in Figure 2.4. The organisational process (i.e. organisational boundary) takes physical and human resource inputs from the environment, as well as being generally influenced by environmental variables, converting them in the process into inputs of goods, services or other impacts upon the environment. Internal feedback mechanisms refer to the information directly used in the process for control and guidance via the decision-making processes. External feedback mechanisms represent the impact of the organisation upon the environment and the information feedback via organisational members. This provides a basis for examining the organisational knowledge which is available from such disciplines as sociology, macro-economics, cultural anthropology and political science which have studied organisations as a part of society or the general environment. Recognising the goals of the formal organisation, we develop strategies for achieving these in terms of organisational design. This has implications for specialisation in the allocation of activities to people, horizontally for production tasks and vertically for different levels of responsibility or authority. Specialisation has implications for co-ordination or integration of the diverse

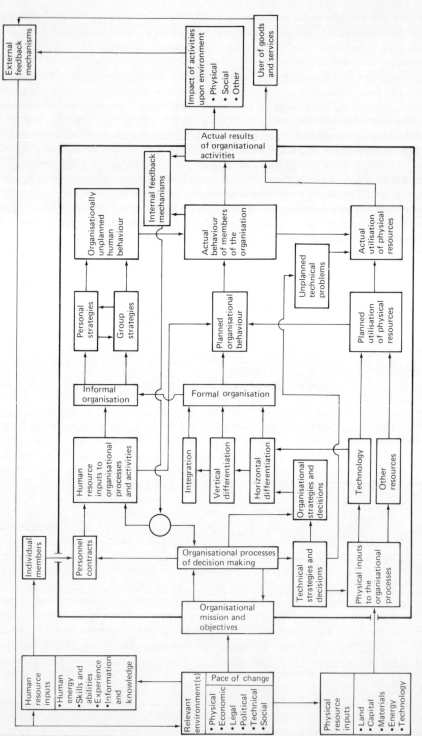

Figure 2.4. Conceptual model of an organisation as the context for human behaviour

activities, particularly with procedures for communication and control to achieve the planned results. The concepts of organisational design are discussed in Lawrence and Lorsch,[33] Dalton et al,[34] Lorsch and Lawrence,[35] and Galbraith.[36] For a comprehensive treatment of the design of formal organisations the reader is referred to Child.[37]

All the functional areas of organisation determine their technical strategies for the planned utilisation of physical or technological resources, with implications for formal organisational design and the required task behaviour of people involved. The contributions of psychology, particularly industrial psychology, are relevant to the planned behaviour of individuals. Similarly social psychology provides insights to assist with planning interpersonal and group behaviour of people collectively.

So far this analysis has referred to the formal organisation, whereby behavioural activities are directed towards the goals of the organisation. A further important element is that the formal organisation provides a framework within which informal organisations, or social organisations, develop. The informal organisation is commonly used to describe the processes whereby individuals collectively act to satisfy needs or goals different from those of the organisation, the typical organised behaviour to adjust productivity in relation to incentive schemes as identified by Whyte[38] and others being a prime example. Similarly social organisations develop to meet a variety of needs of individuals which can be best satisfied through interaction with others, as discussed by many researchers since the classic Hawthorne Studies reported by Roethlisberger and Dickson.[39] These personal and collective goals lead to individual, interpersonal and group activities or behaviour which is not planned by the formal organisation and may well interfere with the achievement of organisational goals.

In order to understand, explain and possibly predict such activities the research by social psychologists and organisational/industrial psychologists is particularly relevant. From the viewpoint of management such unplanned behaviour is dysfunctional, leading to attempts to eliminate or reduce the consequences by procedures aimed at control of behaviour. The weight of evidence suggests that such approaches increase the problems involved, leading to the current view that organisations need to accommodate the needs and goals of their employees to achieve overall efficiency and effectiveness. The emphasis on shared goals and mutual consent is the major theme of our book.

5. Different Levels of Analysis of Human Behaviour

Our conceptual model indicates components of the overall formal organisation, both structural and dynamic, but systems theory provides the basis for detailed analysis of all the sub-systems (human and technical) comprising the whole. To do so, however, requires the knowledge and concepts of many different disciplines concerned with different aspects of human behaviour. Figure 2.5 provides a conceptual framework to illustrate the inter-disciplinary nature of O.B.

Part (a) shows the various levels of analysis, and interactions or relationships, for the study of human behaviour. Each level of analysis is composed of interacting units of lower levels, in a system view of the world. Part (b) provides an approximate indication of the focus of different behavioural science disciplines or sub-disciplines, which examine specific aspects of behaviour and relationships at the different levels of analysis. Individually these disciplines provide partial explanations of different organisational behaviour phenomena, but a move towards greater integration of

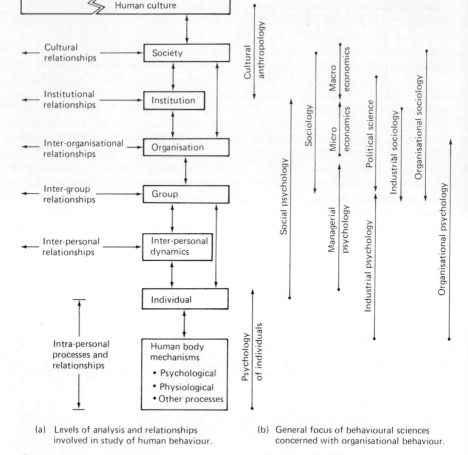

(a) Levels of analysis and relationships
     involved in study of human behaviour.

(b) General focus of behavioural sciences
     concerned with organisational behaviour.

*Figure 2.5. Conceptual framework illustrating the inter-disciplinary
nature of understanding human behaviour in organisations*

research and theory is now generally accepted as necessary to an improved understanding of O.B.

Many of these separate disciplines have developed relatively independently but,
in doing so, have caused boundaries to overlap. This is particularly true of organisational sociology and social psychology, where many common concepts and areas
of study can be identified. As indicated earlier such overlap and need for integration
has resulted in the emergence of O.B. as a distinctive field of study, initially with
collaboration between practitioners trained in different traditions. The process of
integration has developed to the stage where practitioners are increasingly seeing
themselves as O.B. specialists drawing widely upon the knowledge developed in the
related behavioural sciences.

6. The Knowledge Base for O.B.

We have already referred to O.B. as an inter-disciplinary behavioural science concerned
with all aspects of behaviour in organisations.

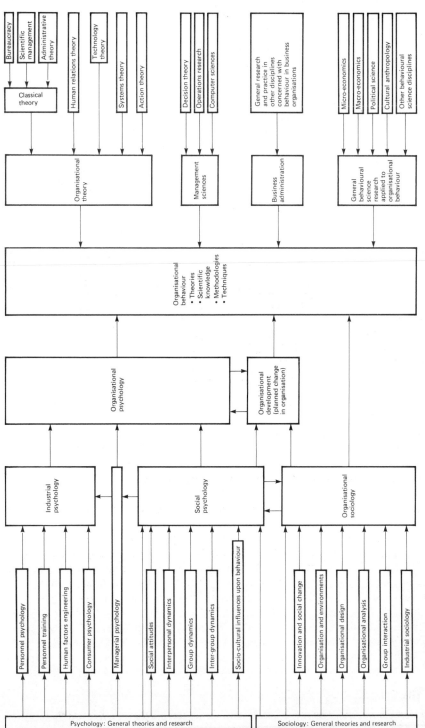

Figure 2.6. General overview of contributions to organisational behaviour — the interdisciplinary behavioural science focusing upon human behaviour in organisations

In Figure 2.6 we illustrate more specifically the different disciplines, sub-disciplines and specific areas of study which comprise the general knowledge base of the O.B. practitioner. *Organisational theory* comprises the various general theories of organisation, in order of their historical emergence (see our references 18 to 27), which have guided different research studies. *Management sciences* includes the methods or techniques developed specifically to guide organisational decision-making. *Business administration* refers to the other business activities, such as financial accounting, marketing, engineering, etc. which influence behaviour within organisations. *General behavioural science* refers to the contributions from several other behavioural disciplines already discussed.

It is from the areas on the left of Figure 2.6 that O.B. derives its primary knowledge base, although also influenced by the above areas. *Organisational psychology* is itself inter-disciplinary in nature, drawing together many areas of psychological research focused upon individual or social behaviour, as illustrated by Schein,[40] Bass,[41] Kolb *et al*,[42] and Seigel and Lane.[43] *Organisational development* has developed with an inter-disciplinary emphasis upon planned organisational change, as indicated by Bennis *et al*,[44,45] although in practice the methodology and techniques are largely derived from social psychology, as indicated by French and Bell,[46] Margulies and Raia,[47] Beer[48] and Huse.[49]

Sociology refers to the science which focusses upon the study of human behaviour that is socially determined, emphasising the total society and its institutional, organisational and group structure with corresponding social influences upon behaviour. Many specialist areas of study have concentrated upon organisational phenomena, often being collectively identified as the sub-discipline of *organisational sociology*. Such studies have had a significant impact upon organisational theory (e.g. references 18 to 27), organisational design (e.g. references 33 to 37), and provided substantial conceptual and analytical contributions to an understanding of social and structural variables affecting behaviour within organisations.

Social psychology is also concerned with human behaviour in a social context, but with an emphasis upon the social phenomena of interaction and taking the individual as the basic unit of analysis. The subsidiary specialist areas identified are of particular help in understanding human behaviour in inter-personal, group and inter-group relationships. Our interaction chapters (numbered 7, 14, 19 and 29) are largely based upon such research, but Bennis *et al*[50] and Argyle[51] provide an overview of 'inter-personal dynamics' studies. Similarly our Chapter 17 on leadership is largely based upon 'group dynamics' research, but general overviews are provided by Cartwright and Zander[52] and Shaw.[53] When considering collective bargaining the 'inter-group dynamics' research is helpful, with overviews provided by Blake *et al*[54] and Lorsch and Lawrence.[55] For more general overviews of social psychology research, Secord and Backman[56] provides a comprehensive examination of the area.

Managerial psychology is concerned with the application of psychology and social psychology research to the problems of managers. The term was introduced by Leavitt,[57] although he used it to describe the wider application of research now referred to as organisational psychology. Current usage is more directly concerned with such areas as job satisfaction, motivation, decision-making and the problems of leading or influencing the behaviour of subordinates. It draws generally upon social psychology research but often comprises an important section of texts covering industrial psychology.

Industrial psychology is the specialist area where psychology research is applied to human problems which arise in the production and distribution of goods or services. As this field of study has developed, psychologists have increasingly specialised further in particular problem areas, but all provide inputs to the activities of the personnel specialist. For an overview the texts of McCormick and Tiffin,[58] Landy and Trumbo,[59] Fleishman and Bass,[60] Howell[61] and Warr[62] all provide a comprehensive examination of the area. The contributions to personnel management are clearly indicated by our references to research in Managerial Psychology (Chapters 8, 10 and 17), Human Factors Engineering (Chapters 8 and 27), Personnel Training (Chapters 9 and 10), and Personnel Psychology (Chapters 5, 6, 7, 28 and 29) in key chapters of our text.

7. O.B. and the Personnel Specialist

The personnel specialist has traditionally been concerned with problems of recruitment, selection, training and development of the people in organisations. To deal with such problems he draws on the knowledge and techniques developed by industrial psychologists. The functions concerned with the welfare of employees are informed by contributions from psychology, social psychology and sociology, as are the functions concerned with payment systems, grievances and discipline.

As the personnel specialist has become increasingly concerned with industrial relations, research by social psychologists and sociologists has become important to understanding, explanation and prediction of the collective behaviour of people. In the capacity of specialist advisor to other managerial specialists, he draws upon knowledge from various behavioural science disciplines.

In responding to legal, political, social, economic, physical or technological changes in the environment, organisations frequently need to introduce corresponding planned changes in structural, technological, task, technique, process or people variables. Such changes have direct implications for the behaviour of people. The personnel specialist is increasingly being called upon to advise. This requires a general understanding of the knowledge which is collectively identified with the discipline of organisational behaviour.

REFERENCES

1. Leavitt H.J., 'Applied Organisational Change in Industry: Structural Technological and Humanistic Approaches', in J.G. March (ed.) *Handbook of Organisations* (Rand McNally) 1965.
2. Leavitt H.J., Dill W.R. and Erying H.B., *The Organisational World: A Systematic View of Managers and Management* (Harcourt Brace Jovanovich) 1973.
3. Chapman J.B., *A General Typology of Approaches to Planned Change within Organisations* (University of Aston) 1979.
4. Porter L.W., Lawler E.E. and Hackman J.R. *Behaviour in Organisations* (McGraw-Hill) 1975.
5. Duncan W.J., *Organisational Behaviour* (Houghton Mifflin) 1978, Chapter 3 (p. 49–77).
6. Labovitz S. and Hagedorn R., *Introduction to Social Research* (2nd ed.) (McGraw-Hill) 1976.
7. Blalock H.M. Jnr., *An Introduction to Social Research* (Prentice-Hall) 1970.
8. Kuhn T.S., *The Structure of Scientific Revolutions* 2nd ed. (University of Chicago Press) 1970.
9. Kerlinger F.N., *Foundations of Behavioural Research* (Holt, Rinehart and Winston) 1964.
10. Gergen K.J., *The Psychology of Behaviour Exchange* (Addison-Wesley) 1969.

11. Bobbit H.R., Breinholt R.H., Doktor R.H. and McNaul J.P., *Organisational Behaviour: Understanding and Prediction*, 2nd ed. (Prentice-Hall) 1978

12. Handy C.G., *Understanding Organisations*, 2nd ed. (Penguin) 1981, pp. 11–22).

13. Tannenbaum T. and Davies S.A., 'Values, Men and Organisations', in *Industrial Management Review*, Vol. 10, No. 2, pp. 69–80, 1969.

14. Benne K.D., 'Some Ethical Problems in Group and Organisational Consultation. Journal of Social Issues', XV, No. 20, pp. 60–67, 1959. (Reprinted in Ref. No. 44.)

15. Kelman H.C., 'Manipulation of Human Behaviour: An Ethical Dilemma for The Social Scientist', *Journal of Social Issues*, XXI No. 2, pp. 31–46, 1965. (Reprinted in Ref. No. 44.)

16. Warwick D.P. and Kelman H.C., 'Ethical Issues in Social Intervention', in Zaltman (ed.) *Processes and Phenomena of Social Change* (John Wiley) 1973. (Reprinted in Ref. No. 45.)

17. Kelman, 1965, *op. cit.*, p. 46.

18. Perrow C., *Complex Organisations: A Critical Essay* (Scott Foresman) 1972.

19. Wexley K.N. and Yukl G.A. (eds.), *Organisational Behaviour and Industrial Psychology* (Oxford University Press) 1975, pp. 192–202.

20. Lichtman C.M. and Hunt R.G., 'Personality and Organisation Theory: A Review of some Conceptual Literature', *Psychological Bulletin*, 1971, Vol. 76 pp. 271–304. (Reprinted in Ref. No. 19.)

21. Hicks H.G. and Gullett G.R., *Organisation: Theory and Behaviour* (McGraw-Hill) 1975.

22. Pugh D.S., Hickson D.J. and Minings C.R., *Writers on Organisation* (Penguin) 1971.

23. Pollard H.R., *Development in Management Thought* (Heinemann) 1974.

24. Pugh D.S. (ed.), *Organisational Theory: Selected Readings* (Penguin) 1971.

25. Silverman D., *The Theory of Organisations: A Sociological Framework* (Heinemann) 1970.

26. Howell W.C., *Essentials of Industrial and Organisational Psychology* (Dorsey) 1976.

27. Schein E.H., *Organisational Psychology*, 3rd ed. (Prentice-Hall) 1979.

28. Weiner N., *Cybernetics* (M.I.T.) 1948.

29. Emery F.R., *Systems Thinking* (Penguin) 1969.

30. Emery F.R., *Systems Thinking* Vol. 1 and Vol. 2 (Penguin) 1981.

31. Katz D. and Kahn R., *The Social Psychology of Organisations* (John Wiley) 1966 and 1978 (2nd Edn).

32. Burack E., *Organisational Analysis Theory and Applications* (Holt, Rinehart and Winston) 1975.

33. Lawrence P.R. and Lorsch J.W., *Organisation and Environment: Managing Differentiation and Integration* (Harvard Business School) 1967.

34. Dalton G.W., Lawrence P.R. and Lorsch J.W. (eds.), *Organisational Structure and Design* (Irwin-Dorsey) 1970.

35. Lorsch J.W. and Lawrence P.R. (eds.), *Studies in Organisational Design* (Irwin-Dorsey) 1970.

36. Galbraith J., *Designing Complex Organisations* (Addison-Wesley) 1973 and *Organisation Design* (Addison-Wesley), 1977.

37. Child J., *Organisation: A Guide to Problems and Practice* (Harper and Row) 1977.

38. Whyte W.F., *Money and Motivation: An Analysis of Incentives in Industry* (Harper and Row) 1955.

39. Roethlisberger F.J. and Dickson W.J., *Management and the Worker* (Harvard University) 1939.

40. Schein, 1979, *op. cit.*

41. Bass B.M., *Organisational Psychology* (Allyn & Bacon) 1965.

42. Kolb D., Rubin I. and McIntyre J., *Organisational Psychology: An Experimental Approach* (Prentice-Hall) 1970.

43. Seigel L. and Lane I.M., *Personnel and Organizational Psychology* (Irwin) 1982.

44. Bennis W.G., Benne K.D. and Chin R. (eds.), *The Planning of Change* 2nd ed. (Holt, Rinehart and Winston) 1969.

45. Bennis W.G., Benne K.D., Chin R. and Corey K.E. (eds.), *The Planning of Change* 3rd ed. (Holt, Rinehart and Winston) 1976.

46. French W.L. and Bell C.H. Jr., *Organization Development: Behavioral Science Interventions for Organization Improvement*, 2nd ed. (Prentice-Hall) 1978.

47. Margulies N. and Raia A.P., *Organisational Development: Values, Process and Technology* (Tata McGraw-Hill) 1975.

48. Beer, M., *Organisational Development* (Goodyear) 1980.
49. Huse E.F. *Organization Development and Change* (West Publishing) 1980 (2nd Edn).
50. Bennis W.G., Berlew D.E., Schein E.H. and Steele F.I. (eds.), *Interpersonal Dynamics* 3rd ed., (Dorsey) 1973.
51. Argyle M., *Social Interaction* (Methuen) 1969.
52. Cartwright D. and Zander A., *Group Dynamics: Research and Theory* 3rd ed. (Harper and Row) 1968.
53. Shaw M.E., *Group Dynamics: The Psychology of Small Group Behaviour* 2nd ed. (McGraw-Hill) 1976.
54. Blake R.R., Shepard H.A. and Mouton J.S., *Managing Inter-Group Conflict in Industry* (Gulf) 1964.
55. Lorsch J.W. and Lawrence P.R. (eds.), *Managing Group and Inter-Group Relations* (Irwin-Dorsey) 1972.
56. Secord P.F. and Backman C.W., *Social Psychology* 2nd ed. (McGraw-Hill) 1972.
57. Leavitt H.J., *Managerial Psychology* (University of Chicago Press) 1958. (3rd ed. 1972.)
58. McCormick E.J. and Tiffin J., *Industrial Psychology* 6th ed. (George Allen and Unwin) 1975.
59. Landy F.J. and Trumbo D.A., *Psychology of Work Behaviour* (Dorsey) 1976.
60. Fleishman E.A. and Bass A.R. (eds.), *Studies in Personnel and Industrial Psychology* 3rd ed. (Dorsey) 1974.
61. Howell, 1976, *op. cit.*
62. Warr, P.B., *Psychology at Work* 2nd ed. (Penguin) 1978.

3

Industrial Relations

In our opening chapter we said that industrial relations is a study that seeks to explain the processes of job regulation. In this chapter we review current ideas and institutions in the field of industrial relations in order to provide the second of our dimensions to the setting of the personnel contract.

In the main we are trying to set up a background to the collective aspects of the contract, but the phenomena of industrial relations will not submit to a simple pigeon-holing of that sort. Although much of what we describe here is to do with trade unions and employers' associations, strikes and agreements on pay, collective bargaining and the like, there is also inevitably an influence of these features on aspects of the individual contract.

1. The Nature of Industrial Relations

One problem about industrial relations is the lack of consensus on what we mean by it, even though we all know what we mean! It is rather like the well-known comment by the visitor to the art gallery: 'I don't know much about art, but I know what I like'.

Comment about industrial relations is so widespread and experience of its manifestations so universal that it is a commonplace in our lives and consciousness. The lack of precision in understanding is not helped by the confusion of academics, who produce definitions as varied as:

> The area of study and practice concerned with the administration of the employment function in modern public and private enterprise . . .

> The study of people in a situation, organisation or system interacting in the doing of work in relation to some form of contract either written or unwritten.

> . . . industrial relations includes any policy action, pay, condition or agreement within a given concern which enables the workforce to continue in a co-operative way. Thus industrial relations have broken down when there is a strike, a go-slow, an overtime ban or work-to-rule or lack of communication.

The definition which most nearly meets our requirements is that of Allan Flanders:

> A system of industrial relations is a system of rules. . . the subject deals with certain regulated or institutionalised relationships in industry. Personal, or in the

language of sociology, unstructured, relationships have their importance for management and workers but they lie outside the scope of a system of industrial relations. The study of industrial relations may therefore be described as a study of the institutions of job regulation.[1]

The orderliness that Flanders saw as central has subsequently been criticised as being not quite the necessity that he believed, but in the context of this book that definition is useful, as it draws a distinction between the institutionalised and the personal type of relationships, as well as incorporating the focus on rules. The sources of rules are various, and are summarised in Figure 3.1. First are those that come from *statute*, rules of the employment relationship that are laid down by government and imposed on all parties to that relationship, whether they be willing or reluctant. The number and importance of rules stemming from this source has certainly increased since 1971. A second source is the *employer*. Although few managers can believe it, most rules about what goes on in the place of work are decided by the employer unilaterally. He decides, for instance, whether the undertaking will manufacturer newspapers or golf balls, and this will have as much impact on employment relationships as any other rules about pay or grievances, because it is so fundamental and influential. The third area of rule-making is *collective bargaining*, where agreements are made between representatives of the employer and others representing the employees. This may be done within a plant employing a few dozen people or it may be done by a confederation of unions bargaining with a federation of employers; the principle remains the same, that each party accepts that it needs the consent of the other for any new rule to become legitimate and therefore operational. With statutory and employer regulation consent helps but is not a pre-requisite. The fourth area has only recently been identified and acknowledged as being important. This is the rules that stem from *custom and practice*.[2] Although not formal and perhaps not even articulated, there are rules of the workplace that are cogent 'because that is the way we do it here'. All participants have certain expectations of what will happen and these provide rules which may be even more inflexible that any from other sources.

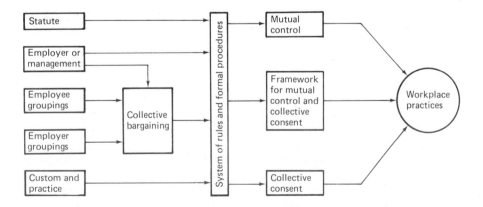

Figure 3.1. Industrial relations as a system of rules and institutionalised relationships

There is a degree of constant movement between these rule sources. Custom and practice rules just grow and tend to emerge as rules without anyone being aware of the development, but there is a tendency for those rules then to be moved into a different area. Some safety rules, for instance, are custom and practice taken over by employer regulation when they are enshrined in a training manual or similar edict. Some collective bargaining is taken up with formalising custom and practice. This is often accompanied by phrases like 'getting it clear', 'tying them down' or 'making them stick'. Although this suggests an attempt to make the rules firmer and more immutable, it can have the effect of making them weaker, as everything in a collective agreement is seen as being negotiable and subject to change some time.

Statutory regulation usually confirms existing practice in some areas and extends it to others, so that much of the employment legislation of recent years has been giving statutory force to practices deriving from employer regulation or collective bargaining in specific industries and making them applicable universally. Also, of course, statutory regulation can suspend other types of rule temporarily. The various effects of incomes policy are the obvious example in which the 'free-wheeling laissez-faire' of voluntary collective bargaining is regularly interrupted by governmental decrees of statutory minima or norms for pay adjustments.

There is also variation in the scope of the different categories of rules in different organisations. British Leyland has more rules derived from collective bargaining than IBM, and the various branches of the armed forces have more statutory regulation than the CEGB.

Our main interest in this chapter is the rules that are produced by collective bargaining, because of our need to provide a setting for the numerous ways in which two sets of representatives — those of management interest and those of employees' interests — confront each other, negotiate, agree and then make their agreement operate as a determinant of future behaviour. The main vehicle for this mutual accommodation is the collective agreement. We have a chapter devoted to this later in the book (Chapter 11), but it is necessary to make the point here that procedures are used as a means of *mutual control* in a situation that all regard as hazardous. Participants are concerned at the trouble that may be caused by the other — unfettered. They are also concerned at the possible dangerous fall-out of their conflictual relationship. Peter Anthony sums up the attitude:

> The procedures of industrial relations are, for the most part, concerned to protect the parties from inflicting an unacceptable degree of damage upon each other in a relationship which is often hostile. The parties thus seek to control each other's behaviour in two ways: by applying power to prevent the other from getting what he wants and by mutually agreeing to limit the extent and the manner in which power can be so applied.[3]

2. Stages in the Development of Industrial Relations Understanding

Although some people like to attribute the beginning of industrial relations to Moses leading a strike of brick-makers (glum fundamentalists, of course, say it all began with Adam's rejection of authority in the Garden of Eden), our most logical and convenient reference point is the development of trade unionism in the aftermath of the Industrial Revolution. This was the time when 'industry' came to mean the large-scale manufacture of goods as well as meaning habitual diligence. The size of employing organisations began to grow, industrial cities mushroomed, there was large-scale migration from the country to the city, expanding population, division of labour, ghastly working conditions and the emergence of the new social class, the *bourgeoisie*. Perhaps of greatest importance, there was a degree of speed of change in people's lives that was unprecedented.

The degree of exploitation of the urban proletariat was so extreme, in such a novel form, that its members attempted collective organisation to resist it. The early trade unions were ineffective and seldom lasted, but by 1880 the British trade union movement had established itself and taken on a form that has not been much altered since. Not only were the methods of industrial action set, so too were the subtle class distinctions between the craft and general unions. It was an essentially British invention and the basic intractability of British trade unions today, as they find it so difficult to adapt policies and practices appropriate to the times, can be seen as a problem of a movement that began when employee representation was being thought up for the first time. At the same time that trade unions were becoming established as part of the social order, the revolutionary philosophy of Karl Marx was being propounded. Asserting that social change results from a class struggle for control of the means of production, Marx predicted the eventual, inevitable victory of the proletariat despite the contemporary subjection of the worker whose labour is bought and sold as a commodity under capitalism, with the economic and human interests of employees being sacrificed. He also argued that the conflict in the social relations of industry was a result of the *inherent* exploitation.

Marxism has not had the same effect on the British labour movement as has been seen in other countries of Europe, where it is common to have some unions that are communist and some that are catholic, but it has had an undoubted influence on thinking about industrial relations, mainly because it provides an explanation of the phenomena and an integrating conceptual framework. Strands of this approach can be seen in many writings, but the principal current advocates are Allen[4] and Hyman.[5]

While Marxists argue that change in industrial relations will only be peripheral and unimportant until the complete social revolution has taken place, a more generally accepted view was proposed by Sidney and Beatrice Webb in the late nineteenth century. They concentrated on the industrial order rather than the more general social order and saw trade unions as organisations to further the interests of their members within the system of industrial government, mainly by influencing the wage–work bargain. Any political action is seen as a means towards the end of reforming the way industry is governed rather than transforming the whole society of which industry is a part. This can be described as the mainstream of industrial relations thinking, which reached its apogee in the 1960s in the work of Flanders,[6] Clegg[7] and the recommendations of the Donovan Commission. Through the first half of the twentieth century trade unions, employers' associations and the various institutions of collective bargaining developed steadily. The General Strike of 1926 was a trauma from which two main lessons were learned. The union movement learned that a general strike would bring no miracles of social change in a British context and those who had so implacably opposed it, particularly in the employer ranks, learned that 'beating' the strike did not cause the trade unions to wither and die, even though they suffered considerable losses in membership, funds and morale.

The next major development came in the middle 1960s, but in 1958 there was a new academic explanation of industrial relations. Dunlop[8] set out his idea of industrial relations as a system with different types of relations at the varying levels of plant, enterprise, industry or nation in any political or economic setting. He attempted to put forward a comprehensive model that would aid subsequent research. Initially the reaction was mainly of interested disagreement, but recent years have seen more detailed and constructive attempts to move forward from his position.[9,10]

By the time Dunlop produced his book, most British managers were resigned to a rather defeatist attitude towards the organisation of employment where trade unions were recognised. Bit by bit more and more was conceded to the unions, who had effected a vice-like grip on production around which nothing could be altered. Restrictive or protective practices were deeply entrenched. This coincided with bad news in the product market. Exports were slipping and the economic growth of other countries was outstripping that of Britain. Productivity bargaining became fashionable as managements sought initiatives with trade unions that had previously seemed impracticable. A Royal Commission on trade unions and employers' associations was set up in order to make proposals for change. The title of the commission itself was interesting, as it was set up to look at the collectives rather than the processes in which they were engaged. The report[11] of the commission reflected a significant change in thinking. The trouble lay not with trade unions, nor with employers, but with the processes for their interactions. Collective bargaining itself needed reform. National agreements were frequently inadequate as a framework for employment relationships in a factory as their formality and precision was shadowed by a series of informal, imprecise arrangements that governed what actually happened on the floor of factories.

It was these informal understandings that needed attention in order to improve the disorder of the workplace. They should be reviewed and a greater degree of formality introduced so that everyone knew more reliably where they stood. No dramatic legislative intervention; no fundamental restructuring in the direction of industrial democracy; and no question of the government taking over. The Royal Commission commented favourably on the productivity agreements that were being concluded, seeing in these deals many of the features which it saw as being necessary at plant level: managers and shop stewards taking responsibility for their own affairs and leaving national agreements as a framework for their affairs, and gradually bringing about the changes in employment and working relationships that were so urgent.

Productivity bargaining received another boost from a new body, the National Board for Prices and Incomes. For the first time there was a statutory prices and incomes policy, which sought to control income growth by statute rather than exhortation and example. One of the agents of this policy was an investigative Prices and Incomes Board. This was soon to become politically unacceptable, but for a few years it produced a series of excellent reports on a variety of investigations into employment matters and advocated the extension of productivity bargaining as a means of achieving economic growth as well as improved industrial relations. Although it was to disappear so soon, it helped to develop the idea of plant-level agreement, which was the productivity bargaining inheritance and brought about that major, and apparently, long-term shift of emphasis towards local agreement on the features of the employment contract.

The proposals of the Royal Commission were not universally accepted. A few weeks before it was published another document was produced called *Fair Deal at Work*.[12] This was a statement of policy by the Conservative party; then in opposition. The proposals were radically different in tenor and were not widely discussed or analysed because the Royal Commission report followed so soon afterwards. The importance of *Fair Deal at Work* was seen in 1970, when a change of government brought in draft legislation based on the earlier policy statement. This became the Industrial Relations Act of 1971, one of the most controversial pieces of legislation in the post-war period. There was a fundamental difference between it and the Royal Commission view, that has been described by McCarthy and Ellis.[13] Instead of seeking the reform of collective bargaining and more effective management, *Fair Deal at Work* and the Industrial Relations Act set out to contain collective bargaining and to control trade unions. The resistance of unions was fierce and the reaction of managements generally apathetic or hostile. Within four years the Act was repealed, but there was again an inheritance. First was the law on unfair dismissal, which was set up for the first time by the Act, received little opposition and has become an established part of the industrial relations scene since re-enactment and development in subsequent legislation. Secondly, certain legislative ideas, like cooling-off periods in industrial action, strike ballots and unfair industrial practices, were discounted and have never returned in the same central way as was then proposed. Thirdly there was a complement to the Act in the Code of Industrial Relations Practice.[14] This produced authoritative guidelines on practice that were widely adopted, and other codes have followed. There were other legacies of the Act[15] that it is not appropriate to discuss here, but one rather intangible effect was a further strengthening of the 'establishment' position of unions. The General Strike of 1926 may have demonstrated that unions would not wither on the vine, but the Industrial Relations Act brought a form of official acceptance that had previously been missing. For a Conservative government to introduce legislation conferring the legal right to belong to a union and various other union rights was a significant step, even if the unions did not want most of the rights they were given.

Law had now arrived in industrial relations in a way that had not previously obtained. Although the Industrial Relations Act was repealed in 1974, it was replaced by the Trade Union and Labour Relations Act, followed by the Employment Protection Act a year later. If we add the ingredient of incomes policy we can see how Rubenstein explains the change:

> ... statutory protection against unfair dismissal and the skill developed by the more sophisticated trade unions in representing their members has provided a further and increasingly important string to the trade union bow. This new role has proved particularly important, at a time when the role of full-time officers has been diminished through successive phases of incomes policy limiting the scope for collective bargaining and through the continued devolution of power to shop stewards and lay officials ... Official British trade union policy is now very much geared to strengthening and extending employment rights for individuals through law.[16]

This period also saw a renewal of interest in the idea of industrial democracy, which had received little encouragement from the Royal Commission. A committee of inquiry produced a report[17] in January 1977, which was followed by a White Paper[18] in 1978. We have a section on participation later in this chapter. At this time there were two other developments that should be mentioned. One was the British membership of the European Economic Community, which began to influence the content of British legislation even if it did not have very much effect on the attitude of British industrial relations participants. It was another nudge away from the set and unimaginative acceptance of the voluntarist *status quo* that had existed for so long. The second development was in the academic field. It has already been suggested that mainstream thinking was that centred round the reformist ideas of Flanders and Clegg, stemming from the industrial government focus of the Webbs. A member of this school of thought was Alan Fox, who appeared to depart from it in 1974 when he published a book[19] in which he argued that much more radical change was needed than reformism had visualised: a fundamental shift in the power relations between managers and managed so as to generate a greater degree of trust between the two interest groups.

At the end of the 1970s came the great turning of the tide, for which the 1971 Industrial Relations Act seemed to be a rehearsal. The decline of British productivity and competitiveness in world markets coincided with a trade recession in most western countries; inflation and unemployment were rising. The winter of 1978–79 saw a series of industrial action episodes that caused widespread concern, symbolised by isolated incidents of patients being moved from their hospitals and one case of gravediggers refusing to bury the dead. The period became known as 'the winter of discontent' and, although trade union membership was still increasing, anxiety grew about the role of trade unions in the social structure.

The 1979 General Election brought into office a government with a declared intention of curbing trade union power, and that curb has followed. This has been partly due to new legislation, partly due to other government action, partly due to greater managerial resolution in saying 'no', and partly due to increasing unemployment, which has reduced trade union membership levels and bargaining strength.

George Ward at Grunwick Film Processing Laboratories (see pp. 153–54) had already displayed remarkable resolution in resisting massed pickets, secondary action, ACAS and Lord Scarman to assert his right to run his film processing business the way that he wanted. Other employers followed this example, with the most notable case being the determination with which B.L. imposed below-average pay rises and dismissed the chairman of the shop stewards combine committee.

It is too early to judge the permanence of this changed situation, but it will be a very long time before a situation of full employment is reached again and complaints about the 1980 and 1982 legislative moves have brought forth very little response, especially when one remembers the national campaigns that were mounted against the 1971 Act.

3. A Management Perspective on Industrial Relations

Governments may intervene in, or abstain from, industrial relations affairs, but those directly concerned cannot make a choice. They have to be involved. In a book about management it is worth looking at the position of one such group inescapably on the industrial relations stage: managers. What exactly is their interest in industrial relations affairs and what is their perspective on the matter? In some ways this is as obvious and as obscure as trying to define industrial relations itself.

One of the difficulties lies in the variety of models of management that are used. Thurley summarises them thus:[20]

a.   Management as profit maximisers;
b.   Management as committed to maintaining organisational power;
c.   Management as an agent of capital concerned with the extension of control over production systems;
d.   Management as a source of specialist know-how;

e. Management as an executive function; and
f. Management as a coalition of interests.

As management is so many different things to different people, it is difficult to attribute to it any particular perspective on industrial relations. Another variation is in the type of manager. We have so many convenient general categorisations of managers that throw sand in the eyes of the observer trying to perceive the standard: line and staff; junior, middle, senior and top; public sector/private sector; autocratic/participative; general/specialist; production/non-production; and so the list continues. There are, nonetheless, some outlines that we can discern.

Anthony uses a phrase of Fogarty's to make a fundamental point, often overlooked:

> . . . an important complication over industrial relations objectives as opposed to management objectives are that the latter are in some sense primary objectives while the former are secondary. 'The business of business,' as Dr Michael P. Fogarty once vividly reminded the IPM, 'is business.' The business of the industrial relations specialist is to see to it that business can get done.[21]

Perhaps one could add the phrase 'but not at all costs' to that statement. No organisation can escape from the society of which it is a part, even though the need for 'good' industrial relations in the National Health Service is as a means to the end of providing health care, and the overriding objective of managers with industrial relations responsibilities in British Petroleum is to enable that company to trade profitably.

Because of the primacy of business it is often grandly asserted that industrial relations policies should be developed from – and should influence but not determine – the corporate plan or whatever else it is that governs the overall direction of the organisation. However frequently this is stated, actual inquiry suggests that it rarely happens and that industrial relations objectives of specialist personnel managers may be conceived independently and according to rather different criteria than those used by the corporate strategists.

The objectives of managers are likely to vary according to the type of employee grouping with which the manager is mainly concerned. The main difference is between those managers with responsibility for shop-floor workers, and those in charge of staff or white-collar groups. Batstone and his colleagues found that shop-floor managers were operating in a situation of frequent crisis and constant uncertainty while staff managers were in a situation of bureaucratic calm.

> . . . managers concerned with staff were concerned above all with their own role in industrial relations. They felt that they lacked the freedom, because of company rules and policies, to overcome their problems of labour turnover and inefficiency. Such concerns were far less important in relation to shop-floor workers. Above all shop-floor managers were concerned with what they believed to be a common failure on the part of stewards to control their members, leading to frequent disputes and an ineffective piecework system.[22]

Although this extract is from a book reporting an investigation in one particular organisation it neatly illustrates the way in which managerial objectives differ between groups of employees with strong union affiliation and organisation and those with primarily a management orientation, even though they may be dedicated union members. This has much to do with the method of payment, and is discussed in Chapter 22 at the begining of the section of this book on 'The Contract for Payment'.

More generally much debate has taken place about management prerogative, defined by the Royal Commission as follows:

> ... this holds that matters not settled by collective agreements should be decided by managers, although they can if they wish consult with their employees or representatives of their employees, before taking their decision.[23]

A more folkloristic version of this is 'the manager must be free to manage', as was reported above by Batstone about managers concerned with staff. The perception customarily is that the manager decides what people should do and then tells them to get on with it. If employees seek to constrain that exercise of decision-making and implementation, then managerial prerogative is under attack. It is relatively easy for such a manager to accept collective agreements, because they put his employees under authority, even if it is not his own. What is more difficult is for him to understand and value his role if the self-exercised or at least known authority is missing from the employment relationship. This is usually regarded as making the working situation unpredictable, unreliable and unproductive. Some cynical observers would say that it merely reduces the degree of the manager's personal satisfaction in exercising power over others, and that the managed will exercise their own self-discipline and the necessary amount of co-ordination to be equally or more productive than in a situation of imposed authority. Evidence can be produced to support both points of view, although the first is almost certainly more widely accepted among working people, managerial or otherwise.

There has been one modification in the traditional managerial view of prerogative, and that is the acceptance by many of a *pluralist* rather than *unitary* frame of reference. The best-known exposition of this is in a Royal Commission research paper by Fox.[24] Briefly the unitary frame of reference is that adopted by a manager who sees the organisation as having a single focus of power and loyalty, so that all members of the organisation look for guidance from those more senior to them on all matters. The team analogy is used to argue that any contrary or questioning view is to be deplored because of its adverse effect on efficiency and harmony. The pluralist frame of reference is that of the manager who regards unitarism as unrealistic, although not necessarily undersirable, and sees the managerial position as slightly different:

> While in the long term shareholders, employees and customers all stand to benefit if a concern flourishes, the immediate interests of these groups often conflict. Directors and managers have to balance these conflicting interests . . .[25]

Because power does not effectively exist totally in managerial hands the means to control lies in making the best deals between the different interests:

> The . . . response to the frustration of management's drive to control is to seek a working accommodation which recognises that there are other institutions in command of sufficient resources and power to make management's wish to exercise absolute control unreal and unlikely to succeed, and which recognises that these other institutions are both permanent and proper. This means collective bargaining which is, in one sense, the area in which management's control processes meet forces which management is incapable of controlling.[26]

This has become the position of most enlightened managers, but it has come under sceptical analysis in recent years because of the attitude that it does not permit of any radical change in the power balance, and only such a radical change will enable improvement. An interesting defence of pluralism was provided by Clegg in 1975.[27]

There is no single management perspective on industrial relations. There are variations according to the different types of responsibility managers exercise, the nature of their business objectives and their management philosophy. We can, however, generalise to the extent of saying that virtually all managers are seeking a greater degree of control than they actually have over the area of operations, and will regard with suspicion movements through which subordinates gain a greater degree of control over the same area; as well as feeling unreasonably constrained by the growing 'intervention' of legislation and government.

4. Power in Industrial Relations

Just as there seems to be widespread acceptance of the notion that management must manage, there also seems to be a widespread belief that the balance of power had shifted in industrial relations from managers to trade union officials, so that a recent movement of the power balance in favour of managers is to be welcomed. This has given great satisfaction to those who see themselves as opposed to unions, like the self-employed and proprietors of small businesses, and has reduced the expectations among trade union members. It is also important to point out that some people analyse the distribution of wealth in society and say that trade union power has been illusory.

There are a few detailed features of change in the balance of power that we need to look at. First there is the effect of *technology,* tending to reduce the labour intensiveness of manufacturing. This strengthens the hands of employee groups in one way, as power to disrupt operations through industrial action can lie in the hands of a very small number of men, like railway signalmen. On the other hand technological innovation typically has the effect of reducing the number of employees required and makes the employer less dependent on both employee compliance and employee ability.

Another power shift is from *national to local* level. The lessening dependency on national agreements, the steady democratisation of trade unions and the effect on managements of legislative requirements have shifted power in unions and in companies away from national level towards the local level. In trade unions this means that shop stewards are exercising greater power while national officers are exercising less than they were. Also managerial authority is tending to devolve towards the place of work, making local managers less dependent on head-office decree, and certainly less dependent on the employers' association. This type of shift usually satisfies the performers on the local stage, but it is not easy to see whether this is more to the advantage of one party or the other. Trade unions originally developed national-scale bargaining on the basis that it gave greater strength to the weak, and there was bitter resistance through 1977 within the National Union of Mineworkers to the introduction of *local* productivity schemes 'setting pit against pit; man against man'. Currently shop stewards generally favour local determination not only to get control in their own hands, but also to develop local variations and therefore more points of comparison on which to base claims for improvements in terms and conditions. Such a strategy, however, depends on having stewards who are both able and well informed. Many managers believe that the shift towards local-level agreement helps them more than their shop steward counterparts. A study by the Commission on Industrial Relations (CIR) of the advantages and disadvantages of centralised and decentralised negotiating arrangements in multi-plant companies did not say that one was to be preferred to the other, but provides a useful check-list of pros and cons.[28]

A third change of power has been partly in unions and rather more in managements, and that is a shift from the *generalist to the specialist*. There has come a greater willingness in board rooms to see responsibility for industrial relations as a specialised job, requiring understanding of agreements, statutes and ability to negotiate. This has tended to improve the lot of the personnel manager in terms of status within the management hierarchy, and has made most other managers defer to his guidance on an increasing range of employment matters. It is too early to say whether it has also had the effect of isolating industrial relations responsibility as other managers wash their hands of it instead of sharing it.

5. Participation and Industrial Democracy

One of the main sections of this book is entitled 'The Contract for Collective *Consent*', not collective *control*. Although that very shrewd and practical personnel manager Richard Stokes was speaking in 1975 of the *controlling* worker and the *consulting* manager we believe that employee control is still far distant, although the need for employee consent is clearly here. The former union leader Hugh Scanlon frequently spoke of the fundamental constraint on trade unions as being the employer simply saying no. Although that still exists, the constraint on managements by the employees simply saying no is increasing, and we believe it has reached the point where most managerial action has to receive the explicit or implicit consent of the employees before it becomes viable.

There has, however, been an extremely lively debate on industrial democracy and various forms of participation.

The most controversial is generally known as *industrial democracy*. This can take various forms, but essentially it is a form in which the participation of employees is developed via representative democracy at the board-room level to influence, or to make, the major strategic decisions of the organisation. Two long-running British success stories of this type are the John Lewis Partnership with 23,000 employees (or partners) and the Scott Bader Commonwealth with 450. In each of these the employees not only share all the profits; their representatives also have a controlling interest in the board room.

Minority representation rather than control has run for some years in the British Steel Corporation and was introduced in the Post Office Corporation.

The main focus of the debate has been the Committee of Inquiry on Industrial Democracy referred to earlier in this chapter. Their majority proposal was that boards of companies should be reconstituted to give equal representation to shareholder and employee representatives, with a smaller number of independents holding the balance. It is worth quoting at some length their opinion on the effect this would have on the efficient management of companies:

> At the other end of the spectrum is the view that employee representation on boards would not only improve efficiency but was indeed essential to developing new forms of co-operation between labour and capital and a new legitimacy for

the exercise of the management function, which are needed if Britain is to overcome its current industrial and economic difficulties . . . . The real benefits, it is argued, will come from the opportunity provided for employee representatives to be involved from the start in the formulation of policy. They will be able to express their concerns before a decision is taken, to point out the implications of a proposal for the interests of employees, to question management on what they are proposing and to suggest alternatives. This will lead to increased commitment to the company on the part of the workforce.[29]

The proposals were met with varying degrees of horror in management circles and less than rapture among trade unions. The eventual government reaction to the ideas was contained in a White Paper[30] over twelve months later which declared that there would not be a standard form of participation, like that proposed by the Committee of Inquiry, imposed by law. Increased participation would result mainly from exhortation, although companies employing 5,000 people or more would be legally obliged to discuss with employees all major proposals affecting the workforce and those employing 2,000 or more would be required to concede a legal right to employee representation a few years later.

The 1979 change of government led to these proposals being shelved, but interest continues among both managers and trade unionists. Dowling *et al* surveyed the attitudes of executives in 25 large private companies and the regional officers of 14 trade unions. Both groups were opposed to worker directors and were relieved that the likelihood of such legislation had receded.

Managers tended to favour forms of 'participation' which emphasised communication and consultation, whereas the trade union officials favoured extensions to the range of issues subject to collective bargaining or joint regulation.[31]

The managerial interest is usually in some form of sharing control in order to regain control and they are clearly committed to the idea that managers are the people to make decisions, although employees may be consulted and have things explained to them in order to obtain their commitment to management objectives. Difficult trading conditions have also increased managerial willingness to disclose information about company affairs. An amendment to the 1982 Employment Act, introduced by the House of Lords, is a requirement for companies with more than 200 employees to include in their annual report a statement of action taken to introduce or develop arrangements for employee participation.

Another view of participation is that it should develop first at *the place of work* itself, with autonomous working groups taking over their own supervision, and with managers giving much more attention to the design of jobs and finding ways in which each individual employee can participate more in the day-by-day decisions that affect his work. The argument supporting this is that board-level decisions are of little interest or immediacy to employees and that their participation will be apathetic or incompetent, while they really care about what they themselves do from day to day.

A third method is one that has been in operation for many years, *joint consultation*. This has been criticised as an avoidance of true participation, as it reserves all authority to decide to the management, who ask for employee comment if they want to. The recent debate has caused some fresh interest in it.[32]

An interesting treatment of industrial democracy in its thoroughgoing sense is to be found in a work by Coates and Topham.[33] It is also appropriate to look at the draft fifth directive of the EEC.[34] Readers who wish to get a broader picture of the historical aspects of industrial relations, and of trade unions in particular, will find helpful material in Halsey[35] and Pelling.[36] Hutt[37] looks at the development of British trade unionism from a fairly extreme position, so that a comparison between his interpretation and that of some of the more orthodox commentators often produces unexpected insights. The best historical treatment is the classic of G.D.H. Cole,[38] but it has the obvious drawback of covering only the period up to 1950. A very stimulating and original treatment of the post-war period is in Hawkins.[39] Any of these works help to get the essential historical perspective on the complex of activities that is contemporary industrial relations, which can only be understood in terms of the past.

REFERENCES

1. Flanders A., *Industrial Relations: What is Wrong With the System?* (Faber & Faber) 1965, p. 10.
2. Best stated by Brown W., 'A Consideration of Custom and Practice' in *British Journal of Industrial Relations,* March 1972.
3. Anthony P.D., *The Conduct of Industrial Relations* (IPM) 1977, pp. 9–10.
4. Allen V.L., *Power and Trades Unions* (Longmans) 1956.
5. Hyman R., *Industrial Relations: A Marxist Introduction* (Macmillan) 1975.
6. Flanders A., *op. cit.,* as well as *The Fawley Productivity Agreements* (Faber) 1964.
7. Clegg H.A., *The System of Industrial Relations in Great Britain* (Blackwell) 1972.
8. Dunlop J.T., *Industrial Relations Systems* (Henry Holt) 1958.
9. Wood S.J. *et al.,* 'The Industrial Relations System Concept as a Basis for Theory in Industrial Relations' in *British Journal of Industrial Relations,* November 1975, pp. 291–309.
10. Walker K.F., 'Towards Useful Theorising About Industrial Relations' in *British Journal of Industrial Relations,* November 1977, pp. 307–316.
11. Royal Commission on Trade Unions and Employers' Associations, *Report* (HMSO) 1968.
12. *Fair Deal at Work* (Conservative Political Centre) 1968.
13. McCarthy W.E.J. and Ellis N.D., *Management by Agreement* (Hutchinson) 1973.
14. *Code of Industrial Relations Practice* (HMSO) 1972.
15. One of the best discussions is in Weekes B., *Industrial Relations and the Limits of Law* (Blackwell) 1975.
16. Rubenstein M., 'Dismissals and the Law' in Torrington D. (ed.), *Comparative Industrial Relations in Europe* (Associated Business Programmes) 1978.
17. Department of Trade, *Report of the Committee of Inquiry on Industrial Democracy* (HMSO) 1977.
18. *Industrial Democracy* (HMSO) 1978.
19. Fox A., *Beyond Contract: Work, Power and Trust Relations* (Faber & Faber) 1974.
20. Thurley K., *The Treatment of Management in Industrial Relations Studies: A New Start?* unpublished paper read to an SSRC Seminar Group on Management Attitudes and Behaviour in Industrial Relations, December 1975.
21. Anthony P.D., *op. cit.* p. 26.
22. Batstone E., Boraston I. and Frenkel S., *Shop Stewards in Action* (Basil Blackwell) 1977, p. 161.
23. Royal Commission on Trade Unions and Employers' Associations, *op. cit.,* p. 93.
24. Fox A., *Industrial Sociology and Industrial Relations,* Research Paper No. 3 (HMSO) 1966.
25. Royal Commission on Trade Unions and Employers' Associations, *op. cit.,* p. 18.
26. Anthony P.D., *op. cit.,* pp. 33–34.
27. Clegg H.A., 'Pluralism in Industrial Relations' in *British Journal of Industrial Relations,* November 1975, pp. 309–316.

28. Commission on Industrial Relations, *Industrial Relations on Multi-Plant Undertakings,* Report No. 85 (HMSO) 1974, pp. 55–58.
29. *Report of the Committee of Inquiry on Industrial Democracy, op. cit.,* p. 49.
30. *Industrial Democracy,* Cmnd 7231 (HMSO) May 1978.
31. Dowling M., Goodman J., Gotting D. and Hyman J., 'Employee Participation: Survey Evidence from the North West' in *Employment Gazette,* April 1981, pp. 185–192.
32. Cuthbert N.H. and Whitaker A., 'The Rehabilitation of Joint Consultation: A Recent Trend in the Participation Debate' in *Personnel Review,* Spring 1977, p. 31–36.
33. Coates K. and Topham T., *The New Unionism* (Penguin) 1974.
34. *Employee Participation and Company Structure,* Bulletin of the European Communities, Supplement 8/75.
35. Halsey A.H., *Trends in British Society since 1900* (Macmillan) 1972. Chapters 3, 4 and 5 especially.
36. Pelling H., *A History of British Trade Unionism,* 3rd ed. (Penguin) 1976.
37. Hutt A., *British Trade Unionism* (Lawrence & Wishart) 1975.
38. Cole G.D.H., *An Introduction to Trade Unionism* (George Allen & Unwin) 1955.
39. Hawkins K., *British Industrial Relations 1945–1975* (Barrie & Jenkins) 1976.

4

Labour Law

Although the knowledge areas of industrial relations and organisational behaviour undoubtedly dominate ideas and practice in the field of employment, labour law is another area requiring some general understanding and perspective. This chapter provides an introduction to the subject, which is developed in a number of chapters. Specialists wanting to investigate this area more deeply are referred to the books mentioned at the end of this chapter.

In seeking first of all to understand what law is we come to some of the most fundamental questions that men ask about their condition. Is it command or obligation? Is it control of the majority by a minority elite for the benefit of the majority or for the benefit of the elite minority? What is the difference between legal rules and moral precepts? We look at two definitions, first that found in a 1919 decree of the Commissariat of Justice of the USSR:

> ... a system (set of rules) for social relationships, which corresponds to the interests of the dominant class and is safeguarded by the organised force of that class.[1]

This, of course, was based on the clear Marxist doctrine that law always represents the interests of the strongest party. It also has the intellectual shortcoming that when the classless society comes, then law logically disappears. Although this definition may be too stark for most of us to accept these days, the intrinsic idea of control for the benefit of a sectional interest is an important one for us to understand in considering some of the legal developments in the United Kingdom during the last century.

Lawyers are usually quick to point out that their laws are different from the *immutable* laws of, say, physics and chemistry in that they are man-made and changeable. They also differ from rules of morality in that they can be enforced. So we find 'lawyers' law' defined as:

> ... a body of rules for the guidance of human conduct which are imposed upon, and enforced among the members of a given State.[2]

'Imposed' and 'enforced' are strong words and it is this feature of law that has for a long time limited its intervention in employment affairs, except as a way of maintaining minimum standards. The law that we have is much more pervasive in its effect on the *individual* contract of employment than it is in its effects on the *collective* relationships between employer and employees. This is the famous 'voluntarist' tradition of British industrial relations, which is so baffling to those of almost every other nationality. There has been minimal regulation of the collective relationship in employment matters, either because that is the most sensible way of conducting industrial affairs, or because the law has attempted to intervene but has failed. Either point of view can be sustained and each has its adherents. By 1975 it was possible to discern a change in this tradition, and the future may be very different from the past, but the voluntarist doctrine remains attractive to most actors on the industrial relations stage and is the basis of most agreements, procedures and practice.

1. Early Developments

Lewis has shown that a key element in the development of labour law has been the tension between two sources of the State's legislative authority: parliament and the courts.[3] In the middle of the nineteenth century judges were in the main strongly and overtly opposed to trade unionism and used two common-law traditions to combat it: conspiracy and restraint of trade. The most famous incident was the sentencing of the Tolpuddle Martyrs to seven years' transportation, despite widespread popular sympathy for their cause and the apparent innocuousness of their offence. The judgement made it clear that they were not only being sentenced for what they had done (to try to form a trade union) but as an example to the rest of the working class of the country. As the years passed pressure on parliament grew to ease the legal attack on trade unions. There was a Royal Commission and then the Trade Union Act of 1871 which provided unions with certain basic protections, strengthening their position *vis-à-vis* the courts. However, the Act did not go the stage further and give unions corporate status, with the capacity to sue and be sued, to own property and to make legally binding contracts. Presumably the infant labour movement would not have welcomed this constraint, and opponents of unionism would have resented the degree of respectability that such further enactment would have conveyed. Whatever the reasons it is this indeterminate legal status that was one of the stumbling blocks over which the Industrial Relations Act of 1971 tripped. Soon after the 1871 Act trade unions were again harried by the courts:

> The new legal threat was based on civil liability for torts (civil wrongs) created by the judges rather than by Parliament. Tortious liability for 'simple' conspiracy replaced criminal liability as judges again condemned trade union objectives as unlawful. This was a fine illustration of judicial bias as employers' trade objectives were regarded by judges as legitimate and perfectly lawful.[4]

The culmination was the *Taff Vale* judgement of 1901 which awarded damages and costs against a trade union of over £40,000 and established that unions could be liable for damages in tort. There was strong reaction to this, which was regarded as a convincing demonstration of the bias of the courts, and again it was parliament that intervened after the election of 1906. A Unionist majority in the Commons of 134 was turned into a Liberal majority of 356. The new government passed the Trade Dispute Act of 1906, which was to be the centrepiece of law relating to trade unions until the 1970s:

> The Act gave trade unions a blanket immunity by prohibiting legal actions in

tort against them, and, for persons acting 'in contemplation or furtherance of a trade dispute', it gave immunities from liability for the torts of simple conspiracy, inducing breach of employment contract and interference, as well as providing them with more legal protection for peaceful picketing. Anomalous privileges and statutory immunities from judge-made liabilities thus became the distinguishing characteristic of the law of industrial conflict in Britain.[5]

Although the 1906 Act was viewed with concern in employer circles, this alarm gradually moderated until most employers were as keen supporters of voluntarism as any trade unionist. Partly this was because employers found that they had little to fear. The preoccupations of the Great War, the post-war economic difficulties in a country fit for heroes to live in and the great debacle of the 1926 General Strike produced a situation in which the balance of power between employer and employees remained tipped strongly in the employer's favour. Trade unions were weakened and the union movement began to adopt more 'reasonable' policies that would enable the development of efficient industries rather than dramatic change of ownership of industry. Trade union members learned to cherish their legal freedoms and employers learned to value a legal framework (or lack of legal framework) that produced a situation in which industry could prosper. Voluntarism became the sacred cow of British industrial relations.

But gradually the position of trade unions became stronger so that the balance of power did begin to tip during the full-employment years of the 1950s and 1960s. The notion of trade unions having 'too much power' became commonplace, as did the complementary notion that small groups of 'politically motivated men' behind the scenes were manipulating the decent, honest, law-abiding and compliant working man into doing terrible things. In comparison with the earlier crucial periods of the late nineteenth and early twentieth centuries, there were now additional tribunals before which trade unionists could be arraigned — newspapers and television, which devoted considerable space to cataloguing the shortcomings of trade unions and their pressure groups. Less conspicuously there was the creation of a new tort by the law lords in the case of *Rookes v. Barnard:* intimidation by threats to break employment contracts. Parliament reacted in the usual way by passing the 1965 Trade Dispute Act to provide protection, but there were other liabilities connected with inducing the breach of *commercial* contracts that began to attract penalties. A skillful analysis of developments in this period is to be found in Wedderburn.[6] The even tenor of the previous half century was being threatened. A Royal Commission was established in 1965, which reported in 1968. The Conservative opposition produced two policy documents, *A Giant's Strength* and *Fair Deal at Work*, while the Labour government introduced legislation based on their own policy document *In Place of Strife*. The most significant chapter in labour law for seventy years was about to begin.

2. The Industrial Relations Act, 1971

In retrospect the Industrial Relations Act of 1971 is perhaps of more interest to the political analyst than to the industrial relations practitioner, who no longer has to concern himself with provisions that have been repealed. We cannot, however, understand the place of law in industrial relations today without understanding what the Industrial Relations Act tried to do and guessing at the reasons for its failure, which was so abject. In the light of the discussion in the last few paragraphs we can see how draconian the measure was, when we realise that it set out to replace the voluntarism of a century with a novel legal framework that would introduce by statute the type of trade union responsibility that parliament had previously restrained the courts from imposing. It also made the legal process, rather than voluntary collective bargaining, the focus of industrial relations, and there was a strong focus on the individual:

> At a time when union power had become controversial, the Act's promotion of individual liberty challenged the dominance of collective as opposed to individual values . . .[7]

The main indicator of the Act's failure was that it was not used. It put great power at the disposal of government and of employers, but they almost completely ignored it. For that matter it put great power at the disposal of trade union general secretaries and they even more resolutely ignored it. The issues that did come before the National Industrial Relations Court were mainly so foolish or basically unjust that the authority of the law was imperilled. After less than three years the Act was repealed.

The reasons for the failure were, first, that it tried to contrive centralised authority and responsibility for trade unions in a highly developed situation of exactly the opposite, and a tradition in which collective agreements were binding in honour but not in law. Secondly the Act depended on the active participation of employers, but did not get it.

> . . . the Act failed because it misjudged the mood of management. There is no getting away from this: had management wanted the Act to work and fought for it, it would have stood a good chance of success. But the truth is that management was almost as unenamoured with a legal structure for industrial relations as their union counterparts.[8]

Thirdly the Act failed because of trade union resistance to employee dependence on law. Trade unionists had become not only wary of the dubious impartiality of the courts, they had seen the absence of law as one of their strengths. If the employee depended on the union for his rights, he would support the union; if those rights were ensured by the law and not the union, would the union still have his support? This argument was to become more interesting shortly after the repeal of the Act, but is also a crucial reason for its failure.

The Industrial Relations Act had two elements that were relatively uncontroversial and which survived repeal. The first was a Code of Industrial Relations Practice,[9] that set out ideas for industrial practitioners to use and shape to their own circumstances on the various aspects of personnel policy and practice for which legally enforceable standards had not been set. The second was legal protection against unfair dismissal. This was carried over and developed in the repealing legislation. Everything else went, including the government that had introduced it. Industrial relations returned to the positions of 1875 and 1906.

Almost at once, however, there were new legislative moves; this time to strengthen the trade union and individual employee position *vis-à-vis* the employer. The Industrial Relations Act had had such a profound effect that it introduced a change rather different from that which was envisaged. The single most significant obstacle had been trade union resistance to more law in the work place. Within months ardent trade unionists were welcoming legislation that previously they would have seen as jeopardising employee dependence on the union.

3. The Aftermath of the 1971 Act

The Trade Union and Labour Relations Act of 1974 and the Employment Protection Act of 1975 removed virtually all the machinery that the 1971 Act had set up: only protection against unfair dismissal and the Code of Practice remained. New measures took the place of the old. Instead of controls on trade union activity there was an extension of individual rights and measures to encourage employers to recognise unions, using a new agency, the Advisory, Conciliation and Arbitration Service, and a new legal body, the Central Arbitration Committee. These measures were part of a new initiative by government to work with the trade unions; in exchange for legislation that would strengthen the hand of union negotiators the Trade Union Congress entered into a Social Contract with the government, undertaking to moderate pay claims to help the fight against inflation.

With these two Acts we could see some swing of the pendulum and some consolidation of change. The first attempt to constrain trade union power had been withdrawn and been replaced with a statute that reinstated the closed shop and made trade union recognition by employers more likely. This had the effect of encouraging the further increase in membership of trade unions. In 1971 49% of all employees were trade union members. This figure reached 52% in 1976 and a peak of 55% in 1979 before unemployment began to take its toll and union membership fell.[10]

The consolidation was in the realm of employee rights. The provisions regarding unfair dismissal were strengthened and new rights were established relating to maternity, guarantee payments, time off work for specified reasons and itemised pay statements. Some modification was to come in 1980, but the pattern seemed to be established of the individual employee being able to look to the law for much greater protection than hitherto. As we shall see shortly, this was contemporaneous with other statutes dealing with individual rights in employment, seeking to protect people against various forms of discrimination.

It is also worth pointing out that two significant pieces of legislation did not reach the statute book. There was no bill in Parliament to introduce industrial democracy, despite the moves we saw in the last chapter, and there was no decisive move in the European Parliament to introduce the draft fifth directive, which was to find a common form of employee participation for European companies.

4. Current Employment Law

If we turn to consider the law we now have, we can group the main statutes under four headings: employment, anti-discrimination, payment and working conditions. We review first the law relating to employment, which is where our review so far has mainly concentrated.

The Contracts of Employment Act of 1963 is the earliest statute to consider in this section, and was introduced to strengthen the position of the individual employee in the employment relationship. The main provisions were to require the employer to provide a written statement of the contractual terms and to specify minimum terms of notice. It was followed by the Contract of Employment Act 1972 and further modifications in 1974 and 1975.

The other end of the employment bargain was covered by the Redundancy Payments Act 1965, which gave employees rights to compensation for loss of employment caused by redundancy but not other causes. The financial compensation is paid by the employer but a proportion of the payment can be recovered from a central redundancy fund. In 1975 further legislation required employers to consult with employee representatives when groups of employees were to be made redundant.

In 1980 came the Employment Act, which repealed sections of 1970s legislation, mainly the legal machinery enabling unions to apply for official investigation of an employer's refusal to recognise or to seek arbitration to secure recognised terms and conditions for groups of their members. The unfair dismissal and maternity provisions were slightly modified to give employers fewer restrictions. The main new features were to establish the right of employees not to be unreasonably expelled from or refused admission to a trade union where a closed shop operates, and limitations (including a code of practice) on picketing. There was also a return to a form of the 1971 procedures for secret ballots, but this time in the relatively innocuous form of providing public money to unions to finance such ballots. A survey of the effects of this provision during the first year suggested that it had had little effect:

> The scheme had failed on important counts. It had been boycotted by the big unions and had been of little help to the small staff associations which had tried to use it.[11]

The 1982 Employment Act further restricted trade union immunities and increased the compensation payable to an employee dismissed unfairly because of non-membership of a union.

ACAS is independent of government and is governed by a council with an equal membership of employer and union representatives, plus three independents. One particular responsibility of ACAS is the development of codes of practice, the idea introduced in conjunction with the 1971 Act. Gradually new codes are being prepared on specific issues, like discipline procedures and time-off work for union and other duties. The *Central Arbitration Committee* is a body with legal powers to determine certain issues. The *Employment Appeal Tribunal* takes appeals from industrial tribunals, that were set up much earlier to deal with problems about redundancy payments, and expanded their scope considerably when it began to hear all the unfair dismissal claims that were not resolved by conciliation.

5. Current Anti-Discrimination Law

There is not quite the same tradition of law in the field of discrimination in employment as there is in the field of employment, but the main statutes are again recent. Each is dealt with elsewhere in this book. The Equal Pay Act 1970 seeks to reduce pay inequities between the sexes, and the Sex Discrimination Act 1975 seeks to eliminate certain aspects of discrimination between the sexes in employment opportunities. These two Acts have their own institution which was set up to administer them — the *Equal Opportunities Commission:*

> The Commission is empowered to give advice and even to intervene on the complainant's behalf if it is not reasonable to expect the individual to take action alone . . . The Commission can initiate inquiries without previous complaints and can compel attendance of witnesses. On finding discrimination it may after one month's warning issue a 'non-discrimination' notice requiring the employer or other party to stop the practice and to inform the Commission and others affected that it has done so and of his new arrangements.[12]

The Race Relations Act 1976 follows earlier legislation in 1965 and 1968 and is designed to protect people against discrimination on the grounds of race, colour, ethnic or national origin. The *Commission for Racial Equality* was set up under the Act and replaces the earlier Race Relations Board. It has similar powers to the Equal Opportunities Commission. At the time of writing we do not have legislation about discrimination against people on the grounds of age. The 'grey power' movement is active in the United States, so this may develop in Europe also.

6. Current Law on Payment

Legislation on payment is quite extensive and long-standing. The first Truck Act was in 1831, and Wages Councils have operated for most of the twentieth century. The main features are covered in the chapter on payment and the law (Chapter 26), but we should note here that the pay of large numbers of employees is determined directly by parliament, e.g. the armed services, and that almost any pay debate has a major element that is controlled by government; that is, the effect of economic policy and strategy, particularly the level of taxation and the level of supplementary benefit. In 1978 a man with two children aged 12 and 14, paying rent and rates of £7 weekly and earning £72.50 a week while working would have a net income of £3195 if he worked continuously and net income of £3027 if he worked for only six in every twelve months.[13]

7. Current Law on Employment Conditions

Another long tradition is in law relating to the physical conditions of work. The pillars here have been the Factories Acts, the first of which was passed in 1833, the most recent in 1961. These determine minimum conditions on many aspects of the workplace, but only in factories. A variety of other premises are covered by the Offices, Shops and Railway Premises Act of 1963. Most recent major legislation in this field has been the Health and Safety at Work Act 1974, with its overseeing institutions, the Health and Safety Executive and the Health and Safety Commission.

8. A Note on Managers and the Law

In this chapter we have looked at union attitudes about law in industrial affairs. What about managerial attitudes? In the era of the Industrial Relations Act managers did not generally seek to use the powers that the Act offered them. This may have been because of the reluctance to get ensnared in legalities, or it may have been due to a reluctance to pick up the hot potato of that particular law. In the time since then, it has become almost normal managerial behaviour to grumble about legal developments, partly because of the headaches which they bring for aspects of managerial practice and partly because of the feeling that managerial hands are tied unreasonably by the new legal constraints upon their freedom of action. In this situation the personnel management specialist has been something of a winner:

> . . . government intervention has not only placed direct constraints on manage-ment's freedom to manage the employment relationship (generally in negotiation with its employees) as it thinks fit, but indirectly it has increased the cost of labour, and consequently the necessity for its efficient utilisation. Theoretically, this process is likely to increase the focus on human resources in that there will be the need for more 'management' of them.[14]

It is perhaps important that those in managerial positions see the opportunities as well as the constraints that growing legislation offers. The effect of the widening floor of rights for the employee certainly reduces the scope for the management of companies to do what they *like*, but enables them better to do what they *can*, because many of the features of the employment relationship become so much clearer.

REFERENCES

1. Quoted by Goodhart A.L. in Pryce-Jones A., *The New Outline of Modern Knowledge* (Gollancz) 1956, p. 581.
2. James P.S., *Introduction to English Law* (Butterworth) 1950, p. 5.
3. Lewis R., 'The Historical Development of Labour Law' in *British Journal of Industrial Relations*, March 1976, pp. 1–17.
4. Lewis R., *op. cit.*, p. 4.
5. Lewis R., *op. cit.*, p. 4.
6. Wedderburn K.W., *The Worker and the Law*, 2nd ed. (Penguin Books) 1971, pp. 361–385.
7. Lewis R., *op. cit.*, p. 12.
8. Rubenstein M., 'Labour Law: Lessons from the Past and Predictions for the Future', article in *Personnel Management*, October 1974.
9. Department of Employment, *Industrial Relations Code of Practice* (HMSO) 1972.
10. Central Statistical Office, *Social Trends 12*, 1982 (HMSO) 1981.
11. Gennard J., 'Chronicle' in *British Journal of Industrial Relations*, March 1982, vol. XX, no. 1, p. 114.
12. Whinchup M., *Modern Employment Law* (Heinemann) 1976, p. 31.
13. Kay J., 'Tax Policy in an Inegalitarian Society', article in the *Guardian*, 3 July 1978, based on material in Kay J. and King M.A., *The British Tax System* (OUP) 1978.
14. Legge K., *Power, Innovation and Problem-solving in Personnel Management* (McGraw-Hill) 1978, p. 70.

Section B
THE CONTRACT FOR WORK

5

The Contract for Work and the Recruitment Overture

Members of organisations are employed to do work and they take employment in order to have work to do. We now take up the theme sketched out in Chapter 1, that the basic contract between organisation and employee is for *work*.

In this area of the contract there are a number of activities that begin by matching the needs of the employee with the needs of the organisation at the point where the individual is still outside and entry is being contemplated by both parties. Thereafter come the activities to develop the capacity for the employee both to perform the tasks assigned to him and to realise his personal aspirations in the organisational context.

To begin our examination we consider what the employee will be seeking in his search for work.

The Place of Work in the Life of the Individual

Work has been traditionally and extensively described as a burden: a duty exacted by an employer in exchange for payment. It has also had strong class association, with work generally being done by the lower social classes in order to sustain the comfort of the privileged. Goffman[1] has traced the development of manners and much of our conventional behaviour to the desire among individuals to demonstrate that they did *not* work. Leisure was a social accomplishment.

This view modified as the physical working conditions of manual labour improved and the hours lessened. At the same time there developed many non-manual occupations carrying a concept of vocation rather than necessity, and idleness became less socially acceptable. Man still *needs* to work, but the reasons for this need are now more varied. Work provides more than payment for expenditure when the work stops, even though the work is done by an employee and therefore someone who relinquishes a degree of personal independence. Any contract of employment has certain implied terms that are legally enforceable:

to work when required to do so, if fit;
to obey lawful orders from the employer;
to compensate the employer for any loss caused to him at the hands of a third

party as a result of the employee's unlawful action in the course of his
employment; and

to act in good faith towards the employer.

Some employees dislike the dependence that this type of working relationship
involves, with the feeling frequently being increased by a sense of dehumanisation
because of the size of the employing organisation and the impersonality of its
operations. Lapel badges have been seen bearing such inscriptions as 'I am a human
being. Do not bend, twist or deface.' The organisation is governed by a system and
this results in work being assigned to individuals not by name but by role; and role
rules.

Mankind survives through organisations, which are designed to perform tasks
beyond the capacity of an individual or small groups. Only the huge corporations
can manufacture the cars, refrigerators and other consumer durables we crave; create
the television service by which we are entertained; and provide the range of social
services on which we depend.

We all need the products and services of organisations, but why does the individual need employment within them, despite the apparent drawbacks? Why is *un*-
employment so fearsome? It is only by producing answers to these questions that it
is possible to approach the personnel management duties like recruitment, selection
and training realistically. The answers can best be seen by thinking in terms not just
of work, nor even of employment, but of *organisational life* − everything that the
organisation does for its members. Here are ten reasons why we need organisational life:

1. Work provides income and therefore determines how much above the minimum
   a person's standard of living can rise.

2. The work that a person does is a major input in the process of him creating a
   personal identity.

3. The work done by a person is a determinant of his social status.

4. Working in an organisation provides opportunities for affiliation and social
   contact not readily found elsewhere, following the decline of extended family
   units and integrated local communities.

5. The organisation provides an area for the playing out of various human
   tendencies − like aggression, competition and teamwork.

6. The organisation provides the opportunity for movement from one social
   position to another.[2]

7. The organisation provides the opportunity to make some contribution to the
   common weal.

8. Organisational life provides a rhythm for the whole of life by determining the
   working span and the leisure span, both short-term and long.

9. The nature of work influences the nature of leisure activities.[3]

10. Employment in an organisation provides some security beyond the basic wage/
    work bargain, by supporting during sickness, holiday and old age, as well as
    providing a variety of other fringe benefits.

The Knowledge Worker

Although much of our thinking and many of our procedures are set up around the idea of the worker as a manual employee, the structure of contemporary employment shows that this is an inappropriate emphasis, as the trend is for manual work to decline and for white-collar work to increase. Grigor McClelland has estimated that no more than 10–15 per cent of the working population can be classified as semi- or unskilled operatives.[4] This has caused some[5,6] to describe the 'standard' employee of the future as the *knowledge worker*.

The crude distinction between manual and white collar work shows how the occupational structure is changing. In 1951 there were 36 per cent of the working population in white collar posts, but this proportion had increased to 53 per cent by 1981.[7] A more specific indicator is qualification. By 1980 63 per cent of people in the 25–29 age group held an educational qualification, compared with 54 per cent in the 30–39 age group. The 25–29 year olds also had 9.5 per cent of their number holding degree or equivalent qualifications, compared with 5.5 per cent in 1971.[8]

In 1969 Drucker provided an illustration of the trend:

> Maintenance of the air fleets of tomorrow – the jumbo jets and jet freighters which, between now and 1980, are likely to become the main carriers of people and freight – will require more workers than now keep all the railroads running. These men, while highly skilled, will greatly differ from the railroad craftsman. First, they will be able to do the entire maintenance operation. They will not, like their predecessors, have been trained in a specific craft, whether sheet metal work or electronics, but in a specific function: keeping an aeroplane operating safely. Second, their skill will rest on theoretical knowledge and formal schooling rather than on an apprenticeship in a craft. While they will work with their hands, they will apply knowledge rather than skill. Manuals, charts and texts will be at least as important to them as the traditional hand tools are to the artisan.[9]

Attitudes to Work

At this stage in our writing we need consider only broad aspects of attitudes to work. The main division is between those to whom work is a central life interest and those to whom it is simply a means towards another end. Although there is no clear generalisation those with relatively unskilled work in specialised, narrow jobs tend to view work as a means towards another end, while knowledge workers tend to find work more important than leisure and non-working life.[10]

When we find a report[11] from the Central Statistical Office that 86 per cent of full-time employees in 1974 were 'satisfied' with their jobs, this means that they were satisfied with what their employment contract provided; it does not necessarily mean that they found the *work itself* satisfying.

Another aspect of attitudes to work that we need to consider is the importance of work as an indicator of social status. Each individual is evaluated by himself and his fellows and assigned a social status as a result. Many factors make up the 'points composition' in this evaluation: education, dress, possessions, behaviour and values. Work is one of the factors and there appear to be certain degrees of rigidity in this classification. Medical practitioners have prestige in the United Kingdom and the United States beyond any other occupation. British civil servants and headteachers have higher social status than their counterparts in America. Among the determinants of occupational status are the following:

1. Responsibility of the job in terms of the results that can flow from decisions made, whether these be a craftsman's decisions on the use of tools or a legal decision to send someone to prison.
2. The amount of education and training required. The doctor has longer education than the schoolteacher; the toolmaker has a longer period of training than the lorry driver.
3. The nature of the work. Is it clean rather than dirty? Does it require the manipulation of words rather than tools? Is it dangerous rather than safe?
4. The amount of authority. The headteacher has considerable power over pupils and teachers; the school caretaker has very little.
5. When the work is done. Shift work and unsocial hours are mainly the prerogative of low-status occupations, despite the exceptions such as doctors, airline pilots and members of parliament.
6. Income.

The related matters of the place of work in the life of the individual and attitudes to work determine two decisions made by people that are essential to the discussion in this chapter:

What do I want to do?
Where do I want to do it?

Individuals choose occupations and they choose organisations in which to follow those occupations. It may be that a person will change both during his working span: it is probable that he will change his organisation several times. The choice of occupation comes first and will be governed by a range of considerations, decisions on what the individual would like to do and decisions on what he sees as possible. Writing in a British context it is more necessary to make that second comment than for the American Drucker:[12]

The society of organisations demands of the individual decisions regarding himself . . . ' What shall I do *with myself?* ' rather than 'What shall I do?' is really being asked of the young by the multitude of choices around them. The society of organisations forces the individual to ask of himself: 'Who am I?' 'What do I want to be?' 'What do I want to put into life and what do I want to get out of it?'

The Employment Contract

In the opening chapter we made brief reference to the work of Enid Mumford. We revert to this now as a way of considering the juxtaposition of employee needs and the needs of the organisation from that employee.

Mumford[13] postulates five areas of the employment contract, in each of which there is a dimension of reciprocal need. Managers representing the organisation are setting up a situation in which an arrangement can be made on working arrangements so that there will be a 'good fit' on each of these dimensions. It may not be the precise match that the engineering analogy implies, but a sufficient accommodation to satisfy both parties to the contract. The five areas are:

	The firm	*The employee*
The Knowledge contract	Needs a certain level of skill and knowledge in its employees if it is to function effectively.	Wishes the skills and knowledge he brings with him to be used and developed.
The Psychological contract	Needs employees who are motivated to look after its interests.	Needs factors which will motivate him. e.g. achievement, recognition, responsibility, status.
The Efficiency contract	Needs to achieve set output and quality standards.	Needs an equitable effort/reward bargain and controls, including supervisory ones, which are seen as acceptable.
The Ethical (Social Value) contract	Needs employees who will accept the firm's ethos and values.	Needs to work for an employer whose values do not contravene his own.
The Task Structure contract	Needs employees who will accept any technical contraints associated with their jobs.	Needs a set of tasks which meet his requirements for variety, interest, targets, feedback, task identity and autonomy.

In those areas of personnel work with an individual focus Mumford's ideas are particularly helpful. The prospective employee as well as the recruiter is looking for the possibility of a 'good fit'. If either party does not see such a possibility then they will not proceed. If the working relationship begins satisfactorily but deteriorates later, there is a 'poor fit', and Mumford's framework can help us identify the reasons for the dissatisfaction with the chance of putting things right.

Job Mobility

Provided that there is the scope for movement, employees are likely to move between organisations a number of times in their working lives, especially in their teens and twenties. The future pattern of job mobility is hard to guess, but it is of great importance to personnel managers, as its provides the basic 'throughput' for their work, so it is necessary to look at the available information. The following table shows the proportions of employees in different categories who changed from one employing organisation to another:[14]

YEAR	PERCENTAGE OF JOB CHANGES FOR EACH GROUP					
	All males	*All females*	*16–24 males*	*16–24 females*	*25–34 males*	*25–34 females*
1973	14	18	30	30	19	21
1976	9	12	20	18	11.5	13
1979	11	13	24	22	15	13

A more recent indicator shows that the number of engagements annually in manufacturing industry as a whole showed little change throughout the years shown above, but *halved* between 1980 and 1981.[15] This suggests that the high unemployment rate in Britain is inhibiting job mobility very strongly. This eliminates in the short term a lot of regular personnel management activity, but there may also be a lot of pent-up demand for job change when the employment situation eases.

Another aspect of the above figures is the light that is shed on the employment of young women. A persistent aspect of recruiting folklore is that young women are a bad recruitment risk as they will not stay, but leave to produce children. The table shows that young men are now leaving employers more frequently than their female counterparts.

The general picture of job mobility is complicated by qualification. The unskilled are more likely to change *occupation* as there is little investment in a particular set of skills or knowledge. The skilled are less likely to change occupation but will have mixed prospects of changing *employer*. The financial accountant has the type of skills that enable him to seek work in a number of different industries, while the radiologist is probably restricted to one.

A recent study of British managers[16] found that managerial mobility had doubled in the previous thirty years and that the better qualified were the more likely to move. It may be that there is now a slight reaction against mobility, with the main reason being the greater dependence of many households on two incomes. If the wife's salary is both a major part of the family income *and* would decline if the family were to move, then a change of location in employment by the husband is less likely. Employers who link promotion to movement – like banks – have begun to notice some reluctance for this reason, but there is not yet evidence that that is likely to become significant.

Employee loyalty has certainly declined, although a more accurate statement would be that employees feel less dependent on a single employer and are acquiring the confidence to change more readily.

Future Patterns of Employment

Our discussion so far, like most discussion on this subject, has been on the basis of people being engaged in full-time employment. This is what we have come to regard as the normal state. It is normal for people to work full-time or more – by overtime or moon-lighting – and it is only those on the fringes of organisational life, like housewives, pensioners and school children, who work part-time if they are lucky.

A rational approach to the future employment patterns in western societies suggests that part-time working should become the norm because not even the most optimistic prophet can foresee full (full-time) employment being a clear possibility. There are some signs of this happening. Although absenteeism is usually criticised, it is one way in which some people settle for less than full pay and full-time employment. The development of the employment agency is a way in which some people, like nurses and secretaries, who have readily transferable skills can arrange to work for six or nine months and then take a long holiday.

We have gradually reduced the proportion of our lives that we spend working, as we defer the age of starting, bring down the age of retirement, extend holidays and clip bits off the normal working week. Is it not logical that we go the step further and all become part-time employees, sharing work out more evenly? This theme is explored in our chapter on Hours of Work (Chapter 31), but it is mentioned here because the part-time employee has a much smaller stake in the organisation of which he is a part, and some of the comfortable assumptions about the dominance of the recruiter in the employment process are made less relevant.

THE RECRUITMENT OVERTURE

We now consider a number of features in recruitment practice of organisations, including suggestions of features needing to be considered in any re-examination of recruiting procedures.

CENTRALISATION OF RECRUITMENT

The process of recruitment must be centred in one place and in the hands of one person or group. Only in this way can there be a sufficient concentration of expertise, knowledge and records to provide the possibility of efficiency in service both to applicants and to the organisation. The obvious inefficiency of decentralisation is illustrated by the situation in which a group of hospitals on a shared site had three different advertisements for the same category of personnel in the same newspaper at the same time offering interviews on the same day — in three different places! The need for centralisation can be summarised:

1. One point of reference for enquiries from, and on behalf of, prospective employees.
2. One stock of records of applicants previously not employed but still interested in future vacancies.
3. The possibility of the 'surprise match'. An applicant for one position is adjudged more appropriate for another.
4. Audit of comparative effectiveness of different media.
5. Advantage in bargaining on terms with suppliers of advertising space etc.
6. The development of job advertising strategy with peripheral advantages like projecting a company image and the use of a special logo.
7. Centralisation of specialised knowledge and skill in advertising copywriting etc.

RECRUITMENT FOR POSTS OR FOR ESTABLISHMENT?

A question that will affect the setting-up of the whole recruitment operation is whether the emphasis is on recruiting people to specific vacancies or for general categories. In banking it is very rare for anyone to join the employer later than the age of mid twenties. The majority are recruited as school-leavers or graduates, and vacancies at higher level are customarily filled from within. A similar system operates in some manual operations, where the only way to start is in the relatively less attractive parts of the process before moving to more acceptable work as others leave. This is quite common on complex assembly lines with clear pecking orders. This is recruiting to provide an establishment, from which all related posts are filled by a process of *developing*, rather than *selecting* people.

In other organisations it is customary to recruit people at all stages of development for posts at many different positions in the organisation. 44 per cent of all those who changed employer in 1974 did so at ages between 25 and 44.[17] In an operation of this type there will be more time spent and expertise required in the recruitment and selection of key personnel and the need to treat applicants who bring with them an understanding of their personal needs in employment shaped by a wide range of previous working experiences.

Most employers probably recruit in both ways, with emphasis varying according to the particular category of employee being considered, but the difference in the type of operation for the two modes is considerable.

THE WORK THAT IS OFFERED AND THE JOB THAT HAS TO BE DONE
Conventional recruitment begins with the definition of needs. In one way or another a document is produced describing the ideal candidate for the position which has to be filled. The inadequacy of this approach is partly shown by reading the personnel specifications or candidate profiles that are written. Very seldom is a candidate envisaged who is more than thirty-five and the combination of other qualities specified usually call for someone who combines the merits of Moses, Oliver Cromwell and the agony columnist of a women's magazine.

The more serious shortcoming lies in the tendency to concentrate on the job to be done, rather than on the work that is offered. Personnel staff conventionally ask for a job description and then regard that as a definitive statement. This is not sufficient. The personnel specialist has to become more concerned with the work that is to be offered to the applicant and with the development of the working package (as well as the remuneration package) so that the offering to the prospective employee will find takers.

Later in this section of the book we consider job design. Frequently this topic is described as job re-design, and perhaps more thought should be given to the opportunities to re-shape individual duties when a vacancy is being filled. Smith and Drake[18] describe this as one of the ways in which personnel work will have to take initiatives relating to tasks in the organisation, not just to people:

> This will require considerable learning on the part of other management in the organisation ... Experiments in specific departments to change jobs to meet both people's needs *and* task requirements more satisfactorily ... will require the full weight of a human resources management team to make it fully effective.

RECRUITMENT IS THE BEGINNING ...
When recruitment is for post rather than for establishment there may be a tendency to think in terms of meeting the immediate requirements of the contract at the expense of longer-term considerations. However a vacancy is described frequently as an expression of an immediate manpower need that is not catered for satisfactorily elsewhere, usually because it calls for specialist skills that have not previously been needed. But organisations change quite rapidly and the continuing contribution of every individual will depend on a potential to contribute in a changing situation, where the initial reasons for the appointment may have disappeared.

Recruitment is the beginning, not of a job, but of a working relationship. When recruited the individual becomes not an addition to the system, but a part of it. The contribution he makes both to the relationship and to the system will be a result of how he interprets his place in both the light of his own skills, abilities and needs. In joining he will also bring change. He will have to adapt to fit in, but the organisation will have to adapt to accommodate his arrival.

This argues against an approach to recruitment based on the *job* and in favour of recruiting to the *organisation*.

THE DIFFICULTY OF DISMISSAL

Until 1972 both employer and employee entered into a contract of employment with the feeling that it could readily be terminated if either party were not satisfied. This perception has altered with the legislation on unfair dismissal that began with the Industrial Relations Act (1971).

The employer's freedom of decision in contract termination is now limited. It is limited not only by the law itself but also by an employer's reluctance to get involved in tribunal proceedings at all. Therefore the mistakes of recruitment and selection cannot be easily put right by dismissal, and such mistakes must be avoided.

THE REMUNERATION PACKAGE

Although payment is dealt with more extensively in Section E of this book, we need here to mention the idea of the remuneration package.

Britain is unusual among western countries in having a tradition of managers and 'senior' employees being remunerated partly by salary and partly by other benefits, of which the company car is the best known and the most envied. But there are also organisations that offer relatively cheap mortgages or subsidised private medical insurance. Many organisations provide the benefit of purchasing their products at favourable terms, and here the airline is a more attractive employer than the bean-cannery. Many potential recruits will expect some non-pay benefits, so the make-up of the package to be offered will be an important feature of the recruitment operation.

RECRUITMENT AND PR

We have already mentioned that people first choose occupations and then they choose organisations in which to undertake their chosen occupation. For this reason the recruiter is interested in the image of the occupations for which he has to recruit and the image of the organisation in which he does it. Largely these are both beyond his control. There is a wide understanding of well-established jobs which are clearly different from anything else and which are accessible to the general public either in reality or in fiction. Most people think they know what is involved in jobs like nurse, postman, teacher, soldier, pilot, judge, electrician and fisherman. Few people think they know what is involved in being a packer, surveyor, systems analyst, turner, local government officer, warehouseman or registrar.

Organisations too have reputations, usually stemming from the quality of their product or service, which will be beyond the control of the recruiter even though being an influence on his activities. Where recruitment is local the image of the organisation will depend much more on local experience of employment in the organisation than on its product, and this can be supported by the active involvement of managers in local affairs — particularly education and employment — and by supplying the local newspaper or radio station with general information.

The recruiter for establishment will depend more on organisation image than occupation image, although they often merge into one — banking and nursing being examples.

INFORMALITY IN RECRUITMENT

We need to remember that it is only a minority of new employees who join organisations as a result of some formal overture by the employer, such as advertising or the use of an employment agency. In 1980 51 per cent of male and 43 per cent of female job changers heard of their new job through friends or by direct approach to the employer.[19] This shows the importance of having information available for the casual enquirer; either the existing employee who is looking for a vacancy for his friend or the passer-by who calls in to see what is possible.

The employee recruited in this way starts his working relationship in the knowledge that the *initiative was his*. He was not wooed; he wanted to come. Also he will probably have some contacts within the organisation that will help him settle.

The Method of Recruitment

The informal methods described in the last paragraph are not sufficient, and there are a variety of recruitment methods that organisations use to increase the number of applicants. The advantages and drawbacks of some of the more common can be summarised.

1. Internal advertisement
ADVANTAGES: a. Maximum information to all employees, who might then act as recruiters.
               b. Opportunity for all internal pretenders to apply.
               c. If an internal candidate is appointed there is a shorter induction period.
DRAWBACKS: a. Limit to number of applicants.
               b. Internal candidates not matched against those from outside.

2. Vacancy lists outside premises
ADVANTAGES: a. Economical way of advertising, particularly if premises are near a busy thoroughfare.
DRAWBACKS: a. Vacancy list likely to be seen by few people.
               b. Usually possible to put only barest information, like the job title, or even just 'Vacancies'.

3. Advertising in the National Press
ADVANTAGES: a. Advertisement reaches large numbers.
               b. Some national newspapers are the accepted medium for search by those seeking particular posts.[20]
DRAWBACKS: a. Cost.[21]
               b. Much of the cost 'wasted' in reaching inappropriate people.

4. Advertising in the local press
ADVANTAGES: a. Recruitment advertisements more likely to be read by those seeking *local* employment.
               b. Little 'wasted' circulation.
DRAWBACKS: a. Local newspapers appear not to be used by knowledge workers in seeking vacancies.

5. Advertising in technical press
ADVANTAGES: a. Reaches a specific population with minimum waste.
               b. A minimum standard of applicant can be guaranteed.
DRAWBACKS: a. Relatively infrequent publication may require advertising copy six weeks before appearance of advertisement.

b. Inappropriate where a non-specialist is needed, or where the specialism has a choice of professional publications.

6. Job centres and Professional & Executive Recruitment
ADVANTAGES: a. Applicants can be selected from nationwide sources with convenient, local availability of computer-based data.
b. Socially responsible and secure.
c. Can produce applicants very quickly.

DRAWBACKS: a. Registers are mainly of the unemployed rather than of the employed seeking a change.

7. Commercial Employment Agencies
ADVANTAGES: a. Established as the normal method for filling certain vacancies, e.g. secretaries in London.
b. Little administrative chore for the employer.

DRAWBACKS: a. Can produce staff who are likely to stay only a short time.
b. Widely distrusted by employers.[22]

8. Management Selection Consultants
ADVANTAGES: a. Opportunity to elicit applicants anonymously.
b. Opportunity to use expertise of consultant in an area where employer will not be regularly in the market.

DRAWBACKS: a. Internal applicants may feel — or be — excluded.
b. Cost.

9. Executive Search Consultants ('Headhunters')[23]
ADVANTAGES: a. Known individuals can be approached directly.
b. Useful if employer has no previous experience in specialist field.
c. Recruiting from, or for, an overseas location.

DRAWBACKS: a. Cost.
b. Potential candidates outside the headhunter's network are excluded.
c. The recruit may remain on the consultant's list and be hunted again.

10. Visiting Universities ('The Milk Round')[24]
ADVANTAGES: a. The main source of new graduates from Universities.
b. Inexpensive and administratively convenient through using the free services of the University Appointments Service.

DRAWBACKS: a. Interviewees are often enquirers rather than applicants.
b. Interviewing schedules can be fatiguing.

11. Schools and the Careers Service
ADVANTAGES: a. Can produce a regular annual flow of interested enquirers.
b. Very appropriate for the recruitment of school-leavers, who seldom look further than the immediate locality for their first employment.

DRAWBACKS: a. Schools and the advisors are more interested in occupations than organisations.

Growing use is now being made of advertising on *television and radio* and this may increase with the development of services like Prestel. The limitation is the very brief amount of information that can be provided. A television advertisement will have to spend a large proportion of its screen time giving details of where those interested should apply. This means that only the most perfunctory particulars of positions can be included. So far this has limited use of this medium to recruitment for establishment.

This adds weight to the argument in favour of placing advertisements through a *recruitment advertising consultant*. This is a source of expert advice on appropriate media and labour markets, and can be used as a way of advertising anonymously. Usually these services are free as the consultant receives a commission payment from the journal or other medium in which the advertisement appears.

Figure 5.1 summarises the main methods of recruitment that are available in terms of the method of providing the information and the increasing cost of reaching a widening labour market.

THE PERSONNEL (OR CANDIDATE) SPECIFICATION

Central to the recruitment process is the personnel specification. This is dealt with fully in Chapter 27 on Job Analysis, as it is a prerequisite that the specification is based on the job description, rather than being thought up independently.

PRESS ADVERTISING

Most employers advertise in the press at some time and become enmeshed in that particular mystique of social classification that seems to obsess the advertising world. The categories used are:

	Social Status	*Head of Household's Occupation*
A	Upper middle class	Higher managerial, administrative, professional.
B	Middle class	Intermediate managerial, administrative, professional.
C1	Lower middle class	Supervisory or clerical, junior managerial, administrative, professional.
C2	Skilled working class	Skilled manual worker.
D	Working class	Semi- and unskilled manual worker.
E	Lowest level of subsistence	State pensioners or widows; casual or lowest grade workers.

However disconcerting this rigid type of classification seems, it is used to justify the competing claims of different media to be able to reach the segment of the population in whom you are interested. For instance 45 per cent of men in social class A and 28 per cent of men in social class B read the *Sunday Times*,[25] compared with 9 per cent and 10 per cent respectively reading the *Guardian*. The logical argument is that your advertisement will reach five times as many social class A men (if that is what you want) in one than the other. The National Readership Survey that is commissioned annually by media owners gives much more detailed figures, based not simply on social class but on occupations – showing, for instance, that 61,000 accountants read the *Daily Telegraph* and 73,000 graduate engineers read the *Daily Express*.

Methods of information provision

Methods of information provision	By employees	By managers	Internal advertising	Board outside premises	University contacts	Schools contacts	Careers service (Local education authority)	Job centre register	Professional and executive recruitment	Commercial employment agencies	Company planned advertising	Recruitment advertising consultant	Management selection consultant	Executive search consultant
National television												●		
Regional television											●	●		
National press											●	●	●	
Technical press											●	●	●	
Professional journals											●	●	●	
Regional radio											●	●		
Local press											●	●	●	
Information package					●	●	●						●	●
Letter or circular	●	●		●	●	●	●		●			●	●	●
Vacancy list			●	●			●	●	●	●				
Vacancy notice			●	●	●		●	●	●	●			●	●
Social interaction	●	●	●			●	●						●	●

Specific recruitment methods commonly used.

General approach(es) used by organisations:
- Informal recruitment: Personal contact (By employees, By managers), Internal advertising
- Relatively informal recruitment: Board outside premises, University contacts, Schools contacts, Careers service
- Employment agencies: Job centre register, Professional and executive recruitment, Commercial employment agencies
- General advertising: Company planned advertising, Recruitment advertising consultant
- Selection consultants: Management selection consultant, Executive search consultant

Formal recruitment

Methods of recruitment

Increasing costs of advertising.
Increasing public relations potential.

Increasing cost of recruitment process.
Widening labour market reached.

Figure 5.1. General typology of approaches to recruitment

The decision on what to include in a recruitment advertisement is important because of the high cost of space and the need to attract attention; both factors will encourage the use of the fewest number of words. The agency placing it will be able to advise on this, as they will on the way the advertisement should be worded, but the following is a short check list of items that must be included.

(a) NAME AND BRIEF DETAILS OF THE EMPLOYING ORGANISATION

If the recruiter is seeking anonymity he will eschew press advertising in favour of some other medium. The advertisement which conceals the identity of the advertiser will be suspected by the reader, not least for fear that he might be applying to his present organisation. If the advertisement conceals the name but gives clues to the identity of the organisation ('. . . our expanding high-precision engineering company in the pleasant suburbs of . . .') then there is the danger that the reader will guess . . . wrongly).

The brief details will fill in some of the uncertainty about what exactly the organisation is and does. The better-known the employer the less important the details.

(b) JOB AND DUTIES

The potential applicant will want to know what the job is. The title will give him some idea, including a subjective assessment of its status, but rarely will this be sufficient. Particularly for knowledge workers some detail of duties will be sought.

(c) KEY POINTS OF THE PERSONNEL SPECIFICATION

If you really believe that the only candidates that will be considered are those between 24 and 29, then this may be included in the advertisement. Not only do you preclude other applicants who would be wasting your time and theirs, you also bring the vacancy into sharper focus for those you are seeking. Other typical key points are qualifications and experience, as long as these can be expressed clearly. 'Highly qualified' and 'considerable experience' are valueless in an advertisement.

(d) SALARY

Many employers are coy about declaring the salary that will accompany the advertised post. Sometimes this is reasonable as the salary scales are well-known and inflexible — as in much public sector employment. Elsewhere the coyness is due either to the fact that the employer has a general secrecy policy about salaries and does not want to publicise the salary of a position to be filled for fear of dissatisfying holders of other posts, or he does not know what to offer and is waiting to see 'what the mail brings'.

Whatever the reasons, the effect of this concealment is to reduce the number of applicants. The most cursory examination of advertisements shows that there is a wide discrepancy in the salaries attaching to apparently similar posts. If the salary is not declared in the advertisement it is inevitable that some of the applicants will be disqualified because of the salary they are currently receiving, and many others will not apply for fear of wasting their time.

(e) WHAT TO DO

Finally the advertisement tells potential applicants what to do. This will vary according to the nature of the post. It is conventional for manual employees to call at the personnel department, while managerial employees will be more disposed to write. Applicants who obey the instruction 'write with full details to . . . ' will be understandably discouraged if the response to their letter is an application form to be completed, giving roughly the same information in a different way. Application forms are now generally accepted, but applicants not only feel it is unnecessary to be asked for the same information twice, they also develop reservations about the administrative efficiency of the organisation that they *had* been thinking of joining.

LEGAL ASPECTS OF RECRUITMENT

There are some legal pitfalls for the recruiter, mainly if he seeks to discriminate on grounds of race or sex. These are discussed in Chapter 15 on Equalising Employment Opportunity, but we should note here that it is unlawful to discriminate in Britain against people on the grounds of sex, marriage, racial or ethnic origin. This does not only mean that advertisements must be free of discriminatory content, but also that the placement of those advertisements must not be discriminatory by selecting, for instance, journals which are predominantly read by men. It would be difficult to justify separate job descriptions for men and women, however well-intentioned such provision might be, and those organising recruiting activities like visits by parties of school-leavers, should not assume that all the girls want to be secretaries and all the boys want to be draughtsmen.

INFORMATION BOOKLETS

It is customary for organisations to produce an information booklet for prospective employees. Partly this provides prepared answers to frequent questions on terms and conditions of employment and partly it 'sells' the organisation as a good employer. Because of this the booklet is often regarded with grave suspicion by the reader, and many of the booklets give the impression that the advertising copywriter, having been severely limited in the advertisement, is allowing creative imagination to take the place of hard information. Such booklets can usefully provide a historical sketch of the organisation and the logical stages of career development for recruits, as well as the details of holiday arrangements, pension plans and the like. Like other aspects of recruitment, the booklet can be as useful in deterring inappropriate applicants as it can be in attracting the appropriate.

THE EFFECTIVENESS OF RECRUITING

Finally we can consider how the effectiveness of recruiting activities can be assessed. We can only consider the effectiveness of different methods in producing candidates who are to be interviewed. If we incorporate an attempt to assess the effectiveness of *selection* we are assessing two activities, and the criteria for the second are less clear than for the first.

Braithwaite and Pollock[26] have described a sophisticated method of measuring effectiveness of job advertising by computer. For most recruiters some more elementary method will suffice which compares the number of respondents with the nature of the advertisement, where it was placed and what it cost.

In the remaining chapters of this section we deal with a number of the features of employment in organisations. The ramifications of employment policies and procedures are extensive, and the reader is referred to the ARCADIA appendix as a framework for his reading of the next few chapters. This model identifies seven phases in the employment process and traces their interconnections. This, with the later ASDICE model, can be used both to plan procedures and as an analytical tool to test the effectiveness of existing practice in organisations. The phases of

ARCADIA are:

1. Analysis and specification of personnel requirements;
2. Recruitment of candidates for employment;
3. Candidate screening;
4. Assessment of candidates;
5. Decision-making for employment;
6. Induction and placement;
7. Appraisal and evaluation.

SUMMARY PROPOSITIONS

5.1.   The management activity of organising recruitment requires an understanding of the meaning of work in the lives of prospective employees. This is not only varied, but also changing, as people become less dependent on a single employer and more willing to seek the type of employment which meets their growing needs.

5.2.   Recruiters need to think not only of the job that has to be done in the organisation but also of the work that is being offered to the applicants.

5.3.   Informal methods of recruitment produce the majority of job changes.

5.4.   The cost and formality of recruitment methods increases with the size of the labour market that has to be reached.

REFERENCES

1. Goffman E., *The Presentation of Self in Everday Life* (Pelican) 1971, pp. 28–82.
2. Drucker P.F., *The Age of Discontinuity* (Heinemann) 1969, pp. 240–243.
3. Clarke A.C., 'The Use of Leisure and its Relation to Levels of Occupational Prestige', *American Sociological Review,* vol. 21, no.3, 1956.
4. McClelland W.G. *And a New Earth* (Friends Home Service Committee) 1976, p. 13.
5. Drucker, *op. cit.* pp. 247–260.
6. du Brin. A.J., *Fundamentals of Organisational Behaviour* (Pergamon) 1974, pp. 8–12.
7. Evans A., *What Next at Work?* (Institute of Personnel Management) 1979, p. 41.
8. Central Statistical Office, *Social Trends 12* 1982 (HMSO) 1981, p. 56.
9. Drucker, *op. cit.*, pp. 250–251.
10. Glueck W.F., *Personnel: A Diagnostic Approach* (Business Publications) 1974, p. 46.
11. Central Statistical Office, *General Household Survey* (HMSO) 1975.
12. Drucker, *op. cit.*, p. 231.
13. Mumford E., 'Job Satisfaction: A Method of Analysis', *Personnel Review,* vol. 1, no.3, 1972.
14. *Social Trends 12,* 1982, *op. cit.* p. 78.
15. Department of Employment, *Employment Gazette,* March 1982.

16. Birch S. and Macmillan B., *Managers on the Move: A study of British Managerial Mobility* (BIM) 1971.
17. *Social Trends No. 7 1976, op. cit.* p. 101.
18. Smith P.J. and Drake R., 'Integrating Personnel and Training', *Personnel Management*, May 1969.
19. *Social Trends 12*, 1982, *op. cit.* p. 67.
20. The *Daily Telegraph* is frequently regarded as the place to find advertisements for sales posts. K.G. Fordham ('Job Advertising' in *Recruitment Handbook*, 2nd edition, published by Gower Press, 1975) reports a 150% increase in the space devoted to recruitment advertising in the *Daily Telegraph* over the ten years to 1973.
21. In April 1982 the *Daily Express* charges for recruitment advertising were £46 per column centimetre in the national edition and £25 per column centimetre in the Northern and Scottish edition.
22. For a comment on this see J.G. Knollys, 'Clerical Staff' in *Recruitment Handbook, op. cit.*, pp. 218–219.
23. A recent treatment of this controversial aspect of recruitment can be found in B. Prentice, 'Head Men and How to Hunt Them', *Personnel Management*, vol. 7, no. 1, January 1975.
24. For further comment see J.S. Gouch, 'Recruitment of Graduates at the Universities,' in *Recruitment Handbook*, op. cit. pp. 295–304.
25. Fordham K.G., 'Job Advertising', *op. cit.*, p..71.
26. Braithwaite R. and Pollock J., 'Analysing Response to Recruitment Advertising', *Personnel Management*, vol. 6, no. 12, December 1974.

6

The Employment Decision and the Induction Step

Usually books have chapters about 'selection': we have elected to have a chapter about 'the employment decision' in order to emphasise the need to see the traditional selection process as one in which potential employers and potential employees are both making decisions.

Employment decisions have long been regarded as a management prerogative and are still widely regarded in this way. With the exception of French,[1] the main current American texts on personnel management[2,3,4,5] all emphasise the management decision and describe the process in terms of hurdles over which prospective employees have to try and leap to avoid rejection.

This view is likely to persist for various reasons:

(i) It is attractive to managers because it underlines their authority, and they frequently feel that the ability to choose their subordinates is a key to their own effectiveness.

(ii) It is supported by much academic research. Psychologists have studied individual differences, intelligence and motivation extensively and have produced a number of prescriptions for those managing selection procedures on how to make sound judgements about candidates.

(iii) Candidates are convinced of their helplessness in selection, which they see as being absolutely controlled by the recruiting organisation.

Despite these features of the situation, we continue to advocate a more reciprocal approach to employment decision-making in the belief that managers will be more effective in staffing their organisations if they can bring about some shift of stance in that direction. We must be concerned not only with the job to be done, but also with the work that is offered.

Who make employment decisions?

The final employment decision is made by the prospective employee. He decides whether to accept or reject the offer of employment he receives.

The stage before — that of deciding to whom the post shall be offered — is more varied in its methods. The most common methods are of individual managers deciding singly or jointly to whom the offer should be made. There are two schools of thought. One is that the manager responsible for the post being filled makes the decision, even though he may receive preliminary advice from colleagues such as personnel specialists. This again shores up the authority of the line manager and makes him responsible for the decision so that he cannot excuse subsequent failure on the grounds that the new employee was wished upon him. The second school of thought is that the decision should be a collective one, with two or three people sharing views and reaching a consensus. The support for this approach is that it ensures justice being done and protects individual managers from charges of favouritism.

We are, of course, talking here of the *final* stage of the management decision-making process on employment; some of the advantages and disadvantages of the two methods outlined have a bearing on what comes earlier.

Head teachers in schools seldom have complete authority to decide to which applicant for a teaching post in the school an offer should be made. The decision will be made in conjunction with officials, both lay and professional, constituting a selection board. This may encourage him to pre-empt the decisions of that panel by lobbying its members beforehand, manipulating the short-list or putting particularly awkward questions to those interviewees he is inclined to disfavour.

Personnel specialists with advisory status regarding employment offers may be sufficiently aggrieved at having their advice disregarded that they sabotage the administrative procedure in some way: the papers are mislaid, references are late in arriving and so on. Also many readers will have encountered this type of comment from a Chief Executive:

'Now you must of course make up your own mind. You have complete responsibility to decide, but I thought you would like to know my opinion . . . and please don't forget who is giving you this advice.'

The simple question for organisational policy is whether decisions to offer should be made by the line managers responsible or by boards. The answer will probably vary for different types of post, but every employment offer needs to proceed by personnel advice or clearance to ensure at the very least that there is no breach of union agreement or statute.

Application Forms

Growing use is being made of the application form as a basis for employment decisions. For a long time it was not really that at all, it was a personal-details form that was intended to act as the nucleus of the personnel record for the individual when he began work. It asked for some information that was difficult to supply, like National Insurance Number, and some that seemed irrelevant, like the identity of the family doctor and next-of-kin. It was largely disregarded in the employment process, which was based on 'a man-to-man chat'. As reservations grew about the validity of interviews for employment purposes, the more productive use of the application form was one of the avenues explored for improving the quality of decisions.

Forms were considered to act as a useful preliminary to employment interviews and decisions, either to present more information that was relevant to such deliberations or to arrange such information in a standard way rather than the inevitably idiosyncratic display found in letters of application. This made sorting of applications and short-listing easier and enabled interviewers to use the form as the basis for the interview itself, with each piece of information on the form being taken and developed in the interview.

More recently the application form has been extended by some organisations to take a more significant part in the employment process. One form of extension is to ask for very much more, and more detailed, information from the candidate. In this way there is some improved prospect of preparing an employment decision *before* the interview by garnering the maximum amount of data for analysis before the incalculable element of the face-to-face discussion comes in. This method has limited application, as there are not many posts for which one can expect the applicants to complete lengthy forms. Candidates are not always as distrustful of the interview as are some analysts, and may feel resentment at being denied an interview in which to put their case.

Another extension of application-form usage has been in weighting. This is an attempt to relate the characteristics of applicants to characteristics of successful job holders. The method is to take a large population of job holders and categorise them as good, average or poor performers, usually on the evaluation of a supervisor. Common characteristics are sought out among the good and poor performers. The degree of correlation is then translated into a weighting for evaluating that characteristic when it appears on the application form. The obvious drawbacks of this procedure are first the time that is involved and the size of sample needed, so that it is only feasible where there are many job holders in a particular type of position. Secondly it smacks of witchcraft to the applicants who might find it difficult to believe that success in a position correlates with being, *inter alia*, the first born in one's family.

Generally application forms are used as a straightforward way of giving a standardised synopsis of the applicant's history. This helps the applicant present his case by providing him with a pre-determined structure, it speeds the sorting and short-listing of applications and it guides the interviewers as well as providing the starting-point for personnel records. Here are some points for a check-list:

(i)   Handwriting is usually larger than typescript. Do the boxes on the form provide enough room for the applicant to complete his information?

(ii) Forms that take too long to complete run the risk of being completed perfunctorily or not being completed at all, as the prospect decides to ignore that possibility in favour of other applications to other employers. Is the time the form takes to complete appropriate to the information needs of the employment decision?

(iii) Some questions are illegal, some are offensive, others are unnecessary. Does the form call only for information that is appropriate to employment decision-making?

Among the most useful references on application forms are Miner,[6] Schuh,[7] Guion[8] and Edwards.[9]

Screening

Preliminary screening of applications is the process of reducing a relatively large number of applicants to a relatively small field of candidates. Assuming that the interview is the climax of the employment process, there will probably be between two and six candidates coming through for that discussion and they will have been drawn from a handful or hundreds of applicants. Apart from preliminary interviews, screening is done by a matching of the declared information on the application form and the features of the candidate specification prepared earlier. If there are far too many applicants a very close match will be required. If the number is few then more flexibility is permitted. Part of the validation of the organisations routines for job analysis and the design of application forms lies in how easily screening can be done.

No matter how skilful the recruiting activities it is unlikely that all applicants will become candidates, as the following extract from a letter of application shows:

'I am interested in your advertisement for a personnel manager. You say you need a man between thirty-five and forty-five with at least five years experience in the personnel field.

I have never worked in personnel before and I am only twenty-three but I have always been interested in personnel matters and feel sure that I could succeed in this post if I were given the opportunity . . .'[10]

Correspondence

As representatives of organisations choose candidates from applicants by screening, applicants choose between organisations and jobs by evaluating the developing relationship between themselves and the prospect. They will decide not to pursue some applications. Either they will have accepted another offer, or they will find something in their correspondence with the organisation that discourages them and they withdraw. Jenkins gives a specific example of how applicants drop out.[11] After newspaper advertising in 1974 booklets and application forms were sent out to 321 applicants: 127 were returned, so 60 per cent withdrew at that point. Dropping out later was only slightly less in percentage terms. Posts were offered to 23 candidates and accepted by 19, of whom only 15 started. 35 per cent dropped out.

This type of example illustrates that the managers in the organisation do not have total control over who is employed and that there are two parties to the bargain. Figures of the type that Jenkins provides can be viewed with pride or alarm. It might be that 194 applicants received the information booklet and were immediately able to make a wise decision that they were not suited to the organisation and that time would be wasted by continuing. On the other hand it might be that potentially admirable recruits were lost because of the way in which information was presented, lack of information, or the interpretation that was put on the 'flavour' of the correspondence.

The frame of reference for the applicant is so different from that of the manager in the organisation that the difference is frequently forgotten. It would not be unrealistic to suggest that the majority of applicants have a mental picture of their letter of application being received through the letter box of the company and immediately being closely scrutinised and discussed by powerful figures. The fact that the application is one element in a varied routine for the recipient is incomprehensible to some and unacceptable to many. The thought that one man's dream is another's routine is something the applicant cannot cope with.

If he has posted an application with high enthusiasm about the fresh prospects that the new job would bring, he is in no mood for delay and he may quickly start convincing himself that he is not interested, because his initial euphoria has not been sustained. He is also likely to react unfavourably to the mechanical response that appears to have been produced on a duplicating machine that was due for the scrapheap. Again there is a marked dissonance between the paramount importance of the application to him and the apparent unimportance to the organisation. Some of the points that seem to be useful about correspondence are:

(i) Reply, meaningfully, fast. The printed postcard of acknowledgement is not a reply, neither is the personal letter which says nothing more than that his application has been received.

(ii) Conduct correspondence in terms of what the applicants want to know. How long will he have to wait for an answer? If you ask him in for interview, how long will it take, what will it involve, do you defray expenses, can he park his car, how does he find you, etc.?

The Use of Tests

The use of tests in employment procedures is surrounded by strong feelings for and against. Those in favour point to the unreliability of the interview as a predictor of performance and the greater accuracy of test data. Those against either dislike the objectivity that testing implies or have difficulty in incorporating test evidence into the rest of the evidence that is collected. The strongest objections of all are about the objectivity of testing, particularly among candidates, who feel that they can improve their prospects by a good interview 'performance' and that the degree to which they are in control of their own destiny is being reduced by a dispassionate routine.

The advocates of testing perhaps concentrate too much on the representatives of the organisation making the right decisions and too little on the importance, to those on both sides of the table, of the interactive ritual that is the interview. Nonetheless, tests *are* used and have a potential beyond their present level of application. There are three main types: tests of intelligence, tests of personality and tests of skills.

Tests of Intelligence

Much of the resistance to this type of test is due to it being perceived as providing a 'yes/no' type of answer; the candidate is found to be either intelligent or stupid. Either candidates regard the idea of testing as an insult or they rationalise a fear that the answer might not be too good. The following reaction is not unusual:

'You should be aware that University examining bodies, which awarded me B.Sc., M.Sc., Ph.D. are quite competent and moreover have the services of some of the country's most eminent people. For a Personnel Officer to presume that he is more fitted for this task may be good for his ego but to me is a repugnant suggestion.[12]

What the tests attempt to do is to sample intellectual development of candidates and then locate the result on a distribution validated for a particular population, such as those with secondary grammar education. In addition they are able to distinguish between different types of mental ability. Theorists differ as to what the observable differences are. The simple distinction between numerical and verbal ability is familiar to many, but another widely regarded interpretation is that of Thurstone,[13] who grouped cognitive abilities under seven headings:

Verbal comprehension
Word fluency
Number aptitude
Inductive reasoning
Memory
Spatial aptitude
Perceptual speed

Tests of Personality

If there is a resistance to tests of intelligence, there is even more to tests of personality, largely because of reluctance to see personality as in any way measurable. Personality is itself susceptible to a variety of definitions. In this context we can use the comment of the Jessups:

> Personality is that which makes one person different from another and includes all the psychological characteristics of an individual ... personality is used to describe the non-cognitive or non-intellectual characteristics of an individual. It refers more to the emotional make-up of a person and is reflected in the style of his behaviour rather than the quality of his performance.[15]

Theories of human personality vary as much as theories of human intelligence. Jung was content to divide personalities into extroverts and introverts; more recently Eysenck[15] regards the factors of *neuroticism* and *extroversion* as being sufficient. The most extensive work has been done by Cattell,[16] who has identified sixteen factors:

reserved . . . . outgoing
less intelligence . . . . more intelligent
affected by feelings . . . . emotionally stable
submissive . . . . dominant
serious . . . . happy-go-lucky
expedient . . . . conscientious
timid . . . . venturesome
tough-minded . . . . sensitive
trusting . . . . suspicious
practical . . . . imaginative
forthright . . . . shrewd
self-assured . . . . apprehensive
conservative . . . . experimenting
group dependent . . . . . self-sufficient
uncontrolled . . . . controlled

The use of personality tests for employment purposes is dependent on two factors. First the general policy decision about whether to incorporate this feature in the recruitment/selection process and second on whether qualified personnel are available to operate the procedures. Considerations on the first point are similar to those about the weighted application form. There needs to be a large number of employment prospects in identical jobs in order to build up sufficient evidence of successful individuals so that correlations can be derived. It is dangerous to assume that there is a standard profile of 'the ideal employee'. Miller[17] quotes the example of two establishments in the same organisation using the Cattell inventory to produce a profile of systems analysts. Though the work of each group was similar, the factors most associated with success in the two locations were different.

Tests of Skills

There is less resistance to the notion of testing skills. Few candidates for a typing post would refuse to take a typing test before interview. The candidates are sufficiently confident of their skills to welcome the opportunity to display them and be approved. Furthermore they know what they are doing and will know whether they have done well or badly. They are in control, while they feel that the tester is in control of intelligence and personality tests as the candidates do not understand the evaluation rationale.

General tests that can be used are for vocabulary, spelling, perceptual ability, spatial ability, mechanical ability and manual dexterity.

References

One way of informing the judgement of managers who have to make employment offers to selected individuals is the use of references. Previous employers or others with appropriate credentials are cited by candidates and then requested by prospective employers to provide information. There are two types: the factual check and the character reference.

(A) THE FACTUAL CHECK

This is fairly straightforward as it is no more than a confirmation of facts that the candidate has presented. It will normally follow the employment interview and decision to offer a post. It does no more than confirm that the facts are accurate. The knowledge that such a check will be made — or may be made — will help focus the mind of the candidate so that he resists the temptation to embroider his story.

(B) THE CHARACTER REFERENCE

This is a very different matter. Here the prospective employer asks for an *opinion* about the candidate *before* the interview so that the information gained can be used in the decision-making phases. The logic of this strategy is impeccable: who knows the working performance of the candidate better than his previous employer? The wisdom of the strategy is less sound, as it depends on the writers of references being excellent judges of working performance, faultless communicators and — most difficult of all — disinterested. The potential inaccuracies of decisions influenced by character references begin when the candidate decides who to cite. He will have some freedom of choice and will clearly choose someone from whom he expects favourable comment, perhaps massaging the critical faculties with such comments as 'I think references are going to be very important for this job', 'You will do your best for me, won't you?'.

Next are the notorious obscurities of reference writers, who say more about themselves than the candidates. The following are some examples of actual references gathered by the authors over the years:

> 'Mr X has clear ideas about what he should be doing and sets himself objectives. By his own standards he succeeds in reaching them.'

> 'Mr Y is always punctual in attending work and has excellent handwriting.'[Mr Y was applying for a senior executive post in charge of a department of fifty people].

> 'Mrs Z, as you will know, has not made progress with us, but I feel that this is because we have not been able to provide her with the appropriate challenge. She is very able, most enthusiastic and reliable with considerable potential. I can strongly recommend her to you without any hesitation.'

Making the Decision

Eventually in the employment process representatives of the organisation have to make a decision about which among several candidates is the most appropriate for the vacancy being considered.

> Typically the line manager or the personnel man (or the two together) look over the application blanks, test results, and interview summaries, and make their decision on the basis of their subjective weighting of these imperfect indices and any other facts (or prejudices) they have at hand. Though this process can be called a *clinical approach*, often it is pure hunch. But most experienced personnel men feel that only in this way can the various important but unmeasurable intangibles be given proper consideration.[18]

More mechanical methods have been devised whereby, for instance, points are awarded for different factors of the candidate specification and candidates are scored on each. The one with the highest score receives the first offer. This method worries many people, who feel that the element of human judgement is too closely proscribed. It can, however, provide useful criteria for judgement. Holman[19] offers ideas on how to treat a range of factors in order to inform a subsequent decision.

The most familiar and popular method of producing decision criteria is the *human attribute classification* approach. The best-known is the *seven-point plan*[20] that was developed by Alec Rodger after extensive research in 1939. Later Fraser developed his *five-fold grading.*[21] More recently Isbister has built on earlier experience with the National Institute of Industrial Psychology to produce his ROGBY scheme.[22] All these provide a basis for consistency and system in making employment decisions. The way in which attributes are classified is shown later in this book, in Figure 28.6 on page 390.

Most selection operations require some sort of diagnostic approach by the organisation's representatives to reach a degree of consistency and logic in the judgements they make. A variety of models or strategies for selection decision-making has been proposed, as indicated in Chapter 28, linking different types of information. Howell[23] provides a conceptual integration of these models linking information obtained about, or provided by, the candidate to performance criteria used for evaluation via intermediate data upon inferred traits and job requirements. This provides an integrated diagnostic approach to dealing with a range of decisions, not only in employment interviewing and decision-making, but also for performance

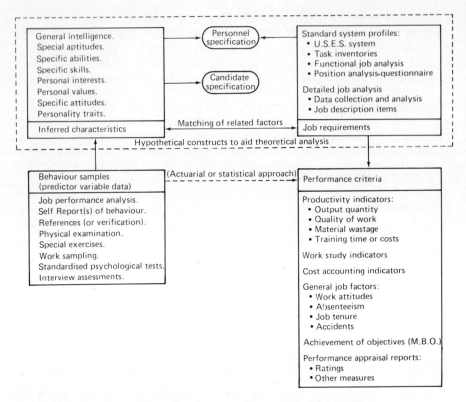

Figure 6.1. The diagnostic approach to employment decision-making

appraisal and similar applications. Figure 6.1 outlines and develops this analytical model.

The Contract of Employment

When someone takes up employment with a new employer a contract of employment is exchanged; this is of major importance in determining the legal rights and obligations of employees and employers. In some other countries the individual contract is of less importance, as the rights, obligations and remedies of the parties to the contract are decided by collective agreement, but in the United Kingdom collective agreements produce *legal* rights and obligations only in so far as they are incorporated into the individual contract.

The present legal basis is the Employment Protection (Consolidation) Act 1978.

(i) Implied terms. As has been mentioned in Chapter 5, certain terms are *implied* in a contract, even if they are not written into it. The employer has a duty to pay agreed wages and to be reasonably careful of the employee's safety, although he is not generally under an obligation to provide work. Employees have a duty to co-operate with the employer by using skill and care, obeying lawful commands and giving faithful service.

(ii) Express terms. The employer has to provide each employee with a written contract within thirteen weeks of his starting work and that will have *express* terms. First there will be those terms that the employer has a statutory obligation to include. In addition he may incorporate other terms, providing that they are lawful and acceptable to the employee, that extend the degree of contractual liability. The contract must include details of the names of the parties to it, when employment began (and a note about continuity of employment where the employer has changed), job title, payment terms, hours of work, arrangements for holidays, sickness payment and pension entitlement, periods of notice, specification of arrangements regarding discipline and the taking up of a grievance.

NAMES OF THE PARTIES
This feature is only likely to cause any difficulty when there is a change of employer in the same employment. If the employer simply changes his *name* the employees must be told of this within one month. If he changes his *identity*, through amalgamation or take-over for example, then the employees' employment ends with one employer and begins with the other, so that new contracts should be issued within thirteen weeks, even if the terms are identical apart from the employer's name.

DATE OF EMPLOYMENT BEGINNING
The contract specifies the starting date for employment so that any subsequent entitlement to a statutory right like maternity pay can be precisely calculated. Where the business of an employer is transferred to an associated employer or a new employer, then employees must be given information about the amount of service with their previous employer that will be regarded as continuous and the date on which it is deemed to have begun.

JOB TITLE
The contract does not only name the parties to the contract, it also names the job of the employee, so delimiting the employer's freedom to move the employee to other work. It is, however, a title and not a job description that has to be provided, so there is some scope for the use of titles that are reasonably broad and flexible, but where there have been tests at tribunal the focus has been on the function that has been performed rather than the title.

PAYMENT TERMS
The contract has to include a statement of how much the employee will be paid, how often and by what means of calculation. Although it is not a feature of the contract, we can mention here that employees must also receive an itemised pay statement when they are paid, that will specify the gross amount of pay, variable or fixed deductions, net pay.

HOURS OF WORK
The employer needs to include in the contract a note of the hours the employee has to work and a note about what are normal hours. This will be referred to if there is to be a statutory payment for redundancy, unfair dismissal or similar.

HOLIDAYS, SICKNESS AND PENSIONS
The wording of the contract should be sufficient for the employee to calculate

accrued holiday pay at any time as well as the arrangements for sickness absence and sickness payment. Where the joining of a pension scheme is a condition of employment, then the details of the scheme must also be included.

PERIODS OF NOTICE

The minimum period of notice than an employer has to give an employee of employment termination is one week after four weeks but less than two years service. This then increases by one week for each additional year up to twelve weeks for twelve years' continuous service. There is no reason why the employer should not undertake to give longer notice. Employees are required to give a minimum period of one week's notice after four weeks' employment. Again the contract may provide for much longer periods. The periods must be in the contract.

DISCIPLINARY AND GRIEVANCE ARRANGEMENTS

The contract has to specify the person to whom an employee can take a grievance and the person to whom he can express dissatisfaction with a disciplinary decision about himself. The contract must also specify either disciplinary rules by which the employee will be bound or refer to a document, reasonably accessible, which specifies the rules. Any later changes in these arrangements must be notified.

Recruitment Policies and Procedures

The practice of organisations in carrying out employment procedures can be illustrated by two sample procedures. First a procedure to ensure general fairness and non-discrimination:

> It is the policy of this Company to recruit the most suitable person for the vacancy concerned, irrespective or nationality, race, colour or religion.
>
> All vacancies will be advertised internally and the same process of selection will apply as would apply to external applicants. (See policy on Transfers and Promotions.)
>
> Applicants will be considered in strict order of application with the exception of those recommended by friends or relatives who are employed by the Company. Such recommendation must appear on the application form and be agreed by the person concerned, but this does not give that applicant any right of employment; the selection process still being applicable. Recommendations will also be treated on a strict order basis.
>
> Where applicants are seeking re-employment they will not be entitled to preferential treatment above that offered to those recommended by existing employees. The decision to re-employ will be made on the basis of the termination report, discussion with the applicant's previous supervisor and in the light of the vacancy for which the applicant is being considered. No person will be offered re-employment without the knowledge of Senior Management and Ex-Supervisor.
>
> Where no immediate vacancies occur, applicants will be placed on a waiting list and will receive an initial interview as soon as possible.
>
> Those who are successful at this stage will be called back for a further interview and, whenever possible, no offer of employment will be made without the applicant having been seen by a member of the Department in which the vacancy occurs.

A more specialised aspect of employment will be in the recruitment of potential employees where a Union Membership Agreement is operating, for instance:

At the time of the first interview, the applicant will be advised that membership of the appropriate Craft Union will be required.

Should it be ascertained at this time that the applicant has either not been a member of the appropriate Union or that his membership has lapsed, he will be advised that, should an offer of employment be made, he will be required to join the appropriate section or to pay his arrears immediately.

Should an offer of employment be made, subject to medical examination, the applicant will be required to bring at the time of the medical examination, his current union card for checking.

The Personnel Department will arrange, through the Engineer in Charge, for the appropriate Shop Steward to be informed that the prospective employee will be on site and that his card may be inspected.

On commencing, the new employee will again bring his card with him and will be introduced to his Shop Steward by the Engineer in Charge if they have not previously met.

THE INDUCTION STEP

It is a commonplace that new employees are most likely to leave the organisation in in the early days and weeks of employment. It is for this reason that the early period is often described as the induction *crisis* before the period of settled connection begins. The approach by managers to this problem is to attempt initiatives which will lead quickly and surely to a settled connection rather than just waiting to see what happens. The costs of unproductive appointments is high and the clinching of the employment decision by integrating the new employee into the organisation is a vital element of the employment process. Induction has been defined as:

> Arrangements made by or on behalf of the management to familiarise the new employee with the working organisation, welfare and safety matters, general conditions of employment and the work of the department in which he is to be employed. It is a continuous process starting from the first contact with the employer.[24]

It is thus different from instruction in that it is concerned not with the specific content of the work to be done, but with the context in which it was carried out. Pigors and Myers[25] provide a checklist of steps in an induction programme, which is abbreviated below.

The organisation — history, development, management and activity.
Personnel policies.
Terms of employment — including disciplinary rules and union arrangements.
Employee benefits and services.
Physical facilities.
General nature of the work to be done.
The supervisor.
Departmental rules and safety measures.
Relation of new job to others.
Detailed description of job.
Introduction to fellow workers.
Follow-up after several weeks.

Although this is comprehensive, it is not likely to turn into an effective programme unless worked out in careful detail about timing, pace and the essence of social adjustment. Some new recruits may be easy to integrate because they have experience of frequent job changes, but others change employment less often and everyone has to start at some time. The induction of school-leavers and graduates has different dimensions because they are entering the world of work for the very first time and will be quite unfamiliar with the myriad of conventions that are common knowledge among all those who have some experience. Other groups who may have special problems are the immigrants, who are probably quite unfamiliar with working routines and customs in a new country, and the married woman returner, who may have lost considerable confidence in her own abilities after a prolonged period of absence. Gomersall and Myers describe an interesting scheme at Texas Instruments where experimentation was carried out under controlled conditions.[26] An experimental group was given an additional period of six hours' social orientation with four elements:

(i) Detailed factual explanations of how long it took to achieve various levels of competence.

(ii) Advice to ignore comments that they would hear from existing employees about the difficulty of achieving standards.

(iii) Instruction to take the initiative in asking for help from the supervisor.

(iv) Detailed description of the sort of person the supervisor was.

The sponsors of the scheme report that training time was halved and training costs reduced by two-thirds as a result of this approach, as it focused on the actual anxieties and reservations of the new employees, instead of concentrating on what it was thought appropriate for them to be told. The key to successful induction is enabling the new employee to be confident of himself in his new situation. However important information about the history of the organisation might be, it is something that is easily deferred until the induction crisis is over. Have you ever met a person who left a new job because nobody had bothered to tell him the history of the company?

SUMMARY PROPOSITIONS

6.1. In employment procedures it is as important to enable the prospective employee to make a wise choice of position as it is for the organisation to make a wise choice among candidates.

6.2. Employment decisions are best made by the use of a mixture of methods. Among these the interview is crucial and character references are of little value.

6.3. The contract of employment is the major determinant of legal rights and obligations in the relationship between employer and employee.

6.4. Effective induction focuses first on the anxieties of the new employee and only later on what the employee should be told.

REFERENCES

1. French W.L., *The Personnel Management Process*, 3rd ed., (Houghton Mifflin)1974,p. 267.
2. Glueck W.F., *Personnel: A Diagnostic Approach* (Business Publications) 1974.
3. Jucius M.J., *Personnel Management*, 7th ed. (Irwin) 1974.
4. Megginson L.C., *Personnel: A Behavioural Approach to Administration* (Irwin) 1972.
5. Pigors P. and Myers C.S., *Personnel Administration*, 7th ed. (McGraw Hill) 1973.
6. Miner J.B., *Personnel Psychology* (Macmillan) 1969, pp. 146–153.
7. Schuh A.J., 'The Predictability of Employee Tenure: A Review of the Literature', *Personnel Psychology*, Spring 1967, pp. 133–152.
8. Guion R.M., 'Employment Tests and Discriminatory Hiring' in *Industrial Relations*, February 1966.
9. Edwards B.J., 'Application Forms' in *Recruitment Handbook*, 2nd ed. edited by B. Ungerson (Gower Press) 1975, pp. 76–94.
10. Torrington D.P., *Successful Personnel Management* (Staples) 1969, p. 32.
11. Jenkins J.F., 'Management Trainees in Retailing' in *Recruitment Handbook, op.cit.*, p. 244.
12. Torrington D.P., *op. cit.*, p. 36.
13. Described in Dunnette M., *Personnel Selection and Placement* (Tavistock) 1969, pp. 47–49.
14. Jessup G. and H. *Selection and Assessment at Work* (Methuen) 1975, p.33.
15. Eysenck H.J. and S.B.G., *The Eysenck Personality Inventory* (University of London Press) 1963.
16. Cattell R.B., *The Scientific Analysis of Personality* (Penguin Books) 1965.
17. Miller K. M., 'Personality Assessment', in Ungerson B. (ed.) *Recruitment Handbook*, 2nd ed. (Gower Press) 1975, p. 134.
18. Strauss G. and Sayles L.R., *Personnel: The Human Problems of Management* 3rd ed. (Prentice-Hall) 1972, p. 430.
19. Holman L.J., 'Deciding the Appointment', chapter in *Recruitment Handbook*, 2nd ed. *op. cit.*, pp. 178–189.
20. Rodger A., *The Seven- Point Plan* (NIIP) 1951.
21. Fraser J.M., *A Handbook of Employment Interviewing* (Macdonald and Evans) 1958.
22. Isbister W.L.T., *Performance and Progress in Working Life* (Pergamon) 1968.
23. Howell W., *Essentials of Industrial and Organisational Psychology* (Dorsey) 1976.
24. Department of Employment, *Glossary of Training Terms* (HMSO), 1971.
25. Pigors P. and Myers C.S. *op. cit.*, p.291.
26. Gomersall E.R. and Myers M.S., 'Breakthrough in On-the-Job Training' in *Harvard Business Review*, July/August 1966, pp. 62–71.

7

Interaction I — the Employment Interview

We now discuss one of the most familiar and forbidding encounters of organisational life — the employment interview. Most people have had at least one experience of being interviewed as a preliminary to employment and few reflect with pleasure on the experience. Usually this is because the interviewer seems more concerned with finding fault than with being helpful.

There is a wide variety of practice in employment interviewing. At one extreme we read of men seeking work in the docks of Victorian London and generally being treated as if they were in a cattle market. In sharp contrast is the attitude of Sherlock Holmes to a prospective employer:

> 'I can only say, madam, that I shall be happy to devote the same care to your case as I did to that of your friend. As to reward, my profession is its reward; but you are at liberty to defray whatever expenses I may be put to, at the time which suits you best.'[1]

There is a neat spectrum of employee participation in the employment process which correlates with social class and type of work. While the London docks situation of the 1890s is not found today, there are working situations where the degree of discussion between the parties is limited to perfunctory exchanges about trade union membership, hours of work and rates of pay: labourers on building sites and extras on film sites being two examples. In most manual employment the emphasis of the interview is largely on the representative of the organisation questioning the applicant to judge his prospective competence. As interviews move up the organisational hierarchy there is growing equilibrium with the interviewer becoming more courteous and responsive to questions from the applicant, who will probably be described as a 'candidate' or 'someone who might be interested in the position'. For the most senior positions it is unlikely that people will be invited to respond to vacancies advertised in the Press. Individuals will be approached, either directly or through consultants, and there will be an elaborate pavane in which each party seeks to persuade the other to declare an interest first. Chairmen of large organisations, retired prime ministers and those of comparable stature apparently just wait for offers.

Another indication of the variety of employment practice is in the titles used. The humblest of applicants seek 'jobs' or 'vacancies', while the more ambitious are looking for 'places', 'posts', 'positions', 'openings' or 'opportunities'. The really high-flyers seem to need somewhere to sit down, as they are offered 'seats on the board', 'professorial chairs' or 'places on the front bench'.

Criticism of the Interview

The interview has been extensively criticised, although the criticism has mainly been of it as a means for managerial selection of candidates rather than as a ritual in the employment process. In his helpful review of recent research, Morgan comments:

> The bald conclusion from all the empirical evidence is that the interview as typically used is not much good as a selection device. Indeed, one might wonder, thinking rationally, why the interview was not long ago 'retired' from selection procedures.[2]

It is difficult to justify the interview as an accurate way of predicting working performance, and there is disturbing evidence of the inability of different interviewers to agree in the evaluation of the same candidates.[3] Some analysts are hopeful about the potential of the interview if it is carried out by trained interviewers:

> Overall the research seems to me compatible with the interpretation that selection interviewing is a very high-level skill which has been ill-treated and taken-for-granted; and that in the *variety* of interviews and the interviewers lies the *possibility* of sufficient improvements.[4]

The most perceptive criticism is contained in the work of Webster,[5] summarising extensive research. The main conclusions were:

(i) Interviewers decided to accept or reject a candidate within the first three or four minutes of the interview and then spent the remainder of the interview time seeking evidence to confirm that their first impression was right.

(ii) Interview seldom altered the tentative opinion formed by the interviewer seeing the application form and the appearance of the candidate.

(iii) Interviewers place more weight on evidence that is unfavourable than on evidence that is favourable.

(iv) When interviewers have made up their minds, very early in the interview, their behaviour betrays their decision to the candidate.

Importance of the Interview

Whatever criticisms are available we must not underestimate the importance of the employment interview. To appreciate its value we must understand its potential.

(i) The interview can be a key part in the process of organisation representatives deciding on which of several candidates is the most appropriate for a particular vacancy.

(ii) Whatever the critics may say few interviewers believe that the criticism can possibly apply to their *own* performance: only other people are poor interviewers. Managers would lose confidence in employment procedures that did not incorporate some element of face-to-face assessment.

(iii) Applicants seem to prefer the face-to-face interview and the opportunity to put their case rather than be judged by more objective methods that deny them the chance to 'sell themselves'. Employment interviews are tough, but the alternatives are worse.

(iv) Both parties need to meet each other before the contract begins to 'tune in' to each other and begin the process of induction.

(v) The interview is important as *ritual* behaviour. It is necessary for the outsider to present himself and display certain performances before the representatives of the organisation as an initiation ceremony. The significance of the ritual is illustrated by the experience of one of the authors who gives a lecture on the interview each year to third-year undergraduates as part of a programme run by the University Careers and Appointments Service. The size of the audience (300–400) is larger than that for any other lecture in the programme, showing the anxiety of those entering the labour market about this feature of their entry. Also the questions asked are usually about behaviour in the ritual: whether or not to shake hands, what to wear, whether to smoke, when to stand up, how formal to be, how to address the interviewer and so forth. There is a clear conviction that there is a set of insider rules, knowledge of which will lead to success.

(vi) Much of the criticism is directed at interviewing that is done badly. Interviews can be effective as means of making sound and consistent judgements, providing that they are conducted properly and guided by the findings of research.[6] It is a flexible means of gathering information, to fill in gaps and to develop points of particular interest. Furthermore, it is a logical conclusion to the employment process, as information from a variety of sources – such as application forms, tests and references – can be discussed together, and some assessment can be made of matters that cannot really be approached any other way – like the potential compatibility of two people who will have to work together, and their social and communication skills.

No matter what other means of making employment decisions there may be, the interview is crucial and when worries are expressed about is reliability, this is not the reason for doing away with it: it is a reason for conducting it properly.

Types of Interview

Employment interviews can be categorised as biographical, stress or problem-solving.

(a) THE BIOGRAPHICAL INTERVIEW

This is the most straightforward and most reliable. It works on the basis that the candidate at the time of the interview is a product of everything in his life that has gone before. To understand the candidate the interviewer must understand the past and he will question the candidate, or talk to the candidate, about the episodes of his earlier life – education, previous employment etcetera.

The advantage of this is that the objectives are clear to interviewer and interviewee, there is no deviousness or 'magic'. Furthermore the development can be logical and so aid the candidate's recall of events. The man who replies to inquiries about his choice of 'A'-level subjects will be subconsciously triggering his recollection of contemporaneous events, like the university course he took, which are likely to come next in the interview. The biographical approach is the simplest for the inexperienced interviewer to use as discussion can develop from the information provided by the candidate on his application form.

(b) THE STRESS INTERVIEW

This is one in which the interviewer becomes aggressive, disparages the candidate, puts him on the defensive or disconcerts him by strange behaviour. The Office of Strategic Services in the United States used this method in World War II to select men for espionage work and subsequently the idea was used by some business organisations on the premise that executive life was stressful, so a simulation of the stress would determine whether or not the candidate could cope.

The advantage of the method is that it may demonstrate a necessary strength or a disqualifying weakness that would not be apparent through other methods. The disadvantages are that evaluating the behaviour under stress is problematical, and those who are not selected will think badly of the employer. The likely value of stress interviewing is so limited that it is hardly worth mentioning except that it has such spurious appeal to many managers, who are attracted by the idea of injecting at least some stress into the interview 'to see what he is made of', 'to put him on his mettle' or some similar jingoism. Most candidates feel that the procedures are stressful enough, without adding to them.

(c) THE PROBLEM-SOLVING INTERVIEW

This is the amateur method of presenting the candidate with a hypothetical problem and evaluating his answer, like the king in the fairy tale who offered the hand of the princess in marriage to the first suitor who could answer three riddles.

This method is most applicable to testing elementary *knowledge*, like the colour coding of wires in electric cables or maximum dosages of specified drugs. It is less effective to test understanding and ability, like the following intriguing poser put to a candidate for the position of security officer at a large department store:

> 'If you were alone in the building and decided to inspect the roof, what would you do if the only door out on to the roof banged itself shut behind you and the building caught fire?'

The retired police superintendent to whom that question was posed asked, very earnestly and politely, for six pieces of additional information, like the location of telephones, time of day, height of building, fire escapes. The replies become progressively more uncertain and the interviewer hastily shifted the ground of the interview to something else. Even if that pitfall can be avoided and the candidate produces an answer that can be assessed, there is no guarantee that he *would* do what he *says* he would. The quick thinker will score at the expense of the person who can take action more effectively than he can answer riddles.

Number of Interviewers

There are two broad traditions governing the number of interviewers. One tradition says that effective frank discussion can only take place on a one-to-one basis, so candidates meet one interviewer, or several interviewers, one at a time. The other tradition is that fair play must be demonstrated and nepotism prevented so the interview must be carried out, and the decision made, by a panel of interviewers.

(a) THE INDIVIDUAL INTERVIEW

This method gives the greatest chance of establishing rapport, developing mutual trust and the most efficient deployment of time in the face-to-face encounter, as each participant has to compete with only one other speaker. It is usually also the most satisfactory method for the candidate, who has to tune in only to one other person instead of needing constantly to adjust his antennae to different interlocutors. He can more readily ask his questions, as it is difficult to ask a panel of six people to explain the workings of the pension scheme, and it is the least formal.

The disadvantages lie in the dependence the organisation places on the judgement of one of its representatives — although this can be mitigated by a series of individual interviews — and the ritual element is largely missing. Candidates may not feel they have been 'done' properly.

(b) THE PANEL

This method has the specious appeal of sharing judgement and may appear to be a way of saving time in interviewing as all panel members are operating at once. It is also possible to legitimise a quick decision — always popular with candidates — and there can be no doubt about the ritual requirements being satisfied.

The drawbacks lie in the tribunal nature of the panel. They are not having a conversation with the candidate; they are sitting in judgement upon him and assessing the evidence he is able to present in response to their requests. Careful jockeying ensures that candidates commit themselves *before* the interview, as a standard opening question is 'are you still a candidate for this position?'.There is little prospect of building rapport and developing discussion, there is likely to be as much interplay between members of the panel as there is between the panel and the candidate. Alec Rodger makes the observation:

> The usefulness of the board interview may depend a good deal on the competence of the chairman, and on the good sense of board members. A promising board interview can easily be ruined by a member who does not appreciate the line of questioning being pursued by one of his fellow-members and who interrupts with irrelevancies.[7]

Panel interviews tend to over-rigidity and give ironic point to the phrase 'it is only a formality'. Ritualistically they are superb, but as a useful preliminary to employment they are questionable.

In this context it is interesting to note Argyle's comment on the social skills that candidates should display:

> Interviewers seem to prefer candidates who are well-washed and quietly dressed, who are politely attentive, submissive and keen, and they are likely to reject candidates who are rude, over-dominant, not interested or irritating in other ways. There seems to be a definite 'role of the candidate' — he is expected to be nicely behaved and submissive — although he may not be expected to be quite like that if he gets the job. There are certain subtleties about being a good candidate — it is necessary for the candidate to draw attention to his good qualities while remaining modest and submissive. He may need to show what a decisive and forceful person he is — but without using these powers on the selection board.[8]

A Structured Approach to the Interview

The candidate expects the proceedings for the employment interview to be decided and controlled by the interviewer and he will anticipate a structure within which he will have to operate. The shortcomings of the interview as a means towards decision-making can be lessened by a patterned approach. The biographical method is one such pattern. Others involve detailed check-lists for the interview itself. Among the helpful outlines developed in recent years is the WASP method of Sidney, Brown and Argyle[9] where the interaction is set in the four stages of Welcome, Aquiring information, Supplying information and Parting.

In the remainder of this chapter we set out a rather fuller structure, that is based on the phases of Preparation, Encounter and Follow-up that are used in other interaction chapters later. This simple formulation has been widely used since it was first put forward in the early 1970s.[10] Although it suggests a sequence, this is intended only as a framework for those responsible for employment procedures to refine and modify to suit their own circumstances and style. It is not a rigid, inflexible structure which people modify at their peril. Figure 7.1 shows it in diagrammatic form.

We appreciate that this model is not suitable for every interview and our working assumption is of interviewing by individuals, meeting candidates for specific posts in permanent employment.

PREPARATION

Interviewer Briefing

We assume that the preliminaries of job analysis, recruitment and shortlisting are complete and the interview is now to take place. The first step in preparation is for the interviewer to brief himself. He will collect and study:

> Job description for the post to be filled
> Personnel specification
> Application forms

He will now have refreshed his memory about the post and the candidates, as well as the specification of the ideal candidate. This will enable him to make his pre-interview notes in line with the requirements of the encounter.

Timetable

If there are several people to be interviewed the interview period needs greater planning than it usually receives. The time required for each interview can only approximately be determined beforehand. A rigid timetable will weigh heavily on both parties, who will feel frustrated if the interview is closed arbitrarily at a pre-determined time and uncomfortable if an interview that has 'finished' is drawn out to complete its allotted span. However the disadvantages of keeping people waiting are considerable and underrated.

Conventional thinking seems to be that candidates are supplicants, waiting on interviewers' pleasure, they have no competing calls on their time and a short period of waiting demonstrates who is in charge. There are a number of flaws in this reasoning. At least some candidates will have competing calls on their time, as they will have taken time off without pay to attend. Some may have other interviews to go to. An open-ended waiting period can be worrying, enervating and a poor preliminary to an interview. If the dentist keeps you waiting you may get distressed, but when the waiting is over you are simply a passive participant and the dentist

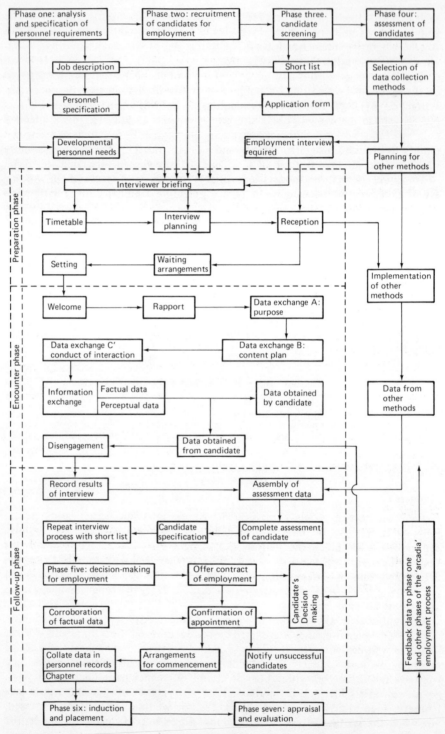

Figure 7.1. The interview as a sub-system of the employment process

does not have the success of his operation jeopardised. The interview candidate has, in a real sense, to perform when the period of waiting is over and the success of the interaction could well be jeopardised.

The most satisfactory timetable is the one which guarantees a break after all but the most voluble candidates. If candidates are asked to attend at hourly intervals, for example, this would be consistent with interviews lasting between 40 and 60 minutes. This would mean that each interview began at the scheduled time and that the interviewer had the opportunity to review and up-date his notes in the intervals.

Reception

The candidate arrives on the premises of his prospective employer on the look out for every scrap of evidence he can obtain about the organisation — what it looks like, what the people look like, and what people tell him. Although no research has been carried out on the subject, it is reasonable to suppose that candidates make judgements as quickly as interviewers and we have already seen that at least one study (Webster, above) found interviewers making their decisions within a few minutes and then using the rest of the time to confirm it. A candidate is likely to meet at least one and possibly two people before he meets the interviewer. First will be the commissionaire or receptionist. There is frequently also an emissary from the Personnel Department to shepherd him from the gate to the waiting-room. Both are valuable sources of information, and interviewers may wish to prime such people so that they can see their role in the employment process and can be cheerful, informative and helpful.

The candidate will most want to meet the interviewer, the unknown but powerful figure on whom so much depends. Interviewers easily forget that they know much more about the candidates than the candidates know about them, because the candidates have provided a personal profile in the application form.

Interviewers do not reciprocate. To bridge this gap it can be very useful for the interviewer to go and introduce himself to the candidate in the waiting-room, so that contact is made quickly, unexpectedly and on neutral territory and the rapport stage of the interview when it begins later is made easier.

Waiting

Candidates wait to be interviewed. Although there are snags about extended open-ended waiting periods, some time is inevitable and necessary to enable the candidate to compose himself. It is a useful time to deal with travelling expenses and provide some relevant background reading about the employing organisation.

Setting

The appropriate setting for an interview has to be considered both from the point of view of what is right for the ritual and from the point of view of what will enable a full and frank exchange of information. It is difficult to combine the two.

Many of the interview horror stories relate to the setting in which it took place, like the candidate for a post as Deputy Clerk of Works who was interviewed on a stage while the panel of 17 sat in the front row of the stalls. The author observed an educational panel in operation on one occasion when a candidate came in and actually moved the chair on which he was to sit. He only moved it two or three inches because the sun was in his eyes, but there was an audible *frisson* and sharp intake of breath from the members of the panel. *They* decided where the chair was going to be: not candidates.

Remaining with our model of the individual interviewer, there are a series of simple suggestions about the setting.

(i)   The room should be suitable for a private conversation.
(ii) If the interview takes place across a desk, as is common, the interviewer may wish to reduce the extent to which the desk acts as a barrier, emphasising the distance between the parties and therefore inhibiting free flow of communication.
(iii) Visitors and telephone calls will not simply interrupt: they will *intrude* and impede the likelihood of frankness.
(iv) It should be clear to the candidate where he is to sit.

ENCOUNTER

Rapport

The opening of the encounter is the time for mutual preliminary assessment and tuning in to each other. Detailed notes on rapport are provided in Chapter 29, but one or two specific points about it in this context can be added.

A useful feature of this phase is for the interviewer to sketch out the plan or procedure for the encounter and how it fits in with the total employment decision process. It is also likely that the application form will provide an easy non-controversial topic for these opening behaviours.

One objective is for the two parties to exchange words so that they can adjust their receiving mechanism in order to be mutually *intelligible*. It also provides an opportunity for both to feel *comfortable* in the presence of the other. If the interviewer is able to achieve these two objectives he may then succeed in developing a relationship in which the candidate trusts the interviewer's ability and motives so that he will speak openly and fully.

The interviewer's effectiveness will greatly depend on his skill with rapport. Bayne regards a pre-requisite as being a 'calm-alert' state of consciousness that can be sustained throughout the interview:

> At times the good interviewer is sharp and in focus, specific and rational; at other times intuitive, picking up nuances and rationalisations; at others stepping back to see the whole interaction, fitting things together and taking note of the amount of time left and the areas to cover . . . the interviewer's calmness helps the candidate to relax and his or her clear perception allows productive silences and the easy asking of questions. The state also counteracts habituation to interviews, when the interviewer is calm but bored. And it allows intuitive processes as well as the usual thinking, evaluating ones.[11]

Data Exchange A — Purpose

The substance of the interview is the exchange of data between the participants.

Remembering again Webster's stricture we must declare that the purpose of this is to exchange data for the basis of judgements *later*. Judgement has to be deferred as long as possible in the interview, preferably until it is over. The interviewer's task is to elicit evidence as a preliminary to judgement and to provide it as required by the candidate for his decision-making.

The purpose of the interview can be summarised as an activity through which:

(i) The interviewer gets to know the candidate;

(ii) The candidate gets to know the work being offered;

(iii) The candidate gets to know the organisation in which the work is done.

The knowledge is not complete at the end of the interview, but it has to be sufficient for two decisions; the interviewer has to decide whether the candidate as he now knows him is the appropriate person for the vacant position and the candidate has to decide whether the position is the one he wants to fill.

Data Exchange B — Plan

The simplest plan for the interview is the one provided by the application form. Here there is information already supplied by the candidate in a logical sequence. Discussion with the candidate to elaborate the points he has made can flow easily from this basis, although it may not be necessary to grind through it in strict chronological order. One American author has produced an interview structure that suggests the interviewer begin with questions about the employment history of the candidate and then goes through his educational record, early home background and present social adjustment.[12] This has the advantage that it begins with what the candidate is best able to handle and later moves to those areas that are not so easy to recall.

Some authorities counsel a more detailed approach by prescribing a check list of questions to be asked. A form designed by Dodd[13] includes a series of boxes at every stage in which the interviewer is asked to check 'acceptable or unacceptable'. This highly structured method does, of course, turn the interview into an interrogation rather than a conversation, making it very difficult to unearth opinions and attitudes, as well as closing certain avenues of enquiry that might appear as the interview proceeded. Furthermore it inhibits the candidate from initiating his own topics for discussion.

Some version of sequential categories like employment, education and training etc. seems the most generally useful, but it will need to have the addition of at least two other categories: the work offered and the organisational context in which it is to be done.

In the preparatory stage of briefing the interviewer will prepare notes on two elements to incorporate in his plan: key issues and check points.

Key issues will be the main two or three issues that stand out from the application form for clarification or elaboration. This might be the nature of the responsibilities carried in a particular earlier post, the content of a training course, the reaction to a period of employment in a significant industry, or whatever else strikes the interviewer as being productive of useful additional evidence.

Check points are matters of detail that require further information: grades in an examination, dates of an appointment, rates of pay and so forth.

Data Exchange C — Method

To handle the interview the interviewer will need to call into play the tactics discussed in Chapter 29. There are five aspects of method.

(a) OBSERVATION

Some data can be collected by simple observation of the candidate. Notes can be made about dress, appearance, voice, height and weight, if these are going to be relevant, and the interviewer can also gauge the candidate's mood and the appropriate response to it by the non-verbal cues that are provided.

(b) LISTENING

The remainder of the interviewer's evidence will come from listening to what is said, so he has to be very attentive throughout. Not only is he listening to the answers to questions, he is listening for changes in inflection and pace, nuances and overtones that provide clues on what to pursue further. The amount of time that the two spend talking is important, as an imbalance in one direction or the other will mean that either the candidate or the interviewer is not having enough opportunity to hear information.

During these first two stages we must remember the danger of making yes/no decisions too quickly.

(c) QUESTIONING

In order to have something to hear the interviewer will have to direct the candidate. This, of course, he does by questioning; encouraging and enabling the candidate to talk, so that the interviewer can learn. The art of doing this depends on the personality and style of the interviewer who will develop his personal technique through a sensitive awareness of what is taking place in the interviews he conducts. Edgar Anstey has described this as the highest stage of interviewing skill:

> Once rapport has been established, the actual questions matter less and less. The candidate senses what one is getting at, without worrying about the form of words, becomes increasingly at ease and responds more spontaneously. This is the ideal . . . [14]

Of the ploys described in Chapter 29, those most appropriate to the employment interview are:

> Reward
> Open-ended questions
> Follow-up questions
> Direct questions
> Summary and re-run
> Probes, and
> Braking.

Closed questions may be needed to check points, or as part of Braking, but are generally to be discouraged in order to avoid a too interrogative style.

(d) NOTES

The best place to make notes is on the application form. In this way they can be joined to information that the candidate has already provided and the peculiar shorthand that people use when making notes during conversations can be deciphered by reference to the form and the data that the note is embellishing. It also means that the review of evidence *after* the interview has as much information as possible available on one piece of paper.

Interviewers are strangely inhibited about note-taking, feeling that it is some way impairs the smoothness of the interaction. This apprehension seems ill-founded as candidates are looking for a serious, business-like discussion, no matter how informal, and note-taking offers no barrier providing that it is done carefully in the form of jottings during the discussion, rather than pointedly writing down particular comments by the candidate. This *does* make the interviewer seem like a policeman taking a statement.

(e) PACE AND CONTROL

Data exchange marks a change of gear in the interview. Rapport is necessarily rather rambling and aimless, but data exchange is purposeful and the interviewer needs to control both the direction and the pace of the exchanges. The candidate will be responsive throughout to the interviewer's control, and the better the rapport the more responsive he will be. The interviewer closes out areas of discussion and opens fresh ones. He heads off irrelevant reminiscences and probes where matters have been glossed over. He can never abandon control. Even when the time has come for the candidate to raise all his queries he will do this at the behest of the interviewer and will look to him constantly for a renewal of his mandate to enquire by using conversational prefixes like 'Can I ask you another question . . . ?','If it's not taking up your time, perhaps I could ask . . . ?', 'I seem to be asking a lot of questions, but there was just one thing . . . '

Disengagement

The standard drill for disengagement can be used, but the explanation of the next step needs especial attention. The result of the interview is of great importance to the candidate and he will await the outcome with anxiety. Even if he does not want the position he will probably hope to have it offered. This may strengthen his hand in dealings with another prospective employer — or his present employer — and will certainly be a boost to his morale. The great merit of convention in the public sector is that the chosen candidate is told before the contenders disperse: the great demerit is that he is asked to say yes or no to the offer at once.

In the private sector it is unusual for an employment offer to be made at the time of the interview, so there is a delay during which the candidate will chafe. His frustration will be greater if the delay is longer than expected and he may start to tell himself that he is not going to receive an offer, in which case he will also start convincing himself that he did not want the job either! It is important for the interviewer to say as precisely as possible when the offer will be made, but ensuring that the candidate hears earlier rather than later than he expects, if there is to be any deviation.

FOLLOW-UP

Decision

When all the candidates have been interviewed the interviewer(s) decide to whom an offer will be made. They do not decide during the interviews themselves, nor do they weigh up the evidence after an individual interview and decide that that candidate will not do, because there is then growing pressure on the interviewers to find later candidates favourable.

The decision requires the integration and analysis of the evidence acquired and a matching of that against the job description and candidate specification. Various methods of reaching the decision are outlined in Chpaters 6 and 28, but here we must emphasise the discipline needed to decide on the basis of the whole of the evidence, eliminating prejudice and preconception as far as possible.

•

Corroboration

Unless references are taken up before the interview there will be the need to confirm the salient points of the candidate's story. Usually this is limited to checking the dates of the previous period of employment, the position held and — perhaps — the salary. If the candidate knows that this is done as a formality later on it may help him avoid any temptation to be over-imaginative in telling his story. As long as the requests are for corroboration of *facts* and not eliciting opinions there is no reason why the offer of employment cannot be made first and corroboration done after acceptance.

SUMMARY PROPOSITIONS

7.1.   Although it has been extensively criticised, the interview is an essential and valuable part of the employment process.

7.2.   Effective interviews are most likely to be those conducted by one person using a biographical or similar logical pattern.

7.3.   Effective interviewing depends on preparation, acquired skill, self-discipline and interview control by the interviewer. Sensitivity and flair are useful additions, but not alternatives to those four requirements.

7.4.   The most important aspect of self-discipline is to avoid making decisions during (instead of after) interviews.

REFERENCES

1. Conan Doyle A., *The Adventures of Sherlock Holmes* (John Murray) 1966, p. 171, (First published by George Newnes, 1892.).
2. Morgan T., 'Recent Insights into the Selection Interview' in *Personnel Review*, Winter 1973, p. 5.
3. See, for instance, Wagner R.F., 'The Employment Interview: A Critical Appraisal' in *Personnel Psychology*, Vol. 2, 1949, pp. 17–40.
4. Bayne R., 'Can Selection Interviewing Be Improved?', paper presented to the British Psychological Society Annual Occupational Psychology Conference, Sheffield, 1977.
5. Webster E.C., *Decision-making in the Employment Interview*, Industrial Relations Center, McGill University, 1964.
6. Among the most helpful researches are Mayfield E.C., 'The Selection Interview: A Re-evaluation of Published Research' in *Personnel Psychology*, No. 17 (1964), pp. 239–260; Wright O.A., 'Summary of Research on the Selection Interview since 1964', *Personnel Psychology*, Vol. 22, 1969, pp. 391–413; Grant D.L. and Bray D.W., 'Contributions of the Interview to Assessment of Management Potential' in *Journal of Applied Psychology*, No. 53 (1969) pp. 24–34.; and Lopez F.M., *Personnel Interviewing* (McGraw-Hill) 1965.
7. Rodger A., 'Interviewing Techniques' in *Recruitment Handbook*, 2nd ed. edited by B. Ungerson (Gower Press) 1975, p. 157.
8. Argyle M., *The Psychology of Interpersonal Behaviour* (Penguin Books) 1972, p. 201.
9. Sidney E., Brown M. and Argyle M., *Skills with People* (Hutchinson) 1973, pp. 80–87.
10. In Torrington D.P., *Face to Face* (Gower) 1972.
11. Bayne R., *op. cit.*
12. Fear R.A., *The Evaluation Interview* (McGraw-Hill) 1958.
13. Dodd J.H.B., 'Personnel Selection – Interviewing' in *Applied Ergonomics*, September 1970.
14. Quoted in Bayne R., *op. cit.*

8

Job Design

Job design is the central feature of the contract for work. For the individual employee, the design of his job specifies the content and nature of his contribution to work activities and many of the conditions within which the work is carried out. For the organisation job design determines the allocation of work, including supervision and integration between the different job holders in the organisation. For both parties to the contract job design is important for the utilisation of individual abilities and skills, satisfaction with mutual expectations about work, and the achievement of goals and objectives through work.

People are not akin to machines designed for specific functions nor is their behaviour capable of complete control or prediction by others. Techniques have been developed to improve assessment of employee potential (Chapter 28), analysis of job requirements in terms of human behaviour (Chapter 27) and employment decision-making (Chapters 6 and 7), all emphasising improved matching of people to job requirements. Training (Chapter 9) and management development (Chapter 10) seek to improve the 'fit' between an individual and his organisation.

Leadership (Chapter 17) and other behavioural research has focused on influencing, guiding or directing human behaviour towards organisational goals. None of these, however, focus on fitting the job to the person.

INDIVIDUAL MOTIVATION AND JOB DESIGN

A body of research evidence and theory, directly influencing job design, is concerned with human motivation and satisfaction at work. Psychologists have consistently studied motivation as a process by which the individual is activated or energised to produce specific activity. For this research the reader is referred to Atkinson,[1] Atkinson and Birch,[2] Bindra and Stewart,[3] Cofer and Appley,[4] Murrell[5] or our later references for useful reviews. Much research has focused on three questions: why people choose a particular work role, the extent of their satisfaction with a chosen work role, and why people of apparently similar abilities produce different levels of performance in their roles. Overviews are provided by Vroom,[6] Vroom and Deci,[7] Howell[8] and Landy and Trumbo,[9] including references to primary sources.

Despite frequent managerial assumptions to the contary, there is no universally accepted theory of motivation, rather a proliferation of theories — many now discredited and others generally accepted as a partial explanation of the processes involved. Campbell *et al*[10] make a useful distinction between two broad classes: 'content theories' and 'process theories', a distinction followed in reviews by Miner and Dachler[11] and other recent reviewers.

1. Content Theories

Content theories describe human motive systems in terms of needs, drives and goals of the individual. The assumption is that people work to satisfy needs, and apply drive or effort towards goals which provide the means of satisfying those needs. Thus the greater the need and the more relevant the goal object to need fulfilment, the harder people work; so the individual is motivated by the extent to which a job provides need-related rewards. Whilst early theories emphasised economic incentives as the general means to satisfy human needs, a variety of needs were subsequently identified and related to other aspects of work.

Perhaps the best known and most influential theory is that of Maslow,[12] who provided a framework for integrating many preceding content theories. He provided a five-category classification of needs: Physiological (to be satisfied in order to sustain life), Safety (protection against threat, danger or deprivation), Social (needs for friendship, belonging, etc. satisfied by association with others), Esteem (needs concerned with self-esteem or the esteem of others) and Self-actualisation (self-fulfilment, creativity, personal development and realisation of one's potential). He arranged these categories in a hierarchy of importance to the individual, as illustrated by Figure 8.1. A number of related propositions have been represented diagrammatically by Krech *et al*[13] upon which our Figure 8.2 is based. Economic rewards are considered to satisfy lower-order needs, whilst the higher-order needs are satisfied by factors more closely related to the working relationships and nature of the work itself — with clear implications for job design.

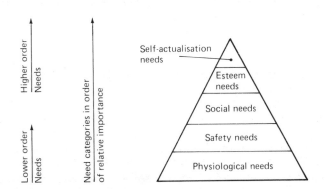

Figure 8.1. Maslow's hierarchy of needs

Another widely known content theory has been outlined by Herzberg *et al*[14] and developed by Herzberg,[15] which directly influenced 'job enrichment'

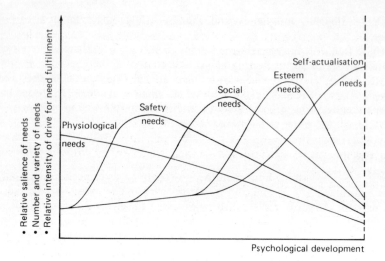

*Figure 8.2. Diagrammatic representation of progressive changes
in the organisation of needs according to Maslow's theory*

approaches to job design. They suggested that two largely independent categories
of factors were important influences upon work behaviour: 'Hygiene factors' (company policy and administration, supervision, relationship with supervisor, work
conditions and salary) and 'Motivators' (achievement, recognition, work itself, responsibility, advancement and growth). Hygiene factors were considered important
influences on the level of dissatisfaction experienced, while motivation was
influenced by the satisfaction experienced through instrinsic factors of the work
itself. The implication is that improvements in extrinsic aspects of work, the
hygiene factors, have limited value in creating a neutral condition whereby the individual is not dissatisfied. In order to motivate people it is necessary to build on this
condition by improving the motivator factors, or re-designing jobs to make the
work more interesting, allowing the scope for responsibility or autonomy, and providing opportunities for advancement and personal growth.

The accumulated weight of research supports the general propositions arising
from the examples of Maslow and Herzberg. Whilst economic and similar rewards
are essential to the satisfaction of lower-order needs, the higher-order needs can be
more readily satisfied by the design of job content. In this way content theorists
suggest that employees will be satisfied and motivated towards efficient work performance.

2. Process Theories

The second category of theories concentrates on the cognitive, motivational and
more general 'mental' processes, through which job satisfaction and performance
are achieved. Motivation is considered to be more complex than simple explanations
in terms of satisfaction of needs. Added explanations include the effects of factors
which influence the cognitive processes by which the individual controls the direction and intensity of his effort. For example a need may be important to a person

but he fails to apply effort because he sees limited 'pay off' from his effort; or his job may provide opportunity for satisfaction of his needs, but he applies less effort because he considers a colleague earns similar rewards for inferior work.

These theories began to develop in the mid-1960s following growing dissatisfaction with content theories, which were simplistic and failed to explain many complexities of human behaviour, as well as largely ignoring the individual capacity for self-determination of behaviour. In particular accumulated evidence, as indicated by the reviews of Brayfield and Crockett[16] and Vroom,[17] indicated that job satisfaction and motivation were different concepts with different relationships to various aspects of work performance — a finding inconsistent with the propositions of content theories.

A number of process theories focus on concepts of equity or perceived fairness of outcomes of work in relation to personal inputs, as represented by the 'Equity Theory' of Adams.[18] Others focus on the setting of work-related goals, as represented by the 'Goal Setting Theory' outlined by Locke[19] and developed by the research of Locke et al,[20] a theory particularly relevant in the context of managerial jobs as indicated by Locke.[21] Another group of theories are referred to as 'VIE (Valence, Instrumentality, Expectancy) Theory', using concepts identified by Vroom,[22] the most influential being introduced by Porter and Lawler[23] and subsequently developed as outlined by Nadler and Lawler.[24]

Whereas content theories suggested generalisable approaches to the motivation of large groups of employees, process theories emphasise the individualistic and cognitive features influencing personal motivation. Further complexity is added by the nature of the processes identified and the differentiation between concepts of job satisfaction (reflecting attitudes to various features of the working situation), with *potential* implications for work behaviour, and motivation reflecting more directly the influences on individual determination of direction, quality and intensity of effort towards work.

Research shows that many of the content and process theories offer useful partial explanations of work behaviour but, being incomplete, action based on them cannot be certain to achieve the required results. The move to more complex, integrative theories also presents problems as indicated by proponents of the Porter–Lawler theory:

> At this point it seems that the theory has become so complex that it has exceeded the measures which exist to test it.[25]

What is clear from the research is that the needs and goals of individuals must be accommodated within the contract for work, and that both motivation and satisfaction are only partially influenced by economic variables. Whilst these are important, the evidence is that job design influences job satisfaction and the resulting attitudes towards work and such behaviour as co-operation with management, quality of work, absences, and remaining a party to the employment contract.

As evidence accumulated to indicate that traditional approaches to job design can produce dissatisfaction and dysfunctional human behaviour, new methods were developed to make work more satisfying for the individual. The methods have varied according to the theory of motivation, and related assumptions about man and his work, guiding managerial action. This relationship between job design methods, motivation and satisfaction is specifically reviewed by Davis and Taylor,[26,27] Cooper[28] and Weir.[29]

MANAGERIAL ASSUMPTIONS

The management of personnel within organisations, both generally and with regard to job design, is strongly influenced by assumptions about people and theories regarding their motivation. These assumptions and theories are rarely explicit, usually being implicit in managerial behaviour and practices. As Schein comments:

> Every manager makes assumptions about people. Whether he is aware of it or not, they operate as a theory in terms of which he decides how to deal with his superior, peers and subordinates. His effectiveness as a manager will depend upon the degree to which his assumptions fit empirical reality.[30]

The nature of these assumptions is important to all areas of the personnel contracts — to the setting, the small print and to the contracts for work, collective consent, individual control and for payment. Assumptions about what motivates people, and about the nature of the people involved, underlie most managerial behaviour and employment practices. Douglas McGregor,[31] an exponent of Maslow's theory in relation to motivation, makes the important point that assumptions can represent a self-fulfilling prophecy, an observation that has significant research support. In other words if one assumes a person to be lazy and uninterested in work, the resulting managerial actions (e.g. simplified work tasks coupled with coercion, close control and supervision) may well be the cause of employee behaviour which appears to confirm the original assumptions. Equally, if one assumes a person to be responsible and seeking fulfilment in work, the resulting managerial actions (e.g. design of work to stimulate interest and challenge, coupled with helpful supervision and a degree of autonomy) may encourage behaviour in accordance with these assumptions.

Most theories and prescriptions for human behaviour contain explicit and implicit assumptions, as illustrated by Duncan's[32] analysis of different approaches in the behavioural sciences generally. Schein[33] has produced a useful analysis of managerial assumptions, identifying four general sets (Rational-Economic Man, Social Man, Self-Actualising and Complex Man) together with related strategies of management and supporting research evidence.

Our own text is developed in the light of 'complex man' assumptions, as are most current approaches to understanding and explaining human behaviour. This implies that all managerial approaches to job design are potentially valid, if appropriate to the people and circumstances involved. Consequently we do not advocate any particular managerial strategy for general use, nor do we suggest any job design method to be universally applicable. We do suggest that managers (and others) should explicitly recognise their own theories and assumptions, thereby being able to question their relevance, validity and influence upon their own behaviour and the behaviour of others. Such questioning can alter assumptions or behaviour which appear inappropriate in particular circumstances.

PHILOSOPHY OF JOB DESIGN

Organisations develop their own culture or ideology which influences the attitudes, values, and behaviour of members. Likert[34] identifies four types of organisational climate arising from managerial behaviour and practices, whilst Harrison[35] identifies four types of ideology which influence such practice. Similarly we consider that different job design methods reflect differences in philosophy relating to attitudes and assumptions about the nature and objectives of work and of people in their working environment.

The traditional, and probably still the most influential, job design philosophy is based on Scientific Managment ideas. Using 'rational-economic man' assumptions, the 'Job-Centred Philosophy' suggests that individual jobs should be specified by management, quite independently of particular job holders, for the satisfaction of organisational goals. This philosophy is seen in customary approaches to employing personnel: identify specific jobs as designed, analyse them, determine job requirements in human terms and then select people with matching physical and psychological characteristics. The person is fitted to the job, which is viewed as relatively fixed. Much research and management practice has developed on this philosophical basis.

However, research evidence and practical experience has pointed to many inadequacies of this traditional philosophy. We have referred to studies of motivation and job satisfaction which point to a need for jobs to be designed to suit their occupants. Studies of the effects of work upon mental health, such as Kornhauser[36] and Gardell,[37] or the many studies relating to employee well-being as summarised by Warr and Wall,[38] all support new approaches to matching people and their work. Selection procedures have been criticised as denying equal opportunities, discriminating by abilities (n.b. a specific objective of selection) or by unfair discrimination on ethnic or other prejudicial grounds. Research by Kirkpatrick et al.[39] Parrish et al[40] and others has shown unintentional discrimination within selection testing procedures arising from sub-cultural differences.

As our social life and values have developed, such evidence has assumed increasing importance resulting in pressure towards different organisational philosophies and action. This is apparent in recent legislation, in the United Kingdom and other developed countries, to restrict organisational freedom of action.

Thus a distinctly different philosophy may well be developing, which could be termed a 'Social Planning Philosophy', to encompass a variety of theoretical positions, political ideas and social values. This implies that wider social needs and objectives (e.g. full employment, job security, employee health and well-being, equal opportunities, job satisfaction) should take precedence over narrowly defined organisational objectives. Further development in this direction, if carried to a logical conclusion, would suggest that employees should be selected upon a basis of societal considerations with jobs designed to suit the characteristics of the individual. This remains a theoretical possibility at present, except for limited adoption within organisations such as sheltered workshops or factories for the handicapped operated by charities or government agencies.

A social planning philosophy will be strongly resisted by most organisations because of the implicit lack of concern for organisational objectives or the needs of shareholders, and the potential consequences for the survival of particular organisations as employers. Equally the purely job-centred philosophy is increasingly being rejected due to lack of concern for individual and social needs. A different approach, a 'Person-centred Philosophy', has developed which recognises both organisational and individual needs to be important. This implies selection of people, perhaps on wider considerations than specific jobs, but viewing job characteristics as flexible so that they can be designed or re-designed to accommodate the abilities and needs of the individual.

Where early approaches to job design represented the traditional philosophy, later approaches have developed towards a person-centred philosophy. Different methods reflect variations in mix of the two philosophies, or different views of the relative importance of the needs of individual and organisation. At an extreme there may well be a primary emphasis on individual needs, just as the traditional philosophy puts primary emphasis on organisational needs.

The pressure towards greater flexibility in job design are many, not least being the general improvements in educational levels and other social changes resulting in increased employee expectations from the work environment. Evidence of the inadequacies of the traditional approach are a definite force towards greater consideration of individual and social needs by management. Related to this there is the so-called Human Relations movement, with organisational theorists and behavioural scientists reacting against Scientific Management by advocating management practices based on a recognition of the importance of human psychological and social needs (i.e. assumptions about 'social man' or 'self-actualising man'). There is the additional, more pragmatic approach of the managers and theorists who recognise long-term organisational advantages in ensuring the improved attitudes or motivation of the workforce.

Although supporting the social and pragmatic advantages of the greater attention to individual needs implied by a person-centred philosophy, we do not consider that this must necessarily imply that organisation needs are less important than those of the individual. The contract for work provides the opportunity for an optimal satisfaction of the needs and expectations of both parties, rather than maximising the satisfaction of either party at the expense of the other. With 'complex man' assumptions this would imply job design on an individual basis for total satisfaction of individual needs. Whilst this would be desirable, there will often be technical reasons, problems arising from homogeneity or heterogeneity of employee characteristics, or problems of identifying individual needs which prevent achievement in practice. An optimal solution involves considering all possible alternatives and selecting one which represents the best balance in the circumstances for satisfying both organisational and individual requirements.

JOB DESIGN APPROACHES: AN OVERVIEW

Whilst various approaches to job design have been advocated and practised, especially in the past two decades, most published material has derived from case studies or research using specific approaches rather than comparative analysis. An early comparative study by Davis[41] and a more recent study by Birchall[42] indicate the development of job design during the decade 1965—1975. Similarly two books of readings by Davis and Taylor[43,44] provide an overview and extracts from influential publications.

Our objective is to provide a broad overview together with references for further study. A major difficulty is the recent and rapid changes in theory and practice, resulting in changing or contradictory definitions of key concepts such as 'job en-

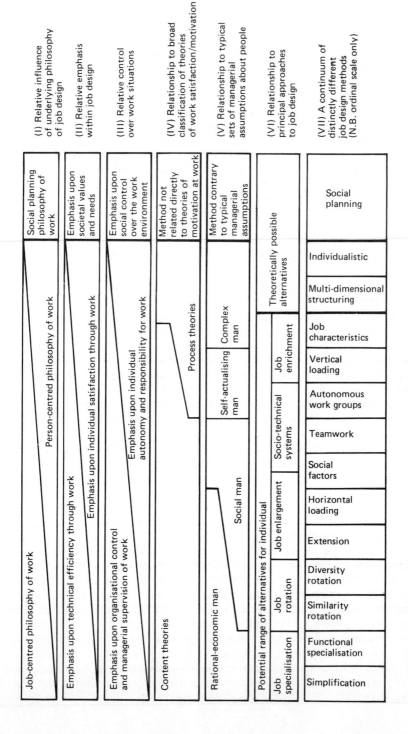

Figure 8.3. A taxonomy of job design methods and some underlying differences between the methods

largement' or 'job enrichment'. To counteract this problem we have identified the principal approaches and sub-divided these to develop a taxonomy of fourteen distinct job design methods.

This is extended into a general model in Figure 8.3, which shows the differences between the methods identified. These relate to job design, philosophy, relative emphasis on organisational and individual needs, and relative control over working situations. The methods are also related to the theories of motivation and general management assumptions discussed earlier. Taking a starting point of job specialisation (*circa* 1900), leading to job simplification (*circa* 1920 onwards), the continuum indicates a general process of development — although not a time scale — to current practices of job enrichment. Further identified are theoretically possible alternatives which have not yet been practically applied except upon a very limited experimental or restricted basis. Although our continuum of methods and associated dimensions is illustrated as a scale, this is considered ordinal only — relative differences will vary considerably on different dimensions.

GENERAL APPROACHES TO JOB DESIGN

1. Job Specialisation

Since the Industrial Revolution manufacturing organisations have emphasised the efficient use of technology (material, tools, machinery, power sources) and people through division of labour and co-ordinated activities. Up to 1900 the understanding and application of technology had developed considerably, but the division and co-ordination of work relied largely on rule-of-thumb methods. Economists since Adam Smith emphasised the productivity benefits of division of labour, but such specialisation was broadly based. Management (or owners) usually exercised a variety of planning and control functions, whilst workers specialised broadly by technology considerations.

During the period 1890 to 1920 several theorists advocated new ideas of organisation, significantly influencing the working environment and stimulating subsequent research and new techniques. Weber[45] produced his analyses of bureaucracy; Fayol's 1916 book[46] outlined principles of administration which advocated systematic planning of organisation and management. Organisational planning and design suggested a variety of managerial roles based on specialisation by function, authority and responsibility.

In the same period others examined production organisation and work activities, stimulating related theories and practices now collectively identified as Scientific Management. The work of F.W. Taylor[47] is popularly recognised as the foundation of this field, identifying many inadequacies of production management and developing new principles and practices which were successfully applied. Whilst an examination of Scientific Managment is inappropriate here, some brief comment is necessary in view of current suggestions that 'Taylorism' can be blamed for many contemporary industrial problems. Many of his ideas were consistent with a person-centred philosophy as he advocated development of employees, full utilisation of skills and abilities, maximum promotion opportunities, and unlimited pay related to performance. Whilst such ideas were largely ignored in practice, other techniques were developed and applied enthusiastically. In the context of job design some of the widely adopted practices are:

Science of Work. The need for scientific methods of observing, measuring and analysing work activities to replace existing unsystematic approaches.

Standardisation. Using the resulting knowledge efficient working methods and performance levels can be set for work.

Selection. Systematic and scientific approaches to selecting workers with relevant qualities and abilities, together with planned training for the work involved.

Specialisation. Both Management and workers to concentrate upon specific functional activities, involving a limited range of tasks for which the individual's abilities and training enable expert performance.

Other contemporary researchers focused upon the science of work, like F. and L. Gilbreth, with their emphasis on motion study, and Bedeaux, who emphasised time study. Personnel psychology, work study or industrial engineering, and ergonomics are all directly concerned with the scientific study of different (but related) aspects of people at work to make work behaviour more efficient.

The application of these ideas and techniques has led to two distinct job design methods:

(a) FUNCTIONAL SPECIALISATION

Individual job content is determined by a rational sub-division of organisational work activities, and is associated with precisely defined limits of responsibility and discretion. Managerial work involves specialisation by administrative functions of planning, control co-ordination, and expert knowledge. Production work involves specialisation in a limited range of defined and pre-planned tasks. Essentially this method involves specialisation by individuals upon a range of tasks which their knowledge, abilities and skills enable them to perform in the manner of an expert.

(b) SIMPLIFICATION

Individual job content is limited as much as possible, by minimising the number of tasks and restricting variations in method and timing of operations. This is mainly directed at production or clerical work, with emphasis on technical efficiency and cost reduction by maximising specialisation and minimising variety, discretion, skill requirements and training time. Essentially this method involves an extreme degree of specialisation, based upon the individual's regular repetition of a very limited range of tasks or physical operations, so that requirements for expert knowledge or skill are minimal.

This approach is common in semi-skilled jobs, particularly production-line work, using work study and man-machine systems design. Work activities are planned and specified, with efficient methods regularly repeated over a fairly constant and short time cycle. The work is closely supervised and largely programmed, leaving the individual employee little variety, discretion over methods, control over work place, or opportunity to exercise skill.

A 1955 study by Davis et al[48] showed clearly that the ideas of job design by simplification were widely accepted as 'best practice' in United States manufacturing industry. Current texts in work study and production management emphasise the design of jobs for maximum specialisation by simplification, technical efficiency, and the corresponding cost minimisation.

As job simplification became widespread a gradual increase of behavioural problems became apparent in the form of industrial disputes and unco-operative working attitudes. Similarly low motivation, reduced quality of work, high absenteeism, and high labour turnover were associated with simplified jobs. It is over-simplistic to explain such problems entirely in terms of job design, but an increasing weight of evidence suggests that they are the psychological consequences of jobs designed as though man can be treated as akin to complex machinery.

Thus job specialisation represents a job-centred philosophy of technical efficiency but little concern for people or social values. Short term cost-efficiency can be achieved, but the behavioural problems interfere with continuity and have long-term costs and consequences for organisational effectiveness. Consequently, a number of alternative job design methods have emerged which aim to balance organisational needs with individual needs to be satisfied at work. This chapter now concentrates on such alternatives, viewing job simplification as a datum point for comparison.

2. Job Rotation

Job rotation increases the variety of activities performed by the individual by allowing him to move from one job to another, perhaps at specified intervals. The rotation may be voluntary, implying some degree of personal choice, but is usually obligatory with specification of time intervals and the tasks involved.

From the organisational viewpoint, this has several advantages, notably that basic work processes remain undisturbed and an increase in flexibility results. Having people experienced in different jobs permits staggering of rest periods and provides cover for lateness and absenteeism, particularly on production lines. Similarly, when specific jobs require uncomfortable working positions or environmental conditions these can be more widely shared. With supervisory or management staff it may make work more interesting, for those unlikely to achieve further promotion, or it may be a basis for training in preparation for promotion. A study of job rotation on an assembly-line by Miller et al[49] indicated that job rotation resulted in higher overall efficiency than when operators carried out a single simplified job.

Consistent with 'Human Relations' approaches to motivation, rotation potentially provides the individual with opportunities for increased responsibility, work variety, experience of greater totality of the work output, stimulation of interest or reduced boredom, and uses a wider range of abilities. In practice, however, such opportunities may be more apparent than real as indicated by the two distinctive methods:

(a) SIMILARITY ROTATION
The different jobs are generally similar tasks and rotation introduces spatial and/or temporal variations. The nature of production-line technology makes this often the only practical form of rotation, and voluntary rotation usually is restricted to similar work activities.

(b) DIVERSITY ROTATION
The duties are dissimilar and rotation involves diversity of work in addition to spatial and/or temporal variations. This has greater potential for employee job satis-

faction and flexibility of working, but there is usually limited scope for diversity or for the rotation to be other than pre-planned.

These methods apply to production-line work designed on a job simplification basis, with people exchanging work stations. Production processes are little affected, with organisational advantages of flexibility often offset by higher pay and training costs. The individual may have more variety and opportunities for wider skill utilisation, but only marginal improvement in job satisfaction can be expected from work comprising different simplified operations.

3. Job Enlargement

Job enlargement represents a definite movement away from simplified jobs, by extending the job content to include a wider range of tasks. As with rotation, the aim is to increase task variety but by changing job content instead of moving occupants between different jobs. There is also potential for greater involvement of the individual in his work, by greater skill and increased identification with the product of personal work.

The stimulus for this approach came from studies of assembly-line work. Studies repeatedly pointed to the alienation of workers through repetitive, simplified jobs which were boring, monotonous, undemanding, with little scope for identification of a product of one's work due to the minor operations involved. Case studies such as Walker and Guest[50] suggested that interest in work was related to the number and variety of operations included in the job. Many of the motivation theorists pointed to needs for esteem, both self-esteem and recognition by others, which can be related to the total contribution and significance of one's work.

Job enlargement is primarily aimed at reduction of boredom and stimulation of interest in work, with some opportunity for improved satisfaction of esteem needs. With a larger number of tasks per worker, the time cycle of work increases so reducing repetition and monotony. Interest is considered to be developed by broader skill utilisation and the ability to identify a definite product of one's work due to the larger contribution made. Esteem needs may be at least partially satisfied, by the recognition that one's work and skill represent a significant contribution, whilst self-evaluation of quality and the increased responsibility also improve the perceived meaningfulness of work. In addition to the advantages associated with more satisfied and involved workers, there are other potential benefits. Broadened work skills of employees improve flexibility. The smaller number of people contributing to a finished product reduces problems of task interdependence (e.g. the effects of inadequate work upon subsequent job activities) and enables sources of poor workmanship to be more easily located. It is easier to introduce product changes or new models, and to modify the production rate by changing the number of employees working on specific products. A consistent finding of case studies is that improvements in quality usually result from enlarged jobs.

There are organisational problems which must be recognised. Reducing the degree of specialisation has consequences for working efficiency in many cases. Enlargement frequently requires greater factory space, duplication of certain machinery and tools, additional materials handling facilities, and other increases in costs. Similarly additional training is usually required, and employees expect their higher skill to be recognised by increased wages. Most organisations have limited ability to enlarge jobs due to product complexity, the technical processes or machinery involved, or characteristics of components. A case study by Biggane and Stewart[51] provides a useful analysis of the advantages and problems of job enlargement, as well as typical results.

We list three broad methods of job enlargement:

(a) EXTENSION

This involves the addition of very similar tasks to the job content, which increases the number of operations but has little impact on the variety and skill of the individual.

(b) HORIZONTAL LOADING

Further tasks are added to the job, increasing the variety for the individual.

(c) SOCIAL FACTORS

Tasks are added to the job, or other changes in working relationships and environment are made both to increase variety and to provide greater opportunity for social interaction. This increases the potential for satisfaction of social needs at work. Typical examples are the enlargement of jobs by including tasks which require regular social interaction with others in the organisation, or with clients and suppliers.

Enlargement is a further improvement over rotation, but the scope for satisfying higher-order needs of individuals remains limited — the increase in variety is real, but scope for genuine intrinsic motivation is restricted. The effects on job satisfaction depend on individual characteristics and requirements, but research consistently reports improvements. Better-quality work and increased interest in work activities are also reported in most cases. Such improvements are significant in relative terms, but in absolute terms further improvements remain possible.

4. Socio-Technical Systems

In the socio-technical systems approach, design of production work focuses on the working group rather than the individual. Based on world-wide research this conceptual and theoretical framework for work design has been particularly identified with work by members of the Tavistock Institute during the 1950s and 1960s.

Their early stimulation came from research into changing methods of production in the coal industry, where improvements in technical methods failed to achieve the expected improvements in efficiency and productivity. Analysis and explanation has been provided by Trist and Bamforth,[52] showing the psychological and social consequences of the changes in production on individuals and working groups. Eventually a compromise production method was developed, with less emphasis on technical efficiency and more attention paid to the needs of members of the working groups. Substantial gains in productivity and job satisfaction were demonstrated, with reductions of 10 to 20 per cent in costs per unit production and decreased absenteeism, negligible labour turnover and improved health records.

A summary of the theoretical framework has been provided by Emery and Trist,[53] also in reports of further research and practice by Trist et al[54] and Miller and Rice.[55] They point out that any production organisation consists of two elements: a technical system and a social system. The technical system comprises the equipment and plant, with particular characteristics and requirements, and their layout and operation. The social system comprises people, with their particular characteristics and requirements, and their formal and informal organisation in the work situation. Most organisational design and planning had been directed at maximising the efficiency of the technical system, applying the principles of Scientific Management and manipulating the social system to satisfy technical requirements. At the same time various Human Relations theorists appeared to be advocating design of the social systems so as to maximise the satisfaction of human needs by manipulating the technical system. As these approaches are incompatible the organisation should be seen as a *socio-technical system* with joint optimisation of the needs of both systems.

This was a change in the philosophy of job design, which brought the Scientific Management and Human Relations ideas together in a framework acceptable to management. By appropriate design of the work organisation both the needs of employee and the needs of the technical system could be optimally satisfied. In reality the emphasis remains on organisational needs but indicates pragmatic benefits to be gained from satisfying individual needs.

In practical applications the unit of analysis has remained the working group rather than individuals, building on the research stimulated by the Hawthorne Studies (see Chapter 2). The consequences of technical requirements in terms of group behaviour has been the primary emphasis, starting from human needs for social relationships and esteem through social interaction and group identification. Compromise in the design of technical systems and associated work activities is considered necessary to develop working groups which are socially satisfying and produce co-operative behaviour.

Three general methods can be identified:

(a) SOCIAL FACTORS

As discussed under the heading of job enlargement, this method involves re-organisation of work activities to provide opportunities to satisfy various social needs at work. Such job enlargement can be provided in this context by work organisation stimulating the individual's identification and interaction with formal and informal groups.

(b) TEAMWORK

This method involves allocating work to groups so that the tasks are identified with the group, with performance achieved by co-operative working activities because of the interdependence of members. As well as providing opportunities for social interaction the objective is to encourage the formation of group norms which influence member behaviour — within the group so as to maintain co-operative and harmonious relationships, and collectively to encourage appropriate work attitudes and performance.

Many of the publications examining group dynamics research and theory, referred to elsewhere in this book, provide useful guidance about the characteristics and behaviour of groups. Wild[56] provides an overview specifically related to alternative forms of group working within industry. In referring to the single method of 'Teamwork' we are actually including a general category covering many alternative forms of work design in practice.

Essentially this method involves substantial job enlargement, together with greater attention to individual needs which are commonly satisfied in a group setting.

Improved job satisfaction is consistently reported to be significant in both relative and absolute terms with improvements in such behaviour as absence, health, turnover, and co-operation. The effect on costs and productivity is less certain, varying considerably with specific applications and people. It appears safe to conclude that the method has potential for improved intrinsic motivation, but realisation depends upon the specific people and work design involved.

(c) AUTONOMOUS WORKING GROUPS

As with teamwork methods, this involves the allocation of work to groups so that tasks and goals are identified with the group, and performance is achieved by co-operative working. The important addition here is that the groups have autonomy and responsibility for their work and organisation. In addition to the benefits associated with teamwork and job enlargement, the group operates with many of the benefits of job enrichment as discussed below.

The duties of the group include some of the responsibilities normally associated with specialists and superiors in the management structure. Within pre-determined limits they are collectively allowed a degree of autonomy, implying independence, relative freedom from controls and authority to make decisions concerning the working activities of members. Having been allocated their tasks and facilities, autonomous groups are typically allowed to scope to:

(i) Regulate the work content allocated to individual members.

(ii) Organise their working activities and determine methods.

(iii) Conduct production planning and adjust to changes required by technological consideration and variations.

(iv) Carry out self-evaluation of quality and level of performance.

(v) Participate in the setting of goals, objectives and standards for the work of the group.

(vi) Conduct decision-making on a participative basis.

This method is currently receiving popular attention for several reasons. Pressures for greater industrial democracy and wide publicity for the purpose-built factory of Volvo at Kalmar in Sweden (see Gyllenhammer[57] for example) have popularised the idea of autonomous group working. The application of job enrichment schemes during the past twenty years has mainly been with selected groups of employees, whereas this method enables a wider application to production workers. However this approach is not as new as many people appear to believe.

We have referred above to the work of Emery, Trist and others based at the Tavistock Institute. From the late 1950s they have advocated greater autonomy for working groups. A large number of organisations throughout the world have implemented such practices but systematic examinations have not always been published. The major applications have been notably those of Philips in Holland, Saab-Scania in Sweden, and Volvo in Sweden, all concerned with mass production factories, and usefully summarised by Dowling,[58] which were all implemented during the period 1960 to 1970. Similarly a number of applications in Norway have been examined by Gulowsen,[59] and were also implemented prior to 1970.

There is little doubt that this approach provides for the satisfaction of a wide range of individual needs at work on a collective basis, with similar potential on an individual basis, depending upon the allocation of work to group members. The impact on job satisfaction, as indicated by interview and attitude survey, is generally significant and better than with other job design methods discussed so far.

One problem for organisations is that it may not be feasible to apply this method in all areas of work, and selective application can increase the dissatisfaction of workers remaining on traditionally designed jobs. For this and other practical reasons, many applications have been in specific factories often purpose-built for the new method of work organisation. A new approach to management is also necessary, with traditional managerial responsibilities allocated to groups and similar problems of co-ordinating the activities of a number of autonomous groups.

From the individual point of view the potential for satisfaction and motivation is moderated by the group decisions. Individual jobs can be allocated according to preferences, or by applying any of the alternative job design methods. This potential may well be affected by limits of flexibility imposed by the work involved, or by allocation of less desirable work on a basis of member popularity. Evidence suggests that group norms develop to influence behaviour towards group and organisational goals, and that groups can be more demanding of members than management. Whilst evidence has accumulated showing increases in collective job satisfaction, this may not necessarily apply to all individuals. Lower labour turnover, absences and sickness are typical as are improvements in grievance and disciplinary incidents. Quality of work is usually reported as improved and, at worst, unchanged. Reduced operating costs and improved productivity are frequently demonstrated, although such improvements are sometimes marginal or debatable due to the capital investment involved. In general, however, this method appears to offer significant benefits to both the individual and organisation.

5. Job Enrichment

Job enrichment extends the content of jobs to provide for greater satisfaction of the individual's needs and goals, and greater intrinsic motivation, by a combination of enlargement, autonomy and responsibility. This method also develops the discretionary aspects of work by adding aspects of planning, normally carried out by specialists, and control, normally associated with management.

We distinguish between two methods which, although having a similar basis, represent differences in technique and underlying theory. The methods are:

(a) VERTICAL LOADING

This method is the now well-established approach to job enrichment whereby individual jobs are developed to provide increased scope for personal achievement and recognition, more challenging and responsible work, and greater opportunity for personal advancement and development. The term 'vertical loading' refers to the addition of discretionary aspects of work, as compared with the horizontal addition of tasks, although both types of change are commonly involved.

Maslow, McGregor and many others have pointed to individual needs for esteem and self-actualisation which can be satisfied at work, as indicated earlier. However, job enrichment is particularly associated with the work of Herzberg discussed earlier, suggesting that the motivational content of work could be increased by improving the work content to satisfy higher-order needs and provide greater discretion and responsibility.

A large number of job enrichment schemes have been implemented over the past two decades, particularly in the USA and UK, many being reported in our earlier references (e.g. Herzberg, Davis and Taylor, Weir, and others). Notable early applications were reported by Myers,[60] at the Texas Instruments Corporation, and by Ford,[61] at AT & T Corporation. All produced many practical and behavioural problems to be overcome, resulting in a number of guidelines and techniques to assist implementation.

The common features of early applications was a basic assumption that Herzberg's theory is universally applicable to all employees. Thus by enriching a job, the individual's higher-order needs would be met at work, resulting in improved job satisfaction and motivation. In general the evidence supported this view with collective improvements in job satisfaction, in labour turnover, absences, sickness, grievances, disciplinary problems, etc. commonly reported. Most studies report improved quality of work and many report improved productivity.

Organisations have even greater problems than with other methods in providing opportunities for job enrichment. Practical problems of enrichment have resulted in selective applications often, but not always, limited to managerial and clerical jobs. For many production operations it is difficult or impossible to enrich individual jobs, hence the growing attention to autonomous work groups discussed earlier. Higher-calibre individuals may need to be selected, additional training will be needed, and payment levels inevitably increased to recognise more responsible work. By definition an enriched job implies significant loss of the technical efficiency provided by simplified jobs. Despite such problems, researchers and management consistently report organisational benefits in overall cost-productivity improvements.

Many applications have failed to produce the benefits claimed, but these are less well publicised. The reasons are usually considered to be failures of management rather than of the method, because of inadequate preparation, planning and implementation of changes. Often management are reluctant to permit realistic autonomy and responsibility, thus undermining the essential features. Such explanations are usually valid, but growing evidence suggests that the basic assumptions are often over-simplistic. As indicated in our discussion of process theories, individual needs and motivation differ considerably. Consequently a general application of job enrichment may well be inappropriate in some situations.

(b) JOB CHARACTERISTICS
This method includes all aspects of job enrichment, as discussed above, but is concerned with developing criteria and techniques for the design of jobs in terms of the satisfaction and intrinsic motivation of the individual job holder. A summary of the essential features, based on several years of research, is provided by Hackman.[62] This summary identifies five important core job dimensions: skill variety, task identity, task significance, autonomy and feedback. These are incorporated in a theoretical model derived originally from previous research, but specifically tested and developed by their own research, relating them to 'critical psychological states' (e.g. meaningfulness of work, responsibility for outcomes, and knowledge of actual results) as experienced by the individual. These in turn are related to 'personal and work outcomes', in terms of satisfaction and motivation, as moderated by the individual's 'strength of needs for growth'. Two practical applications of the theoretical framework are:

(i) A set of action principles relating to the job dimensions, to guide the design and implementation of enriched jobs.

(ii) Diagnostic measuring instruments to assess the characteristics of existing jobs, current employee reactions to the job, and 'growth needs strength' of the employee. These permit careful diagnosis of existing jobs and employees, to guide the planning of enriched jobs, and the evaluation of the impact of changes afterwards.

The result is a practical approach to job enrichment which permits closer attention to the specific needs of individuals or groups. As such it is an improvement upon the general prescriptive approach to job enrichment and provides the guidance needed for effective job design. However, this framework is relatively new and untried in practice, although the research support is currently impressive, so it must be considered developmental and applied with caution.

6. Theoretically Possible Alternatives

The above approaches represent the development of job design practice to the present time, but three further possibilities can be envisaged:

(a) MULTI-DIMENSIONAL STRUCTURING

A survey of the literature indicates many job dimensions and psychological factors which appear important to job design. Job enrichment is concerned with the larger number of variables, but it seems reasonable to expect further improvements. As behavioural science knowledge develops, and psychological measurement techniques improve, so improved theoretical and practical frameworks will be developed. With such guidance a larger number of job dimensions will be capable of manipulation, to achieve a more precise optimisation of organisational and individual needs.

(b) INDIVIDUALISTIC

This method refers to the selection of an individual on more general considerations than the job requirements, then designing the particular job to suit his abilities and personal characteristics, with greater emphasis upon individual needs and goals than those of the organisation. This represents a pure 'person-centred philosophy' emphasis on individual needs, but with the organisation determining the general considerations or criteria for employment. As a voluntary method this is only likely to suit organisational needs in special cases — such as maintaining the interest and employment of an individual appointed in advance of future requirements for knowledge, skills, or management succession.

(c) SOCIAL PLANNING

This method refers to the possibility, currently only theoretical and likely to be strongly resisted by organisations, mentioned earlier as consistent with a social planning philosophy. If adopted in practice it would involve selecting employees in accordance with socially determined criteria, then designing jobs to suit their abilities, personal characteristics and needs. The only current applications are for government-sponsored workshops, or those operated by charities, intended to provide subsidised but real employment for the mentally or physically handicapped.

SUMMARY PROPOSITIONS

8.1.   Although jobs have traditionally been designed to meet technical and cost criteria, it is now clear that failure to meet employee needs in job design reduces the likelihood of meeting organisational needs.

8.2.   Some newer approaches put employee needs first and those of the organisation second, but the ideal is to aim for a 'best fit' between the two sets of needs.

8.3.   None of the newer approaches provides the single answer to the question of how best to design jobs. All methods, traditional and novel, are potentially useful depending on the particular organisation, employee and working requirements.

8.4.   The further developments that are expected will probably all move away from the principle of job simplification.

REFERENCES

1.   Atkinson J.W., *An Introduction to Motivation* (Van Nostrand) 1964.
2.   Atkinson J.W. and Birch D., *An Introduction to Motivation* 2nd ed. (Von Nostrand) 1979.
3.   Bindra D. and Stewart J.W. (eds.), *Motivation* 2nd ed. (Penguin) 1971.
4.   Cofer C.N. and Appley M.H., *Motivation: Theory and Research* (Wiley) 1964.
5.   Murrell H., *Motivation at Work* (Methuen) 1976.
6.   Vroom V.H., *Work and Motivation* (Wiley) 1964.
7.   Vroom V.H. and Deci E.L., *Management and Motivation* (Penguin) 1970.
8.   Howell W.C., *Essentials of Industrial and Organisational Psychology* (Dorsey) 1976.
9.   Landy F.J. and Trumbo D.A., *Psychology of Work Behaviour* (Dorsey) 1976.
10. Campbell J.W., Dunnette M.D., Lawler E.E., III and Weick K.W. Jr., *Managerial Behaviour, Performance and Effectiveness* (McGraw-Hill) 1970.
11. Miner J.B. and Dachler H.P., 'Personnel Attitudes and Motivation', *Annual Review of Psychology,* Vol. 24, 1973, pp. 379–402.
12. Maslow A.H., 'A Theory of Human Motivation', *Psychological Review,* Vol. 50, 1943, pp. 370–396.
13. Krech D., Crutchfield R.S. and Ballachey E.L., *Individual in Society* (McGraw-Hill) 1962.
14. Herzberg F., Mausner B. and Snyderman B., *The Motivation to Work* (Wiley) 1959.
15. Herzberg F., *Work and the Nature of Man* (Cleveland: World Publishing) 1966.
16. Brayfield A.H. and Crockett W.H., 'Employee Attitudes and Employee Performance', *Psychological Bulletin,* Vol. 52, 1955, pp. 396–424.
17. Vroom V.H., *op. cit.* (ref. 6).
18. Adams J.S., 'Inequality in Social Exchange' in L. Berkowitz (ed.), *Advances in Experimental Social Psychology* (Vol. 2.) (Academic Press) 1965, pp. 267–79.
19. Locke E.A., 'Towards a Theory of Task Motivation and Incentives', *Organisalional Behaviour and Human Performance,* Vol. 3, 1968, pp. 157–189.
20. Locke E.A., Cartledge N. and Kerr C.S., 'Studies of the Relationship between Satisfaction, Goal Setting and Performance', *Organisational Behaviour and Human Performance,* Vol.5, 1970, pp. 135–158.
21. Locke E.A., 'The Ubiquity of the Technique of Goal Setting in Theories of and Approaches to Employee Motivation', *Academy of Management Review,* July 1978.
22. Vroom V.H., *op. cit.* (ref. 6).
23. Porter L.W. and Lawler E.E., *Managerial Attitudes and Performance* (Irwin-Dorsey) 1968.
24. Nadler D. and Lawler E.J., Motivation: 'A Diagnostic Approach' in Hackman J.W., Lawler E.A. and Porter L.W., *Perspectives on Behaviour in Organisations* (McGraw-Hill) 1977.

25. Lawler E.E., and Suttle J.L. 'Expectancy Theory and Job Behaviour' *Organisational Behaviour and Human Performance*, Vol. 9, 1973, p. 502.
26. Davis. E. and Taylor. C. (ed.), *Design of Jobs* (Penguin) 1972.
27. Davis L.E. and Taylor J.C. (eds.), *Design of Jobs* 2nd ed., (Goodyear) 1979.
28. Cooper R., *Job Motivation and Job Design* (Institute of Personnel Management) 1974.
29. Weir M. (ed.), *Job Satisfaction: Challenge and Response in Modern Britain.* (Fontana/Colling),1976.
30. Schein E.H., *Organisational Psychology*, 3rd ed., (Prentice-Hall) 1979.
31. McGregor D., *The Human Side of Enterprise* (McGraw-Hill) 1960.
32. Duncan W.J., *Organisational Behaviour* (Houghton Mifflin), 1978, Chapter 2, pp. 19–48.
33. Schein E.H., *op. cit.* (ref. 30), 1979.
34. Likert R., *The Human Organisation* (McGraw-Hill) 1960.
35. Harrison R., 'Understanding your Organisation's Character,' *Harvard Business Review*, May-June, 1972, pp. 119–128.
36. Kornhauser A., *Mental Health of the Industrial Worker* (John Wiley) 1965.
37. Gardell B., *Alienation and Mental Health in the Modern Industrial Environment.* Apr. 1970. W.H.O. Symposium on Society, Stress and Disease, Stockholm.
38. Warr P. and Wall T., *Work and Well-being* (Penguin) 1975.
39. Kirkpatrick J.J. *et al., Differential Selection among Applicants from Different Socio-Economic or Ethnic Backgrounds,* Final Report to the Ford Foundation by Research Centre for Industrial Behaviour, New York University, 1967.
40. Parrish J.A., *et al., The Industrial Psychologist: Selection and Equal Employment Opportunity* (A Symposium). *Personnel Psychology*, Vol. 19, 1966, pp. 1–40.
41. Davis L.E., 'The Design of Jobs', *Industrial Relations*, Vol. 6, 1966, pp. 21–45.
42. Birchall, D. *Job Design: A Planning and Implementation Guide for Managers* (Gower Press) 1975.
43. Davis L.E. and Taylor J.C., *op. cit.* (ref. 26) 1972.
44. Davis L.E. and Taylor J.C., *op. cit.* (ref. 27) 1979.
45. Weber M., *The Theory of Social and Economic Organisation*, translated by A.M. Henderson and T. Parsons (Oxford University Press) 1947.
46. Fayol H. *General and Industrial Management*, translated by C. Storrs (Pitman) 1949.
47. Taylor F.W., *Scientific Management: A Collection of Material* (Harper and Bros.) 1947.
48. Davis, *et. al.,* 'Current Job Design Criteria', *Journal of Industrial Engineering*, Vol. 6, No. 2, 1955, pp. 5–11. (Reprinted in Ref. No. 26, pp. 65–82.)
49. Miller F.G., Dhaliwal T.S. and Magas L.G., 'Job Rotation raises Productivity', *Industrial Engineering* (U.S.A.), Vol. 5, No.6, 1973, pp. 24–26.
50. Walker C.R., and Guest R.H., *The Man on the Assembly Line* (Harvard University Press) 1952.
51. Biggane J.F. and Stewart P.A., *Job Enlargement: A Case Study*, College of Business Administration, State University of Iowa Research Series, No. 25, July 1963.
52. Trist E.L. and Bamforth K.W., 'Some Social and Psychological Consequences of the Longwall Method of Coal Mining', *Human Relations*, Vol.4, 1951, pp. 1–38.
53. Emery F.E. and Trist E.L., 'Socio-Technical Systems' in C.W. Churchman and M.Verhulst (eds.) *Management Science, Models and Techniques*, Vol. 2 (Pergamon) 1960.
54. Trist E.L., Higgin G.W., Murray H. and Pollock A.A., *Organisational Choice* (Tavistock) 1963.
55. Miller E.J. and Rice E.K., *Systems of Organisation* (Tavistock) 1970.
56. Wild R., *Work Organisation: A study of manual work and mass production* (Wiley Interscience) 1975.
57. Gyllenhammar P. 'How Volvo adapts Work to People'. *Harvard Business Review*, July-August, 1977, pp. 102–113.
58. Dowling W.F., 'Job Design on the Assembly Line: Farewell to Blue Collar Blues?' *'Organisational Dynamics'*, Autumn 1973, pp. 51–67.
59. Gulowsen J. *Sevstyrte Arbeidsgrupper (Autonomous Work Groups)* (Tanum Press) 1971.
60. Myers M. 'Who are your Motivated Workers?', *Harvard Business Review*, Jan-Feb. 1964, pp. 73–88.
61. Ford, N., Job Enrichment Lessons from A.T. & T., *Harvard Business Review*, Jan-Feb. pp. 73–88.
62. Hackman J.R., 'Designing Work for Individuals and Groups', in J.R. Hackman, E.A. Lawler and L.W. Porter (eds), *Perspectives on Behaviour in Organisation* (McGraw-Hill) 1977.

9

The Development of Training Programmes

After the process of matching the needs of the employee with the needs of the organisation through the employment process, the next stage of the contract for work is training: developing the employee's capacity to perform. By this means he is enabled to carry out the tasks assigned to him and to realise his personal aspiration in the organisational context.

We are all exposed to training from birth, first within the family and later in both the family and the setting of formal education. When starting work employees already have long experience of learning and being trained *for their own good*. Even though they may have resisted some of the phases in the process, it will have been clear to most of them that the objective of those organising the training was the development of the trainee for the sake of the trainee.

On entering organisational life the individual is therefore experienced in learning and expects to be trained. Traditionally company training programmes have been a disappointment to recruits, partly because they have tended to be perfunctory and partly because they are often geared so completely to the requirements of the organisation that the trainee has found it an unsatisfying and inadequate preparation for what lies ahead of him. Gradually the nature of training programmes is altering, as the contract principle in employment becomes more generally accepted, and programmes are designed to meet the expectations of the trainee as well as to equip him with specific knowledge and skill. The constructive working relationship with a high degree of mutual trust and commitment is dependent on an approach to training that is as much concerned with the quality of working life as it is with meeting short-term organisational goals. All training is directed at 'changing people' – their knowledge, experience, attitudes and other elements of their behaviour. Only if they see the change process as being to their advantage are they likely willingly to co-operate with the change process.

The Place of Training in Organisations

The training function has long had low status in organisations, and many studies have shown it to be poorly planned, badly conducted and rarely evaluated properly. Typical studies are those of French[1] and Shafer[2] showing that only 2½ per cent of companies carried out systematic evaluation of supervisory training and that most organisations spent less than 5 per cent of their training time and budget on evaluation.

Recent years have seen greater attention being given to training provisions. Rapid technological advance has caused many unskilled jobs to disappear and an accompanying need for knowledge about new technology. New methods of control for more complex organisations – like operations research and computer systems – require employee training orientation, as do the new legislation, trade union involvement and the prescriptions of behavioural science for fresh management initiatives. Behind all these have been growing governmental concern about unemployment and productivity, resulting in a powerful Training Services Agency with a very large budget, as well as Industrial Training Acts in 1965 and 1973.

Along with other personnel activities, training is receiving that increased attention and emphasis within organisations that the professional trainer has so long sought. The need brings the opportunity to organise training that is thorough and effective in meeting the needs of both employee and employer.

Systematic Training Programme Development: An Overview

The primary objective of training is to promote human learning, which is best described in the operational definition of Bass and Vaughan:

> . . . learning is a relatively permanent change in behaviour that occurs as a result of practice or experience.[3]

The independent variable (practice or experience) and dependent variable (change in behaviour) are operational in that they are susceptible to observation and verification. An effective training programme depends upon assessment of what is to be learnt, how this may be achieved, the provision of relevant practice or experience, and evaluation of results.

The process should be systematic, carefully designed and planned, well conducted and cost-effective, and the results should be evaluated for efficient achievement of objectives. Several models of instructional systems have been published, such as that of Goldstein,[4] whilst military and business organisations have developed their own systems. After a survey of published data, one of the authors has developed the ASDICE system model of training programme development,[5] this name being an acronym for the six principal phases.

Many components of the model have been suggested by other systems and it is generally compatible with most current systems. The essential difference is the inclusion of sub-systems indicating the principal components involved and their inter-relationships. This provides a useful checklist of the major components of programme design and permits a more dynamic application of evaluation data, for feedback and control applied to appropriate components of the systems. The ASDICE model is reproduced in Appendix II and provides the overview for this chapter, in addition to links with other related chapters.

The development of a training programme begins with a perceived need, arising from personnel or other organisational processes such as employment, performance appraisal, job design or manpower planning. This may visualise a unit of instruction, a module of several units dealing with specific skills, or a course of modules concerned with a combination of different skills. In each case a formal process of programme development is advisable although individual components may receive varying amounts of detailed attention.

Phase One: Assessment of Training Needs

It appears obvious that a training programme will not be successful unless one knows in advance why the programme is needed. Surprisingly a detailed and explicit assessment is less common than the fairly subjective and operationally vague judgement of individual managers. The more careful the assessment and explicit statement of training needs, the more likely it is that the programme will satisfy those needs.

Four main stages are involved:

(a) ORGANISATIONAL ANALYSIS AND DIAGNOSIS

Whilst decisions of individual managers will often incorporate an analysis of organisational features, or diagnosis of organisational problems, this may not be formally recognised and recorded. In training programme development such data informs all phases of the process and activities involved, so some record of relevant analyses or diagnosis is necessary. In particular the analysis and diagnosis may reveal general or specific training needs, or factors which may affect the effective design and conduct of the training programme.

Chapter 2 provides an overview of the O.B. knowledge area which involves analysing organisational systems and components with a view to understanding the influences upon human behaviour, planned and unplanned, including diagnosis of problems or opportunities for effective operation. Clearly our references provide sources for a wide variety of analyses and diagnoses, which may have implications for training.

The internal design or formal organisation indicates the flow of communications, authority and promotion pathways. Resources, both financial and material, indicate training limitations, whilst comparison of current resources with manpower planning may suggest developmental training requirements. The goal systems, reflected in short- and long-term goals, such as internal promotion and expansion, may suggest training needs. As indicated by many studies, including the classic research by Fleishman et al[6] and Likert,[7] the organisational climate or general philosophy can have a significant impact upon retention or transfer of learning. A comprehensive guide by Likert[8] indicates how climate can be measured and analysed.

Information upon employee attitudes may be particularly helpful in identifying problem areas, needs for training or other action, or in assessing the attitudinal results of a training programme. A guide by Oppenheim[9] provides useful information upon the design of questionnaires and surveys, and upon techniques of attitude measurement.

Various organisational health indicators, such as workforce characteristics, job tenure, absenteeism and productivity data, may indicate general training needs. External factors, such as changes in governmental policies or legislation, may create a general or specific need for training. For example the UK Industrial Training Acts had a major impact on training provisions generally, whilst Employment Protection and Anti-Discrimination legislation has created specific training needs within organisations.

(b) JOB ANALYSIS (See Chapter 27)

When training moves beyond orientation and into the development of job-related skills, job analysis is essential. Such analysis is usually particularly detailed for training purposes, identifying the component tasks and responsibilities of a job with detailed analysis of the activities or operations necessary to these component tasks. This information identifies the key elements of training – the particular operations, abilities, skills and other characteristics which are necessary for effective performance of specific tasks. In addition to identifying what is to be taught, the data is useful for the design and conduct phases, and relevant to specification of objectives and criteria for evaluation.

A formal presentation of data is incorporated within the training specification. The job description provides a written statement of the purpose, scope, component tasks, duties and responsibilities of a focal job which may be supplemented by detailed data upon important tasks. A personnel specification provides a detailed statement of the physical and physiological characteristics, qualities, abilities, etc., which are required by a fully trained job holder, and is often supplemented by similar data on characteristics considered necessary for a trainee.

(c) EMPLOYEE ASSESSMENT (See Chapter 28)

A further essential feature is the assessment of individual candidates for training. The candidate specification provides a detailed statement of the individual's current physical and psychological qualities and development. For a new employee this will be a product of the employment process (Chapter 6, 7, 8), whilst an existing employee's specification would be updated after further assessment and performance appraisal.

An organisation-centred approach would consider this data sufficient. Increasingly, however, organisations are accommodating individual needs for career planning and development. Thus training may be provided in response to individual needs and/or in relation to immediate work activities.

(d) IDENTIFICATION OF SPECIFIC TRAINING NEEDS

The above analyses will identify a mixture of general and specific training needs, possibly supplemented by specific planning or operational diagnosis of problems, which must be formally collated and recorded. These needs may be focused on the training or development of individuals, groups, departments, or on the organisation as a whole.

Phase Two: Specification of Training Objectives

Following this thorough diagnosis of needs, the training objectives must now be specified. Well-written objectives state clearly what the trainee should be able to accomplish following completion of the training programme, and an indication of the conditions under which performance must be maintained and the standards by which this will be evaluated. In this way the goals are made explicit to the designer, and subsequently to trainer and trainee, to assist in designing the relevant learning situation and identification of evaluation criteria.

The principal activities of this phase are:

(a) EDUCATIONAL OBJECTIVES

Education has traditionally focused on provision of knowledge and development of general intellectual abilities, with difficulty in specifying objectives in precise terms. This problem was approached by Bloom,[10] who developed a taxonomy of objectives in the development of cognitive skills. Subsequent taxonomies by Krathwohl[11] and Simpson[12] focused upon the development of emotional commitment and of psychomotor skills respectively. Each taxonomy focuses upon a different domain or area of skill acquisition, although inter-related to some extent; several current research programmes are attempting to develop a similar taxonomy in the area of social skills.

The taxonomies offer a classification system for identifying and specifying educational objectives, all being particularly useful for the common areas of training provision. All objectives are arranged in a hierarchy of levels, each of which (and also specific levels in the other related taxonomies) must be reached before the next level can be achieved. The objectives become more complex as one progresses through the levels, and each level is capable of some sub-division. Thus the taxonomies provide a useful basis for specifying general or fairly precise training objectives.

(b) BEHAVIOURAL OBJECTIVES

Ideally all training objectives should be translated into behavioural objectives to be achieved by the trainee upon completion of training. One approach, suggested by the critical incident technique, developed by Flanagan and others,[13] is to identify clearly any behaviour to be avoided or to be demonstrated. More detailed objectives are useful as indicated by Cicero, who provides an example relating to training in a particular aspect of Xerox-machine servicing:

> Given a tool kit and a service manual, the technical representative will be able to adjust the registration (black line along paper edges) on a Xerox 2400 duplicator within 20 minutes according to the specification stated in the manual.[14]

This indicates to trainee and trainer what must be achieved, the relevant conditions, and the standard by which performances of behaviour will be evaluated.

(c) CRITERIA DEVELOPMENT

A key problem in training evaluation, indeed of all aspects of human assessment, is in the identification and measurement of relevant criteria for evaluating behaviour or performance. Useful research reviews by Goldstein[15] and Landy and Trumbo[16] show the problems, alternatives and requirements to be satisfied by criteria. Any criterion should have the following characteristics:

Relevance	— it should be a relevant measure of efficiency;
Acceptability	— it should be acceptable to those who use it;
Measurable	— it should be capable of measurement;
Freedom from bias	— it should not be affected by factors outside individual control;
Reliability	— all measures should be consistent in relation to temporal and measurer variations.

Although some compromise may be necessary, any criterion for assessing behaviour or specific results must meet these requirements and must be developed in relation to the needs and objectives identified.

(d) PRE-REQUISITE EXPERIENCE AND ABILITIES

Most training programmes are based upon trainees having some prior experience, development of appropriate abilities, or specific aptitudes relevant to the training provisions. If so, these should be explicitly recognised.

(e) TRAINING SPECIFICATION

A formal training specification is desirable, summarising the data from phases one and two as a guide to both programme designer and trainee. For a comprehensive programme an appropriate format is in Figure 9.1. For particular units or modules a similar format is desirable with depth of analysis and specification depending on circumstances and limitations of resources.

Section	Broad heading	Summary of information included
A	Organisational data	Aspects of organisation relevant to training provisions
B	Job description	Description of relevant features of occupation, job or tasks included
C	Personnel specification data	Details of relevant human requirements for effective performance of job or tasks
D	General training provision	General outline of training needs to be satisfied by programme
E	Specific training provisions	Details, for each unit or module of instruction, of: (a) Educational objectives (b) Behavioural objectives (c) Evaluation criteria and standards (d) Pre-requisite experience and abilities (e) Other relevant data (such as specific training activities necessary)
F (or in form of supplements).	Candidate specification(s)	Current level of development of experience and abilities for each potential trainee

Figure 9.1. General format of comprehensive training specification

Phase Three: Design of Training Programme

For a unit or module the design features may be shown by job analysis and the experience of the trainer. Complex learning situations or complete programmes usually require more specialised knowledge and training. Such expertise can come from specialists in the personnel department, or from commercial or academic consultants.

Alternatively, it may be possible to utilise a generally designed programme to achieve particular objectives. A standard programme offered by a college may be suitable and a wide variety of courses is available for educational and industrial training at all levels. Many organisations such as professional bodies, employers' associations and Government sponsored agencies offer specialised training programmes. In the UK, the Manpower Services Commission, through its Training Services Division,[17] provides training advice and specific instructional programmes for both individuals and industrial organisations. In recent years the Commission has been allocated considerable and increasing funding to encourage and sponsor training programmes mainly intended for the unemployed, especially young people and school leavers, to develop work related skills and experience. Some of the result-ing schemes involve work in industry whilst a substantial proportion involve special courses at local colleges of education where, due to cuts in traditional education finance provision, there has been significant transfer of resources to the various M.S.C. schemes.

During the past two decades, a large number of Industrial Training Boards were established for many industries, to generally improve the standard of training provision for all employees. Using an imposed levy system, they provide financial incentives to employers to develop effective and well-designed programmes. In addition they usually provide specialist advice, by expert staff and published materials, upon training provisions as well as encouraging group schemes, sponsorship of specific courses and establishing standards. In 1981 the Government carried out a major review and decided to eliminate many of the boards, the remainder being viewed as successfully providing a quality service to major industries and in a cost-effective manner. The Engineering Industry Training Board,[18] for example, has established an effective reputation within the industry and publishes a comprehensive guide to training, together with many well-designed standard instruction modules covering a wide range of skill areas, which are most useful in designing programmes.

Consequently various inputs can be provided by such sources, contributing to phases three, four or five of programme development. A well-designed programme will be based upon several factors:

(a) TRAINING DESIGN EXPERIENCE

An effective programme will utilise the previous experience of the designer and feedback from past organisational programmes. As training is concerned with modifying the behaviour of people, knowledge of psychology research will help to improve all aspects of design and conduct phases. More specifically we are concerned with human learning, so research-based theory and experience must be applied to the process.

A discussion of learning research and theory is not feasible here, but several of the references include reviews which can provide an introduction, as will the publications by Hill,[19] Borger and Seaborne,[20] and Holding.[21] For more detailed discussion the reader is referred to Hilgard and Bower,[22] Gagne,[23] McKeachie,[24] and to other publications in the educational and industrial psychology fields. Such research provides guidance for all phases and the following steps in particular:

(b) ORGANISATION OF TRAINING MATERIALS

In order to learn, the trainee must receive and understand new knowledge, thus the relevant information inputs must be identified and presented in a manner which aids the learning process. Similarly the organisation of materials can inhibit or assist the human memory, which needs to retain and recall this information. The relationship between information inputs, practice with application, and feedback upon achievements, all need careful planning.

The quantity and pace of material presented depend upon differences in intellectual skills and memory. The order of presentation can be important, with some materials easily remembered and others requiring presentation immediately prior to a practice session. Sequencing of data helps to make materials meaningful to the trainee, assisting in turn the processes of understanding and memory.

With short, simple or integrated materials and tasks, the information generally needs to be presented and practised as a whole. On the other hand, complex materials are usually more efficiently learned by successive presentation and practice of parts or sub-tasks. When a combination of complexity and integration is involved, the 'progressive part learning' approach (i.e. learning materials A, then A + B, then A + B + C, and so on) aids memory and understanding processes.

Some information may best be communicated directly and explicitly, whilst other requires the trainee to carry out guided self-discovery.

(c) ORGANISATION OF PRACTICE

In addition to new knowledge, learning involves the application of this in practice in order to develop experience and enable behaviour to be modified. There is general agreement that a quantity and frequency of practice assist learning, but the organisation of practice sessions can affect learning efficiency.

As mentioned above, the use of whole, part or progressive part methods of practice depends upon the nature of tasks involved. Massed practice, where practice is steady until task is mastered, and spaced practice, where breaks are planned between sessions, both have advantages and disadvantages for different skills. The timing of practice and rest, or alternative sessions, may also be important. Degree of practice, for example overlearning of materials, may result in discouragement of some trainees or improved retention of skills in others.

In general some degree of self-discovery assists learning, as we usually find it easier to retain, recall and understand facts which we personally discover. A primitive method is trial and error learning, whilst modelling behaviour on observation of others can be useful, but both imply self-instruction rather than training. The other extreme is relatively unsupervised research and experimentation which, though effective, is rarely relevant to a training programme as such.

A well-organised training programme will include carefully planned practice involving application experience and some guided self-discovery. Careful structuring and organisation of practice sessions can encourage varying degrees of self-discovery whilst minimising the inefficient aspects of unguided or unstructured experience.

(d) LEARNING ENVIRONMENT

The learning environment must create the conditions in which trainees are able to learn efficiently, in accordance with the objectives, and are properly motivated to do so.

Physical environment may include the general approach discussed below in phase four, having implications for transfer of learning into the working situation. At the most immediate level environmental conditions such as noise, temperature, humidity, ventilation, etc., may affect both information communication and practice efficiency. Similarly efficiency of learning may be influenced by the type and layout of learning equipment, seating positions or other features of physical organisation of people and equipment.

The psychological environment is largely created during conduct of the programme, discussed below as phase five. However the degree of homogeneity of heterogeneity of trainees, and the staff—student ratio, need to be planned carefully. In a general sense the relative characteristics of trainers and trainees need to be considered, in order to ensure suitable compatibility.

(e) GENERAL DESIGN AND SEQUENCING

The above general steps relate to detailed planning of individual instruction units or modules. In a similar manner the general design and sequencing of all separate modules need to be organised and planned with care, to produce an effective training programme.

To a large extent phases three and four are integrated, because individual modules

may utilise different instruction methods. Thus, in developing a complete programme, the instruction methods for each module will be selected (phase four) and
incorporated in the overall design at this stage.

Phase Four: Instruction Methods Selection

Essentially part of the design process, this phase is identified separately because it
follows the general learning design of each module of instruction. In many programmes one general method may be considered suitable, for all or most of the
programme. Ideally, however, the methods will be selected to suit the specific
requirements of each unit or module.

The choice of instruction methods is often left to the trainers; for certain
materials, or for experienced trainers, this may be appropriate. The disadvantage of
this approach is the risk of ineffective methods, due to inexperience or to the selection of methods to suit the *trainer*, particularly with regard to 'off the job' techniques.
Effective training requires methods which are suitable for the materials and trainees.

The general approaches to training, and corresponding methods or techniques,
are as follows:

(a) 'ON THE JOB' TRAINING

For practical reasons this is a common approach to job training, with trainees working directly in the production or operating environment. Special space and equipment are unnecessary, controls and reinforcements are operational and real, and the
trainee is considered to earn as he learns. The practice is totally realistic and, as it is
under true working conditions, little or no 'transfer of training' problems are expected.

On the other hand, expensive space and equipment may be under-utilised,
wastage may be significant or costly, and skilled production workers may have to
devote considerable time to trainee activities. The effects upon learning may be
disadvantageous because of the need to work at a pace and in conditions set for fully
experienced personnel, and appraisal is likely to be on a production basis with
limited explanation of reasons for mistakes. Also a skilled person may not be a
skilled coach. In short, the primary emphasis is upon production and not upon
training.

Thus the general approach has advantages in relation to practice and experience,
with disadvantages for efficient learning. Whilst most research focuses upon
particular methods (e.g. job instruction, apprenticeship and assistantship), a variety
of methods is potentially available. The general typology is illustrated in Figure 9.2.

Significant variations arise from particular combinations of alternative methods
of development and coaching. Development methods indicated are self-explanatory,
referring to different approaches to job practice and experience, with each having
the potential for achieving certain objectives. Coaching methods refer to different
approaches to instruction in job related knowledge, as briefly shown below:

Orientation. This method is necessary when personnel need introduction to a
new or changed working environment, in the form of information upon procedures, etc., and introduction to relevant people. This involves 'sponsorship' by
an experienced worker or supervisor, provision of information, open responses to
questions, and an overall helping, guiding relationship.

Primary objective of development method	Development method (provision of relevant practice and experience)	Coaching method (provision of job related knowledge)					
		Orientation	Modelling	Job instruction	Apprenticeship	Assistantship	Skilled coaching
Familiarisation	Introduction to new job situation, product or process	•					•
Economical job instruction	Observation, trial and error (method not recommended)		•				
Specific job training	Single job placement			•	•	•	•
Variety of job experience	Multiple job placement			•		•	•
	Job rotation			•	•		•
Variety of operations or tasks	Job enlargement				•	•	•
	Job enrichment				•	•	•
	Committee representation						•
Development of specific skills or experience	Group project assignment				•	•	•
	Individual projects assignment				•	•	•

Figure 9.2. General typology of 'on the job' training techniques of coaching and development

Modelling. As a coaching method this is usually of the 'sitting next to Nellie' type and is unsatisfactory; in a general sense, however, trainees can be strongly influenced to model their own behaviour upon that of people they admire. Therefore by implication, the examples set by skilled, effective colleagues are desirable factors.

Job Instruction. This is generally applied to 'semi-skilled' jobs or operator training, comprising a carefully designed programme and coaching by an instructor trained for this specific purpose. Close supervision gradually decreases over a short period of training.

Apprenticeship. This term refers to a trainee following a long term programme for learning a skilled trade, under the supervision of a craftsman skilled in that particular occupation. This approach varies considerably, from unsystematic coaching to a carefully planned programme combining classroom instruction and varied supervised practice.

Assistantship. Also known as 'internship', this involves the allocation of a trainee to act as assistant to a departmental head who provides supervision and guidance, whilst the trainee carries out a variety of assignments with gradually increasing personal responsibility. This is the common approach to postgraduate management training or development.

Skilled Coaching. This method can be any form of instruction where the trainer has the qualities, communication abilities, and social skills necessary for effective teaching and guidance of the trainee. Ideally all training would involve skilled coaching but in practice the necessary combination of skills and personal characteristics is not easily available to all trainees, as illustrated by the differing achievements of apparently similar apprentices or assistants.

Many of the combinations on the above typology are not mutually exclusive, thus permitting the possibility of varying periods of 'on the job' training under different conditions in order to satisfy various training objectives.

(b) 'VESTIBULE' TRAINING

This may involve a company training school, a specific training department, or an annexe area within a production department. The equipment, materials and environment are close simulations of the production situation, but with the primary emphasis upon training rather than production. A programme may last for a few days or some months, depending upon the complexity of the tasks or job involved, and training is conducted by a specialist instructor or skilled coach.

Vestibule training can be expensive, with duplication of specialised facilities. The obvious advantage is providing realistic job experience with minimum 'training transfer' problems, whilst eliminating the disadvantages of 'on the job' training. Skilled instruction and carefully designed training conditions, combined with active participation by the trainee, encourages and enables efficient learning to take place.

When justified by available resources, regular needs for training relevant personnel and the training requirements, this approach is strongly recommended. It is particularly appropriate for operator training, early stages of apprentice training, or for providing workshop experience to graduate trainees. When the training objectives involve learning and practice, vestibule training provides a useful basis which can be subsequently followed by 'on the job' development of experience.

(c) 'OFF THE JOB' TRAINING

Most training programmes include a significant element of 'off the job' training in classroom situations. In some cases this comprises training prior to placement in the working environment, and 'on the job' or 'vestibule' training is usually supplemented by 'off the job' instruction. As indicated earlier, many organisations offer courses to suit general or specific training needs, with a variety available which is beyond the scope of any one company. Similarly companies may organise individual courses incorporating contributions from internal staff and external specialists. Such courses may vary from a short course upon a particular technique to an extended executive development programme, but the common feature is an emphasis upon training and specifically designed learning situations.

It is often difficult to provide relevant practice with work-related activities in a classroom situation, however it may be a useful preparation for a period of 'on the job' training. The major weakness, usually, is a lack of specific attention to overcoming 'learning transfer' problems or the effective application of principles learnt. Such problems should receive careful attention in the overall training design by provision of practice and experience, the opportunity to apply new ideas, and an awareness that organisational climate or human resistance may discourage the practice of new ideas in the working environment.

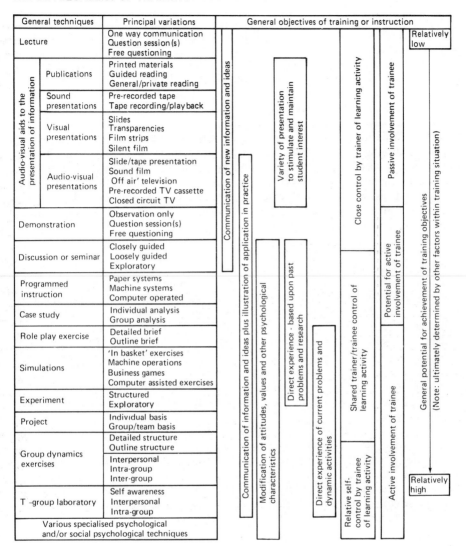

Figure 9.3. General typology of 'off the job' training techniques

The advantages are many, notably the opportunity to expose trainees to information, ideas and experience beyond the confines of the working environment. When separated from the pressures of work activities, trainees can devote their full attention to learning, may experiment with new ideas and generally undertake the self-analysis which is necessary for permanent behaviour change. Professional training staff, with coaching and communication skills, may be supplemented by various technical specialists and the learning situation is designed actively to facilitate learning.

The potential for varying educational technology and techniques to suit different tasks and learning situations is considerable. This is illustrated by Figure 9.3 which provides a general typology of techniques, with principal variations, indicating some of the objectives for which they may be useful. Most professional trainers will be aware of these techniques and their potential advantages or disadvantages in different situations.

Other readers will find useful overviews in Bass and Vaughan,[25] Goldstein[26] and other references. New methods or variations, and new applications for existing techniques, are being developed constantly by researchers and practitioners. Often new developments have been overpromoted, creating a succession of fashionable techniques advocated as generally effective.

It is futile to advocate any method as universally effective. All have advantages and disadvantages depending upon the people, materials and the situation in which they are applied. Empirical verification by research and experience will provide a guide to usefulness, and is yet another reason for the emphasis upon systematic evaluation as part of a continuous process. Professional trainers and programme designers should have knowledge and experience to ensure an appropriate matching of techniques and learning situations.

(d) COMBINATION OF TECHNIQUES

We have clearly emphasised the view that the general approach, specific techniques and media must be selected for the particular training or learning situations diagnosed. A similar emphasis is provided by Belbin and Belbin[27] in advocating a particular approach to skills training based upon their CRAMP mnemonic for the human processes necessary to learning – namely comprehension, reflex development, attitude formation, memorising and procedural learning. Where analysis of needs suggests that these processes are involved, specific guidance upon relevant methods is provided on a basis of psychological research, facilitating an effective combination of methods to achieve the learning objectives appropriate to each of the processes. This approach is considered useful to incorporate within the systems advocated here.

Most modules and all complete programmes are likely to involve a combination of different approaches and techniques, to meet the needs and objectives of the training as identified in phases one and two above. This selection of instruction methods should be integrated with the design phase, rather than left to personal preferences of the trainer, although the skills of the trainer do need to be considered in the selection process. Selection needs to be well informed by both research and practical experience, in conjunction with careful diagnosis.

Phase Five: The Conduct of Training

Although the previous design and planning phases are important, effective training depends crucially on the conduct of the training programme. A common assumption is that persons with relevant knowledge and skills are capable of teaching others, but research and experience indicate that this is frequently not true. An appreciation of learning processes, social and communication skills, and specific personal characteristics are needed for effective teaching or coaching behaviour.

Among the features to be considered are:

(a) SELECTION OF PARTICIPANTS

Prior to conduct of the programme, the participants need to be selected, although this may be carried out during earlier phases. The trainer's personal characteristics and skills need to be appropriate to the learning situation. Trainees similarly must be selected according to their needs, characteristics and abilities. As a group the number of trainees, relative homogeneity of characteristics and abilities, relative status, and other factors need to be related to potential consequences within the conduct phase.

For subsequent evaluation and monitoring of progress, it is necessary to assess or pre-test the trainees prior to commencement of training.

(b) THE SOCIAL INTERACTION PROCESS

The conduct of training may be considered as a process of interaction within a social context, often involving multiple relationships between trainer(s) and trainees. Social psychology research offers useful guidance, particularly the work of Argyle,[28, 29] Shaw,[30] and other writers. Readers are also referred to our Chapter 29. An obvious objective of the conduct phase is for the trainer to communicate information and influence behaviour change in the trainees, but it would be a serious mistake to assume the communication and influence to be wholly uni-directional. Indeed effective training often involves harnessing group and individual influences to facilitate learning activity.

(c) MOTIVATION AND FACILITATION OF LEARNING

The trainer has a responsibility to provide the necessary conditions under which the trainee is able to learn efficiently. General organisation of materials, practice and the physical environment are clear starting-points. Provision of guidance in the correct quantity and manner at the appropriate times, balancing the potential advantages and disadvantages of the trainee experiencing poor methods or making errors, calls for judgement in relation to the trainee's particular needs at any specific point in the training programme.

Similarly the trainer can influence the psychological environment significantly so as to motivate the trainee to learn. The arousal of interest, stimulation of curiosity, encouragement of questions or debate, and similar behaviour are all helpful. Using real problems, or relating learning activity to problems the trainee may ultimately face, and stressing the value of materials to be learnt are practical means of maintaining interest and motivation.

(d) COMMUNICATION OF INFORMATION

All learning involves communication of new information to the trainee in a manner which encourages effective reception, understanding and acceptance of the information and ideas concerned. This facilitates action by the trainee in practice or application of new ideas, developing experience and the relatively permanent change of behaviour appropriate to training objectives. Thus effective presentation, explanation, discussion and general efficiency of communication need to be promoted by the interaction process.

(e) PRACTICE AND EXPERIENCE DEVELOPMENT

The role of practice or application of new ideas and techniques has been considered in earlier discussion. It is during the conduct of training that the trainee is encouraged to undertake practice, with appropriate guidance, to develop understanding and experience. Practice continues until a satisfactory level of performance is achieved.

(f) FEEDBACK AND REINFORCEMENT

The provision of feedback upon the results achieved in practice enables the trainee to correct mistakes. As a control mechanism, feedback is important to learning. Optimally this is given by the trainer as soon as possible after the activity is completed.

At suitable points in the programme the trainees' progress should be monitored, providing the means of assessing how well training objectives are being achieved. In addition to enabling the conduct of the programme to be modified, if necessary, this provides the opportunity to inform the trainee (in a non-evaluative manner) of his general progress.

Feedback discourages inappropriate behaviour, and reinforces appropriate behaviour by encouraging its repetition. Reinforcement is related directly to motivation and learning, and the reader is referred to earlier references for detailed guidance. In addition to general or specific feedback of results, appropriate behaviour is encouraged by provision of rewards – which may involve money or other material rewards, but non-material rewards (praise, recognition of competence, indicators of approval, etc) are important and effective. On the other hand punishment (negative reinforcement) in the form of penalty or disapproval, has many adverse consequences and so should be used sparingly, and in the mildest form practical.

(g) TRAINER SKILLS AND PREPARATION

The trainer clearly needs to have a detailed knowledge and understanding of the materials and skills to be taught. Similarly the trainer must be fully and carefully prepared, by familiarisation with all the information from previous phases together with a clear understanding of the training programme design and the instruction methods to be utilised. All of the methods indicated in Figures 9.2 and 9.3 will be more or less effective, according to the skills and experience of the trainer in those methods.

Sections (a) to (f) above indicate specific considerations in relation to the conduct of training and most of our chapter references provide partial guidance to the trainer. More specific guidance to trainer behaviour is provided by the Industrial Training Research Unit[31,32] and by Winfield[33] in relation to teaching practical skills. In fact training involves a 'helping relationship' as usefully examined in detail by Brammer,[34] whilst the development of coaching skills is likely to be assisted by Megginson and Boydell[35] and a training package developed for the Training Services Division[36] of the Manpower Services Commission.

It is in this phase, the conduct of training, that the careful planning and design of the training programme is applied in practice. The efficiency of the training, and effectiveness in achieving the training objectives, is significantly affected by the skills and behaviour of the trainer or coach. Commonly the training process is considered completed when the conduct phase is finished – but it is essential to move into a further phase, to evaluate the efficiency and effectiveness of the overall process and of the individual stages of the development of the programme.

Phase Six: Evaluation of Training Programme

We have referred earlier to two American studies which indicated that about 2½ per cent of companies attempted scientific evaluation of training provisions and less than 5 per cent of financial and human resources were applied to such evaluation that did occur. This is generally true today in the UK, despite a remarkable consistency of research findings indicating that evaluation is essential. Often it appears to be assumed that specific techniques necessarily achieve particular objectives, a dangerous over-generalisation, and that the reported judgements of training staff and/or trainees after the event is suitable evaluation.

To be useful and effective, evaluation must involve rigorous procedures based upon relevant research, properly integrated with all other aspects of programme development. Although some outcomes of training are difficult to anticipate, predict or measure, problems often occur due to ambiguous or unstated goals. Hence the emphasis in phase two on clear and explicit specification of objectives. Also, as indicated earlier, suitable criteria should be established at an early stage, with pre-testing of trainees to enable progress to be monitored and subsequent assessment of how well these objectives have been achieved.

Kirkpatrick[37] recommends the consideration of four levels of criteria for evaluation of training programmes — reaction, learning, behaviour and results. *Reaction* refers to what trainees thought of the programme, usually measured by questionnaire. *Learning* refers to objective indicators or measures of the learning of principles, facts, techniques and attitudes specified as training objectives. *Behaviour* refers to measures of job performance, whilst *results* is a category relating consequences of training for general organisational objectives. Whilst other categories may be appropriate to a specific programme, these provide a useful general basis for evaluation.

Principal steps in evaluation procedures would normally include:

(a) FEEDBACK FROM TRAINEES
The reactions and opinions of trainees may provide useful data relating to design and conduct of the programme. This may be gathered in group discussion or interview, but such responses may be inhibited. A well-designed questionnaire, providing pre-determined information in a manner which can be quantified and analysed, permits anonymity and free response comments. Such feedback will provide data relevant to features of the learning situation to guide future design, but favourable reactions do not necessarily guarantee effective learning.

(b) POST-TESTING OF TRAINEES
The 'post-testing only' approach is widely used and provides an indication of the adequacy of preparation of the trainee for his job placement. As a measure of training effectiveness it is totally inadequate as the results may be affected by prior experience, motivation, or other factors relatively independent of the training programme.

(c) BEFORE–AFTER COMPARISON
A comparison of the test results before and after training, on a basis of the pre-determined criteria, is a distinct improvement upon the previous method. It reduces the possibility that post-training performance is a function of conditions existing before training, providing a useful indication of behaviour change during the training period.

(d) EXPERIMENTAL DESIGN
For detailed evaluation of training some form of experimental design is necessary and useful reviews of alternative approaches are provided by Goldstein,[38] and Campbell and Stanley.[39] Essentially such designs usually obtain 'before–after

comparison' results for both a trainee group and a control group. To evaluate a specific programme the control group would not be exposed to the training, whilst to evaluate a new programme the control group would be exposed to the previous programme. In practice various designs are possible according to the specific evaluation data required, essentially attempting to control major factors which might affect the validity of evaluation conclusions.

(e) EVALUATION OF TRAINING RESULTS
Using data such as the above, supplemented by the reports and judgements of training staff, the training programme can be evaluated. The conclusions from the data should indicate behaviour change achieved through training provisions, effectiveness in meeting objectives, and the means for a general evaluation of all phases of the programme development.

(f) EVALUATION OF JOB PERFORMANCE
Upon satisfactory completion of the training, trainees usually receive a job placement which requires the knowledge and skills developed. After a suitable time interval a performance appraisal, again using the pre-determined criteria, will indicate how well the training has been applied under working conditions. This enables the trainees' retention of learning, and the specific transfer of training to be evaluated.

(g) FEEDBACK TO PROCESS
All the data obtained by evaluation procedures provides useful feedback to the complete system or process of training. This may indicate some inadequacies in the trainees' development which suggests further training needs, hence a re-cycling of the process. At a general level it may provide useful data to assist subsequent training design. More specifically it will indicate where modification needs to be made at the different phases, or to components or practices during the sub-processes involved, for future programmes.

SUMMARY PROPOSITIONS

9.1.   The development of employee capacity through training is becoming more important due to a range of changes affecting organisations: technological advances, increasing organisational complexity, legislation, union intervention, employment levels, need for higher productivity and the application of behavioural science knowledge, together with changing social values and employee expectations.

9.2.   The trainee must see the benefits to himself, as well as to the organisation, in the training he receives.

9.3.   Training programmes are best developed in the six phases of the ASDICE formula: assessment of trainee needs, specification of trainee objectives, design of the training programme, selection of training methods, conduct of training, evaluation of the training programme.

9.4. Training will be more efficient and effective if viewed as an explicit, systematic and integrated process which incorporates elements and decisions based upon current research and practical experience. The ASDICE model is suggested as a basis for modification to suit particular needs or new developments.

9.5. An explicit system model such as ASDICE is useful for fault-finding or redesign of existing programmes, as problem areas can be readily identified with the sub-systems or elements which need to be examined in detail.

REFERENCES

1. French S.H. 'Measuring Progress towards Industrial Relations Objectives', *Personnel,* 1953, Vol. 30, pp. 338–347.
2. Shafer C.I., 'A Study of Evaluation in Management Education and Development Programs in Selected US Companies', Doctoral Dissertation, Michigan State University, 1961.
3. Bass B.M. and Vaughan J.A., *Training in Industry: The Management of Learning* (Wadsworth) 1966.
4. Goldstein I.I., *Training: Program Development and Evaluation* (Brooks/Cole) 1974, p. 21.
5. Chapman J.B., *ASDICE: A Systematic Approach to Training Programme Development,* University of Aston, 1978.
6. Fleishman E.A., Harris E.F. and Burtt H.E., *Leadership and Supervision in Industry,* Ohio State University, Bureau of Educational Research, 1955.
7. Likert R., *New Patterns of Management* (McGraw-Hill) 1961.
8. Likert R., *The Human Organisation* (McGraw-Hill) 1967.
9. Oppenheim A.N., *Questionnaire Design and Attitude Measurement* (Heinemann) 1966.
10. Bloom B.S., *Taxonomy of Educational Objectives – Cognitive Domain* (Longmans) 1956.
11. Krathwohl, *Taxonomy of Educational Objectives – Affective Domain* (Longmans) 1964.
12. Simpson E.J., *Taxonomy of Educational Objectives – Psychomotor Domain* (University of Illinois) 1966.
13. Flanagan J.C., 'The Critical Incident Technique', *Psychological Bulletin,*1954, Vol. 51, pp. 327–350.
14. Cicero J.P., 'Behavioural Objectives for Technical Training Systems', *Training and Development Journal,* Vol. 28, 1973, pp. 14–17 (p. 15).
15. Goldstein I.I., *Ibid.* (Chapter Four, pp. 49–66).
16. Landy F.J. and Trumbo D.A., *Psychology of Work Behaviour* (Dorsey Press) 1976, Chapter 4, pp. 87–130 and Chapter 8, pp. 256–290.
17. Manpower Services Commission – Training Services Division. Various publications available from head office (1–2 Cambridge Gate, Regent's Park, London NW1 4LA) or from regional offices.
18. Engineering Industry Training Board. Various publications available from head office (140 Tottenham Court Road, London W1) or from regional offices.
19. Hill W.E., *Learning: A Survey of Psychological Interpretations* (Methuen University Paperbacks) 1964.
20. Borger R. and Seaborne A.E.M., *The Psychology of Learning* (Penguin) 1966.
21. Holding D.H., *Principles of Training: Research in Applied Learning* (Pergamon) 1965.
22. Hilgard E.R. and Bower G.H., *Theories of Learning,* 3rd ed. (Appleton-Century-Crofts) 1966.

23. Gagne R.M., *Conditions of Learning* (Holt, Rinehart and Winston) 1965.
24. McKeachie W.J., 'Instructional Psychology', *Annual Review of Psychology*, 1974, Vol. 25, pp. 161–193.
25. Bass B.M. and Vaughan J.A., *Ibid.*, Chapter 7, pp. 85–137.
26. Goldstein I.I., *Ibid.*, Chapters 8 and 9, pp. 139–195.
27. Belbin E. and Belbin R.M., *Problems in Adult Retraining* (Heinemann) 1972.
28. Argyle M., *Social Interaction* (Methuen) 1969.
29. Argyle M., *The Psychology of Interpersonal Behaviour* (Penguin) 1972.
30. Shaw M.E., *Group Dynamics: The Psychology of Small Group Behaviour*, 2nd ed. (McGraw-Hill) 1976.
31. Industrial Training Research Unit, *Choose an Effective Style: A Self-Instructional Approach to the Teaching of Skills*, ITRU Publications, 1976.
32. Belbin and Belbin, *op. cit.*, 1972.
33. Winfield L., *Learning to Teach Practical Skills* (Kogan Page) 1979.
34. Brammer L.M., *The Helping Relationship: Process and Skills* (Prentice-Hall) 1973.
35. Megginson D.F. and Boydell T.H., *A Guide to Management Coaching* (B.A.C.I.E.) 1979.
36. Training Services Agency, *Coaching For Results*. A Package of two films and instructor's notes, distributed by Millbank Films Ltd.
37. Kirkpatrick D.L., 'Techniques for Evaluating Programs', *Journal of the American Society of Training Directors* 1959, Vol. 13, pp. 3–9 and 21–26.
38. Goldstein I.I., *Ibid.*, Chapter 5, pp. 67–88.
39. Campbell D.T. and Stanley J.C., *Experimental and Quasi-Experimental Designs of Research* (Rand McNally) 1963.

10

Management Development

The history of management development is one of constant changes of direction and emphasis as one unsatisfactory approach is changed in favour of another. The term 'management development' itself is an indication of this uncertainty. It came into common usage when 'management training' sounded too narrow or too plebeian, and many people already feel that it is out-dated and should be replaced by 'organisation development' or even 'development management'.

> What is likely to happen to management development in the seventies? I believe that it will become closely linked with a newly evolving branch of management – development management. Development management is concerned with building new forms of organisation that will enable the enterprise to cope effectively with change. This contrasts with operations management, which is concerned with the efficient use of existing resources to make the goods and services currently required, and with the rapid restoration of steady state whenever a breakdown occurs.[1]

There is a strong myth-making tradition attached to the development of effective management as those senior in organisations have sought to preserve their elite status. Initially there was no question of acquiring skill; entry to a management position came as part of the right of ownership, the favour of the owner or the natural entitlement of those in a particular social position. As the size of organisations and the number of managers began to increase there was a move to professionalisation to justify managerial status, with the development of professional or quasi-professional bodies, controlling entry by examination and election. This, together with organisational complexity, produced specialisation and the longest-running feature of management development: management training courses. Run by educational establishments, professional bodies, employers or consultants, there is a wide range of courses which seek to communicate some distilled wisdom relating to the management task. Although the training course is well established, it was joined during the 1960s by a fresh idea – that of developing individuals. Instead of managers being fed information in a course, their managerial capacity and potential would be developed by a wide variety of experiences, through which they would acquire greater understanding, awareness, sensitivity, self-confidence and those other aspects of effectiveness that were regarded as most important but which could not be inculcated. This change of emphasis was accompanied by growing use of employee appraisal to determine individual development needs, rather than leaving trainers to produce universal programmes. There was also some move towards putting the control of the development programme in the hands of the individual being developed, instead of the experts. In reporting on one such experiment Graves concludes:

> '... managers are better able to develop their own skills if given development opportunities rather than training ... training should be based on managerial needs as perceived by the managers rather than development needs perceived by the trainers.[2]

Furthermore such development may well take place on the job in the everyday ebb and flow of events rather than in the specially-contrived circumstances beloved by trainers. In this way the learning is not only relevant to the job being done, it may also alter the manager's approach to his work as he becomes more questioning of events and more analytical of processes:

> The remarkable and persuasive reason for saying that nonetheless managers can become more effective as learners lies in the dedication to doing things, being active, that is the hallmark of so many of them . . . ask them to undertake activities associated with learning which build on existing managerial processes and rewards.[3]

One recent emphasis has been that on innovation and organisation development, based on the premise that managers can only develop if the organisation develops with them (and *vice versa*). Organisation development takes various forms, but usually there is a focus on team-building exercises whereby the members of a team develop their capacity to work together, their strategies for future development and the organisational change that this will involve.

A feature of management for thirty years in Britain has been growing specialisation, partly caused by an ever-increasing number of graduates joining companies who were put in specialist groups on the assumption that specialisation would pay off. However, the economic difficulties of so many companies in the early 1980s has reduced demand for managerial specialists and increased interest in flexibility.[4]

The Goals of Management Development

What broadly does management development set out to do? In what way is it different from other types of vocational preparation? Why have a separate chapter in this book on the subject as well as the comprehensive treatment of the training process that we have already offered? Most answers tend to state the obvious, like this extract from a company manual of procedures:

> Management development is the system of interrelated activities necessary to ensure that the Company has an effective management structure and managers in appropriate quantity and quality to achieve its current and future business objectives.

Apart from the chilling phrase 'appropriate quantity and quality' this does not help us as there is so much uncertainty about the nature of managerial work. Among the mass of recent theorising has been the research of Rosemary Stewart[5] in analysing work in terms of the type of relationships involved; Mintzberg's analysis of managerial work as comprising various combinations of ten distinct roles in three general categories: decision making, inter-personal and information-processing.[6] A little earlier Scholefield had produced the suggestion that managers should do three things: operate the firm, make innovations and stabilise the organisation.[7] Much of this type of analysis and speculation links with assessments of leadership, which we discuss fully in Chapter 17. A useful counterblast is the iconoclasm of Alistair Mant,[8] whose scepticism is so perceptive and persuasive that one is left with the feeling that he might just be right when he argues that we tend to undervalue a large number of jobs that are of true social and economic importance, such as salesman and house-wife, while ascribing enormous significance to the job of manager, which seems non-existent in some of the world's more successful industrial societies:

> The puzzle, then, is to understand why we downgrade so many of the jobs that really matter whilst building around the idea of 'management' a plethora of myths, shibboleths and incantations which our most successful competitors seem able to do without.[9]

An equally stimulating but less sceptical piece of writing is that of Morris and Burgoyne,[10] who survey the type of metaphors that are used in describing management development and then set out a model around the ideas of dramas, rituals and routine in management development.

Finally we can see one of the results of recent research about the learning goals of course organisers:

> Immediately striking is the priority which is given to developing social skills and the skills of analysis, problem-solving and decision-making; of equal impact is the lack of attention paid by most organisers to the development of the managers' basic understanding of situational facts and professional knowledge. Increasing productivity is also low on the list of the organisers' learning goals.[11]

The goals of management development are often uncertain and frequently spurious. The goals of the organisers of development may differ markedly from those undergoing the process. Among the generalisations we can make are:

(i) Management development is an elitist process.
(ii) Emphasis will be on skills at *doing*, rather than knowledge *about*.
(iii) Dominant will be the capacity of the individual manager to be socially adroit and to evaluate information as a preliminary to making choices between alternatives.

The Elements of Management Development

The organiser of management development programmes will, we hope, find material to help him in various parts of this book, especially Chapter 9 on training and Chapter 17 on leadership. It is not therefore our aim to make specific suggestions here about how to conduct the process, but to provide notes on some of aspects of organising training that apply especially to this form.

(a) SELECTION

Those who undergo management development are nearly always selected by organisational superiors as being in need of the process. An undergraduate may take a degree in business studies without anyone else ever posing the question as to whether or not he is suited to a management post, and some people work very diligently at night school or on correspondence courses to obtain a qualification for some management specialism in an attempt to improve their employment prospects. These, however, are not processes of management development, to which entry depends on being chosen, but choice is sometimes made on strange criteria.

The greatest problems are those where someone is trying to correct a mistake for which management development is not the remedy. If a job-holder is under-performing because the job is beyond his basic ability or will, then the solution lies in rectifying the basic error — that he was appointed in the first place — rather than in elaborate procedures of courses, objective-setting and appraisal so that months later his continued inadequacy can be blamed on *him* ('We really have done all we can to bring him up to scratch') and not on the people who wrongly appointed him in the first place.

Apart from the requisite ability and other qualities that are needed, it is impor-tant that the employee should be committed to the programme, seeing the benefits that will flow from it, and should have the opportunity to use and practise quickly the skills he hopes to acquire.

(b) APPRAISAL

Gradually performance appraisal is being used in organisations more as a means of determining development needs — or training needs — than as a preliminary to a salary review. In this way the person appraised is more likely to participate frankly and positively in the appraisal procedures so that his development programme is begun by an assessment, by himself and others, of where he is and what he needs do to prepare for the type of future he would like. Guidance on appraisal schemes is to be found in Chapter 28 and readers will be interested in the work of Andrew and Valerie Stewart in diagnosing what makes for effective management performance in different jobs, as they have concluded from their experience and research that effectiveness varies enormously from one job to another, but can be defined in be-havioural terms.[12]

(c) EDUCATION AND TRAINING COURSES

As we have already mentioned, the training course will usually feature strongly in a programme of development. We need to develop one or two points about courses provided as standard offerings by various specialist bodies in comparison with those that are developed within organisations for their own specified needs.

First are the *pre-experience* courses: full-time education leading to academic qualification with a management sciences or business studies label and undertaken by young people as a preliminary to a career. These have been developing in the United Kingdom since the middle 1960s and have proved very popular with students at universities and polytechnics. They are often described as 'vocational' and inten-ded to be a practical preparation for a management-type occupation on completion. They can never, however, be vocational in the same sense as degrees in areas such as medicine or architecture because there is relatively little practical element in the course. The sandwich courses that incorporate periods of work in the 'real' world may help to bring the feet of students nearer to the ground, but they cannot give any meaningful experience in, and practice at, managerial work. The courses provide an education, normally based on a study of the academic disciplines of economics, mathematics, psychology and sociology and incorporating some work in the more specialised disciplines like industrial relations and organisational behaviour, as well as an introduction to the practical areas like accounting, marketing, personnel and production. The student should emerge with a balanced understanding of the workings of an industrial society and an industrial economy, and he will have some useful blocks of information which may well be at the frontiers of knowledge in management thought. He should also have developed the more traditional qualities of maturity and the ability to analyse and debate that university education purports to nurture: he will not be trained to be a manager.

Second are the *post-experience* courses: full-time education usually leading to a diploma or master's degree with a management or business label and undertaken during a career. Although such courses were being run in this country early in this century, the great boom came after the establishment of the London and Manchester Business Schools and other management centres in the 1960s. The main difference is not only that students are older, but that they study on the basis of experience they have had and with the knowledge of the work to which they will return. Typically the member of a course at a business school will be seconded by his employer at a time when he has already held a management post. The material of the course may not be very different from that of the pre-experience course, but the student's perception will be very different and his application of any new insights or skills will be more immediate.

Neither pre-experience nor post-experience courses of the type described here will feature strongly the skills element mentioned on page 136 in the listing of management development goals. It is interesting to see the quite different emphasis that is asserted by the Principal of the London Business School:

> I would argue that an essential basis for a flexible and adaptable industrial and commercial base must be a flexible and adaptable management . . . This . . . takes various forms. The first, which is evidently related to our place in the world economy, requires a greater awareness of the position of organisations in world markets and an increased capacity to think through problems on a wider canvas than in the past. Parochialism will not do as a basis for future prosperity. At the same time management will have to become more sensitive to changes in its immediate social environment.[13]

The third category can be generally described as *consultancy* courses. Varying from a half-day to several weeks in length, they are run by consultants or professional bodies for all comers. They have the advantage that they bring together people from varying occupational backgrounds and are not therefore as introspective as in-house courses and are popular for topical issues. They are, however, often relatively expensive and superficial, despite their value as sources of industrial folklore, by which we mean the swapping of experiences among course members.

The most valuable courses of this type are those which concentrate on specific areas or knowledge, like developing interviewing skills or teaching special technical methods. This short-course approach is probably the only way for managers to come to terms with some new development, such as a change in legislation, because they need not only to find an interpretation of the development, they also need to share views and reactions with fellow managers to ensure that their own feelings are not idiosyncratic or perverse.

(d) LEADERSHIP

Management development is largely connected with developing those qualities in a person that can be described as leadership qualities, although this is a term that has caused some difficulty in recent years, as some have caricatured it as a simple disguise for crude manipulation and others have seen it in essentially charismatic terms. We obviously regard it as crucial to the management process and we have a comprehensive treatment of it as part of the contract for individual control. The ideas of some of the leadership theorists feature largely in management development programmes, probably the most influential being Likert, Blake and Mouton, Reddin, and Tannenbaum and Schmidt in recent years. These ideas are discussed in our chapter on leadership.

(e) ACTION LEARNING

The iconoclasm of Mant, referred to earlier in this chapter, is mild compared with that of Revans, one of the great original thinkers to study management. After an industrial career that included moments of dramatic insight, he became a professor of management and used his prodigious statistical skills to demonstrate, for instance, a relationship between the management style of hospital matrons and both the turnover of student nurses and the speed of recovery of patients in the hospitals that the matrons supervised.[14] While occupying his chair he became more and more disenchanted with the world of management education that he saw developing around him. Among the many aphorisms attributed to him was: 'If I teach my son to read, how do I know he will not read rubbish; if I teach him to write, how do I know that he will not write yet another book on management education?' Despairing of the way in which the London and Manchester Business Schools were established, Revans resigned his chair in Manchester and moved to Belgium to start his first action learning project. This was based on his conviction that managers need not education but the ability to solve problems. His method has been basically to organise exchanges, so that a manager experienced in one organisation is planted in another to solve a particular set of problems that is proving baffling. He brings a difference of experience, a freshness of approach, and he is not dependent on his new, temporary organisational peers for his career growth. He works on the problem for a period of months, having many sessions of discussion and debate with a group of other individuals similarly planted in unfamiliar organisations with a knotty problem to solve. The learning stems from the immediate problem that is presented, and from all the others that emerge, one by one, in the steps towards a solution. This presents a need that the student has to satisfy and all the learning is in terms of what he discovers he needs to know rather than what someone else feels is necessary. It is an idea of startling simplicity. Its relative unpopularity in academic circles is easy to understand, but in management circles there has been some diffidence because the action learning approach nearly always stirs something up, and not all organisations have the nerve to risk the soul-searching and upheaval that is caused.[15]

(f) COACHING

In our training chapter (Chapter 9) we refer to various features of the conduct of training as comprising a 'helping relationship'. Closely allied to this is the idea of coaching, whereby the developing manager is helped by his one-to-one relationship over a long period with someone else – usually his superordinate. This is not a subject extensively dealt with in the literature (although we provide some useful references in Chapter 9) as it is so imponderable and not susceptible to measurement and analysis. It is a close working relationship in which the coach works to improve the performance of the trainee by discussion, exhortation, encouragement and understanding. This is a job to be performed by someone who has done it before and can in some way share in the experience. That most elegant of writers on management, Henry Boettinger, makes the point:

> Only someone who can actually perform in an art is qualified to teach it. There is no question that constructive criticism from an informed bystander is helpful; actors, for instance, can learn a great deal about human motivation from psychiatrists. Nevertheless, this kind of procedure is different from the one an actor goes through to show another how to express human feelings . . .

> To learn the art of management entirely on one's own is impossible, even in a master–student relationship. Higher managers must, therefore, assume some responsibility for the training of those who will succeed them . . . There is an apparent perversity in the obligation to assist others to destroy, or at least to make obsolete, one's current operational vision, and yet that is the noble imperative for the best teachers of management.[16]

Coaching is the most informal of activities, that cannot be set down in manuals and controlled by administrative procedures. The main component activities of the coach will be constructive criticism, listening, counselling and delegation.

(g) MANAGEMENT BY OBJECTIVES

A particular formula that has been widely used as a vehicle for management development has been management by objectives, conveniently abbreviated to MbO. It is based on the elementary premise that unless you know where you are going you are unlikely to arrive, and unless you know what results you want to achieve you will not achieve them. This is applied to developing the effective management of an organisation by a simple sequence of procedures which define objectives for individual managers in the context of a set of objectives for the organisation as a whole. Once these have been established, and agreed by those who have to meet them, ways of meeting them are set down in statements with names like management guides and job improvement plans; the management guide specifying key results areas. Later comes the review of performance and the setting of fresh objectives. The initial attractiveness of this approach lay in the fact that it was relatively uncommon for such objectives to be set down for any individual in an organisation and unlikely that any such individual would receive systematic feedback on the performance he was producing. One protagonist of MbO summarised the needs of the individual manager as follows:

  (i) 'Agree with me the results I am expected to achieve.'
 (ii) 'Give me an opportunity to perform.'
(iii) 'Let me know how I am getting on.'
 (iv) 'Give me guidance and training where I need it.'
  (v) 'Reward me according to my contribution.'

In many situations this was a major step forward to autonomy and self-control, and the excellent sense of the approach has influenced the nature of management development far beyond the number of organisations who formally adopted it. The difficulty lies in the tendency to expect too much and base future plans on specified performance standards of individuals rather than collectives. A set of objectives linked to sales volume of a new product for a sales manager will be of little value — perhaps harmful — if a technical defect develops that the designers had not foreseen and cannot rectify. Every manager is vulnerable to the operation of *force majeure* in the form of the unpredictable and unexpected. Other difficulties are those of joint goal-setting between those who are not equal, so that the 'shared' objectives can easily be 'imposed' objectives. There is also a tendency to focus on short-term specific targets, like productivity targets or sales figures, at the expense of longer-term considerations that cannot be so precisely defined.

(h) ORGANISATION DEVELOPMENT

The last method of approach to mention here is also the most recent to find popularity. The interaction between organisational structure and employee performance, as well as the interaction between organisation and employee well-being, has been studied so closely as to bring a shift in thinking towards the idea that teams of managers and their organisations have to be developed simultaneously. This is much influenced by the concern with planned organisational change and the fear of organisational obsolescence because the methods of an organisation are appropriate only for a situation that no longer exists. This brings us back very close to the idea of 'development management' and the comments of John Morris at the beginning of this chapter. It also brings us, of course, right back to the argument, with which we began this book, of the interdependence between man and the organisation. Compared with some of the approaches we have been discussing – like action learning and MbO – organisation development lacks the basic simplicity to appeal to the imagination of many people, and its acceptance has been much bedevilled by uncertainty about what it is. This difficulty is compounded because organisation development (inevitably abbreviated to OD) has a variety of gurus, each of whom has received a revelation about its nature that differs from all the others. One of the best summaries is by Bristow, Carby and Thakur,[17] who trace its development back to the United States (where else?) in the thirties.

OD's method of operation centres round not only objectives and aims, but on interpersonal behaviour, attitudes and values in the organisation. There is usually an emphasis on openness between colleagues, improved conflict resolution methods, more effective team management and the collaborative diagnosis and solution of problems. The training strategy typically centres on groups of managers, or directly on organisational processes with the assistance of the change agent or consultant, who helps the participants to perceive, face up to and resolve the behavioural problems experienced.

Definitions of OD vary considerably, often according to the limited perspective of the particular writer concerned. A broadly acceptable definition is the following:

> ... it focuses on assisting individuals, groups and organisations *to learn how to develop* rather than relying on formal 'training' for individuals and seeking expert advice for organisational improvement. As we have seen, OD efforts are usually centred on groups but individual differences are taken into account. Indeed, it is believed essential that the 'whole man' should be considered; his feelings as well as his thoughts; and his relationships as well as his actions ... It questions the validity of conventional hierarchical structures and suggests options for alternative forms based on task demand.[18]

Two other quotations help to fill out the picture:

> OD is a response to change, a complex educational strategy intended to change the beliefs, attitudes, values and structures of organisations so they can better

adapt to new technologies, new markets and challenges, and the dizzying rate of change itself.[19]

OD is a long range effort to improve an organisation's problem-solving and renewal processes, particularly through a more effective and collaborative management of organisational culture . . . with the assistance of a change agent, or catalyst, and the use of the theory and technology of applied behavioural science.[20]

But Do We Know What Management Is?

The management development movement has been a bandwagon for a quarter of a century and a gloomy view would be that its most apparent result has been to make British management ineffective.[21,22] Some critics argue that management ineffectiveness is the key reason for Britain's industrial decline and that this, in turn, is due to inappropriate ideas about management nurtured by the managers themselves, copied slavishly from American practice without being in an American context.[23]

One other problem is the assumption that management is homogeneous: middle management is senior management writ small and junior management is written smaller still. In practice the duties undertaken by people at different levels varies significantly and one of the effects of microtechnology applications in business has been to make senior management less dependent on those in the middle. This is one of several factors leading to a 'middle management problem'. Middle management can not be seen simply as a training ground for more senior positions; it is now a whole career for most people in that category. One very large, and expanding, company produced data in 1981 to show that the average age at which managers reached the grade in which they eventually retired was between 43 and 48 for middle managers and between 46 and 53 for senior managers, so that the career development escalator stops earlier for middle managers. That was in an *expanding* company: in most the situation is one of fewer promotion opportunities.

Technological advance means that many middle managers find their technical skills obsolete and there are several studies[24,25] showing growing dissatisfaction in their ranks. White[26] conducted a participant observation study in an electrical company on the South coast and explained middle management's resistance to change by the facts that they are structurally dissociated from the satisfaction of ownership, technically dissociated from the technique of production and socially dissociated from the work force. Perhaps the most positive approach to this situation is the rather romantic view of Nancy Foy:[27]

Every ten years or so the average middle manager ('the backbone of his organisation') might be sent on a short course, but his chances to have a voice in his own development are low at best, and as a result many managers have stopped thinking of themselves as developable. Turning them back on may be one of the most important steps towards revitalising organisations . . . their power is immense, based on deep knowledge of how the organisation really works; thus, while they may not be able to bring about change themselves, they nonetheless have tremendous capacity to block changes other people want, to paralyze an organisation, consciously or unconsciously.

SUMMARY PROPOSITIONS

10.1. Continuing uncertainty about how managerial competence should be developed is partly due to an uncertainty about the nature of managerial work.

10.2. The main difference between management development and management training is that the latter is centred on increasing ability to perform a particular role in a specific organisational context, usually involving other contiguous members of the organisation in the process.

10.3. Organisation Development is a method of management that is gaining in popularity and concentrates on collaboration and team-working by members of a working group as a means towards innovation and organisational renewal.

10.4. The development needs of managers vary not only according to their individualism, but also according to their level in the management hierarchy.

REFERENCES

1. Morris J. 'Management Development and Development Management' in *Personnel Review*, Autumn 1971, p. 30.
2. Graves D., 'The Manager's Job and Management Development', in *Personnel Review,* Autumn 1976, p. 15.
3. Mumford A., 'What Did You Learn Today?' in *Personnel Management*, August 1981, p. 38.
4. Savage A., 'Selecting Managers for a Permanent State of Flux' in *Personnel Management*, October 1981, pp. 38–42.
5. Stewart R., *Contrasts in Management* (McGraw-Hill), 1976.
6. Mintzberg H., *The Nature of Managerial Work* (Harper and Row) 1973.
7. Scholefield J., 'The Effectiveness of Senior Executives' in *Journal of Mangement Studies,* May 1968, pp. 219–234.
8. Mant A., *The Rise and Fall of the British Manager* (Macmillan) 1977.
9. *Ibid*, p. 3.
10. Morris J. and Burgoyne J.G., *Developing Resourceful Managers* (IPM) 1973, especially Chapters 1 and 3.
11. Stuart R. and Burgoyne J.G., 'The Learning Goals and Outcomes of Management Development Programmes' in *Personnel Review*, Winter 1977, p. 10.
12. Stewart A. and V., *Tomorrow's Men Today* (IPM) 1976.
13. Ball R.J., 'Britain's Economy: Some Implications for Management and Management Education' in *Personnel Review*, Autumn 1976, p. 8. There is also a very helpful comment on business schools in Morris and Burgoyne, *op. cit.,* pp. 67–78.
14. Revans R.W., *Standards for Morale* (Tavistock) 1969.
15. Statements on the action learning approach can be found in Revans R.W., 'Action Learning —A Management Development Programme', in *Personnel Review,* Autumn 1972, pp. 36–44, and in Revans R.W., 'Action Learning Projects' in Taylor B and Lippitt G.L., *Management Development and Training Handbook* (McGraw-Hill) 1974, pp. 204–217.
16. Boettinger H.M., 'Is Management Really an Art?' in *Harvard Business Review,* January/February 1975.
17. Bristow J., Carby K. and Thakur M., 'An Introduction to Organisation Development' in Thakur M., Bristow J. and Carby K., *Personnel in Change* (IPM) 1978, pp. 1–25.

18. *Ibid.,* p. 25.
19. Bennis W. *Organisational Development: its Nature, Origins and Prospects* (Addison-Wesley) 1969.
20. French W.L. and Bell C., *Organisational Development* (Prentice-Hall) 1973.
21. Pratten C.F., *A Comparison of the Performance of Swedish and United Kingdom Companies* (Cambridge University Press) 1981.
22. Fores M. and Sorge A., 'The Decline of the Management Ethic' in *Journal of General Management*, Spring 1981.
23. Glover I., 'Executive Career Patterns: Britain, France, Germany and Sweden' in *Manufacturing and Management* (HMSO) 1978.
24. Arbrose M., 'The Changing Life Values of Today's Executive' in *International Management*, July 1980.
25. Cooper M.R., Gelford P.A. and Foley P.M., 'Early Warning Signals: Growing Discontent Among Managers' in *Business*, Jan/Feb 1980.
26. White C., 'Why Won't Managers Co-operate?' in *Industrial Relations Journal*, March/April 1981.
27. Foy N., *The Yin and Yang of Organizations* (Grant McIntyre) 1981.

Section C
THE CONTRACT FOR COLLECTIVE CONSENT

11

The Contract for Collective Consent and Organisation for Recognition

The contract for employment between man and his organisation is for the employment of an individual, but that contract is reached within a framework of collective consent. In this next section we turn to the theme of collective agreement between representatives of employees and representatives of the organisation which gives *collective consent* to a general framework of rules and guidelines for the individual contract.

The collective agreement is the outcome of that most precious and contentious process of western societies, collective bargaining, which has a significance beyond the scope of this book:

> Collective bargaining occupies a critical interchange position in Western European societies, influencing and being influenced by a myriad of characteristics of each society — economic, political, cultural, social historical. It is related most fundamentally and directly to the pluralist political structures of Western democracies.[1]

In this dimension to the employment contract we consider first the arrangements for mutual recognition between the parties to the agreement, and the organisation of management to meet the challenge of recognition and then administer the subsequent activities. We then examine the procedural aspects of the resultant working relationship and the interactive process of negotiating agreement. The position of the employee representative is discussed in a separate chapter (Chapter 13) and we close the section by reviewing the situation about the equalisation of employment opportunity for certain large minority groups.

The Nature of Collective Consent

In this section of the book we talk about collective consent rather than collective agreement. The difference in emphasis is that consent implies the acceptance of a situation, while agreement has the more positive connotation of commitment following some degree of initiative in bring the situation into existence.

We are not therefore necessarily describing active employee participation in managerial decision-making. The range is wider, to include the variety of circumstances in which employees consent collectively to managerial authority, so long as they find it acceptable.

This may well fall far short of the notion of employee participation as advanced *inter alia* by Bullock[2] or the McCarthy and Ellis formula[3] for management by agreement that was described briefly in the opening chapter. In order to couch the discussion in terms which can embrace a variety of styles, we set out seven *categories of consent*, in which there is a steadily increasing degree of collective employee involvement. This is illustrated in Figure 11.1. We begin with a category in which there is straightforward and unquestioning acceptance of management authority, and then move through various stages of increasing participation in decision-making and the necessary changes in management style as the power balance alters and the significance of bargaining develops and extends to more and more areas of organisational life.

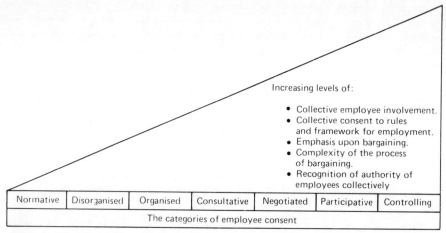

Figure 11.1. Alternative categories of collective consent

(a) NORMATIVE

We use this term in the sense of Etzioni,[4] who described 'normative' organisations as being those in which the involvement of individuals was attributable to a strong sense of moral obligation. Any challenge to authority would imply a refutation of the shared norms and was therefore unthinkable.

(b) DISORGANISED

In organisations that are not normative there may be collective consent simply because there is no collective focus for a challenge, so disorganised consent is where there may be discontent but consent is maintained through lack of employee organisation.

(c) ORGANISED

When employees organise it is nearly always in trade unions and the first collective activities are usually in dealing with general grievances. It is very unlikely that there will be any degree of involvement in the management decision-making processes. Employees simply consent to obey instructions as long as grievances are dealt with.

(d) CONSULTATIVE

Consultation here is seen as a stage of development beyond initial trade union recognition, even though some organisations consult with employees before — often as a means of deferring — trade union recognition. Here is the first incursion into the management process as employees are asked for an opinion about management proposals before decisions are made, even though the right to decide remains with the management.

(e) NEGOTIATED

Negotiation implies that both parties have the power to decide and the power to withhold agreement, so that a decision can only be reached by some form of mutual accommodation. No longer is the management retaining all decision-making to itself; it is seeking some sort of bargain with employee representatives, recognising that only such reciprocity can produce what is needed.

(f) PARTICIPATIVE

When employee representatives reach the stage of participating in the general management of the organisation in which they are employed, there is a fundamental change in the control of that organisation, even though this may initially be theoretical rather than actual. Employee representatives take part in making the decisions on major strategic issues like expenditure on research, the opening of new plants and the introduction of new products. In arrangements for participative consent there is a balance between the decision-makers representing the interests of capital and those representing the interests of labour, though the balance is not necessarily even.

(g) CONTROLLING

If the employees acquire control of the organisation, as in a workers' co-operative, then the consent is a controlling type. This may sound bizarre, but there will still be a management apparatus within the organisation to which employee collective consent will be given or from which it will be withheld.

All of the above categories require some management initiative to sustain collective consent. In categories (a) and (b) it may be exhortation to ensure that commitment is kept up, or information supplied to defer organisation. In each subsequent category there is an increasing bargaining emphasis that becomes progressively more complex. The discussion in this section of the book is centred around an assumption that organisations will be roughly between categories (c) and (e). This appears to be the most common situation and is that for which organisations in categories (a) and (b) may need to prepare. We see little difference in substance for categories (f) and (g).

The implication of the last few paragraphs is that there is a hierarchy of consent categories, through which organisations steadily progress. Although this has frequently been true in the past, it is by no means necessary. Some may begin at (f) or (g): there is no inflexible law of evolution and change can move in the opposite direction as well.

Trade Union Recognition and Bargaining Units

When a trade union has recruited a number of members in an organisation it will seek *recognition* from the employer in order to represent those members. The step of recognition is seldom easy but is very important as it marks an irrevocable movement away from unilateral decision-making by the management. We can examine some of the questions to be considered.

(a) WHY SHOULD A UNION BE RECOGNISED AT ALL?

If the employees want that type of representation they will not readily co-operate with the employer if he refuses. In extreme cases this can generate sufficient antagonism to cause industrial action in support of recognition. A more positive reason is the benefits that can flow from recognition: there are employee representatives with whom to discuss, consult and negotiate so that communication and working relationships can be improved. The 1980s have, however, certainly seen a decline in union membership and effectiveness in resisting management initiatives. Employers are considering recognition claims more carefully and collective consent can be achieved by other means in some situations, providing that the management work hard at the job of both securing and maintaining that consent.

(b) WHEN SHOULD A UNION BE RECOGNISED?

When it has sufficient support from the employees. There is no simple way of determining what is sufficient. The 1971 Industrial Relations Act[5] specified that 51 per cent of the employees must be in membership, but current legislation lays down no percentage. The first thirteen cases brought to ACAS after the passing of the Employment Protection Act 1975 produced recommendations for recognition where the level of membership varied from 21 to 100 per cent and in five cases the figure was below 40 per cent.[6] Among the factors that have influenced ACAS in whether or not to recommend recognition have been the degree of union organisation and efficiency, the number of representatives, the size of constituency and the degree of opposition to recognition from non-union employees. A frequent encouragement for the management of an organisation to recognise a union relatively quickly is where there is the possibility of competing claims, with some employees seeking to get another union established because they do not like the first.

(c) FOR WHOM SHOULD A UNION BE RECOGNISED?

For that group of employees who have a sufficient commonality of interests, terms and conditions for one union to be able to represent them and the management be able to respond. This group of employees are sometimes described as those making up a *bargaining unit;* the boundaries of the units need careful consideration by the management to determine what is most appropriate and what consequent response to recognition claims they will make. There are a number of boundaries that are generally acknowledged: manual employees are usually represented by different unions from white-collar employees, and skilled employees are usually represented by a different union from semi-skilled and unskilled as well as from those possessing different skills. Other boundaries are less easy, particularly where a distinction may be drawn on the grounds of hierarchical status, as between those who are paid monthly and those paid weekly. Where status is related to responsibility for subordinates there appears to be another accepted boundary: the supervisor will not be represented by the same union as the supervised, although one or two levels may be included sometimes in the same unit.

(d) FOR WHAT SHOULD A UNION BE RECOGNISED?

The terms and conditions of employment of the employees who are members of

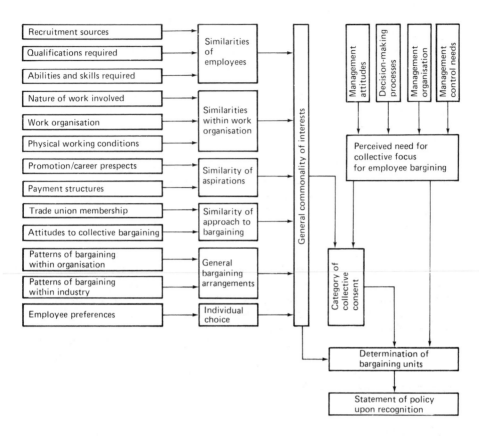

*Figure 11.2. General factors influencing the determination
of bargaining units and recognition*

the bargaining unit. A union can seek recognition on anything that might be covered in a contract of employment, but the employer may agree to recognition only for a limited range of topics. The irreducible minimum is assistance by a union representative for members with grievances, but the extent to which matters beyond that are recognised as being a subject of bargaining depends on which consent category (see page 147) the organisation is in. It also depends on the possible existence of other agreements that could take some matters out of the scope of local recognition.

The general factors influencing the determination of bargaining units and recognition are summarised in Figure 11.2.

The Legal Position on Recognition

Trade unions seek recognition from employers by the traditional means of recruiting members and making representations to the management. If they are not successful then they have to take risks by, for instance, calling on their members to take industrial action to persuade the employer into a position where he will grant recognition.

The Employment Protection Act provided an alternative method for trade unions to seek recognition via ACAS from an employer who was reluctant to recognise. These provisions were so unpopular that they were repealed by the 1980 Employment Act, but it is worth a brief review to consider why the measures were originally introduced and what led to their repeal.

The 1975 legislation was based on the premise that an employer's right to refuse recognition to a trade union should be open to some question other than that of union bargaining power, in order to ensure basic rights of representation to employees and union members employed in situations where trade union organisation was weak. Many unions ignored the 1975 measures entirely and most employers objected to the one-sided nature of the legislation, whereby unions could ask for an investigation of an issue but employers could not. ACAS became concerned about the variety of hats they were being asked to wear. Their main duties are to improve industrial relations and to extend collective bargaining, but it was difficult to reconcile that with the compulsory arbitration that the 1975 provisions involved.

The issue of ACAS and trade union recognition was greatly publicised by the extraordinary affair of the Grunwick Film Processing Laboratories, where the management not only refused union recognition, but also dismissed all of a substantial number of employees who took strike action, refused to co-operate with an ACAS ballot of employee opinion, refused to accept the recommendation and then refused to accept the suggestion of a government Court of Inquiry. Despite every form of persuasion, including mass picketing and union attempts at blacking supplies, the management remained firm in refusing to recognise and in the end the state agencies were as powerless as the trade union movement to produce union recognition in a situation where the management was determined to deny it.[7,8]

Although unions can no longer seek recognition by this method, it is still vital for them to be recognised if they are to enjoy other legal rights. The remaining provisions of the 1975 Act include rights for recognised trade unions only to receive collective bargaining information, time off for industrial relations, trade union and public duties, and consultation of proposed redundancies. The Health and Safety Act provisions for safety representatives only apply to recognised unions, as do the planning information rights under the 1975 Industry Act and the workplace facilities and secret ballot provisions of the Employment Act 1980.

During the time that the statutory powers were in force 1,610 claims for recognition were submitted to ACAS. Over 1,100 of these were withdrawn, although half resulted in some form of union recognition. Investigations by ACAS were completed and final reports issued on 247 claims: the remaining 248 were unresolved when the provisions were repealed. 158 of the 247 final reports recommended recognition but only one third of those were implemented and covered only 16,000 employees. The level of achievement in obtaining union recognition by compulsory means is therefore poor, especially when compared with the success rate of other methods. Apart from the cases withdrawn (mentioned at the beginning of this paragraph) ACAS has cases submitted to it constantly for *voluntary* conciliation: in the same period that compulsory measures produced recognition for 16,000 people, the voluntary route produced full recognition for 55,000 people and limited recognition for a further 22,000.[9]

The Union Membership Agreement ('the Closed Shop')

Another matter to consider is not only whether a trade union should be recognised but whether the employer should go further and make an agreement that all employees in a particular category should be members of that union. The principle is that of the closed shop; the technical term being 'union membership agreement.' A union membership agreement can be reached between an employer and a trade union that makes it a condition of employment for each employee in a particular category within the organisation to be a member of that trade union. It is an aspect of employment practice that causes more interest than most outside the small world of the specialists. When the Trade Union and Labour Relations Act was making its way on to the statute book it was on this single point that modifications had to be made to satisfy members of the Commons who expressed serious alarm about individual freedom and the independent judgement of newspaper editors.

Those who are not industrial relations practitioners therefore have an interest in this matter which ranges more broadly than considerations that are appropriate for the more specialised purview of this book. For those managing organisations we can see the issue of the closed shop as recognition writ large. To some extent it is the logical step beyond recognition in establishing the union as the mode of communication with, and representation of, employees. If this is the situation, runs the logical argument, every employee should support his union financially, exercise his right to vote and speak, and then be bound by the discipline of democratic control of the individual. Everyone is in the same position and there is no ill-feeling between members and non-members.

The other view of the matter is to question whether employees should be obliged to join a trade union against their will, especially if they have strong ideological objections, and whether there are some members of the organisation for whom trade union membership provides serious role conflict, because their occupational life usually puts them in the position of representing employer interests in opposition to employee collective interests.

The 1980 and 1982 Employment Acts established new rights for the individual in relation to the closed shop. Previously the individual employee was obliged to be a member of the union if a union membership agreement existed between his employer and a recognised trade union, which made membership of that union a condition of employment. Anyone refusing to join or resigning from membership while employed in a category of work covered by the UMA had no defence against dismissal by his employer on that ground. The single exception – long honoured by trade unions – was the employee who had genuine religious objections to trade union membership, and which has now been widened to include grounds of conscience or other grounds of deeply-held personal conviction as a basis for objecting either to membership of any union or to membership of a particular union.

Also those who are not members of a union specified in a union membership agreement, but who are employees of the employer, cannot be dismissed for remaining non-members. Furthermore any UMA coming into existence after August 1980 has to be approved by an 80% vote in a secret ballot: furthermore the 80% must be of those entitled to vote rather than of those actually voting. Dismissal for non-membership of a union will be unfair if there has not been a secret ballot before November 1983 or within intervals of five years after that date. In conjunction with the Act ACAS have issued a code of practice which sets out how the ballot should be conducted.

Management Organisation for Recognition

The 'category of consent' for an organisation will influence its style of management and the structure of its management organisation, with the most important change coming when an organisation moves from category (b) to (c). That is the point at which there is some guarantee of commitment by management to procedure and the acknowledgement that a limited range of management decisions could be successfully challenged by the employees, causing those decisions to be altered. We have already said that we see the majority or organisations as being between categories (c) and (e), and that the argument of this section of the book is based on that assumption.

Most of the surveys of managerial duties in industrial relations, like those of Anthony and Crichton[10] and Marsh,[11] show negotiations with trade union representatives being carried out mainly by production managers or others in line positions, while personnel specialists provided advice or some other service. Although it seems certain that this picture has changed in very recent years and that the personnel specialist is much more likely to be the dominant figure in negotiations, there is still a notional distinction between the roles of personnel and line managers. The Commission on Industrial Relations has made this comment:

> a. The line manager is necessarily responsible for industrial relations within his particular area of operations. He needs freedom to manage his plant, department or section effectively within agreed policies and with access to specialist advice.
> b. The personnel manager should help by supplying expert knowledge and skill and by monitoring the consistent execution of industrial relations policies and programmes throughout the company. He needs the backing of top management and must establish the authority which comes from giving sound advice.[12]

The same publication indicates elsewhere[13] that the simple distinction between advisory and executive roles is more useful as an instrument of analysis than as a means of describing current practice, which varies so much. Some organisations give full executive authority to industrial relations specialists. Parker, Hawes and Lumb illustrate the variation with two quotations from company policy statements:

> 'management responsibility for the conduct of industrial relations is . . . delegated by the accountable line manager to his senior industrial relations executive who will make industrial relations decisions or review such decisions and ensure their consistency with established policy, practices and procedure . . . '

> 'the management of employees is the responsibility of line management; the role of personnel specialists is to advise and assist line management in the exercise of that responsibility and to provide requisite supporting services.'[14]

The issues underlying this dilemma are most recently and extensively discussed by Thomason[15] in the introduction to his work on personnel management. In our present writing we have to acknowledge that there is no clear, single answer, as so much depends on the traditions of the particular organisation, the personalities involved, the nature of the working processes and the extent of recognition. However, we believe that recent developments have strengthened the case for the *dominance* of a personnel specialist in employee relations matters; and we are careful to use the word 'dominance' in preference to some of the popular alternatives like 'authority', 'executive', 'power', 'responsibility' and others. The development that has potentially enhanced the personnel specialists' status most since 1974 is the access of power to the employee's position in the employment relationship, through the underpinning of his employment rights by evolving legislation. This makes the employer more dependent on specialist advice and internal administrative controls to ensure consistency. Both of these are crucial to the personnel role.

If we consider first the question of advice, we may say that the conception of advice used to be of the type offered by a well-meaning mother-in-law. It was thoughtful, genuinely intended to be helpful, and was sometimes welcome, but its basis was simply general experience and good intentions. The recipient could use or ignore it at will, depending on his commonsense assessment of its value. Legislation has caused the need for advice of the type offered by a professional. This is thoughtful, intended to be helpful, but may not be welcome. It will be based on an informed examination of statute and precedent, and will carry a quite different type of authority. It may also be that people see the need not only for advice, but also for representation by someone who knows the esoteric rules of procedure and behaviour in a highly stylised form of discussion.

As well as advice the employer needs to see that all employment matters are administered in a way that is consistent with the legislative framework, and part of that requirement is that managerial actions should be consistent with each other.

In many management decisions in relation to employees the correctness lies not only in the intrinsic quality of the decision but also in the consistency of management handling of similar matters previously and in other parts of the organisation. In labour law consistency is an important feature of justice, and it can be achieved in an organisation either by having inflexible rules or by having a single source of control on decisions made.

The need for specialist advice based on a sound knowledge of the law and the need for an associated control over a wide range of management decisions have changed the range of options open to the employer in deploying personnel expertise. The personnel officer may be charged with the task of deciding action on all employment matters and then implementing those decisions. Alternatively he may monitor tentative decisions by others, which he agrees or vetoes before they are confirmed and implemented by those who formulated them. What seems to us essential is that this type of specialist element should dominate management thinking and action on employee relations, whatever the detailed method may be. There is no place for mothers-in-law.

A specialist focus that is less readily ceded to the personnel officer by his line colleagues is that of negotiating skill. This is not as tangible as knowledge of the law and many people in line management positions find it difficult to countenance a situation in which someone else negotiates with 'their' staff. Also we should not paint too simplistic a picture of the management process by implying that one person decides on issues with Olympian disregard for the opinions of others. Many decisions will be by consensus, some will be obvious and others will be complex. It is for this reason that we have chosen the word 'dominance' as the most helpful to describe the personnel involvement.

Organisational Strategy for Union Recognition

Finally in this chapter we need to consider the strategy of an organisation's management for union recognition. There are a sequence of steps.

(a) MANAGEMENT ATTITUDES

However dominant the personnel specialist may be in an organisation on employee relations matters, the other members of management do not simply leave him to get on with trade union recognition while they pursue their other and more interesting preoccupations. The step of recognition, or the extension of recognition, and all that follows from such a step can affect other policy matters like the introduction of new products, investment in new plant, the manning of equipment and the opening or closure of establishments.

Equally, policy decisions to do with marketing, manufacturing, financing or new technology are likely to have employment repercussions. Union recognition or extension of recognition represents the introduction of change that can have major implications in all parts of the life of the organisation. Because of this it is important that collective management attitudes towards recognition should have as wide a degree of consensus as possible. Then policy on recognition and its consequences can be fully integrated with other aspects of policy.

The previous three sentences represent a homily that has been repeated in innumerable different ways for years, and managers are frequently sceptical about such bland exhortations to do something which they know to be extremely difficult. Some of the problems lie in the specialised nature of the issue. The very existence of trade unions is resented by some and the alleged behaviour of trade unionists has been given as the reason for the fall of governments, let alone managerial ineffectiveness. The reasons justifying trade union recognition in general, and on some contentious matters in particular, are not readily appreciated, and when understood may still be disputed. Another difficulty is the need for a positive rather than grudging approach to recognition. If the management of an organisation recognise a trade union only because they feel there is no alternative, then they will derive scant benefit from the arrangement. As with other aspects of change in organisations it can be an initiative towards improvement and development or it can be a defensive reaction to something distasteful and unwanted. It is also typical for the new convert to trade union recognition to be disappointed with the outcome. The conventional illustration of this attitude is where management have been persuaded that rank-and-file employees will make a contribution to better management decisions if they are involved through their union being recognised for negotiation and consultation. A few months later there are bitter, disillusioned remarks about the unwillingness of the employees to discuss anything other than trivial matters like the colour of their overalls.

These and other problems about the integration of policy and a management consensus on recognition can probably only be resolved by full and lengthy discussion by members of management to find and then 'own' a collective view.

(b) PREPARING TO RECOGNISE

Does a management respond or initiate on recognition? Does it wait for a claim and then treat it on its merits or does it invite a claim? The answer to this question will come from a consideration of timing. It has already been suggested in this chapter that care has to be taken with a recognition claim that the time is ripe, not too soon or too late. There is always a danger that recognition will be harder if deferred. The CIR found several situations like this:

> the success of the company's products in the markets of the world meant that management had to concentrate, to the virtual exclusion of all else, on increasing output . . . The problems arising from the needs and aspirations of a large number of people had been largely shelved under the presence of the more immediate need to meet production targets.[16]

Another argument in favour of a recognition initiative by the management is that most of the areas of employment where recognition has not yet been granted are white-collar; one of the traditional reasons for white-collar employees not joining unions is their feeling that the management do not approve. They may tend to identify with the members of management and do not want to do things that are disliked.

Preparing to recognise requires a decision on whether to wait or to initiate. It also requires decisions on strategy about which union would be most 'appropriate', what the boundaries of the bargaining units could be and on what matters recognition would be contemplated.

(c) ORGANISATION, COMMUNICATION AND RESPONSIBILITY

How are the management to organise themselves to make recognition work? This process will involve a re-examination of the decision-making processes so that the additional input of employee consent can be incorporated with the other variables to be evaluated. It does not mean that managers have to get permission from their employees before they do anything — even though this is how union recognition is often caricatured. Management activity within a framework of collective consent is discussed in more detail throughout the rest of this section of the book. Here it will suffice to say that the decision-making processes have to be examined and the boundaries of managerial roles re-drawn. Any recognition step involves moving one or more items off the list that are customarily a subject for unilateral decision and on the the list of those for joint regulation; when that happens it will involve not only a different approach but also a different process of discussion and validation within the management ranks.

Associated with the considerations in the previous paragraph are those of personal power and responsibility. We have argued for the dominance of a personnel specialist, but how is that to be deployed? Will it be in the form of a clearing-house for personnel decisions or will it be a decision-*making* function? Will it make decisions which are then communicated to employees by others or will the implementation of decisions be an additional dimension to the specialisation?

(d) THE CONTRACT FOR RECOGNITION

Our next chapter will describe the procedure agreement as the cornerstone of the contract for collective consent. We anticipate that analogy by describing the agreement to recognise as the foundation stone for that contract.

PM - L

There will ideally be some written statement to which both parties assent; this will include the basic factual information about which union is a party to the agreement, what the bargaining unit is and what the subjects of recognition are. It may include much more, as it is an opportunity to declare aspects of the policy of the organisation — either the policy of the organisation's management or the policy of management and employee representatives combined. This can pave the way for openness between the parties, awareness of what is happening and consistency in management.

Such a statement will also have the advantage of focusing the attention of policy-makers on the purposes and implications of it. The drafting of the statement could well be the basis of the full and lengthy discussion suggested earlier in this chapter. The CIR give us a useful summary of the benefits of a written statement of policy:

Firstly, the processes involved in producing the document will themselves have been valuable in focussing minds on the purpose of the policy. They clarify intentions and eliminate uncertainties which may exist when reliance is placed on custom and practice or when policy is a matter of surmise. Secondly, a written document provides an objective reference point in the communication of policy to managers, employees and their representatives. Thirdly, by making clear the starting point of policy it provides a basis for change. A written policy need not be inflexible but should be reviewed and adapted as circumstances require. By being written it should, in fact, be easier to change than policies which are embedded in custom and practice, tradition and precedent.[17]

SUMMARY PROPOSITIONS

11.1.   Employee acceptance of management authority may be strengthened if the management recognise a trade union to provide a focused, collective questioning of that authority.

11.2.   Management need to decide what bargaining units there should be, which union should be recognised for each unit and when, what the scope of recognition should be.

11.3.   The step of recognition requires re-examination of managment decision-making processes and will involve the dominance of a personnel specialist in management of employment matters.

11.4.   A written statement of policy on recognition can provide the basis for mutually beneficial development of collective consent.

REFERENCES

1. Goodman J.F.B., 'Trade Unions and Collective Bargaining Systems', in Torrington D., *Comparative Industrial Relations in Europe*, (ABP) 1978, p. 31.

2. Dept. of Trade, *Report of the Committee of Inquiry on Industrial Democracy* (HMSO) 1977.
3. McCarthy W.E.J. and Ellis N.D., *Management by Agreement* (Hutchinson) 1973.
4. Etzioni A., *A Comparative Analysis of Complex Organisations* (Free Press) 1961.
5. Industrial Relations Act 1971, p. 44.
6. Reported in IDS Brief No. 105 (Incomes Data Services Ltd) March 1977, p. 3.
7. Rogaly J., *Grunwick* (Penguin) 1977.
8. Department of Employment, *Report of a Committee of Inquiry Under the Chairmanship of Lord Chief Justice Scarman into the Affairs of Grunwick Film Processing Laboratories and APEX* (HMSO) 1977.
9. Advisory, Conciliation and Arbitration Service, *Annual Report 1980* (HMSO) 1981.
10. Anthony P. and Crichton A., *Industrial Relations and the Personnel Specialists* (Batsford) 1969.
11. Marsh A.I., 'The Staffing of Industrial Relations Management in the Engineering Industry'. *Industrial Relations Journal*, vol. 2, no. 2, Summer 1971.
12. Commission on Industrial Relations, *The Role of Management in Industrial Relations* (HMSO) 1973, p. 26.
13. *Ibid.,* p. 16.
14. Parker P.A.L., Hawes W.R. and Lumb A.L., Department of Employment Manpower Paper No. 5, *The Reform of Collective Bargaining at Plant and Company Level* (HMSO) 1971, p.23.
15. Thomason G.F., *A Textbook of Personnel Management*, 2nd ed. (IPM) 1976, pp. 9–46.
16. Commission on Industrial Relations, *BSR Ltd* (HMSO) 1972, p. 12.
17. Commission on Industrial Relations, *The Role of Management in Industrial Relations, op. cit.*, p. 6.

12

Collective Procedures

The cornerstone of the contract for collective consent is the procedural agreement. In developing a behavioural theory of the business enterprise Cyert and March [1] considered standard operating procedures as being at two levels — the general choice procedure and the specific. Three basic principles for general choice were suggested:

1. Procedures are intended to minimise the need for predicting future events.
2. Once feasible procedures are established the organisation will abandon them only under duress.
3. Rules are simple, depending on individual judgement to provide the necessary flexibility.

Cyert and March regarded specific operating procedures as being of four major types:

1. Rules governing the performance of tasks in the organisation.
2. Continuing records and reports.
3. Drills for handling information.
4. Plans for the intended allocation of resources among alternatives.

All these elements are present in various types of collective procedures in the field of employment which are used to regulate the relationships between the employees collectively and the representatives of the organisation to which they are contracted. Some rules of the working relationship derive from statute, some from unilateral employer decree and some from custom and practice, but in this chapter we are considering those rules which derive from collective bargaining. They provide a framework within which the parties can engage each other in discussion, problem-solving and negotiation at the same time as exercising some decree of control over each other by specifying what the other party will and will not do in certain specified circumstances. The procedural structure *prescribes* certain actions by the actors in the arena (that, for instance, an employee takes a grievance first to his first-line supervisor) and *proscribes* others (like changing a payment scheme without prior consultation). They are described as *collective* procedures because they usually come into existence as a result of negotiation and are monitored by representatives of the collectives, even though some of the principal procedural issues — such as discipline and grievance — are essentially individual matters.

General Arguments Supporting Procedures

Although procedural arrangements have existed in British industrial relations for decades, it is only since the publication of the Donovan Report[2] in 1968 that their significance has been widely appreciated and their extension has been authoritatively advocated. A variety of reasons are advanced in their support.

(a) CLARITY AND ORDER

The development of procedures brings under public examination a greater degree of the activities by the parties, so that those involved know more clearly what is going on and what will happen in certain future eventualities. During the 1960s there was extensive productivity bargaining, which usually had some procedural element, and McKersie and Hunter express the following view:

> Prior to productivity bargaining, decisions were made in terms of precedent, customary practice or the dictates of stewards and foremen. Such a control system could be characterised as haphazard and personal. By contrast, under productivity bargaining, the control system becomes much more deliberate, rational and professional. It remains just as much a product of joint influence, but the process of joint regulation has been placed on a much more systematic and impersonal basis.[3]

(b) FAIRNESS

In reducing the degree of irrationality in actions, procedures can also contribute to a fairer working situation at the workplace, making nepotism or overbearing supervision less likely and ensuring that all employees discharge the obligation of their contracts.

(c) CONSISTENCY

Through the inherent monitoring facility, procedures tend to ensure managerial consistency in actions. Not only does this help towards the fairness already mentioned, it also acts as a safeguard against legal repercussions, as consistency in treatment is one of the cardinal criteria of the tribunals in examining a case presented to them.

(d) DISORDER CAUSES TROUBLE

The advocates of procedures claim not only that greater clarity and order in the employment relationship is 'a good thing' but that the lack of procedures and contingent benefits is one of the main causes of poor industrial relations.

Reservations about Procedures

There are at least two points of reservation about procedures that must be made to reach a balanced appreciation of their potential:

(a) THE INHIBITING OF CHANGE

As we have already seen, procedures will not be readily abandoned, as those who have created them will cling to them for the security they offer. The industrial relations actors have working lives of considerable uncertainty and tend to be very anxious to sustain procedures. As they have the effect of freezing the action at the time they were devised, they can inhibit change by becoming sacrosanct.

This can be a particular frustration for managers seeking a swift change of working arrangements to cope with a shift in the company's affairs. Part of the tradition of procedures is that they are a means whereby employees reduce the extent to which they are the sole element in managerial flexibility to meet changing circumstances, so procedural discussion becomes a way of buying time in the face of endangered job security. Through 1981 and the early part of 1982 the management of Times Newspapers in London made various attempts to reach agreement with employee representatives on necessary redundancies. Union officials did not agree with the number that were 'necessary' and the employer eventually went to the lengths of, apparently, abrogating the procedure by declaring redundancies in order eventually to reach (or force) an agreement.

(b) THE SIGNIFICANCE OF CUSTOM AND PRACTICE

Some would regard the view of McKersie and Hunter, quoted earlier, as naively optimistic; the claim that the control system becomes 'much more deliberate, rational and professional' is seen as more shadowy than substantial. Employees may not welcome the procedural restraints on their individuality and the real control of the workplace lies in the sense that people have of convention and tradition in the workplace — custom and practice — which produces rules having a greater cogency. Just as managers may not like to get involved in procedures because they lose freedom of action, employees may circumvent procedures for the same reason. Terry has suggested the following reasons:

> The workers may not like the new rules, or at least may consider they can be improved. Secondly, workers may be more prepared to challenge formal plant-level rules than they were to challenge the same understandings in a C & P form. This preparedness is tied up with . . . a feeling of loss of personal control over their working lives. Thirdly, where these conditions apply, and the workers are in a position to put pressure on foremen, this tactic will be the most logical and likely one for them to apply. Fourthly, the likely outcome of such low-level negotiations will be informal rules and understandings.[4]

So collective procedures are one element in the structure of relationships and they provide positive benefits so long as the expectations of the actors do not exceed what the procedures themselves can offer.

> . . . the procedure ought to be closely related to the actual behavioural process, but just how formal it is, along what dimensions, and how closely it should be followed are key issues in contingency analysis. In essence we would argue that informality has increasing disadvantages with increasing conflict and a deteriorating attitudinal climate. It is also important to note that a conflict relationship can change in degree and kind so that the procedures for resolution become out of date.[5]

THE NATURE OF PROCEDURES

The Industrial Relations Code of Practice gives a useful summary to provide a starting point in the discussion of what procedures are in practice:[6]

Procedural provisions should lay down the constitution of any joint negotiating body or specify the parties to the procedure. They should also cover:

(i) the matters to be bargained about and the levels at which bargaining should take place;

(ii) arrangements for negotiating terms and conditions of employment and the circumstances in which either party can give notice of their wish to re-negotiate them;

(iii) facilities for trade union activities in the establishment and the appointment, status and functions of shop stewards;

(iv) procedures for settling collective disputes and individual grievances and for dealing with disciplinary matters;

(v) the constitution and scope of any consultative committees.

In this book we are dealing with the third item of that list in the next chapter, and the remaining procedural elements can be combined and re-stated as:

(i) Negiotiation/consultation,

(ii) Dispute/grievance,

(iii) Discipline.

1. Procedures for Negotiation and Consultation

If an organisation recognises a trade union, such recognition brings with it a need to establish a way or working. If the parties are to negotiate and consult on a range of matters, they need to agree the mechanisms. This will usually be in a negotiating procedure. A pre-requisite is a constitution, which will usually specify some central committee or body to act as the focus for negotiation. This will provide the main piece of machinery for differing employer/employee interests to be resolved in relation to all the bargaining units affected. The membership of the committee will be agreed by the parties but will, of course, be joint. The constitution will also spell out the scope of the committee, specifying which groups of employees are covered by its deliberations, what the matters are that come within its orbit and — often more significant — which do not.

The range of coverage will normally have been settled at the recognition stage, but there can be a number of complications. For instance, if the committee is negotiating on behalf of the members of more than one union, then it may be that the topics to be negotiated about will vary from one union to another. Also there may be an agreement that supervisors will be excluded from the outcome of certain aspects of negotiation, as newly negotiated rules might produce role conflict for them but not for other union members.

The matters to be bargained about will be under the general umbrella phrase 'terms and conditions of employment' but there may be extensive exclusions. Some of this will derive from negotiations elsewhere, so that it is common for plant-level negotiating committees to rule themselves out of discussing issues like the length of the standard working week or the number of days of annual holiday, because these matters are discussed by national negotiating teams. There is usually a vague statement about the union recognising the right of the management 'to manage their business'. This indicates a tacit acceptance that there are certain things that are management prerogative, but they are seldom described in any more detail. This is an interesting aspect of the formality versus informality debate. Once the scope of the negotiating committee is set down by specifying what it *cannot* do, then there is a windmill to tilt at and someone is likely to challenge the limit. This is less likely when the arrangement is less formal and the subtleties of the relationship are left to 'understanding'.

If the organisation is a large one the central committee may spawn sub-committees as replications of itself to deal with similar matters on a smaller scale, often with an increasing degree of informality. The naming of these groups as *negotiating* committees describes them as committees set up to resolve differences of interest, where there is a basic conflict or divergence between that which is in the *employer* interest and that which is in the *employee* interest. This does not call for a particular operational procedure, although we consider later in this book the question of negotiating skill. Singleton makes the comment:

> There has to be a way in which negotiations are carried out which constitutes the negotiating procedure, however simple, however lacking in explicit formulation. In time, however, with the repetition of previous practice, with the adoption of methods for handling new problems as they are encountered, even the least sophisticated negotiating arrangements take on the character of an established procedure, the accepted method of conducting negotiation.[7]

2. Procedures for Dispute and Grievance

> A grievance procedure is commonly thought of as the method by which an individual raises some query or complaint about his or her pay or working conditions and the steps which are laid down for dealing with the matter.[8]

Because of its individual focus, and because of the legal requirement for a grievance procedure that the Contracts of Employment Act lays on employers, grievance procedure exists in many organisations where there is no trade union recognised. In such a situation it will be devised unilaterally by the management, even though they may take advice on how to frame it.

The grievance of an individual can, nevertheless, have collective implications of the 'there but for the grace of God go I' type, quite apart from the fact that the grievance expressed by one person may actually be aggrieving others at the same time. For this reason there is customarily an extension of grievance procedure where trade unions are recognised, to allow for collective endorsement of an individual grievance with which an individual employee has not been successful. At that time it has turned itself into a collective dispute. But dispute can also arise from a failure to agree within the negotiating procedure, so we need to consider the processing of grievances as a separate issue from disputes procedure even though one may develop into the other.

Although grievance procedure has been extensively studied in the United States,[9,10] those discussions do not necessarily help a consideration of the British situation because of the different legal basis of agreements in the two countries. One very helpful discussion of British procedures is in the treatment of McCarthy and Marsh[11] but more recently there has come an excellent and thorough investigation by Thomson and Murray,[12] that enables us to understand the operation of procedure more clearly. They succeeded in interviewing 268 managers in thirty-five plants about their views on grievance procedure and their experience with it, and they present their analysis of this fieldwork in a wider perspective to develop both a composite view of the process and a contingency-based approach to procedural structure. The book is also very agreeable to read. One invaluable chapter in it[13] deals with the practical issues in development of procedures, describing the elements as being in five main areas:

(i) Basic structure. The number of steps; the final stage; time limits; recording of grievances; written or oral presentation and answers; co-operation clause.

(ii) Roles of participants. Line management; staff management; employers' association representatives; shop stewards; senior shop stewards; full-time union officials; grievance committee; the individual grievant.

(iii) Scope of procedure.

(iv) Procedural differentiation.

(v) Impact of procedure. Formalisation of procedural usage, status of the grievance decision; no-strike clause; sanctions; external impact; procedural review.

They also present six alternative organisational scenarios, suggesting the type of procedural elements appropriate for each.

A less rigorous and more simplistic approach can be found in Naylor and Torrington[14] where the individual grievance procedure is seen as having three essential steps:

Preliminary. The aggrieved employee discusses his grievance with the immediate superior and serves notice that he is not satisfied with the answer and would like his case to be heard at the next stage.

Hearing. The aggrieved duly presents his case to a more senior manager, the rationale for this being that this manager will be able to take a broader view than the aggrieved's immediate superior because he has a wider span of responsibility, and he may be able to view the issue more dispassionately.

Appeal. The final step of the individual procedure is challenging the result of the hearing by going to appeal, when some greater authority is invoked to examine the first two decisions. This is likely to be a further move up the management hierarchy, but it could be a move to a grievance committee or, conceivable, to external arbitration.

This is suggested as the basic structure, although it is for individual grievances only. The collective-disputes dimension is seen as being built on to the top. Most procedures in practice have more steps, although all that is happening is a development of the appeal stage. A relatively sophisticated procedure agreed between Shell Chemicals UK Ltd and the Association of Scientific Technical and Managerial Staffs[15] has a 'Differences Procedure' which starts in the way outlined above, but continues through a total of seven stages, which progressively involve full-time union officers, national officials of both sides, the National Negotiating Committee and, finally, external adjudication.

In passing it is interesting to note the preference for items which are not so stark as those of the textbooks. 'Grievance' is often regarded as too harsh a word to describe the gentlemanly debates that ensue, so one finds euphemisms like 'differences', 'issues', 'complaints', 'questions' or 'points'.

One commonplace of these procedures is that the aggrieved employee shall have the right to be accompanied at each stage — although not always at the first. This not only acknowledges that the employee on his own is likely to be at a disadvantage in contending with management representatives; it also is necessary because of the conventional reluctance of individual employees to pursue grievances, especially when they see themselves as complaining about their own supervisor.

Another procedural commonplace is to specify time limits between stages. The argument is either that the management representatives will prevaricate unless tied down or that aggressive shop stewards will be demanding the final stage within hours of the grievance first being lodged unless they are held back. The time-limit principle ensures that matters are dealt with at reasonable speed, but also that the manager to whom the grievance is presented at the preliminary and the hearing has time to investigate and deliberate in order to find a solution. Singleton indicates that not all organisations find this time-limit principle very helpful.[16]

3. Procedures for Discipline

A disciplinary procedure is in many ways the converse of a grievance procedure. In a grievance procedure an employee is concerned with something unsatisfactory in the employer's performance or at least within the employer's power to alter; in a disciplinary procedure the employer is concerned with something unsatisfactory in the employee's performance.[17]

The complementary nature of grievance handling and discipline is explored further in Chapter 18, dealing with those processes of mutual control. Here we are concerned only with the collective procedural aspects of the activity. Employees collectively may wish to agree to or modify the arrangements whereby disciplinary matters will be dealt with by the management. It is very rare for them to share the task of enforcing discipline, but quite common for them to participate in preparing an acceptable judicial framework of procedure, which will constrain the activities of individual managers and help to underpin the employment rights of the individual. It can also have the effect of legitimising dismissal decisions by management as it provides some guidelines for managers in disciplinary situations involving individuals, who are judged according to principles agreed with the majority.

... whereas so-called group 'indiscipline' normally results from a widespread rejection of a working arrangement or rule and the resolution of any conflict lies in the negotiation of new work standards, individual indiscipline indicates merely a personal deviation from standards generally accepted by other employees.[18]

The original 1972 Code of Practice[19] had one of its most comprehensive sections devoted to disciplinary procedures, specifying the following key elements: rules, offences, penalties, procedural steps, location of responsibility. Although those sections have been superseded by an ACAS code in 1977[20] we use the first formulation for our consideration of disciplinary procedures.

(a) RULES

Working rules and arrangements that are broadly acceptable to the employer and the employees provide a framework of organisational justice, thereby ensuring general compliance with the rules, which are seen as fair and worthy of moral support by the majority. Some rules come from statutes, like the unfair dismissal legislation, but the majority come from the organisation in which they operate, for the obvious reason that many of the disciplinary requirements stem from the processes undertaken in that situation but not elsewhere, like rules on personal hygiene that would be essential in a food factory, but bizarre on a building site. Although more general rules on matters like absence, lateness and smoking in prohibited areas are more widespread, they will still need to vary in flexibility according to working circumstances. This type of rule may be jointly determined, but it is more likely that the management will formulate rules and the employee representatives will concur with them.

(b) OFFENCES

It is necessary to distinguish between rules — which are general principles — and offences indicating a degree of severity that can later be linked to a particular penalty. Only typical offences can be cited in the organisational justice framework. One reason is that it would not be possible to list every variation. The other is the danger of suggestion. Maier quotes a neat example:

The other is the danger of suggestion. Maier quotes a neat example:

> ... the vice-president of personnel in a utility anticipated some problems in connection with a forthcoming strike. He realised that the strikers could do a lot of damage if they shot bullets through some of the cables. As soon as the strike was on, he announced that anyone who shot a rifle bullet through a cable would be dealt with by the law. The company never had so many bullets shot through cables.[21]

The Department of Employment paper provides a general categorisation.[22]

Negligence. Failure to do a job properly, but distinguished from *incompetence* (not a disciplinary matter) by the assumption that the employee is able to do the job properly but has not.

Unreliability. Failure to comply with job attendance requirements, like lateness and absenteeism.

Insubordination. Refusal to obey an instruction or deliberate disrespect in the form of abuse.

Interfering With The Rights of Other Employees. A wide range of behaviours including fighting, intimidation, pernicious gossip and practical jokes.

Safety Offences. Employee behaviour likely to cause a hazard.

Theft. Stealing from the organisation or from fellow employees.

(c) PENALTIES

Various penalties will be possible and for minor offences there may well be a standard scale that could be agreed with employee representatives. Singleton[23] quotes an example from a company in the engineering industry of specific penalties for specific offences relating to lateness and absenteeism:

First occasion: caution by the unit manager, to be recorded in departmental records.

Second occasion: warning by unit manager in presence of shop steward and a written warning sent to the offender by the personnel manager.

Third occasion: suspension of two days without pay by the unit manager in presence of shop steward.

Fourth occasion: dismissal by unit manager in presence of senior shop steward.

In many working situations this degree of formality would be unwelcome and inappropriate, but it indicates the penalties available to any employer:

Caution. An authoritive indication that an offence has been committed, of which a record is to be held.

Warning. A formal statement that a more serious penalty will follow if the offence is repeated. In the example quoted here there is only one warning before the likelihood of more severe penalty. In many situations there is a hierarchy of warnings, like 'verbal', 'written' and 'final'. Because of the potential problem of a later dismissal being challenged, the warnings not only have to be recorded but — at least in the later stages — have to be given to the employee in writing.

Suspension With Pay. The employer has a contractual obligation to provide pay, but not to provide work, so it is feasible to suspend someone from attendance at work for two or three days while a possible offence is being investigated. This is not done lightly as it is a penalty for the individual suspended in all but a strict legalistic sense.

Suspension Without Pay. A more severe punishment and can only be used if the contract of employment permits such a measure. In some cases it is seen as an alternative to dismissal. The right for an employer to suspend without pay only exists where there is a specific express term in the individual contract of employment permitting him to do so, or where there is a clear implied right due to established custom and practice.

Dismissal. The contract is terminated. Dismissal is dealt with fully in Chapter 20.

Two other penalties can be mentioned. Occasionally employees are *fined*, usually by a deduction from wages to compensate for lateness. Charges for breakages or damage are sometimes used but are beset with legal pitfalls and seldom warrant the administrative time involved in their collection. The employee's contract of employment must permit fines for them to be lawful.

The 1977 Code of Practice mentions *disciplinary transfer*,[24] whereby an employee is transferred to work within the organisation that he does not want to do: it may be of lower status, physically less agreeable or less remunerative. Again the contract must permit this type of change.

(d) PROCEDURAL STEPS

The procedural steps themselves will first specify the operational drills associated with imposing penalties for offences that break the rules, and then they will set out the arrangements for the individual to challenge the penalties if he feels them inappropriate.

The operational drills will specify *who* has the responsibility and authority to make the relevant decisions, usually ensuring that the immediate superior does not have the power to dismiss — or at least does not have the power to make the decision — even though his managerial colleagues may be quite happy for him to be the one to give the information to the person to be sacked. The drills will also specify the *mode* of imposing various penalties; which are to be given in writing, or simply recorded, by whom, with or without witnesses and so on. It is in the operational drills that personnel specialists are now having a key part to play, largely because of the legal aspects of dismissal which impose clear requirements for certain types of skilled advice and record-keeping. If a dismissal is challenged at a tribunal hearing, the judgement may well hang on questions of precedent and consistency. Personnel usually records all formal warnings and would certainly be consulted before a dismissal decision to ensure that the dismissal was in line with the law and with organisational rules and practice.

The arrangements for challenging a disciplinary decision follow a similar hierarchical sequence to those of grievance procedure, except that the appeal should be heard by someone not involved in the original decision. This will often rule out the preliminary step of grievance procedure, where that involves the immediate superior. It is essential that the appeal procedure should operate quickly.

The 1977 Code provides the following summary:[25]

'Disciplinary procedures should

(a) Be in writing.
(b) Specify to whom they apply.
(c) Provide for matters to be dealt with quickly.
(d) Indicate the disciplinary actions which may be taken.
(e) Specify the levels of management which have the authority to take the various forms of disciplinary action, ensuring that immediate superiors do not normally have the power to dismiss without reference to senior management.
(f) Provide for individuals to be informed of the complaints against them and to be given an opportunity to state their case before decisions are reached.
(g) Give individuals the right to be accompanied by a trade union representative or by a fellow employee of their choice.
(h) Ensure that, except for gross misconduct, no employees are dismissed for a first breach of discipline.

(i) Ensure that disciplinary action is not taken until the case has been carefully investigated.

(j) Ensure that individuals are given an explanation for any penalty imposed.

(k) Provide a right of appeal and specify the procedure to be followed.'

Other Types of Procedure

The substance of any procedure agreement will be in the areas we have now examined: negotiation; grievance; discipline. There will often, however, be collectively endorsed procedures for dealing with other matters where there is a policy that needs collective support, which will only be conceded if the policy is codified as a procedure. The procedure then becomes an instrument of control on both employees and the management. In some cases there are agreed procedures for recruitment and promotion, but the most common other procedures are for redundancy or aspects of payment.

In industrial relations 'redundancy' is a word like 'dispute' that is frequently disguised by a euphemism such as 'temporary surplus of manpower', 'reduction of labour requirement' or even 'redeployment'. Whatever it is called it is likely to have the same procedural features. First, agreed measures to obviate the need to make anyone redundant; and second, the categories of employee who will be selected for redundancy, should it be unavoidable. The most common agreed ways of avoiding redundancy at all are to stop recruiting and to use sub-contractors. Other possibilities are to introduce short-time working or work-sharing. If redundancy becomes inevitable there are certain categories of employee who may be selected for termination earlier than others. Those over retiring age, part-time employees and volunteers for early retirement are the most common. Other volunteers are likely to come next and then those with the shortest period of employment with the organisation, though sometimes a redundancy procedure specifies 'those with a poor working record' to leave before the new recruits. Between these categories there are other possible strategies, such as re-training existing employees for new work in the organisation or providing access for re-training to take up employment elsewhere. There is no legal decree on who goes first, as long as it is not a category that breaches a statute like 'all immigrants' or 'all married women with working husbands.' The arrangements are for determination within the organisation.

A specialised type of grievance procedure sometimes operates on matters of payment, usually where there is a system of job evaluation and an employee feels that his job is not correctly graded and he wishes to appeal against it. This is again a collective procedure and the setting up of the job evaluation scheme will incorporate appeal provisions.

SUMMARY PROPOSITIONS

12.1. Collective procedures articulate aspects of policy and declare how the policy is to be carried out. They are likely to bring clarity, fairness, consistency and the avoidance of trouble.

12.2. Procedures are limited in the extent to which they can countermand custom and practice and they may inhibit change.

12.3. The most common procedures are to do with negotiation, grievance and discipline.

REFERENCES

1. Cyert R.M. and March J.G., *A Behavioural Theory of the Firm* (Prentice-Hall) 1963, pp. 101–113.
2. Royal Commission on Trade Unions and Employers' Associations Cmnd 3632 (HMSO) 1968.
3. McKersie R.B. and Hunter L.C. *Pay, Productivity and Collective Bargaining* (Macmillan) 1973, p. 287.
4. Terry M., 'The Inevitable Growth of Informality' in *British Journal of Industrial Relations,* March 1977, p. 87.
5. Thomson A.W.J. and Murray V.V., *Grievance Procedures* (Saxon House) 1976, p. 124.
6. Industrial Relations Code of Practice (HMSO) 1972, p. 21.
7. Singleton N., 'Industrial Relations Procedures' Department of Employment *Manpower Paper No. 14* (HMSO) 1975 pp. 8–9.
8. *Ibid.* p. 16.
9. Kuhn J.W., *Bargaining in Grievance Settlement* (Columbia University Press) 1961 and 'The Grievance Process' in Dunlop J.T. and Chamberlain N.W. (eds) *Frontiers of Collective Bargaining* (Harper and Row) 1967.
10. Slichter S.H., Healy J. and Livernash E.R., *The Impact of Collective Bargaining on Management* (Brookings Institution) 1960.
11. Marsh A.I., *Disputes Procedures in British Industry* and Marsh A.I. and McCarthy W.E.J., *Disputes Procedures in Britain,* parts 1 and 2 of Research Paper No. 2 for Royal Commission on Trade Unions and Employers' Associations (HMSO) 1966.
12. Thomson A.W.J. and Murray V.V., *op. cit.*
13. *Ibid.,* pp. 134–163.
14. Torrington D.P., 'Individual Grievance Procedures' in Naylor R. and Torrington D.P., (eds) *Administration of Personnel Policies* (Gower) 1974, pp. 441–458.
15. ASTMS and Shell Chemicals UK Ltd *A National Procedure Agreement,* 1974, pp. 9–10.
16. Singleton N., *op. cit.,* pp. 23–24.
17. *Ibid.,* p. 30.
18. 'In Working Order – A Study of Industrial Discipline', Department of Employment Manpower Paper No. 6 (HMSO) 1973. p. 2.
19. Industrial Relations Code of Practice, *op. cit.,* p. 28.
20. Advisory, Conciliation and Arbitration Service, Code No. 1, *Disciplinary Practice and Procedure in Employment* (HMSO) 1977.
21. Maier N.R.F., 'Discipline in the Industrial Setting' in *Personnel Journal,* April 1965, p. 190.
22. 'In Working Order', *op. cit.,* pp. 10–15.
23. Singleton N., *op. cit.*
24. ACAS Code No. 1, *op. cit.* S. 12, c.
25. *Ibid.* S. 10.

13

The Employee Representative and his Facilities

The contract for collective consent is negotiated between those who represent management interests and those who represent the interests of employees. The nature of the contract that is reached will be influenced by the ability and effectiveness of the representatives from both parties. Elsewhere we have considered aspects of developing managerial effectiveness; in this chapter we look at the representative of the employees.

Management Responsibility for Employee Representative Effectiveness

A question frequently raised is why the management should give any aid and comfort to the enemy. The argument runs that the employee representative is challenging management authority and that it is illogical to render assistance so that his challenge becomes more effective. The answer to that sort of question lies in the argument about recognition. If a trade union is recognised for the purposes of collective bargaining, then management authority is going to be challenged anyway, so it is helpful for this to be done as constructively as possible.

Another version of the same question is to ask whether the management can destroy the representative's effectiveness by insidious indoctrination with the 'right' ideas so that he becomes their puppet. This is much more difficult to answer because the danger is so great: one of the main objections to worker directors is that the employee representative becomes isolated once he reaches the boardroom and the door closes behind him. It is unusual for managers to weaken the position of employee representatives deliberately, but when it happens there is the risk that the employees repudiate the representative seen as being 'in the management's pocket' and seek other representation, usually outside any understood and agreed procedures.

The employee representative depends on management provision for his work to be productive, and the management depends on employee representatives for a workable contract of collective consent.

Functions of the Representative

Except for the minority of instances where the employee representation is arranged outside of trade union machinery, the representative or shop steward is a lay union official acting as spokesman and negotiator for the work group.

This points up one of the main conflicts which the representative has to contend with. He is a member of the work group *and* an official of the union to which the members of the work group belong, and the interests of the union will sometimes run counter to the interests of the work group. This is rarely the sort of problem faced by his management counterpart.

Although the main function of the representatives is to act as spokesman and negotiator, there are other aspects to the job. He is responsible for *recruitment* of union members from among the employees. In the earliest stages this means building up a kernel of support for the union before recognition. Later it is maintaining and developing the number of union members by approaching new employees. In most situations he will also have to maintain the membership of existing employees to ensure no reduction of support or, the real nightmare, defection to another union. In some situations there is no recruitment task as the recruiting is done via a closed-shop agreement and an arrangement whereby union dues are deducted from wages by the management instead of being collected by the stewards. It is not surprising that unions have tried so hard to protect the closed-shop principle and have advocated collection of union dues by the management; but the latter has been with some reservation. The engineers resisted check-off (the jargon phrase for deduction of dues) for a long time on the basis that it impaired the branch life of the union and reduced the reliability of its democratic processes.

Another duty of employee representatives is the dissemination of *information*. They pass on to their members information about the union and its policy. They also feed in to their full-time officials information on current working practices as they develop.

The information channel is one for which there is little substitute and many stewards regard it as important to counteract the effect of the media — generally regarded as antagonistic to trade unionism. Not only do newspapers and television not bother with carrying details of union policy in their coverage, but also they provide extensive coverage of the more dramatic and melodramatic aspects of trade union activity and involvement in national issues. If the membership are going to hear their union policy on a particular matter, it is from their steward that they are most likely to hear it, although some will also read of it in their union journal. If full-time union officials are to be up-to-date in representing and interpreting the views of their members, they depend mainly on their shop stewards to tell them what is happening.

Other steward duties stemming from his position in the union are dealing with advice to members about services available from the union and ensuring compliance with union rules.

In their study of shop stewards Goodman and Whittingham pointed out that management also uses the steward as an important communications link:

> He will be expected to state grievances from the shop floor and, having reached an agreement with the management, will be expected to carry his members with him. As such, management may have a vested interest in his strength, regarding him as both representative and advocate. Additionally he will be expected to lead, as well as reflect, shop floor opinion. The steward's representative role may be further emphasised by participation in joint consultative committees, about which he should also disseminate information.[1]

That quotation leads us to consider the more obvious aspects of the steward's role:

negotiating with management. Although practice varies so widely, it is common for stewards to initiate *negotiations* with management, even though an initial recognition claim is more likely to be put by a full-time official. Once a union is recognised most managers prefer to deal with their 'own' stewards rather than with full-time officials. Either because of personal inclination or because of difficulty in getting the time of an official, many stewards prefer the arrangement of dealing with their own negotiations, and carry their members' support on such a policy.

One of the main effects of recent legislation has been to strengthen and clarify the role of the steward in *grievance procedures,* where the possibility of advocacy on behalf of an aggrieved employee is specifically written in. An interesting piece of work by Batstone *et al.* provides us with some insights into how stewards see the fullness of their role. Stewards in a large company were studied, one set representing

Table 13.1

	Staff	Shop-floor
	%	%
Promote socialism, trade union principles	12	16
Protect members, improve wages and conditions	31	100
Maintain unity and union organisation	12	13
Ensure harmony with management	38	19
Solve problems in accordance with agreements	6	23
Act as communications channel with the membership	50	16
Total respondents	100%	100%
No. of respondents	16	31
No. of responses	24	58
No answer	3	—

Table 13.2

	Staff %	Shop-floor %
Supportive:		
Protect/defend members	10	27
Limit management behaviour	6	21
Represent members	14	8
Ensure fairness	—	16
Pursue union principles	—	8
Improve wage-effort bargain	6	16
Critical:		
No relevance to us	31	—
Cause trouble — prevent management working properly	34	4
Total	101%	100%
No. of references	102	183

staff employees and one representing shop-floor employees. Views on their role differed between the two sets as shown in Table 13.1.[2] The staff stewards clearly saw their role as essentially maintaining either a harmonious relationship with the management or maintaining communications. Less than a third of the staff responses were concerned with protecting members and improving wages and conditions, while every one of the shop-floor stewards saw this as part of their role.

Table 13.1 shows the result of questioning stewards about how they saw their role. Another finding from the same study suggested that some of the reasons for this difference in view could be attributed to the views held in the group of employees represented. The researchers categorised union members' expectations of the union, as shown in Table 13.2.[3] The comments from the shop-floor union members are roughly consistent with those of their stewards. They are looking for some degree of protection – which they feel they need – and the union to provide some sort of rough justice in relation to what the management want. In contrast the staff members have apparently little sympathy with the union, nor do they feel much need for it. It is not surprising that their representatives show greater concern for maintaining an equable relationship with the management than for resisting their apparent depredations.

At the close of this chapter there is a brief comment on the images that stewards have of managers, and vice versa in which the management view of the steward is shown to be generally unflattering. Part of the conventional wisdom is that stewards seek office either because they desire power or to satisfy a personal need that has not been satisfied by promotion within the organisational hierarchy of the company. A thorough investigation by Moore[4] found little support for this line of reasoning and offered an alternative conclusion:

> 'Perhaps the greatest single characteristic that emerged from the study, as under-lying the motives of the respondents in becoming shop stewards, was the inability to stand the stress of the disorganisation that results from ineffective or non-existent shop-floor leadership. This characteristic appeared to be linked to two others: (a) a sense of responsibility mainly to self, but partly to others, and (b) a desire to have some measure of control over the matters which are of immediate personal concern in the workplace.'

The Management/Steward Relationship

In the examples quoted above the nature of the relationship between managers and stewards will naturally differ. Although the two situations analysed by Batstone and his colleagues can be regarded as typical, there are other points on the spectrum of employment situations which would call for a different type of relationship. The two samples we have, however, help to indicate the main differences.

If stewards represent employees who are not particularly interested in, or sympathetic with, the labour movement and socialism, and who may be in many ways hostile to the union – as might be the case with some staff groups – then the employees represented will identify closely with the management and see their interests as similar. Stewards will become almost an extension of the management, working in a harmonious relationship and very dependent on management to sustain them in their position: any general opposition would not be supported by the members, who would regard such opposition as either irrelevant or trouble-making.

Where a steward represents employees who do not identify so readily with the management, one might expect a different type of relationship. It is still very close, but with a greater degree of mutual dependence. William Brown sums it up:

> The bargaining relationship that exists between a manager and a shop steward consists in the confidence each can have about his expectations of the other's behaviour. This depends upon their mutual trust and respect and upon the extent to which they share common assumptions and a common language. A 'good' bargaining relationship may be said to exist to the extent that these things help reduce the uncertainty of the relationship.[5]

In the next chapter we examine the bargaining behaviour of negotiators and notice its ritualistic nature, with aggressive, hostile statements always being made *on behalf of* the party being represented by the negotiator. Their representative nature is carefully expressed so as to preserve appropriate rapport between the negotiators themselves; otherwise movement in negotiations becomes unlikely. Managers and shop stewards engaged in a situation where there is clear conflict of interests, and adversary positions between the two parties, carry this type of schizophrenic behaviour away from the bargaining table and allow it to suffuse the whole of their working relationship. There will be frequent testing out of the other's reaction to certain possible courses of action and the passing of information to the other so as to avoid unwelcome initiatives or to speed up otherwise protracted interchanges. They both have power and high uncertainty as a context for their activities. If they are able to establish a strong bargaining relationship with each other they are able to balance each other's power and develop a degree of trust in how they will behave towards each other. This reduces some of the uncertainty and makes their parties more dependent on them. The manager becomes the man 'who has a way with old Bert' while the steward is the man 'who has the management's ear'. Any manager in this situation needs to remember how perilous is the tightrope that the steward walks. Having the ear of the management is useful to his members: being 'in their pocket' makes him suspect. A good working relationship with the steward must never prevent him from representing effectively the members' interests as *they* see them.

The Representative's Training

The difficulty for the employee representative in maintaining independence of thought was shown in the content of recommendations from the CIR[6] on industrial relations training in 1972. Among many other suggestions the report advocated that employers should join with trade unions in training stewards, including payment towards costs, on the basis that the efficiency of the organisation would increase as a result of the improved industrial relations that would follow. The TUC criticised the flavour of the report as being too much concerned with management problems rather than trade union duties. They argued[7] that employee representatives were essentially union officers and that their first allegiance and terms of reference should be related to union organisation, objectives and procedures. They should be trained within that framework and not within the framework of the management problems of individual organisations. Control of training should be with the TUC and not the employer and should be provided by developing existing links with the further and adult education sector. Since that time there has been no major change in industrial relations training for employee representatives, although the training requirement increases. The trade union movement has had to accept the need for their workplace lay officials to receive training in legislation generally, health and safety in particular, pension fund administration and – perhaps – the operation of worker directors. By 1977 the number of tutors working full-time in teaching trade union studies had reached 100, although the predicted need for 1982 is 600. The TUC[8] believe that they will need 180,000 training places a year: 120,000 being the estimate of new representatives appointed annually and 60,000 for those who have not so far had the opportunity for training. The Department of Education and Science provides an annual grant towards the cost of TUC training. It was £1,674,000 in 1980/81.

Notwithstanding the reservations expressed by the TUC Education Committee, the CIR report neatly summarises the training need of the employee representative:

> Principally [the shop steward's] role is to represent, in negotiations with management, the individual members of the work group who have elected him and to represent his union in the establishment in his contact both with union members and with management. In carrying out these tasks effectively the steward has to acquire considerable knowledge of his union, its policies and practices, and his part in them, and of the institutions and procedures of industrial relations in his establishment. Particularly he needs to understand clearly his part in operating the procedures and the limits of his authority in settling issues. It is necessary for him to combine the skills of negotiation with those involved in communicating not only with management but with his members, fellow stewards, and full-time officers. He needs analytical abilities in preparing cases and dealing with problems; and understanding of techniques such as work study and job evaluation.[9]

Later the report summarises minimum training standards for shop stewards:[10]

(i) Training related to the steward's role as a representative of the work group. Knowledge of trade union organisation in the establishment, including arrangements for inter-union co-operation and joint working. Knowledge of the establishment's industrial relations policies, agreements and practices.
  Understanding the roles of managers, personnel staff and supervisors in industrial relations at the workplace.
  Knowledge of his own specific role and responsibility in disputes, grievance and disciplinary procedures and consultative and negotiating machinery.
  Understanding the limits of his authority in industrial relations. Knowledge of payment systems and methods of wage determination employed in the establishment.
  Skill in preparing cases, handling grievances and negotiating.
  Communication skills.

(ii) Training related to the steward's role as a representative of his union. Knowledge of the structure and rules of the union at national, regional and local level.
  Understanding his role in the union in formulating and carrying out policy, the scope and limitation of his authority in relation to union rules, legal provisions and the union organisation at the workplace.
  Knowledge of the role of union full-time officers at national, regional and local level.
  Knowledge of union services.

This list provides a useful starting point for anyone wishing to set up a programme of training for employee representatives. Many of these matters will be covered in courses run by, or sponsored by, the TUC, but it may be that a manager in a particular organisational setting will wish to extend what is provided from elsewhere by setting up additional training to deal with matters not included in the more general TUC-approved course. Although an employer cannot influence or vet the content of a TUC course, he can always obtain a copy of the programme to see what has been covered and what has been left out.

Time Off

Closely related to the issue of training is the question of time off for the discharge of union duties, including attendance at training courses. The Employment Protection Act established various rights to time off work for employees, and two of the rights are for time off for industrial relations duties and time off for trade union activities. The Trade Union and Labour Relations Act defines a trade union *official* as

> . . . a person elected or appointed in accordance with the rules of the union to be a representative of its members or some of them.[11]

This therefore includes shop stewards and all other employee representatives appointed by a union to represent union members, including safety representatives. The Act and the ACAS Code of Practice on time off[12] draws a clear distinction between the *industrial relations* duties of officials and their *trade union* activities. The importance of the distinction being that the employee has a legal right to payment from his employer during time off for the former, but not for the latter. Industrial relations duties are:

> . . . those duties pertaining to his or her role in the jointly agreed procedures or customary arrangements for consultation, collective bargaining and grievance handling, where such matters concern the employer and any associated employer and their employees.[12]

For the proper performance of these the representative is entitled to time off for collective bargaining; meetings to inform members of the outcome of negotiations; meetings with other union officials to discuss industrial relations business; dealing with matters of grievance and discipline; appearing before outside bodies on behalf of members on industrial relations matters; explanations to new employees about union role and industrial relations structure.

Trade union activities relate to the running of, and participation in, the affairs of the union. For these activities there is a right to time off for all union members, not just officials, provided that it is recognised by the employer for collective bargaining. There is no right to payment for the time off for trade union activities.

Officials should also receive time off with pay for industrial relations training, if it is relevant to the official's industrial relations functions and approved by the TUC or relevant union.

> An official who has duties concerned with industrial relations should be permitted to take reasonable paid time off work for initial basic training . . . [and] for further training relevant to the carrying out of his or her duties concerned with industrial relations where he or she has special responsibilities or where such training is necessary to meet circumstances such as changes in the structure or topics of negotiation at the place of employment or legislative changes affecting industrial relations.[13]

The way in which the general question of time off for officials' industrial relations duties and their trade union activities is handled could well be a subject for collective agreement between the employer and recognised trade unions. Also our old friend 'reasonableness' is not to be forgotten. The trade union official is only entitled by the Act to *reasonable* time off. Disputes about what is reasonable can be referred to an industrial tribunal by a dissatisfied employee.

These time off rights apply only to officials of unions that are *recognised*, even though the recognition may be only partial, and time off for trade union activities is only allowed under the Act for members of *appropriate* trade unions, so that the union must not only be recognised by the employer, it must be recognised for that category of employees to which the person seeking time off for union duties belongs.

The amount of time off that is 'reasonable in all the circumstances' is difficult to determine, although some employers have long had the practice of allowing certain stewards to be completely free of normal duties so as to be available for constant attendance to their industrial relations duties. The employer can, however, set conditions for any time off, such as specifying the amount of notice to be given to supervisors and requiring some attempt to make up lost time on other occasions.

The same piece of legislation gave all employees the right to reasonable time off for the performance of public duties, such as magistracy, membership of a local authority, a board of school governors, a health or water authority, or a statutory tribunal. There is no right to pay for this time off, but the amount of time can be considerable. One helpful example is from the Civil Service, which allows up to eighteen days special leave a year for public duties. A problem arose about one of their employees who was employed by the Department of National Savings and was elected a local councillor. He asked for fifty days special leave during 1981, but his employer regarded this as being unacceptable, so he complained to an industrial tribunal and his employer agreed that, if his application succeeded, they should ask the tribunal to *recommend* the amount of time off that would be appropriate. After hearing all the facts of this individual case, including the normal provision for cover during absence made by the employer, the tribunal recommended that the councillor should receive thirty-six days special leave in 1981, of which eighteen would be unpaid.[14]

Other Facilities

Beyond time off and training the employee representative may operate more effectively if he has available to him certain other types of facility, such as:

(i) Access to new employees for the type of explanations about industrial relations and union membership referred to above;
(ii) Noticeboards and opportunities to distribute literature from the union;
(iii) Clerical and administrative support, such as facilities for typing and duplicating, postage, filing and storage of material;
(iv) The use of a telephone;
(v) Places for meetings.

Images

To conclude this chapter we briefly consider the ways in which managers and employee representatives see each other, as this is a means towards mutual understanding. There is a considerable problem of stereotyping as both managers and shop stewards are so regularly caricatured in television programmes. Cooper and Bartlett give the result of an exercise in image exchange they conducted with a group of managers and shop stewards to see how each perceived the other.[15]

Shop Stewards' Perception of Managers	Managers' Perception of Shop Stewards
Cunning	Sincere
Anti-union	Aggressive
Cost-conscious	Mixed-up
Worried	Democratic
Dedicated	Trusting
Forward-looking	Emotional
Consultative	Friendly
Trusting	Understanding
Decisive	

Another vignette is the classic story from Tyneside:

Joe, an old labourer, is trudging through the shipyard carrying a heavy load on his shoulders. It is a filthy, wet day and the sole of his shoe is flapping open. The shipyard manager, passing at the time, stops him, saying, 'Hey, Joe, you can't go around with your shoe in that state on a wet day like this' and reaching into his back pocket takes out a bundle of bank notes. Joe beams in anticipation. 'Here', says the manager, slipping the elastic band off the bundle of notes, 'put this round your shoe, it will help keep the wet out.'[16]

SUMMARY PROPOSITIONS

13.1. Management depend on the employee representative for the initiation and maintenance of a mutually acceptable contract for collective consent.

13.2. The employee representative has responsibilities and duties to the union outside the organisation, as well as to union members within it.

13.3. The industrial relations attitudes of work groups vary considerably, producing commensurate variations in attitude and behaviour of employee representatives.

13.4. The employer has a legal obligation to provide reasonable time off for trade union activities and reasonable time off with pay for industrial relations duties of trade union officials.

REFERENCES

1. Goodman J.F.B. and Whittingham T.G., *Shop Stewards in British Industry* (McGraw-Hill) 1969, p. 6.
2. Batstone E., Boraston I., Frenkel S., *Shop Stewards in Action* (Basil Blackwell) 1977, p. 25.
3. *Ibid*, p. 121.
4. Moore R.J., 'The Motivation to Become a Shop Steward' in *British Journal of Industrial Relations*, March 1980, p. 98.
5. Brown W.A.., *Piecework Bargaining* (Heinemann) 1973, p. 134.
6. Commission on Industrial Relations, Report No. 33 *Industrial Relations Training* (HMSO) 1972.
7. Chairman of TUC Education Committee, *Shop Steward Education and Training,* opening statement at meeting with the Secretary of State for Education, May 1973.
8. *Report to Congress* (TUC) 1977.
9. Commission on Industrial Relations, Report No. 33, *op. cit.,* pp. 28–29.
10. Commission on Industrial Relations, Report No. 33, *op. cit.,* p. 68.
11. Trade Union and Labour Relations Act 1974 (HMSO).
12. Advisory, Conciliation and Arbitration Service, *Time Off For Trade Union Duties and Activities* (HMSO) S. 30 13.
13. *Ibid.*, 16, 17.
14. Anderson v. Department of National Savings, COIT 1062/48, reported in *IDS Brief*, 212, September 1981.
15. Cooper B.N. and Bartlett A.F., *Industrial Relations: A Study in Conflict* (Heinemann) 1976, pp. 161–164.
16. Murray J., 'The Role of the Shop Steward in Industry' in Torrington D. (ed.), *A Handbook of Industrial Relations* (Gower) 1972, p. 279.

14

Interaction II — Negotiating the Collective Agreement

Management and academic interest in the negotiating encounter has been slow to develop. It has been a relatively specialised activity in which few managers have been engaged, and some managers have not been keen to accept that they were involved in negotiating at all; preferring the idea that they were listening to grievances, explaining problems, giving information or being diplomatic (saying 'no' in a roundabout way). Academics have been more interested in the economic and social factors giving rise to conflict situations.

Recently, however, interest has grown considerably, starting in the United States and developing in the United Kingdom since the middle 1960s. Much of the development has been as a result of increasing interest by psychologists in the behavioural aspects of the interaction itself, as well as the growing sense of need by managers because of the increasing requirement for a negotiating style in a variety of interactive situations. Knibbs[1] quotes a survey he has conducted of what managers consider to be the characteristics of the effective negotiator. He identifies four clusters of abilities:

1. *Knowledge* — Thorough understanding of the facts and issues involved in the negotiations.
2. *Communications* — The ability to speak clearly and concisely, thinking and responding quickly.
3. *Objectivity* — An ability to be fair by sifting information and making judgements without bias or too much emotional involvement.
4. *Social Skill* — Tact, diplomacy, flexibility, empathy, coolness, ability to control emotions etc.

Here, as with other interactions like the employment interview, we see a concern with behaviour that is 'correct' and well-mannered. It is doubtful whether it is a set of characteristics that makes for effectiveness in negotiation, which depends on an appreciation of the *conflict of interest* that is the basis of bargaining.

The Nature of Conflict in the Employment Relationship

The approach outlined later in this chapter depends on the view that conflict of interests is inevitable between employer and employee because there is an authority relationship in which the aims of the two parties will at least sometimes conflict.[2] A further assumption is that such conflict is not necessarily dysfunctional for that relationship.[3]

This has led a number of commentators to discuss negotiation in terms of equally-matched protagonists. The power of the two parties may not actually be equal, but they are both willing to behave as if it is. The negotiation situation thus has the appearance of power equalisation, which can be real or illusory, due to the search for a solution to a problem. When both sides set out to reach an agreement which is satisfactory to themselves and acceptable to the other, then their power is equalised by that desire. Where the concern for acceptance by the other is lacking, there comes the use of power play of the forcing type described later in this chapter.

The relative power of the parties is likely to fluctuate from one situation to the next; this is recognised by the ritual and face-saving elements of negotiation, where a power imbalance is not fully used, both to make agreement possible and in the knowledge that the power imbalance may be reversed on the next issue to be resolved.

The classic work of Ann Douglas[4] produces a formulation of the negotiating encounter that has been little modified by those coming after her. Blake, Shepard and Mouton are very well-known exponents of this view,[5] and Walton has written a most helpful book, too little known in the United Kingdom, about the application of this thinking to the interpersonal relationships between equals in the management hierarchy.[6] However, this needs further thought if it is to be applied to the negotiations that take place between representatives of management and representatives of employees about terms and conditions of employment. Cooper and Bartlett point out the difficulty:

> If equality is available to all . . . conflicting groups can meet. All they need to shed are their misperceptions and their prejudices. Any differences are psychological rather than economic.
>
> The truth of the matter is, of course, that . . . there are glaring inequalities of wealth and power. Each society contains its own contradictions which arise from the distribution of money, of status and control. So conflict resolution is not just a matter of clearing away mistrust and misunderstanding replacing them with communication. It is also concerned with political matters such as the re-allocation of power.[7]

Fox[8] would make a clear distinction between the type of bargaining situation which forms the basis of the propositions set out by Walton and Blake *et al* on the one hand and British collective bargaining on the other. He describes the relationships between senior managers as relationships of *social exchange,* with high trust and discretion and tight specification of roles. An interesting marginal note, as it were, on conflict is the suggestion by Harvey that managers too often set out to manage a conflict situation that does not actually exist, but is agreement misinterpreted. He argues that the level of potential agreement is usually much higher than managers realise.[9]

Sources of Conflict in the Collective Employment Relationship

Focusing our attention on the collective contract we can list some of the sources of conflict endemic in that situation.

(a) THE AGGRESSIVE IMPULSE

Those who have charted the evolution of *homo sapiens,* such as Konrad Lorenz[10] and Robert Ardrey,[11] demonstrate for us the innate aggressiveness of man. Although the processes of civilisation tend to constrain it there is a natural impulse to behave aggressively to some degree at some time. It has a number of outlets, like football matches, televised wrestling and the more masochistic aspects of gardening, and one of its opportunities for expression is in negotiations within the employing organisation, which is a splendid arena for the expression of combat.

(b) DIVERGENCE OF INTERESTS

Probably the main source of industrial relations conflict is divergence of interests between those who are classified as managers and those who are seen as non-managers. One group is seeking principally such things as efficiency, economy, productivity and the obedience of others to their own authority. The members of the other group are interested in these things, but are more interested in features like high pay, freedom of action, independence of supervision, scope for the individual and leisure. To some extent these invariably conflict.

(c) CLASH OF VALUES

More fundamental is the possible clash of values, usually about how people should behave. These may be variations of allegiance to the positions of different political parties on questions like 'What is production for?', or differences of social class attitude to what constitutes courtesy. Most frequently the clash is about the issue of managerial prerogative. Managers are likely to believe and proclaim that management is their inalienable right, so that those who question the way their work is done are ignorant or impertinent. Non-managers may regard management as a job that should be done properly by people who are responsive to questioning and criticism.

(d) COMPETITIVENESS

One of the most likely sources is the urge to compete for a share of limited resources. Much of the drive behind differential pay claims is that of competing with other groups at a similar level, but there may also be competition for finance, materials, security, survival, power, recognition or status.

(e) ORGANISATIONAL TRADITION

If the tradition of an organisation is to be conflict-prone, then it may retain that mode obdurately, while other organisations in which conflict has not been a prominent feature may continue without it. It is axiomatic that certain industries in the United Kingdom are much more likely to display the manifestations of extreme conflict in industrial relations than others. Indicators like the number of working days lost through strikes show a stable pattern of distribution. The nature of the conflict can range between the extremes of pettiness, secrecy, fear and insecurity on the one hand to vigorous, open and productive debate on the other, with many organisations exhibiting neither.

Potential Benefits of Such Conflict

It is widely believed that conflict of the type described here — and described frequently and more luridly in the newspapers — is counterproductive, and that all should make strenuous efforts to eliminate it. There are, however, some advantages:

(a) CLEARING THE AIR
Many people feel that a conflict situation is improved by getting bad feelings 'off their chests' and bringing the matter into the open. Sometimes combatants feel closer together as a result.

(b) INTRODUCING NEW RULES
Employment has a number of rules that govern it. Formal rules that define unfair dismissal and the rate of pay for various jobs, as well as informal rules like modes of address. Management/union conflict is usually about a disagreement over the rules and the bargain that is struck produces a new rule: a new rate of pay, a new employment practice or whatever. It can be the only way of achieving that particular change, and it is a very authoritative source of rule-making because of the participation in its creation.

(c) MODIFYING THE GOALS
The goals that management set can be modified as a result of conflict with others. Ways in which their goals will be unpopular or difficult to implement may be seen for the first time and modifications made early instead of too late. A greater range and diversity of views are brought to bear on a particular matter so that the capacity for innovation is enhanced.

(d) UNDERSTANDING OF RESPECTIVE POSITIONS
Combatants will come to a better understanding of their position on the issue being debated because of their need to articulate it, set it forth, develop supporting arguments and then defend those arguments against criticism. This enables them to see more clearly what they want, why they want it and how justifiable it is. In challenging the position of the other party, they will come to a clearer understanding of where they stand, and why.

Potential Drawbacks of Such Conflict

These advantages may not be sufficient to balance the potential drawbacks:

(a) WASTE OF TIME AND ENERGY
Conflict and the ensuing negotiations take a great deal of time and energy. Conflict can become attritive when over-personalised, and individuals become obsessed with the conflict itself rather than what it is about. Negotiation takes a lot longer than simple management decree.

(b) EMOTIONAL STRESS FOR PARTICIPANTS
People vary in the type of organisational stress to which they are prone. The need to be involved in negotiation is a source of stress which some people find very taxing, while others find it stimulating.

(c) ORGANISATIONAL STRESS
Accommodating conflict often causes some inefficiency through the paraphernalia

that can accompany it: striking, working to rule, working without enthusiasm, withdrawing co-operation, or the simple delay caused by protracted negotiation.

(d) RISKS
Engaging in negotiation may be necessary as the only way to cope with a conflictual situation, but there is the risk of stirring up a hornet's nest. When conflict is brought to the surface it may be resolved or accommodated, or the way it is handled may make the situation worse.

(e) WORSENING COMMUNICATIONS
The quality and amount of communication is impaired. Those involved are concerned more to confirm their own viewpoint than to convey understanding, and there are perceptual distortions like stereotyping and cognitive dissonance. The attitudes behind the communications may also become inappropriate as there are greater feelings of hostility and attempts to score off others.

Bargaining Strategies

A reading of Schmidt and Tannenbaum,[12] and Lawrence and Lorsch[13] helps us to identify various strategies that are adopted to cope with conflict and some of the likely effects:

(a) AVOIDANCE
To some extent conflict can be 'handled' by ignoring it. For a time this will prevent it surfacing so that it remains latent rather than manifest: the danger being that it is harder to deal with when it eventually does erupt. Opposing views cannot be heard unless there is apparatus for their expression. The management of an organisation can fail to provide such apparatus by, for instance, not having personnel specialists, not recognising trade unions and not recognising employee representatives. If the management organise the establishment as if conflict of opinion does not exist, any such difference will be less apparent and its expression stifled. This is a strategy that is becoming harder and harder to sustain due to the developing legal support for employee representation.

(b) SMOOTHING
A familiar strategy is to seek the resolution of conflict by honeyed words in exhortation or discussion where the emphasis is on the value of teamwork, the assurance that 'we all agree really' and an overt, honest attempt to get past the divergence of opinion, which is regarded as a temporary and unfortunate abberration. This is often an accurate diagnosis of the situation and represents an approach that would have broad employee support in a particular employment context.

(c) FORCING
The opposite to smoothing is to attack expressions of dissent and deal with conflict by stamping it out. This is not easy and has innumerable political analogues in the past and present.

(d) COMPROMISE
Where divergence of views is acknowledged and confronted, one possibility is to split

the difference. If employees claim a pay increase of £10 and the management say they can afford nothing, a settlement of £5 saves the face of both parties *but satisfies neither*. However common this strategy may be — and sometimes there is no alternative — it has this major drawback: that both parties lose, or fail to win.

(e) CONFRONTATION

The fifth strategy is to confront the issue on which the parties differ. This involves accepting that there is a conflict of opinions or interests, exploring the scale and nature of the conflict and then working towards an accommodation of the differences which will provide a greater degree of satisfaction of the objectives of both parties than can be achieved by simple compromise. We suggest that this is the most productive strategy in many cases and offers the opportunity of both parties winning.

It is this fifth strategy which we consider in the remainder of this chapter.

Bargaining Tactics

In preparing for a bargaining encounter there are a number of preliminary aspects that are mentioned here as things for bargainers to set in their minds before they begin.

(a) RESOLUTION OR ACCOMMODATION

Conflict can be *resolved* so that the original feelings of antagonism or opposition vanish, at least over the issue that has brought the conflict to a head. The schoolboy story of how two boys 'put on the gloves in the gym' after a long feud and thereafter shook hands and became firm friends is a theoretical example of a conflict resolved. This type of outcome has a romantic appeal and will frequently be sought in industrial relations issues because so many people feel acutely uncomfortable when involved in relationships of overt antagonism.

Alternatively the conflict may be *accommodated*, so that the differences of view persist, but some *modus vivendi*, some form of living with the situation, is discovered. In view of the inevitability of the conflict that is endemic in the employment relationship, accommodation may be a more common prospect than resolution, but it is an interesting question for a bargainer to ponder when approaching the bargaining table: which is it — resolution or accommodation?

(b) TENSION LEVEL

Most bargainers feel that they have no chance to determine the timing of encounters. This is partly due to reluctance; managers in particular tend to resort to negotiation only when necessary, and the necessity is usually a crisis. A more pro-active instead of reactive approach is to initiate encounters, to some extent at least trying to push them into favourable timings.

A feature of timing is the tension level. Too much, and the negotiators get the jitters, unable to see things straight and indulging in excessive interpersonal vituperation: too little tension, and there is no real will to reach a settlement. Ideal timing is to get a point when both sides have a balanced desire to reach a settlement.

(c) POWER BALANCE

The background to any negotiation includes the relative power of the disputants. *Power parity is the most conducive to success.*

> Perceptions of power inequality undermine trust, inhibit dialogue, and decrease the likelihood of a constructive outcome from an attempted confrontation. Inequality tends to undermine trust on both ends of the imbalanced relationship, directly affecting both the person with the perceived power inferiority and the one with perceived superiority.[14]

The greater the power differential, the more negative the attitudes.

(d) SYNCHRONISING

The approaches and reciprocations of the two parties need a degree of synchronising to ensure that an approach is made at a time when the other party is ready to deal with it. Management interpretation of managerial prerogative often causes managers to move quickly in the search of a solution, virtually pre-empting negotiation. When what they see as a positive overture is not reciprocated, then they are likely to feel frustrated, discouraged and cross; making themselves, in turn, unready for overtures from the other side.

(e) OPENNESS

Conflict handling is more effective if the participants can be open with each other about the facts of the situation and their feelings about it. The Americans place great emphasis on this and we must appreciate that openness is more culturally acceptable in the United States than the United Kingdom, but we note their concern that negotiators should own up to feelings of resentment and anger, rather than masking their feelings behind role assumptions of self-importance.

A Structured Approach to Negotiating

As with the employment interview in Chapter 7, we now suggest a structured approach to the negotiating encounter. This is advanced as a framework for understanding and handling the dynamics of the situation: it is not suggested as an inflexible model. The phases are again Preparation, Encounter, Follow-up. Figure 14.1 shows the outline of the sequence but, unlike the employment sequence, there are three parallel phases of development. Items on the left-hand side are aspects of activity by management representatives, while those on the right-hand side are activities of employee representatives. In the middle are the things they do together.

PREPARATION

Agenda

The meeting needs an agenda or at least some form of agreement about what is to be discussed. In some quarters a naive conviction persists that there is some benefit in concealing the topic from the other party until the encounter begins, presumably because there is something to be gained from surprise. In fact this only achieves a deferment of discussion until the other party have had a chance to consider their position.

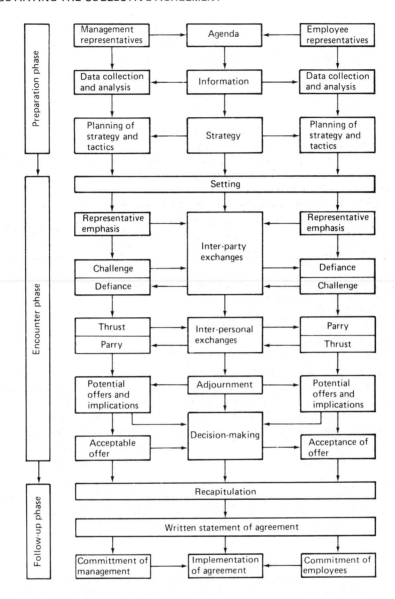

Figure 14.1. Outline of the negotiation process

There may be some advantages in having an agenda which provides relatively easy topics before relatively hard ones so that the negotiators can have the satisfying experience of producing agreement. This can then increase the motivation of negotiators to find solutions to the more intransigent problems on which they are divided.

Information

Both parties will need facts to support their argument in negotiation. Some information will be provided to employee representatives for the purposes of collective bargaining (see Chapter 30) and both sets of negotiators need to collect what they need, analyse it so that they understand it and confirm that the interpretation is shared by each member of their team.

Strategy

The main feature of preparation is the determination of strategy by each set of negotiators. Probably the most helpful work on negotiation strategy has been done by Atkinson,[15] with his careful analysis of bargaining conventions and possibilities. In this chapter we limit our considerations to four aspects of strategy.

(a) OBJECTIVES

What do the negotiators seek to achieve? Here one would ask them to produce clear and helpful objectives. When the question has been put to management negotiators entering either real or contrived negotiations in recent years the following have been some of the statements of objectives:

'Get the best deal we possibly can.'
'Maintain factory discipline at all costs.'
'Remain dignified at all times.'
'Look for an opening and exploit it to the full.'

Apart from their general feebleness, all these declarations have a common negative quality. The initiative is with the other party and the only strategy is to resist manfully for as long as possible and to concede as little as possible. If this is the best management negotiators can contrive, then their prospects are indeed bleak. They are bound to lose, the only unresolved question is how much. They cannot gain anything because they do not appear to want anything.

More positive objectives are those that envisage improvements that could flow from a changing of the employment rules — changes in efficiency, working practices, manning levels, shift-work patterns, administrative procedures, flexibility, cost control and so forth. Unless both parties to the negotiations want something out of the meeting there is little scope for anything but simple attrition.

(b) ROLES

Who will do what in the negotiations? A popular fallacy is that negotiation is best conducted by 'everyone chipping in when they have something to say' and 'playing it by ear'. This is the style for a brain-storming, problem-solving group discussion, and negotiation is quite different. Problem-solving implies common interests; negotiation implies conflicting interests between groups who are opposed in debate. Negotiators need a specific role, that they stay in. The roles are:

(i)Chairman. In the majority of cases the management provides this function, and one of the management team will chair the discussion and control the meeting.

(ii)Lead Spokesman. Each party requires one person who will be the principal advocate to articulate the case and to examine the opposing case. This pro-

vides focus to the discussion and control of the argument. Although it is common for the roles of chairman and lead spokesman to be combined in one person for status reasons, this can put a great strain on the individual, who is bowling and keeping wicket at the same time.

(iii)Specialists. The third role is that of specialist. One person who fully understands the incentive scheme, another to provide expert comment on any legal points, and so forth. The important emphasis is on what the specialist does *not* do. He does not get involved in the general debate, as this is confusing and moves control from the lead spokesman. He is there to deal with specialist matters, when required. Negotiating does not benefit from free-for-all, unstructured discussion.

(iv)Observers. There is no need for all those attending to speak, in order to justify their presence. There is an important part to be played by those who do no more than observe the discussions. They get less emotionally involved in the interplay and point-scoring and are able to evaluate the situation as it develops. When there are adjournments the observers often initiate the discussions within their team as strategy is re-defined and further tactics considered.

(c) PREDICTING COUNTER-CLAIMS

No strategy altogether survives the first encounter with the opposition, but its chances are improved if the negotiators have tried to predict what they will hear from the opposition. In this way they will be prepared not only to advance their own arguments, but also to respond to arguments put to them.

(d) UNITY

Because negotiations are the confrontation of different sets of interests, each team works out a united position before negotiations begin and expresses that unity in negotiation. If the position is to be modified, then they will agree the modification. This is another aspect of the vital difference between this activity and problem-solving. It is the differences *between* the parties that have to be handled; differences *within* the parties are simply a nuisance.

ENCOUNTER

(a) SETTING

The number of people representing each side will influence the conduct of negotiations. The larger the number the greater the degree of formality that is needed to manage the meeting; this is an argument in favour of negotiations between very small teams. On the other hand meetings between two or three people in 'smoke-filled rooms' give rise to allegations of manipulation and are difficult for members of trade unions to countenance in view of their dependence on democratic support. Another problem is that different phases of negotiation call for different arrangements. Relatively large numbers can be an advantage at the beginning, but are a hindrance in the later stages.

When asked to suggest an appropriate number, most experienced negotiators opt for three or four per side.

The nature of the seating arrangements needs to reflect the nature of the meeting, and that means that the sides face each other, with the boundaries between the two being clear. The importance of the physical arrangements was demonstrated by the Paris peace talks that were intended to bring an end to the Vietnam war. The start of talks was delayed for some weeks due to the delegations not being able to agree about the shape of the table.

(b) CHALLENGE AND DEFIANCE

The somewhat melodramatic term 'challenge and defiance' is used to describe the opening stage of the negotiations, for the deliberate reason that there is a deal of theatricality about the various processes of what Alec Irvine has described as the 'elaborate pavanes' of bargaining.

Negotiators begin by making it clear that they are representing the interests of people whose will and desire transcends that of the representatives themselves. They also emphasise the strength of their case and its righteousness as well as the impossibility of any movement from the position they are declaring. The theatricality lies in the realisation by both sides that there will be movement from the relative positions that they are busy declaring to be immovable. The displays of strength are necessary for the negotiators to convince themselves that they are right and that they understand their position, and to convince the opposition.

The substantive element of this phase is to clarify what the differences are. By the time it draws to a close the negotiators should be quite clear on the matters which divide them, where and how. This, of course, is an important part of the process: differentiation precedes integration.

It is important for the participants to keep the level of interpersonal animosity down. This is a part of the emphasis on their representative role that has already been mentioned. Different behaviours are needed later that depend on an open, trusting relationship between the negotiators, so this must not be impaired by personal acrimony at the opening. It is similar to the ritual whereby the lawyer describes his legal adversary as 'my learned friend'.

(c) THRUST AND PARRY

After the differences have been explored, there is an almost instinctive move to a second, integrative stage of the encounter. Here negotiators are looking for possibilities of movement and mutual accommodation.

> Douglas distinguishes between the public role-playing activities of the first stage and the 'psychological' (individual) activities of the second stage as being concerned, respectively, with *inter-party* and *interpersonal exchange*. Behaviourally the inter-party exchange is characterised by *official* statements of position, ostensibly committing the party or parties to some future action congruent with that position. The interpersonal exchange, on the other hand, is characterised by *unofficial* behaviours which do not so commit the parties in question.[16]

Thus the statements made by negotiators are of a much more tentative nature than earlier, as they sound out possibilities, float ideas, ask questions, make suggestions and generally change style towards a problem-solving mode. This has to be done without any commitment of the party that is being represented, so the thrusts are couched in very non-committal terms, specifically exonerating the party from any responsibility. Gradually the opportunities for mutual accommodation can be perceived in the background of the discussion. We can now incorporate the idea of target points and resistance points advanced by Walton and McKersie.[17]

The *target point* of a negotiating team is the declared objective; what they would really like to achieve. It will be spelled out in challenge and defiance. The *resistance point* is where they would rather break off negotiations than settle. This point is never declared and is usually not known either. Although negotiators frequently begin negotiations with a feeling of 'not a penny more than . . . ', the point at which they would *actually* resist is seldom the same as that at which they *think* they would resist. Normally the resistance points for both parties slide constantly back and forth during negotiations.

(d) DECISION-MAKING

Through thrust and parry all the variations of integration will have been considered and explored, even though negotiators will have veered away from making firm commitments. The third phase of their encounter is when they reach an agreement, and it is interesting to pause here with the comment that agreement is inevitable in all but a small minority of situations, because the bargainers need each other and they have no-one else with whom to negotiate. The employees want to continue working for the organisation. Even if they take strike action they will eventually return to work. The management need the employees to work for them. Employees collectively cannot choose a different management with whom to negotiate and managers cannot choose a replacement workforce with whom to bargain. They have to reach agreement, no matter how long it takes.

After an adjournment the management will make an offer. The decision about what to offer is the most difficult and important task in the whole process, because the offer can affect the resistance point of the other party. The way in which the other's resistance point will be affected cannot be pre-determined. A very low offer could move the other's resistance point further away or bring it nearer; we cannot be sure until the negotiations actually take place.

The offer may be revised, but eventually an offer will be accepted and the encounter — not the negotiation — is over.

Negotiations on the contract for collective consent are thus significantly different from those other types of bargaining in which people engage. The negotiations to purchase a second-hand car or a house may seem at first sight to be similar, but in both those situations either party can opt out at any stage and cease to deal any further. The possibility of losing the other is always present, just as is the possibility of negotiating with a different 'opponent'. For this reason the political analogies are more helpful. A peace treaty has to be agreed between the nations that have been at war, and no-one else.

FOLLOW-UP

(a) RECAPITULATION

Once a bargain has been struck the tension of negotiation is released and the natural inclination of the bargainers is to break up and spread the news of the agreement that has been reached. It is suggested that they should first recapitulate all the points on which they have agreed and, if necessary, make agreements on any minor matters still outstanding that everyone had forgotten.

In the wake of a settlement there are usually a number of such minor matters. If they are dealt with there and then they should be dealt with speedily because of the overriding feeling for agreement that has been established. If discussion of them is deferred because they are difficult, then agreement may be hard to reach later as the issues stand on their own instead of in the context of a larger settlement.

(b) WRITTEN STATEMENT

If it is possible to produce a brief written statement before the meeting is ended, both parties to the negotiations will be greatly helped. The emphasis here is on producing a brief written statement *before* the meeting ends, not as soon as possible afterwards. This will help all the negotiators to take away the same interpretation of what they have done and make them less dependent on recollection. In most circumstances it can also be used to advise non-participants: re-typed as a memorandum to supervisors, put up on notice boards, read out at union meetings and so on. This will reduce the distortion that can stem from rumour. Until the agreement is in writing it rests on an *understanding* and understanding can easily change.

(c) COMMITMENT OF THE PARTIES

So far agreement has been reached between negotiators only and it is of no value unless the parties represented by those negotiators accept it and make it work. This requires acceptance at two levels, first in words and then in deeds.

Employee representatives have to report back to their membership and persuade them to accept the agreement. To some extent management representatives may have to do the same thing, but they customarily carry more personal authority to make decisions than do employee representatives.

Although this is a difficult and uncertain process it is no more important than the final level of acceptance, which is where people make the agreement work. Benefits to the employees are likely to be of the type that are simple to administer — like an increase in the rates of pay — but benefits to the organisation, like changes in working practices and the variation of demarcation boundaries, are much more difficult. They may quickly be glossed over and forgotten unless the changes are painstakingly secured after the terms have been agreed.

Boulwarism: A Cautionary Tale

Lemuel Boulware, Vice-President for Employee Relations in the General Electric Company of the United States, tried to side-step the ritual dance described above by developing a strategy which he called 'truth in bargaining'. The essence was that his first offer was also his last. He claimed that in conventional bargaining everyone knew that the first offer would be improved, so it was artificially low. He intended to be direct and truthful, making one offer that would not be varied so as to save time and speculation about the final outcome.

This policy had short-run success, but trade unions objected to 'Boulwarism' on the grounds that it eliminated the constructive interchange of normal bargaining and diminished the importance of union representatives in negotiation. Eventually they challenged the policy successfully in the American courts on the grounds that it was not bargaining in good faith.[18]

Lemuel Boulware is an interesting footnote to the history of collective bargaining. He acted as though the only thing in negotiation that mattered was the result, and he ignored the fact that employee representatives and some specialist managers justify their existence by negotiating. He also overlooked the fact that people join trade unions in order to obtain from the management of their organisations improvements in terms and conditions that the management will not willingly give. Negotiations are won or lost; the most useful negotiations are those where both parties win by reaching a mutually satisfactory agreement.[19]

SUMMARY PROPOSITIONS

14.1. Conflict is inevitable in the employment relationship, but need not be dysfunctional for that relationship.

14.2. The optimum bargaining strategy is likely to be to confront the issue on which the parties differ, to explore the reasons for the difference and to work towards an accommodation of those differences that will be acceptable to both parties.

14.3. Compared with other encounters at work, negotiating has a very high degree of ritualistic content, involving elaborate and artificial behaviours from the participants.

REFERENCES

1. Knibbs J.R., 'Negotiating Skills Training and Industrial Relations Development' in *Personnel Review*, Winter 1977, p. 29.
2. As argued in Dahrendorf R., *Class and Conflict in Modern Society* (Routledge and Kegan Paul) 1959.
3. See Coser L.A., *The Functions of Social Conflict* (Free Press of Glencoe) 1956.
4. Douglas A., *Industrial Peacemaking* (Columbia University Press) 1962. As this text is difficult to obtain, readers can find a brief summary in Morley I.E. and Stephenson G.M., 'Strength of Case, Communication Systems and the Outcomes of Simulated Negotiations' in *Industrial Relations Journal*, Summer 1970, pp. 19–20.
5. Blake R.R., Shepard H.A. and Mouton J.S., *Managing Intergroup Conflict in Industry* (Gulf Publishing) 1964.
6. Walton R.E., *Interpersonal Peacemaking: Confrontations and Third Party Consultation* (Addison-Wesley) 1969.
7. Cooper B.M. and Bartlett A.F., *Industrial Relations: A Study in Conflict* (Heinemann) 1976, p. 167.
8. Fox A., *Work, Power and Trust Relations* (Faber & Faber) 1974.
9. Harvey J.B., 'The Abilene Paradox: The Management of Agreement' in *Organisation Dynamics*, Summer 1974, pp. 63–80.
10. Lorenz K., *On Aggression* (Methuen) 1966.
11. Ardrey R., *The Territorial Imperative* (Collins) 1967.
12. Schmidt W. and Tannenbaum R., 'Management of Differences' in *Harvard Business Review*, November/December 1960, pp. 107–115.
13. Lawrence P.R. and Lorsch J.W. *Managing Group and Intergroup Relations* (Dorsey) 1972.

14. Walton R.E. *op. cit.*, p. 98.
15. Atkinson G., 'Bargaining: The Rules of the Game: in *Personnel Management,* February 1976, pp. 21—24, 39. Also his book *The Effective Negotiator* (Quest Research Publications) 1975.
16. Morley I.E. and Stephenson G.M., *op. cit.*, p. 20.
17. Walton R.E. and McKersie R.B., *Towards a Behavioural Theory of Labour Negotiations* (McGraw-Hill) 1965.
18. Lowndes R., *Industrial Relations: A Contemporary Survey* (Holt, Rinehart & Winston) 1972, pp. 116—118.
19. Further reading that can be suggested on this theme is Warr P., *The Psychology of Collective Bargaining* (Hutchinson) 1973, or Morley I.E. and Stephenson G.M., *The Social Psychology of Bargaining* (George Allen & Unwin) 1977.

15

Equalising Employment Opportunity

In this chapter we consider moves towards the equalisation of opportunities in employment, mainly in dealing with discrimination on the grounds of sex or race, although we shall also consider the less topical types of discrimination against people on the grounds of age or disability.

The General Argument Against Discrimination

The most pervasive argument against discrimination in employment or anywhere else is the argument based on an appreciation of *rights* and *obligation*. From the Universal Declaration of Human Rights and similar statements of principle, those who see themselves at a disadvantage are likely to assert their rights and point out that the discrimination from which they suffer is unjust and probably unlawful. Many of those who do not personally suffer from the effects of discrimination will still support the rights argument, claiming that the more fortunate have an obligation to level up opportunities.

Practical arguments are less well-known and need stating here. We have already suggested that work is central to the life of man, even if the reason for that centrality has changed. We posit that work is an important means towards personal fulfilment and that this attitude is widely supported. In that context those members of the community who are denied the opportunities of work will both become second-grade citizens and hold back the development of the society because they have no stake in the benefits that change is intended to produce. If their restricted employment opportunities are accompanied by limited access to education then they will be less able to take part in programmes of social action like education and health care. The under-privileged woman may seek refuge in producing too many children; the deprived urban Negro or under-privileged youth may find an outlet in street violence. A society develops through the will of its members and if the will is lacking, then the development is arrested.

It is also possible for a society to move too quickly in equalising opportunities. If women are pushed too systematically into employment such an imperative may produce problems of anxiety, overwork and guilt so that the domestic/employment balance is wrong, leading to social malaise and a steeply declining birthrate.

Another practical consideration is the balance between the economically active and inactive members of the community. At each end of their lives people are spending more time economically inactive, so that it is not uncommon for an individual to be gainfully employed for only half of his total life-span — forty years in employment, preceded by twenty years of childhood, education and training, followed by twenty years of retirement. If the proportion of those in the middle period who are economically inactive is too great there is an imbalance between the producers and consumers. At least until recently such an imbalance has been regarded as unsatisfactory.

We sometimes overlook the fact that for married women to be economically inactive is a relatively recent development in western cultures. Previously women had a major economic justification for themselves because of their productivity on behalf of the family. They were almost completely responsible for making clothes, preparing food and extensive housework. Gradually these duties have been whittled away as clothing is purchased rather than made, food is purchased ready-prepared and housework becomes steadily easier both through the development of labour-saving appliances and the domestication of husbands.

Many members of the management fraternity complain that social problems like equalising opportunity fall outside the responsibility of employing organisations:

'When social attitudes have changed sufficiently for men to work willingly for a coloured supervisor, we will employ them, but at the moment we have to comply with the prevailing mood. It's not our job to bring about social change.'

'The women we've got at the moment seem happy enough in the jobs they're doing and we hardly ever get a woman applying for a senior post. Why should we go looking for trouble?'

Some social reformers would agree with this line of thinking and say that it is not for managers to exercise social responsibility according to their sense of what is right: it is for society to exact through legislation what managers ought to provide. The problem for both groups, however, is that legislation appears to have a poor track record where social change is involved. The place of employment is crucial to racial and sexual equality. That is where there needs to be a will and belief in the need for change that goes beyond simply obeying the law. Other provisions like better educational opportunities and certain legal protections against discrimination will have only a marginal effect. The employing organisation depends on the surrounding society not only in the obvious sense as a source of prospective employees, but also in the sense that those employees import attitudes and experience into their employment from the world outside. A company that discriminates directly or indirectly against women or coloured people will first be curtailing the potential of available talent (and employers are not well-known for their complaints about the *surplus* of talent), but secondly they will be contributing to a situation in which social stability is put at risk and economic growth may be held back. Employer inaction aggravates discrimination as it is principally through employment that progress can be made. If employers open up employment opportunities for women, then women will acquire the confidence to follow the lead and gradually broaden their social role. If employers open up employment opportunities for black people, then they too will grow in confidence and achieve social integration. The employer cannot necessarily expect gratitude and certainly not immediate short-term miracles, but in the longer run he improves the effectiveness of his organisation.

Progress in achieving equality of opportunity in employment seems slow. The Equal Opportunities Commission and the Commission for Racial Equality have both expressed disappointment at the rate of improvement and the Equal Opportunities Commission have asked for changes in the legislation in order to speed up development. Some indication is provided by the statistics on cases taken to industrial tribunals under the employment provisions of the Race Relations Act, Sex Discrimination Act and Equal Pay Act.[1]

Race	1977/8	1978/9	1979/80	1980/81	
Number of cases	146	364	426	332	
Percentage upheld	8	31	11	12	

Sex	1976	1977	1978	1979	1980
Number of cases	1985	980	514	441	271
Percentage upheld	29	25	26	20	19

LAW AND THE EMPLOYMENT OF WOMEN

Women are not only numerous in the working population, they are increasing as a proportion of the whole. There were nearly ten million working women in 1976. The official estimate is that the number of men in the working population will increase by 700,000 by 1986, while the number of women will rise by 1,300,000, making up well over 40 per cent of the total.

For how long will women continue to occupy the fairly small number of occupations which are effectively open to them, and for how long will the economy be able to manage without using their skills more widely? Women's employment tends to be heavily concentrated in certain occupations:[2]

Of all women workers:
29.1 per cent are clerical workers (including secretaries, typists etc.)
23.2 per cent are in service, sports and recreation (including canteen assistants, office cleaners etc.)
11.9 per cent are professional, technical or artistic workers (including teachers, nurses etc.)
10.7 per cent are sales workers.

Furthermore, *within* occupations, women account for:
96.8 per cent of all canteen assistants, counterhands etc.
91.7 per cent of all charwomen, office cleaners etc.
91.6 per cent of all nurses.

Legal developments to protect the employment of women are mainly in three recent enactments:

Sex Discrimination Act 1975
Employment Protection (Consolidation) Act 1978 (Maternity provisions)
Equal Pay Act 1970

1. Sex Discrimination Act

The Act has four objectives:

(i) To make illegal certain types of disrimination between the sexes,
(ii) To make illegal discrimination on the grounds of marriage,
(iii) To promote equality of opportunity between the sexes, and
(v) To establish an Equal Opportunities Commission.

Discrimination is not removed entirely as it is not unlawful to discriminate against someone on the grounds of their family status – such as the number of dependents. The 1975 Act recognises two types of discrimination on the grounds of sex:

Direct discrimination is where an employer treats a man or women less favourably than he treats a person of the opposite sex in the same circumstances.
Indirect discrimination is where an employer applies a condition equally to both sexes but the proportion of one sex which can comply is considerably smaller than the proportion of the other which can comply, and the condition is not justifiable on non-sex grounds and the complainant suffers through not being able to comply.[3]

Direct discrimination is sufficiently obvious for it to be easy to recognise. Indirect discrimination may not be so readily identifiable and is where the greatest difficulties occur. It should be remembered that all the elements (disproportionate ability to comply, non-justifiability of condition and suffering of complainant) have to be present to substantiate a claim. Furthermore sex discrimination is not like unfair dismissal in that discrimination is for the complainant to *prove;* not for the employer to disprove.

Discrimination on the grounds of marriage is made illegal by requiring men and women again to be treated alike:

If a person treats or would treat a man differently according to the man's marital status, his treatment of a woman . . . is to be compared to his treatment of a man having the like marital status.[4]

It is thus possible to treat a married man more favourably than a single woman, but not than a married woman, because it is not unlawful to discriminate in favour of married people, but it is unlawful to discriminate against them. It is, therefore, possible to offer free or subsidised housing to married couples without being under a legal obligation to offer similar facilities to single people of either sex. One interesting tribunal judgement on discrimination against married people has been that it can be fair to discriminate if a husband and wife work in the same or closely competing organisations where there could be a conflict of interest.[5]

The main likelihood of discrimination arises at the *pre-employment* stage, and there are a number of ways in which an employer could get into difficulty.

RECRUITMENT

Activities like school visits should not assume a preference among school leavers, so that the employer who arranges for parties of school leavers to visit his premises could be accused of discrimination if the party were divided arbitrarily, with the boys being shown round the laborarory and the vehicle maintenance area while the girls were taken to see the offices and the computer.

ADVERTISEMENTS

The recruiter faces two problems with advertising vacancies: *wording* and *placement.* The wording must avoid either direct or indirect discrimination. Specific terms like 'manageress' and 'barmaid' are taboo because they exclude one sex and certain terms that have strong associations with only one sex like 'engineer', 'manager' and 'nurse' must either be avoided or qualified in some way such as the prefix 'male or female' or the phrase 'applications invited from men and women'. Also the recruiter cannot bias the wording of the advertisment to discourage one sex or to make it feasible for members of only one sex to apply. Disproportionately long periods of *unbroken* previous employment would discriminate against women because of the likelihood that they would interrupt their careers to bear and rear children. Age limits can also be discriminatory:

> A woman applied for employment in the Executive Grade of the Civil Service but her application was refused on the grounds that she was over the age limit of 28 for first entry. After failing with a complaint to a tribunal she appealed to the EAT, claiming that few women could meet the age limit as it was set at an age when many women were having babies or looking after children. The finding was in her favour.[6]

INTERVIEWING

Interviewing methods can be discriminatory in a number of ways if the recruiter does not take care. Application forms must not, for instance, have sections for women only to complete, and job descriptions should not assume that women wish to receive different information than men. In the interview itself there is some peril for the interviewer in asking questions that appear to discriminate. *Prima facia,* for instance it is discriminatory to ask women applicants questions about domestic circumstances (like 'who will look after the children') if these same questions are not also put to married men applicants. The Employment Appeal Tribunal has, however, ruled that it is not necessarily unlawful to put such questions.

> A woman applied for the position of golf professional with a local authority. Although short-listed she was not appointed and regarded three of the men who went for final interview to be less well qualified than she was. She made a claim at tribunal that discrimination was apparent in the questions put to her at interview, e.g.:
> 'Do you think men respond as well to a woman golf professional as to a man?'
> 'Are there any women golf professionals in clubs?'
> The Employment Appeal Tribunal found that the questions might indicate an out-of-date attitude but did not in themselves constitute a violation of the Act. They also said that superior qualifications do not give an automatic right to employment over other candidates, as interviewers are entitled to take factors like personality into account.[7]

From this judgement it appears that it is in practice very difficult for a complainant to make a complaint stick on the grounds that the interview and subsequent decision were discriminatory.

The main interest in the Act and its effect on employment has been at the point of recruitment, but it also restrains employers from discriminating in matters of promotion, transfer and training. Again it is difficult for a complainant to succeed at tribunal unless the discrimination is clear, because no employee has a right to promotion.

A well-qualified woman store detective complained when a promotion opportunity was not advised to her. She only heard about the vacancy after it had been advertised in 'The Police Review'. The tribunal found in her favour as she was denied an equal opportunity for promotion.[8]

There are, however, many examples of women failing in claims.

A woman and her husband were employed by the same company and the woman was not considered for a more senior position because her husband was a subordinate of the person for whom she would be working. The tribunal found this discrimination to be not unlawful.[9]

GENUINE OCCUPATIONAL QUALIFICATIONS
To avoid the bizarre, the Act includes a range of genuine occupational qualifications that make discrimination lawful.

(i) *Physiological reasons.* These do not include strength or stamina, but other physiological reasons which make only one sex appropriate. Hamlet does not have to be played by a woman and men do not have to be given the opportunity to model women's clothes.

(ii) *Privacy or decency.* Jobs which require physical contact or working when people are undressed can be limited to one sex. Examples would be baths and lavatory attendants.

(iii) *Accommodation.* If the job makes it impracticable for the employee to live elsewhere and there are sleeping and sanitary facilities for only one sex, it would be permissible to discriminate, providing that it is *unreasonable* to expect the employer to make extra provision.

(iv) *Character of the establishment.* Employment in an establishment with a basic character making the employment of one sex appropriate. The normal example is of male warders in male prisons and female wardresses in female prisons. However, gardeners in prisons could be of either sex.

(v) *Education and Welfare.* If the job holder provides individuals with 'personal services promoting welfare or education' that can best be provided by members of only one sex, then discrimination is possible. This would make it reasonable to appoint only men to be housemasters in boys' boarding schools, but would not make it reasonable to prevent women from being appointed as secretary to the headmaster. It is difficult to see how extensive is the range of jobs to which this provision can apply, as the Act permits men to become midwives.

(vi) *Statutory bar.* This section relates to the restrictions of statute — mainly the Factories Act provisions already mentioned — which do not permit women to be employed in certain categories of employment.

(vii) *Married couples.* Although we have seen that discrimination against wives can be condoned by the Act, there is legal discrimination in their favour when the job to be filled is one of two held by a married couple. If a man and wife are to be employed as joint stewards of a social club it is possible to appoint the husband and then discriminate against other women by appointing his wife.

(viii) *Overseas working.* Where the job involves working in countries overseas where the laws and customs are such that the work could not be performed by a woman, it would not be unlawful to discriminate against them. This feature was an amendment to the original Bill and is designed for jobs that require working in Muslim countries.

EQUALITY OF OPPORTUNITY AND THE COMMISSION
The Act is designed to promote equality of opportunity between men and women in employment; this is to be achieved partly by the legal restraints described, partly by the example of legislation in shaping attitudes and partly by the Equal Opportunities Commission which has been set up with three principal duties:

(i) To work towards the elimination of discrimination,
(ii) To promote equality of opportunity between men and women generally, and
(iii) To keep under review the workings of the Sex Discrimination and Equal Pay Acts.

The Commission can bring proceedings on discrimination issues, even where there has not been a complaint, so that some of the deeply entrenched discrimination practices can be tackled.

Despite legislation and an Equal Opportunities Commission, discrimination will persist until there is a will for it to be discontinued.

> The woman entering a predominantly male sector of work . . . will have her performance judged alongside that of her male colleagues. Yet, although she has formal membership of the organisation, she may find it difficult to function effectively unless she is received into the informal network of work relationships in the same way as her male counterparts. It is precisely at this informal level that it is most difficult to generate true equality and acceptance because of the attitudes and psychological effects of sexual differences both in the conscious and the sub-conscious.[10]

2. Employment Protection (Consolidation) Act

The Act establishes three rights for women in employment:

(i) The right not to be unfairly dismissed because of pregnancy,
(ii) The right to maternity pay, and
(iii) The right to return to work following maternity leave.

Some aspects of these rights have been modified by the 1980 Employment Act.

DISMISSAL AND PREGNANCY
Pregnant women have the right to work for as long as the law permits, providing that they are capable and have completed the normal qualifying period of fifty-two weeks that is a prerequisite for all employee rights against unfair dismissal. A pregnant woman dismissed for any other reason will be unfairly dismissed and

entitled to the remedies that such dismissal confers. Even if she is incapable of continuing her duties due *specifically* to her pregnancy, then she will still be unfairly dismissed if her employment is terminated at a time when there is suitable alternative employment available in the organisation but not offered to her.

MATERNITY PAY

Whether or not a woman intends to return to her employer after her pregnancy, she is entitled to six weeks' maternity pay at the beginning of her maternity leave. This is calculated as 90 per cent of a normal week's pay, multiplied by six, less the statutory amount of maternity allowance. It is payable by the employer, but the full amount is reclaimable from a Maternity Pay Fund financed by a part of National Insurance contributions so that the cost is spread over all employers and not only those employing young women. The qualifications for receiving maternity pay are:

   (i) The employee must work up to the 11th week before the expected date of confinement,

  (ii) She must advise her employer at least three weeks before her absence begins, and

 (iii) She must have completed two years' continuous employment by the beginning of the 11th week referred to in (i) above.

MATERNITY LEAVE

A woman has a right to return to her work for up to 29 weeks after the date of confinement. If her employer does not re-engage her she will be considered either unfairly dismissed or redundant. The qualifications for maternity leave are the same as those for maternity pay with the addition of a declaration of an intention to return to work made at least three weeks before the period of absence begins. The employer may write to the employee seven weeks after the expected confinement date, asking her to confirm in writing her intention to return, advising her that if she does not reply within fourteen days she will have forfeited her return right. The work to which the Act confers the right of return is:

> the job in which she was employed under the original contract of employment and on terms and conditions not less favourable than those which would have been applicable to her if she had not been so absent.[11]

This does not limit the employer to giving her precisely the same job back. He can use whatever flexibility the contract of employment permits in re-employing the woman in similar work.

Because of the need, sometimes, to recruit a replacement, the Act provides for the fair dismissal of such a replacement, providing that the replacement is informed in writing, on appointment, that he or she will be dismissed when the woman on maternity leave returns. The replacement employee cannot be fairly dismissed for any other reason, so if the woman returns from maternity leave and is placed in other work, the temporary replacement cannot be fairly dismissed for incompetence.

The 1980 Act also confers a right to paid time off for ante-natal care, but removes the 'job-back' right from women working in undertakings with five or fewer employees if her return to work is not reasonably practical.

When maternity provisions were introduced there was a widespread view that they would prove onerous on employers. The Policy Studies Institute have surveyed the experience of 300 employers, all of whom have had at least one employee who has stopped work to have a baby. The conclusion of their study is that maternity rights actually cause very few problems for employers and the problems caused are seldom more than minor irritations.[12]

3. Equal Pay Act, 1970

Although the Act came on the statute book in 1970 it did not come into full effect until the end of 1975. This was to give employers time to make progressive changes in payment arrangements so that the costs of up-grading could be spread over several years. The Act establishes the right of a woman to terms and conditions of employment equal to those of a man when she is employed on:

a. The same work or broadly similar work, or
b. Work which has been given an equal value to men's jobs in a job evaluation exercise.

THE SAME OR BROADLY SIMILAR WORK

The work does not have to be identical to that done by men to justify equal pay: it has to be either the same or of a broadly similar nature. Any difference in pay or terms of employment can only be justified if there is a difference in the work done that is substantial or of *practical importance*. The frequency with which the difference occurs will influence the assessment of what is 'like work'. If, for instance a male supervisor is better qualified and therefore able to exercise a greater flexibility and mobility of supervision than a woman supervisor doing the same job, there could be a case for a discriminatory payment as the difference can be judged as of practical importance.[13] Another justification for discriminatory payment is where there is a *material difference:*

> A man and a woman were employed on broadly similar work as audit clerks, but she complained because she was paid less. The man carried more responsibility and did more complex work (difference of practical importance) but there was also a material difference in that clients of the employer could be charged more for the services of the man than the woman, thus entitling him to be paid more.[14]

WORK OF EQUAL VALUE

This relates to jobs which are substantially different, but which are rated as equivalent by the process of job evaluation, which is intended to provide a standard method of comparing the contents of widely differing jobs. In this situation the job content is not important in justifying or resisting an equal pay claim. It is important that the scheme of job evaluation should be fair and without sex bias. Section 1 (5) of the Act provides the definition of job evaluation to be used:

> A woman is to be regarded as employed on work rated as equivalent with that of any man if her job and their job have been given an equal value, in terms of the demand made on a worker under various headings (for instance, effort, skill, decision), on a study undertaken with a view to evaluating in those terms the jobs to be done by all or any of the employees in an undertaking . . . or would have been given an equal value but for the evaluation being made on a system setting different values for men and women on the same demand under any heading.[15]

Despite the legislation, effective equality of pay for women makes slow progress. Their average earnings are only some 73 per cent of average earnings for men.[16]

OTHER ASPECTS OF THE EMPLOYMENT OF WOMEN

There are other ways in which employment opportunities for women are limited. One is their dependence upon part-time work. Approximately one third of women workers work less than 30 hours a week so that their choice is limited and their level of pay and benefits will be less also. As most women working part-time do so because of domestic and family convenience, they are also handicapped by the shortage of nursery provision by both employers and local authorities. There are special problems for an employer contemplating the establishment of a day nursery. A helpful publication is available from the Institute of Personnel Management.[17]

LAW, RACE AND EMPLOYMENT

The number and proportion of coloured people in the community have been the subject of some controversial statements, largely because of the above-average birthrate among women living in the United Kingdom but born elsewhere. A detailed examination of the statistics takes the 1971 population census as a starting point:

> Black people form a small but growing proportion of the labour force in Britain. In 1971, people who were born outside the UK accounted for just under six per cent of all economically active persons: 2.2 per cent (555,520) were from the New Commonwealth, 1.7 per cent (421,130) from Ireland and two per cent from elsewhere.[18]

The percentage of immigrants in the work force varies from one part of the country to another, being highest in the large conurbations and reaching 15 per cent in Greater London. Of particular concern is the fact that unemployment among blacks increases more rapidly than among the rest of the population. Between 1973 amd 1980 the number of unemployed people doubled while the number of unemployed black people increased fourfold.

The Race Relations Act 1976 replaces the earlier Act of 1968 and seeks to make discrimination unlawful with a similar approach to that of the Sex Discrimination Act. It deals with three kinds of discrimination:

(i) Direct discrimination
(ii) Indirect discrimination
(iii) Victimisation

DIRECT DISCRIMINATION

It is unlawful if an employer discriminates against an employee or prospective employee if on racial grounds he treats that person less favourably than he treats or would treat other people. The term *on racial grounds* is defined as being on the grounds of colour, race, nationality or ethnic or national origin. Although the Act is concerned mainly with the rights of coloured people, it also affects, for instance, Europeans. A German who believed he was being discriminated against on the grounds of his nationality could seek the protection of the Act.

Less favourable treatment includes such actions as isolation, providing that the action is deliberate, like separate Asian and European canteens, even though facilities were equal. The simple fact that one particular working group is made up entirely of one racial group may not necessarily be less favourable treatment, although such situations are dangerous.

> . . . employers who allow entirely Asian night shifts to develop in their factories are not as such in breach of the Act. If the single race shift has developed because Asians have asked to go on the night shift there is — probably — congregation rather than segregation. Discrimination will only have occurred if Asians have had no other option open to them; or have been prevented from going on to other shifts; or if a member of the night shift asks to be transferred to the day shift and is refused on racial grounds; or a member of the day shift asks to go on nights and is similarly refused.[19]

INDIRECT DISCRIMINATION

The tests for indirect discrimination are exactly the same as for discrimination on grounds of sex: disproportionate number of persons who can comply, not justified on non-racial grounds, and some disadvantage to a complainant.

VICTIMISATION

Those who experience racial discrimination have been reluctant to complain and there is the fear of reprisals if one does complain. For this reason the Act gives the right of complaint to an industrial tribunal to those who feel they have been victimised in their employment because of bringing proceedings under the Act against the discriminator, giving information for proceedings or making allegations against the discriminator.

REMEDIES

The pattern of remedies for racial discrimination are again similar to those for sex discrimination and unfair dismissal. The tribunal can make an order asserting the rights of the parties or can recommend action to be taken in the future to put things right. If neither of those remedies are appropriate, then the tribunal can award compensation as for unfair dismissal. It is different in one important particular: compensation can be awarded for hurt feelings.

The 1976 Act also set up a Commission for Racial Equality, with similar powers to the Equal Opportunities Commission, which can bring complaints to a tribunal where there may be indirect discriminatory practices but no particular casualty, or in the cases of discriminatory advertising.

GENUINE OCCUPATIONAL QUALIFICATIONS

(i) *Entertainment.* If it is necessary to have a person of a particular racial group to achieve an authentic presentation.

(ii) *Artistic or photographic modelling.* If it is necessary to use a person from a particular racial group to provide authenticity for a work of art, visual image or sequence.

(iii) *Specialised restaurants.* If it is necessary to have a person from a particular racial group to sustain the special setting of an establishment where food or drink is served to the public (like the Chinese restaurant).

(iv) *Community social workers.* If a person provides personal services to members of a particular racial group and the services can best be provided by someone of the same racial group.

These genuine occupational qualifications permit an employer to be selective in recruiting, training, promoting or transferring. They do not permit discriminatory treatment in terms and conditions of employment.

As with discrimination on the grounds of sex, employers frequently feel that they should wait until public opinion has changed before they make changes in employment conditions, but with racial discrimination in particular one can argue that it is the place where public opinion is formed. Tom Connelly, the Chief Executive of the Commission on Racial Equality, put it this way:

> What happens in employment is crucial for the whole issue. A person's job and employment prospects obviously determine his current and material welfare, the well-being of his family and his status in the community . . . An indispensable condition for fuller acceptance is the breakdown of the association between colour and inferiority. If coloured workers are seen mainly in low status jobs and in poor housing, the association will be sustained and strengthened. The more they are seen in higher status jobs, particularly those which involve the exercise of authority, the weaker the association with inferiority will become. The experience of coloured workers in industry will therefore influence crucially the attitudes and behaviour of the host society.[20]

There has been much exhortation on the question of improving employment prospects for racial minority employees, but few signs of advance and many of prejudice.[21] In attempts to stimulate progress two administrative devices have been authoritatively advocated by the CRE.[22] One is the development of equal opportunity policies in companies and the other is monitoring. Research has not succeeded in showing the introduction of policy 'from the top' as being effective except in situations where the employment of minority employees has produced major problems that needed to be resolved.[23]

The idea of monitoring is that records should be kept of those in racial and ethnic minorities who are employed in the organisation. This produces the immediate reaction that it is a discriminatory act in itself. However, the potential dangers are offset by the need to take positive steps to check what the penetration into the more attractive areas of the organisation actually is. The tentative list of classifications to be used is:

African	those born in, or whose recent forbears were born in, Africa.
Asian	the same for the Indian sub-continent.
Caribbean	the same for the Caribbean.
UK & Irish	English, Welsh, Scottish, Irish.
Other European	
Others	including those of mixed descent.

LAW AND THE DISABLED

It has been estimated that there are 600,000 people registered as disabled in the United Kingdom.[24] The law requires that at least 3 per cent of the employees of each organisation employing more than 20 workers should be registered as disabled, so as to enhance the general employment prospects of the disabled. Once on the register the disabled person can use the services of the Disablement Resettlement Officer (DRO) at the local Jobcentre to help in obtaining employment.

Two occupations − lift attendants and car park attendants − are reserved for the registered disabled under the terms of the Disabled Persons (Designated Employments) Order of 1946. That order gives the Secretary of State power to designate other occupations, but this has not been done. Some aspects of work with computers are particularly appropriate for the blind, and many jobs in manufacturing may be so noisy as to make deafness an occupational advantage. Nevertheless, most of the people on the disabled register feel that they do not want special treatment or reserved occupations, they merely want an opportunity to take up normal employment for which they feel perfectly competent and from which they often feel excluded because of ignorance or prejudice on the part of employers, or similar resistance from employees. 1981 was The International Year for Disabled People and produced a lot of publicity, including an account by Len Peach of action taken in one major company.[25]

AGE

This chapter began with a general discussion of discrimination; one of the arguments mentioned was the balance between the economically active and the economically inactive. This is exemplified mainly by married women resenting their dependence on their husband's income, and popular (usually ill-informed) feelings about the cost of unemployed immigrants to the Department of Health and Social Security. We end the chapter with a brief comment about a section of the community who may resent economic inactivity, yet who so far have virtually no legal rights against discrimination: the older employees.

The main protection for the older employee is against redundancy, for which he will be financially compensated, but there is no protection for him in seeking fresh employment, training or promotion (unless *she* happens to be black!). The problems of unemployment in the 1980s have tended to militate against the employment prospects of those who are older, because the working population appears to be too large for our total employment requirements. People have been under pressure to retire early in many circumstances and find it very difficult to continue working after normal retirement age.

In the United States recent legislation has been introduced to prevent discrimination in employment on the grounds of age. There are no signs of this spreading to the United Kingdom, but we need to consider not only whether citizen's rights are being impaired because of the lack of such legislation, but also − as with other types of anti-discrimination legislation, − whether the effectiveness of organisations is being impaired by people suggesting to older employees that they are becoming less effective and that they may be standing in the way of the legitimate career aspirations of others.

Megginson put some of the reasons to favour people over forty years of age:

... greater experience and better judgement in decision making; more objectivity about personal goals and abilities, as the older men have already satisfied many of their needs for salary and status and are able to concentrate more on job responsibilities; increased social intelligence and the ability to understand and influence others; decreased risk, as the older person's potentialities can be more easily determined from their performance record; reduced training time, as their previous experience is easily transferable, especially into management positions; and proven value as the older workers have proven their abilities . . .[26]

SUMMARY PROPOSITIONS

15.1.   Equality of opportunity is not only to be supported on grounds of social justice, but also because of the practical advantages to employers that stem from avoiding people feeling disadvantaged.

15.2.   The opening up of opportunities for women, racial minorities, the disabled and older employees in the organisation will increase the range of talent that can be deployed.

15.3   Assumptions about prejudice in others are seldom found to be significant when tested by managerial action.

15.4   For those who experience discrimination — particularly racial minorities — the place of employment is crucial to their overcoming discrimination in the wider society.

REFERENCES

1.   Central Statistical Office, *Social Trends 1982* (HMSO) 1981, p. 204.
2.   Hunt J., *Organising Women Workers* (Workers Educational Association) 1975, p. 6.
3.   Sex Discrimination Act 1975, p. 6.
4.   *Ibid.* pp. 1 and 2.
5.   Established in *McLean* v. *Paris Travel Service,* 1977.
6.   *Price* v. *Civil Service Commission and Society of Civil and Public Servants,* 1976.
7.   *Saunders* v. *Richmond upon Thames Borough Council,* 1977.
8.   *Woodcock* v. *Boots Ltd,* 1976.
9.   *Martin* v. *National Car Parks,* 1976.
10. Richbell S., 'De Facto Discrimination and How to Kick the Habit' in *Personnel Management,* November 1976.
11. Employment Protection Act 1975.
12. Policy Studies Institute, *Maternity Rights: The Experience of Employers* (PSI) 1981.
13. *Sampson and others* v. *Polikoff Universal Ltd,* 1976.
14. *Oakes* v. *Lester Beasley & Co.,* 1976.
15. Equal Pay Act 1970.
16. Equal Opportunities Commission, *Annual Report 1980.*
17. Day C., *Company Day Nurseries* (IPM) 1975.
18. The Runnymede Trust, 'A Profile of Black Employment' in Braham P., Rhodes E., and Pearn M. (eds.), *Discrimination and Disadvantage in Employment* (Harper & Row) 1981, p. 97.
19. Incomes Data Services, *Handbook No. 4 The New Race Law and Employment* (Incomes Data Services) 1976, p. 7.

20. Connelly T.J., 'Racial Integration in Employment' in Torrington D.P. (ed.), *A Handbook of Industrial Relations* (Gower) 1972, pp. 194,5.
21. See for instance, Smith D.J., *Racial Disadvantage in Britain* (Penguin) 1977.
22. Commission for Racial Equality, *Equal Opportunities in Employment* and *Monitoring an Equal Opportunity Policy* (CRE) 1978.
23. Torrington D.P., Hitner T.J. and Knights D., *Management and the Multi-Racial Workforce* (Gower) 1982.
24. Broadhurst A., 'Disabled Persons and the Law' in *Industrial and Commercial Training,* December 1973.
25. Peach L.H., 'A Realistic Approach to Employing the Disabled' in *Personnel Management*, January 1981, pp. 18–21.
26. Megginson L.C., *Personnel: A Behavioural Approch to Administration* (Irwin)1972, pp. 235,6.

Section D
THE CONTRACT FOR INDIVIDUAL CONTROL

16

Authority and the Contract for Individual Control

The workplace of the individual is controlled by the decisions which are made on what to do, by what methods, for what purpose and within what time. We contend that this is an area of occupational life in which our notion of the contract is not only valid but also one where there seems to be the greatest degree of uncertainty.

Our focus is the *individual*. In this section of the book we are not investigating the collective aspects of exercising or challenging authority, but the one-to-one superior/subordinate relationship. We will not be entering the debates about power in organisations and in society, but feel it necessary to refer the reader to this area for further investigation. Organisational control as a school of thought is to be found in the work of Perrow[1] and Tannenbaum.[2] A different analysis is that of Cyert and March[3] with their notion of a 'dominant coalition'. Hyman and Brough[4] provide a more detached critique of power and its connection with inequality. Charles Handy has a most comprehensive and practical treatment of power and influence.[5]

Blau analyses authority as the legitimate exercise of power:

> Collective approval of power legitimates that power. People who consider that the advantages they gain from a superior's exercise of power outweigh the hardships that compliance with his demands imposes on them tend to communicate to each other their approval of the ruler and their feelings of obligation to him. The consensus that develops as a result of these communications finds expression in group pressures that promote compliance with the ruler's directive, thereby strengthening his power of control and legitimizing his authority.[6]

He later explains that authority can be destroyed by the reverse process involving collective disapproval or shared discontent. His work is useful both as an analysis of power and authority, and as a link between the collective and individual superior/subordinate power relations.

In Chapter 11 we summarised the legal basis of the contract of employment, which authorises the employer to give instructions to his employees. In organisations with more than a handful of employees there will be a chain of command in which superiors pass instructions on to subordinates. The subordinates will react to those instructions in ways which will satisfy or dissatisfy the superior. If he is dissatisfied he finds it easy to correct the situation — by, for instance, asking a typist to correct a spelling mistake in a letter she has typed — or he may find it virtually impossible because effective compliance cannot come from obeying orders – like the advertising agency executive who directed a copywriter to write about the latest hair spray with more 'conviction'.

The subordinate will be making competing bids for control of his own working situation. He will want to work at a pace that suits him, he will seek to have flexible meal breaks, his own choice of methods of working, the chance to 'produce' overtime or influence incentive earnings and so forth. These competing claims for control reach an accommodation in a form of contract between the superior and subordinate, although the superior is immeasurably more powerful, as we shall demonstrate.

Power and Authority in the Organisation

Man creates organisations as power systems, and the individuals who become employees of the organisation surrender a segment of their personal autonomy to become relatively weaker, making the organisation inordinately stronger. The benevolence of the organisation cannot be guaranteed, so man seeks to delimit its power in relation to himself.

Usually the authority to be exercised in an organisation is impersonalised by the use of *role* in order to make it more effective. New recruits to the armed services have an early lesson from their drill sergeant who points out to them a young and unimpressive officer in the distance with colourful, disparaging remarks about him as a *man* before the sergeant calls the recruits to attention and presents an immaculate salute to the *uniform* of the officer. Quality-assurance staff in factories (who are no longer called quality *controllers*) are likely to wear white coats and send unfavourable reports in writing so as to deploy the authority of their role rather than test the authority of their own selves.

Dependence on role is not always welcome to those in managerial positions, who are fond of using phrases like 'I can handle men', 'I understand my chaps', and 'I have a loyal staff'. Partly this may be due to their perception of their role as being to persuade the reluctant and command the respect of the unwilling by the use of personal charismatic qualities because there is no other source of authority in their position; therefore there is no other source of self-confidence.

The Milgram Experiments with Obedience

Obedience is the reaction expected of people by those in authority positions, who prescribe actions which otherwise may not necessarily have been carried out. Stanley Milgram[7] has conducted a series of experiments to investigate obedience to authority and has highlighted the significance of obedience and the power of authority in our everyday lives.

Subjects were led to believe that a study of memory and learning was being carried out which involved giving progressively more severe electric shocks to a learner when he produced incorrect answers. If the subject questioned the procedure he received a standard response from the authority figure conducting the experiment, viz:

(i) 'Please continue' or 'Please go on'.
(ii) 'The experiment requires that you continue'.
(iii) 'It is absolutely essential that you continue'.
(iv) 'You have no other choice: you must go on'.

These responses were given sequentially; (ii) only after (i) had failed, (iii) after (ii) and so on.

The 'learner' was not actually receiving shocks, but was a member of the experimental team simulating progressively greater distress as the shocks were made stronger. Eighteen different experiments were conducted with over a thousand subjects, with the circumstances varying between each experiment. No matter how the variables were altered the subjects showed an astonishing compliance with authority even when administering 'shocks' of 450 volts to a screaming victim. Up to 65 per cent of subjects continued to obey throughout the experiment in the presence of a clear authority figure and as many as 20 per cent continued to obey when the authority figure was absent.

Milgram has been extensively criticised for this study, largely because of questions about the ethics of requiring subjects to behave in such a distressing way, but we cannot evade the fact that he induced a high level of obedience from a large number of people who otherwise considered their actions to be wrong. Understandably the reaction of Milgram to his own results was of dismay, that:

> With numbing regularity good people were seen to knuckle under to the demands of authority and perform actions that were callous and severe. Men who are in everyday life responsible and decent were seduced by the trappings of authority, by the control of their perceptions, and by the uncritical acceptance of the experimenter's definition of the situation into performing harsh acts.[8]

Our interest in Milgram's work is simply to demonstrate that individuals have a predilection to obey instructions from authority figures, even if they do not want to.

Milgram explains the phenomenon of obedience for us by an argument which he summarised thus:

> (1) organised social life provides survival benefits to the individuals who are part of it, and to the group; (2) whatever behavioural and psychological features have been necessary to produce the capacity for *organised* social life have been shaped by evolutionary forces; (3) from the standpoint of cybernetics, the most general need in bringing self-regulating automata into a co-ordinated hierarchy is to suppress individual direction and control in favour of control from higher level components; (4) more generally, hierarchies can function only when internal modification occurs in the elements of which they are composed; (5) functional hierarchies in social life are characterised by each of these features, and (6) the individuals who enter into such hierarchies are, of necessity, modified in their functioning.[9]

He then points out that the act of entering a hierarchical system causes a man to see himself acting as an agent for carrying out the wishes of another person, and this results in the individual being in a different state, described as the *agentic state*. This is the opposite to the state of *autonomy* when a person sees himself as acting on his own. Milgram then sets out factors which lay the groundwork for obedience to authority.

(a) FAMILY

Parental regulation inculcates a respect for adult authority. Parental injunctions form the basis for moral imperatives as commands to children have a dual function. 'Don't tell lies' is a moral injunction carrying a further implicit instruction 'And obey me!' It is the implicit demand for obedience that remains the only consistent element across a range of explicit instructions.

(b) INSTITUTIONAL SETTING

The child emerges from the family into an institutional system of authority: the school. Here he learns how to function in an organisation. He is regulated by teachers but he can see that they themselves are regulated by headmaster, local authority and central government. Throughout this period he is in a subordinate position and when he goes to work he may find a certain level of dissent is allowable, but the overall situation is one in which he is to do a job prescribed by someone else.

(c) REWARDS

Compliance with authority is generally rewarded, while disobedience is frequently punished. Most significantly promotion within the hierarchy not only rewards the individual but ensures the continuity of the hierarchy.

(d) PERCEPTION OF AUTHORITY

Authority is normatively supported: there is a shared expectation among people that certain institutions do, ordinarily, have a socially controlling figure. Also the authority of the controlling figure is limited to the situation. The usher in a cinema wields authority which vanishes on leaving the premises. As authority is expected it does not have to be *asserted,* merely presented.

(e) ENTRY INTO THE AUTHORITY SYSTEM

Having perceived an authority figure, he must then be defined as relevant to the subject. The individual does not only take the voluntary step of deciding which authority system to join (at least in most of employment) he also defines which authority is relevant to which event. The fireman may expect instant obedience when he calls for everybody to evacuate the building but not if he asks employees to use a different accounting system.

(f) THE OVERARCHING IDEOLOGY

The legitimacy of the social situation relates to a justifying ideology. Science and education formed the background to the experiments Milgram conducted and therefore provided a justification for actions carried out in their name. Most employment is in realms of activity regarded as legitimate, justified by the values and needs of society. This is vital if the individual is to provide willing obedience, as it enables the obedient person to see his behaviour as serving a desirable end.

Legitimising Authority

All our discussion in the last few pages leads us to the assertion that employees are predisposed to obey rather than defy instructions from authority, providing that there are certain conditions like a hierarchical setting, identification of authority figures, a voluntary entry to the system and a justifying ideology. We can now look at some aspects of organisational life that can be developed in order to support the effective exercise of authority.

(a) THE CONTRACT PRINCIPLE

The main thrust of our argument in this book is the need for a series of contracts to which the parties are willing. The willing entrant to the authority system who regards his employment as legitimate will be predisposed to obey.

(b) COLLECTIVE CONSENT

The particular feature of the contract that was dealt with in the chapter on collective consent further legitimises the management of the organisation by providing the reassurance of some check on its activities.

(c) DISCIPLINARY PROCEDURES

Later in this section of the book we examine grievance and disciplinary procedures, which are a way of enabling authority to be perceived and of defining authority systems.

(d) JOB DESCRIPTIONS

Another way in which authority systems are defined is by the use of job descriptions which clarify the boundaries between different roles, confirming where particular segments of authority lie.

(e) JUSTIFICATION FOR ROLE INCUMBENTS

If organisations impersonalise authority by assigning it to those in roles, then the role incumbent has to be seen as justifying his tenure of the authority position by reference to *impersonal* qualities like experience, knowledge or qualification rather than to personal qualities like poise, understanding or 'the common touch'.

The crucial question here is whether the incumbent has a blend of *position* power and *expert* power that is appropriate. There is a strange tendency for managers to abandon their specialist (non-managerial) expertise as they rise through the management hierarchy in favour of more nebulous management expertise, so that they tend to lose the power of being *an* authority in favour of becoming someone *in* authority.[10]

Sources of Power and Influence

No matter how much we emphasise the impersonalisation of authority through role, it is evident to all of us that some authority figures are more effective than others in influencing the behaviour of others. Shortly we list some 'lineaments' of authority figures, but first we consider how French and Raven[11] identified five main bases of power to influence others. In the following summary the person seeking to wield influence is person A and the one to whom he is making the attempt is person B.

Base 1. Reward: the ability of A to control the incentives or rewards administered to B.

Base 2. Coercive: the ability A to provide penalties or punishments to B.

Base 3. Legitimate: where the influence of A is considered to be legitimately exercised and acceptable, due to common norms and values.

Base 4. Referent: where B wishes to identify with A.

Base 5. Expert: where B perceives A as being more knowledgeable on the subject about which the influence is exercised.

Ways in Which Authority is Demonstrated

The next two sections of this chapter are based on a small piece of unpublished research carried out by C.R. Bedford and L. Brown in 1976. It was designed to investigate perceptions of authority in everyday life expressed by sixty-five respondents in different groupings from schoolboys to pensioners. In analysing their results Bedford and Brown were able to derive a list of ways in which their respondents identified attempts by others to demonstrate an authority relationship.

(a) SPATIAL POSITION

Many situations present a space for the authority figure to occupy. Once the space is taken up the occupant becomes a focus for the expression of authority. The extremes are the conductor's rostrum, the pulpit, the head of the table or the referee's chair; but there are other spaces, like the separation of one desk in an open-plan office or the foreman's cubicle in the machine shop.

(b) TITLE

Titles can be explicit in that they define the precise position of the individual in the hierarchy — Commanding Officer, Second Ballerina, Despatcher, Secretary to the Managing Director — or they may be imprecise in a hierarchical sense but give credence to expertise — Professor, Doctor, Accountant, Chemist. Both are means of emphasising the role of the job holder.

(c) UNIFORM

One of the strongest of personal signals is the uniform that submerges the individuality and personality of the wearer while declaring the authority of his role. The extremes are the armed forces and the police, but there are many examples in organisational life. One of the most obvious is the white shirt and dark suit of the sales representative, the dirty overalls of the mechanic (anyone can have clean overalls), the dark coat of the toolmaker and the pristine white of the technician.

(d) SYMBOLS

Many accoutrements have a symbolic inference of authority and may be eagerly sought as a result. The busy and *important* manager carries with him a small radio transmitter when he tours the factory and it will squeak at him when he is wanted on the telephone. The slide rule, the pocket calculator, the short-hand notebook, the micrometer and keys all are attractive symbols of expertise or hierarchical status.

(e) DRESS

The researchers found some tendency to associate the style of dress with authority in that respondents expected authority figures to be conventionally dressed in a sober and smart manner. They did not regard authority as unacceptable if emanating from someone dressed differently; simply that they expected a particular, conventional type of dress.

(f) EQUIPMENT

A particular type of accoutrement that has connotations of authority is that of a functional nature which can be associated with the authority role. Part of the authority of the dentist is regarded as being the chair and associated paraphernalia, while there may be reservations about the psychiatrist because of his relative lack of equipment. Some people are more impressed by the systems analyst's computer than by the accountant's balance sheet.

(g) BACKGROUND ORGANISATION

Standing behind the individual in the authority role is the whole of the environment in which the authority operates. It includes sign boards, buildings, television commercials, offices, letter headings, furniture, location and all the other indicators by which organisations, as opposed to people, exhibit their power. An authority figure operating within the environment created by the organisation he represents will acquire some of the aura of authority created by that environment.

(h) PHYSIOLOGY

Some people expected authority figures to be taller, older and well-spoken. Tallness can be seen as enabling physical dominance while maturity is connected with the wish to see those holding authority positions as being expert with the associated assumption that wisdom increases with age. The view about people being well-spoken was partly a social class connection and partly an opinion that authority should be comprehensible.

Lineaments of Acceptable Authority Figures

Just as there is no single, generalised method of demonstrating authority, equally there is no single form of authority being exercised that finds universal acceptance. From the research, however, it was possible to derive a list of the attributes most frequently mentioned by respondents as enhancing the effectiveness of authority figures in making their authority more acceptable. The list is very similar to those that have been produced by generations of writers trying to define the ideal leader.

(a) CONSISTENTLY FAIR IN DEALINGS WITH OTHERS

This was mentioned so often by respondents that it could almost be considered as an ideology for anyone exercising authority. People seemed willing to forgive much for the sake of consistency so that they knew accurately where they stood. This protects the individual from the whim of the superior. In tribunal and similar cases on dismissal, equal pay and sex discrimination we can see the principle of consistency dominating the judgements that are produced.

(b) EXPERT IN THE FIELD

Compliance with authority usually stems from some power to coerce, although this is seldom welcomed. An alternative or complementary basis for authority is knowledge, and superiors who were regarded as expert were also described as people whose instructions would be accepted rather than questioned, with the expertise being in a specific area, different from general wisdom. None of the respondents described expertise as being 'the ability to handle folk' or 'knowing what makes people tick'.

(c) MATURE

Different from expertise was an appreciation of experience, and here there was some flavour of wordly-wisdom in the attribute that was being described, although 'mature' was the word used most frequently. Respondents were willing to entrust themselves to decisions by, and instructions from, those who had a store of experience to temper their judgement.

(d) POISE

A quality frequently described in an acceptable authority figure was self-confidence or poise, so that respondents felt their uncertainty or doubt about the wisdom of a proposed course of action being removed by the sheer confidence of the way in which it was expressed. This particularly related to matters where there was an apparent complexity that was difficult to unravel or where there was little to choose between one line of action and another. It indicated the extent to which people saw themselves as dependent on authority for clarification and support in the face of dilemmas. A similar point has been made by some observers (for instance, Sidney, Brown and Argyle[12]) about effectiveness in interpersonal behaviour.

(e) LACK OF PREJUDICE

Not only did respondents emphasise the desire to see authority behaving consistently in all dealings with others, they also sought an unprejudiced approach. A matter should not be approached with a set of assumptions about the appropriate decision, but rather with an open mind in order to decide on the merits of individual situations.

(f) CONSIDERATE BUT NOT FRIENDLY

There was general, if not unanimous, support for authority being dispensed by someone who maintained a judicious degree of social distance from those subject to his authority. This was described as a somewhat paternalistic consideration for the well-being of his subjects without being too friendly with them. This attitude was further delineated as involving a degree of polite formality in exchanges between the parties without losing accessibility. The majority of the respondents thought that a difference in modes of address was desirable: 'I like him to call me Fred, but I don't want to call him Charlie.'

(g) CLEARLY SPOKEN

A surprising attribute mentioned was the need for the person exercising authority to speak clearly. This stemmed from various reasons. One was the wish to receive instructions that could be understood and another was a wish by some to receive instructions that were precise to the point of removing any potential initiative from the recipient, but some people expressed irritation about superiors who disguised their own lack of confidence by giving instructions that were equivocal or vague. A further problem manifesting itself under this heading was jargon and technical language, often seen as a smokescreen to protect insubstantial authority from disagreement.

(h) RESPONSIBLE

Those receiving commands from authority like to feel that the person issuing the instructions is willing to be held responsible for the decisions he makes, so that if anything goes wrong and the decision has to be modified the locus of responsibility is clear and action will be taken. There were a number of cynical comments about buck-passing and one neat opinion:

> 'It is bad enough trying to get a decision: usually no-one will give you one, and you can be damned sure that no-one will have it back when it turns sour.'

The Other Side of the Bargain

This chapter has so far considered the reaction of the individual to authority from those seeking to control his activities and has suggested how the prospective controllers may approach their function. What is the other side of the contract? In what way does the subordinate control authority meted out to him?

Whatever the legal standing of the contract of employment document and its implied terms, the individual employee has a degree of control over his own place of work that will be greater than a strict interpretation of the law permits and greater than is usually perceived.

The more sophisticated the level of knowledge the worker deploys in his duties, the greater degree of control he will have over the organisation of his work. The performance desired by superordinates will require willing co-operation, initiative, commitment and enthusiasm. These are incompatible with any form of compulsion. The desire of managers to control the managed has produced a range of devices to limit the scope for the individual to control his own work situation. Most obvious is the use of schemes of performance appraisal, and management by objectives (see Chapter 28). In both of these arrangements employees yield up a degree of control or scope in setting and changing personal objectives in return for information that is always most anxiously sought: 'How am I getting on?' In recent years there have been a growing number of examples, particularly in public sector employment, of performance appraisal schemes not being implemented because of union resistance.

More recent and more substantial support for the control by the individual of his own place of work is that stemming from legislation. Employers now have a legal duty to open up grievance channels through which employees can challenge managerial decisions, and there is an increasing floor of employment rights for the individual.

In the remaining chapters of this section of the book we discuss various dimensions to the contract for individual control. Our next chapter deals with the subject that has long loomed large in the management literature: leadership, which includes ways to support the compliance of subordinates with the objectives of the organisation as described by the management. The grievance and disciplinary processes are the subject of Chapter 18, in which we examine the procedural arrangements whereby one or the other party to the employment contract can try and restore a 'good fit' when there is a breakdown. Our interaction episode is the interview that takes place within that procedural framework. Then we have a chapter on dismissal and one on working safely in healthy conditions.

SUMMARY PROPOSITIONS

16.1.   Superior and subordinate make competing bids for control of the working
        situation, but the superior usually has greater power in the competition.

16.2.   Authority within organisations is generally more dependent on formal role
        or position in the hierarchy than on personality.

16.3.   An effective superior will exercise authority derived from his positional
        power, together with that derived from his personal qualities, in relation to
        the needs and expectations of his subordinates, who will accept his authority
        as legitimate.

REFERENCES

1. Perrow C., *Complex Organisations* (Illinois) 1972.
2. Tannenbaum A.S., *Control in Organisations* (McGraw-Hill) 1968.
3. Cyert R.H. and March J.G., *A Behavioural Theory of the Firm* (Prentice-Hall) 1963.
4. Hyman R. and Brough I., *Social Values and Industrial Relations* (Blackwell) 1975, especially
    pp. 184–228.
5. Handy C.B., *Understanding Organizations* (Penguin Books) 1976, especially pp. 111–144.
6. Blau P.M., *Exchange and Power in Social Life* (Wiley) 1964.
7. Milgram S., *Obedience to Authority* (Tavistock) 1974.
8. *Ibid.*, p. 123.
9. *Ibid.*, p. 132.
10. Torrington D.P. and Weightman J.B., 'Technical Atrophy in Middle Management' in
    Journal of General Management, Summer 1982.
11. French W.L. and Raven S., 'The Bases of Social Power' in Cartwright D. (ed.) *Studies in
    Social Power* (Michigan) 1959.
12. Sidney E., Brown M. and Argyle M., *Skills with People* (Hutchinson) 1973, pp. 11–30.

17

Leadership

In the contract for individual control managers seeking the compliance of others frequently attempt to do this by exercising leadership. It does not sound so heavy-handed as authority and implies that effectiveness derives from personal qualities rather than role. Its importance to our discussion is that leadership depends on voluntary response from the followers.

There has been extensive research, which is usefully summarised in the work of Stogdill,[1] Gibb[2] and Bass,[3] and a range of theoretical perspectives has been developed.

Definitions of leadership vary according to the theoretical perspective adopted and Stogdill has observed:

> there are almost as many different definitions of leadership as there are persons who have attempted to define the concept.[4]

A more general definition is distilled by Tannenbaum *et al* as a process of

> Interpersonal influence exercised in situation and directed, through the communication process, towards the attainment of a specified goal or goals.[5]

This definition is generally acceptable today and embodies the key concepts, although individual theoretical viewpoints may elaborate further.

Thus a leader is a person who exerts a dominant influence, in an interpersonal or group situation, over other individuals and directs their behaviour towards the accomplishment of goals. He may exercise leadership by formal appointment or by the voluntary consent of others, on a temporary or relatively permanent basis, and in any specific relationship the roles of leader and follower may vary over time. Furthermore, a view of leadership as involving process or function, rather than a prescribed role, permits the notion of shared leadership in a group setting.

The terms 'leader', 'manager' and 'supervisor' are sometimes used interchangeably but they are not synonymous.

A foreman or supervisor is usually viewed as the first level of management, an organisational position involving the direct supervision of workers, whilst a manager is an organisational position responsible for the activities of lower levels of management, although occasionally the title is applied to specialists without responsibility for the behaviour of others. The occupants of these positions are usually expected to exercise leadership of others towards organisational goals. The effectiveness of their leadership behaviour will vary and leadership is only one way in which the manager or supervisor contributes to organisational effectiveness.

His duties will include liaison and co-ordination with other units, obtaining resources and maintaining records, but leadership remains a central feature. In a comprehensive analysis of managerial activities, Mintzberg is quite explicit:

> leadership permeates all activities; its importance would be underestimated if it were judged in terms of the proportion of a manager's activities that are strictly related to leadership.[6]

A manager's effectiveness is usually evaluated in terms of the achievement of his unit (e.g. units produced, sales achieved, profit level), but this does not necessarily show his leadership effectiveness since bias may be introduced by other factors such as the age of machinery, sales territory or the quality of subordinates.

OVERVIEW OF LEADERSHIP RESEARCH

Dissatisfaction with the current state of leadership theory is summarised in a recent review by Schriesheim and Kerr:

> We are without instruments with demonstrated reliability, validity, etc., we seem to test only one or two 'dominant' theories (and ignore all others) and even our 'dominant' theories suffer from problems of theoretical inadequacy ... until new or improved theories are developed, we shall not be able to integrate whatever findings we obtain.[7]

Leadership research currently has a major focus on several dominant theories – outlined below as interaction approaches. However, some more complex theories are being developed which attempt to integrate and build upon the diversity of past research. This involves recognising leadership as multidimensional, with personal and situational variables, and involving complex, dynamic interactions between such variables.

Most theoretical formulations in leadership research have been directed towards practical organisational applications, notably:

(i) Selection of individuals likely to be effective in organisational leadership positions.
(ii) Placement of individuals in organisational positions where they will develop their leadership potential.
(iii) Training individuals in effective leadership behaviour, thus requiring the identification of such behaviour.
(iv) Organisational engineering of situational variables surrounding a given position, to facilitate effective leadership behaviour by the incumbent of that position.

The variety of theoretical perspectives and methodology has presented problems of interpretation and integration. The current position is disappointing for most organisational applications. The least disappointment is in training, where research has indicated fruitful areas of education and behaviour to develop the effectivness of individuals in their exercise of leadership functions.

Figure 17.1 shows a simplified overview of the major theoretical perspectives

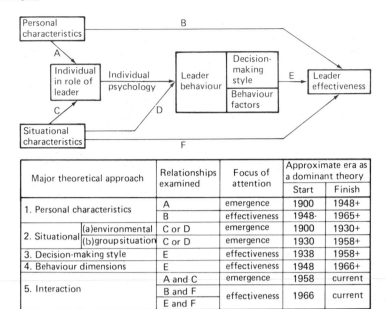

Figure 17.1. An overview of major theoretical approaches to the study of leadership

and relationships examined. The diagram indicates the main variables involved in the process of leadership: an individual occupying a leader role, the situational context in which leadership is exercised, and the effectiveness of the leader in that situation. Any individual brings with him particular personal characteristics, both physical and psychological, and exhibits observable behaviour which may be more or less effective than that of another individual occupying the same role.

Research has usually focused upon either *emergence*, the factors leading to the individual occupying a leader role, or *effectiveness,* the factors which distinguish between more or less effective leaders. Some studies have examined initially leaderless groups, whilst many have taken an organisational position as indicative of leadership — which may or may not involve leadership, as indicated above, since emergence or occupancy of the role may be determined by 'non-leadership' factors such as technical qualifications, patronage or performance in a different role context.

Five general theoretical approaches are shown, based on an implicit or explicit assumption of relationship between classes of variable. The first four approaches dominated past research in the eras shown — the end points being derived from important publications which led many researchers towards a different perspective. Finally we identify the interaction approach, which views leadership as an interaction between personal characteristics and situational variables. This is currently dominant.

We will now outline some of the major contributions to leadership research, under each theoretical approach indicated in Figure 17.1.

1. Personal Characteristics Approach

Historical and biographical studies of 'Great Men' created a general assumption that such individuals possessed personal qualities of physique, intellect or personality which differentiated them from the many. With the development of the science of psychology, *circa* 1900, it is not surprising that considerable attention was devoted to identifying and measuring individual differences between leaders and non-leaders.

The emphasis was to identify leaders who were viewed as successful, using criteria which seemed appropriate to the researcher, and then to identify the particular characteristics appearing to determine success. Some researchers studied *emergence* by measuring success as achieving a leader role, others studied *effectiveness* by using organisational indicators of success, whilst confusion was added by researchers studying one and interpreting results in terms of the other.

Several reviews attempted to evaluate the research generally by comparing and analysing the diverse findings, including the following:

(a) STOGDILL (1948)

The most influential widely quoted review was Stogdill,[8] following analysis of 124 studies. Several factors were considered to be positively associated with leadership positions, as shown in Figure 17.2. This particular review marks the decline of the personnel characteristics approach in favour of viewing leadership as a social process relating characteristics of individuals to situations. However, subsequent reviews were still able to incorporate additional research concerned with personal characteristics.

Classification	Factors associated with occupancy of leader role
1. Capacity	intelligence, alertness, verbal facility, originality, judgement
2. Achievement	scholarship, knowledge, athletic accomplishments
3. Responsibility	dependability, initiative, persistence, aggressiveness, self-confidence, desire to excel
4. Participation	activity, sociability, co-operation, adaptability, humour
5. Status	socio-economic position, popularity
6. Situation	mental level, status, skills, needs and interests of followers; objectives to be achieved, etc.

Figure 17.2. A summary of Stogdill's 1948 review findings

(b) OTHER REVIEWS

A review of the relationship between personality factors and group performance was reported by Mann[9] in 1959, finding that several factors were positively associated with leadership in 71 to 80 per cent of the studies examining these factors. Correlation with leadership was extremely significant and positive for some personal characteristics (intelligence, adjustment and extroversion), positive for others (dominance masculinity, interpersonal sensitivity), and negative for conservatism.

Gibb concluded that:

numerous studies of the personalities of leaders have failed to find any consistent pattern of traits which characterise leaders.[10]

One potential explanation of this failure was that combining studies of different types of group may obscure relationships which could exist within relatively homogeneous groups or situations. To examine this possibility several studies examined the performance of effective and less effective managers.

Dunette[11] suggested that the effective manager has a forceful, dominant personality and tends to be intelligent and high in needs for achievement, power, autonomy and money. Ghiselli[12] and his associates consider that the traits of intelligence, supervisory ability, initiative, self-assurance and perceived occupational level differentiate between successful and less successful managers.

(c) STOGDILL (1974) REVIEW

This later review considered research since his 1948 review and combined the results as indicated in Figure 17.3.

General clusters of personality characteristics	Differentiations provided
1. Strong drive for responsibility	These clusters of characteristics are considered to differentiate:
2. Strong drive for task completion	
3. Vigour and persistence in pursuit of goals	
4. Venturesomeness and originality in problem solving	(1) Leaders from Followers
5. Drive to exercise initiative in social situations	(2) Effective from Ineffective leaders
6. Self-confidence and sense of personal identity	
7. Willingness to accept consequence of decision and action	(3) Higher Echelon from Lower Echelon leaders
8. Readiness to absorb interpersonal stress	
9. Willingness to tolerate frustration and delay	
10. Ability to influence other person's behaviour	
11. Capacity to structure social interaction systems to purpose	

Figure 17.3. A summary of Stogdill's 1974 review findings

His review concludes that:

> the characteristics, considered singly, hold little diagnostic or predictive significance. In combination it would appear that they interact to generate personality dynamics advantageous to the person seeking the responsibilities of leadership.[13]

The conclusion of an examination of 'personal characteristics' research must be that such characteristics alone have limited usefulness in prediction of a person's leadership potential. Clearly the dynamics of personality interact with other characteristics of the situational context to determine the emergence or effectiveness of leaders.

2. Situational Approach

Another early approach also derived from historical and biographical analyses of
'Great Men' which suggested that such people were an expression of the needs of
their time. The assumption of the 'environmental approach' was that if a particular
individual had not fulfilled the needs of that social context, then another individual
would emerge to do so. This approach was not influential, as leadership was generally viewed as reflecting qualities of individual people.

With the growth of interest in Social Psychology and Group Dynamics in the
1930s a modified 'group situation' approach is clearly evident. Whilst some studies
focus on the personal characteristics of leaders, many researchers adopt an overriding perspective which views leadership as emerging from group processes. This
viewpoint is clearly illustrated by Gibb,[14] who differentiates between 'leadership'
and 'headship' — the former a function of group processes and the latter referring
to occupancy of an organisational role determined from outside the group.

Our view is that such a distinction is misleading, arising from the methodology
used in group dynamics research. In an effort to create conditions akin to those of a
laboratory, many researchers studied initially leaderless groups — thus it is hardly
surprising that studies based upon leader emergence should emphasise features of
the group situation or context. To distinguish between leadership and headship is to
suggest that managers, whose source of status and influence is outside the group, are
not exercising leadership. This narrow view of leadership is not generally accepted
and our view of leadership as a process of interpersonal influence recognises the importance of group situational factors, including the source of influence and status,
in determining the limits or degree of acceptance of the leader's authority and
influence. The distinction also obscures the fact that such research has generated
much knowledge which is useful for the education and training of managers.

An important body of research has been conducted by Bales and his associates at
Harvard, studying small group behaviour. Bales and Slater[15] reported a study of
thirty five-member experimental groups involved in problem solving. They showed
that two separate leaders tend to emerge. The 'task specialist' has high task ability
and is active in assisting others to achieve the group problem-solving goals, whilst
the 'social-emotional' specialist has high likeability and is active in establishing and
maintaining cordial and socially satisfying relationships. They consider it rare for
any one person to combine high task ability with high likeability and so satisfy both
the task and social needs of the group.

Subsequent research has identified types of behaviour which facilitate the task
activities of groups, and others which maintain the group as an effective social unit.
These behaviours are discussed in the survey by Collins and Guetzkow[16] and have
obvious implications for management training in the awareness and practice of
effective behaviour for leading groups in task activities and developing the group as
a co-operative social unit.

An understanding of the dynamics of group interaction, decision making and
problem solving can be found in books by Cartwright and Zander[17] and Shaw,[18]
which provide surveys of group dynamics research and theory. These insights are
valuable to managers in exercising their leadership functions with subordinates, and
in relation to their contributions as members of other groups.

3. Decision-making Style Approach

The originator of the 'decision-making style' approach is Lewin, who conducted his famous studies with White and Lippitt,[19] starting in 1938 by organising boys' clubs and subjecting these to three leadership styles.

The styles were carefully specified and each researcher operated the styles with different groups, observing the member reactions. With the 'authoritarian' style the leader controlled and directed all activities, the 'democratic' style emphasised group discussion and shared decision making, whilst the *'laissez-faire'* style had no participation by the leader. The authoritarian style produced hostility, and discontent among members, discouraged individuality and encouraged dependence. It was clearly the least-liked style. The democratic style was the most popular, encouraging group mindedness, friendliness and motivation to work. *Laissez-faire* was less popular than democratic and characterised by less work of poorer quality. Group productivity was slightly greater for the authoritarian style than the democratic, but the latter was viewed as potentially efficient because of greater interest, motivation and originality demonstrated.

Gradually a view became widely adopted that a democratic style was ideal for all situations. The implication was that managers trained to adopt such a style would be more effective because team spirit, member satisfaction and group productivity would all improve.

Stogdill[20] examines many of the studies of leadership styles which are 'person oriented' or 'work oriented'. We have summarised and adapted this data in Figure 17.4, the numbers referring to studies identifying the associations indicated.

'Person oriented' styles are clearly associated with member satisfaction. Such styles also appear to foster team spirit. For productivity, however, the association is less certain, indicating that this more common indicator of leader effectiveness involves an interaction of leader style with situational variables.

Many business decisions require acceptance by those responsible for efficient execution or implementation, whilst other decisions involve less need for acceptance. Also there are many problems where the manager has insufficient time for group decisions to be practical, or where he has insufficient knowledge and needs the involvement of subordinates. Maier[21] is quite clear that the effective manager utilises a variety of styles for the particular needs of the situational context. This is early advocacy of what we now refer to as an 'interaction approach'.

It is the classic paper by Tannenbaum and Schmidt[22] that provides the most influential advocacy of an 'interaction approach'. They identify a range of styles and the various combinations of managerial authority and subordinate freedom from which a leader may select his behaviour. Figure 17.5 illustrates the continuum of decision-making styles identified.

The appropriate choice of style depends upon three classes of variables — personal characteristics of the manager, personal characteristics of the subordinates and characteristics of the situation (time, problem, work group and organisational variables). The effective manager is aware of the forces relevant to his behaviour, is able to select the most appropriate style, and is flexible enough to be able to behave accordingly. Figure 17.6 provides a pictorial representation of the factors which Tannenbaum and Schmidt considered important within these three classes of variable.

Variable	Productivity			Follower satisfaction			Group cohesiveness		
Direction of relationships	Pos. (+)	Zero. (0)	Neg. (−)	Pos. (+)	Zero. (0)	Neg. (−)	Pos. (+)	Zero. (0)	Neg. (−)
Leadership style									
person oriented Democratic	3	11	−	7	1	1	2	1	−
Permissive	7	3	4	8	2	3	2	1	3
Follower oriented	19	5	4	13	2	1	3	−	2
Participative	10	5	3	8	3	1	8	2	1
Considerate	8	8	3	12	1	1	5	1	−
Totals	47	32	14	48	9	7	20	5	6
work oriented Autocratic	3	10	1	−	1	3	−	1	2
Restrictive	2	3	1	−	−	3	−	1	−
Task-oriented	3	3	3	2	1	1	−	1	−
Socially distant	16	1	1	−	1	1	1	1	−
Di.ective	10	4	1	2	2	2	2	−	1
Structured	13	5	−	10	3	1	6	−	−
Totals	47	26	7	14	8	11	9	4	3

Figure 17.4. Associations with leadership style (adapted from Stogdill (1974))

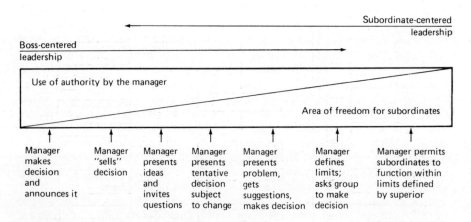

(A)   The decision-making style continuum

Reprinted by permission of the Harvard Business Review. Exhibit 1 from 'How to Choose a Leadership Pattern' by Robert Tannenbaum and Warren H. Schmidt, May–June 1973. Copyright © by the President and Fellows of Harvard College; all rights reserved.

Figure 17.5. The Tannenbaum–Schmidt continuum of decision-making styles

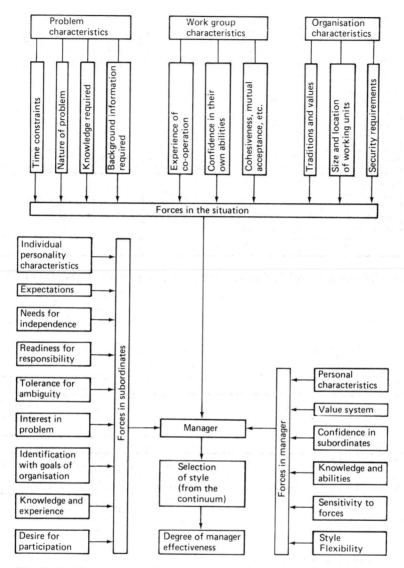

(B)   A pictorial representation of the analytical discussion

Figure 17.6. A pictorial representation of the Tannenbaum—Schmidt analysis of influences upon style selection

4. Behaviour Dimensions Approach

The lack of success of the 'personal characteristics' approach led to several research programmes being directed towards the identification of behaviour dimensions to distinguish between effective and less effective leaders. The major programmes are summarised below:

(a) OHIO STATE UNIVERSITY STUDIES

The research developed general measures of manager behaviour and is described in a collection of papers published by Stogdill and Coons[23] in 1957.

Fleishman devised a 150-item questionnaire – the leader behaviour description questionnaire (LBDQ) – which measured nine dimensions: initiation, communication, production emphasis, representation, fraternisation, organisation, evaluation, initiation and domination. Halpin and Winer conducted a factor analytical study and found that four dimensions covered the behaviour sample provided by the LBDQ. Their findings are summarised in Figure 17.7. Because the two dimensions,

Behaviour measured by LBDQ		Percentage of total variance accounted for by dimension	
Dimension	Brief behaviour description		
Consideration	Behaviour indicative of friendship, mutual trust, respect and warmth	49.6%	83.2%
Initiating structure	Behaviour that organises and defines relationships and roles, establishes well-defined patterns of organisation, communication and ways of getting job done	33.6%	
Production emphasis	Behaviour which makes up a manner of motivating the group to work by emphasising the mission or job to be done	9.8%	16.8%
Sensitivity	Social awareness and sensitivity of the leader to social inter-relationships and pressures inside or outside the group	7.0%	

Figure 17.7. Summary of results of Halpin and Winer study[29]

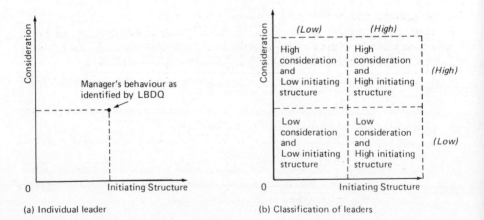

Figure 17.8. Two-dimensional representation of leader behaviour

consideration and initiating structure, account for most of the variance, many subsequent researchers have utilised a two-dimensional representation, as indicated in Figure 17.8.

Fleishman and Harris[24] examined the relationship between these dimensions and satisfaction, labour grievances and labour turnover. Both high turnover and grievances were related to supervisors showing low consideration or high structure or a combination of both, but high consideration leaders could sharply increase structuring behaviour with only marginal impact. Member satisfaction was related to high consideration, a finding confirmed by most other studies.

(b) MICHIGAN STUDIES

A similar research programme was undertaken by the Survey Research Center of the University of Michigan.[25] Studying a variety of organisations they found that supervisors of high producing departments tended to exhibit behaviour characterised as 'employee centred', whilst supervisors of low producing departments exhibited 'production-centred' behaviour, the former involving consideration and concern for subordinates whilst the latter emphasised close supervision and direction towards task activities.

The findings originally were conceptualised as a unidimensional behaviour continuum of leader effectiveness, from 'employee-centred' (most effective) to 'production centred' (least effective). In 1960 they were re-cast as two independent dimensions, recognising that supervisors could exhibit varying degrees of both types of behaviour. Thus the result was a two-dimensional representation of leader behaviour, similar to the findings of the Ohio State studies.

(c) BLAKE AND MOUTON — THE MANAGERIAL GRID

A book by Blake and Mouton[26] developed a framework for classifying managerial styles, using the dimensions 'concern for people' and 'concern for production'. The 'ideal style' is clearly that of the manager high (on a nine-point scale) on each of the two dimensions. A comprehensive training programme was offered for manager development aimed at changing behaviour to this ideal style, thus suggesting that managers can and should improve their style in order to improve their effectiveness.

(d) BOWERS AND SEASHORE — FOUR FACTOR THEORY

In their classic paper, Bowers and Seashore[27] review the research on leader behaviour generally with a view to integration in a common framework. They identify four factors which appear to comprise the basic structure of leadership.

  (i) *Support.* Behaviour which emphasises someone else's feeling of personal worth and importance.
 (ii) *Interaction Facilitation.* Behaviour that encourages members of the group to develop close, mutually satisfying relationships.
(iii) *Goal emphasis.* Behaviour that stimulates an enthusiasm for meeting the group's goal or achieving excellent performance.
 (iv) *Work facilitation.* Behaviour that helps achieve goal attainment by such activities such as scheduling, co-ordinating, planning, and by providing resources such as tools, materials and technical knowledge.

Developing measures of these behavioural factors they investigated a variety of assumptions and relationships. Whilst establishing the usefulness of the dimensions, their general conclusion was that a theory of leadership conceived in terms of leader behaviour alone is insufficient to predict effectiveness. Additional and/or intervening constructs are required to improve prediction. They identify three distinct types of additional construct — leadership related (e.g. expert power, influence and acceptance), work patterns, personal and motivational (relating to manager, his subordinates and the organisation generally). A consequence of this study and others referred to earlier, was to direct the mainstream of leadership research towards more complex and integrative theories of the determinants of leadership effectiveness.

5. Interaction Approach

The common perspective of current theories of leadership is that the effectiveness of leaders is not determined solely by their personal characteristics or behaviour, nor by the characteristics of the situation, but by the interaction of all these.

Whilst sharing a common overall perspective, wide differences in approach and subsidiary assumptions are apparent. All attempt to integrate past research, at least to some extent, but some utilise simplistic analytical frameworks whilst others attempt to come to terms with the demonstrated complexities of influencing leadership effectiveness. Difference conceptualisations of leader behaviour or style are utilised, and different assumptions are made about the relative rigidity or flexibility of such behaviour. Even greater differences are apparent in the identification of situational variables, and assumptions about their relative importance and variability. Some of the more influential current approaches to leadership include:

(a) TANNENBAUM AND SCHMIDT — CONCEPTUAL FRAMEWORK

Tannenbaum's work, which was discussed earlier in this chapter, was subsequently revised in 1973.[28] This later view recognises additional factors involved — the societal and organisational environments, relative power of subordinates and leaders, and the interrelationships between all the different classes of variable. Strictly speaking this is not a theory of leadership, but a combination of diagnostic model and conceptual framework which integrates diverse research findings, analysing the determinants of leader effectiveness. It has been influential upon much research and management training, because of its simple analysis of a complex and dynamic interaction of leader characteristics and the situational variables.

(b) FIEDLER — CONTINGENCY THEORY

An early interaction theory was presented by Fiedler in 1967, based upon his earlier research since 1951.[29] Much of this research was focused on a particular measuring instrument which, in its current form, consists of sixteen bipolar adjectival scales (e.g. pleasant — unpleasant), each with an eight-point rating scale, on which the individual evaluates his least preferred co-worker (LPC). Initially conceived as a personality measure, the LPC score was redefined as an indicator of leadership style.

The research indicated that high LPC leaders were more considerate and their groups were lower in anxiety, with more harmonious relationships and the members more satisfied. Low LPC leaders were considered to be more concerned with tasks, more punitive towards poor co-workers, with more efficient and goal oriented behaviour. Thus Fiedler considers that a high LPC leader gains his major satisfaction from successful interpersonal relations, whilst the low LPC leader derives his major satisfaction from task performance — the 'style' being relatively permanent and difficult to change in any individual.

The theory was based upon a typology of situations measured upon three dimensions: task structure, leader–member relations and position power. These situation types were identified with a composite scale of 'favourableness of the situation' to the leader. A low LPC (task oriented) style was viewed as most effective in most and least favourable situations, whilst high LPC (human relations oriented) was most effective in intermediate situations. Fiedler provides a theory and measuring instruments which he considers sufficiently developed for practical application. Using the LPC measure he suggests that organisations can select or place individuals according to the situational conditions measured or, as style is difficult to modify by training, by 'organisational engineering' the situation can be modified to suit the leader. A subsequent publication[30] in 1974 developed further aspects of the theory and reported evidence from subsequent research.

Fiedler et al[31] have now introduced the Leader Match Concept, essentially a programmed self-teaching manual with questionnaires to enable individuals to identify their own LPC style and the dimensions of their job. The manual teaches the theory and how to diagnose situations, and how to change aspects to optimise the style/situation match to maximise leader effectiveness. Support for this approach is reported by Fiedler and Mahar[32] but much independent research is critical of the theory and its application in practice.

Ashour[33] provides a critical evaluation whilst Graen et al[34,35] criticise the research strategy, the statistical analysis, limited number of statistically significant results, failure to meet scientific standards of reliability, and unsatisfactory features of the studies used to validate the theory. The reliability and validity of the LPC measure is strongly criticised by Schriesheim and colleagues[36,37] and by other researchers. Other critiques have focused upon the measures and definition of situations, relation of LPC to other measures, and the value of LPC as an indicator of leader behaviour. The most favourable verdict at present is that many serious criticisms remain to be answered before we would recommend any practical application of this theory.

(c) THREE DIMENSIONAL THEORIES OF LEADER EFFECTIVENESS

We have referred to Blake and Mouton, who utilised a two-dimensional analysis as a basis for integrating much previous research, incorporating this in a training programme designed to develop an 'ideal style' of leader behaviour. Subsequently[36] they added a third dimension of effectiveness, based on the ability to maintain a given style under pressure. By the mid-1960s, however, a substantial body of research seriously questioned notions of an ideal style, suggesting that effective leader behaviour involved a need to develop flexibility or otherwise achieve an appropriate interaction with the needs of specific situations.

Two current theories both use a two-dimensional representation of leader style, adding a third dimension of effectiveness by which behaviour is related to situational variables. This integrates a variety of previous research in leadership and organisational behaviour, provides the basis for a style diagnosis measuring instrument and a training programme for management development.

The emphasis of training is on diagnosing situational variables and demands, developing flexibility and matching behaviour to the circumstances of particular situations.

Credit for the first such theory must go to W. J. Reddin, who published papers in 1966[37] and 1967[38] outlining key features of what he termed the '3–D Theory of Managerial Effectiveness'. A subsequent book[39] elaborated on the theoretical framework.

A second theory was introduced in 1969 by Hersey and Blanchard[40] as 'Life Cycle Theory of Leadership', later retitled but based upon the 'Tridimensional Leader Effectiveness Model'. Whilst recognising the influence of Reddin's work, they consider their approach to represent a separate theory. Their measuring instrument is different, as is their analysis in many respects, but the broad approach is sufficiently similar for us to outline the key features of both simultaneously.

Figure 17.9 is a diagrammatic representation of the basic elements of both conceptual frameworks. Basic styles are determined by two dimensions of behaviour, which are then related by an analysis of situational variables to circumstances

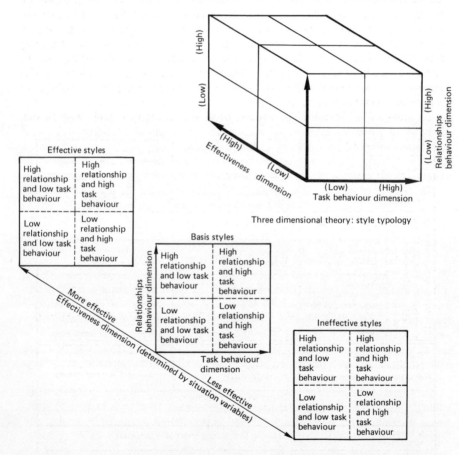

Figure 17.9. Three-dimensional theories: a diagrammatic representation of key elements

where each style is more or less effective. This results in a three-dimensional style typology which is related to the measuring instrument developed to match the individual theories.

Figure 17.10 extends the analysis comparing the principal features of both theories. Reddin's behaviour dimensions are said to represent a synthesis of several different approaches, whilst Hersey and Blanchard base their dimensions upon the Ohio State research programme. The situational variables related to effectiveness are essentially similar, comprising group member factors and other more general classes.

Using the relevant measuring instrument, managers are provided with a diagnosis of their personal style, including a profile of the eight styles identified, ability to vary behaviour and relative use of different styles.

A number of criticisms can be made. The effectiveness dimension is determined by theoretical analysis, albeit based upon research evidence, thus involving individual judgement of the situational variables. Ideally direct measurement would permit the effectiveness dimension to be tested. The other dimensions are also suspect, first because they represent perceptions of behaviour rather than actual behaviour and secondly because previous research has shown other aspects of behaviour to be important. However, the main criticism must be directed at the measuring instruments, which cover selected examples of situations that may or may not be relevant to the individuals concerned. More importantly the test development also appears to be judgemental and little or no data upon interpretation, reliability or validity has been published.

As theories of leader effectiveness, both are incomplete and need further

Factors included in theory and measuring instrument		3–D Theory by W J Reddin	Tri-dimensional theory by Hersey and Blanchard
Leader style or behaviour dimensions		(1) Task orientation (2) Relationships orientation	(1) Task behaviour (2) Relationships behaviour
(3) Effectiveness dimension. Environment and situational variables influencing effectiveness of behaviour	Group members	Subordinates	Followers
	Other role interactions	Co-workers Superiors	Associates Superiors
	General organisational climate	Organisational philosophy	Organisational values and goals
	Technical factors	Technology	Job demands Other variables (technical)
Diagnosis factors for examining style of leader or manager		Style profile Style flex Style synthesis	Style range Style adaptability Dominant and supporting style(s)
Key features of theory		Diagnosis of situational demands Matching style to situation Integration of previous research	
Intended theory application		Training and development of managers	

Figure 17.10. Principal features of three-dimensional theories

research and development. We would not consider either to be suitable as a basis for placement of individuals in organisational positions. Whilst the authors do not make claims to such applications, any claim to present a theory of leader effectiveness should assist with such problems and is likely to be so utilised by organisations.

We would favour the Hersey and Blanchard approach because their book, currently in its third edition, incorporates a wider range of research into organisational behaviour and provides greater detail of analysis of situations. In addition their measuring instrument is published, making it available for testing by others, their work thus lends itself to self-development and adoption in training programmes other than those conducted by the designers.

(d) VROOM—YETTON NORMATIVE MODEL OF DECISION-MAKING BEHAVIOUR

A completely different approach to leadership effectiveness has been described by Vroom and Yetton,[41] based upon a research review and programme commenced in 1968. Their intention was to develop a normative model of decision-making behaviour which would be of practical use to managers.

Effectiveness of decisions is defined in terms of three criteria: (1) the technical quality or rationality of decisions; (2) the acceptance or commitment by subordinates to executing decisions effectively, and (3) the time required to make the decision. Leader behaviour is defined in a taxonomy of decision-making process or styles, based on the relative participation of leader and subordinates, which are likely to result in different outcomes. The situation is analysed in terms of seven variables, or problem attributes, and their behavioural requirements are analysed in terms of effectiveness. The logic for style selection was represented in a decision tree format.

Figure 17.11 outlines the key elements of the normative model. Part A is the taxonomy or continuum of decision-making styles, as applied to problems involving groups or individual subordinates. Part B lists the diagnostic questions by which managers identify relevant problem attitudes. Figure 17.12 provides the normative model by which yes or no responses to the diagnostic questions eliminate less effective styles and identify specific problem types; each resulting problem type has prescribed styles which will result in effective decisions in terms of both quality and acceptance. Where a choice of styles is considered feasible, the selection is made of the style most economical in terms of man-hours.

The problem attributes and decision rules produce a typology of problems or decision-making situations, for either group or individual problems, which are related to the most effective decision-making behaviour. The diagnosis and prescription of effective leader behaviour is relatively simple and specific for a manager to apply. The normative model is clearly presented as a prescriptive device, describing what managers should do in various circumstances. This approach is explicitly directed towards the training of managers.

It would have been easy to develop a training programme based on mechanistic application of the model, but Vroom and Yetton reject this approach. Their training programme is based on group activities directed towards understanding the research foundations, flexibility of behaviour and direct experience of problem solving situations. An important feature is the emphasis on self-discovery and insight learning by individual managers, assisted by group feedback on their behaviour and its consequences.

This model is an improvement over most others for several reasons. It is relatively easy to understand and apply, as well as providing a wider base for training based

Group Problems

AI. You solve the problem or make the decision yourself, using information available to you at the time.

AII. You obtain the necessary information from your subordinates, then decide the solution to the problem yourself. You may or may not tell your subordinates what the problem is in getting the information from them. The role played by your subordinates in making the decision is clearly one of providing the necessary information to you, rather than generating or evaluating alternative solutions.

CI. You share the problem with the relevant subordinates individually, getting their ideas and suggestions without bringing them together as a group. Then *you* make the decision, which may or may not reflect your subordinates' influence.

CII. You share the problem with your subordinates as a group, obtaining their collective ideas and suggestions. Then you make the decision, which may or may not reflect your subordinates' influence.

GII. You share the problem with your subordinates as a group. Together you generate and evaluate alternatives and attempt to reach agreement (consensus) on a solution. Your role is much like that of a chairman. You do not try to influence the group to adopt 'your' solution, and you are willing to accept and implement any solution which has the support of the entire group.

Individual Problems

AI. You solve the problem or make the decision by yourself, using information available to you at the time.

AII. You obtain the necessary information from your subordinate, then decide on the solution to the problem yourself. You may or may not tell the subordinate what the problem is in getting the information from him. His role in making the decision is clearly one of providing the necessary information to you, rather than generating or evaluating alternative solutions.

CI. You share the problem with your subordinate, getting his ideas and suggestions. Then you make a decision, which may or may not reflect his influence.

GI. You share the problem with your subordinate, and together you analyze the problem and arrive at a mutually agreeable solution.

DI. You delegate the problem to your subordinate, providing him with any relevant information that you possess, but giving him responsibility for solving the problem by himself. You may or may not request him to tell you what solution he has reached.

(A) Decision-making style taxonomy

A. Is there a quality requirement such that one solution is likely to be more rational than another?
B. Do I have sufficient info to make a high quality decision?
C. Is the problem structured?
D. Is acceptance of decision by subordinates critical to effective implementation?
E. If I were to make the decision by myself, is it reasonably certain that it would be accepted by my subordinates?
F. Do subordinates share the organizational goals to be attained in solving this problem?
G. Is conflict among subordinates likely in preferred solutions? (This question is irrelevant to individual problems.)
H. Do subordinates have sufficient info to make a high quality decision?

(B) Diagnostic questions for problem attributes

Figure 17.11. The Vroom & Yetton style taxonomy and diagnostic questions

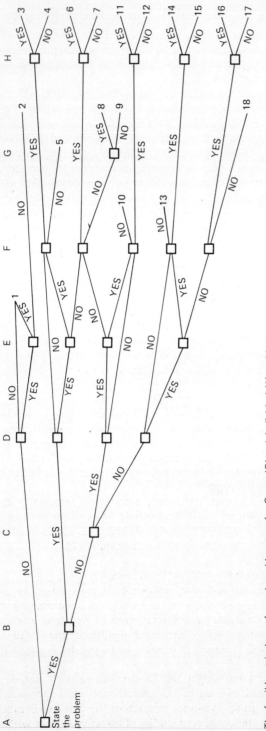

The feasible set is shown for each problem type for Group (G) and Individual (1) problems.

1 { G: AI, AII, CI, CII, GII
    I: AI, DI, AII, CI, GI

2 { G: GII
    I: DI, GI

3 { G: AI, AII, CI, CII, GII
    I: AI, DI, AII, CI, GI

4 { G: AI, AII, CI, CII, GII
    I: AI, AII, CI, GI

5 { G: AI, AII, CI, CII
    I: AI, AII, CI

6 { G: GII
    I: DI, GI

7 { G: GII
    I: GI

8 { G: CII
    I: CI

9 { G: CI, CII
    I: CI

10 { G: AII, CI, CII
     I: AII, CI,

11 { G: AII, CI, CII, GII
     I: DI, AII, CI, GI,

12 { G: AII, CI, CII, GII
     I: AII, CI, GI

13 { G: CII
     I: CI

14 { G: CII, GII
     I: DI, CI, GI

15 { G: CII, GII
     I: CI, GI

16 { G: GII
     I: DI, GI

17 { G: GII
     I: GI

18 { G: CII
     I: CI

Figure 17.12. The Vroom & Yetton normative model of style selection

on understanding leadership and group processes. It is sufficiently precise to permit rigorous testing of all key features and predictions whilst, being based on empirical research rather than esoteric theory, it is easily modified to accommodate new evidence. More importantly the designers themselves recognise actual and potential deficiencies, and are both conducting and encouraging research designed to test and, if necessary, modify their framework.

Initial reports of research testing the model by Hill and Schmitt,[42] Jago[43] and Vroom and Jago[44] appear to provide useful evidence of validity and utility of the model, although Field[45] questions the validity after examining the methodology used. As an aid to managerial decision-making, it is a clear improvement on notions of ideal styles, or more arbitrary choice of styles. As a basis for training, involving a wide basis of understanding rather than mechanistic application, it provides a most useful bridge between theory and practice and compares very favourably with other approaches.

(e) OTHER THEORIES OF CURRENT INTEREST

Path-Goal Theory was proposed separately by Evans[46] and House[47] with later developments reported by House and Mitchell[48] and House and Dressler.[49] Operating within the expectancy framework of motivation theory, this theory views leadership as a process of motivating subordinates so that the effective leader is one who can select appropriate styles with different subordinates and circumstances. The leader attempts to influence the subordinate's perceptions and motivation in accordance with the theoretical framework provided. Reviews by Filley *et al*[50] and Mitchell[51] suggest supporting findings, but other studies by Greene[52] and Schriesheim and DeNisi[53] appear more pessimistic. Thus the theory promises useful guidance to leaders and managers, but more research is needed as is further refinement, before that point is reached.

The Vertical Dyad Model was proposed by Graen[54] and Graen and Cashman,[55] recognising that leaders and subordinates exert reciprocal influence upon each other and that leaders have to play multiple roles with different activities at different times with different subordinates. The leader is viewed within a two-person relationship with each subordinate, effectiveness being dependent upon leader flexibility in perceiving and adapting to the relevant characteristics of subordinates and circumstances according to Graen and Scheimann.[56]

A number of new directions, tentative theories, analyses of leadership, and empirical researches have been reported to the Carbondale series of conferences in the U.S.A. The interested reader is referred to the published texts edited by Hunt and Larson[57, 58, 59, 60] for details of recent work in the leadership field.

(f) GROUP DYNAMICS RESEARCH AND INTERACTION THEORY

Our earlier discussion of the 'group situation' approach drew attention to the important contribution of social psychology researchers to an understanding of group dynamics relevant to the emergence and effectiveness of leaders in working groups. The group dynamics research has contributed significant knowledge of value in the training of leaders and managers in relevant social and diagnostic skills for team and group work.

The reviews of such research by Cartwright and Zander[61] and Shaw[62] include a diversity of research, much related to each of the general theoretical approaches identified above. However, most group dynamics research of the past two decades has clearly adopted an interaction approach, even studies of leader emergence within an overall 'group situation' approach. Similarly, leader effectiveness has more often been conceived from an interactional viewpoint, despite differences in conceptualisation of both leader behaviour and effectiveness. Thus a leader is considered more or less effective according to how appropriately the leader's behaviour interacts with group variables.

As a practical assistance to leaders and managers in diagnosing group characteristics and processes, understanding the behavioural factors which help or hinder group functioning etc., the group dynamics research and theory has perhaps had most significance for training of management. The commercial and practical success of training programmes based upon the theories or conceptual frameworks we have discussed, are all related directly to the incorporation of group based knowledge in the framework and training design.

LEADER EFFECTIVENESS: A SUMMARY

Despite some 80 years of intensive research, a comprehensive theoretical understanding and explanation of leadership remains to be developed. The currently accepted view is that leader effectiveness depends upon the interaction between variables associated with the leader (i.e. personal characteristics and behaviour factors) and situation variables. It seems apparent that leader emergence, or acceptance if appointed from outside the working group, depends upon the interaction of similar variables. Thus current theories of leader effectiveness attempt to identify a 'best fit' between leader behaviour style indicators and situational variables.

The problems facing current theory development are illustrated in Figure 17.13, which provides a simplified summary of the principal classes of variable which

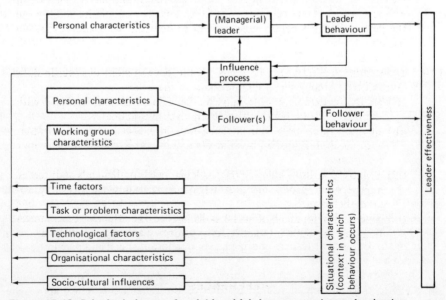

Figure 17.13. Principal classes of variable which interact to determine leader effectiveness

interact to determine leader effectiveness. Any comprehensive leadership theory, attempting to integrate past research usefully, will have to develop the means to cope with this complexity.

The most significant contribution of the current leadership theory is in the development and training of managers in skills relative to their behaviour in practice. Research in leadership, group dynamics and social psychology generally has provided useful knowledge and technology for improving managerial effectiveness in influencing their followers towards appropriate goals.

However improved leader effectiveness does not guarantee managerial effectiveness, which may well be influenced by lack of other skills and abilities in technical or other non-leadership functions of the particular role.

SUMMARY PROPOSITIONS

17.1.   There are no combinations of personal characteristics which accurately predict effectiveness of any individual in a particular leader role. However, there are several clusters of personality factors and abilities which generate personal dynamics advantageous to a person seeking to be an effective leader.

17.2.   There is no general mode of behaviour, or ideal style, which will be consistently effective in a variety of situations. The leader needs appropriate flexibility to vary behaviour according to the needs of varying situations.

17.3.   Leadership involves a dynamic interaction between characteristics of the leaders, of the followers and of more general situational variables. An effective leader is one who possesses the knowledge and ability to diagnose the demands of the context, meeting these demands with appropriate behaviour.

17.4.   Leadership training needs to focus on the development of specific skills and abilities. Among the more important of these are:
(i) ability to exhibit a wide range of behaviour patterns, coupled with the flexibility to deploy these alternatives in practice;
(ii) an understanding of human behaviour in a social context, together with an appreciation of possible consequences of one's own behaviour for others;
(iii) diagnostic skills to identify the particular needs or demands of different interpersonal, group and organisational situations in terms of appropriate behaviour;
(iv) general development of social skills needed for effective communication, interpersonal interaction, group activity and social influence.

REFERENCES

1. Stogdill R.M., *Handbook of Leadership: A Survey of Theory and Research* (The Free Press) 1974.

2. Gibb C.A., 'Leadership', chapter 31 of *Handbook of Social Psychology*, Vol. IV (second ed.), edited by Lindzey G., and Aronson E. (Addison-Wesley) 1969.
3. Bass. M., *Leadership, Psychology and Organisational Behaviour* (Harper) 1960.
4. Stogdill, *op.cit.*, p. 7.
5. Tannenbaum R., Weschler I.R. and Massarik F., *Leadership and Organisation: A Behavioural Science Approach* (McGraw-Hill) 1961.
6. Mintzberg, H. *The Nature of Managerial Work* (Harper and Row), 1973.
7. Schriesheim C.A. and Kerr S. *Theories and Measures of Leadership: A Critical Appraisal of Current and Future Directions*, Faculty of Administrative Sciences, Graduate School of Business Administration, Kent State University, Working Paper No. 77–01, 1977, p. 57. Reprinted in ref. 59.
8. Stogdill R.M., 'Personal Factors associated with Leadership: A Survey of the Literature', *Journal of Psychology*, Vol. 25, 1948, pp. 35–71 (reprinted as Chapter 5 of ref. no. 1, 1974, pp. 35–71).
9. Mann R.D., 'A Review of the relationships between Personality and Performance in Small Groups', *Psychological Bulletin*, Vol. 56, 1959, pp. 241–270.
10. Gibb, *op. cit.*, 1969, p. 227.
11. Dunnette M.D., 'The Motives of Industrial Managers', *Organisational Behaviour and Human Performance*, Vol. 2, 1967, pp. 176–182.
12. Ghiselli E.E., 'Managerial Talent', *American Psychologist*, Vol. 18, No. 10, October 1963.
13. Stogdill, *op.cit.*, 1974, p. 81.
14. Gibb C.A. (ed), *Leadership* (Penguin) 1969.
15. Bales R.F. and Slater, P.E., 'Role Differentiation in Small Decision-Making Groups', in Parsons T. and Bales R.F. (ed), *Family, Socialisation and Interaction Process* (Free Press) 1955, Chapter 5.
16. Collins B.E. and Guetzkow H., *A Social Psychology of Group Processes for Decision Making* (Wiley) 1964.
17. Cartwright D. and Zander A. (eds.), *Group Dynamics: Research and Theory*, third ed. (Tavistock) 1968.
18. Shaw M.E. *Group Dynamics*, second ed. (McGraw-Hill) 1976.
19. White R. and Lippitt R., 'Leader Behaviour and Member Reaction in three 'Social Climates'', abridged from chapters 3 and 5 of *Autocracy and Democracy* (Harper) 1960, and published in ref. no. 17, pp. 318–335.
20. Stogdill, *op.cit.*, 1974, pp. 363–407.
21. Maier N.R.F., *Psychology in Industry* (Harrap) 1955 (second ed. 1959).
22. Tannenbaum R. and Schmidt W.H., 'How to choose a Leadership Pattern', *Harvard Business Review*, Vol. 36, No. 2, 1958, pp. 95–101 (also reprinted as Chapter 5 of ref. no. 5).
23. Stogdill R.M., and Coons A.E., *Leadership Behaviour: Its Description and Measurement* (Ohio State University, Bureau of Business Research) 1957.
24. Fleishman E.A., and Harris E.F., 'Patterns of Leadership Behaviour related to Employee Grievances and Turnover', *Personnel Psychology*, Vol. 15, 1962, pp. 43–56.
25. Likert R., *New Patterns of Management* (McGraw-Hill) 1961.
26. Blake R.R. and Mouton J.S., *The Managerial Grid* (Gulf) 1964.
27. Bowers D.G. and Seashore S.E., 'Predicting Organisational Effectiveness with a Four-Factor Theory of Leadership', *Administrative Science Quarterly*, Vol. 11, 1966, pp.258–263.
28. Tannenbaum A.S., 'Retrospective Commentary', *Harvard Business Review*, May/June 1973, pp. 166–168.
29. Fiedler F.E., *A Theory of Leadership Effectiveness* (McGraw-Hill) 1967.
30. Fiedler F.E. and Chemers M.M., *Leadership and Effective Management* (Scott Foresman) 1974.
31. Fiedler F.E., Chemers M.M. and Mahar L., *Improving Leadership Effectiveness: The Leader Match Concept* (Wiley) 1976.
32. Fiedler F.E. and Mahar L. 'The Effectiveness of Contingency Model Training: A Review of the validation of Leader Match' *Personnel Psychology*, Spring 1979.
33. Ashour A., 'The Contingency Model of Leadership Effectiveness: An Evaluation' *Organisational Behaviour and Human Performance*, June 1973, pp. 339–355.

34. Graen G., Alvares K.M., Orris J.B. and Martella J.A., 'Contingency Model of Leadership Effectiveness: Antecedent and Evidential Results' *Psychological Bulletin*, Vol. 74, 1970, pp. 285–296.
35. Graen G., Orris J.B. and Alvares K.M., 'Contingency Model of Leadership Effectiveness: Some Experimental Results' *Journal of Applied Psychology*, June 1971, pp. 196–201.
36. Blake R.R. and Mouton J.S., 'The Managerial Grid in Three Dimensions', *ASTD Journal*, January 1967, pp. 2–5.
37. Reddin W.J., 'The Tri-Dimensional Grid', *The Canadian Personnel and Industrial Relations Journal*, January 1966, pp. 13–20.
38. Reddin W.J., 'The 3–D Management Style Theory', *Training and Development Journal*, April 1967, pp. 8–17.
39. Reddin W.J., *Managerial Effectiveness* (McGraw-Hill) 1970.
40. Hersey P. and Blanchard K., *Management of Organisational Behaviour* (Prentice-Hall) 1969 (Third Ed. 1977).
41. Vroom V. and Yetton P., *Leadership and Decision Making* (University of Pittsburgh Press) 1973.
42. Hill T.E. and Schmitt N., 'Individual Differences in Leadership Decision Making' *Organisational Behaviour and Human Performance*, Vol. 19, 1977, pp. 353–367.
43. Jago A.G., 'A Test of Spuriousness in Descriptive Models of Participative Leader Behaviour' *Journal of Applied Psychology*, Vol. 63, 1978, pp. 383–387.
44. Vroom V.H. and Jago A.G., 'On the Validity of the Vroom-Yetton Model', *Journal of Applied Psychology*, vol. 63, 1978, pp. 151–162.
45. Field R.H.G., 'A Critique of the Vroom-Yetton Contingency Model of Leadership Behaviour', *Academy of Management Review*, April 1979, pp. 249–257.
46. Evans M.G., 'The Effect of Supervisory Behaviour on the Path-Goal Relationship', *Organisational Behaviour and Human Performance*, May 1970, pp. 277–298.
47. House R.J., 'A Path-Goal Theory of Leader Effectiveness', *Administrative Science Quarterly*, September 1971, pp. 321–338.
48. House R.J. and Mitchell T.R., 'Path-Goal Theory of Leadership', *Journal of Contemporary Business*, vol. 3, 1974, pp. 81–97.
49. House R.J. and Dessler G., 'The Path-Goal Theory of Leadership: Some *post hoc* and *a priori* tests' in Hunt and Larson (eds.), *Contingency Approaches to Leadership* (Southern Illinois) 1974.
50. Filley A.C., House R.J. and Kerr S., *Managerial Process and Organizational Behaviour*, 2nd ed. (Scott, Foresman) 1976.
51. Mitchell T.R., 'Organizational Behaviour', *Annual Review of Psychology*, vol. 30, 1979, pp. 243–281.
52. Greene C.N., 'Questions of Causation in the Path-Goal Theory of Leadership', *Academy of Management Journal*, vol. 22, 1979, pp. 21–41.
53. Schriesheim C.A. and DeNisi A., 'Task Dimensions as Moderators of the Effects of Instrumental Leader Behaviour: A Path-Goal Approach', *Academy of Management Proceedings*, 1979.
54. Graen G., 'Role making processes within complex organisations' in M.D. Dunnette (ed.), *Handbook of Industrial and Organisational Psychology* (Rand McNally) 1976.
55. Graen G. and Cashman J.F., 'A role making model of leadership in formal organisations' in Hunt and Larson (eds.), *Leadership Frontiers* (Southern Illinois) 1975.
56. Graen G. and Scheimann W., 'Leader member agreement: a vertical dyad linkage approach' *Journal of Applied Psychology*, vol. 63, 1978, pp. 206–212.
57. Hunt J.G. and Larson L.L., *Contingency Approaches to Leadership* (Southern Illinois) 1974.
58. Hunt J.G. and Larson L.L., *Leadership Frontiers* (Southern Illinois) 1975.
59. Hunt J.G. and Larson L.L., *Leadership: The Cutting Edge* (Southern Illinois) 1977.
60. Hunt J.G. and Larson L.L., *Crosscurrents in Leadership* (Southern Illinois) 1979.
61. Cartwright and Zander, *op. cit.*, 1968.
62. Shaw, *op. cit.*, ref. 18, 1976.

18

Grievance and Disciplinary Processes

In this chapter we develop further the arguments that have been put forward in Chapter 16 about the complementary nature of the grievance and disciplinary processes and the material about procedures included in Chapter 12.

Our basic position is that employer and employee are seeking a good fit on the employment contract and that this is the foundation of the employment relationship. Both employer and employee have the opportunity to remedy their dissatisfactions with each other. As a last resort either can terminate the contract, but before such severance there are considerable possibilities of adjustment in order to resolve or come to terms with perceived dissatisfactions. Employer seeks adjustment through processes of *discipline:* employee seeks adjustment through processes of *grievance.*

Towards an Understanding of Discipline in Employment

Megginson[1] suggests that in looking at employment issues it is appropriate to limit consideration of discipline to three areas of meaning:

Self-discipline: concerned with the self-control of the individual to adjust himself to certain needs and demands;

Esprit de corps: concerned with orderly behaviour within an organisation, controlling individual behaviour within a group;

Judicial process: concerned with monitoring performance and applying correctives to avoid a future recurrence of an undesirable act.

Accepted orthodoxy in management thinking appears to be moving towards ideas of discipline which rely little on penalties and coercion in favour of self-discipline. Slichter, Healy and Livernash quote the tenet:

> ... effective discipline is that training which makes punishment unnecessary.[2]

It is reasonable to argue that self-discipline is the most effective, as well as the most dignified, method whereby employee behaviour will be consistent with organisational objectives, and in many cases will be the only means available. All management thinking on disciplinary matters should be towards enabling and encouraging self-discipline among employees and the reduction of supervisory control. If we have another look at Megginson's three areas we can slightly reorganise them into a hierarchy:

   (i) Working rules and arrangements that are broadly acceptable to the employer and employees, to provide a *framework of organisational justice* that will ensure general compliance with rules because they are seen as fair and worthy of moral support.

   (ii) *Managerial control* of individual and small group performance to ensure compliance with the rules and to correct deviations.

   (iii) *Individual control* of own performance to meet organisational objectives within a framework of organisational justice.

The hierarchical principle in (iii) is only possible where (ii) already exists, and (ii) is only possible in the presence of (i). All three are necessary elements of a disciplined situation with self-control, autonomy and responsibility being the pinnacle.

Towards an Understanding of Grievance in Employment

Pigors and Myers[3] give us a helpful approach to the question of grievances by drawing a distinction between the terms *dissatisfaction, complaint* and *grievance* as follows:

Dissatisfaction:	anything that disturbs an employee, whether or not he expresses his unrest in words;
Complaint:	a spoken or written dissatisfaction, brought to the attention of the supervisor and/or shop steward;
Grievance:	a complaint which has been formally presented to a management representative or to a union official.

This provides us with a useful categorisation by separating out *grievance* as a formal, relatively drastic step, compared with commonplace grumbling. Most important for management to know about are the *dissatisfactions*. Although nothing is being expressed, the feeling of hurt following failure to get a pay rise or the frustration about shortage of materials can quickly influence performance. Dissatisfaction can lead to serious unrest or high staff turnover without necessarily being expressed as a complaint or grievance. The fact that it is not expressed does not always mean that it is not important. The employee may withold complaint because he does not want to cause trouble, because he is apprehensive about repercussions, or perhaps because he is not clear on what it is that he is dissatisfied about.

   Complaint is a midway point: dissatisfaction is being expressed, but not in a procedural way. It is a straightforward request for action to be taken by someone else to solve a working problem, even though the request may be expressed in forceful or colourful terms.

   The *grievance* step is when the complaint is presented formally and triggers the procedural machinery, moving the issue out of the narrow confines of the particular workplace in which it began. The word carries with it the idea that the complaint has been ignored or unfairly treated, or that there is a difference in interpretation of the working rules. Although this may seem unreasonable in many circumstances, it is a feature of judicial process, which requires the differences between two positions to be made clear as a preliminary to arbitration.

   Roethlisberger and Dickson[4] differentiated three types of complaint, according to content.

   The first kind referred to tangible *objects* in terms that could be defined by any competent worker and could be readily tested:

'The machine is out of order . . . '
'This tool is too dull . . . '
'The stock we're getting now is not up to standard . . . '
'Our cement is too thin and won't make the rubber stick . . . '

Secondly were those complaints based partly on sensory experience, but primarily on the accompanying, *subjective* reactions:

'The work is messy . . . '
'It's too hot in here . . . '
'The job is too hard . . . '

These statements include terms where the meaning is biologically or socially determined and can therefore not be understood unless the background of the complainant is known; seldom can their accuracy be objectively determined. A temperature of 18 degrees centigrade may be too hot for one person but equable for another.

The third type of complaint they differentiated were those involving the *hopes and fears* of employees:

'The supervisor plays favourites . . . '
'The pay rates are too low . . . '
'Seniority doesn't count as much as it should . . . '

These complaints proved the most revealing to the investigators as they showed the importance of determining not only what employees felt but also why they felt as they did; not only verifying the facts ('the manifest content') but also determining the feelings behind the facts ('the latent content').

Roethlisberger and Dickson concluded, for instance, that one employee who complained of his supervisor being a bully was actually saying something rather different, especially when he gave as his reason the fact that the supervisor did not say 'good morning'. Later it was revealed that the root of his dissatisfaction was in his attitude to any authority figure, not simply the supervisor about whom he had complained.

Each of the types of dissatisfaction manifested in this analysis are important for the management to uncover and act upon, if action is possible. Action is likely to be prompt on complaints of this first type, as they are neutral: blame is being placed on an inanimate object and individual culpability is not an issue. Action may be taken on complaints of the second type where the required action is straightforward — such as opening a window if it is too hot — but the problem of accuracy is such that there may be a tendency to smooth over an issue or leave it 'to sort itself out' in time. The third type of complaint is the most difficult and action is therefore less likely to be taken. A supervisor will often take the complaint as a personal criticism of his competence, and employees will often translate the complaint into a grievance only by attaching it to a third party like a shop steward, so that the relationship between employee and supervisor is not jeopardised.

Another dimension to this problem is the feeling frequently expressed by managers that grievance machinery encourages petty grumbles from people who had previously been content:

'These are parts of the job that they just have to accept . . .'
'We can't always do what they want, just like that . . .'

A further perspective on grievances is suggested by Gellerman in considering morale:

... morale depends far more on whether employees feel able to influence management decisions that affect them than on any specific decision itself ... prompt responsiveness to evidence of employee dissatisfaction will help to sustain morale even if management decides, upon investigation, not to make any changes. Morale depends, in other words, upon the existence of adequate grievance channels.[5]

For grievances to be dealt with effectively there needs to be the same framework of organisational justice that is needed for discipline: the rules, the clarity of roles, the steps to be taken and an implication that individual whim will not distort the framework; but — again like discipline — grievances depend greatly on the relationship between the employee and the immediate superior, where much is done without recourse to procedure, although both are confident that the procedure is there if necessary.

The Framework of Organisational Justice

The elements of the organisational justice framework are set out in Chapter 12, where there is discussion of rules, offences, penalties, procedural steps etc. We now consider some of the ways in which such a framework is made to work.

(a) PREVENTING THE BREAKING OF RULES

The value of rules is that people know what to do: it is not to have a reason for imposing penalties. Here are some ways of helping people to obey the rules:

(i) *Information.* Employees need to know what the rules are. The simple publication of a disciplinary code will not be sufficient; thought will be needed on presentation, penetration and reiteration. Reasoned argument has more impact than pontifical emphasis, but employees must *know*.

(ii) *Placement.* Initial placement can reduce the risk of rule infringement. The heavy smoker is best not working in a strict non-smoking situation. Skilled employment interviewing can reduce the chance of someone being placed in a situation where working competence is unlikely.

(iii) *Training.* Training improves the chances of a recruit knowing the rules. It also increases his self-discipline, deriving from his sense of competence, self-confidence and responsibility.

(iv) *Example.* Many aspects of behaviour are socially determined and the individual copies the behaviour of those around him, especially those with high status. If these people observe the letter and spirit of the law scrupulously then the rules will have general support, but one law for the rich and one for the poor will produce a situation in which rules are a challenge to avoid rather than a challenge to accept.

(b) CORRECTING DEVIANT BEHAVIOUR

We can now examine ways of putting things right that do not involve punishment, although penalties may eventually become necessary. There is a note on penalties in Chapter 12.

(i) *Relocation.* If indiscipline occurs through placement not being right, one corrective is to re-locate the person causing the difficulty. This is *transfer,* not *demotion,* trying to find a more satisfactory arrangement of work.

(ii) *Probation.* Where new employees are clearly unsuitable there is the possibility of terminating the contract before the expiry of a probationary period, providing that the length of such period is known to the parties beforehand.

(iii) *Training.* Just as some disciplinary difficulties can be *prevented* by training, others can be overcome by training or re-training. New working procedures or new equipment will require that employees are trained to operate the new system accurately. Mistakes can be analysed to establish whether the problem is lack of training at all, need for more practice with a procedure that is understood but not perfected, or need for performance feedback to rectify misunderstanding or misapplication.

Managers will also need training on disciplinary matters, as there are often difficult matters to handle both in deciding who, if anyone, is to blame and in having to face the unpopularity that usually follows the implementation of penalties. Maier and Danielson conducted an experiment that showed over half of a group of 172 foremen as not being prepared to persist with a disciplinary decision once it was challenged by a steward. This was despite the fact that it was a safety offence in which there was no doubt about guilt.[6]

(c) MANAGERIAL DISCIPLINE

An important feature of the justice framework is the behaviour of its custodians and their respect for it.

(i) *Short-circuits.* A senior manager sustains those junior to him in the hierarchy by enabling and encouraging them to deal with matters of discipline and grievance. The so-called 'open-door' policy ('. . . my door is always open . . . call in and see me any time you think I can help you . . . ') among senior managers may have great advantages and in some matters may be necessary, but will devalue the justice framework. First it encourages the by-passing of a section of the framework; secondly it develops a reliance on the goodwill of an individual instead of on rights.

(ii) *Grievances.* Grievances are to be *encouraged* not avoided as they are the tip of the dissatisfaction iceberg. If they are dealt with, quickly and without hauteur, they will reduce dissatisfaction. Gradually too the manifest content will increase and the latent reduce as people are more ready to be frank. In passing we should point out that there is not always a latent content to a grievance. The lady who says she does not want to work week-ends any longer because she has had enough is not necessarily concealing some deep personal trauma and issuing a cry for help!

(iii) *Discipline.* Only as a last resort does discipline involve punishment. It is much more concerned with prevention and correction.

Managerial Control of Performance

The way in which managers control the performance of their working group will influence both discipline and the level and nature of grievances.

(a) MANAGER'S PHILOSPHY AND STYLE

A manager's beliefs about discipline and grievances will crucially govern his behaviour in relation to them. If he sees discipline as punishment and grievances as employees getting above themselves, then he will behave in a relatively autocratic way. We suggest that he could more realistically view 'disciplinary problems' as obstacles to achievement that do not necessarily imply incompetence or ill-will by the employee, but as matters needing analysis for cause and then appropriate initiatives to eliminate the cause. The necessary action may sometimes require much from the management and little from the employee, because it is caused by operational problems rather than subversive employees.

(b) ANALYSIS FOR CAUSE OF UNSATISFACTORY WORK.

If we are tackling operational problems there is the need for some analysis. As a preliminary we can quote Glueck's suggestion of three kinds of employees whose behaviour can be described as difficult:[7]

Class I. Those whose personal problems off the job begins to affect job productivity. These problems can be alcoholism, drugs or family relationships.

Class II. Those who violate laws while on the job by such behaviour as stealing from the organisation or its employees and by physical abuse of employees or property.

Class III. Those whose quantity or quality of work is unsatisfactory due to lack of abilities, training or motivation.

Miner[8] provides a scheme for analysing deficient behaviour which produces a checklist of possible causes. Indicators like absence and turnover, well analysed and used, will point out departments or occupational categories where some sort of morale loss can be expected and sought out with a view to remedy. Where there is a disciplinary 'offence' there is need to look for the cause of the deviant behaviour before any rebuke or penalty is invoked. When the work of an employee becomes lacklustre there is a further need for inquiry to establish reasons and try to remove them. The main feature of analysis will be interviewing of employees, which is dealt with in the next chapter.

(c) FEEDBACK ON WORKING PERFORMANCE

A potential preventer of both indiscipline and dissatisfaction is information to the employee on how his working performance compares with managerial expectation:

In recent years there has been considerable interest in the values and problems associated with feeding back appraisal information to the employee with a view to stimulating greater effort and helping him to perform more effectively.[9]

The use of performance appraisal schemes as modifiers of performance is still not widespread, although growing, and the performance modification objective makes different demands of the scheme than does the more traditional objective of assessing performance for reasons of possible promotion. There is the need to establish realistic performance norms with an emphasis on developing the present working performance, followed by discussion with the job holder of the work being done and agreed decisions by job holder and manager on action to enhance the performance. This might involve a change in working arrangements, persuasion by the manager, further training, re-definition of objectives or some other strategy appropriate to the particular situation.

(d) LEADERSHIP

The final dimension to management control of performance to mention here is the amalgam of behaviours and style that can be lumped under the heading of leadership exercised by the manager in relation to the employee: encouragement, explanation, stimulus, guidance, coaching and the rest. The nature of the manager/subordinate relationship can influence employee attitudes to compliance with managerial authority as well as their ability to comply, and the same relationship can contribute towards the ready expression of dissatisfaction or its suppression. The whole question of leadership is, of course, dealt with fully in Chapter 17.

Individual Control of Own Performance

At the opening of this chapter we suggested that self-control, autonomy and responsibility represent the pinnacle of the hierarchy of discipline, and that it was only likely to flourish when there was a setting of organisational justice and management control. Management control and employee autonomy are not incompatible and the basis for individual control of own performance is already established if the organisational justice framework is firm and the style of management control appropriate and consistent.

Megginson argues that self-analysis is an essential pre-requisite to self-discipline:

> The ability of an individual to analyse himself objectively in order to discover possible areas of improvement in his work is the *sine qua non* of self-discipline.[10]

The need for self-analysis may be partly met by managerial provision of appropriate performance appraisal arrangements. Some schemes incorporate specific arrangements for self-analysis or self-assessment. There are other managerial initiatives to make self-discipline more likely. Training, for instance, can produce varying degrees of independence and self-sufficiency. Thorough selection procedures, including the use of selection tests, can ensure that employees are placed in jobs within the range of their own self-discipline, both actual and potential.

Perhaps the most important contribution of the manager to the self-discipline of the individual employee lies in *reducing supervision*. Self-discipline requires the need for self-discipline and the right to the autonomy that goes with it. The learner driver is absolutely dependent on the instructor during the first lesson, but gradually he lessens that dependence until the very presence of the instructor is unnecessary and may actually inhibit his driving performance. In any occupation there is a proper area for external control — like quality sampling or the annual audit of the books — but there is also the area for self-control that cannot be invaded by the superior without jeopardising performance and imparing the manager/subordinate relationship. Mostly this distinction is drawn between 'what' and 'how'. Seldom does any employee query instructions on what he is required to do. In a cricket team the bowler will normally start and stop bowling when instructed by the captain, and may well bowl fast or medium, on the leg stump or the off stump according to

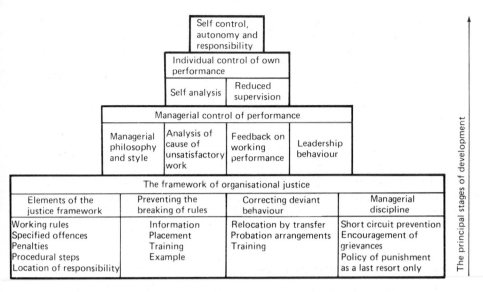

Figure 18.1. Features in the development of effective individual control

what is required of him; but he would take strong exception to being told *how* to bowl an off-cutter or a leg-break.

This point needs some emphasis because so many managers derive much of their job satisfaction from the authority relationship and may relinquish close supervision only reluctantly. Indeed a situation of extensive employee autonomy is often described by managers as 'lacking discipline'. Figure 18.1 summarises the features that are found in the development of self-control.

Are Grievance and Discipline Processes Equitable?

For these processes to work they must command support, and they will only command support if they are seen as equitable, truly just and fair. At first it would seem that it is concern for the individual employee that is paramount, but the individual cannot be isolated from the rest of the workforce. Fairness should therefore be linked to the interests that all workers have in common in the organisation, and to the managers who must also perceive the system as equitable if they are to abide by its outcomes.

Procedures have a potential to be fair in that they are certain. The conduct of industrial relations becomes less haphazard and irrational; people 'know where they stand'. The existence of a rule cannot be denied and opportunities for one party to manipulate and change a rule are reduced. Procedures also have the advantage that they can be communicated. The process of formalising a procedure that previously existed only in customs and practice clarifies the ambiguities and inconsistencies within it and compels each party to recognise the role and responsibility of the other. By providing pre-established avenues for responses to various contingencies there is the chance that the response will be less random and so more fair. The impersonal nature of procedures offers the possibility of removing hostility from the work place, since an artificial social situation is created in which the ritualism marks displays of aggression towards managers as not intended as personal attacks.

The achievement of equity may not match the potential. Procedures cannot for instance import equitability into situations that are basically unfair. Thus attempting to cope with an anomalous pay system through grievance procedure may be alleviating symptoms rather than treating causes. It is also impossible to overcome accepted norms of inequity in a plant, such as greater punctuality being required of manual employees than of white-collar employees.

A further feature of procedural equity is its degree of similarity to the judicial process. All adopt certain legalistic mechanisms, like the right of the individual to be represented and to hear the case against him, but some aspects of legalism, such as burdens of proof and strict adherence to precedent may cause the application of standard remedies rather than the consideration of individual circumstances.

Notions of fairness are not 'givens' of the situation; they are socially constructed and there will never be more than a degree of consensus on what constitutes fairness. Despite this the procedural approach can exploit standards of certainty and consistency which are widely accepted as elements of justice. The extent to which a procedure can do this will depend on the suitability of its structure to plant circumstances, the commitment of those who operate it and the way that it reconciles legalistic and bargaining elements.

A THEORETICAL FORMULATION FOR THE DISCIPLINE
AND GRIEVANCE PROCESSES

Having reviewed approaches to the processes of dealing with disciplinary and grievance processes we can offer a formulation which combines these ideas with those on the employment contract, using Mumford's basic idea that was described in the first chapter.

1. A good fit on the different dimensions of the employment contract produces *satisfaction* for the employee and for the management.

2. If the fit becomes bad there is *dissatisfaction*, either of the employee or of the management.

3. Dissatisfaction does not necessarily break the contract, as there are a series of *containing walls* reducing the likelihood of total breakdown.

4. The first containing wall is the feeling of *commitment* and mutual tolerance which both employee and management bring to the contract.

5. If the first is broken, the second containing wall is the *self*. The dissatisfaction is latent but not yet expressed, either by employee to management or by manager to employee.

6. The third containing wall is the *superior/subordinate* relationship. Once the second wall is breached by the dissatisfaction being manifest, there is a further containment within the employment relationship between the employee and his immediate superior. Dissatisfaction has changed to complaint or caution.

7. The final containing wall is *procedural discussion*. The issue threatening the

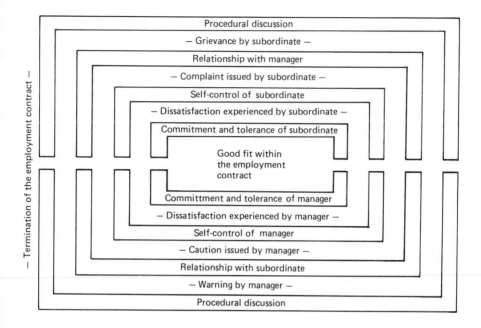

Figure 18.2. Theoretical formulation for grievance and discipline processes

employment contract now involves others than the superior and subordinate in seeking a remedy. Dissatisfaction has now become either grievance or warning.

8. At each stage the initiator (dissatisfied employee or dissatisfied manager) has a choice:
   (a) Resolve dissatisfaction and restore good fit, or
   (b) Move to next stage.
   The employee has a further option that is not normally available to the manager until the later stages:
   (c) Terminate employment contract.

9. Both discipline and grievance are similar in seeking the accommodation of conflicting interests: those of the organisation with those of the employee.

Figure 18.2 illustrates this theoretical formulation and the series of containing walls that reduce the likelihood of a total breakdown of the employment contract.

REFERENCES

1. Megginson L.C., *Personnel – A Behavioural Approach to Administration* (Irwin) 1972, p. 632.
2. Slichter S.H., Healy J.J., Livernash E.R., *The Impact of Collective Bargaining on Management* (Brookings Institution) 1960, p. 630.
3. Pigors P. and Myers C.A., *Personnel Administration* (McGraw-Hill) 1973, p. 229.
4. Roethlisberger F.J. and Dickson W. J., *Management and the Worker* (Harvard) 1939, pp. 225–269.

5. Gellerman S.W., *Motivation and Productivity* (American Management Association) 1963, p. 251.
6. Maier N.R.F., Danielson L.E., 'Two Approaches to Discipline in Industry', in *Journal of Applied Psychology,* vol. 40, 1956, pp. 319–323.
7. Glueck W.F., *Personnel: A Diagnostic Approach* (Business Publications) 1974, p. 609.
8. Miner J.B., *The Management of Ineffective Performance* (McGraw-Hill) 1963.
9. Miner J.B., *Personnel Psychology* (Macmillan) 1971, p. 7.
10. Megginson L.C., *op. cit.,* p. 634.

19

Interaction III — Grievance and Disciplinary Interviewing

We now consider the interviews that managers carry out with employees during disciplinary and grievance processes, as it is in these encounters that any managerial or employee initiative succeeds or fails. Procedures can do no more than force meetings to take place: it is the meetings themselves that provide answers.

In his profound and simple book of 1960, Douglas McGregor advocated an approach to management based on the strategy of *integration and self-control.*[1] He regarded forms and procedures as having little value and emphasised the importance of social interaction as well as the difficulty of achieving any change in people's interactive behaviour:

> Every adult human being has an elaborate history of past experience in this field, and additional learning is profoundly influenced by that history. From infancy on, his ability to achieve his goals and satisfy his needs — his 'social survival' — has been a function of his skills in influencing others. Deep emotional currents — unconscious needs such as those related to dependency and counterdependency — are involved. He has a large 'ego investment' and his knowledge and skill in this area, and the defences he has built to protect that investment are strong and psychologically complex.[2]

Managers undoubtedly spend a great deal of their time in interviews of one type or another with subordinates, potential subordinates and with peers. It may be that the ability of the manager to handle the grievance/discipline interview will be the most important test of his effectiveness in organising the efforts of his working group.

The Nature of Grievance and Disciplinary Interviewing

Many of the interviews that take place are simple: giving information, explaining work requirements and delivering rebukes, but from time to time every manager will need to use a problem-solving approach, involving sympathy, perception, empathy and the essential further feature that some managers provide only with reluctance: time.

We are not concerned in this chapter to provide guidance on how to deliver a 'dressing down', nor how to give fatherly advice. We are seeking to offer suggestions about the conduct of those analytical, constructive types of interview that are built in to the grievance and discipline process as a means of treating *dissatisfaction*, not only in procedure, but also in avoiding recourse to the rigid formality of procedure. We see such interviews as one of the means towards *self-discipline* and *autonomy* of employees, reducing the need for supervision.

As we have shown in the previous chapter, a grievance may be expressed only in manifest form, requiring interviewing to understand its latent content in order that appropriate action is taken to remove the underlying dissatisfaction. Discipline problems will have underlying reasons for the deviant behaviour and these need to be discovered before solutions to the problems can be attempted.

Much work has been done to analyse the nature of the problem-solving interview, mainly based on the work of Carl Rogers[3] and set out in prescriptive form by such British writers as Argyle,[4] Bessell[5] and Beveridge.[6] Our structures in this chapter are largely based on their insights, as well as on our experience in running training courses for varied groups of managers. Readers may find interest in another text which considers the method of another type of problem-solving interview: patients consulting a doctor,[7] where the attitudes of the parties are very different, yet the methods involved are similar.

A Structured Approach to the Interviews

As with the other interactive episodes examined in this book, we now offer a model for a structured approach that may help both to understand the situations and to handle them in practice. Although we use the formula of Preparation, Encounter and Follow-up, there is a variation at the encounter stage, where there is one suggested sequence for the grievance interview and another for discipline. Preparation and follow-up are seen as being common for either type. Figure 19.1 is a model of the interviews we are going to describe.

PREPARATION

(a) PROCEDURAL POSITION

The first requirement is to check the procedural position and to ensure that the impending interview is appropriate. In a grievance situation, for instance, is the employee pre-empting the procedure by taking his case to the wrong person or to the wrong point in procedure? This is most common when the first-line supervisor is being by-passed, either because the employee or his representative feel that it would be a waste of time, or perhaps because the supervisor is unsure of the appropriate action and is conniving at the procedure being side-stepped. It is also possible that the supervisor knows what to do but is shirking the responsibility or the potential unpopularity of what has to be done. Whatever the reason for such by-passing it is usually to be avoided because of the worrying precedents that it can establish.

In disciplinary matters even more care is needed about the procedural step, as the likelihood of penalties may already have been set up by warnings, thus reducing the scope for doing anything else in the impending interview apart from a further penalty.

In the majority of cases we believe that interviews will precede procedure, in which case the parties to the interview are less constrained by procedural rules. In

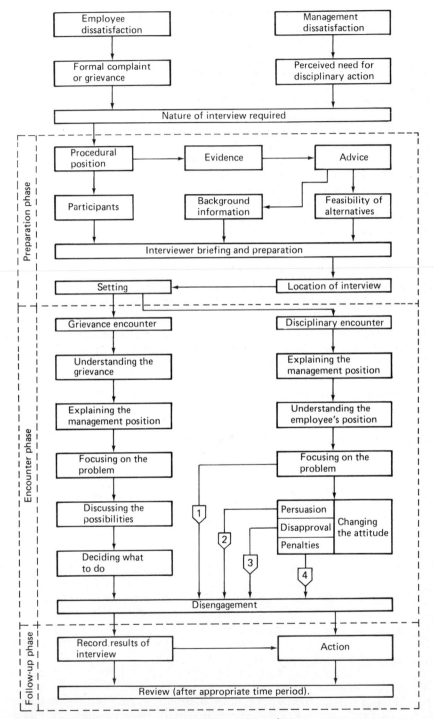

Figure 19.1. The grievance and disciplinary interviews

these situations managers will be at pains to establish that the interview is informal and without procedural implications.

(b) PARTICIPANTS

Who will be there? Here there are similar procedural considerations. *In* procedure there is the likelihood of employee representation, *out* of procedure there is less likelihood of that, even though the employee may feel anxious and threatened without it. If the manager is accompanied in the interview, the employee may feel even more insecure, and it is doubtful how much can be achieved informally unless the employee feels reasonably secure and able to speak frankly.

(c) EVIDENCE

What are the facts that the interviewer needs to know? In grievance he will want to know the subject of the grievance and how it has arisen. In discipline he will need similar information, plus more details on such matters as previous working record, cautions, warnings or penalties. Perhaps he will also need to establish the feasibility of dismissal being the outcome of the interview.

(d) BACKGROUND INFORMATION

What more general information is needed? For both types of interview there will be more general information required. Not just the facts of the particular grievance or disciplinary situation, but knowledge to give a general understanding of the working arrangements and relationships, will be required. Other relevant data may be on the employee's length of service, type of training, previous experience and so forth.

(e) ADVICE

Most managers approaching a grievance or disciplinary interview will benefit from advice before starting. It is particularly important for anyone who is in procedure to check his position with someone like a personnel executive before starting, as the ability to sustain any action by management will largely depend on maintaining consistency with what the management has done with other employees previously. He may also have certain ideas of what could be done in terms of re-training, transfer, assistance with a domestic problem etc. He will need to check the feasibility of such actions before broaching them with an aggrieved employee or with an employee whose work is not satisfactory.

(f) LOCATION AND SETTING OF INTERVIEW

Where is the interview to take place? However trivial this question may seem it is included for two reasons. First because we have seen a number of interviews go sadly awry because of the parties arriving at different places; this mistake seems to happen more often with this type of encounter than with others. Secondly because there may be an advantage in choosing an unusually informal situation — or an unusually formal one. A discussion over a pie and a pint in the local pub may be a more appropriate setting for some approaches to grievance and disciplinary problems, although they are seldom appropriate if the matter has reached procedure. Also employees frequently mistrust such settings, feeling that they are being manipulated, or that the discussion 'does not count' because it is out of hours or off limits. If, however, one is trying to avoid procedural overtones, this can be a way of doing it.

Unusual formality can be appropriate in the later stages of procedure, especially in disciplinary procedure, when proceedings take on a strongly judicial air. An employee is not likely to take seriously a final warning prior to probable dismissal if it is delivered over a pint in a pub. The large impressive offices of senior managers can make an appropriate setting for the final stages of procedure.

1. GRIEVANCE ENCOUNTER

(a) UNDERSTANDING THE GRIEVANCE

The first step in the grievance encounter is for the manager to be clear about what the grievance is; a simple way of doing this is to state the *subject* of the grievance and get confirmation from the employee that it is correct. The importance of this lies in the probability that the manager will have a different perspective on the affair from the employee, particularly if it has got beyond the preliminary stage. A supervisor may report to a superior that Mr X has a grievance and ' . . . will not take instructions from me . . . ', but when the interview begins Mr X may state his grievance as being that he is unwilling to work on Saturday mornings. In other situations it might be the other way round, with the supervisor reporting that Mr X will not work Saturday mornings and Mr X saying in the interview that he finds the style of his supervisor objectionable. Even where there is no such confusion, an opening statement and confirmation of the subject demonstrate that they are talking about the same thing.

Having clarified or confirmed the subject of the grievance the manager will then invite the employee to state his *case*. This will enable the employee to explain why he is aggrieved, citing examples, providing further information and saying not just 'what' but also 'why'. Seldom will this be done well. The presentation of a case is not a particularly easy task for the inexperienced and few aggrieved employees are experienced at making a case of this type. Furthermore there is the inhibition of questioning the wisdom of those in power and some apprehension about the outcome. After the declaration of case the manager will need to ask questions in order to fill in the gaps that have been left by the employee and to clarify some points that were obscure in the first telling. As a general rule it seems better to have an episode of questioning after the case has been made, rather than to interrupt on each point that is difficult. Interruptions make a poorly argued case even more difficult to sustain. There may, however, be disguised pleas for assistance that provide good opportunities for questioning to clarify: ' . . . I'm not very good with words, but do you see what I'm getting at . . . ?', ' . . . do you see what I mean . . . ?' or ' . . . Am I making myself clear . . . ?'

Among the communication ploys that the manager will need in this stage is *summary and re-run,* described in Chapter 29. Another that might be appropriate is *reflection* that is described by Beveridge:

> . . . a selective form of listening in which the listener picks out the emotional overtones of a statement and 'reflects' these back to the respondent without making any attempt to evaluate them. This means that the interviewer expresses neither approval nor disapproval, neither sympathy nor condemnation. Because the respondent may be in an emotional state, sympathy is liable to make him feel resentful and angry. Any attempt to get the respondent to look objectively and rationally at his problem at this stage is also likely to fail; he is still too con-

fused and upset to be able to do this and will interpret the very attempt as criticism.[8]

After all the necessary clarification has been obtained the manager will re-state the employee grievance, together with an outline of his case and ask the employee to agree with the summary or to correct it. By this means the manager is confirming and demonstrating that he understands what the grievance is about and why it has been brought. He is not agreeing with it or dismissing it. The grievance is now understood.

This phase of the interview can be summarised in sequential terms:

Manager	*Employee*
1. States subject of grievance	
	2. Agrees with statement
	3. States case
4. Questions for clarification	
5. Re-states grievance	
	6. Agrees or corrects

The grievance is now understood

(b) EXPLAINING THE MANAGEMENT POSITION

The next phase is to set out the management position on the grievance. This is not the action to be taken but the action that has been taken with the reasons for it, and may include an explanation of company policy or the detail of collective agreements, safety rules, previous grievances, supervisory problems, administrative methods and anything else which is needed to make clear why the management position has been what it has been. Having set out his case, the manager will then invite the employee to question and comment on the management position to ensure that it is understood and the justifications for it are understood, even if they are not accepted. The objective is to ensure that the parties to the discussion see and understand each other's point of view.

The management position is now understood

(c) FOCUSING ON THE PROBLEM

The setting out of the two opposed positions will have revealed a deal of common ground. The parties will agree on some things, though disagreeing on others. In the third phase of the interview the manager and employee sort through the points they have discussed and identify the points of disagreement. At least at this stage the points on which they concur can be ignored as the need now is to find the outer limits. It is very similar to the differentiation stage in negotiation.

Points of disagreement are now in focus

(d) DISCUSSING THE POSSIBILITIES

As a preliminary to taking action in the matter under discussion, the various possibilities can be put up for consideration. It is logical that the employee puts forward his suggestions first. Probably this has already been done either explicitly or implicitly in his development of the case. If, however, he is invited to put specific suggestions at this stage he may be able to make different ones, as he now understands the management position and is seeing the whole matter clearly due to the focusing that has just taken place. As he is bringing the grievance it is logical that his suggestions for overcoming the problem are given first. Then the manager will put forward alternatives or modifications, and such alternatives may include — or be limited to — the suggestion that the grievance is mischievous and unfounded so that no action should be taken. Nevertheless in most cases there will be some scope for accommodation, even if it is quite different from the employee's expectation. Once the alternative suggestions for action are set forward, there is time for the advantages and disadvantages of both sets to be discussed.

Alternatives have now been considered

(e) DECIDING WHAT TO DO

A grievance interview is one that falls short of the mutual dependence that is present in negotiation, so that the decision on action is to be taken by the manager alone; it is not a joint decision even though the manager will presumably be looking for a decision that all parties will find acceptable. In bringing a grievance the employee is challenging a management decision and that decision will now be confirmed or it will be modified, but it remains a management decision.

Before making the decision the manager may deploy a range of behaviours to ensure his decision is correct. He may test the employee's reaction by thinking aloud ' . . . well, I don't know, but it looks to me as if we shall have to disappoint you on this one . . . '. He may adjourn for a while to seek further advice or to give the employee time to reflect further, but he will have little opportunity for prevarication before he has to make his decision and then explain it to the employee. In this way he is not simply deciding and announcing, he is supporting the decision with explanation and justification in the same way that the employee developed the case for his grievance at the beginning. There may be employee questions and he may want time to think, but eventually he will have to accept the decision or take the matter to the next stage.

Management action is now clear and understood

2. DISCIPLINARY ENCOUNTER

(a) EXPLAINING THE MANAGEMENT POSITION

Discipline arises from management dissatisfaction rather than employee dissatisfaction with the employment contract, so the opening move is for a statement of why such dissatisfaction exists, dealing with the *facts* of the situation rather than managerial feelings of outrage about the facts. The importance of this is that the interview is being approached by the manager as a way of dealing with a problem of the working situation and not — yet — as a way of dealing with a malicious or indolent employee. If an employee has been persistently late for a week, it would be unwise for a manager to open his disciplinary interview by saying ' . . . your lateness this week has been deplorable . . . ' as the reason might turn out to be that the employee has a seriously ill child needing constant attendance through the night. Then the manager would be seriously embarrassed and the relationship with the employee would be jeopardised. An opening factual statement of the problem ' . . . you have been at least twenty minutes late each day this week . . . ' does not prejudge the reasons and is reasonably precise about the scale of the problem. It also circumscribes management dissatisfaction by implying that there is no other cause for dissatisfaction: if there is, then it should be mentioned.

(b) UNDERSTANDING THE EMPLOYEE'S POSITION

Now the manager needs to know the explanation and he asks the employee to say what he sees as the reasons for the problem. He may also ask for comments on the seriousness of the problem itself, which the employee may regard as trivial, while the manager regards it as serious. If there is such dissonance it needs to be drawn out. Getting the employee reaction is usually straightforward, but the manager needs to be prepared for one of two other types of reaction. Either he may need to probe — as described in Chapter 29 — because the employee is reluctant to open up, or he may encounter angry defiance. Disciplinary situations are at least disconcerting for employees and are frequently very worrying and surrounded by feelings of hostility and mistrust, so that it is to be expected that some ill-feeling will be pent up and waiting for the opportunity to be vented.

(c) FOCUSING ON THE PROBLEM

If the employee sees something of the management view of the problem and if the manager understands the reasons for it, the next requirement is to seek a solution. We have to point out that a disciplinary problem is as likely to be solved by management action as it is to be solved by employee action. If the problem is lateness one solution would be for the employee to catch an earlier bus, but another might be for the management to alter his working shift. If the employee is disobeying orders, one solution would be for him to start obeying them, but another might be for him to be moved to a different job where he receives orders from someone else. Some managers regard such thinking as unreasonable, on the grounds that the contract of employment places obligations on individual employees that they should meet despite personal inconvenience. The answer to this type of query seems to lie in the question not of how people *should* behave, but how they do. Can the contract of employment be enforced on an unwilling employee? Not if one is seeking such attitudes as enthusiasm and co-operation or behaviour such as diligence and carefulness. The disenchanted employee can always meet the bare letter rather than the spirit of his contract. He can also terminate his contract with a week's notice.

The most realistic view of the matter is that many disciplinary problems require some action from both parties, some require action by the employee only and a small proportion require management action only.

The problem-solving session may quickly produce the possibility for further action and open up the possibility of closing the interview.

First possible move to disengagement

(d) CHANGING THE ATTITUDE AND BEHAVIOUR OF A RELUCTANT EMPLOYEE

The simple, rational approach that we have outlined so far may not be enough, due to the unwillingness of the employee to respond. He may not want to be punctual or do as he is instructed, or whatever the particular problem is. There is now a test of the power behind management authority. Three further steps can be taken, one after the other, although there will be occasions when it is necessary to move directly to the third.

(i) Persuasion. A first strategy is to demonstrate to the employee that he will not achieve what he wants, if his behaviour does not change:

'You won't keep your earnings up if your output doesn't meet the standard.'
'It will be difficult to get your appointment confirmed when the probationary
period is over if . . . '

By such means the employee may see the advantages to himself of changing his
attitude and behaviour. If he is so convinced, then there is a strong incentive for
him to alter, because he believes it to be in his own interests.

Second possible move to disengagement

(ii) Disapproval. A second strategy is to suggest that the continuance of the
behaviour will displease those whose goodwill the employee wishes to keep:

'The Management Development Panel are rather disappointed . . . '
'Some of the other people in the Department feel that you are not pulling your
weight.'

A manager using this method will need to be sure that what he says is true and
relevant. Also he may be seen by the employee as shirking the issue, so he should
always consider a version of

'I think this is deplorable and expect you to do better . . . '

We asked for a restraint from judgement in the early stages of the interview, until
the nature of the problem is clear. The time for judgement has now come, with
the proper deployment of the *rebuke* or *caution,* as described in Chapter 18,
during the discussion of penalties.

Third possible move to disengagement

(iii) Penalties. When all else fails or is clearly inappropriate — as with serious
offences about which there is no doubt — penalties have to be invoked. In rare
circumstances there may be the possibility of a fine, but usually the first penalty
will be a formal warning as a preliminary to possible dismissal. In situations that
are sufficiently grave summary dismissal is both appropriate and possible within
the legal framework.

Fourth possible move to disengagement

(e) DISENGAGEMENT

We have indicated possible moves to disengagement at four different points in the
disciplinary interview. Now we come to a stage that is common for both grievance
and disciplinary encounters, from the point of view of describing the process,
although the nature of disengagement will obviously differ. Essentially the manager
needs to think of the working situation that will follow. In a grievance situation can
the employee now accept the decision made? Are there faces to be saved or reputations to be restored? What administrative action is to be taken? In closing a disciplinary interview, the manager will aim for the flavour of disengagement to be as
positive as possible so that all concerned put the disciplinary problem behind them.
In those cases where the outcome of the interview is to impose or confirm a dismissal, then the manager will be exclusively concerned with the fairness and accuracy
with which it is done, so that the possibility of tribunal hearings is reduced, if not
prevented.

It can never be appropriate to close an interview of either type leaving the
employee humbled and demoralised.

FOLLOW UP

For both types of interview we can outline a common follow-up sequence.

(a) RECORD
Some written record of what has transpired must be made unless the interview has been of an extremely informal nature. In disciplinary situations there has to be the notes to enable further action, perhaps leading to dismissal, and to advise anyone else who may be involved. In grievance situations there is the need of a note of what has happened in case the matter goes further in procedure, in which case the next manager in line will be seeking advice on what has gone before. At the more informal stages of both types of procedure there is the need for the employee to have a note of what has been agreed, at least as an *aide-memoire*.

(b) ACTION
The time spent on these interviews is wasted unless there is action to follow them up. The manager must make sure that whatever action he has agreed shall be taken by the organisation is in fact taken.

(c) REVIEW
Each situation needs to be reviewed after a period to see what change has transpired. Is the employee now satisfied where he was previously dissatisfied, or does the dissatisfaction persist? Alternatively, has the undisciplined behaviour altered as a result of effective solving of the problem, or is it still a difficulty?

In disciplinary matters there will be another aspect of review; that is, to look at the warning situation. Most procedures allow for some type of 'clean slate' provision, whereby the employee's record is wiped clean after a prescribed period of blameless work.

The 'Red Hot Stove' Rule

In closing this chapter we relate the advice contained in the 'red hot stove' rule, originally formulated by Douglas McGregor, but developed by Strauss and Sayles. The rule offers the touching of a red hot stove as an analogy for disciplinary action, as it is immediate, with warning, consistent and impersonal:

1. The burn is immediate. There is no question of cause and effect.
2. You had warning. If the stove was red hot, you knew what would happen if you touched it.
3. The discipline is consistent. Everyone who touches the stove is burned.
4. The discipline is impersonal. A person is burned not because of who he is, but because he touched the stove.[9]

Although not claimed by its inventors, one could suggest a fifth benefit of this rule: it works — people who touch red hot stoves *always* stop! It is not possible, however, for us to guarantee the same reliability for all disciplinary action taken by managers.

REFERENCES

1. McGregor D., *The Human Side of Enterprise* (McGraw-Hill) 1960, p. 75.
2. *Ibid.*, p. 219.
3. Rogers C., *Client-Centred Therapy* (Houghton Mifflin) 1952.
4. Argyle M., *Social Interaction* (Tavistock) 1969.
5. Bessell R., *Interviewing and Counselling* (Batsford) 1971.
6. Beveridge W.E., *Problem-Solving Interviews* (Allen & Unwin) 1968.
7. Byrne P.S. and Long B.E.L., *Doctors Talking to Patients* (HMSO) 1976.
8. Beveridge W.E., *op. cit,*, pp. 57—8.
9. Strauss G. and Sayles L.R., *Personnel: The Human Problems of Management,* 3rd ed. (Prentice-Hall) 1972, pp. 267—8.

20

Terminating the Employment Contract

If efforts in the grievance and discipline process do not succeed in restoring a good fit on the employment contract, then the contract is terminated. The dissatisfied employee gives notice and leaves; or the dissatisfied employer dismisses the unsatisfactory employee. Either party may terminate the contract for reasons other than dissatisfaction with the other — retirement and redundancy being examples. In this chapter we look at the various aspects of dismissal of employee by employer, including redundancy. In the United Kingdom a formidable literature on this subject has grown up since the Redundancy Payments Act of 1965 and the Industrial Relations Act of 1971. In these few pages we cannot claim to be comprehensive in our treatment of the subject, but hope to be adequate for most purposes.

The Scale of Dismissals

In 1967 the Ministry of Labour calculated that there were approximately 3 million dismissals each year, of which nearly one third were due to sickness and slightly fewer due to redundancy. The next most common reason was unsuitability, followed by misconduct.[1] It is important to bear this scale in mind when we look at the current situation.

In most cases dismissal of an employee is logical and unavoidable; the straightforward culmination of various attempts to put things right. It is uncomplicated, even though it is seldom pleasant. In a small number of cases the employer may be acting unlawfully so that the employee complains to an industrial tribunal that he has been unfairly dismissed. The tribunal may then have to test the fairness of the employer's decision and actions. In 1980 there were 28,624 applications to tribunals (compared with 33,383 in 1979) claiming unfair dismissal. One third of these were withdrawn by the applicant after conciliation and a further third were withdrawn after the employee had accepted compensation from the employer before the hearing, indicating either that the employer was in the wrong or that he did not feel the case worth defending at tribunal. Of the 10,037 tribunal hearings the employee's case was dismissed in 7,259 and upheld in 2,778 cases, or 9.7%. Remembering that unfair dismissal claims are only a minority of all dismissals, we see that the scale of decisions against the employer is very small indeed.[2]

Wrongful Dismissal

There is a long-standing common-law right to damages for an employee who has been dismissed *wrongfully,* that is, when the employer has not given proper notice: either the notice period is incorrect or the dismissal has been summary when the behaviour of the employee did not warrant such peremptory treatment. This remains a form of remedy that is used by very few people, but it could be useful to employees who have not sufficient length of service to claim unfair dismissal, so the employer who has learned that he can dismiss people unfairly if they do not have six months' service needs to remember that this does not permit him to dismiss them wrongfully. There may also be cases where a very highly paid employee might get higher damages in an ordinary court than the maximum that the tribunal can award.

Unfair Dismissal

Every employee who has been with his employer for twelve months has the right not to be unfairly dismissed; the fairness being determined by the provisions of the Trade Union and Labour Relations Act 1974 and the Employment Protection Act 1975, re-enacted in the Employment Protection (Consolidated) Act in 1978, though the main structure of unfair dismissal legislation has remained unaltered since it was first introduced in the Industrial Relations Act of 1971. In some areas of employment the legal provisions have made little difference, as the existing personnel policies of the employer have provided a similar or better degree of protection. The protection of the employee is due to a specific set of rules and precedents that have developed in his particular place of work and which are particularly relevant to it.

Obtaining a legal remedy from the tribunal involves a dependence on interpretation of the law and the situation by outsiders, and this may not necessarily be in the best interests of either or both participants. The tribunal members are concerned with precedents and fairness for employment as a whole; not within one industrial concentration. Tribunals are most likely to be used by white-collar and management employees as well as coloured employees and women. Furthermore the compensation ordered by tribunals seldom approaches the maximum figures stated in the Acts and, of course, the tribunal can only act when the dismissal is a fact. It cannot prevent in specific instances.

This does not means that the law can safely be ignored by employers, as the level of complaints to tribunals remains low only as long as practice is ahead of legislation. Even a 'cheap' unfair dismissal could be costly in terms of the unfairness stigma which will influence employee relations generally, can have a damaging public relations effect and could jeopardise the career of the manager to blame. Thus the law determines management practice.

Determining Fairness

The novel legal concept of fairness relating to dismissal is determined in two stages — *potentially fair* and *actually fair*.

A dismissal is potentially fair if there is a fair ground for it. Such grounds are:

(a) LACK OF CAPABILITY OR QUALIFICATIONS

If the employee lacks the skill, aptitude or physical health to do the job for which he is being paid, then there is a potentially fair ground for his dismissal.

(b) MISCONDUCT

This category covers the range of behaviours that we examined in considering the grievance and discipline processes — disobedience, absence, insubordination and criminal acts. It can also include taking industrial action.

(c) REDUNDANCY

Where an employee's job ceases to exist, it is potentially fair to dismiss him for redundancy.

(d) STATUTORY BAR

When employees cannot continue to discharge their duties without breaking the law, they can be fairly dismissed. Almost invariably the operation of this category is for drivers who have been disqualified from driving for a period.

(e) SOME OTHER SUBSTANTIAL REASON

The most intangible category is introduced in order to cater for genuinely fair dismissals that were so diverse that they could not realistically be listed. Examples have been security of commercial information (where an employee's husband set up a rival company) or employee refusal to accept altered working conditions.

Having decided whether or not a fair ground existed, the tribunal then proceeds to consider whether the dismissal is fair in the circumstances. Here there are two questions. The first is 'was the decision a *reasonable* one in the circumstances?' and the second is 'was the dismissal carried out in line with the *procedure*?' The second is the easier question to answer as procedural actions are straightforward, and the dismissal should be procedurally fair if the procedure has been carefully followed without any short cuts. Here is a cautionary tale:

> A charge nurse in a hospital attacked a hospital official, punched him and broke his glasses. He was dismissed for misconduct. Later he was convicted of assault and causing damage. A tribunal found his dismissal to be unfair because he was not given a chance to state his case and because his right of appeal was not pointed out.[3]

The questions about decisions that are reasonable in the circumstances is a more nebulous one and the most reliable guide is a common sense approach to deciding what is fair. It would, for instance, be unreasonable to dismiss someone as incapable if the employee had been denied necessary training; just as it would be unreasonable to dismiss a long-service employee for incapacity on the grounds of sickness unless his future incapacity had been carefully and thoroughly determined.

Automatic Decisions

Although fairness usually has to be judged, there are some defined situations in which dismissal is automatically fair or unfair.

It is automatically fair to dismiss an employee who refuses to join a trade union designated in a union membership agreement, unless there are genuine grounds of conscience or other deeply-held personal conviction, provided that the union membership agreement meets the requirements of the 1980 Act, described in Chapter 11. It is also fair to dismiss strikers, providing that they are *all* dismissed while the strike is in progress. If only some of the strikers are dismissed, then the reason must be one of the fair grounds listed above. The 1982 Act varies this by allowing the employer to discriminate between those who remain on strike and those who return to work, providing that he gives four days notice of his intention.

A dismissal will automatically be adjudged unfair if no reason is given, or if an employee is selected for dismissal or redundancy on the grounds of trade union membership. Selection for redundancy would also be automatically unfair if an employee were selected in breach of a customary arrangement or procedure.

Fair Grounds Re-visited

Having mentioned the potentially fair grounds for dismissal, we can now look again at the first three — incapability, misconduct and redundancy — in more detail.

(a) LACK OF CAPABILITY OR QUALIFICATIONS

The first aspect of capability relates to *skill or aptitude.* Although employers have the right and opportunity to test an applicant's suitability for a particular post before he is engaged, or before he is promoted, the law recognises that it is possible that mistakes will be made and that dismissal can be an appropriate remedy for the error, if the unsuitability is gross and beyond redemption. Normally there should be warning and the opportunity to improve before the dismissal is implemented, but there are exceptions if the unsuitability of the employee is based on an attitude that the employee expresses as a considered view and not in the heat of the moment. Another exception is where the employee's conduct is of such a nature that his continued employment is not in the interests of the business, no matter what the reasons for it might be.[4]

> An employee of a shop-fitting company tended to irritate the customers, lacking 'the aptitude and mental quality to be co-operative with, and helpful to, important clients'. His employer dismissed him and the tribunal accepted the fairness of the ground but not the procedural fairness of the decision. On appeal the tribunal judgement was overturned as specific warnings of the procedure type would not have altered the employee's performance. He had known for some time that he was at risk because of his difficulty in getting on with the customers and was not able to change his attitude.[5]

Nevertheless, the employer will have to demonstrate the employee's unsuitability to the satisfaction of the tribunal. This will involve evidence of unsuitability and the evidence must not be undermined by providing the employee with, for instance, a glowing testimonial at the time of his dismissal.

Although we have seen that dismissal without specific warnings can be fair, it is normal for procedural fairness to be required, especially in giving the employee the chance to state his case and to improve.

The 57-year old sales manager of the very small English subsidiary of a German distributing company was receiving £3,000 a year in 1972. In the first year of operations the sales results were poor and there was an overall loss of £15,000. The employee was dismissed and given three months salary and commission in lieu of notice. On appeal this was found unfair, on the grounds that there was no warning nor chance for him to state his case and improve. This decision was made even after it was accepted that the employee was not really capable of the duties.[6]

If the employee is grossly incompetent, so that any action taken by way of investigation, warning and opportunity to improve would be unlikely to have any effect, then the dismissal may be regarded as fair:

An employee who admitted that he was in the wrong job and that improvement by him was unlikely was found to have been fairly dismissed, despite the fact that the employer had not provided a period to see if improvement could be made.[7]

Lack of skill or aptitude is a fair ground when the lack can be demonstrated and where the employer has not contributed to it — by, for instance, ignoring it for a long period — but normally there must be the chance to state a case and/or improve before the dismissal will be procedurally fair.

The second aspect of capability is *qualifications*; the degree, diploma or other paper qualification needed to qualify the employee to do the work for which he has been employed. The simple cases are those of misrepresentation, where an employee claims qualifications he does not have. More difficult are the situations where the employee cannot acquire necessary qualifications:

A Post Office recruited a telegraph officer. In order to guard against dilution the Union of Postal Workers had negotiated an agreement with the Post Office that all those recruited would have to pass a special aptitude test by a specified date, providing that their practical work was acceptable. They would be allowed three attempts at the test. The officer failed the test three times and was dismissed after five years service. An Industrial Tribunal and the National Industrial Relations Court both judged the dismissal fair.[8]

The third aspect of capability is *health*. It is potentially fair to dismiss an employee on the grounds that he is incapable because of ill-health, but it must not be too hasty and there must be the consideration of alternative employment. Not only is the procedure followed important, but also the way in which medical evidence is used:

While employers can not be expected to be, nor is it desirable that they should set themselves up as, medical experts, the decision to dismiss or not to dismiss is not a medical question, but a question to be answered by the employers in the light of the available medical evidence.[9]

Normally absences through sickness have to be frequent or prolonged, although absence which seriously interferes with the running of a business may be judged fair even if it is neither frequent nor prolonged, but in all cases the employee must be consulted before being dismissed.

A man had been employed by a company for eighteen years before his dismissal in 1975, but had had long periods of sickness; twenty weeks in 1972—73 and 29 weeks in 1973—74. He returned to work in February 1974 but was unable to resume his original duties, so clerical work was found for him. Two months later he asked to return to his old job and was told that he could do this provided that he was able to demonstrate his fitness during the following six months, while continuing his temporary clerical work. He was then absent for six weeks and dismissed by his employer. This was held to be fair.[10]

It is appropriate to mention here that dismissal for pregnancy is unfair, unless the employee is unable to carry on doing her job or unless continuing to employ her would be contravening a statute, such as the Ionising Radiation Regulations. This is dealt with more fully in Chapter 15.

The first successful claim for unfair dismissal on the grounds of pregnancy, following the provisions of the Employment Protection Act, was in November 1976.

A woman with a poor record of sickness absence was given time off for a gynaecological operation. She was also warned that any further time off in the following six months would lead to dismissal. Two months later she was dismissed after going in to hospital where she had a miscarriage. The employer contended that the dismissal was fair because pregnancy was not the principal reason for the dismissal. The tribunal found the dismissal unfair on the grounds that she would not have been dismissed if she had not had a miscarriage, which was a reason connected with pregancy.[11]

(b) MISCONDUCT

The range of behaviours that can be described as 'misconduct' is so great that we need to consider different broad categories, the first being *disobedience*. As we saw in Chapter 5 it is implicit in the contract of employment that the employee will obey lawful instructions; but this does not mean blind, unquestioning obedience in all circumstances: the instruction has to be 'reasonable' and the employee's disobedience 'unreasonable' before the dismissal can be fair. The tribunal would seek to establish exactly what the employee was engaged to do and whether the instruction was consistent with the terms of employment.

A woman was employed on the understanding that she could have leave during her children's holidays. After a period she was informed that it was not feasible to continue her employment on these terms and she was given twelve month's warning of the need to make alternative arrangements. She did not make any such arrangements and was then dismissed for refusing to work during school holidays. This dismissal was found to be fair as the company had shown it needed her services during the holidays, the nature of her work had not changed and she had been unreasonable in rejecting the new terms. We must also note that her trade union had agreed to the change.[12]

Although it is generally fair to dismiss the employee for *absence*, including lateness, the degree of the absence will be an issue. Lateness will seldom be seen to justify dismissal, unless it is persistent and after warning. Absence may be appropriate for dismissal if the nature of the work makes absence unsupportable by the employer. It will normally be expected that the employer will take account of an employee's previous record before taking extreme action.

The third area of misconduct is *insubordination* or rudeness:

. . . words or conduct showing contempt for one's employers — deserved or otherwise, and as distinct from disagreement or criticism — may make it impossible for the employer to exercise the authority which the law regards as his or to assume that the job in hand will be properly done.[13]

It is important that the insubordination should be calculated rather than a single moment of hysteria. The willingness of the employee to apologise can also be important.

> A woman employee with five years of satisfactory service called her manager a 'stupid punk' in a heated moment and in front of other employees. Later she refused to apologise. The tribunal held that the dismissal was unfair as it was based on a single episode in a substantial period of service. The compensation for the employee was, however, reduced to £20 because she would not apologise.[14]

Rudeness to customers is more likely to result in dismissal that a tribunal will find fair.

Another area of misconduct is *criminal action*. Tribunals are not courts for criminal proceedings, so that they will not try a case of theft or dishonesty, they will merely decide whether or not dismissal was a reasonable action by the employer in the circumstances. If a man is found guilty by court proceedings this does not justify automatically fair dismissal, it must still be procedurally fair and reasonable, so that theft off-duty is not necessarily grounds for dismissal. On the other hand strong evidence that would not be sufficient to bring a prosecution may be sufficient to sustain a fair dismissal. Clocking-in offences will normally merit dismissal. Convictions for other offences like drug handling or indecency will only justify dismissal if the nature of the offence will have some bearing on the work done by the employee. For someone like an apprentice instructor it would almost certainly justify summary dismissal, but in other types of employment it would be unfair, just as it would be unfair to dismiss an employee for a driving offence when there was no need for him to drive in the course of his duties and he had other means of transport for getting to work.

(c) REDUNDANCY

Dismissal for redundancy is now covered in the Employment Protection (Consolidation) Act of 1978 and ensures compensation for the employee who is made redundant, provides the opportunity of compensation for unfair redundancy, and for consultation prior to redundancy. There is a helpful definition of redundancy in the 1965 Redundancy Payments Act:

> ... redundancy occurs where the employer has stopped or is about to stop carrying on business in the place or for the purpose for which the employee in question was employed, or where the requirements of the business for work of a particular kind, or in a particular place, have ceased or diminished or are likely to do so.[15]

Apart from certain specialised groups of employees anyone who has been continuously employed for two years or more is guaranteed a compensation payment from his employer if he is dismissed for redundancy. The compensation is not assessed in the same way as compensation for unfair dismissal, but on a sliding scale relating length of service, age and rate of pay per week. If the employer wishes to escape the obligation to compensate, then he must show that the reason for dismissal was something other than redundancy. When the compensation payment is made the employer is able to recover some of it from the Department of Employment's Redundancy Fund, so the Department too will wish to be satisfied that the redundancy is genuine.

One of the most important aspects of redundancy from the employer's point of view is the procedure that is followed in redundancy situations. The Employment Protection Act introduced new rules relating to redundancy by stating that if ten or more employees are to be made redundant, and if those employees are in unions that are recognised by the employer – or have been recommended for recognition by ACAS – then the employer must give written notice of intention to the unions concerned and the Department of Employment at least 60 days before the first dismissal. If it is proposed to make more than 100 employees redundant within a three-month period, then 90 days' advance notice must be given. Having done this the employer has a legal duty to *consult* with the union representing the employees on the redundancies: he is not obliged to negotiate with them, merely to explain, listen to comments and reply with reasons. The Employment Protection Act also gives employees the right to reasonable time off with pay during their redundancy notice.

A further provision is in the Trade Union and Labour Relations Act to alter the burden of proof location. Originally it was for the employee to show that he was redundant if there was any dispute, now the burden of proof lies with the employer.

Probably the most difficult aspect of redundancy for the employer is the selection of those who should be declared redundant, rather than the question whether or not redundancy is justified. The obvious points here are that selection would not be in contravention of an agreed procedure and, in default of any other agreed principle for selection, that the general rubric of 'last-in-first-out' should operate. Also selection should not be on grounds of sex or race.

Part-time employees can be in a vulnerable position, as they can be made redundant if their jobs are to be made full-time and they are not able to comply with the revised terms:

> A part-time secretary did work for two directors of a chain of garages, but reorganisation involved the job being reclassified as full-time with a need to travel. The part-time scretary was willing to move to a full-time basis for her contract but refused the position as she did not hold a driving licence. She was dismissed as redundant and, on appeal, this was held to be fair.[16]

Behaving so that the employee says 'I quit' instead of the employer saying 'You're fired' equally makes the employer liable. This is known as constructive dismissal. Following decisions under the Industrial Relations Act the principle was set out in the Trade Union and Labour Relations Act.

> . . . an employee shall be treated . . . as dismissed by his employer if . . . the employee terminates that contract, with or without notice, in circumstances such that he is entitled to terminate it without notice by reason of his employer's conduct.[17]

The type of employer behaviour that might justify such employee action is where the employee makes changes unilaterally in status, pay, benefits, working arrangements or place of work of the employee that can be construed as a serious breach of contract, although the tendency in judgements has been to widen that test, for instance:

> . . . the perception of the facts by which the test has to be applied has changed
> . . . employer conduct may properly fall within para. 5 (2) (c) notwithstanding

that it is not expressly in breach of contract, if it is of a kind which, in accordance with good industrial practice, no employee could reasonably be expected to accept.[18]

This widening does not, however, inevitably increase the burden upon the employer as the same judgement says later:

> ... the conduct of both parties has to be looked at when assessing whether or not the employer's conduct was such that the employee is entitled to . . . say that he was forced to go.[19]

During 1978 the employer's position in constructive dismissal cases was somewhat strengthened by the decision that the 'constructively dismissed' employee has to prove a substantial breach of contract by the employer. There is also the rarely-heard doctrine of 'constructive resignation' whereby the employee behaves in such a way that his employer can reasonably assume that he has resigned, even though he may not have formally done so. This becomes important when the employee challenges the assumption. For constructive resignation to be established, there must be a clear breach of the terms of contract and intention by the employee not to continue to be bound by the contract.

Unauthorised absence usually will be construed as constructive resignation, especially in situations, for instance, where an employee asks for leave at a particular time and has it turned down. If he proceeds to take the leave he has been denied, then he will almost certainly be constructively resigning.

Some of the cases that have been through tribunal will illustrate the complexity of this issue:

> An employee was employed by a construction company and was moved to a different working location. He left and claimed constructive dismissal due to unilateral change of his workplace. His claim was upheld on the grounds that his contract of employment did not define his employment as a mobile operator under the terms of the Company's working rule agreement.[20]

> A rota was agreed between trade union representatives and the management of an organisation under which day workers would work nights. One of the employees who was asked to change to nights, in line with the agreement, refused, left work and claimed that he had been constructively dismissed. This dismissal was found fair on the grounds that the collective agreement was an implied term of the contract and that changes in working practice arising therefrom were not a breach.[21]

Figure 20.1 is a summary of the main unfair dismissal provisions and Figure 20.2 is an algorithm for estimating the fairness of a dismissal.

Compensation for Dismissal

Having considered the various ways in which the employee might have some legal redress against his employer when his contract is terminated, we now consider the remedies. If an employee believes that he has been unfairly dismissed he has to complain to an industrial tribunal. The office of the tribunal will refer the matter first to ACAS in the hope that an amicable solution between the parties can be reached. As was indicated at the beginning of this chapter a number of issues are settled in this way. Either the discontented employee realises that he has no case or the employer makes an arrangement in view of the likely tribunal finding. If an agreement is not reached the case will be heard by an industrial tribunal and if either party is not satisfied with the finding they can appeal to the Employment Appeal Tribunal.

The tribunal can make two types of award; either they can order that the ex-employee is re-employed or they can award him financial compensation from his ex-employer for the loss that he has suffered. The Employment Protection (Consolidation) Act makes re-employment the main remedy, although this was not previously available under earlier legislation. They will not order re-employment unless the dismissed employee wants it and they can choose between *re-instatement* or *re-engagement*. In re-instatement the employee gets his old job back under the same terms and conditions, plus any increments etc. to which he would have become entitled if he had not been dismissed and any arrears of payment that he would have received if his employment had not been interrupted. The situation is just as it would have been, including all rights deriving from length of service, if the dismissal had not taken place. The alternative of re-engagement will be that the employee is employed afresh in a job comparable to the last one, but without continuity of employment. The decision as to which of the two to order will depend on assessment of the practicability of the alternatives, the wishes of the unfairly dismissed employee and the natural justice of the award taking account of the ex-employee's behaviour.

If the employer disagrees with the tribunal award of re-employment so strongly that he refuses to comply he will incur a penalty award of between 13 and 26 weeks' pay depending on the circumstances, and if the dismissal was based on discrimination arising from union membership, race or sex the penalty must be between 26 and 52 weeks' pay, subject to a maximum. In addition to this the employee would be entitled to a two-tier award as compensation for his dismissal. The first tier is a *basic award* calculated in the same way as redundancy compensation on each full year of service in various brackets:

Each year of service wherein the employee is aged 41 or over — 1½ weeks' pay
Each year of service between the ages of 22 and 41 — 1 week's pay
Each year of service between the ages of 18 and 22 — ½ weeks's pay

The second tier is the *compensatory award,* depending on the tribunal's assessment of the employee's financial loss suffered as a result of his dismissal. The loss may be actual in terms of loss of earnings or potential in, for instance, loss of pension rights, and is subject to reduction if the ex-employee has not taken due steps to mitigate his loss.

The tribunal may well decide that an award of re-employment would be impracticable and in this case they would award financial compensation only: a basic and compensatory award. Before leaving the subject of compensation we should re-iterate that it is only due if the tribunal finds the employee to have been unfairly dismissed after conciliation between the parties has failed; they will not necessarily award re-employment and it is very unlikely that they will make maximum awards, save in the most flagrant defiance of the law by the employer.

In 1980 the maximum compensatory award was made in only eight cases. The fact that the employee can only seek redress after dismissal makes the number of re-instatements and re-engagements low. In other countries the situation differs in that the dismissal does not take effect until its fairness is determined, so that there is less likelihood of the employment relationship having broken down. Research by Paul Lewis among people who have been dismissed indicates that most applicants to

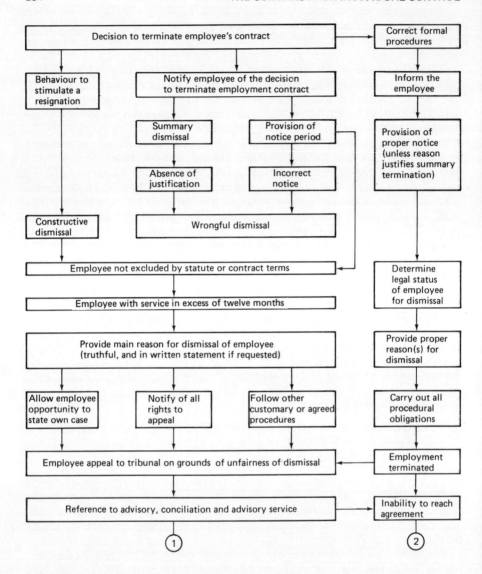

tribunal want their old jobs back at the time of making their claim, but want cash compensation instead by the time the hearing takes place. Even those still wanting re-instatement and having it ordered by the tribunal will still probably not be re-instated by their employer, who will prefer enhanced compensation. Only six of Lewis's 343 respondents achieved re-instatement or re-engagement.[22]

Written Statement of Reasons

The Employment Protection (Consolidation) Act gives employees the right to obtain from their employer a written statement of the reasons for their dismissal, if they

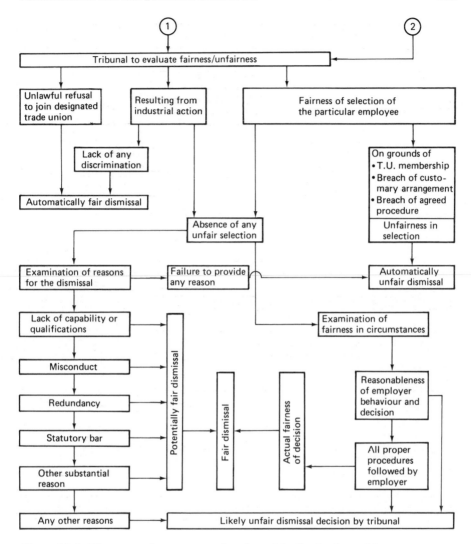

Figure 20.1. Diagrammatic summary of main unfair dismissal provisions

are dismissed after at least 26 weeks' service. If asked, the employer must provide the statement within 14 days. If it is not provided the employee can complain to an Industrial Tribunal that he has been refused and the tribunal will award him two weeks' pay if they find the complaint justified. The employee can also complain, and receive the same award, if the employer's reasons are untrue or inadequate – provided, again, that the tribunal agrees.

Such an award is in addition to anything the tribunal may decide about the unfairness of the dismissal, if the employee complains about that. The main purpose of this provision is to enable the employee to test whether he has a reasonable unfair dismissal complaint or not. Although the statement is admissible as evidence in

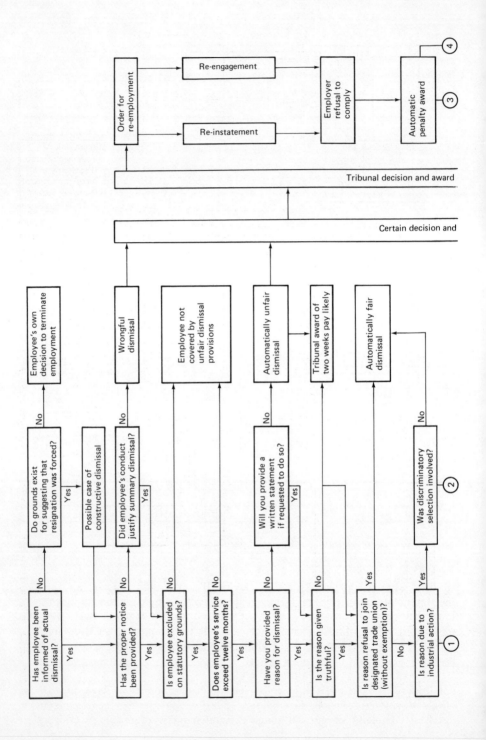

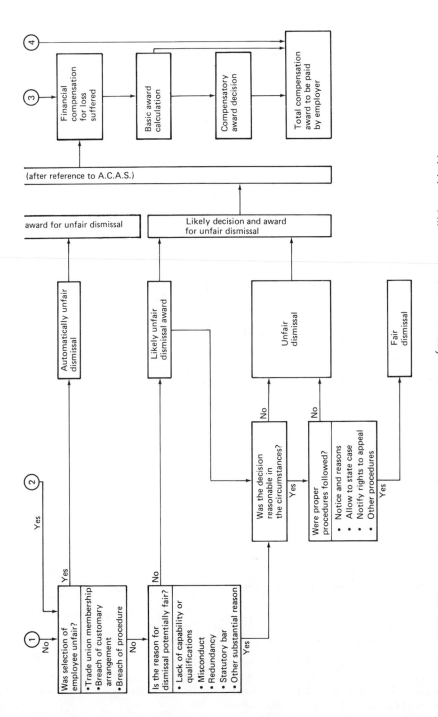

Figure 20.2. An algorithm for estimating fairness of dismissal { Note: many answers will be guided by current legal provisions and cases of precedent

tribunal proceedings, the tribunal will not necessarily limit their considerations to what the statement contains. If the tribunal members were to decide that the reasons for dismissal were other than stated then the management's case would be jeopardised.

Notice

An employee qualifies for notice of dismissal when he has completed four weeks of employment with an employer. At that time he is entitled to receive one week's notice. This remains constant until he has completed two years' service, after which it increases to two weeks' notice, thereafter increasing on the basis of one week's notice per additional year of service up to a maximum of twelve weeks for twelve years' unbroken service. These are minimum statutory periods. If the employer includes longer periods of notice in the contract, which is quite common with senior employees, then they are bound by the longer period.

The employee is required to give one week's notice after completing four weeks' service and this period does not increase as a statutory obligation. If an employee accepts a contract in which the period of notice he has to give is longer, then he is bound by that, but the employer may have problems of enforcement if an employee is not willing to continue in employment for the longer period.

Neither party can withdraw notice unilaterally. The withdrawal will only be effective if the other party agrees. Therefore, if an employer gives notice to an employee and wishes later to withdraw it, this can only be done if the employee agrees to the contract of employment remaining in existence. Equally the employee cannot change his mind about resigning unless the employer agrees.

Notice only exists when a date has been specified. The statement 'We're going to wind up the business, so you will have to find another job' is not notice: it is a warning of intention. The warning could, however, be classified as repudiation of the contract by the employer, thus justifying the employee in bringing a constructive dismissal complaint.

The employer retains the right to dismiss summarily, without notice, if the employee's conduct merits summary termination. Difficulties occur with the interpretation of certain phrases:

> There have been half a dozen cases on the precise meaning of 'fuck off' — apparently a common industrial salutation. In *Futty v. Brekkes*, 1974, a foreman in the course of a discussion with a fish filleter on Hull docks said to him, 'If you don't like the job you can fuck off'. He made no bones about it! The filleter took him at his word and then claimed damages for unfair dismissal. The tribunal held that what the foreman actually meant was, 'if you are complaining about the fish you are working on; or the quality of it, or if you do not like what in fact you are doing then you can leave your work, clock off, and you will be paid up to the time when you do so. Then you can come back when you are disposed to start work again the next day'. His remark was therefore no more than 'a general exhortation' whose precise effect the filleter had failed to appreciate.[23]

In another case (brought, believe it or not, against the Humberside Erection Company) a supervisor was held to have been constructively dismissed when his employer told him to 'fuck off and get some overalls on'.[24] This remark was to be construed as a demotion, repudiating the contract!

REFERENCES

1. Ministry of Labour, *Dismissal Procedures* (HMSO) 1976, p. 57.
2. Department of Employment, *Gazette* (HMSO) January 1982, p. 539.
3. *Amar-Ojok v. Surrey Area Health Authority*, 1975.
4. In the judgement of the National Industrial Relations Court on the case of *James v. Waltham Holy Cross U.D.C.*, 1973.
5. *A. J. Dunning & Sons (Shop Fitters) Ltd v. Jacomb*, 1973.
6. *Winterhalter Gastronom Ltd v. Webb*, 1972.
7. *Matthews v. F.L. Sanderson & Sons Ltd*, 1979.
8. *Blackman v. Post Office*, 1974.
9. In the judgement of the Employment Appeal Tribunal on the case of *East Lindsey District Council v. Daubney*, 1977.
10. *Coulson v. Felixstowe Dock and Railway Co.*, 1975.
11. *George v. Beecham Group Ltd.*, 1976.
12. *Moreton v. Selby*, 1974.
13. Winchup M., *Modern Employment Law*, (Heinemann) 1976, pp. 85–86.
14. *Rosenthall v. Butler*, 1972.
15. Redundancy Payments Act, 1965, Section 1.
16. *Cant v. James Edwards (Chester) Ltd.*, 1981.
17. Trade Union & Labour Relations Act 1974, Sch. 1, part II, para. 5(c).
18. E.A.T. judgement in *Geo. Wimpey & Co. Ltd. v. Cooper*, 1977.
19. *Ibid.*
20. *Aldridge v. Dredging and Construction Company Ltd*, 1972.
21. *Dudar v. Leys Malleable Castings Company Ltd*, 1972.
22. Lewis P., 'Why Legislation Failed to Provide Employment Protection for Unfairly Dismissed Employees' in *British Journal of Industrial Relations*, November 1981, pp. 316–326.
23. Whinchup M., *op. cit.*, p. 72.
24. *Walker v Humberside Erection Company*, 1974.

21

Working Safely in Healthy Conditions

Through ignorance or carelessness an employer may endanger his employees' health by exposing them to hazard in the working conditions that are provided. Through ignorance or carelessness an individual employee may endanger his colleagues or those using the product or service he provides. Both have responsibilities in the employment contract.

An impression of the scale of accidents and health hazards at work is given by the fact that 360,000,000 working days were lost due to certified incapacity for sickness and invalidity benefit in 1980.[1] This number is increasing and many of the days are lost due to sickness caused or exacerbated by aspects of working conditions. There is, of course, a difference between this feature of occupational life and the other activities we consider in this book, due to the nature of the social responsibility that is involved. Lives rather than satisfaction are at stake, and the problems to be avoided are those of injury or long-term incapacity, rather than a drop in earnings or an arrested cash flow.

In the area of safety and health legislative intervention has existed continuously for longer than in any other matter we consider. It was in 1842 that Parliament approved Lord Shaftesbury's bill to protect children from being put to work in mines and factories, while the factory inspectorate was established as long ago as 1833. There is now a strong body of detailed law. The principal current statutes are:

The Factories Act 1961
The Offices, Shops and Railway Premises Act 1963
The Health and Safety at Work Act 1974

There are a host of minor statutes and orders which are to be gradually superseded by Part I of the Health and Safety at Work Act (hereinafter referred to by the inevitable shorthand of HASWA).

The Factories Act 1961

This statute applies to all factories where two or more persons are employed in manual labour by way of trade or for the purpose of gain in a range of operations that are set out in Section 175 of the Act. This list is very wide and includes, for instance, building sites, dry docks, gas holders of over 5,000 cubic feet and the production of films.

The Act sets out to ensure that minimum standards are maintained in factories on cleanliness, space for people to work in, temperature and ventilation, lighting, conveniences, clothing, accommodation and first-aid facilities. Many of the standards are fairly obvious, like keeping factories clear of the effluvia from drains, but some of them provide very precise levels that have to be met. Workshops must be so organised that every person employed has a minimum of 410 cubic feet of space excluding any air space more than 14 feet from the floor. That means that employees must have at least 29 square feet of space to work in, or more if the ceiling is less than 14 feet from the floor.

Another very specific figure is for working temperature, which must be at least 60° fahrenheit (15.5° centigrade) after the first hour if a substantial proportion of the work of employees in a work room is to be done sitting and does not involve serious physical effort. Lavatories must be provided in the proportion of at least one for every twenty-five men and one for every twenty-five women, and first-aid boxes must be provided on the scale of one for every 150 employees. If a factory employs more than 50 people there must be at least one person trained in first-aid.

There are further requirements relating to general safety, fire precautions and various statutory registers and reports that have to be kept on things like reportable accidents and industrial diseases. Although there are excellent guides to the legislation available from Her Majesty's Stationery Office, these only deal with the main points in the Act.[2] In every factory there needs to be readily available the standard work of reference, originally produced by Redgrave.[3] The 1961 Factories Act is the most recent of a succession of such statutes, so that most factory managers are familiar with the provisions. Part of the enforcement machinery is the factory inspector, to whom we have already referred. He has a statutory right of entry to factory premises, without any obligation to give notice of his impending arrival. HASWA reinforced his authority by empowering him to issue improvement notices requiring remedial action by the employer within a specified time or prohibition notices to stop a particular operation or process forthwith. Although both these notices can be the subject of appeal to an industrial tribunal, the prohibition remains in force until the appeal has been decided.

Offices, Shops and Railway Premises Act 1963

The Offices, Shops and Railway Premises Act was introduced to extend to these buildings protection similar to that provided for factories. The legislation covers the type of premises described, but does not include offices in which fewer than twenty-one man-hours are worked in a week or movable offices in which people will work for less than six months.

The general provisions are very similar to those of the Factories Act, and deal with cleanliness, lighting, ventilation and so on. There is a difference in the minimum space provision for employees. This is set at at least 40 square feet of floor space for each person employed, or 400 cubic feet for each person if the ceiling height is less than 10 feet. The temperature requirement is slightly higher than for factories: 61° fahrenheit (16.0° centigrade) after the first hour. The detailed provisions are obtainable in explanatory booklets.

Health and Safety at Work Act 1974

The Health and Safety at Work Act of 1974 is an attempt to provide a comprehensive system of law, covering the health and safety of people at work.

> Its objectives, which are very ambitious, include both raising the standards of safety and health for all persons at work, and protection of the public, whose safety and health are put at risk by the activities of persons at work. Thus, because of its general application, it brings within statutory protection many classes of persons who previously were unprotected.[4]

The Act is based largely on the recommendations of the Robens Committee on Safety and Health,[5] and has various institutions. *The Health and Safety Commission* has a Chairman and between six and nine other members appointed by the Secretary of State to represent employers, employees and local authorities. The Commission then appoints three people to form the *Health and Safety Executive,* one of whom is the Director, to undertake the daily administration of affairs. The Commission is responsible for carrying out the policy of the Act and providing advice to local authorities and others to enable them to discharge the responsibilities imposed upon them by the Act. It issues codes of practice and regulations, as well as having the power to make investigations and inquiries.

The Employment Medical Advisory Service was set up in 1972 to provide general advice to the government on industrial medicine matters and a corps of employment medical advisors to carry out medical examinations of employees whose health may have been endangered by their work. Responsibility for this service can now be delegated by the Secretary of State to the Health and Safety Commission.

The Factory Inspectorate has already been mentioned and has a large part to play in the monitoring of the Act. In 1976 there were 830 inspectors, compared with 681 in 1973.[6] They specialise in the problems of different industries, so that there is, for instance, an Alkali Inspectorate responsible specifically for chemical plants. Inspection under the Offices, Shops and Railway Premises Act is normally the responsibility of the local authority.

We now review the ways in which HASWA requirements are enforced.

(a) EMPLOYER HEALTH AND SAFETY POLICY

Each employer is required to declare a policy on safety and health in the organisation, including details of the organisation to carry out the policy. All employees must be advised of what the policy is. It is perhaps inevitable that many employers have regarded this as a statutory chore and have gone through the motions of articulating a policy in terms of the bare minimum that is possible, rather than thinking out a policy statement that will have genuine impact on safe working. The report of the inspectorate for 1976 is very critical of companies where this happens, especially where the policy is a hollow statement without action to implement the declared intentions. Other specific criticisms were the lack of information in policy statements about particular hazards and how they could be dealt with, and a failure to stress management responsibility for safety as strongly as those of safety representatives.[7] Another requirement of the Act is up-dating:

> ... it is the duty of every employer to prepare, and as often as may be appropriate revise, a written statement of general policy with respect to the health and safety at work of his employees ...[8]

If a safety policy is produced as something then to be filed away and forgotten, there is little chance that arrangements for coping with new hazards or changed working conditions will be made. The need for safety policy statements to be specific to the circumstances makes it difficult to offer models, but a useful starting point is provided by Armstrong:

> The general policy statement should be a declaration of the intention of the employer to safeguard the health and safety of his employees. It should emphasise four fundamental points: first, that the safety of employees and the public is of paramount importance; second, that safety will take precedence over expediency; third, that every effort will be made to involve all managers, supervisors and employees in the development and implementation of health and safety procedures; and fourth, that health and safety legislation will be complied with in the spirit as well as the letter of the law.[9]

(b) MANAGERIAL RESPONSIBILITY

The management of the organisation carry the prime responsibility for implementing the policy they have laid down, but they also have a responsibility under the Act for operating the plant and equipment in the premises safely and meeting all the Act's requirements whether these are specified in the policy statement or not. In the case of negligence proceedings can be taken against an individual, responsible manager as well as against the employing organisation. The appointment of a safety officer can be one way of meeting this obligation. He does not become automatically responsible for all managerial failures in the safety field, but he does become an in-house factory inspector.

(c) EMPLOYEE RESPONSIBILITY

The management cannot be totally responsible for operations within the organisation, and the Act requires employees to take due care of their own safety and that of others, as well as their *health*, which appears a more difficult type of responsibility for the individual to exercise. The employee is, therefore, legally bound to comply with the safety rules and instructions that the employer promulgates. Rose reported that nine employees had been prosecuted under this section of the Act.[10]

Employers are also fully empowered to dismiss employees who refuse to obey safety rules on the grounds of misconduct, especially if the possibility of such a dismissal is explicit in the disciplinary procedure.

> An employee who refused to wear safety goggles for a particular process was warned of possible dismissal because the safety committee had decreed that goggles or similar protection were necessary. His refusal was based on the fact that he had done the job previously without such protection and did not see that it was now necessary. He was dismissed and the tribunal did not allow his claim of unfair dismissal.[11]

(d) SAFETY REPRESENTATIVES

One of the more radical features of HASWA is to rely on involvement of the workforce as one of the normal means of keeping the place of work safe, instead of relying completely on the strict enforcement of standards by external bodies. A controversial aspect of this is the provision for safety representatives: either elected by the employees or appointed by recognised trade unions to represent the employees in consultations with the employers in promoting and developing measures to ensure the safety and health of employees.

Originally HASWA provided for the alternative of election by employees or appointment by recognised trade unions for safety representatives, but the Employment Protection Act repealed section 2 (5) of HASWA, making appointment by recognised trade unions the only method. These representatives have the right to paid time-off for training and to carry out the functions, such as inspecting plant and equipment and copies of documents kept by the employer in connection with the legislation. Furthermore the inspectorate is charged with a duty to inform employees of matters of fact about the premises in which they work and any action to be taken concerning them. Logically the duty to inform employees usually means their representatives:

> In the absence of safety representatives, the inspector may find himself in an embarrassing situation, for, without them, it may be difficult for him to communicate with the employees. It is true that the statute does not stipulate that the representative with whom the inspector communicates must be a safety representative, presumably a trade union official, or even a person selected as representative for this single purpose, could be a medium through whom the inspector could discharge his duty. If, however, the employee's representative were not an appointed safety representative, problems might arise in establishing that he was properly representative of all the employees entitled to receive the information concerned.[12]

(e) SAFETY COMMITTEES

Although the Act does not specifically instruct employers to set up safety committees, it comes very close:

> ... it shall be the duty of every employer, if requested to do so by the safety representatives ... to establish, in accordance with regulations made by the Secretary of State, a safety committee having the function of keeping under review the measures taken to ensure the health and safety at work of his employees and such other functions as may be prescribed.[13]

The safety representatives also have to be consulted about the membership of the committee, and detailed advice on the function and conduct of safety committees is provided in the guidance note on safety representatives.[14]

Research by Leopold and Coyle has shown that there has been a great increase in the number of safety committees in operation since the passing of the Act, especially in companies employing fewer than 200 people and in those industries where there was previously a low level of accidents.[15] They also found the effectiveness of such committees to be much dependent on the employment of trained safety officers. This was generally confirmed by the work of Donnelly and Barrett,[16] but Codrington and Henry are less sanguine in looking at the accident-prone construction industry:

> The innovations of (HASWA) can only produce significant improvements in the construction industry's apalling safety record if there are improvements in trade union site organisation, for without it safety representatives have very little real power or authority . . . With a declining membership and increasing fragmentation of employment relationships on site, the construction unions will only have limited resources available to encourage the development of safety representatives' activities.[17]

(f) SAFETY TRAINING

There is a general requirement in the Act for training to be given, along with information, instruction and supervision, to ensure 'the health and safety at work of his employees'. There is thus fairly wide scope to determine what is appropriate in the differing circumstances of each organisation.

(g) CODES OF PRACTICE

The Commission is empowered to follow the growing practice of issuing codes for people to follow in various situations. Where it is not feasible to specify precisely, there is the possibility of offering general guidance. If the Commission does not wish to prepare a code itself it can approve a code prepared by another body. It is most likely that such approvals will be used for codes prepared by professional bodies or specialised consultants, but it may be that codes prepared by an employer for use in his own premises could be so approved, if the Commission thought that its endorsement was both necessary and appropriate. There remains in the Act the provision for health and safety *regulations* on a wide range of matters, but the power to issue these lies with the Secretary of State and not the Commission.

(h) IMPROVEMENT NOTICES

Inspectors can serve improvement notices on individuals who they regard as being in breach of the HASWA provisions, or earlier legislation, like the Factories Act. This notice specifies the opinion of the inspector and the reasons for it, as well as requiring him to remedy the contravention within a stated period. Most frequently this will be issued to a member of the management of an organisation, depending on which individual the inspector regards as being appropriate, but such a notice could also be issued to an employee who was deliberately and knowingly disobeying a safety instruction.

(i) PROHIBITION NOTICES

An alternative, or subsequent, power of the inspector is to issue a prohibition notice, where he believes that there is a risk of serious personal injury. This prohibits an operation or activity being continued until specified remedial action has been taken.

From the implementation of this section of the Act up until the middle of June 1976, inspectors issued 6,598 improvement notices and 3,414 prohibition notices. There were twenty successful prosecutions for failure to comply with notices.[18]

It is possible for employers to appeal against both improvement and prohibition notices. In 1978 an employer appealed successfully against a prohibition notice issued against a hand-operated guillotine that had been used — as had nine similar machines — for 18 years without accident. Another successful appeal was against an improvement order that was issued requiring safety shoes to be provided free of charge to employees. The tribunal found that the cost of £20,000 in the first year and £10,000 a year thereafter was disproportionate to the risk involved, and that the fact of the shoes being provided free did not make it more likely that they would be worn.[19]

Management Organisation for Safety and Health

Having considered the legal framework, we can now look at ways in which managerial responsibility can be discharged to implement the policy statement. The responsibility of individual members of management has to be circumscribed as accurately as possible to ensure that everyone is not the father of success while failure remains an orphan. This requires a health and safety element in every job description and that needs planning to produce a situation in which the areas of responsibility fit together like pieces of a jig-saw. In looking through job descriptions we have found a number of sections like this:

> The prime responsibility of the supervisor is the safe-working of his subordinates. This cannot be over-emphasised and he should use his very best endeavours to achieve a safe working environment and strict adherence to safety procedures.

The main value of that is simply its emphasis. It makes the issue of safety sound important. The danger is that it does not specify the extent of the responsibility and how the duties interlock with those of the safety officer, production engineer and so forth.

There is an important distinction to be drawn between making the work safe and working safely. The first is the realm mainly of the designer and production engineer. Everyone concerned in the design and manufacture of plant and equipment, as well as those who engineer the working environment, has a responsibility to make the operations as safe as is possible, by removing hazards or controlling them. These may be the hazards intrinsic to the production process, like manufacturing explosive gas; or a side effect of it, like workers operating unsafely because of a noisy atmosphere. As this is essentially the province of the engineer it lies outside the competence of this book, but we should point out that a process that is designed to be safe by engineering standards can still be unsafe in practice because of the ways in which employees will respond to the requirements of the plant. Engineering design may need to be guided by, or tempered by, judgement of a 'human' kind. This will probably be a job for the safety representatives, but it may need the safety officer or a personnel officer to act as midwife. Making the work safe is completely a management responsibility.

Working safely is principally a management responsibility, but the individual employee may contribute his own negligence to work unsafely in a safe situation. The task of the management is two-fold; first the employee must know what to do, secondly he must translate knowledge into action: he must comply with safe working procedures that are laid down. To meet the first part of the obligation the management need to be scrupulous in communication of drills and instructions and the analysis of working situations to decide what the drills should be. That is a much bigger and more difficult activity than can be implied in a single sentence, but the second part of getting compliance is more difficult and more important. Employee failure to comply with clear drills does not absolve the employer and the management. When an explosion leaves the factory in ruins it is of little value for the factory manager to shake his head and say 'I told him not to do it.' We examine the way to obtain compliance shortly under the discussion about training.

The initiative on safe working will be led by the professionals within the management team. They are the safety officer, the medical officer, the nursing staff and the safety representatives. Although there is no legal obligation to appoint a safety officer, more and more organisations are making such appointments. One reason is to provide emphasis and focus for safety matters. The appointment suggests that the management mean business, but the appointment itself is not enough. It has to be fitted in to the management structure with lines of reporting and accountability which will enable the safety officer to be effective and which will prevent other members of management becoming uncertain of their own responsibilities – perhaps to the point of thinking that they no longer exist. Ideally the safety officer will operate on the two fronts of both making the work safe and ensuring safe working, although this may require an ability to talk constructively on engineering issues with engineers as well as being able to handle training and some industrial relations type arguments. Gill and Martin have demonstrated[20] that there is usually a clear dissonance between what is prescribed and what takes place, because the engineering approach produces complex and detailed manuals based on the belief that safety is a technical rather than human problem, whereas the people who do the work tend to produce different working practices based on experience.

> When we came to study the chemical plants we found an apparent paradox. On the one hand there existed a comprehensive body of written safety practices and procedures to cater for every conceivable contingency, and on the other hand actual working practice often differed considerably from the rules specifying safe working practices. Nevertheless the plants ran well and both the frequency of dangerous incidents and accidents were very low by national standards.[21]

If this is the reality it will be a remarkable safety officer who can deal in both areas without jeopardising his own mental health and safety.

Although not all companies have safety officers, even fewer have medical officers, but there are a number now employed. Their main activity is ususally in dealing with issues of general health and well-being or with very specific industrial hazards like radiation or lead dust. The value of their contribution lies in two directions. First their qualification and expertise is probably unique within the organisation. If it is big enough to employ a medical officer in the first place it will also be big enough to have a variety of technical expertise of the engineering type as well as those familiar with the strength of custom and practice in employment rules. The doctor will almost certainly be the only medically qualified person and can therefore introduce to the thinking on health and safety discussions a perspective and a range of knowledge that is both unique and relevant. Secondly, the doctor speaks with a rare authority. In the eyes of most employees he will probably carry more social status than the managers dealing with health and safety matters, and he will be detached from the management in their eyes and his own. He has his own ethical code, which is different from that of the managers. He is an authoritative adviser to management on making the work safe and can be an authoritative adviser to employees on working safely. He is an invaluable member of the safety committee and a potentially important feature of training programmes.

The medical officer will probably be part-time in employment with the organisation; nurses will probably be a mixture of part-time and full-time. Although their whole training and experience gears them up to taking instructions from doctors rather than from managers, they have to fit in to the normal management structure for responsibility and accountability. They deal more directly with working safely than with making the work safe, and they will often play a part in safety training as well as symbolising care in the face of hazard. Employees will be prepared to discuss with nurses matters that they will not be prepared to discuss directly with managers or safety representatives, so that they become an invaluable source of information about employee concerns and anxieties. This is not to suggest that nurses will disclose to managers matters about   individuals that those individuals wish to preserve as confidential, but that they will provide an interpretation about employee attitudes and apprehension that will not be available in quite the same way from other sources.

Safety representatives are much more recent on the industrial scene than the other professionals mentioned here and their role is different. Although the legislation confer rights upon them, they cannot be held responsible for unsafe working situations. The safety representatives should normally have worked for their employer for two years prior to appointment or have had at least two years experience in similar employment elsewhere. Although the nature of their inspections is to be agreed with the employer, three different methods are recommended for consideration. First are *safety tours,* or general tours of the establishment, and secondly *safety sampling,* which would be examining especially dangerous processes, activities or areas within a factory. This would need to be done systematically rather than randomly in order to keep a running check on potential trouble spots. The third activity recommended is what are termed *safety surveys,* in which there is a general inspection of trouble spots.

Safety Training

The approaches to training we have advanced earlier in this book relate to safety training as well as to other types, but there are one or two special points to be made. We have already referred to the conclusions of Gill and Martin about actual operation being different from prescribed operation, but still safe. The purpose of safety training is that people shall work safely: not that they shall obey the rules. This may sound a dangerous premise but we would argue that rules make no distinction between persons and are frequently produced in such detail as to eliminate thought and therefore become a challenge to people. The important thing is that people should *understand* the nature of hazards and be told the rules and drills. Then they will modify the rules to suit their own — safe — convenience. Without the understanding the modification will be disastrous: with understanding it can lead to working that is responsible and thinking rather than the robotic, mindless following of drills. The trainer cannot, of course, condone the short-cut or he implies a general flexibility in the rules. He has to emphasise the strictness of the rules and the danger of their violation, so that any modification is only taken by the skilled and knowledgeable with a full sense of the responsibility they are assuming. However heretical this may sound, it is consistent with the experience of all of us. The skilled are able to take risks that are beyond the capacity of novices. Adults can cross busy roads when children cannot; advanced motorists can complete driving manoeuvres safely that would be beyond the average driver. The real danger lies in the attempt of the tyro to emulate the expert before he has acquired the skill and knowledge that are needed, and this is another reason why we emphasise the need for understanding so that people can calculate the risks they might take.

Although we seek understanding for employees, there is also a need for *conviction.* This may seem hair-splitting but there is a difference between a skilled man taking calculated risks at a process in which he is expert and the more general ignoring of basic safety drills that are easy to understand, like wearing safety goggles, but which so many people do not believe to be important. Pirani and Reynolds have conducted an interesting investigation[22] into the problem of how to persuade employees to wear safety helmets, goggles, gloves and boots. They soon discovered that the management view was that the reluctance could be attributed to ignorance, lack of concern and lack of self-discipline among the employees. The managers differed, however, in their view of the solution to the problem. Some saw it as a communications problem, while others saw the need for discipline to be imposed. Using the repertory grid technique they obtained from both management and employees a construct of the ideal, safety-conscious employee.

> ... the management sample saw this 'ideal' safety-conscious operative as a half-witted, slow but reliable person who gave little trouble. They saw him as a worker who could be left safely alone but prone to making trivial complaints. He certainly was not depicted as a worker to be respected.
>
> The major construct to emerge from the operatives' data alone was that the ideal safety conscious man was rather a 'cissy' and somewhat unsociable. It is important to note however, that individual operatives did not see him in these terms but felt that this was how the rest of the operatives would view him — a feeling substantiated by a large sample of operatives.[23]

Is it surprising that there was an unwillingness to be seen as a safety-conscious employee?

The project then went on to test the effect of different methods of persuasion: poster campaigns, film shows, fear techniques, dicussion groups, role-playing, and disciplinary action. The effect of these on employee behaviour were tested after two weeks and after four months. The results after two weeks were dramatic, showing a considerable increase in the wearing of all types of safety equipment from all methods of persuasion, with disciplinary action being the most effective. After four months this initial improvement had virtually disappeared with all the persuasion techniques except for role-playing, where it was sustained at almost exactly the same level.

This investigation was at two smallish factories and it would be difficult to make sweeping assumptions on its basis, but it suggests two lines of action. First a management initiative on safety will produce gratifying results in the obeying of rules, but a fresh initiative will be needed at regular and frequent intervals to keep it effective. Secondly the technique of role-playing appears to produce results that are longer-lasting. We also note one of the authors' concluding comments:

> Management must also be prepared to stick rigidly to safety rules whatever the tempo of production. The credibility of management and their policies, whether safety or otherwise, rests only on their fairness and consistency. It is also clear that we cannot isolate attitudes towards safety from other general attitudes and especially at workshop level operatives seem to see safety as part and parcel of the general employer/employee relationship.[24]

Occupational Health

So far the focus of our discussion has been on safety, largely because of the legislation, but there is a much broader facet to the subject: occupational health. This is largely an educational function in that there is the opportunity for employees to be counselled on smoking and diet, and given prior warning on potential health problems. The medical officer in the employing organisation can probably do little that the general practitioner cannot do just as well, but he has the advantage of being accessible and of knowing at least something of the particular working situation — which may be a principal contributor to whatever ails the employee. He will also have experience of the industrial world and specialised knowledge of industrial health hazards. One of the main current interests in occupational health is stress, about which a substantial literature is growing.[25]

With effect from July 1982 there is new legislation relating to provision for first aid in factories, to ensure that there are sufficient 'first-aiders' in the organisation and that there is full information for employees on the location of first aid materials.

SUMMARY PROPOSITIONS

21.1.   Compared with other features of organisational life, employees have a high degree of responsibility for safe working, although the management have prime responsibility for this and near-total responsibility for healthy conditions.

21.2.   Management initiatives to ensure safe working by employees require regular repetition and 'freshening'.

21.3.   Role-playing by employees is the learning technique most likely to produce long-lasting changes in safe working behaviour.

21.4.   Safety is a part of the whole employer/employee relationship and cannot be isolated from other aspects of that relationship.

REFERENCES

1. Central Statistical Office, *Social Trends 1982*, (HMSO) 1981, p. 70.
2. Health and Safety Executive, *The Factories Act 1961: A Short Guide*, 2nd ed. (HMSO) 1977.
3. *Redgrave's Health and Safety in Factories* (Butterworth) 1976.
4. Howells R. and Barrett B., *The Health and Safety at Work Act: A Guide for Managers* (IPM) 1975, p. 9.
5. Department of Employment, *Report of the Committee on Safety and Health at Work* (Robens Report) Cmnd. 5034 (HMSO) 1972.
6. Quoted in Rose P., 'Surveying the New Safety Structure' in *Personnel Management*, November 1976, p. 34.
7. Health & Safety Commission, *Health and Safety in Manufacturing and Service Industries, 1976* (HMSO) 1978.
8. Health and Safety at Work Act 1974, section 2 (3).
9. Armstrong M., *Handbook of Personnel Management Practice* (Kogan Page) 1977, p. 337.
10. Rose P., *op. cit.* p. 34.
11. *Mortimer v. V.L. Churchill*, 1979.
12. Barrett B., 'Safety Representatives, Industrial Relations and Hard Times' in *The Industrial Law Journal*, September 1977, p. 168.
13. Health and Safety at Work Act 1974, section 2 (7).
14. Health and Safety Commission, *Safety Representatives and Safety Committees* (HMSO) 1976.
15. Leopold J. and Coyle R., 'A Healthy Trend in Safety Committees' in *Personnel Management*, May 1981.
16. Donnelly E. and Barrett B., 'Safety Training Since the Act' in *Personnel Management*, June 1981.

17. Codrington C. and Henley J.S. 'The Industrial Relations of Injury and Death' in *British Journal of Industrial Relations*, November 1981, p. 308.
18. Rose P., *op. cit.*, p. 35.
19. Both cases are summarised in *IDS Brief* No. 145 (Incomes Data Services Ltd) November 1978, p. 20.
20. Gill J. and Martin K. 'Safety Management – Reconciling Rules with Reality', in *Personnel Management*, June 1976.
21. *Ibid.*, p. 37.
22. Pirani M. and Reynolds J., 'Gearing up for Safety' in *Personnel Management*, February 1976.
23. *Ibid.*, p. 26.
24. *Ibid.*, p. 29.
25. See, for instance, Torrington D. P. and Cooper C. L., 'The Management of Stress and the Personnel Initiative' in *Personnel Review*, Summer 1977.

Section E
THE CONTRACT FOR PAYMENT

22

Fairness and the Contract for Payment

A quotation from George Thomason usefully introduces our discussion in this chapter;

> Any society, and any employing organisation within it, faces the need to determine two questions about the remuneration or reward of those who make some contribution to production:
>
> First, what in absolute terms shall be the level of wages and salaries, or, alternatively, how the value of production is to be distributed through the ranks of the contributors?
>
> Secondly, what differences in relative payment will be admitted within the system, that is, given the answer to the first question, what differentials are to be given recognition?[1]

The Concept of Fairness

The basic principle informing the thinking of both parties to the employment contract can be expressed in the age-old axiom: 'A fair day's pay for a fair day's work.' The employer, and his managerial agents, feel it is reasonable that the employee should be compensated or rewarded for the skill and effort that he has to exercise. The employee feels there is a reasonable payment that he can expect in exchange for his contribution. When both sets of expectations can be satisfied there is the basis for a payment contract.

The axiom is not necessarily either equitable or just. Karl Marx described it as 'a conservative motto' and more recently a number of commentators have pointed to the way in which the application of this idea impedes the types of change that seem to be needed in some payment arrangements. We can see the comment of Barbara Wootton:

> That every wage bargain must be 'fair' or 'reasonable' now goes without saying. Also unspoken — though for a different reason — is the rubric by which the fair and the reasonable are defined; nobody knows in this context what justice is, and no Socrates walks the streets pestering us to find out. That is where conservatism comes to the rescue. Change — always, everywhere, in everything — requires justification: the strength of conservatism is that it is held to justify itself. It is not therefore surprising that the maintenance of standards, absolute or comparative, should be woven as warp and woof into the texture of wage

discussions; or, to change the metaphor, that history should be summoned to fill the void when moral actions must be performed without moral principles to guide them.[2]

So one criticism of the fairness convention in payment is that, in inhibiting change, it could impede restructuring.

Another critism is implicit in Thomason's second point. Namely, that the differences in relative payment should be according to the differences in the *work* undertaken. As Hyman and Brough[3] point out, there is no intrinsically more logical justification for that argument than there is for the quite different concept of 'from each according to his ability, to each according to his needs'.

Even though the way in which the fairness principle tends to operate in payment can be exposed to criticism, we can as a basis for our discussion accept its pervasiveness. Despite the reservations it is quite clear that the conventional notion of fairness is the basis on which employers and employees, whether individually or collectively, approach the acceptability of the contract for payment.

Fairness involves comparison. Individual employers are anxious to determine whether they pay more or less than their competitors, both within their own industry and within their own locality, while trade union negotiators and individual employees or prospective employees carry out their own comparative studies of the good and bad buys in employment. Much research has been directed to assessing the influence of comparability studies on wage determination. Studies by Addison[4] and by Brown and Sisson[5] suggest that there is a growing significance of the comparability principle in determining acceptable wage levels. In the United States there have been attempts to refine the general wisdom of comparability by demonstrating not only that perceived fairness is necessary for an acceptable wage bargain, but also to identify the specific effects on the quantity or quality of output of the employee perceiving himself to be *un*fairly remunerated. A tentative working hypothesis was that the employee who saw himself to be overpaid would become more diligent and effective, whereas the employee who saw that he was underpaid would produce less quality and quantity of work.

Various attempts have been made by, among others, Adams[6] and Lawler[7,8] to test this hypothesis. Although the results tend to confirm the second part, they are equivocal regarding the first part. Furthermore, of course, they are the results of studies carried out in the United States rather than in Europe, and the culture and prevailing attitudes towards payment are by no means necessarily the same.

Two of the leading British analysts of payment arrangements, Angela Bowey and Tom Husband, have both pointed out the need for a change in traditional managerial attitudes towards pay, because of a change in the realities surrounding the management process which is not often reflected in the arrangements for payment.

They see a general movement in the managing of organisations away from authoritarianism and paternalism towards a greater degree of employee participation in the management process, and they argue that this change in emphasis should be reflected more positively in payment arrangements. Quotations from both observers make the point:

> As firms change their management styles from authoritarian/paternalistic to consultative/participative they must review the nature of their payment strategies. Hopefully the management style will match the mood of the firm's employees, and, in turn be reflected in the determination of an equitable payment structure.

It is obviously wrong to apply techniques, however sophisticated, which call for a management style which does not exist in the Company. Equally it is just as wrong to persevere with techniques which were right for the management style and mood of the employees ten years ago but inappropriate today.[9]

Wherever the time and resources can be made available, and the management style can cope with it or learn to, the most effective way of changing a payment system is to involve in its design and introduction representatives of all those who will have to work with the changed system. In this way they would understand and be committed to the aims of the scheme from the outset, provided the attempt to involve them succeeds.[10]

In the whole field of payment some of the changes taking place are the following:

(a) GROWING INTEREST IN SALARY SYSTEMS

The traditional preoccupation of payment administrators has been with *wages*, but in recent years we have seen growing interest in *salary* systems. This is partly because of the increasing proportion of employees in white-collar posts who therefore are more likely to be salaried, but also because salary administration is coming under closer scrutiny.

The convention has been that wages may be negotiated, but decisions on salaries are made unilaterally by management. Progressively that unilateralism has been challenged by union negotiators and questioned by individual employees. To meet such questioning and challenge, the scheme has to be carefully planned and meticulously administered. *Ad hoc* decisions are dangerous.

(b) GROWING INTEREST IN SECURITY

Payment to managers has a long tradition of elements other than a simple remuneration for the time and effort and skill spent working. Pensions, sickness payment schemes, possibly payment for private medical treatment and many other benefits have become commonplace. Until recently there was relatively little interest in such provisions among manual employees, where the tradition has been to focus on the direct and immediate benefits.

We now see nearly all employees taking a greater interest in the full spectrum of pay and benefits available to them, or potentially available. This is not only the *embourgeoisement* process at work; it is also the result of some income policy initiatives to defer pay increases. This is partly shown in the work of Elliott and Steele,[11] revealing the increasing proportion of weekly earnings that is provided by the basic wage rate.

(c) THE PACKAGE PRINCIPLE

A development of fringe benefits, particularly for executives, has been the so-called cafeteria or package arrangement of 'total remuneration'. These schemes attempt to produce arrangements for remuneration acknowledging the difference in aspiration and personal need between individuals, largely because of their varying tax positions. Instead of general arrangements about company cars, low-interest personal loans, discount purchase facilities and the like, a choice of such benefits is devised and costed so that individuals can make up the particular 'trayful' that suits them. One may relinquish a company car in order to enhance his pension, while another elects to take a large loan from the company at low interest.

Although there is a superficial attraction in such an arrangement, it can be difficult for the employee to understand the scheme in sufficient detail to make the most appropriate choice. It can also be criticised on the grounds that it is the type of provision offered only to a privileged minority in most organisations and will cause resentment among the majority of employees, who feel unfairly disadvantaged. It also has a tendency to be seen, and used, as a means of avoiding legal requirements. Gilling-Smith describes the need for the planner of remuneration strategies to be able:

> ... to think in terms of net-of-tax receipts by the individual as well as of every conceivable method by which the adverse effects on motivation of statutory intervention in the form of salary and wage controls, can be minimised.[12]

(d) THE NATIONAL INTEREST

Payment is an aspect of employment in which there are interests that go beyond those of the employer and employee. The nature of pay bargains is crucial to a country's social and economic development because the bulk of its purchasing power comes from wages and salaries. Much socially disruptive industrial action also stems from dissatisfaction with pay. Moreover there is the inescapable problem of inflation and the wage-price spiral that is an inevitable result if pay rises more quickly than productivity.

EMPLOYEE OBJECTIVES FOR THE CONTRACT FOR PAYMENT

Those who are paid, and those who administer payment schemes, have objectives for the payment contract to which they are a party. Not surprisingly the objectives differ according to whether one is the recipient or the administrator of the payments. There is also some variation in objectives between different recipients, as is shown by the development of remuneration packages. The contract for payment will be satisfactory insofar as it meets the objectives of the parties. Therefore we consider the range of objectives, starting with employees.

(a) FIRST OBJECTIVE: PURCHASING POWER

The absolute level of weekly or monthly earnings determines the standard of living of the recipient, and will therefore be the most important consideration for most employees. How much can I buy? It is apparent that employees are rarely satisfied about their purchasing power, and the annual pay adjustment will do little more than reduce dissatisfaction. The two main reasons for this are inflation and rising expectations.

(b) SECOND OBJECTIVE: 'FELT-FAIR'

We have already discussed the notion of fairness in payment. Here we have the term 'felt-fair' that was devised by Elliott Jaques,[13] who averred that every employee had a strong feeling about the level of payment that was fair *for his job*. Here we move away from the absolute level of earnings to the first of a series of aspects of *relative* income. In most cases this will be a very rough personalised evaluation of what is seen as appropriate.

If the employee feels underpaid he is likely to demonstrate the conventional symptoms of withdrawal from his job: looking for another, carelessness, disgruntlement, lateness, absence and the like. If he feels that he is overpaid, he may simply feel dishonest, or may seek to justify his existence in some way, like trying to *look* busy, that is not necessarily productive.

(c) THIRD OBJECTIVE: RIGHTS
A different aspect of relative income is that concerned with the rights of the employee to a particular share of the company's profits or the nation's wealth. The employee is here thinking about whether the division of earnings is providing fair shares of the Gross National Product. 'To each according to his needs' is overlaid on 'a fair day's pay . . .' This is a strong feature of most trade union arguments and part of the general preoccupation with the rights of the individual, although it is seldom going to enter into negotiations by individuals. Mainly this is the long-standing debate about who should enjoy the fruits of labour.

(d) FOURTH OBJECTIVE: RELATIVITIES
'How much do I (or we) get relative to . . . group X?' This is a slightly different version of the 'felt-fair' argument. It is not the question of whether the employee feels the remuneration to be reasonable in relation to the job that *he* does, but in relation to the jobs other people do.

There are many potential comparators, and the basis of comparison can alter. The Pay Board[14] pointed out three. First is the definition of pay. Is it basic rates or is it earnings? Over how long is the pay compared? Many groups have a level of payment that varies from one time of the year to another. Second is the method of measuring the changes: absolute amount of money or percentage. £5 is ten per cent of £50 but five per cent of £100. Third is the choice of pay dates. Nearly all employees receive annual adjustments to their pay, but not at the same time and the period between settlements can be crucial to perceived relativities.

The simple example in Figure 22.1 shows first the effect of a six-month gap between the annual settlement dates for the two groups, then the effect of a one-month gap and finally the effect of a one-month gap in the opposite direction. The value of the annual adjustment, £5, is the same in absolute terms for both groups in each situation, and Group B starts and finishes at a higher point than Group A, yet it is interesting to see the effect of the varying settlement dates, when compared at the year end. In situation I each group is ahead of the other for six months, but the superficially lower-paid group A actually receives slightly more money in the full year than Group B. Assuming twelve four-week months for simplicity, Group A members receive £2560 compared with £2536 received by members of Group B. In situation II the settlement date is shifted so that A is always behind B. Members of B group still receive £2536, but Group A drops to £2420. Situation III again puts Group A at an advantage. Their members enjoy a higher pay rate for ten months and an annual income of £2620 compared with B's £2516.

(e) FIFTH OBJECTIVE: COMPOSITION
How is the pay package made up? The growing complexity and sophistication of payment arrangements raises all sorts of questions about pay composition. Is £100 pay for 60 hours' work better than £70 for 40 hours' work? The arithmetical answer that the rate per hour for the 40 hour arrangement is marginally better than for 60 hours is only part of the answer. The other aspects will relate to the individual, his

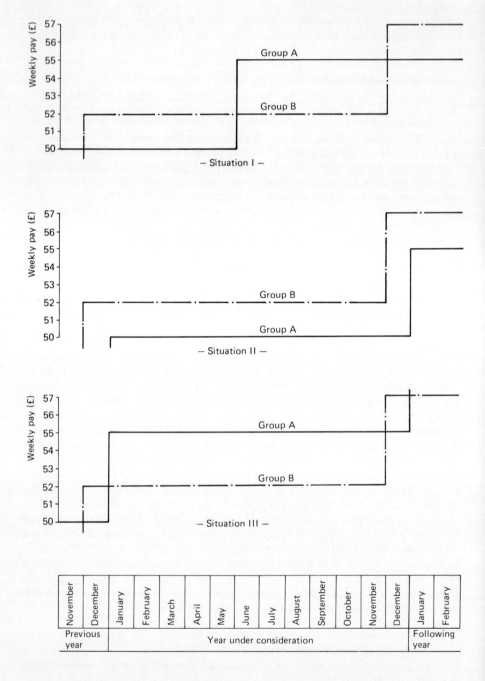

Figure 22.1. An illustration of the effects of different settlement dates

circumstances and the conventions of his working group and reference groups. Another question about composition might be: Is £70 per week, plus sickness payment and a pension, better than £90 per week without? Such questions are not able to produce universally applicable answers because they can be quantified to such a limited extent, but some kernels of conventional wisdom can be suggested as generalisations:

(i) Younger employees are relatively more interested in high direct earnings at the expense of indirect benefits, like pensions and sick pay, which will be of relatively more interest to older employees.

(ii) Incentive payment arrangements are likely to interest employees who either see a reliable prospect of enhancing earnings through the ability to control their own activities, or who see an opportunity to wrest control of their personal activities (which provide little intrinsic satisfaction) away from management by regulating their earnings.

(iii) Married women are seldom interested in payment arrangements that depend on overtime.

(iv) Overtime is used by many men to produce an acceptable level of purchasing power; particularly among the lower-paid.[15]

(v) Pensions and sickness payment arrangements beyond statutory minima are a *sine qua non* of white-collar employment, and are of growing importance in manual employment.

White quotes a study[16] which sheds interesting light on managerial views of payment. 2,500 senior executives in one company were interviewed or asked to complete questionnaires. When the results were analysed six distinct groupings emerged, each having members who shared a common set of values in terms of the rewards which they regarded as of major or minor importance. An important proportion of the respondents were potentially responsive to financial motivators, but others showed little interest in them, other than the 'dissatisfying' effect that Herzberg has noted.

Another implication is that managers are not a homogeneous group as far as attitudes to payment are concerned, but have quite widely differing requirements of the payment contract. The reader may then draw his own inference from this that other employees have equally differing requirements and that the traditional social solidarity of manual employees represented by trade unions could mask individual aspirations for variation that would not in any way undermine that solidarity.

EMPLOYER OBJECTIVES FOR THE CONTRACT FOR PAYMENT

In looking at the other side of the picture we consider the range of objectives in the thinking of employers, or those representing an employer interest *vis-à-vis* the employee.

(a) FIRST OBJECTIVE: PRESTIGE
There is a comfortable and understandable conviction among managers that it is 'a

good thing' to be a good payer. This seems partly to be simple pride at doing better than others, but also there is sometimes a feeling that such a policy eliminates a variable from the contractual relationship. In conversation with one of the authors a chief executive expressed it this way:

> I want to find out the highest rates of pay, job-for-job, within a fifty-mile radius of my office. Then I will make sure that all my boys are paid twenty per cent over that. Then I know where I am with them as I have taken money out of the equation. If they want to quit they can't hide the real reason by saying they're going elsewhere for more cash: they can't get it. Furthermore, if I do have to fill a job I *know* that we won't lose a good guy because of the money not being right.

Whether high pay rates succeed in getting someone the reputation of being a good employer is difficult to see. What seems much more likely is that the low-paying employer will have the reputation of being a poor employer.

(b) SECOND OBJECTIVE: COMPETITION

More rational is the objective of paying rates which are sufficiently competitive to sustain the employment of the right numbers of appropriately qualified and experienced employees to staff the organisation. A distinction is drawn here between competition thinking and prestige thinking, as the former is more calculated, designed to get a good fit on one of the employment contract dimensions rather than simply overwhelm it. It permits consideration of questions such as: How selective do we need to be for this range of jobs? and: How can we avoid over-paying people and inhibiting them from moving on? Every employer has this sort of objective, even if only in relation to a few key posts in the organisation.

(c) THIRD OBJECTIVE: CONTROL

There may be ways of organising the pay packet that will facilitate control of operations and potentially save money. The conventional approach to this for many years has been the use of piecework or similar incentives, but this has become difficult due to the unwillingness of most employees to see their payment fluctuate wildly at the employer's behest. Theoretically overtime is a method of employer control of output through making available or withholding additional payment prospects. In practice, however, employees use overtime for control more extensively than employers. Gradually other ways in which employers could control their wages costs are being eliminated or made more difficult by legislation. Redundancy, short-term lay-off and dismissal are all now more expensive, women are less readily seen as a reservoir of inexpensive, temporary labour, and part-time employees now have to be nationally insured on the same basis as full-time employees.

(d) FOURTH OBJECTIVE: MOTIVATION AND PRODUCTIVITY

There is a widespread conviction about the motivational effect of payments that rests on over-simplistic assumptions about amounts and methods of payment. Motivation is explored more fully in Chapter 8, but some features of payment and its influence on productivity are worth mentioning here.

Incentive payment schemes are extensively used in manufacturing as the basis for paying manual employees, and they have a built-in bias towards volume rather than quality of output. Two extreme examples indicate the weakness of this approach. Someone engaged in the manufacture of diamond-tipped drilling bits would serve his employer poorly if his payment were linked to *output*. If it were possible to devise a payment system that contained an incentive element based on high quality of workmanship or on low scrap value that might be more effective. If school-teachers were paid a 'quantity bonus' it would presumably be based either on the number of children in the class or on some indicator like the number of examination passes. The first would encourage teachers to take classes as large as possible, with probably adverse results in the quality of teaching. The second might increase the proportion of children succeeding in examinations, but would tend to isolate those who could not produce impressive examination performance.

(e) FIFTH OBJECTIVE: PROFITABILITY

Just as employees are interested in purchasing power, the absolute value of their earnings, so employers are interested in the absolute cost of payment, and its bearing on the profitability or cost-effectiveness of the organisation. The importance of this varies with the type of organisation and the relative cost of employees, so that in the refining of petroleum employment costs are minimal, in teaching or nursing they are substantial. The employer interest in this objective obviously increases with the significance of employment costs in the organisation, but he is considering not what he can afford to pay in the short-term, but in the long-term. Not only do employees expect their incomes to be maintained and carry on rising, rather than fluctuating with company profitability, but also a pay settlement of x per cent will set up an expectation of at least x per cent the following year.

Recently accountants have been developing new methods of assessing the true costs of employment. As this topic is not treated elsewhere in this book, readers wishing to pursue the matter may find help in the work of Flamholtz,[17] Hopwood[18] and Giles and Robinson.[19]

MATCHING OBJECTIVES WITHIN THE CONTRACT FOR PAYMENT

The differing objectives of the parties for the contract for payment can be summarised:

Employee	*Employer*
Purchasing power	Prestige
'Felt-fair'	Competition
Rights	Control
Relativities	Motivation and productivity
Composition	Profitability

These two sets of five objectives do not directly match each other and do not integrate in the way Mumford's contract areas are shown in the opening chapter. Nevertheless there is some consensus between employee and employer representatives regarding the area of debate about payment. Glendon, Tweedie and Behrend[20] sampled the opinions of trade union and management negotiators about, among other things, arguments used in pay negotiations. The first question put to trade union negotiators was:

What do you think are the arguments for pay increases which are the most important to your members?

The first question put to management negotiators was:

Which arguments, put forward by your employees' representatives in an attempt to increase your employees' pay, have you personally found to be acceptable?

Many respondents mentioned more than one argument to produce the following results:

Argument	Trade union (per cent)	Managers (per cent)
1. Cost of living; need to improve standard of living	82	55
2. Comparability; parity with other workers	30	25
3. Productivity; increased production; cost saving.	23	31
4. Profitability of the company; full order book; they can afford it.	20	1½
5. Conditions of work; hours; danger; shift work.	17	1½
6. Responsibility; special skills	8	2
7. Differentials within the company	7	4
8. Others	10	18

The Elements of Payment

The payment of an individual will be made up of one or more elements from those shown in Figure 22.2. Fixed elements are those that make up the regular weekly or monthly payment to the individual, and which do not vary other than in exceptional circumstances. Variable elements can be varied either by the employee or the employer.

(a) BASIC

The irreducible minimum rate of pay is the basic. In most cases this is the standard rate also, not having any additions made to it. In other cases it is a basis on which earnings are built by the addition of one or more of the other elements in payment. In 1975 one group of employees — women operatives in footwear — had little more than half of their earnings in basic, while primary and secondary schoolteachers had 99.9 per cent of their pay in this form.

(b) PLUSSAGE

Sometimes the basic has an addition to recognise an aspect of working conditions or employee capability. Payments for educational qualifications and for supervisory responsibilities are quite common. There are also an infinite range of what are sometimes called 'fudge' payments, whereby there is an addition to the basic as a start-up allowance, mask money, dirt money and so forth.

Bonus	Profit allocation		Variable elements
	Discretionary sum		• Irregular
Incentive	Group calculation basis		• Variable amount
	Individual calculation basis		
Overtime payment			• Usually discretionary
Premia	Occasional		
	Contractual		
Benefits	Fringe benefits		Fixed elements
	Payment in kind	Other	• Regular
		Accommodation	• Rarely variable
		Car	• Usually contractual
	Benefit schemes	Other	
		Pension	
		Sick pay	
Plussage	"Fudge" payments		
	Special additions		
Basic rate of payment			Basic

The total potential pay package

Figure 22.2. The potential elements of payment

(c) BENEFITS

Extras to the working conditions that have a cash value are categorised as benefits and can be of great variety. Some have already been mentioned; others include luncheon vouchers, subsidised meals, discount purchase schemes and the range of welfare provisions like free chiropody and cheap hairdressing.

(d) PREMIA

Where employees work at inconvenient times, like shifts or permanent nights, they receive a premium payment as compensation for the inconvenience. This is for inconvenient rather than additional hours of work. Sometimes this is built in to the basic rate or is a regular feature of the contract of employment so that the payment is unvarying. In other situations shift working is occasional and short-lived, making the premium a variable element of payment.

(e) OVERTIME

It is customary for employees working more hours than are normal for the working week to be paid for those hours at an enhanced rate, usually between 10 and 50 per cent more that the normal rate according to how many hours are involved. Seldom can this element be regarded as fixed. No matter how regularly overtime is worked, there is always the opportunity for the employer to withhold the provision of overtime or the employee to decline the extra hours.

(f) INCENTIVE

Incentive is here described as an element of payment linked to the working performance of an individual or working group, as a result of prior arrangement. This includes most of the payment by results schemes that have been produced by work study, as well as commission payments to salesmen. The distinguishing feature is that the employee knows what he has to do to earn the payment, though he may feel very dependent on other people, or on external circumstances, to receive it.

(g) BONUS

A different type of variable payment is the gratuitous payment by the employer that is not directly earned by the employee: a bonus. The essential difference between this and an incentive is that the employee has no *entitlement* to the payment as a result of his contract of employment and cannot be assured of receiving it in return for a specific performance. The most common example of this is the Christmas bonus.

Secrecy in Payment

Our last comment in this chapter is on the widespread but declining practice of keeping a high level of secrecy on who gets what in payment, usually in order to avoid odious comparisons and to give more scope to those who administer payment schemes. There are at least four disadvantages to such a policy:

(i) In the absence of facts most people will over-estimate what others earn, particularly when the occupational life-style of the others supports such an over-estimate. Sales representatives are frequently thought by their colleagues to be better paid than they are.

(ii) If there is some form of industrial action by employees to express dissatisfaction when pay levels are *known*, the management can argue their case and perhaps redress a perceived inequity. Employee dissatisfaction is just as likely when pay rates are *not known*, sometimes for that very reason, yet the management can then do little but give assurances: nothing can be clearly demonstrated.

(iii) A secret policy enables individual managers to be capricious, unfair and nepotistic in the treatment of subordinates. (This, of course, is one of the reasons that secrecy policies exist.)

(iv) Secrecy enables the organisation to continue without a coherent, articulated policy that can be generally accepted as a fair basis for payment.

SUMMARY PROPOSITIONS

22.1. Differences in relative payment to individuals should be according to the differences in the work they do.

22.2. Changing management perceptions of the employment relationship should be reflected in management perceptions of payment.

22.3. Employee objectives for the payment contract will vary from one employee to another, as well as differing from employer objectives.

22.4. Managers and employee representatives give strong support to three criteria for payment discussions: purchasing power, relativity and productivity.

22.5. There is no single prescription for a universally effective payment system. The system should be geared to organisational circumstances.

22.6. Pay secrecy encourages managerial capriciousness and unfair practice, as well as undermining the 'felt-fair' basis for the payment contract.

22.7. The payment system should accommodate both employer and employee objectives within the framework of a pay policy that is seen as fair, understandable, consistent and published.

REFERENCES

1. Thomason G., *Textbook of Personnel Management*, 2nd ed. (IPM) 1976, p. 262.
2. Wootton B., *The Social Foundation of Wages Policy* (Allen and Unwin) 1955, p. 162.
3. Hyman R. and Brough I., *Social Values and Industrial Relations* (Basil Blackwell) 1975, p. 31.
4. Addison J.T., 'The Role of Comparability in Wage Determination' in *British Journal of Industrial Relations*, November 1975, pp. 388–395.
5. Brown W. and Sisson K., 'The Use of Comparisons in Workplace Wage Determination', in *British Journal of Industrial Relations*, March 1975, p. 23–54.
6. Adams J.S. and Rosenbaum W.B., 'The Relationship of Worker Productivity to Cognitive Dissonance about Wage Inequities' in *Journal of Applied Psychology*, June 1962, pp. 161–164.
7. Lawler E.E. and O'Gara P.W., 'Effects of Inequity Produced by Underpayment on Work Output, Work Quality and Attitudes towards the Work', *Journal of Applied Psychology*, October 1967, pp. 403–410.
8. Wood I. and Lawler E.E., 'Effects of Piece Rate Overpayment on Productivity', *Journal of Applied Psychology*, June 1970, pp. 234–238.
9. Husband T., 'Management Style and Fair Payment' in *Personnel Review*, Autumn 1975, p. 26.
10. Bowey A.M., 'Pay Systems in Perspective' in *Personnel Management*, April 1976, p. 32.
11. Elliott R.F. and Steele R., 'The Importance of National Wage Agreements', in *British Journal of Industrial Relations*, March 1976, p. 53.
12. Gilling-Smith D., 'The Total Remuneration Concept' in *Handbook of Pensions and Employee Benefits*, edited by Hymans C. (Kluwer Harrap) 1973.
13. Jaques E., 'Objective Measures for Pay Differentials' in *Harvard Business Review*, January/February 1962, pp. 133–137.
14. Pay Board, *Relativities*, Advisory Report No. 2, Cmnd 5535 (HMSO) 1974, pp. 7, 8.
15. A helpful analysis of this phenomenon is to be found in Leeslie D., 'Overtime, the Institution that Will Not Die' in *Personnel Management*, July 1977, pp. 34–36.
16. White M., *Motivating Managers Financially* (IPM) 1973, pp. 10–19.
17. Flamholtz E., *Human Resource Accounting* (Dickenson) 1974.
18. Hopwood A.G., *Accounting and Human Behaviour* (Haymarket/ Prentice-Hall) 1974.
19. Giles W.J., and Robinson D., *Human Asset Accounting* (IPM) 1972.
20. Glenson A.I., Tweedie D.P. and Behrend H., 'Pay Negotiations and Incomes Policy: a Comparison of views of managers and trade union lay negotiators' in *Industrial Relations Journal*. Autumn 1975, pp. 4–8.

23

Relativities and Differentials

As we saw in the quotation which opened the last chapter, one of the main tasks in payment administration is setting the differential gap. Only partly can the employer decide this in terms of the *contribution* made by different groups of employees; much more significant will be a range of *comparisons:*

> In a society such as ours most groups look to the pay levels and the pay increases of others for guidance on the 'fair' level of pay or expected increase of pay for themselves. In pay matters no man and no group is an island.[1]

If pay adminstrators and pay recipients are going to use comparison as a means of deciding what is acceptable, they have a growing problem in the choice of the comparator. We considered some of these in the last chapter. There is, for instance, the range of elements that make up the total pay package, the different settlement dates and the nature of what is compared. Is it the basic rate or the total income? When we reach the stage of actually making decisions, as opposed to developing attitudes, there is the difficulty of comparison caused by obscure job titles and vagueness about function. In traditional hierarchies there is little problem. Most people would assent to the Police Inspector being paid more than the Sergeant and the Sergeant being paid more than the Constable. Theirs is a single hierarchical system with a strong tradition of authority justifying both pay and perquisites increasing with rank. In most employment, however, the differences are confused. A glance through the employment advertisements in any newspaper illustrate the problem. Should a Development Officer, for instance, be paid more than a Development Engineer? What are the differences between Sales Office Managers, Branch Managers, Area Managers, Product Managers, Sales Development Managers, Warehouse Managers, Technical Sales Managers, Depot Managers, Regional Managers, Regional Sales Managers, Distribution Managers, Marketing Managers and Sales Promotion Managers — advertisements for all of which posts appear on a single page in one newspaper?

Not only does such proliferation of titles complicate the task of the employer in determining what is appropriate, it also makes the job holder anxious to justify his employment and project his own status by appropriate comparison with other jobs.

In this chapter we consider various aspects of the processes of comparison and the methodology of job evaluation, which is management's best attempt so far to tackle the problem and produce a satisfactory pay structure.

Relativities, Differentials and Identification

In their examination of 1974 the Pay Board identified three separate categories of pay relationship: differentials, internal relativities and external relativities.[2] We look now at those three, plus a fourth of our own — external identification.

(a) DIFFERENTIALS

Differentials are used to describe pay differences within a single negotiating group, where any comparison involves reaching agreement between one set of negotiators representing management interests and one representing employee interests — the simple model of the bargaining relationship. If the management of an organisation negotiates with one bargaining agent on behalf of, say, manual employees who are skilled, semi-skilled and unskilled, then any disagreement about different levels of pay between the different categories of employee are for those two parties to resolve. The resolution is normally within their competence, unless there is some external constraint like incomes policy, or unless the negotiators are so unresponsive to the feelings of their members that one category of employees withdraws its support and seeks separate representation.

(b) INTERNAL RELATIVITIES

A more difficult type of pay relationship to control is that of internal relativity. Here the employer is constant, but the employees are represented by different agents as a result of being identified in differing bargaining units. The most common internal relativity problem is between manual and non-manual employees, where one union or group of unions represents the manual employees and another represents the non-manuals, although bargaining may be much more fragmented in many organisations — the problem of multi-unionism. Although more difficult to control than differentials, there is at least one common factor, the employer.

In one way the managerial problem of internal relativities seems to be easing, and that is the relativity between skilled and unskilled manual employees. Halsey points out that the advantage of the skilled man reduced from 100 per cent in 1867 to 50 per cent in 1915 and 16 per cent in 1952.[3] In 1980 this had narrowed further to 12 per cent, and in the chemical industry it was as low as 4 per cent.[4]

(c) EXTERNAL RELATIVITIES

Employees do not, however, restrict themselves to making comparisons between their own pay and that of others within their organisations, even though this may be the most cogent comparison. They will compare themselves with those in other companies, industries and services. Occasionally there will be a common element in the union, which negotiates better terms with one employer than another for groups of employees who see themselves as being similar. More often the comparison is with completely different groups of employees. Perhaps the most pervasive comparator in external relativities is the national average, which is dutifully published monthly by the Department of Employment and elaborated in the New Earnings Survey. Those politicians and academics who look at problems of differentials and internal relativity in a comfortable patrician way and say that 'the unions and the employers ought to be able to sort it out' have some difficulty in applying that simple formula to external relativities, as the various sets of negotiators are independent of each other and probably in competition with each other.

(d) EXTERNAL IDENTIFICATION

In one specialised category the employee identifies with an external employee grouping for purposes of determining the appropriate pay level. These people are usually taken out of intra-organisational bargaining. The obvious examples are company doctors and nurses, where the appropriate rates of pay are determined by bodies external to the company which proceeds to pay on that basis, unless there is some wish to pay above that rate. Other examples would be such professional groups as solicitors, surveyors and architects, although there will be many others where the number of employees will be so small as well as specialised that some external reference is the most appropriate way of determining the rate. The company employing one or two chemists or actuaries or other specialists would probably accept scales of pay published by the appropriate professional body rather than try to produce a pay structure that accommodated a range of specialists all identifying with an external professional grouping. The acceptance of the external identification principle can also cope with the sort of problem that can otherwise occur when people are working within the organisation under contract and invariably appear to be better off that the regular employees. Figure 23.1 illustrates these points.

Limitations on Management Action

If managers can accept and understand the range of limitations upon their actions in connection with pay comparisons, they can begin to develop a strategy to deal with them. There are six major constraints upon management action.

(a) STATUTORY REGULATION

As we see in Chapter 26, there are a number of legal constraints on management action regarding differentials and relativities. The most dramatic is incomes policy, which usually has the effect of freezing problems and prohibiting solutions, but at least the external relativity situation is frozen as well. Moving in to a period of incomes policy is fairly straightforward, moving out of it is invariably much more difficult.

Other statutory features of constraint are wages council orders and equal pay provisions.

(b) THE PRODUCT MARKET

The influence of the product market varies according to how important labour costs are in deciding product cost, and in how important product cost is to the customer. In an industry like catering, labour-intensive and low-technology, there will usually be such pressure on labour costs that the pay administrator has little freedom to manipulate pay relationships. In an area like magazine printing, the need of the publisher to get his product on time is so great that labour costs, however high, may concern him relatively little. In this situation the pay negotiators have much more freedom to deal at least with differentials.

In their analysis of the footwear industry[5] Goodman and his colleagues found that a major reason why the industry was characterized by peace rather than conflict was the need for employer collaboration on labour matters because of the intensive competition between them in the product market.

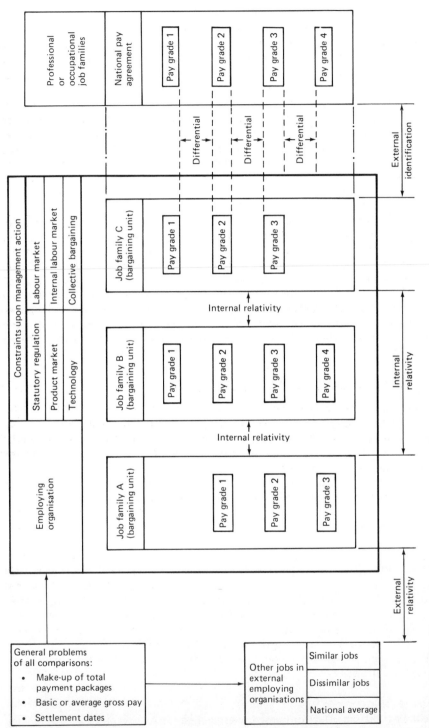

Figure 23.1. The bases of job comparisons and pay relationships

(c) THE LABOUR MARKET

We have suggested that the most intractable type of pay relationship for the personnel specialist is the external relativity because it is so completely beyond his control. It may not be beyond his understanding, and understanding could offer the opportunity at least to pre-empt some problems so as to deal with them before or when they arise rather than being taken by surprise. Craftsmen, for instance, come very close in our categorisation to those who identify with an external employee grouping, as their assessment of their pay level will be greatly influenced by the 'going rate' in the trade or the district. A similar situation exists with jobs which are clearly understood and where skills are readily transferable, particularly if the employee is to work with a standard piece of equipment. Driving heavy goods vehicles is an obvious example, as the vehicles are common from one employer to another, the roads are the same, and only the loads vary. Other examples are typists, telephone operators, card punchers and computer operators. Jobs which are less sensitive to the labour market are those which are organisationally-specific, like most semi-skilled work in manufacturing, general clerical work and nearly all middle-management positions.

Lupton and **Bowey**[6] have devised an interesting method for comparing jobs in different organisations in order to identify whether or not like is being compared with like. It is a method of identifying similar job types, rather than a method of measuring and structuring differences, which is the task of job evaluation. The method aims to identify benchmark jobs in different companies that are sufficiently similar for a comparison of pay rates to be valid; by extension, a comparison of other rates becomes more realistic. The authors are cautious in their claims for this system, but it does provide a mechanism for understanding better the type of pay relationship described as external relativity.

(d) COLLECTIVE BARGAINING

Perhaps the most obvious constraint for management is the operation of collective bargaining. Employees do not join trade unions in order to comply with managerial wishes, but to question them, and the differential structure that fits in with management requirement will not necessarily fit in with employee expectations. The study by Metcalf[7] tries to assess the effect of unionisation on relative wages and concludes that it is significant, even if less dramatic than some have argued previously.

One of the best-known aspects of union influence on differentials and relativities has been the long-running Toolroom Agreement in the engineering industry, which has guaranteed a fixed pay advantage for toolroom workers compared with those engaged on production in the same establishment or district.[8]

Gradually, however, the extension of collective bargaining to white-collar and managerial groups has reduced the scope for unilateral decisions about differential structures. One of the influences of collective bargaining is in the use of internal relativities as the basis for negotiations. The members of a low-pay group will narrow the gap between themselves and those in a high-pay group; whereupon the higher-paid will seek to widen the gap again by 'restoring the differential'. Before long there will follow more arguments from the lower-paid that the gap has widened — and should be narrowed.

(e) TECHNOLOGY

Technology has an effect on most things, and pay is no exception. As technology changes there will arise the need for new skills in the organisation and people who are recruited possessing those skills will tend to import a pay level with them. The external identification principle may justify special treatment for one or two such employees, but once the numbers begin to increase, then they must be assimilated into the pay structure, almost certainly upsetting it in the process.

(f) INTERNAL LABOUR MARKET

Just as there is a labour market of which the company is a part, so there is a labour market within the organisation. This is mainly in the constraining influence of custom and practice, so that any substantive and permanent change in the internal relativities needs considerable justification. One pair of commentators[9] has classi-fied different types of internal labour market. First is the *enterprise* market, so-called because the enterprise or organisation defines the boundaries of the market itself. Such will be the situation of manual workers engaged in production processes, for whom the predominant pattern of employment is one in which jobs are formally or informally ranked, with those jobs of the highest pay or prestige usually being filled by promotion from within and those at the bottom of the hierarchy usually being filled only from outside the enterprise. It is therefore those at the bottom which are most sensitive to the external labour market. Doeringer and Piore point out that there is a close parallel with managerial jobs, the main ports of entry being from management trainees or supervisors in the organisation, and the number of appointments from outside gradually reducing as jobs become more senior. This *modus operandi* is one of the main causes of the problems attaching to executive redundancy. The second type of market is the *craft*, where there are rigid rules of entry — usually a combination of time-served apprenticeship plus an appropriate union card — but the allocation of jobs to people tends to be much more flexible, emphasising equality of employment experience among the work force rather than the considerations of seniority and ability which are predominant in enterprise markets.

The situation in internal labour markets may be the most important in attitude formulation on pay relationships:

> . . . feelings of being inadequately paid usually arise as a result of highly localised anomalies. The macro-system of pay differentials, the argument runs, is generally accepted as just. Therefore, in evaluating their own pay, individuals make the critical comparisons not with levels of earnings throughout society as a whole, but with more restricted 'reference groups'. Individuals compare their earnings against those of people in the same or broadly similar occupations.[10]

The authors of the article from which that extract is taken go on to question this assumption, on the basis that people are generally ill-informed on what relative pay levels are, but concede that the view expressed represents 'conventional wisdom'. Coates and Silburn[11] have demonstrated that even the poorest are able to feel satisfaction with their lot if they select appropriate comparators. An opinion, advanced with little supporting argument, suggests that the internal labour market may still be the most important influence on attitudes about pay relationships:

> It seems to us at least arguable that most people are little interested in whether other people are better off, or whether they have become better off than others, provided they themselves are treated fairly in relation to most of those with whom they work. No grand design here.[12]

Management Policy Decisions and Pay Relationships

Although there are limitations to managerial freedom of action on pay relationships, there is still a need for managerial initiative in policies to influence differentials and relativities. These are mostly to do with employee groupings or deciding on *job families*.

The job family is a collection of jobs which have sufficient common features for them to be considered together when differential gaps are being set. What are the management decisions to be made?

(a) WHY NOT ONE BIG (HAPPY) FAMILY?

The first question is whether there should be sub-groupings within the organisation at all, or whether all employees should be paid in accordance with one overall salary structure. Internal relativities disappear; there is only a *differential* structure. This arrangement has many attractions, as it emphasises the integration of all employees and may encourage them to identify with the organisation as a whole, it is administratively simple and can stimulate competition for personal advancement. Two well-publicised schemes of pay structuring have been built on the principle of a single pay structure, and each have used a single-factor scheme of job evaluation to determine the differentials. In Paterson's decision-band method[13] the single factor is the nature of the decisions taken by the employee, in Jaques' scheme[14] it is the time-span of the discretion that the employee is expected to exercise.

There are undoubtedly organisations with a single pay structure, and the Paterson and Jaques methods of determining differentials have been adopted, but they remain rare because of the reservations that are expressed about such integration. The more diverse the skills, values and union affiliation of the employees, the more difficult is such a single job family. In the National Health Service, for instance, there is a diversity of skill that can probably not be matched in any other area of occupational life. While it *might* be possible to structure a single system of payment to encompass doctors, nurses and ancillary staffs, it would be extremely difficult to extend such a scheme to include administrators and para-medical *cadres*. The factors used to compare job with job will always tend to favour one grouping at the expense of another: one job at the expense of another. The wider the diversity of jobs that are brought within the purview of a single scheme, the wider will be the potential dissatisfaction, with the result that the payment arrangement is one that at best is tolerated because it is the least offensive rather than being accepted as satisfactory. The limitations of the single-factor evaluation scheme have been pungently criticised by Alan Fox on the grounds that it discriminates in favour of those in posts that are traditionally better paid anyway and therefore inhibits change of pay differentials towards a more broadly acceptable structure.[15]

Other difficulties about a single, integrated system of payment are those of responding to the external labour market and the impact of collective bargaining. If the only variables to control were within the organisation, it would be easier to sustain than in a situation where sectional interests are actively seeking to alter the structure specifically in their favour.

The single job family is probably best suited for the organisation that is not too large, where trade unions are not recognised for collective bargaining purposes, where all employees are engaged on work where there are a very small number of crucial job factors present in each job, for which the particular labour market is not too volatile.

(b) BARGAINING UNITS

In our chapter on trade union recognition (Chapter 11) there was mention of the need to decide the boundaries of bargaining units. A job family and a bargaining unit will normally coincide, as the matter principally being discussed — pay — is common to both concepts. However, job families are created to deal with differential gaps rather than internal relativities even though they influence the internal relativity structure, and it is quite feasible to have bargaining units with more than one job family within them. A company might, for instance, negotiate with a trade union to determine a single salary scale for clerical, computer and administrative staff and then evaluate jobs in two separate families in the bargaining unit to determine the place within the scale for the different jobs. This procedure would be justified by the argument that the skills and requirements of computing staff are specialised, so that *differentials* are appropriately decided only by comparison with other computing jobs, while the *relative* position of computing staff is settled by collective bargaining.

(c) THE FAMILY STRUCTURE

Another decision to be made is whether there will be any degree of overlap on the pay scales that relate to each family. There is no right answer to this question. No overlap at all (a rare arrangement) emphasises the hierarchy, encouraging employees to put their feet on the ladder and climb, but the clarity of internal relativities may increase the dissatisfaction of those on the lower rungs and put pressure on the pay system to accommodate the occasional anomaly. Overlapping grades blur the edges of relativities and can reduce dissatisfaction at the bottom, but introduce dissatisfaction higher up the ladder.

Usually pay scales for different families overlap, not only to 'blur the edges' but also to accommodate the appropriateness of different-length scales for different families. A family with a flat hierarchy will tend to have a small number of scales with many steps, while the steep hierarchy will tend to have more scales, but each with fewer steps. One of the main drawbacks of overlapping scales is the problem of migration, where an employee regards his job as technical at one time and makes a case for it to be re-classified as administrative at another time, because he has got as far as he can in the first classification. Another aspect of migration is the more substantive case of employees seeking transfer to other jobs as a result of changes in the relative pay scales, which reduce rigidity in the internal labour market.

(d) ARE EXECUTIVES A SPECIAL CASE?

It is usual for executive pay to be discussed and administered differently from the pay of other employees. This is largely because traditional theoretical formulations of economists have no place for executives, who are neither wage earners in the normal sense nor owners, yet they are both earners and acting on behalf of the owner(s).

A further reason for regarding executives as a special case is the result of a number of investigations which have demonstrated a relationship between executive pay and organisational features such as sales turnover and number of employees. An admirable summary is to be found in Husband[16] of work by analysts who argue that there is a typical relationship between the number of earners and the number of salaries at different levels.

The simplest, if not the cheapest, guide available to this type of approach is in the annual surveys of AIC/Inbucon in which an extensive survey of salaries and other benefits being received by executives in British organisations is presented in relation to two variables, sales turnover and number of employees, with separate scales for different managerial specialisms and hierarchical levels.[17]

(e) PAYMENT METHOD

Both differentials and internal relativities will be affected by the method of payment that is adopted. In Chapter 25 there is more detailed consideration of the incremental principle, but here we need to point out the distinction between *fixed rate, incremental scale* and *open-ended* methods of payment.

The fixed rate applies to two types of employee. First is the type like the craftsman for whom there is a rate of pay for the job; the only way it increases is by adjustment for increases in the cost of living or some advance relative to other groups. Secondly there is the person who has reached the top of an incremental scale. For these people the only point of comparison is their current earnings and they will be particularly sensitive to relativities.

The person with an incremental scale of pay, the top of which he has not yet reached, can foresee a third possibility of improvement in addition to the two available to those on fixed rates: he has further incremental steps, so 'his' rate of pay will have the extra dimension of what it will become as well as what it is. He will be slightly less sensitive on relativity questions as he still has some headroom, but may be sensitive on differentials.

The third type of earner is the one for whom there is neither pre-determined rate nor pre-determined scale. His income is at a level fixed either by unilateral decision from his superiors or by his negotiating with them. It is *ad hoc,* so that his pay could rise to an undefined point at any time. His sensitivity to differentials and relativities will relate not so much to his method of payment but to his degree of control over its alteration.

With both incremental scale and open-ended methods of payment there is some scope for management to manipulate the differential position of employees by accelerating or slowing down the rate at which an employee's pay moves up in relation to other employees.

Job Evaluation

Job evaluation is the most common method used to compare the relative values of different jobs in order to provide the basis for a rational pay structure. Among the many definitions are:

British Institute of Management (1961)
> 'Job evaluation is the process of analysis and assessment of jobs to ascertain reliably their relative worth, using the assessments as the basis for a balanced wage structure.'

Trade Union Congress (1964)
> 'Job evaluation may be described, in broad terms, as a process used at company — but sometimes at industry — level in order to determine the relationship between jobs and to establish a systematic structure of wage rates for them.'

It is a well-established technique, having been developed in all its most common forms by the 1920s. In recent years it has received a series of boosts. First various types of incomes policy between 1965 and 1974 either encouraged the introduction of job evaluation or specifically permitted expenditure above the prevailing norm by companies wishing to introduce it. More recently the use of job evaluation is the hinge of most equal pay cases. Despite its popularity it is often misunderstood, so the following points have to be made:

(i) Job evaluation is concerned with the *job* and not the performance of the individual job holder. Individual merit is not assessed.

(ii) The technique is *systematic* rather than *scientific*. It depends on the judgement of people with experience, requiring them to decide in a planned and systematic way, but it does not produce results that are infallible.

(iii) Job evaluation does not eliminate *collective bargaining*. It determines the differential gaps between incomes; it does not determine pay level.

(iv) Only a structure of *pay rates* is produced. Other elements of earnings, such as premia and incentives are not determined by the method.

There are many methods of job evaluation in use and they are summarised in Husband[18] and Thomason.[19] We have already seen the problems connected with the single-factor schemes, like those of Jaques and Paterson. Some of the more complex schemes have been developed in order to improve the reliability of the outcome, usually by the use of a computer, but they have the problems of being harder to understand and depending on mechanical decision-making rather than human judgement. This may produce 'better' decisions which are less acceptable. Cynical, and possibly unfair, criticisms of complex schemes range from accusations that they are means for consultants to make money to statements that they are devices to blind shop stewards with science.

The most popular scheme is that of *points rating,* under which a number of factors (such as skill, effort and responsibility) are identified as being common to all the jobs being evaluated. Each factor is given a weighting indicating its value relative to the others and for each factor there are varying degrees. A job description is prepared for each job and a committee then considers each description in turn, comparing it, factor by factor, with the degree definitions. Points are allocated for each factor and the total points value determines the relative worth of each job. The best-known set of factors, weightings and degrees is that devised for the National Electrical Manufacturers Association of the United States.[20] The points values eventually derived for each job can be plotted on a graph or simply listed from the highest to the lowest to indicate the ranking. Then — and only then — are points ratings matched with cash amounts, as decisions are made on which points ranges equate with various pay levels.

A typical variation of the NEMA scheme was used in part of a British television programme to compare actual earnings in selected jobs with earnings that would result from job evaluation. Using the scheme set out in Figure 23.2 a panel of shop stewards and personnel officers evaluated a heterogeneous range of jobs. After the evaluation the results were matched against a prepared set of pay rates to produce 'ideal' rates for each job and then compared with the prevailing actual earnings of the job holders. The results illustrate the principle and show one of the snags in job evaluation — what happens about the job holder who is overpaid according to the findings of the evaluators?

It is virtually inevitable that some jobs will be found to be paid incorrectly after job evaluation has been completed. If the evaluation says that the pay rate should

Factors	Weight (per cent)	Degrees									
		1st	2nd	3rd	4th	5th	6th	7th	8th	9th	10th
SKILL											
1. Education	14	14	28	42	56	70	84	98			
2. Experience	22	22	44	66	88	110	132	154			
3. Initiative/ Judgement	14	14	28	42	56	70	84	98	112	126	
EFFORT											
4. Physical demand	10	10	20	30	40	50	60	70	80	90	
5. Mental stress	5	5	10	15	20	25	30	35	40	45	50
RESPONSIBILITY											
6. Material & Process	10	10	20	30	40	50	60	70			
7. Safety of others	5	5	10	15	20	25	30	35			
8. Work of others	5	5	10	15	20	25	30	35	40	45	50
CONDITIONS											
9. Working conditions	10	10	20	30	40	50					
10. Unavoidable hazards	5	5	10	15	20	25					

Job title*	Points awarded by panel	Suggested 'ideal' rate £'s per week	Actual rate £'s per week
Personnel Officer (National Health Service)	471	115	150
Personnel Officer (Engineering Industry)	497	130	110
Toolmaker in Motor Industry	365	78	76
Car assembly Worker	327	66	72
Wages Clerk	245	42	45
Copy typist	228	36	35
Farm labourer	336	69	42

* To provide a realistic comparison the first two were specific, with almost identical characteristics in terms of level of responsibility, scope, number of employees etc. and the rates of actual pay quoted were salaries being received by the incumbents. For the other jobs current rates of pay were provided by trade unions or employers' associations.

Figure 23.2. A Scheme of Job Evaluation by Points Rating

be higher then the rate duly rises, either immediately or step by step, to the new level. The only problem is finding the money and introducing job evaluation always costs money. More difficult is the situation where evaluation shows the employee to be overpaid. It is not feasible to reduce the pay of the incumbent. There have been two approaches. The first, which was never widespread and appears almost to have disappeared, is *buying out*. The overpaid employee is offered a large lump sum in consideration of the fact that he will henceforth be paid at the new, lower rate. The second and more general device used is that of the personal rate or *red circling*. In the example of the Health Service Personnel Officer above, the rate for the job would be re-established at £115 instead of £150, but the rate for the present incumbent would be circled in red on the salary administrator's records to show that he should continue at his present level all the time he remained in that post. His successor would be paid £115. There have been many instances where unequal pay has been justified by employers before tribunals on the basis of red circling.

We have identified a general process of job evaluation, capable of incorporating specific modifications and techniques, which is illustrated in Figure 23.3.

Employee Participation in Job Evaluation

The degree of participation by non-managerial employees in job evaluation varies from one organisation to another. In some cases the entire operation is conducted from start to finish without any employee participation at all. Some degree of participation is more common. Apart from negotiating on pay levels and bargaining units, the main opportunities for employee contribution are:

(a) JOB FAMILIES
Employees collectively need to consent to the family structure and they can probably add to the deliberations of managers about what that structure should be, as they will be well aware of the sensitive points of comparison.

(b) JOB DESCRIPTION
Job descriptions are crucial to the evaluation and it is common for job holders to prepare their own, using a pro-forma outline, or for supervisors to prepare them for jobs for which they are responsible. Superficially this is an attractive method, as there is direct involvement of the employee, who can never claim that he has been misrepresented if he has prepared the statement himself. Also it distributes the work of job describing, enabling it to be completed more quickly. The drawback is similar to that of character references in selection. Some employees write good descriptions and some write bad ones: some overstate while others understate. Inconsistency in job descriptions makes consistency in evaluation difficult.

An alternative is for job descriptions to be compiled by job analysts after questioning supervisors and incumbents, who subsequently initial the job description the analyst produces, attesting to its accuracy.

(c) EVALUATION
The awarding of points is usually done by a panel of people who represent between them the interests and expertise of management and employee. This is not only being 'democratic', it is acknowledging the need for the experience and perspective of job holders as well as managers in arriving at shrewd judgements of relative worth.

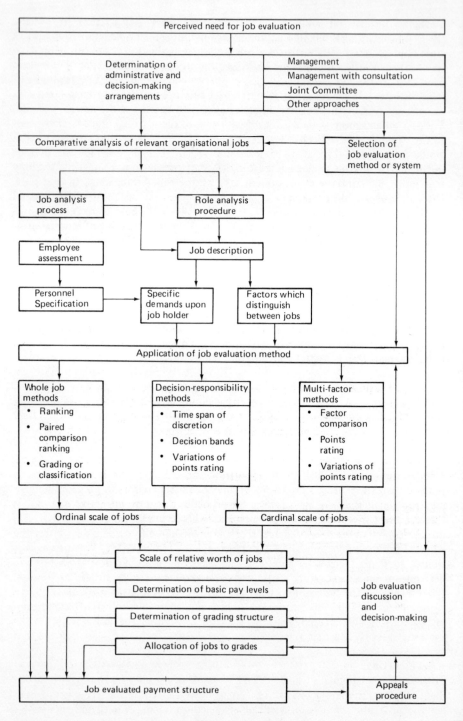

Figure: 23.3. A General model of the job evaluation process

Naturally panel memberships alter so that employees are not asked to evaluate their own jobs. Although there is an understandable general tendency for employee representatives to push ratings up, whereupon management representatives try to push them down, this usually smoothes out because both parties are deriving differential rankings and not pay levels. The only potential conflict of interest will be if employee representatives and managers have divergent objectives on the shape of the eventual pay structure, with big or small differential gaps.

SUMMARY PROPOSITIONS

23.1. Differentials and internal relativities are largely controlled within the organisation. External relativities and external identification are features of pay relationships which managers need to understand, even though they are beyond their control.

23.2. The key management policy decisions on differentials and internal relativities are those grouping jobs in families, with executives possibly being classed as a special case.

23.3. The most successful method so far devised to structure differentials and internal relativities is job evaluation, of which the most widely accepted technique is points rating.

23.4. Job evaluation provides a number of practical opportunities for employee participation in management decision-making, bringing knowledge and expertise as well as contributing to the equity of the result.

REFERENCES

1. Pay Board, *Anomalies,* Advisory Report 1, Cmnd 5429 (HMSO), 1973.
2. Pay Board, *Relativities,* Advisory Report 2, Cmnd 5535 (HMSO), 1974.
3. Halsey A.H., *Change in British Society* (OUP) 1981, p. 52.
4. Department of Employment, *Employment Gazette,* January 1982, p. 54.
5. Goodman J.F.B., Armstrong E.G.A., Wagner A., Davies J.E., *Rule-Making and Industrial Peace* (Croom Helm) 1977.
6. Lupton T. and Bowey A.M., *Wages and Salaries* (Penguin) 1974, pp. 50–69.
7. Metcalf D., 'Unions, Incomes Policy and Relative Wages in Britain' in *British Journal of Industrial Relations,* July 1977, pp. 157–175.
8. For an account of the working of this agreement see Clegg H.A., *The System of Industrial Relations in Great Britain* (Blackwell) 1976, pp. 245–48.
9. Doeringer P.B. and Piore M.J., *Internal Labour Markets and Manpower Analysis* (Heath Lexington Books) 1971.
10. Roberts K., Clark S.C., Cook F.G., Semeonoff E., 'Unfair or Unfounded? Pay Differentials and Incomes Policy' in *Personnel Management,* August 1975, p. 29–37.
11. Coates K. and Silburn R., *Poverty: The Forgotten Englishman* (Penguin) 1970.
12. IDS Focus, *The Pay Merry-go-Round* (Incomes Data Services Ltd) 1977, p. 17.
13. Paterson T.T., *Job Evaluation II – A Manual for the Paterson Method* (Business Books) 1972. (See also Volume I of this work.)

14. Jaques E., *Equitable Payment* (Heinemann) 1961.
15. Fox A., 'Time-span of Discretion Theory: An Appraisal' in Lupton T. (ed.) *Payment Systems* (Penguin) 1972, pp. 347–365.
16. Husband T.M., *Work Analysis and Pay Structure* (McGraw-Hill) 1976, pp. 167–193.
17. AIC/Inbucon *Executive Salary Survey*.
18. Husband T.M., *op. cit.,* pp. 48–64.
19. Thomason G.F., *A Textbook of Personnel Management*, 4th ed. (IPM) 1981, pp. 490–494.
20. The scheme is described in Husband T.M., *op. cit.,* pp. 51–52.

24

Financial Incentives —
Manipulation or Luck?

When introducing the section of this book on aspects of payment, we made the suggestion in Chapter 22 that changing managerial attitudes to the employment relationship should be reflected in management attitudes towards payment, and that one attitude towards payment needing modification was the view of incentives. An incentive was defined as 'an element of payment linked to the working performance of an individual or working group, as a result of prior arrangement'.

The period since the mid-1950s has generally been a time of moving away from individual piecework incentive schemes. They have been based on a well-tried principle that he who works harder deserves more money, but the schemes have lost popularity because of problems connected with that very principle. On the one hand research on human motivation has cast doubt on the reliability of the necessary adjunct to the principle from a management point of view — that opportunity to earn more money produces greater productive effort. On the other hand the changes that have been taking place in technology have thrown up innumerable situations where productivity would be increased as a result of less effort rather than more. Many changes in manufacturing method have made the outstanding individual performer an embarrassment, as the system has called for consistency in pace and application among a group of people rather than competitive striving.

The key ideas in the disenchantment are those in the title of this chapter — manipulation and luck. Those receiving incentive payment have had a clear, unshakeable conviction that the scheme was a managerial manipulative device to do the worker down. Those administering payment schemes have developed an equally clear conviction that workers have manipulated payment schemes to frustrate managerial objectives for efficiency and increased productivity in order to optimise employee earnings 'unfairly'. The idea of luck has been used both to explain and to rationalise variations in incentive payment by attributing the variation not to effort but to chance events like the level of orders, the share-out of the jobs that can produce high levels of earnings and those that do not, availability of materials, administrative delays and so on.

Despite the disenchantment incentive schemes persist, and it is unrealistic simply to suggest that they will go away if ignored long enough. The reasons why they persist include some of the reasons why they have lost favour, such as the way in which so frequently managements avoid a problem by buying a way past it through juggling with the incentive arrangement. If there were not an incentive pay scheme in existence it could not be used for that sort of short-circuiting operation. Other reasons are their use to overcome resistance to change, the attractiveness sometimes to employees who feel they are gaining an element of control over their own workpace, the possible help from a supervisory point of view and — probably more important than any of these — a deepseated conviction in the minds of many managers that incentive schemes *ought* to work as they seem basically sensible.

Managerial Expectations of Incentive Schemes

There is no single managerial view and there is no standard working situation in which managers have to organise payment arrangements. The need for managers to adopt varying opinions is set out by Lupton and Bowey:

> . . . in order to be sure of the outcome of a scheme the manager needs to consider the particular circumstances of his firm.
>
> From a 'contingency' perspective we are now able to understand the apparently conflicting prescriptions of people like R.M. Currie who advocated incentive-bonus schemes of various kinds, and Wilfred Brown who recommended that piecework be abandoned. They had each been observing situations in which the particular system they were proposing had been successful, but were not aware that there was something peculiar about those circumstances which contributed to the success of the scheme.[1]

(a) MOTIVATIONAL THEORIES

The opinion of a manager will be first influenced by the personal theory of motivation that he holds. If his views coincide with those of McGregor's Theory X, then he will tend to regard incentive payment schemes as necessary to control the workers, who will otherwise loaf and rip off the management at every possibility. Deploring the mollycoddling effect of recent developments in individual employment rights he may well feel that incentives are the only device left to a manager to extract a reasonable day's work from the labour force. If the manager's views are more consistent with McGregor's Theory Y, then he will be less likely to look to incentives for control and will be more concerned with clarity, reasonableness, security and employee involvement.[2] Husband[3] suggests that the norm in managerial thinking is moving from X to Y on payment matters.

(b) CONTROL

Control thinking is expressed in the view that the output of individuals has to be measured for incentive payments to be made, and that these measurements provide a useful set of control information for the manager, either to see who is working hard and who is idling, or in order to build up data on how best to distribute tasks among a group of people so that they can all work optimally. This type of information can also demonstrate where there are weaknesses in departmental organisation, and provide some basis for controlling labour costs.

There is much managerial cynicism about control through incentive schemes because employees, individually or collectively, set out to beat the system. A control system implies rules, and most human beings accept the validity of rules at the same time as they seek to test their flexibility. Especially if the incentive scheme is a management scheme with limited employee involvement in its creation and maintenance, the controlling rules will stimulate a competitive claim for control from the employee seeking to optimise *his* benefits from the scheme rather than those of the management.

(c) COST

Incentive arrangements are built on the principle that the cost of increasing output through incentive payments will decline with volume, so that the unit cost for each of 100 units of output will be less than the unit cost for each of 99 such units. There can be a situation in which this only appears to happen, as the scheme is manipulated to produce a rather different result. A remark attributed to a Midlands shop steward sums up the reason:

> 'When we get control of the piecework scheme, management lose control of their labour costs.'

All but the most crude methods of incentive payment incorporate an element to compensate the worker for an inability to earn an incentive because of delays beyond his control, usually known as waiting time. Few schemes can get round the problem of the worker assigning as much output as possible to the productive periods of the day at the same time as recording as much waiting time as possible. There are many other ways in which direct labour costs can increase as a result of incentive arrangements, not least of which is the bargaining of local representatives to increase the cash pay-off. Also the scheme may require high indirect labour costs in clerical and related staff to keep all the records that the scheme requires.

Employee Expectations of Incentive Schemes

Just as there is no single set of managerial expectations, so there is no single set of employee expectations surrounding incentives. The contingency approach is as relevant for them as it is for managers:

> It is dangerous to make broad generalisations regarding British workers' attitudes to incentive systems. In some industries their use is taken for granted by the workers. This is probably the case, for example, with female operatives in the hosiery industry. In other industries there is great suspicion of incentive schemes on the part of workers. A typical case is probably the printing industry.[4]

(a) ORIENTATION TO WORK

Earlier in this book we have mentioned the spectrum of attitudes to employment as ranging from the *instrumental* ('work is just a means to another end') to the *central life interest*. What the employee expects from his work will influence what he expects of his payment arrangements. If there is a strong instrumental orientation, then there will be a stronger interest in the financial arrangements, although the interest may lead to compliance with management objectives for the scheme or frustration of those objectives, according to whichever provides the best pay-off. Lawler examined a wide range of research studies before producing the conclusion:

> ... pay can be instrumental for the satisfaction of most needs but it is most likely to be seen as instrumental for satisfying esteem and physiological needs, secondarily to be seen as instrumental for satisfying autonomy or security needs and least likely for satisfying social or self-actual needs.[5]

(b) AUTONOMY

Incentive pay programmes can give the employee his best scope for autonomy in providing him with a satisfactory basis on which he can determine his rate and level of application rather than having it determined for him mediated via close supervision. It may sound contradictory in view of earlier remarks about management control to suggest here that it can be the employee who gains control of his work as well as of the payment scheme, but the reason is that the incentive scheme takes the form of objective setting. It is somewhat analogous with Management by Objectives in that the scheme will normally provide an open-ended objective with the implication 'It's up to you: you can earn as much as you like.' The responsibility for exactly when the work is done and how the individual work space is organised is partly transferred from the management to the employee, and supervision is more remote.

(c) INTEREST

It is not always recognised that the incentive pay structure can be welcome as a source of interest in an otherwise monotonous occupation. Casual conversation with anyone holding a job with a strong element of routine shows how they tend to set up milestones to look forward to. The coffee break is not just a break and a chance to drink coffee; it is also a marker that the morning is half over. Others are such events as the arrival of the post, the bell sounding at the nearby school, the plane from New York flying overhead, the Pullman going past on the way to London, and many more. Financial incentives can build another marker element into the day's routine as the employee regularly checks his progress against what he has set himself as a target.

Typical Problems with Incentive Schemes

From the foregoing discussion it can be seen that the satisfaction of one party may be the dissatisfaction of the other, so that, for instance, the expectation of the management that control of labour costs will be improved will be disappointed if that control is lost to the union negotiators. There are, however, various other problems to mention.

(a) OPERATIONAL INEFFICIENCIES

For incentives to work to the mutual satisfaction of both parties there has to be a smooth operational flow, with materials, job cards, equipment and storage space all readily available exactly when they are needed, and an insatiable demand for the output. Seldom can these conditions be guaranteed and when they do exist they seldom last without snags. Raw materials run out, job cards are not available, tools are faulty, the stores are full or customer demand is fluctuating. As soon as this sort of thing happens the incentive-paid worker has an incentive to fiddle the scheme so as to protect himself against operational vagaries.

(b) FLUCTUATION IN EARNINGS

Any payment method which is truly linked to performance must result in a level of earnings which will fluctuate in all but the most unusual circumstances, as demand will vary, operations will be spasmodically inefficient or the operator's effectiveness will alter from time to time. If the fluctuations are considerable then the employees will be encouraged to try to stabilise them, either by pressing for the guaranteed element to be increased, or by storing output in the good times to prevent the worst effects of the bad, or by social control of high-performing individuals to share out the benefits of the scheme as equally as possible. Any one of these tactics reduces the potential management advantages quite considerably, but has relatively less effect on the employee advantages suggested above.

(c) QUALITY OF WORK

The stimulus to increase volume of output can adversely affect the quality of output, as there is an incentive to do things as quickly as possible. If the payment scheme is organised so that only output meeting quality standards is paid for, there may still be the tendency to produce expensive scrap. Two very simple examples illustrate the possibilities. Operatives filling jars with marmalade may break the jars if they work too hurriedly. This means that the jar is lost and the marmalade as well, for fear of glass splinters. On the other hand people operating machines casting lead grids for battery plates produce little net scrap, as grids that do not meet quality standards can be 'put back in the pot' for re-processing.

(d) QUALITY OF WORKING LIFE

. . . financial incentives in industry today probably yield a net gain in productivity, but most of them fail to release more than a small fraction of the energy and intelligence workers have to give to their jobs. Even when the financial incentive yields higher productivity, it may also generate such conflicts within the organisation that we must wonder whether the gains are worth the costs.[6]

In our industrial consciousness payment by results is associated with the worst aspects of rationalised work: routine, tight control, hyper-specialisation and mechanistics. The worker is characterised as an adjunct to the machine, or as an alternative to a machine. Although this may not necessarily be so, it is usually so, and generally expected. The quality of working life for the individual employee is impaired. In a more general way the quality of working life is impaired because of the mechanical element in the control of working relationships.

(e) THE SELECTIVE NATURE OF INCENTIVES

Seldom do incentive arrangements cover all employees. Typically groups of employees are working on a payment basis which permits their earnings to be geared to their output, while their performance depends on the before or after processes of employees not so rewarded, such as craftsmen making tools and fixtures, labourers bringing materials in and out, fork-truck drivers, storekeepers and so forth. This type of problem is illustrated most vividly by Angela Bowey's study of a garment factory, where employees 'on piecework' were set against those who were not, by the selective nature of the payment arrangement.[7]

One conventional way round the problem is to pay the 'others' a bonus that is linked to the incentive earned by those receiving it. The reasoning for this is that those who expect to earn more (like the craftsmen) have a favourable differential guaranteed as well as an interest in high levels of output, while that same interest in sustaining output is generated in the other employees (like the labourers and the storekeepers) without whom the incentive-earners cannot maintain their output levels. The drawbacks are obvious. The labour costs are increased by making additional payments to employees on a non-discriminating basis, so that the storekeeper who is a hindrance to output will still derive benefit from the efforts of his colleagues, and the employees whose efforts are directly rewarded by incentives feel that the fruits of their labour are being shared by those whose labours are not so directly controlled.

(f) OBSCURITY OF PAYMENT ARRANGEMENTS

Because of the difficulties we have described, incentive payment schemes are constantly being modified or refined in an attempt to circumvent fiddling or to get a fresh stimulus to output, or in response to employee demands for some other type of change. This leads to a situation in which the employees find it hard to understand what behaviour by them leads to particular results in payment terms. This was a problem mentioned by Donovan[8] and more recently in a number of investigations.[9] Few schemes can be more pointless than those where cause cannot be related to effect.

Payment by Results Schemes

There are many variations on the theme of incentive payment, which is still widely used as a feature of at least the work done by manual employees. The most comprehensive surveys undertaken have been those of the Ministry of Labour in 1961[10] and the National Board for Prices and Incomes in 1967.[11] The conclusion of the NBPI was that there had been little change between the two dates, indicating that 42 per cent of manual employees in manufacturing were employed on some form of incentive basis and four million employees altogether being paid in such a way. In Chapter 22 we referred to the recent work of Elliot and Steele suggesting a drop in the number of workers paid by this means, but whatever the drop, the number is still substantial and there is renewed interest in such arrangements because of concern about how productivity can be stimulated. The main types of incentive payment arrangement are set out here.

(a) INDIVIDUAL TIME-SAVING

The type of scheme most in use, and the type against which most of the foregoing criticisms have been levelled, is one whereby the incentive is paid for time saved in performing a specified operation. It is rare for a scheme to be based on the payment of x pence per piece produced, as this provides no security against external influences which depress output. For this reason a standard time is derived for a work sequence and the employee receives an additional payment for the time he saves in completing a number of such operations. If he is unable to work due to shortage of materials or some other reason, the time involved is not counted when the sums are done at the end of the day.

The standard times are derived by the twin techniques of method study and work measurement which are the skills of the work study engineer. By study of the operation, the work study engineer decides what is the most efficient way to carry it out and then times an operator actually doing the job over a period, so as to measure the 'standard time'.

For individual incentive schemes to be effective there need to be trained staff to carry out the measurement and studies. Despite the criticisms a payment method of this sort could be appropriate in a situation where people are employed on short-cycle manual operations where the volume of output is variable between individuals

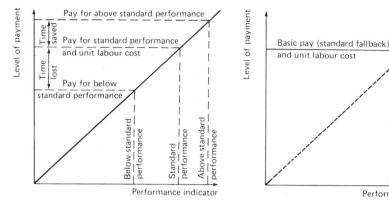

(a) P.B.R. or piecework scheme
(b) P.B.R. with standard fallback

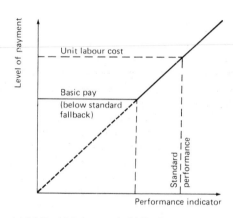

(c) P.B.R. with below standard fallback

Figure 24.1. Widely used payment by results (P.B.R.) schemes

depending on their skill or application. It would also be necessary for changes to be relatively few, with the prospect of employees being able to sustain a productive working rhythm and not be constantly set back by delays.

Figure 24.1 illustrates some of the widely used schemes for payment by results.

(b) GROUP INCENTIVES

Sometimes the principles of individual time-saving are applied to schemes where the payment is made for group output rather than individual output. The argument is that in many circumstances, like assembly lines, it is fruitless to operate a scheme encouraging individuals working in harmony to increase their collective output. Where jobs are interdependent a scheme of this nature may have benefits, but it may also put great pressure on the group members, aggravating any interpersonal animosity that exists and increasing the likelihood of stoppages for industrial action. It is also difficult for a new recruit to be incorporated into the scheme, as the existing members feel that they will have to compensate for his inexperience.

(c) MEASURED DAYWORK

To some people the ideas of measured daywork provide the answer to the short-comings of individual incentive schemes. Instead of the employee receiving a variable supplement to his basic pay in accordance with the output he achieves, he is paid a *fixed* sum as long as he maintains a predetermined and agreed level of working. A useful summary of this method was provided by the Office of Manpower Economics.[12]

Theoretically this deals with the key problem of other schemes by providing for both stable earnings and stable output instead of 'as much as you can, when you can, if you can', but the NBPI found that productivity declined in some instances when this method was introduced, although there were also instances of lower labour cost per unit.[13] It seems that there is a greater degree of effective management control of these schemes than there is of conventional payment by results arrangements. IDS quote from a TUC working party on productivity techniques:

> There can be no doubt that management techniques reduce significantly workers' control over some important aspects of their employment, e.g. the pace and method of work. A payment scheme such as MDW involves the use of several of these techniques including work study and job evaluation, and trade unions are right to be cautious in their acceptance of it. There is good reason to conclude that the growth in the use of MDW indicates its value, whether real or apparent, permanent or temporary, for employers.[14]

Husband, however, speaks of 'a happier industrial relations climate' and 'less expenditure on dealing with grievances' as being among the many benefits that can come from MDW. He then sounds a note of caution:

> Unless sound production engineering, production scheduling and supervisory practices are developed there is no reason to suppose that a measured daywork pay structure will remain undistorted over time. The pay structure is subject to many of the same pressures under measured daywork as it is under conventional bonus systems. Measured daywork provides a sound base, but management need to strengthen the base by effective training of foremen and careful analysis of their production control systems.[15]

Figure 24.2 illustrates measured daywork schemes.

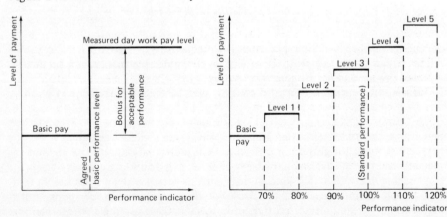

(a) Basis for measured daywork schemes   (b) Basis for effective step measured daywork schemes

Figure 24.2. Measured daywork schemes

(d) PLANT-WIDE SCHEMES

A variant on the group incentive is the plant-wide bonus scheme, under which all employees in a plant or other organisation share in a pool bonus that is linked to the level of output, the value added by the employees collectively or some similar formula. The best-known schemes are those of Scanlon and Rucker,[16] both developed and mainly applied in America. The attraction of these methods lies in the fact that the benefit to the management of the organisation is 'real' because the measurement is made at the end of the system, compared with the measurements most usually made at different points within the system, whereby wages and labour costs can go up while output and profitability both come down.

Theoretically also employees are more likely to identify with the organisation as a whole, they will co-operate more readily with the management and each other, and there is even a whiff of workers' control.

The difficulties are that there is no incentive as there is no tangible link between individual effort and individual reward, so that those who are working hard can have their efforts nullified by others working less hard or by misfortunes elsewhere.

(e) COMMISSION

The payment of commission on sales is a widespread practice about which surprisingly little is known as these schemes have not come under the same close scrutiny that has been put on incentive schemes for manual employees. They suffer from most of the same drawbacks of manual incentives, with the added problem that those earning sales commission are more likely to be members of pension schemes or holding mortgages, in which case the fluctuating proportion of their income is an embarrassment to them. The New Earnings Survey shows that the number of people receiving commission is falling and that the proportion of their earnings constituted by commission is also declining.[17]

(f) TIPS

The practice of tipping is generally criticised as being undesirable for those receiving tips — it requires them to be deferential and obsequious — and for those giving them — because it is an unwarranted additional charge for a service they have paid for already. It is also often described as an employer device to avoid the need to pay realistic wages. Despite the criticism the practice persists, although it is of varying significance in different countries of the world.

The attraction of tipping is the feeling of the employee that he can personally influence the level of his remuneration by the quality of service he is able to give to individuals with whom he comes in contact, and the feeling of the tipper that he is providing personal recognition of service that he has received. This does not, of course answer the criticism that tipping is usually for reasons of convention rather than direct acknowledgement of special service. From the employer's point of view the tipping convention can be a helpful way of ensuring application to customers' wishes by employees, but can present problems in coping with known 'bad tippers'.

(g) SUGGESTION SCHEMES

A specialised form of incentive payment is that resulting from suggestion schemes. These are now rare, but provide the opportunity for employees to make suggestions about cost-saving, increases in efficiency or any other matter. If the suggestion is adopted the employee receives a payment. Theoretically these arrangements provide the opportunity to influence the decision-making process and encourage employees to identify with the organisation.

Suggestion schemes fell into disfavour for many reasons, but principally because they were difficult to operate satisfactorily. Who is excluded from making suggestions? Can a personnel officer be rewarded for making a suggestion about improving personnel records? It may take some time to evaluate a suggestion, only to find that it is of no value. Many suggestions have to be turned down, but those making them may feel disgruntled unless they receive detailed explanations of the reasoning, which may not be acceptable to them. What is an appropriate reward?

Notwithstanding the criticisms, schemes persist and some are successful, but their success depends on suggestions actually being welcome and not simply tiresome. If they are genuinely welcomed then there needs to be an understood basis of payment, like 20 per cent of the anticipated net savings in the first year, and a systematic way of evaluating suggestions and providing feedback quickly. Suggestion schemes provide an excellent opportunity for using a management/employee committee to oversee the scheme.

SUMMARY PROPOSITIONS

24.1. Although individual incentive schemes have been widely criticised, they still form a major part of the payment of many manual employees.

24.2. There is no single best method of incentive payment that will work in all situations, but a growing number of variations that will be appropriate for different objectives and circumstances.

24.3. Incentives schemes provide one of the conventional ways in which the parties to the employment contract play out the conflict in their relationship. Failure of either party to meet his expectations of the scheme will be rationalised as bad luck or as unfair manipulation by the other.

The best way to close this chapter is with a quotation from Douglas McGregor:

> The practical logic of incentives is that people want money, and that they will work harder to get more of it. Incentive plans do not, however, take account of several other well-demonstrated characteristics of behaviour in the organisational setting: 1) that most people also want the approval of their fellow workers and that, if necessary, they will forgo increased pay to obtain this approval; 2) that no managerial assurances can persuade workers that incentive rates will remain inviolate regardless of how much they produce; 3) that the ingenuity of the average worker is sufficient to outwit any system of controls devised by management.[18]

REFERENCES

1. Lupton T. and Bowey A.M., *Wages and Salaries* (Penguin) 1974, p. 79.
2. As described in McGregor D., *The Human Side of Enterprise* (McGraw-Hill) 1960, and subsequently reiterated in summary form by innumerable commentators.
3. Husband T.M., *Work Analysis and Pay Structure* (McGraw-Hill) 1976, pp. 15–17, 75–76.
4. *Ibid.*, pp. 73–74.
5. Lawler E.E. Jnr, *Pay and Organisational Effectiveness* (McGraw-Hill) 1971.
6. Whyte W.F., 'Economic Incentives and Human Relations' in *Payment Systems*, ed. Lupton T. (Penguin) 1972, pp. 115–116.
7. Lupton T. and Bowey A.M., *op. cit.*, pp. 76–78.
8. *Royal Commission on Trade Unions and Employers' Associations* (HMSO) 1968 p. 18.
9. Mainly in reports of the Commission on Industrial Relations, for example the CIR Report on Electrolux in Luton.
10. Ministry of Labour, *Gazette* (HMSO) September 1961.
11. National Board for Prices and Incomes, *Payment by Results Systems,* Report No. 65 (HMSO) 1968.
12. Office of Manpower Economics, *Measured Daywork* (HMSO) 1973.
13. National Board for Prices and Incomes, *op. cit.,* pp. 37–38.
14. IDS Study 140, *Incentive Pay Schemes 1* (Income Data Services Ltd) 1977, p. 6.
15. Husband T.M., *op. cit.,* p.81.
16. See, for instance, Industrial Relations Counsellors Inc. 'Group Wage Incentives' in *Payment Systems, op. cit.* pp. 200–214. Also British Institute of Management, Information Note 26, *Notes on Some Company-Wide Incentive Schemes: Scanlon, Rucker & Kaiser Steel.*
17. Department of Employment, *New Earnings Survey 1977* (HMSO) 1978, p. 35.
18. McGregor D., *op. cit.,* p. 100.

25

Salary Administration

In the previous chapter, on financial incentives, the underlying assumption was that those receiving incentives were likely to be wage-earners. In this chapter we look at salaries, and immediately face the question: what is the difference? The question is surprisingly difficult to answer, because the differences are largely those of attitude and convention, so that many dictionaries give 'wages' as a synonym for 'salary'. However difficult the answers are to find, they are important due to the differences in expectation that are held of wage bargains and salary bargains.

The Differences Between Wages and Salaries

Some of the more obvious differences between the two methods of payment can be outlined here. An alternative discussion can be found in Lupton and Bowey.[1]

(a) PERIODICITY

Conventionally wages are paid more frequently than salaries, so that most wage-earners will be paid weekly while most salary-earners are paid monthly. The unit of time for which the wage-earner is paid will probably, however, be much shorter, so that five or ten minutes lateness will often be penalised by a deduction of pay for that period. Rates are usually expressed as hourly rates, with that figure remaining the standard reference point in any discussion or negotiation, so that weekly earnings are seen as a variable figure based on the rate multiplied by forty (or whatever the normal weekly hours are) with possible subtractions for lateness or absence and possible additions for overtime, shift-working, incentives and the like.

The salaried employee's monthly payments are usually expressed as an annual figure, which is the reference point in comparisons and negotiations. Implicit in this arrangement is that he cannot provide services to his employer that are readily susceptible to division into small segments. It is very rare for lateness and short-term absence to be penalised by salary deductions, leading to the wage-earner's assertion that the salaried are paid 'work or play'.

(b) PENSIONS AND FRINGE BENEFITS

The difference in the periodicity of payment leads to another variable: the importance that is attached to benefits other than cash-in-hand. Until the 1970s pension provision, other than by the state, for the wage-earner was unusual outside public-sector employment, whereas it was the *sine qua non* for the salaried and could be the main consideration in appointment to some highly paid positions due to the marginal improvement in income of even higher salaries. There are other common fringe benefits that usually feature in the remuneration package for the salaried, as was mentioned in Chapter 22, such as luncheon vouchers, additional payments for extra qualifications, company cars, and the generally murky area of 'expenses'. Those receiving wages are less likely to have these fringe advantages and have traditionally been very unwilling to receive them instead of cash.

(c) METHOD OF PAYMENT
Another great divider is the way in which the payment is made. Virtually all salaries are paid by bank transfer or by cheque, while most wages are paid in cash, clearly emphasising the expected dominance of short-term thinking on financial matters by the wage-earner in contrast to the longer-term concern with financial security of the salariat.

(d) THE NATURE OF THE INCENTIVE
Incentives for wage-earners are required to be precise, comprehensible, fair and quick. Apart from the minority of the salaried who receive add-on incentives of this type, the incentive principle for them is of a fundamentally different nature: *prospects.* Salaries are geared to the career principle so that their recipients are always encouraged to look ahead to the possibility of the salary going up. Like their wage-earning colleagues they expect increases to compensate for changes in the cost-of-living, but they are encouraged to look to the future in three other ways. First, they will probably be on incremental scales carrying definite expectations of a future salary level with a precise cash value. Secondly, there is a stronger element of discrimination between salary-earners on the basis of a merit assessment than with wage-earners, where consistency or uniformity are more common. Thirdly, salary scales are the visual representation of career growth. There is always a better paid job in the future with the individual reaching his ceiling relatively late and the different career ladders being adjacent to each other, requiring little more, in the eyes of the employee, than persistence, hard work and good behaviour to ensure access. The wage-earner will see himself reaching the peak of his earning power much earlier, probably in his twenties, and will see the initiatives required of him to get onto another ladder as being very demanding because the social system does not define him as a ladder climber.

(e) IDENTIFICATION
The last difference to mention is probably the most important, as it is a part of all the others. Those receiving salaries are likely to identify with the management interest in the organisation. This was suggested by the studies by Batstone and his colleagues that were reported in Chapter 13, and Bain[2] has pointed out that management encouragement is one of the features that needs to be present before white-collar unions expand. Salaried employees are most likely to see themselves doing a piece of the job of management, that has had to be split up because it — and the

organisation – have grown too big for top management to handle alone, but unquestionably it is a part of management. Wage-earners see themselves as doing the work that the management would never do and which is independent of management apart from the labour-hiring contract.

The identification of the salaried with management interests is closely related to their dependence on those senior to them in the hierarchy. The fringe benefits will sometimes depend on the favour of someone else, who will query an item on an expense sheet or let it pass; or who will decide the priority sequence for company cars to be replaced. Principally, however, the salary-earner depends on his superiors for the most significant determinants of his future: *merit payments* and *promotion*. These will result from hard work and good behaviour, as was mentioned above. There are no absolute standards of good behaviour. Work study officers do not measure it and produce a standard for the employee to use. Merit lies in the eye of the beholder, whose subjective evaluation will dominate any system of peer-rating, management by objectives or any other scheme which can only modify – not eliminate – the degree of subjective judgement. Also promotion depends not on merit alone, however it is judged, but on competition; this makes the competitors dependent on those who declare the winner.

Implications for the Employment Contract

The foregoing paragraphs show us that the difference in the nature of salary against wages reflects a difference in attitude to the employment contract. The contract of the wage-earner emphasises insecurity and the here-and-now, while the contract for the salaried employee emphasises a long-term relationship between employer and employee. The employee looks forward to his terms and conditions of employment steadily improving over a long career path, and the employer can anticipate ready compliance with employer objectives for the organisation because of the employee's interest in the future.

The relationship also reflects the difficulty of measuring the performance of salaried employees, whose contribution is usually not immediate and tangible. Some critics would argue that the emphasis on the career growth is counter-productive because it encourages job holders to behave in a way which will demonstrate their potential for the next job rather than their competence in the current position. A slightly different version of this question is posed in the famous Peter Principle, which states that 'each employee is promoted to the level of his own incompetence'.[3] In attacking the hierarchical idea, Dr Peter argued that the effect of the career pyramid on employees was to encourage performance that would ensure promotion, which was sensibly based on competence, so that compentence in one job led to the incumbent being promoted out of it. If he succeeded in the next job his competence would lead to further promotion and the growth would only stop when he reached a position in which he could not cope – the level of his own incompetence. Because his performance now became incompetent it would not justify further promotion, meaning that he stuck in a job he could not do. Most of those engaged in organising schemes of management development and making promotion decisions would argue that this is too simplistic a criticism, since the criteria for promotion are more those of potential for the future than past performance, even though the evidence of future potential must be distilled from achievements so far.

ISSUES IN SALARY POLICY

We now move to a discussion of the main issues in salary policy of an organisation, as it is in these areas that the main decisions have to be taken and here lie the keys to policy success.

1. The Location of Control

The broad outlines of the salary policy and annual budget will usually be decided by the most senior committee, coalition or individual in the organisation, who will approve major structural changes in salary arrangements, the annual budget and any drastic alterations. Within that framework there will, however, be a number of operational decisions on the salary position of particular individuals. These two types of decision-making raise various questions, the first being the extent to which salaries are negotiated with trade unions. Although relatively uncommon until recently, the salary framework and general levels are gradually being more pervasively (and persuasively) negotiated. This has long been standard practice in the public sector and is becoming much more common in the private. There is usually a cut-off point towards the top of the salary hierarchy where trade unions do not negotiate actual rates, which are more likely to be determined by negotiation between the individual job holder and his superior. In large areas of the private sector of industry that cut-off point is after quite junior posts. In 1973 Jean Cothliff reported the results of a survey of 190 British companies. One of the pieces of information was the extent of negotiation or representation for different staff categories. Out of these companies, 66 negotiated staff salaries with trade unions and 26 received representations from staff associations, as follows:[4]

	Trade union negotiation (per cent)	Staff association representation (per cent)
Senior and middle management	14	39
Junior management	49	81
Technical and specialist	85	85
Clerical	79	81

Smaller companies are less likely to negotiate with trade unions on salaries. They are also less likely to have staff associations.

Even if salary levels are not negotiated directly with trade unions, they will still be strongly influenced by negotiations with other groups, so that negotiations with trade unions on behalf of the manual employees in an organisation will set the pace for salary increases to compensate for cost of living increases at around the same level.

Although the most senior committee, coalition or individual in the organisation will decide the broad outlines of salary policy and the annual budget, large elements of the package may only result from negotiation or from response to the effect of negotiations elsewhere.

At the level of implementation there is a different argument. Should the salary position of individuals be determined by a central salary administration department or individual, or should it be determined by the appropriate line manager to whom the individual reports? Very rarely is the decision made by the line manager alone. Frequently all the decisions are centralised, but sometimes schemes operate whereby the line manager either makes part of the overall decision or influences that decision. As organisations become steadily more bureaucratic in their form, so salary decisions are more likely to become standardised and beyond the control of *any* individual in the hierarchy. The move towards the remuneration package, mentioned in Chapter 22, provides the employee with some choice of payment method: not a choice in deciding payment level.

2. The Salary Structure

The salary levels of those holding senior positions outside the range of collective bargaining are likely to be decided by marking off differential points from the salary of the chief executive at the same time as keeping an eye on the competition. Husband[5] describes how the AIC/Incubon annual salary survey[6] develops a set of suggested salary levels for different organisations using organisational distance from the chief executive as the criterion. Two choices are offered: one according to the number of employees in the company and one according to the sales turnover. In large organisations this type of approach will govern the salaries of few. Most will be encompassed in a structure of *groups, ladders and steps.*

(a) GROUPS

The first element of the structure is the broad groupings of salaries, each group being administered according to the same set of rules. The questions in making decisions about this are to do with the logical grouping of job holders, according to their common interests, performance criteria, qualifications and – perhaps – bargaining arrangements and trade union membership. The BIM study, already mentioned, used a framework of four groups:[7]

> *Senior and middle management:* directors, heads of major functions and their immediate subordinates.
> *Junior management:* responsible to the above and including supervisory staff.
> *Technical and specialist:* personnel with technical or professional skills and/or qualifications (excluding those working in a managerial capacity), e.g. work study officer, technician, draughtsman.
> *Clerical:* all clerical occupations including secretarial staff.

There are various alternatives to this type of arrangement, such as separating senior and middle management; incorporating technical and specialist personnel into appropriate management groups according to seniority; including manual employees as a salaried group. Another alternative is not to have groups at all, but simply a single system of ladders and steps, so that all salaried employees have their payment arrangements administered according to one set of criteria. This is the type of system described by Bowley,[8] but he is concerned with management careerists only. The argument against such a system is that it applies a common set of assumptions that may be inappropriate for certain groups. In general management, for instance, it will probably be an assumption that all members of the group will be interested in promotion and job change; this will be encouraged by the salary arrangements, which will encourage job holders to look for opportunities to move around. In contrast the research chemist will be expected to stick at one type of job for a longer period and movement into other fields of the company's affairs, like personnel or marketing, will often be discouraged. For this reason it will be more appropriate for the research chemist to be in a salary group with a relatively small number of ladders, each having a large number of steps; while his general management colleague will be more logically set in a context of more ladders, each with fewer steps. The broad salary ranges are then set against each group, to encompass either the maximum and minimum of the various people who will then be in the group or — in the rare circumstance of starting from scratch — the ideal maximum and minimum levels.

As the grouping has been done on the basis of job similarity, the attaching of maximum and minimum salaries can show up peculiarities, with one or two jobs far below a logical minimum and others above a logical maximum. This requires the limits for the group to be put at the 'proper' level, with the exceptions either being identified as exceptions and the incumbents being paid a protected rate or being moved into a more appropriate group.

Salary groups will not stack neatly one on top of another in a salary hierarchy. There will be considerable overlap, recognising that there is an element of salary growth as a result of experience as well as status and responsibility. A typical set of groups could be as illustrated in Figure 25.1.

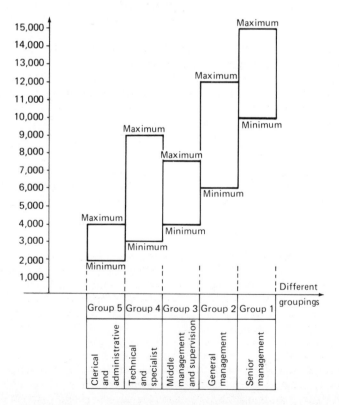

Figure 25.1. Typical salaried staff groupings

Another way of dealing with specialists is to take them out of the corporate salary structure altogether and pay them according to salaries prescribed by an acknowledged outside body. This is done most frequently for nurses working in industry, who are often paid according to scales published by the Royal College of Nursing. A device like this can solve the problem of one or two specialised employees whose general rank or standing in the organisation is not consistent with the necessary level of payment.

The grouping stage in salary administration has thus identified a number of employees whose remuneration will be organised along similar lines.

(b) LADDERS AND STEPS

In 1969 the National Board for Prices and Incomes surveyed employers and found that in companies employing 250 people or more some type of salary structure using maxima and minima was applied to 60 per cent of managerial, executive, professional and technical staff, while the percentage was approaching 75 in larger companies.[9]

Because the salaried employee is assumed to be career-oriented, his salary arrangements have the same assumption, so each salary group has several ladders within it and each ladder has a number of steps (often referred to as 'scales' and 'points'). As with groups there is considerable overlap, the top rung of one ladder being much higher than the bottom rung of the next. Taking the typical general management group that was mentioned above, we could envisage four ladders, as shown in Figure 25.2. The size of the differential between steps varies from £200 to £600 according to the level of the salary and the overlapping could be used in a number of ways according to the differing requirements. Steps 6 and 7 on each ladder would probably be only for those who had reached their particular ceiling and were unlikely to be promoted further, while steps 4 and 5 could be for those who are on their way up and have made sufficient progress up one ladder to contemplate seeking a position with a salary taken from the next higher ladder.

The figures attached to the ladders in this example are round, not having been influenced by incomes policies. They are expressed in this way in the belief that salaries are most meaningful to recipients when they are in round figures. However, ladders are sometimes developed with steps having a more precise arithmetical relationship to their relative position, so that each step represents the same percentage increase. Equally some ladders have the same cash amount attached to each step.

Some commentators place importance on the relationship of the maximum to the minimum of a ladder, described as the *span*, and the relationship between the bottom rung of adjacent ladders, referred to as the *differential*. Both Bowley[10] and Armstrong[11] suggests that the most logical arrangement is a 50 per cent span and a 20 per cent differential. There is no inscrutable logic behind those precise figures, so that 49 per cent and 21 per cent would not be 'wrong', but they have a similar value to the use of round figures referred to in the last paragraph. There is a neatness and symmetry about the method which can commend itself to salary recipients.

3. Timing of Increases

Salaries go up. The salaries of individuals may go up at any time in the year if they change jobs. The salaries for jobs will go up probably once a year as a response to increases in the cost of living. Salaries of individuals *not changing* jobs may go up as a result of performing particularly well, and this is also most likely to happen annually — if at all.

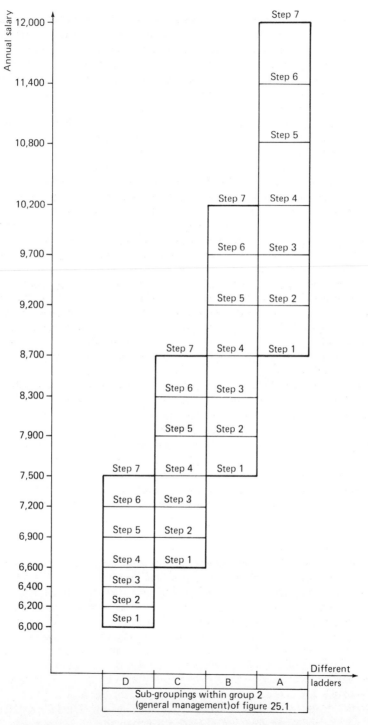

Figure 25.2. Ladders and steps within staff grade or grouping

Salary change following job change is something we need consider no further here, as the decision being made is primarily on whether or not the job should change, not whether the salary should change. Is there an especially appropriate time for general increases? The two main determinants will be the timing of the company's financial year and the timing of union negotiations with other groups of employees in the same organisation. The financial planners in the organisation will wish to have an accurate salary figure to include in their budgets, so that it might suit them for salaries to be adjusted at the same time as their budgets are being finalised. If there are other negotiations in the organisation it might be appropriate for salary discussions to follow those.

Some months appear to be more popular than others. BIM found that most companies reviewed around Christmas, with 37 per cent carrying out reviews in either December or January and a further 17 per cent reviewing in April.[12] Variations are to review different sections of the organisation at different times, or to review individuals on the anniversary of their appointment. Both these methods have the advantage that salary speculation is spread over twelve months instead of being concentrated into one short spell, but it is almost impossible to work this way if salaries are negotiated with trade unions and difficult to ensure that treatment is consistent over twelve months.

4. The Elements of Increases

The Office of Manpower Economics have set out the most comprehensive categorisation of how different organisations arrange for increases or increments, which is summarised below.[13] (In this chapter we use the word 'ladder' in exactly the same way as OME use the word 'scale'.)

(i) *Fixed scales with automatic progression.* The individual progresses automatically up a salary ladder on the basis of service or age, so that annual increases are pre-determined up to the maximum of the ladder and cost-of-living increases are added to the figures when negotiated. This method is standard through much of public sector, white-collar employment.

(ii) *Fixed scales with limited flexibility.* Flexibility in operation can sometimes be found whereby outstanding performance can be rewarded with two or three increments instead of one. Particular qualifications allow for entry at a higher point on the ladder than normal. It is also possible that increments could be withheld to penalise poor performance.

(iii) *Fixed but parallel scales.* Very similar to (ii) above, this arrangement has two or three parallel ladders that are of the same length, but with differing sizes of step for varying levels of potential and performance.

(iv) *Automatic progression to a specified point in the salary range.* Another minor variation is to guarantee progression to a specified point only, so that further progression depends on outstanding performance.

(v) *Variable progression according to definite guidelines.* The incremental points are not fixed, so there is need for considerable management discretion in deciding who gets what, but this discretion is circumscribed by clear guidelines from the centre on how increases are to be organised. The ladder will have a top and a bottom, but the rate of progress between the two will not be pre-determined, although the guidelines may well include a statement of the period normally taken to reach the maximum.

(vi) *Variable progression without definite guidelines.* Management discretion will here be limited only to the maximum of the range and general financial constraints limiting the total amount of potential disbursement. These are usually only found at senior levels in organisations.

(vii) *Variable progression without defined ranges.* There is no structure, simply *ad hoc* decisions made according to operational requirements.

All these variations require some form of control, although it may be slight in the last method cited. Not only is there a need to ensure consistency, but also it is necessary in all but the first of the methods to distinguish between that proportion of a salary increase that is to compensate for increases in the cost of living and that proportion which is in recognition of personal achievement. Although many salary administrators tend to blur this distinction and just deal with increases without specifying the proportions, such a strategy takes away the point of using salary as an incentive because the individual does not know whether his salary increase is 90 per cent cost-of-living and 10 per cent merit or the other way round. One reason for blurring recently has been that inflation has made for such large across the board adjustments that the merit element has been trivial in comparison and could have the effect of damning with faint praise.

5. The Salary Budget

The Prices and Incomes Board tells us what sort of information companies examined before setting the size of their salary budget. Of the respondent companies, 23 per cent said they could not answer the question as they did not have a salary budget, but for the other companies the factors were:[14]

Information examined	Percentage of firms
Movement of salaries in other companies	49
Movement of wages against salaries in the company	49
Movement of salary bill since last year	36
Profit targets	32
Compa-ratios (see page 344)	4
Other information	12

The information about salary movements in other companies is difficult to gather because it is traditionally treated as secret. Also information that is made available relates to a job title that will have varying connotations in different organisations. Most information comes from the ever-increasing number of salary surveys that are published annually. Some of these are produced by consultants and others by professional bodies. Typically they give a range of salaries actually being received by people of various ages and degrees of qualification within a professional field. Alternatively they try to identify the nature and level of responsibility within a management function that rates a particular salary.[15]

Study of job advertisements is notoriously unreliable as a measure of market rates, as not all organisations include the salary being offered in the advertisement they place, and often jobs that are advertised have what Bowley describes as a 'buying-in' factor included in the salary:

Salaries for jobs quoted in public advertisements, and buying-in rates for staff who have been persuaded to leave other companies, should never be confused with current market rates for individual jobs. There is almost always an 'x' factor necessary to persuade people to leave a job and a personal niche in another company; so that the buying-in rate must be higher than the market rate except in times of high executive unemployment.[16]

6. The Self-financing Increment Principle

It is generally believed that fixed incremental payment schemes are self-regulating, so that introducing incremental payment schemes does not mean that within a few years everyone is at the maximum. The assumption is that just as some move up, others retire or resign and are replaced by new recruits at the bottom of the ladder:

> The position can best be illustrated in terms of a single group of staff paid within the same salary range. The normal movement of salaries for the individual members of such a group set up what might be described as a circular process. While some individuals progress upwards, others leave the group by retirement or resignation or promotion and are replaced by newcomers who usually start lower down the pay range. This process of 'attrition' can mean that in certain circumstances the payment of increments is completely self-financing and leads to no increase in the salary bill.[17]

This thinking was born in a period when salary-earners were moving relatively frequently in an active labour market. Once the buoyancy of that market lessens then the effect of attrition is less also and the incremental pay scheme becomes an escalator not only for the individual, but also for the salary costs of the organisation. The Office of Manpower Economics surveys suggests that the level of attrition will fluctuate more with variable schemes than with fixed schemes,[18] and an article by Boddy[19] produces evidence of incremental payment schemes showing considerable increases in cost.

The way is which such movements are measured is by a device known as the compa-ratio, which compares all the salaries being received by individuals on a particular ladder with the middle point of the ladder, viz:

$$\frac{\text{Average of all salaries on the ladder}}{\text{Middle rung of the ladder}} \times 100$$

Assuming that all salaries should average out at the mid point, this provides a means of control.

7. Salary Decisions

Who decides where in the salary structure the individual fits? The answer to that question at one extreme is 'job evaluation and fixed increments' and at the other extreme it is the capricious whim of another individual. The first means that decisions are not made about individuals but about systems, and the individual salary emerges from the inexorable process of increments. The second means that decisions on salaries are made without constraint and, perhaps, without logic. Between these two extremes we can list the sequence of decisions that are involved in a typical annual salary review:[20,21]

(i) *How much the salary budget for the next year will be.* Decision made by the senior decision-making individual or coalition after submissions of evidence from personnel, finance and other specialists, including an interpretation of labour market indicators and trade union negotiations, if any.

(ii) *How the additional budget provision is to be divided between general increases (cost-of-living) and individual increases (merit).* This decision probably made at the same time as the first, but evidence and advice from personnel given more weight than any other. Possibly a wholly personnel decision.

(iii) *How merit increases are decided.* Recommendation from individual's superior, according to clear-cut rules, vetted by personnel to ensure consistency of approach by all superiors and that no previous undertakings are overlooked.

(iv) *How individuals hear the news.* Face-to-face by line superior, written confirmation from personnel.

SUMMARY PROPOSITIONS

25.1. Salaried status reflects and reinforces the commitment of the salaried to career orientation and identification with management interests.

25.2. Salary structures can be developed to emphasise those patterns of career growth and movement within the organisation that coincide with organisational objectives.

25.3. The idea that incremental salary systems keep the total cost of salaries stable around the mid point of scales is less likely to be correct when there is little activity in the relevant labour market.

REFERENCES

1. Lupton T. and Bowey A.M., *Wages and Salaries* (Penguin) 1974, pp. 106–115.
2. Bain G.S., *The Growth of White Collar Unionism* (Clarendon Press) 1970. Also *White Collar Unions: A Review* (IPM) 1972.
3. Peter L.J. and Hull R., *The Peter Principle: Why Things Go Wrong* (Morrow) 1969.
4. Cothliff J., *Salary Administration,* Management Survey Report No. 16 (BIM) 1973, p. 15.
5. Husband T.M., *Work Analysis and Pay Structure* (McGraw-Hill) 1976, pp. 179–180.
6. AIC/Inbucon Executive Salary Survey, published annually.
7. Cothliff J., *op. cit.,* p. 1.
8. Bowley A., *Salary Structures for Management Careers* (IPM) 1972.
9. National Board for Prices and Incomes Report No. 132, *Salary Structures* Cmnd 4187 (HMSO) 1969, p. 9.
10. Bowley A., *op. cit.,* pp. 10–12.
11. Armstrong M., *A Handbook of Personnel Management Practice* (Kogan Page) 1977, p. 217.
12. Cothliff J., *op. cit.,* p. 12.
13. Office of Manpower Economics, *Incremental Payment Schemes* (HMSO) 1973, pp. 14–16.
14. National Board for Prices and Incomes, *op. cit.,* p. 73.
15. A helpful guide to salary surveys is by Murlis H., 'Making Sense of Salary Surveys' in *Personnel Management*, January 1981.

16. Bowley A., *op cit.*

17. National Board for Prices and Incomes, *op. cit.,* pp. 25–26.

18. Office of Manpower Economics, *op. cit.* pp. 36–38.

19. Boddy D., 'Salary Payment Systems and Salary Costs' in *British Journal of Industrial Relations.* March 1977, p. 18.

20. The detailed functioning of such a scheme can be found in Torrington D.P. and Sutton D.F., *Handbook of Management Development* (Gower) 1973, pp. 71–90.

21. A system of salary administration for small companies is described in Swannack A.R., 'Small Firm Salary Structures' in *Personnel Management,* January 1975, pp. 31–34.

26

Payment and the Law

In this chapter we pull together various aspects of payment and legal requirements, that are not covered elsewhere but which have an effect on the contractual relationship.

The Truck Acts 1831—1940

Although the Truck Acts were brought on to the statute book at a time when workers needed protection of the type they are less likely to need to-day, the effect of these Acts is still considerable.

The original purpose of the legislation was to restrain employers from paying employees in kind rather than in money, so that workers have to be paid in coin of the realm. We use the word 'workers' instead of 'employees' in the previous sentence because the protection is not universal; it only applies to *manual workers, other than domestic or menial workers,* employed under a contract of service. Those automatically excluded from protection by this definition include all managers and staff employees. Some of those conventionally classed as manual workers may also be excluded. For instance the workshop clerk who makes out job cards or time sheets may be employed on an hourly rate as a manual employee but be excluded from Truck Act protection because his work is no longer manual.

For those enjoying the protection the Act requires that they be paid in coin of the realm. This does not only mean that the employer is barred from paying them in kind, but also that he cannot pay them by cheque or bank transfer, unless they provide written permission. If payment, or any part of payment, is made in any other way the contract has not been fulfilled and the worker can demand payment in cash. O'Higgins suggests one way in which the well-meaning employer may get in difficulty:

> The term 'wages' is very widely defined in the 1831 Act and . . . would include, for example, in certain cases the gold watch or other award given to a long-service employee. The effect of payment in any form other than cash is that the payment is void and the employee can demand its cash value, so in our example the long-service employee could keep the watch and demand its cash value as well.[1]

In 1980 there was a surprising judgement in a county court that a cheque made

357

out to cash could be used by an employer to pay a workman. The judge reasoned as follows:

> . . . all the recipient need do is go to the bank or post office, hand in the cheque and draw his money in 'current coin of the realm' over the counter. The Acts do not specify where wages shall be paid. In a large organisation the workman might have to go some distance to obtain his money . . . I can not see any distinction between that and the handing of cash cheque or Girocheque to the workman so that he may go to the bank or post office and draw his wages in cash. It might not be as convenient for the workman, but the Acts do not stipulate that he may not be inconvenienced.[2]

This should be regarded with some caution as a mandate for employers as the judge had earlier decided that the particular workman was not covered by the Trucks Act anyway. Also it was a county court judgement which is not therefore binding precedent.

A further feature of this legislation is that the employer may not make deductions from a worker's pay, so it is extremely doubtful that an employer can legally 'fine' an employee for bad workmanship by withholding payment. Certain deductions are permitted by the Act, such as those made to cover the cost of meals on the premises and the provision of tools. A deduction of particular interest is deduction of union dues. This is permitted by the Acts, providing that the employee gives written authorisation for the deduction to be made. The important principle here is that the employer is not receiving the benefit of the payment: he is merely conveying it to a third party. The same applies to the range of deductions that are either statutory, like income tax and national insurance, or as a result of a court order. If the employer is deducting union dues and receiving payment from the union to cover administrative costs, he may then be committing a criminal offence.

It is commonplace for employees to be able to purchase at reduced prices the goods in which the employer deals, but payment for them cannot be deducted from wages and the contract of employment cannot contain a clause requiring the employee to spend some of his wages in this way.

None of these protections apply to non-manual workers, even though the employer will usually extend them to manual and non-manual alike. The main difference being in the method of payment. While the manual employee has the right to payment in cash unless he authorises payment by another method (and he can change his mind, if he wishes), the non-manual employee has no such right and will be paid by bank transfer, cheque or cash according to employer decision.

There is the possibility that the Truck legislation will be modified as it is seen as a stumbling block to the development of 'cashless pay'. More than half the British employed population is paid in cash, which poses growing security problems and is a costly way to deal with payments to employees.[3]

Wage Councils

An element of the British industrial system which has been criticised from most quarters for a very long time is the setting of legally binding rates of pay and conditions by Wages Councils. These have been set up by the Secretary of State for Employment (or his predecessors) for what have usually been described as 'poorly organised trades' with the objective of providing in those areas of employment some of the protection for workers that has come elsewhere from trade union representation. Statutory intervention has been deemed necessary because the collectivisation of both employers and employees is not practicable due to the employment being largely in small units, widely dispersed. The main Wages Council areas have been retail distribution, road haulage, catering and hairdressing, though there have also been Wages Councils for the more esoteric byways of employment such as coffin-furniture and cerement-making; and pin, hook, eye and snap-fastener manufacturers.

The form of Wages Councils has been tri-partite, with those representing employer interests facing those representing employee interests, with one or more independents holding the ring. All representatives have, however, been appointed by the Secretary of State, rather than elected by those they represent. In some circumstances the appointment by the Secretary of State is a rubber-stamping of some democratic process, but the *power* to appoint or not remains with him.

Councils meet to discuss terms of pay, holidays and holiday pay for the industry. If there is a failure to agree, such failure is resolved by the independent members in order to produce a set of recommendations, which are then put to the Secretary of State for incorporation in a wages regulation order. Thereafter the terms become the statutory minima for the particular industry within the purview of the Council.

Although Wages Councils have been responsible for as many as 3.5 million workers, their operations have been unpopular because of their undemocratic nature and because they produce results which keep the workers concerned at the bottom of the wages table. Attempts have been made for some time to eliminate them, or to improve their effectiveness if they cannot be discontinued. The most recent move has been in the Employment Protection Act 1975, which extended the powers of Wages Councils, so that the Council and not the Secretary of State will now issue wages regulation orders, and they will be able to determine other terms and conditions: not simply pay and holidays. These changes speed up the machinery and provide the opportunity for introducing statutory minimum standards in areas such as sickness payment for the first time.

A further development is to provide for Wages Councils to be transformed into Statutory Joint Industrial Councils by eliminating the independent members. In this way the employer and employee representatives acquire greater responsibility and power over their own affairs and move towards the halcyon state of free collective bargaining, whilst still retaining the statutory framework for their operations. When appropriate voluntary machinery is established the Secretary of State can abolish either a Wages Council or a Statutory Joint Industrial Council. One recent abolition has been of the Road Haulage Wages Council, following the decision by the Secretary of State that adequate voluntary machinery existed.

Incomes Policy

Perhaps the most drastic way in which law has entered the area of pay in recent years has been incomes policy, with legal controls coming and going, voluntary controls coming and going, and the nature of the controls also changing. Different policies have different effects, but some of the inevitable results are these:

(a) LOSS OF CONTROL
The employer loses control of the payment system operating within his organisation, and recognised trade unions lose their prime function. The loss in both cases is not

always total, but is invariably considerable and affects the attitudes of all parties. Managers feel that they are losing one of the few controls they have over employee behaviour. This is particularly their feeling when they are looking at their relationship with salaried employees, where managers have much more scope for manipulation than with manual employees. As we saw in our discussion of salary administration, one of the prime differences between salaries and wages is the mode of administration in which the employer is directing the employee to look toward the future and a variety of improvements which will be provided or withheld by more senior people in the hierarchy according to the employee's behaviour. In a time of incomes policy that scope for manipulation is reduced and managers will seek out other variables to manipulate to compensate for the loss.

The loss to trade union officials may be greater, particularly to full-time officials. The main reason why people join union ranks is to improve their level of payment, through union negotiations with the employer. At a time of statutory control of incomes or a national agreement that is universal and unalterable, that function has been taken completely away from the union negotiator. Will employees feel the same need for the union? Will they be as ready to comply with union discipline? Like his managerial counterpart the union official will look for other matters on which to represent his members — otherwise he is useless.

(b) PAY STRUCTURE DISTORTION AND INFLEXIBILITY

Not only do managers and employee representatives lose control over payment arrangements: they are also faced with problems in the pay structure itself resulting from external control. Incomes controls are intended to affect all the employed population equally and for this reason it is the apparently simple formulae — like no pay rises at all for anybody for six months, or £6.00 a week supplement for everyone — that are the easiest for governments to implement, because they seem fair and reasonable to at least most people. These simple arrangements have the difficulty for individual organisations, however, that payment arrangements are seldom stable. There is a sequence of events in a year, with different bargaining units settling at different times, salary reviews, performance reviews, promotions, pay 'birthdays', increases promised, others held back for a further three months, or six months, and so on. Incomes policy has the effect of freezing this pattern of interaction or altering it in a way which is not appropriate to the policy or traditions which are being followed within the organisation.

Whatever the problems of the apparently uncomplicated incomes policies, the problems of the deliberately flexible policies may be greater. The most intricate policy was that of the period 1972–74, when there was a policy with detailed provisions for additional payments beyond the norm, but frequently the flexibility permitted and the *way* it was permitted made it quite impracticable for companies to produce the type of results that were intended.

The periods of voluntary incomes control are easier for employers because the 'volunteers' are really members of the TUC General Council, who agree to specific or general limitation to the level of wage claims, leaving the employers somewhat freer to manipulate the details of payment arrangements at the same time as enjoying the protection of official TUC policy in keeping the general level of settlements down.

(c) THE LOW-PAID

Periods of incomes policy benefit the lower-paid at the expense of the better-paid, at least while the incomes policy is operating, because there is a tendency to equalise benefits and reduce the advantage of those with negotiating strength or with skills in current demand.[4] Although there has historically been a tendency for differentials to widen in the period following a spell of incomes constraint, at least some of the lower paid achieve a permanent narrowing of the gap, so that non-manual earnings have increased at a slightly lower rate than those of manual employees and earnings of women have increased at a greater rate than those of men. Although the latter increase is due mainly to the effect of the Equal Pay Act, it is also due to incomes policy.[5] The provisions of the Equal Pay Act are set out in Chapter 15 on Equalising Employment Opportunity.

Employment Protection (Consolidation) Act — Miscellaneous Provisions

Although we consider elsewhere in this text the main elements of the Employment Protection (Consolidation) Act 1978, there are several miscellaneous provisions dealing with pay that require treatment here.

(a) GUARANTEE PAYMENTS

In some areas of manual employment there is a practice of laying employees off when the employer is unable to provide work. Until 1975 the employer had no obligation to pay the employee during these periods except where there was a collective agreement with a trade union specifying levels and conditions of lay-off pay. The 1975 Act introduced an entitlement of employees to limited guarantee payment from the employer for any day or part of a day on which the employer is unable to provide work. The amount of the payment is the normal daily earnings, up to a maximum of £9.15 a day (February 1982) and a maximum of five days in any period of three months.

To be eligible the employee must have been continuously employed for at least four weeks and for at least sixteen hours in each week, and must not have unreasonably refused alternative work outside his normal contractual duties. There is no obligation on the employer to make the payment if the lay-off is caused by an industrial dispute involving employees of the same or an associated employer.

This provison is potentially an expensive one; estimates made when the Act was first being implemented suggested that the cost to employers of this single requirement would be four times the cost of all the other provisions together.[6]

A complicating factor is that in many industries there is already a collective agreement providing for guaranteed *weekly* payments, compared with the Act's provision for *daily* payments. It is therefore necessary for the employer to arrange the lay-off for short-time periods of working so as to reduce his costs, as the employees will clearly, and legitimately, seek the payment that produces the most money.

There is a tendency to think of lay-off as being a feature only of large-scale employment, but some of the early cases before tribunals have involved very small organisations. An intriguing example was *Gregory and Pailing* v. *Hodgkinson & Son.* Mr Hodgkinson's business was decorating but he laid off Mr Gregory and Mr Pailing because of shortage of work. When they sought compensation from him (they actually requested redundancy) he offered them the business in settlement of their claim! The tribunal awarded them guarantee pay.[7]

The Act provides for exemption of those employees who are covered by a collective agreement that confers benefits matching or exceeding those of the Act, providing that both parties to the agreement apply for such exemption. There have been relatively few such exemptions.

Obviously these provisions only apply to manual workers in most cases. White-collar employees will normally have a contract of employment that protects them from vagaries of payment due to shortage or work.

The Act requires that an employee shall not refuse alternative work that is reasonable in the circumstances. In *Purdy* v. *Willowbrook International Ltd,* Mr Purdy was asked to work in the finishing shop of his plant, where he had worked previously for a short period though he was now employed as a coach trimmer. The tribunal found that the work in the finishing shop was reasonable in terms of skill and payment and was not likely to be a permanent transfer, so Mr Purdy lost his claim for guarantee pay on the grounds of his refusing alternative work.[8]

The employer is not liable for guarantee pay on a day when the employee's contract does not entitle him to work and payment:

> no guarantee payment shall be payable to an employee in whose case there are no normal working hours on the day in question.[9]

So an employee who is contracted to work for two or three days a week cannot claim guarantee pay for the other days of the week.

(b) ITEMISED PAY STATEMENT

Section 81 makes it compulsory for the employer to provide each employee with an itemised pay statement before or at the time he is paid. The obligatory features of the statement are:

(i) The gross amount of salary or wages. There is no requirement for this to be detailed to show how it is made up of different elements of basic rate, incentive, premia etc. Most employers will do this anyway, but it is not a statutory obligation.

(ii) Details of *variable* deductions that have been made. These are mainly the statutory deductions for national insurance contribution and income tax.

(iii) Details of *fixed* deductions, such as trade union subscriptions, attachment of earnings and many more. As the details can be lengthy, the Act provides for the employer to take the option of providing a standing statement of what they are. This needs to be up-dated annually and any alteration has to be notified to the employee and a fresh standing statement prepared, even when the alteration is at his request.

(iv) The net amount of wages payable.

All employees are entitled to such an itemised statement providing that they work at least sixteen hours a week, or eight hours a week when they have been with the employer for more than five years.

The remedies for the employee are complaint to a tribunal; if the tribunal finds that the employer is not complying with the requirements of the Act it is empowered to order the employer to pay back to the employee up to thirteen weeks of un-notified deductions, even if they are statutory deductions like income tax.

For most employers this obligation is no greater than that which they meet anyway, but there is the important point of detail that any alteration in fixed deductions has to be notified to the employee in writing and a fresh standing statement compiled. One of the most common fixed deductions is contributions to an occupational pension scheme, and these customarily alter with salary increases. Every alteration has to be notified and a new standing statement prepared.

Sick Pay

In 1982 a change in legislation removed the provision by doctors of medical certificates authorising absence from work by employees for short periods. These have been relied on by employers and employees to justify absence and the payment by the employer of sick pay, where the contract of employment called for such payments. The notes became even more important after 1972 and the introduction of unfair dismissal legislation.

With effect from April 1983 Statutory Sick Pay is introduced, whereby the responsibility for paying benefits to employees during the first three days of sickness absence will pass from the Department of Health and Social Security to the employer.

SUMMARY PROPOSITIONS

26.1. The law provides the right, not enjoyed by salary earners, for manual workers to be paid in cash.

26.2. Wages Councils set legally binding minimum rates of pay and conditions in industries where there is not satisfactory voluntary machinery for determining pay matters.

26.3. Within organisations the effects of government incomes policies are to reduce employer control of the pay system, to distort its structure and to narrow differentials.

26.4. Among the miscellaneous provisions of the Employment Protection (Consolidation) Act are guarantee payments during lay-off and itemised pay statements to employees.

REFERENCES

1. O'Higgins P., 'Truck Legislation' in *Encyclopaedia of Personnel Management,* ed. Torrington D. (Gower Press) 1974, p. 439.
2. *Brooker v. Charringtons Fuel Oils Ltd.*, 1980. A discussion of this case and its implications is to be found in *IDS Brief no. 205,* May 1981, pp. 10/11.
3. Retail banks are obviously interested in encouraging these changes, and there is a report by the Central Policy Review Staff entitled *Cashless Pay* (HMSO) 1981.

4. For a detailed, if difficult, analysis of this phenomenon see Metcalf D., 'Unions, Incomes Policy and Relative Wages in Great Britain' in *British Journal of Industrial Relations*, July 1977.
5. Central Statistical Office, *Social Trends, No. 8* (HMSO) 1977, pp. 102, 3.
6. Quoted in Rubenstein M., *A Practical Guide to the Employment Protection Act* (IPM) 1975, p. 22.
7. *Gregory and Pailing v. Hodgkinson and Son*, 1977.
8. *Purdy v. Willowbrook International Ltd*, 1977.
9. Employment Protection Act 1975, Section 23.

27

The Job Analysis Process

Our consideration of the many facets of the personnel contract has been developed on an explicit assumption that the parties involved are aware of all relevant details of particular jobs or organisational positions. The purpose of this chapter is to examine the methods by which job information can be collected, analysed, recorded and used in various managerial activities.

Our general theme is that important personnel management activities should be well planned and systematic, being carefully designed after consideration of requirements and alternatives. This is particularly true of the activities associated with analysis of jobs and we introduce the 'ADAIRE' model as a basis, together with our discussion, for consideration of the activities involved. We provide an overview of the Job Analysis Process indicating various applications, methods of data collection and analysis, approaches to recording and reporting information, together with appropriate references to sources of more detailed information. This should enable the reader to design a particular process according to the needs of the situation and the resources available.

The job analysis process provides important information to management generally and the personnel specialist in particular, but the application of this information often raises problems, especially when it is prepared for general use as part of a rather bureaucratic system of defining the different jobs in an organisation. For example, an inadequate job description permits the currently prevalent industrial sanction of 'working to rule', and is unlikely to provide sufficiently detailed information for training applications. Similarly, an over-detailed job description will have been expensive to produce and may result in unnecessary complexity and rigidity in situations where more general job-related information is required.

Job Analysis Definitions

Job analysis has been described as:

> a sort of handmaiden serving in various ways a variety of needs and all the while floundering in a mass of semantic confusion.[1]

Written in 1955, this comment refers to conventional essay-type job descriptions, and is relevant when organisations adopt practices without a clear understanding of the needs to be satisfied by the process.

A 1920 definition describes job analysis as:

the scientific study and statement of all the facts about a job which reveals its content and all the modifying factors which surround it.[2]

A more recent publication, currently widely used in the UK, adopts the same definition, observing that:

it is difficult to improve upon it, though equally difficult to refrain from the comment that much work we now accept as job analysis is not particularly scientific.[3]

Job analysis is often used as a heading for describing one method of analysis, whereas it is actually a generic term under which a variety of methods may be subsumed.

The Department of Employment Glossary of Training Terms defined job analysis as:

the process of examining a job in detail in order to identify its component tasks. The detail and approach may vary according to the purpose for which the job is being analysed.[4]

We use the following key terms:

Job Analysis: The process of systematic and logical examination of a job in detail sufficient to identify the nature, component tasks, other job content information, demands on the job holder and other modified factors relative to the purpose of the analysis.

Occupation: All jobs which have sufficient similarity of their major tasks and requirements to enable them to be grouped together for the purpose of a generalised job description.

Job: A collection of tasks which are assigned to one person and constitute the work of that person. Associated with an organisational position or role, a job usually has a title, organisationally defined relationships and contractual implications.

Task: A major element of work which can usually be identified in terms of its objectives or end results.

Job Description: A broad statement of the purpose, scope, component tasks, duties and responsibilities which constitute a particular job. The quantity and detail of information contained will vary according to the purpose for which it is to be used.

Personnel Specification: A detailed statement of those physical and psychological characteristics, qualities, abilities, etc., which are required by the job holder in order to fulfil the requirements of that particular job.

THE JOB ANALYSIS PROCESS: AN OVERVIEW

Our definition of job analysis as a systematic process of inter-related activities leads to the identification of six distinct stages or phases, as follows:

(i) Assessment of objectives and requirements.
(ii) Data collection.
(iii) Analysis of data.

(iv) Information assembly and recording.
(v) Reporting the job-related information.
(vi) Evaluation and feedback of results.

The initial letters for each phase provide the acronym ADAIRE for our overview model of the process. During each phase of the process a number of inter-related activities are involved, although the depth and detail of consideration of each will vary according to decisions about requirements and the resources which can be invested in a particular process.

Figure 27.1 provides the ADAIRE model of the general process as an overview of the main activities which may be required, as a checklist and a guide to planning. It must be emphasised that the model indicates activities involved in a particularly thorough process of job analysis, whereas many particular applications will be adequately dealt with by a more simplified process. It is our view that it is preferable to consider all the possibilities and make a conscious decision to omit specific activities when not necessary or justified in a particular case.

The following discussion will focus upon each of the distinct phases of the process and the relevant activities in the collection, analysis, recording, reporting and utilisation of job-related information. The selection of activities and design of the final process will depend upon the purpose of the investigation, the human and other resources available, and the judgement of the job analyst or personnel officer involved.

PHASE ONE: ASSESSMENT OF OBJECTIVES AND REQUIREMENTS

Job analysis is usually initiated by needs for job-related information in other organisational processes or activities. The purpose indicates the objectives and the specific information requirements, and obviously influences the type and amount of resources which it is appropriate to invest in a particular job analysis process. These factors in turn influence decisions about the feasibility of activities within the process, so this initial phase is one of preparation and planning based upon the identification and assessment of relevant objectives and requirements. Particular considerations include the following aspects.

Purpose of Job Analysis

As the purpose influences decisions about resources, selection of activities and methods, and presentation of the information, the starting point must be a clear identification of the purpose to be served. Figure 27.2 indicates some of the major purposes and applications of job-related information, within personnel management activities discussed in other chapters and also more general management activities involving other users.

The particular organisational user(s) will have different needs for type and detail of information and the form in which it is presented. Different applications justify different resource investment and demand variable types and quality of information provision. These aspects of purpose influence many features of planning and decision-making within the process, so are crucial to effective provision and utilisa-

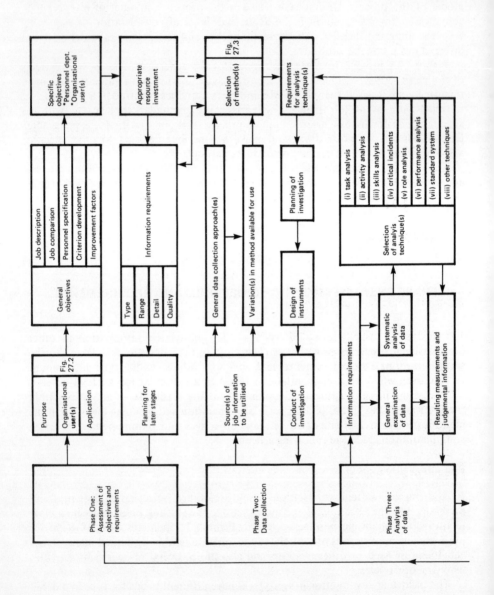

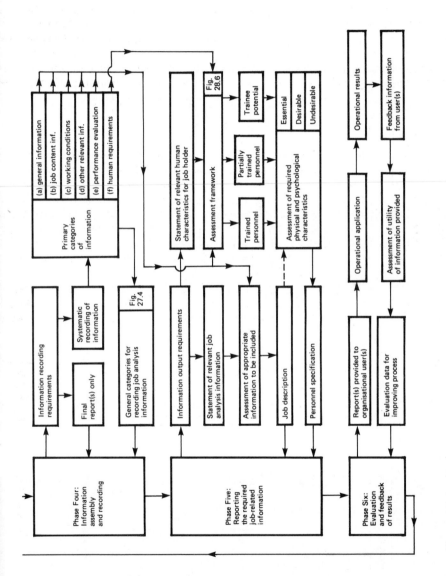

Figure 27.1. 'ADAIRE': a systematic approach to job analysis

Major Applications of Job Related Information

Personnel Management work activities				General management activities	
The Contract for work	The Contract for collective consent	The Contract for individual control	The Contract for payment	Operations management	Policy and planning
Recruitment	Industrial relations	Grievances	Wages administration	Working conditions	Corporate planning
Selection	Negotiation processes	Disciplinary procedures	Salary administration	Equipment design	Manpower planning
Placement		Dismissals	Job evaluation	Plant layout	Manpower utilisation
Training:		Redundancies		Methods design and improvement	Organisational development
— on the job		Safety administration		Job design	Management decision-making
— off the job		Vocational counselling		Setting standards of performance	Career programming
Management development					
Job design					
Performance appraisal					

Figure 27.2. The management activities served by job analysis

tion of the information. These observations may appear self-evident but most problems and criticisms of job descriptions and personnel specifications can be traced to their use by people or for purposes other than originally intended.

General and Specific Objectives

Job analysis usually involves one, or a combination, of the following five general objectives:

(a) JOB DESCRIPTION
Information, to enable decisions to be made about a job, which may be completely or relatively unfamiliar to the parties involved in making the decision. The obvious examples are recruitment and selection.

(b) JOB COMPARISON
Information is commonly required in order to compare a particular job with others inside or outside the organisation. The obvious example is job evaluation, but job comparison data is also useful for such applications as grievance procedures, career programming and manpower utilisation decisions.

(c) PERSONNEL SPECIFICATION
It is often necessary to be able to provide an assessment of the hypothetical person required to carry out a job satisfactorily, either immediately or after undergoing a development or training programme. Typical examples are in selection and training, management development, vocational counselling and manpower planning.

(d) CRITERION DEVELOPMENT
Information is often required to assist the development of appropriate criteria for assessing the performance, or potential, of job occupants. Such criteria are needed for recruitment and selection decisions, in addition to performance appraisal systems, payment administration and productivity negotiation.

(e) IMPROVEMENT FACTORS
The job analysis may also identify aspects of organisational activities which can be improved. The improvement of personal competence (education, training, developmental experience), working activities (methods design, job design), working situations (working conditions, plant lay-out, equipment design) and total organisational functioning (corporate planning, manpower planning, organisational development) are common objectives of job analysis activities.

A consideration of the *general objectives* has implications for the nature of information to be provided in each case, but it must be emphasised that the relevance and importance of these objectives will vary according to the different applications involved. Having identified the purpose, organisational user and general objectives the *specific objectives* of those involved can be made explicit where these have implications for the process.

Information Requirements

Arising from these considerations, we should now have a clear knowledge of the job-related information required. The *type* or nature of information, the *range* covered, the amount of *detail*, etc., all need to be understood together with the *quality* aspects of the information required. These features, and the methods to be utilised, are clearly moderated by the decision about appropriate investment of resources in relation to the objectives and purpose.

The completion of this phase is a detailed consideration of methodology for later phases, with relevant preparation and planning of these activities.

PHASE TWO: DATA COLLECTION

This second phase in the process involves the gathering of job-related information for subsequent analysis and processing. Data collection usually receives only brief attention in the personnel management literature, but the quality of job analysis depends upon appropriate choice of methods and relevant application to the gathering of useful information.

Two important areas for consideration are:

Sources of Job Information

A critical decision is the choice of source(s) of information relating to the focal job and the accuracy, relevance, significance or reliability of information from the source(s). Roff and Watson, in their influential manual, observe: 'there is only one really satisfactory source of job information and that is the man who is doing the job.'[5] They were arguing against another common assumption that a superior, by virtue of his position and/or experience, should be the source of information. A number of separate research studies including those of Heller,[6] Heneman[7] and Thornton,[8] have all demonstrated that different members of a 'role set' (i.e., those organisational positions with which the role holder is in regular interaction such as superiors, subordinates and peers) often have significantly different perceptions of the work or behaviour which comprises any focal job.

The point is neatly emphasised by Singleton who observes:

> inevitably the various people associated with a particular job have different frames of reference and different ideas about what the job should be . . . this gives at least four different answers to the question of what a particular worker is doing.[9]

In selecting a particular method, therefore, one has to consider the source of the information which the method is designed to collect. Each source has a different information potential and different problems. The major sources of information are:

(a) INCUMBENTS

The occupant of a particular job has the most detailed knowledge of the job requirements. However, he may provide distorted information by exaggeration to boost his self-esteem, omission of items taken for granted, inclusion of own idiosyncratic methods, or through caution regarding the purpose he perceives the information as serving.

(b) SUPERIORS

The superior or supervisor has his own view of what the job involves and, in particular, of the organisational expectations. However, a superior is unlikely to be fully aware of all job details, even if he previously occupied a similar position himself. Changes in the job over time, faulty memory for critical details, or a biased view of the job incumbent are likely to affect the viewpoint of the most knowledgeable supervisor. The variety of different jobs in organisations often results in supervisors having only a superficial knowledge of the jobs in their charge but, during an investigation, there is a human tendency to exaggerate such knowledge to avoid a charge of ignorance about the subject of one's supervision.

(c) OTHER MEMBERS OF THE 'ROLE SET'
The subordinates, peers and others with whom the job holder is in regular interaction may also provide useful information for job analysis. They know about different aspects of the work behaviour of a particular job incumbent, through their direct observation and experience. Once again one has to be extremely cautious because of the likelihood of bias or error being introduced, intentionally or unintentionally, for personal reasons.

(d) TECHNICAL EXPERTS
This term is used here to describe organisational members who are aware of the tasks or behaviour which the organisational systems require the job incumbent to carry out.

(e) SPECIALIST OBSERVERS
We use this term for trained observers, such as job analysts or work study practitioners, who can provide an independent view of the work being carried out by an incumbent. The major problem here is that the incumbent, knowing he is being observed, is able to adjust the behaviour which he makes available for observation. This is a problem particularly noted by work study practitioners, whose training includes a variety of observational techniques and analytical methods designed to minimise such inaccuracies.

More detailed analysis of the relative advantages and disadvantages of alternative sources of job information may be found in the research and other publications of industrial psychology and work study, many being listed as references for this chapter. Once again, the purpose and objectives of the investigation are important to the selection decision, as the sources vary in the significance, relevance and reliability of information according to the perceived application. As a general rule, we consider that variety of sources is preferable in providing a wider data base for analysis, although increasing the need for informed judgement by the analyst.

Data Collection Approaches

The general approach to data collection may be one or a combination of several approaches to collecting usable data from the source(s) utilised. Each of the general approaches has a number of variations, the principal ones applicable to job analysis being indicated in Figure 27.3 below. A brief summary of the general data collection approaches is as follows:

(i) *Self Report Methods.* Maintaining a work diary of activities, writing an essay or narrative about one's own view of a particular job, and completing checklists and questionnaires are all common data collection methods. The reference in the figure to standard instruments includes the possibility of applying

General data collection approaches	Principal variations commonly used	Potential sources of job information				
		Incumbent(s)	Superior(s)	Other members of 'role set'	Technical experts	Specialist observers
Self report	Work diary	√				
	Written narrative	√	√			
	Checklist	√	Δ	Δ		
	Questionnaire	√	Δ	Δ		
	Standard instruments	√	Δ	Δ	Δ	Δ
Interviews	'On the job' questioning	√				
	Critical incidents	√	√	Δ	Δ	
	Structured interview	√	Δ	Δ		
	Unstructured interview	√	√	Δ	√	Δ
Group discussions	Occupational group	Δ				
	Technical conference		Δ		Δ	Δ
	Mixed conference	Δ	Δ	Δ	Δ	Δ
Recorded observation	Continuous commentary	√	Δ			
	Time-lapse photography	√				
	Slow-motion film	√				
	Film or CCTV recording	√				
	Instrumentation	√				
Observation (usually Work Study or Industrial Engineering practitioners)	Direct observation		Δ	Δ	Δ	√
	Method Study techniques					√
	Work Measurement techniques				Δ	√
	Observation and inference				Δ	√
Existing written records	Relevant statistics	Materials — consumed or wasted. Performance/output records Quality Control records, etc.				
	Procedures	Drawing and design data. Organisational analysis.				
	Previous analysis	Past job analysis data (updated or modified to suit new purpose)				

Note: √ indicates more common sources; Δ indicates potential sources

Figure 27.3. Typology of data collection methods

psychological tests, where these will provide useful job-related information. We also include the measuring instruments and manuals for use with standardised job analysis systems such as those indicated in our later discussion of data analysis techniques.

(ii) *Interviews.* The variations and methods of interviewing are dealt with in Chapter 29.

(iii) *Group Discussions.* Essentially these are group interviews or discussions which focus on specific jobs or, more usually, occupational groupings. The variations simply identify different types of participant involvement in these group discussions.

(iv) *Recorded Observation.* There are various methods available for recording directly the job behaviour of particular incumbents, for a more detailed examination and analysis of the work activities so recorded.

(v) *Observation.* Direct observation of the work behaviour of any particular job incumbent may be carried out and reported by any of the non-incumbent sources of information indicated. There are problems of recording, observing over a sufficient time period, and observers as a source of bias or error. The other principal variations listed in Figure 27.3 refer to methods and techniques which are generally examined by the literature of work study or industrial engineering, but which often represent methods available to the job analyst either through special training or by the co-operation of appropriate departments of the organisation.

For further details of the 'recorded observation' and 'observation' approaches and variations the literature of work study or industrial engineering should be studied. Particularly useful texts are by Karger and Bayha,[10] the International Labour Office,[11] Currie,[12] Barnes[13] and Larkin.[14]

(vi) *Existing Written Records.* The written records of an organisation may provide useful data in the form of general statistics or details of procedures. Similarly previous job analysis data or written records should not be ignored.

In Figure 27.3 we provide a typology of data collection methods combining general data collection approaches, the principal variations commonly used, and the potential sources of information to which they may be applied. This provides a basis for selection of those combinations which will provide useful information.

Having decided upon the method to be used, it is essential to consider any requirements arising from particular analytical techniques before completing the planning of the investigation. The design of measuring instruments, including those for assessing potential or performance of job holders as discussed in Chapter 28, is then selected or carried out as appropriate. Data collection is completed by carrying out the investigation as planned.

We have indicated that the job analysis process should be initiated anew whenever job-related information is required for a specific purpose. We do not wish to imply that it is always necessary to carry out a complete process of job analysis, or even that it is essential to initiate new data collection activities. Indeed, where job analysis data or existing written records provide the necessary job information, little further study will be required, other than to ensure that the information has not been overtaken by changes over time. Our emphasis is upon the need to examine existing job analysis data and ensure that this is up-dated or modified to suit the particular purpose for which it is required for a fresh application.

PHASE THREE: ANALYSIS OF DATA

Having collected the necessary data, the next stage is to analyse the information gathered. In our overview we identify data collection and data analysis as two distinct phases in the process, a distinction which may be true in some situations and rather artificial in others. Clearly there will be a considerable amount of integration between 'data collection' and 'data analysis', as the methods to be used in each of the phases will be mutually dependent — that is to say, the method selected may be influenced by the analytical techniques to be used, whilst the analytical technique may depend upon a particular approach to data collection.

For some applications or purposes, it may be sufficient to carry out a general sifting of data to arrive at judgements based upon this general examination. Where more detailed information is required, such as for selection or training, then a more detailed, systematic and logical analysis will be necessary. A variety of specific analytical procedures has been developed:

(a) TASK ANALYSIS

At a simple level task analysis consists of identifying a range of tasks to be carried out by the occupant of a job. Indeed, many writers treat the terms 'task analysis' and 'job analysis' as being synonymous, indicating a concern for identifying the major task composition of jobs. One problem of such a simple analysis is that a job may contain a minor or infrequent task which, although easily overlooked by a superficial examination, is crucial to effective job performance. Another problem is that for some purposes, notably training programme design, greater detail and precision is necessary. Consequently more detailed task analysis methods have been developed.

Many focus upon the recording and analysis of complex activities or inter-related tasks. Logical trees and algorithms are popular methods with advantages and limitations which are discussed by Annett and Duncan.[15] Such methods examine the sequence and inter-relationships between different activities, both physically and psychologically based, which comprise the complete task. Similarly these approaches may be used to examine the sequencing and inter-relationships between separate tasks which comprise particular jobs.

Research at the University of Hull has resulted in a comprehensive method of task analysis, described by Annett et al.[16] A particular job is analysed in terms of the range of tasks which can be identified as comprising the work associated with it. A task in this context is viewed as a collection of operations or activities resulting in a specific end product or task objective. They point out that each task involves a variety of subsidiary operations, activities or sub-tasks designed to achieve the task objective. These operations are arranged in a sequence or plan.

Consequently the next stage involves the diagnosis of the plan which is needed to achieve the task objective, resulting in a hierarchy of operations being identified and defined in terms of subsidiary objectives.

The depth of analysis may be adjusted to suit the information requirements relating to the particular job. Some individual tasks simply require identification and specification, whilst others require a next level of analysis in terms of identifying the primary operations or sub-tasks. There may be further extension to successive levels of analysis of the operations or sub-tasks in the hierarchy.

The basic analysis will, of course, be required for most applications. The more detailed task analysis methods outlined here provide greater depth.

(b) ACTIVITY ANALYSIS

Whilst other approaches are concerned with the analysis of tasks or activities relating to a job, we use the term 'activity analysis' to identify approaches concerned more directly with human activities and the psychological demands of tasks. In practical terms, this approach usually leads directly to a personnel specification rather than a job description. Consequently this is distinctly different from task analysis, although often subsumed under the same heading in the literature.

This approach is represented by the method outlined by Miller[17] using a taxonomy of functions[18] needed for analytical purposes. This approach basically depends on asking what functions would have to be built into a robot in order to enable it to carry out the tasks effectively. Thus the technique emphasises the kinds of activity being performed and their demands upon the human operator, particularly in relation to memory, perceptual and decision-making functions.

The functions identified do not therefore describe the task content relating to differences between individual job incumbents. Description of robot functions only describes part of the situation and does not, for example, account for factors relating to variations in memory, skills, training and experience. Such factors are normally important to the purpose of job analysis so this approach is usually used in conjunction with other methods.

(c) SKILLS ANALYSIS

Current usage appears to sanction this term to describe the techniques outlined by Seymour,[19] and later developed as a specific approach.[20] Skills analysis is particularly orientated towards training problems and concentrates on those aspects of behaviour which are susceptible to learning or modification with experience — the generally accepted description of a 'skill'.

The repertoire of tasks performed by a job holder is identified (i.e. task analysis) and then examined in detail. Subsidiary operations or tasks are identified and analysed to discover the relevant body movements for effective performance. The emphasis of the analysis is on the perceptual aspects of tasks, that is the cues used by the human operator for input and feedback to enable the body motor functions to be ordered, co-ordinated and controlled. Thus this analysis is most appropriate for jobs commonly referred to as 'skilled' or 'semi-skilled', where tasks are primarily the manual operation of tools and machinery. It provides very useful information about the perceptual and motor skills required for efficient performance.

(d) 'CRITICAL INCIDENTS' ANALYSIS

Engineering psychologists used the term 'error analysis' to describe those studies concerned with identifying the types and causes of human error or mistakes. Useful reviews of such work are provided by DeGreene[21] and also by Singleton,[22] who provides a summary of the different error taxonomies.

A major emphasis of such studies has been upon those errors leading to industrial accidents. However, the major problem with accidents is obtaining a useful sample size in view of their relative unpredictability; Fitts and Jones[23] attempted to increase sample sizes by asking subjects to report upon errors they had made or seen others make.

This approach was adopted by Flanagan[24] and others into the 'critical incident' technique which is now widely used. Participants in a study are asked to identify critical incidents, based upon their own experience and observation, relative to the objectives of the investigation. Early studies invited participants to identify behaviours which resulted in accidents. Similarly respondents may be asked to identify those factors related to successful performance of a job or task, and those resulting in failure. Analysis of the responses will identify types of behaviour which should be encouraged or eliminated.

(e) ROLE ANALYSIS

The analysis of managerial jobs has always been a particular problem, as tasks are often difficult to define and measure, and a greater variety of tasks is usually involved. The study by Mintzberg[25] provides a review of research into the nature of managerial work; one major conclusion is that managerial activities are characterised by their brevity, variety and fragmentation rather than being consistent and clearly defined. It is for this reason that job analysis and job description are often treated as a synonymous activity, with descriptions being directly generated by self-report data from incumbents or their superiors. We have already referred to the fact that several studies have identified often substantial discrepancies between the views of the job incumbent, his superior and other employees regarding the precise requirements of a particular job. Other studies have emphasised the problems of ambiguity, or of incumbents not being fully aware of what is expected of them, due to such discrepant perception.

In pointing to inappropriate applications of job descriptions, Douglas McGregor[26] suggested that the most fruitful application could be in stimulating management discussion, so that different members of the role set exchanged perceptions about the nature of particular jobs and differences in their expectations of the job incumbent. As well as identifying areas of overlap or omission of activities, possible needs for organisational change and improvement, the discussion process should improve mutual understanding and efficiency.

Thus for many years personnel specialists have generally recommended some process to arrive at a job description *acceptable* to all parties concerned. This has now developed into the specific technique of 'role analysis', which is built upon the concepts of role theory, as a method for organisational development activities. A variety of specific procedures has been developed, but certain common features can be identified and a useful summary is provided by French and Bell.[27]

The incumbent, his superior and possibly other members of the role set generate their own individual lists of the duties, responsibilities and behaviour expected from the job holder. Discussion and negotiation produce a role description which is satisfactory to all concerned. The participants next explore their expectations of each other until some mutual understanding is reached. The result should be an agreement about most of the important features of the focal job, which can then be used to produce a *useful* job description.

The role analysis approach, as an organisational development technique, assists team building by enabling problems and mutual expectations to be resolved. Further it may enable roles to be redefined as a contribution to improving organisational functioning.

Discussion and negotiation clarify problems and develop mutual concern for appropriate behaviour. As a vehicle for negotiating many aspects of the personnel contract they assist in improving the 'fit' between the individual and the organisation.

(f) PERFORMANCE ANALYSIS

For all applications of job analysis (Figure 27.2) some performance evaluation data is usually required. Indeed, most of the approaches to data collection and analysis discussed here are intended to yield data concerning performance of either individual tasks or complete jobs. However, performance analysis is a significant contribution to the job analysis process.

The ultimate in thoroughness would be to measure performance in every aspect and task of the job, but this is usually impracticable and too detailed. At the opposite extreme is the single criterion, such as the performance rating by a superior or a measure of productivity, which is used to judge the performance of a job holder. This type of measure has limited value, as it does not cover important features of a job or is influenced by factors outside the individual's own control. For example, a salesman judged by his gross sales may have other responsibilities not measured by this criterion and there may be differences in territory, organisational support facilities or other factors.

Different measures may be combined to provide a 'composite criterion' or considered separately as 'multiple criteria' relating to different job dimensions. As Howell observes in reviewing the problems of establishing and measuring performance criteria:

> there is little consensus on the appropriate philosphy for evaluating performance (whether it should be represented as one or many criteria), or the proper kinds of criteria (objective or subjective), or on the ways in which these criteria should be measured.[28]

Performance analysis takes various forms but usually needs to address the following questions:

(i) *What is the appropriate basis for judging job performance?* This requires identification of the dimensions of the job to be evaluated, followed by decisions about whether single, composite or multiple criterion measures are needed.

(ii) *What criteria are relevant?* They may include productivity measures (outputs, time taken, quality wastage, etc.), job factors (judgement, accident rate, absenteeism, etc.), the achievement of objectives, work attitudes or performance ratings. It is necessary to ensure not only relevance but also that the criterion is capable of measurement.

(iii) *How should the criteria be measured?* The measurement method should ensure consistency, independent of who does the measuring. It should also aim to be free from bias or distortion by factors outside the control of the individual. In practice these requirements are difficult to achieve, since subjective measures (like ratings) allow idiosyncratic factors to intervene, whilst objective measures are rarely free of ambiguity.

(iv) *Are the criteria and measurements acceptable?* It is essential that the acceptability is established, from the point of view of the incumbent and those who are to use the performance data, if it is to be useful in practice.

(v) *What constitutes an acceptable performance standard?* We need to determine standards of performance levels to be achieved, in order to evaluate the comparative performance of different job incumbents.

To summarise, the performance analysis should produce information about the appropriate criteria to be used and the method of measuring them, as well as identifying performance standards and performance expectations for evaluating the performance of the job incumbent.

(g) STANDARD SYSTEMS

The whole emphasis of this chapter, so far, has been the study of particular organisational jobs and the design of the process so that job-related information is obtained in sufficient detail to meet the requirements. An alternative approach has been developed in the USA in recent years, which simplifies the preparation of job descriptions by using standard systems, usually comprising standard questionnaires/ instruments, general classification of jobs and instructions for the procedure to be followed in the collection, analysis and recording of data. Examples of standardised systems are as follows:

(i) *USES system.* The US Training Employment Service (USES) is a federal agency which periodically classifies the nation's population of jobs. Results appear in the Dictionary of Occupational Titles (DOT), which lists and briefly defines about 22,000 current job titles,[29] identifying the major tasks and activities for each of the jobs listed. USES has produced a standard system for classifying jobs on the basis of six basic trait dimensions, with different scales for each of the dimensions. The combination of the DOT and the dimensional profile provides a brief job description and a dimensional description of the human requirements for successful performance.[30] Certainly this represents the most widely used standardised system although it is often used, as suggested below, as a preliminary to a subsequent job analysis process.

(ii) *Task inventories.* This approach, which has not been provided with a formal title, refers to the job analysis system adopted by the United States Air Force and described by Marsh.[31] The system comprises a combination of standard check list, open-ended questionnaire and observation interviews using both experts and incumbents as the sources of information. The instruments could be adapted as an approch to industrial job analysis although they suffer from the disadvantage of requiring many people and much time. It would be difficult to implement in anything but a large organisation, such as the armed service for which the system was developed.

(iii) *Functional job analysis.* This is a system currently being developed on a basis of research in USA and described by Fine and Wiley.[32] The method is intended to develop a standard language to describe and evaluate what workers do, using the task as the basic unit of analysis, with the object of ensuring that different analysts will arrive at comparable job descriptions.

Whilst tasks may be described in many ways, the basic premise underlying FJA is that they may be reduced to a few basic behaviour patterns or functions. These functions are viewed as being directed toward one of three possible objects: data, people or things. The functions also vary in complexity, and a taxonomy has been developed for each of the functional orientations.

Thus the process commences by identifying the component and then the component functions of the task. The extent to which each function is oriented towards data, people or things, is estimated in percentages. The resulting description enables the essential features of the job to be described in terms of the work carried out, and at which level of complexity. The research evidence suggests that FJA is a reliable approach, in that different analysts will arrive at similar descriptions, but whether it provides a sufficiently detailed description is uncertain.

(iv) *Position Analysis Questionnaire.* This approach is similar to functional job analysis, with the assumption that all jobs can be reduced to a set of job elements which tend to cluster together to form specific job dimensions.[33] After research a modified PAQ[34] has been developed based upon 194 job elements classified into six major categories and analysed further into 27 more specific job dimensions. Application to ratings of particular jobs seems to have high reliability, with different analysts arriving at much the same descriptive values for each job considered. These and other findings suggest that the concept of the common structure underlying all jobs may be reasonable and that the measurement of jobs in terms of structure is feasible.

Although the above approaches are all based upon research in the USA and are still in the development stage, they can be useful, but we have two reservations. First, due to their being designed for USA applications, the terminology and relevance of the measures must be suspect for application in the UK. Secondly there is the main problem with any standardised system, which is that it cannot encompass all the nuances of any specific job – the duties of a sheet metal worker, foreman, secretary or any other job in one company may be quite different from jobs with similar titles in other companies. Thus we consider it important to conduct individual job analysis to describe the jobs as they actually exist, or are intended to exist, within a particular organisation.

However, the methods and standardised instruments may be adopted or modified for use in a particular organisation. Similarly the job dimensions identified, notably by the FJA and PAQ approaches, may provide a useful basis for analysis to be incorporated within the process. Such approaches, being relatively simple and economical to apply, may form a useful preliminary analysis to assist with the design of a particular job analysis process.

PHASE FOUR: INFORMATION ASSEMBLY AND RECORDING

In certain cases, for example when managerial jobs are examined using some form of role analysis procedure, there will be direct assembly of the information in the form of a suitable job description. Phase 4 in these cases becomes incorporated within phase 5 activities.

It is more common, however, for data to be collected from several sources, by a variety of methods and subjected to multiple analyses as indicated for earlier phases. This introduces a requirement for a systematic approach to assembly and recording of the information available. This is particularly true when some of the data is collected and/or analysed by external specialists, such as a work study department, requiring combination with the information produced within the personnel management departments.

Whilst the compilation and assembly of information in the form of written records depends partly upon the purpose and partly upon the judgement of the analyst, some detailed records will usually be helpful with future investigations for different purposes. It may be sufficient to file copies of data, analyses and reports but the information will be more useful for present and future applications if systematically recorded. We suggest general data categories, corresponding to usual reporting requirements, each being capable of further sub-categorisation as appropriate. The following general headings appear relevant for most purposes:

(a) GENERAL INFORMATION

Most job analyses will require the recording of general information under the following sub-headings:

(i) *Job identification data.* This would include the current title of the job, the department and division of the organisation in which the job is situated and the number of people employed in it.

(ii) *Organisational data.* Here is recorded any general organisational data relevant to the focal job and the precise position of the focal job in relation to others. This will include superior and subordinate positions, preferably also including a statement of the kind and degree of supervision involved. It may also be necessary to include the details of any other positions with which co-ordinatory activities or working contact is made.

(iii) *Job summary.* A condensed statement of the job provides a readily understandable idea of the basic functions and purposes of the job.

(b) JOB CONTENT INFORMATION

This section would include all data about tasks or duties, together with the results of any detailed analyses which have been conducted.

A primary interest will be to identify the Task Composition or the range of tasks and duties involved. In certain circumstances the analysis may also identify a hierarchy of sub-tasks or operations. The analysis may have been concerned with the methods involved and the purpose of tasks should also be identified.

When the job involves repetitive work the job analysis, at least in theory, is a straightforward identification of a definite hierarchy of operations to be repeated over time. Because many other jobs are non-repetitive it is common to classify component tasks into categories of relative frequency such as: routine, periodic or occasional tasks or duties. This provides a useful breakdown of the job but it may be misleading. For example, Mintzberg[25] showed that many managerial jobs involve a large percentage of available time spent on routine matters, but the significant contribution to the effectiveness of the organisation usually occurs when 'occasional' duties are performed. It is for this reason that we suggest identification of the relative importance of tasks to indicate a mix of quantitative and qualitative information.

The job may involve other job duties which are not clearly identifiable, such as tasks which are carried out in conjunction with people in other organisational units. It can also be useful to provide information about the scope of responsibility of the job holder.

(c) WORKING CONDITIONS

It is important to record the working conditions of a job, because of their impact on any job incumbent. The physical environment category will include the physical demands upon the job holder, temperature and other working conditions, accident or health risks and any other physical demands. The social environment category may identify membership of formal groups, associated social pressures or influences, and other relevant social factors. An economic conditions category includes a record of wage or salary details, together with any other direct or indirect financial benefits.

(d) OTHER RELEVANT INFORMATION

For some jobs, or some organisations, additional information may be needed. For example, the prospects of promotion or transfer of the job incumbent may be significant. If the particular job is seen as a proving ground leading to subsequent promotion or transfer, then the incumbent may need to possess abilities or characteristics which are not essential for the focal job but may be important at a later date.

(e) PERFORMANCE EVALUATION INFORMATION

Most job analyses will require at least some performance criteria which can be used to evaluate the performance of the job holder. Performance standards facilitate comparison or judgement of relative effectiveness of performance, whilst it is useful to indicate performance expectations either in the job as a whole or in different component tasks.

(f) HUMAN REQUIREMENTS

The data collection and analysis will provide direct information regarding the physical or psychological characteristics which are needed by the job holder. Whilst this is often recorded in the personnel specification to be discussed later, it may be useful to keep records of any more detailed information gathered during job analysis.

The assembly of information on the lines described above will be useful for two reasons. First, the job analysis process may produce information which is not directly applicable for the current purpose, but potentially useful for future applications. Secondly, assembling information in this way will make the subsequent preparation of job description and personnel specification more straightforward. Finally, the preparation of both the job description and the personnel specification depend upon judgement by the job analyst or personnel specialist. Consequently more detailed records may help in the comparison of these judgements with the results achieved, so assisting organisational learning.

PHASE FIVE: REPORTING THE JOB-RELATED INFORMATION

The first phase identified the information requirements which comprise the output from the job analysis process, which may take the form of a simple statement of the relevant job analysis information. In most cases, however, the requirement is for a report in the form of a job description although the particular form and content may be expected to vary for different purposes, applications or users. For some purposes, usually when concerned with the required capabilities of job holders, an additional report may be provided in the form of a personnel specification.

A general review of these two primary forms of reporting job analysis information identifies the main considerations for phase five of the job analysis process, as follows:

Job Description

The job description should provide a concise and straightforward word picture of the job, appropriate to the purpose for which it is intended. It is usually the means by which the job analyst records the job-related information in a form which enables it to be used by other members of the organisation. The previous section has outlined a number of headings and subsidiary categories for the recording of job-related information. These headings are consistent with most recommendations in the literature for the job description compilation. Figure 27.4 shows the broad outline of a job description prepared on the basis of information assembled and recorded in phase 4 of the job analysis process.

The diagram may be useful as a general checklist for the preparation of a job description. The degree of detail included will depend on the preceding stages of data collection and analysis, the purpose for which the description is intended,

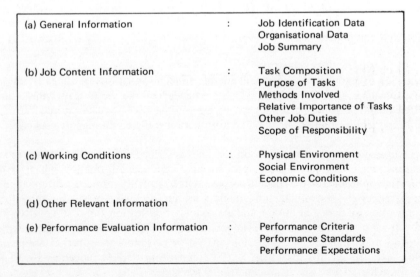

(a) General Information	:	Job Identification Data
		Organisational Data
		Job Summary
(b) Job Content Information	:	Task Composition
		Purpose of Tasks
		Methods Involved
		Relative Importance of Tasks
		Other Job Duties
		Scope of Responsibility
(c) Working Conditions	:	Physical Environment
		Social Environment
		Economic Conditions
(d) Other Relevant Information		
(e) Performance Evaluation Information	:	Performance Criteria
		Performance Standards
		Performance Expectations

Figure 27.4. Compilation of the Job Description

and will vary according to the particular job concerned. For example, a job description intended for a training application requires detailed information under all categories, so that a training programme for that job can be designed; while a job description for productivity negotiations may require broad descriptive information with details of performance evaluation information. However, some description under each of the headings will usually be needed.

Although this general approach has been suggested as a basis, the form of the job description must depend on the particular circumstances of the investgation. We do not reject the notion of a general purpose form for job description, as advocated by many writers, but we do consider that there are some dangers, including the possibilities of oversimplification, omission of important data and a general viewing of job description as a mechanistic process.

There are several problem areas which should be recognised. The job description is a means of communication and is subject to the normal problems of any written communication within organisations. It is also a simplification of reality in that it is rarely possible to include all the essential features of any particular job. An accurate simplification depends on the quality and detail of the data collection and analysis stages. Similarly, as a summary of the data available, the job description represents a judgement about what data is appropriate and the degree of detail which is relevant — a judgement which may be valid, but equally may be biased or inaccurate.

There are problems in the preparation of job descriptions, in particular those of judgement by individuals about what to collect, analyse and record. These judgements are all directly influenced by the purpose for which the information is intended. This is why we identified the job analysis process as commencing with the purpose, from which other consequent actions follow. This does not mean that a repetition of the complete process would be required for a different application, rather to emphasis the need to consider the existing data and if necessary, prepare a new job description for the new purpose.

Despite the problems with job descriptions thay can serve very useful purposes for organisations. Most criticisms can be traced either to technical deficiencies arising from the job analysis process, or to inappropriate use. The use of job descriptions for control purposes, for example, leads to suspicion and deliberate attempts by individuals to manipulate the data provided. The use of general job descriptions, as part of a bureaucratic system of specifying all organisational jobs, leads to rigidity. Systematic job analysis is valuable when designed and used for a specific purpose, recognising possible limitations and the changing nature of jobs over time.

A final point is that a job description, though prepared by a specialist, needs to be acceptable to others involved. The job incumbent, his superior, his subordinates, and others such as training officers and work study practitioners may each have a special knowledge and viewpoint of the job. The personnel contract philosophy argues that a job description should distil the significant features of a job in a way acceptable to all those affected by its specific application.

Personnel Specification

For some purposes a job description is sufficient. However, for the primary personnel functions such as recruitment, employment and training, the job requirements need to be specified in terms of a person who can carry them out. The personnel specification is developed from job analysis and related to job requirements rather than to a specific job incumbent.

The personnel specification will usually be prepared using an assessment framework such as the 'seven-point plan' described in Chapters 6 and 28. Essentially the demands of the job are translated into physical, psychological and experiential characteristics of a hypothetical individual which would enable that individual to carry out the job. The framework may be used intact, or modified if desired and augmented by test scores, but it is essential that the same methods are used for preparing the personnel specification as are used for assessing candidates.

Chapter 28 provides references to several proprietary frameworks. They usually specify several categories of human requirement to be considered in relation to a specific job. Thus the requirements of the job, as identified by job analysis, are translated into human requirements by using the assessment framework. The requirements specified should be accurate and supported by job analysis data, but there can be problems of over-precision. The specified requirements need to be not only accurate but realistic in terms of people normally to be attracted to the job. For example, the recruitment advertising pages of newspapers often produce examples of unrealistic requirements, specifying qualifications and/or experience likely to be found only in candidates already occupying positions of a higher responsibility and salary. Similarly, one has to be careful with any limits specified, to ensure that they are essential and realistic. For example, a reduction of half an inch on the police height requirement would considerably enlarge the number of potential recruits who are otherwise suitable. Thus the personnel specification requires a mixture of scientific method and commonsense judgement.

The personnel specification will usually begin with general information such as job identification data, organisational data and a brief job summary. Then come the categories of the assessment framework relevant to the job. Alongside the assessment framework categories the human requirements may be specified under three headings:

(i) *Essential requirements.* Here the particular requirements are those which are essential for adequate performance.

(ii) *Desirable requirements.* This enables characteristics to be specified which, whilst not absolutely essential, will enhance effective performance and job satisfaction.

(iii) *Undesirable factors.* This enables specification of negative factors when relevant.

Thus for the job of a security guard, it might be considered essential for an incumbent to be a minimum of 5'8" in height, whilst desirable for him to be 5'10" with a build appropriate to this height. For a job of designer a general education to HNC level and practical experience of three years in an allied field may be essential requirements, whilst desirable requirements would be a bachelor's degree and five years' experience. This approach to preparing the personnel specification avoids some of the problems of over-rigidity and enables requirements to be considered realistically and flexibly.

Our emphasis so far has been upon the preparation of personnel specification in terms of an individual who is fully trained and experienced and so able to perform the focal job effectively. For some applications, such as training or the selection of untrained candidates for jobs, the specification may be required to focus on *potential* for effective performance training or experience. In this case, the emphasis would be on physical and psychological characteristics which research and experience have identified as indicating a potential to perform or to learn the job activities. In theory, it is possible to produce two alternative personnel specifications, one for trained and one for untrained personnel. In practice the personnel specification is usually prepared for a fully competent person with the training-related elements specifically identified or covered by a separate section.

PHASE SIX: EVALUATION AND FEEDBACK OF RESULTS

With any systematic process, the final phase must be concerned with evaluation of the results achieved in order to take correcting action if necessary. This evaluation also provides necessary feedback for learning purposes, so that inadequacies within the process are identified and corrected for future activities. There are three areas of activity to be considered:

Application of Reported Information

For many purposes the job description and the personnel specification are used as operational information within the personnel department. In such cases further information about the specific application and its consequences should be readily available.

When the job-related information is provided to other organisational users, however, further details are rarely available unless actively followed up. In practice it is rare for the application to be followed up on any formal basis, but this is essential to the development of effective job analysis.

Evaluation by the Operational User

A starting point for evaluation of the application of reported job-related information is the viewpoint of the operational user(s) involved. This will assist with evaluation of the suitability of the information provided, the appropriateness of the presentation, convenience in use and other relevant user data.

The operational results may be immediately available in some cases, but many applications will involve varying time lags before such results are identified. This data provides the basis for an evaluation of how well the initial objectives have been achieved, and the identification of any deficiencies in the process.

Evaluation by the Job Analyst

The data from operational users provides essential feedback to the job analyst(s) at two levels. It may be possible to correct any deficiencies and improve the utility of the information provided for current use, although this will not always be practical. The evaluative data always provides useful feedback for learning, by enabling advantages or deficiencies of the process activities to be identified. Feedback assists in clarifying uncertainties, modification of activities, improving judgements or decisions, and generally aiding in improving the quality of subsequent job analysis.

The job analysis process does not end with the production of a job description or personnel specification, despite common practice as though this is the case. All organisational processes need to be designed for the gathering of evaluative feedback upon the results, so that effective organisational learning or adaptation by experience can take place. A systematic overview model such as ADAIRE, or a suitable variation, can aid in the planning of the process and in the practical use of feedback for subsequent improvement.

SUMMARY PROPOSITIONS

27.1.   Job analysis has many applications within organisations and the appropriate product of the job analysis process will vary according to the purpose to which it is applied.

27.2.   Job analysis is a continuous process, requiring the products to be developed in line with organisational changes or improvements in information available.

27.3.   The product of the job analysis process is a job description, a personnel specification, or a summary report of job-related information intended for a specific purpose and should not be used for other purposes without a careful check of suitability.

27.4.   When job analysis produces documents for use, it is particularly desirable that all people concerned with the focal job should find the statements and judgements acceptable.

27.5.   An explicit system model such as ADAIRE provides a useful basis for planning a particular job analysis, identification of problem areas, and for incorporation of subsequent evaluative feedback or new knowledge.

REFERENCES

1.   Kershner A.M., *A Report on Job Analysis* (Office of Naval Research) 1955.
2.   Tead O. and Metcalf H.C., *Personnel Administration* (New York) 1920, p. 285.
3.   Roff H.E. and Watson T.E., *Job Analysis* (Institute of Personnel Management) 1961.
4.   Department of Employment, *Glossary of Training Terms* (HMSO) second ed., 1971.
5.   Roff and Watson, *op. cit.,* p. 10.
6.   Heller F.A., *Managerial Decision Making* (Tavistock) 1971.
7.   Heneman H.G., 'Comparison of self and superior ratings of managerial performance', *Journal of Applied Psychology,* Vol. 59, No. 5, 1974, pp. 638–642.
8.   Thornton G.G., 'The relationship between supervisory and self appraisals of executive performance', *Personnel Psychology.* Vol. 28, 1968, pp. 441–455.
9.   Singleton W.T., *Man–Machine Systems* (Penguin) 1974, p. 64.

10. Karger D.W. and Bayha F.H., *Engineered Work Measurement* (Industrial Press) second ed. 1955.
11. International Labour Office, *Introduction to Work Study*, ILO, 1960.
12. Currie R.M., *Work Study* (Pitman) 1968.
13. Barnes R.M. *Motion and Time Study* (Wiley) sixth ed., 1969.
14. Larkin J.A., *Work Study Theory and Practice* (McGraw-Hill) 1969.
15. Annett J. and Duncan K.D., 'Task analysis and training design', *Occupational Psychology*, Vol. 41, 1967, pp. 211–221.
16. Annett J., Duncan K.D., Stammers R.B. and Gray M.J., *Task Analysis*, Department of Employment Training Paper No. 6 (HMSO) 1971.
17. Miller R.B., 'Task Description and Analysis', in R.M. Gagne (ed), *Psychological Principles of System Development* (Rinehart and Winston) 1962.
18. Miller R.B., 'Task taxonomy: science or technology?', *Ergonomics*, Vol. 10, 1967, pp. 167–176.
19. Seymour W.D., *Industrial Skills* (Pitman) 1966.
20. Seymour W.D., *Skills Analysis Training* (Pitman) 1968.
21. DeGreene K.B. (ed), *Systems Psychology* (McGraw-Hill) 1970.
22. Singleton, *op. cit.*, pp. 79–84.
23. Fitts P.M. and Jones R.E. (1947):
    (i) 'Analysis of factors contributing to 460 "pilot error" experiences in operating aircraft controls'
    (ii) 'Analysis of 270 "pilot error" experiences in reading and interpreting aircraft instruments' Reprinted in Sinaiko H.W. (ed), *Selected Papers on Human Factors in the Design and Use of Control Systems* (Dover Publications) 1961.
24. Flanagan J.C., 'The critical incident technique', *Psychological Bulletin*, Vol. 51, 1954, pp. 327–358.
25. Mintzberg H., *The Nature of Managerial Work* (Harper and Row) 1973.
26. McGregor D., *The Human Side of Enterprise* (McGraw-Hill) 1960.
27. French W.L. and Bell C.H., *Organization Development: Behavioral Science Interventions for Organisation Improvement* (Prentice-Hall) 2nd ed., 1978.
28. Howell W.C., *Essentials of Industrial and Organisational Psychology* (Dorsey) 1976, p. 136.
29. United States Training and Employment Service, *Dictionary of Occupational Titles*, third ed., (Superintendent of Documents, Governement Printing Office), 1965.
30. Fine S.A. 'Matching job requirements and worker qualifications', *Personnel Psychology*, Vol. 34, 1958, pp. 411–414.
31. Marsh J.E., 'Job analysis in the United States Air Force', *Personnel Psychology*, Vol. 17, 1964, pp. 7–17.
32. Fine S.A. and Wiley W.W., 'An Introduction to Functional Job Analysis', in E.A. Fleishman and A.R. Bass (eds), *Studies in Personnel and Industrial Psychology* (Dorsey) 1964.
33. McCormick E.J., Jeanneret P.R. and Mecham R.C., 'A study of job characteristics and job dimensions as based on the Position Analysis Questionnaire', *Journal of Applied Psychology*, Vol. 56, No. 4, 1972, pp. 347–368.
34. McCormick, *et al., Position Analysis Questionnaire (Form B)* (Indiana University Bookstore).

28

Assessment of Employee Potential and Performance

Organisational life provides many needs for the potential or performance of employees to be assessed. The two main occasions for such appraisal are prior to initial employment and during considerations about possible promotion or transfer. In this chapter we are bringing together a review of this area. We deliberately put the two main occasions together, even though they are separated in organisational life, because the methods and approach are so similar.

Two main approaches can be identified, as discussed by Howell,[1] the *General Characteristics Approach* and the *Individual Difference Approach*. The former is concerned with the similarities of human characteristics, processes and behaviour — seeking to understand how people in general think and act, under specified conditions, to enable predictions to be made about typical behaviour. In contrast the alternative approach recognises that individuals differ from each other in a relatively consistent manner for certain characteristics, processes and behaviour — leading to efforts to identify, measure and understand these differences. Both approaches are important, but the *General Characteristics Approach* contributes primarily to assessment of typical and collective behaviour, whilst the *Individual Differences Approach* contributes primarily to assessment and comparison of different individuals.

Personnel psychology, as outlined by Miner[2] and Fleishman and Bass,[3] has focused on problems of human assessment. Similarly considerable psychology research has been devoted to identification of individual differences, leading to development of psychometrics or mental measurement. Social psychology has also developed knowledge of the processes of human assessment in interpersonal relationships, groups and other social contexts for reasons summarised by Eiser:

> Our behaviour towards other people depends to a large extent on the impressions we form of them, our interpretation of their past and present actions, and our predictions of what they will do in the future. It is easy to see, therefore, why social psychologists should be so concerned with the judgements people make about one another, since an understanding of social behaviour must depend, in part at least, on an understanding of social perception.[4]

This quotation indicates an important problem which must be faced by specialists in assessment. Because people constantly assess one another in the social context, there is a common human belief expressed in the form: 'I pride myself as being a good judge of people and human nature'.

Although people vary in their level of competence, such expressions of belief usually represent an overestimate. One reason is that judgements may be self-fulfilling prophecies.

There is no infallible means of assessment. At the same time a knowledge of the problems of assessment and the advantages and inadequacies of different methods can improve standards. The assessment of individuals involves an analysis of particular characteristics of the person, which have implications for the behaviour of that person, so that current capabilities and future potential can be estimated. To develop such estimates, and to compare the capacities of different individuals, we need to measure the characteristics and behaviour concerned. The overall assessment needs to be sufficiently accurate and reported in a way which facilitates decision-making by others within the organisation.

1. Planning for Assessment and Measurement

Careful planning improves the quality of assessment and of decisions based on it. One aspect of such planning is understanding and anticipating problems likely to occur in different phases of the process. Another is the more general knowledge and understanding of human assessment and measurement of psychological characteristics or behaviour. Some aspects of specific advance planning are covered in later sections of this chapter, whilst some more general considerations include:

(a) NATURE OF ASSESSMENT

Assessment involves the collection of data about the individual, particularly relating to current behaviour and past experience, so that informed analysis of overall capabilities and future potential can be developed. It requires the identification of differences between individuals, which are relatively consistent for the individual and help to explain behaviour variations between those operating under similar conditions. Relative capacities of different individuals can be compared and reported. In broad terms the assessment is used to understand the individual, to explain current development, to predict future behaviour, and to make comparisons between people.

(b) INDIVIDUAL DIFFERENCES

Observation of human physical characteristics shows many similarities and differences between people. Similarities include the same number of eyes, ears, limbs and other component parts, with a shared configuration of these parts and similar movement patterns. At the same time there are differences in size, shape, weight and other variables for individual features and the body as a whole. These differences represent variations within identifiable limits, which often define a fairly narrow range of alternatives for any particular characteristic. Despite physical similarities and limits to variation, however, it is relatively easy to identify a particular individual within a large group — his uniqueness being assessed by a particular combination of a large number of characteristics.

Psychologists with an 'individual differences orientation' work upon the assumption that people differ on behavioural or psychological characteristics in a similar manner to the more easily observed physical characteristics. The difference is that such psychological characteristics or traits are 'hypothetical constructs'. They have no physical reality which can be observed directly; they represent characteristics attributed to the individual by inference from behaviour which can be observed. Thus it is possible to use different sets of constructs to describe individuals, as illustrated by Eysenck[5] advocating two factors (extroversion and introversion) to account for personality differences whilst Cattell[6] advocates sixteen. The hypothetical nature of such psychological differences presents problems in the literally thousands of constructs which have been identified and used for assessment purposes. A 1936 study by Allport and Odbert[7] identified some 18,000 'trait names' in a standard English dictionary. Although the list included synonyms, many terms represent subtle differences in description — in both cases the alternatives of terminology available present real problems of understanding for different people involved in assessment processes. Similarly the intangible nature of such characteristics presents problems of understanding, and also problems of resentment by people who are assessed upon factors which can be argued to be unreal.

When the primary emphasis is on current performance of a job, such hypothetical constructs are not essential. The performance-related behaviour itself can be directly observed and assessed. However most applications involve assessment without the opportunity for direct observation, as when assessing prospective employees, or assessing individual suitability for different jobs under changed working conditions. In such cases the hypothetical constructs provide a basis for understanding and explanation of the determinants of behaviour.

(c) THE DETERMINANTS OF BEHAVIOUR AND PERFORMANCE

A common formulation for understanding human performance of jobs states that *performance* is a function of the *abilities* and *motivation* of the individual (i.e. $P = A \times M$). This indicates that poor performance may result from inadequate ability (i.e. knowledge, skill and experience), from low motivation (i.e. force or effort directed towards performance), or from a combination of both. Thus attempts to understand motivation were directed to identifying general characteristics which could be influenced, whilst individual differences relating to ability and motivation were studied to assist with guidance, selection, development and placement of people for jobs in which they could be expected to produce satisfactory performance.

This is useful as a description of performance as an individual phenomenon, but is unsuitable as a basis for assessment because of the assumption that *performance* can be directly equated to the actual *behaviour* of the individual. The problem can be related to measurement of performance, often referred to as the 'criterion problem', which is examined in detail by many writers such as Landy and Trumbo.[8] Basically many performance criteria are subjective or judgemental (e.g. supervisor rating) whilst more objective criteria (e.g. productivity indicators) may be subject to influences (i.e. delay in providing materials, age of machinery) not controlled by the individual.

If performance measures are inadequate for assessing actual behaviour, inferences of psychological characteristics based on them will be inappropriate for assessment. Figure 28.1 provides a diagrammatic analysis of the principal factors influencing behaviour and performance. All the hypothetical constructs represent potential differences between individuals, whilst most broad categories (i.e. abilities, aptitudes or latent abilities, intelligence and different aspects of personality) can be subdivided into more specific dimensions. Our identification of 'intention' is to draw attention to the assumption on which inferences are based, namely that the behaviour observed

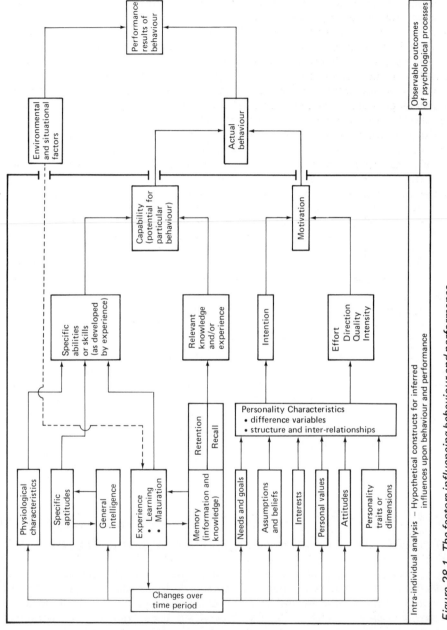

Figure 28.1. The factors influencing behaviour and performance

properly represents the intended behaviour of the individual. It also indicates a problem of assessment based on test procedures, which is the human capacity to discern purposes and intentionally produce less representative behaviour in order to produce a more favourable assessment.

(d) MEASUREMENT OF PSYCHOLOGICAL CHARACTERISTICS

The basis of measurement is the fact that people demonstrate differences in performance-related behaviour. On this several assumptions are developed in the process of attributing psychological characteristics to the individual. It is assumed that regular patterns of specifically defined and observable behaviour can be attributed to specific psychological characteristics. As the behaviour patterns are regular, and if measures are to be useful, it is further assumed that these characteristics are relatively stable over time. This assumption is often debated, particularly with regard to personality traits, as some researchers argue that many traits are fairly permanent characteristics whilst others argue that most measurable characteristics may change over time due to new experiences. A rather obvious assumption is that if people differ in a reliable manner, in performance or psychological characteristics, it is possible to measure these differences.

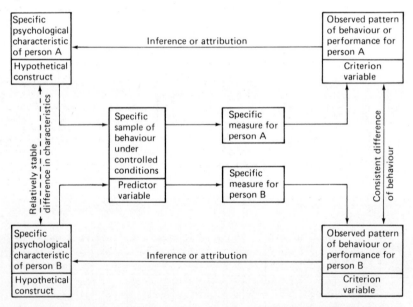

Figure 28.2. Basic assumptions and features of psychological measurement

These assumptions are illustrated in Figure 28.2, which also indicates the basic features of standardised measures of psychological characteristics. A test may be used to obtain a sample of behaviour — the predictor variable — which provides a specific measure for each person directly related to the differences between criterion measures. Thus any assessment device, such as the interview judgement or psychological test, is designed to provide a measure of the predictor variable which is *reliable* (i.e. provides a consistent measure for the individual whenever used, even by different assessors) and *valid* (i.e. measures what it is designed to measure).

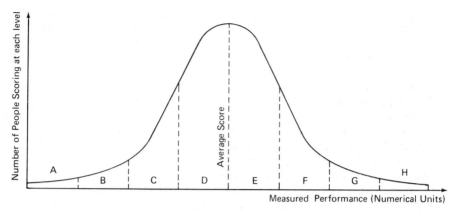

(a) Distribution of Performance Measures in Population or Representative Sample

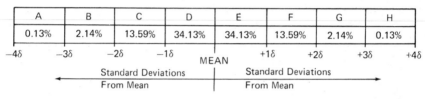

A	B	C	D	E	F	G	H
0.13%	2.14%	13.59%	34.13%	34.13%	13.59%	2.14%	0.13%

$$\delta = \sqrt{\frac{\Sigma\chi^2}{N}}$$

where δ = Standard Deviation
   χ = Deviation of each score from the mean
   N = Number in Population

(b) Percentage of Population under Specific Sections of a Normal Distribution Curve

Figure 28.3. The Normal Distribution Curve

A further important assumption is that individual difference measures for a large number of people will result in a normal distribution, as is the case for distributions of physical characteristics. Figure 28.3(a) shows that relatively few people will be measured at the high or low extremes of the variation range, with the remainder distributed symmetrically around an average. This curve has several properties which assist interpretation, including the identification of percentages of population within particular measurement ranges as indicated in Figure 28.3(b). Another useful property is the potential for identification of the specific curve for a representative sample, which can be generalised for the complete population concerned. In this way a test measure can be used to identify how the individual relates to the average score, and what percentage of the population has a higher or lower score. Population in this sense refers to a relatively homogeneous grouping with pre-determined characteristics (i.e. age, socio-economic classification, occupation, etc.).

The above discussion draws heavily on the research of psychologists specialising in psychological testing or psychometrics. This does not mean that assessment necessarily involves psychological tests, although they will frequently be useful, but such research has identified principles of psychological measurement which apply equally to the interview judgement, interpersonal perceptual judgement, questionnaire or any other method used for assessment purposes. Consequently anyone involved in personnel assessment will be aided by training in psychometrics or, at least, study of relevant texts such as Anastasi,[9] Cronbach,[10] Guion[11] or Tyler.[12]

2. Purpose of Assessment

An important early phase in assessment is to identify the purpose of the process, as this will influence planning and conduct of the necessary activities. It will influence the factors to be assessed, the degree of accuracy needed, the people involved in the process, and the resources which can be utilised. This, in turn, will influence the general approach, data collection methods, measurement techniques, human knowledge and skills, and other features of assessment activities.

Conventionally personnel work deploys assessment in two areas. One is in employment, placement and training, where there is a need to assess current capabilities, motivation and personality in order to predict *future potential for job performance*. The second area is in performance appraisal. Instead of prediction there is assessment of the *current level of job performance*.

Our reason for integrating the two areas of assessment here is that the essential features of understanding and practice are the same; only specific methods and techniques vary in response to different circumstances. Also it is often unrealistic to view assessment as concerned with *either* potential *or* actual performance. Performance appraisal is frequently concerned, implicitly or explicitly, with future potential. Similarly employment decision-making applications would be simpler if it were possible to assess current performance directly. Some applications such as promotion decisions and management development involve both current performance and future potential. Figure 28.4 identifies common assessment purposes and their principal emphasis to illustrate this point.

Decisions affecting existing employees will inevitably be based on reports from the performance appraisal system. With the variety of assessors involved, often unskilled in general assessment practices, such reports may lack reliability or validity for prediction. Similarly the emphasis on current performance is likely to produce inadequate data for assessing future potential. A 1977 survey for the Institute of Personnel Management indicates 26.7 per cent of the companies did not assess potential in their system, and 62.2 per cent simply included a general section, leading to the observation:

> there was little evidence that companies were tending to treat the assessment of potential as a separate exercise from the review of current performance but there was evidence to suggest that potential now has a lower priority in most appraisal schemes than in 1973 [an earlier survey]. A review of both the appraisal forms which included sections on potential and the separate potential assessment forms indicated that, for the most part, such assessments are purely subjective and are largely based on the judgement or opinions of one person — usually the immediate superior. Such methods are notoriously unreliable and have been shown to amount to little more than crystal-ball gazing.[13]

Purpose of assessment		Measurement emphasis	
General	Specific	Future potential	Current job performance
Employment decision making	Recruitment	Yes	Not measurable
	Initial screening	Yes	Not measurable
	Selection	Yes	For internal appointments
	Placement	Yes	For existing employee
Individual development	Training	Yes	For existing employee
	Management development	Yes	Yes
	Career programming	Yes	Possibly
	Vocational guidance	Yes	Possibly
Policy and planning decision making	Manpower planning	Yes	Yes
	Job design	Yes	Yes
	Organisational development	Yes	Yes
	Technical changes	Yes	Possibly
Control activities	Safety administration	Yes	Yes
	Grievances	Possibly	Possibly
	Disciplinary procedures	Possibly	Yes
	Redundancies	Possibly	Possibly
	Dismissal	Yes	Yes
Performance appraisal	Distribution of rewards	Possibly	Yes
	Performance improvement	Possibly	Yes
	Potential for future work	Yes	Yes

Figure 28.4. Different purposes and principal emphases of methods of assessment

Assessment of future potential and appraisal of performance are closely related and need to be considered together. The use of performance appraisal reports for assessment of potential is inadequate. Supplementary data is required, and a more systematic approach is necessary. Similarly a systematic approach to assessing future potential requires the criterion and evaluation data provided by a performance appraisal system. The practices of performance reviews can also benefit from the application of knowledge developed in the more analytical approach to measurement and prediction of individual differences. The ultimate purpose needs to be established early to ensure appropriate design and conduct of assessment processes. If data gathered for a different purpose is to be used then the implications should be recognised and supplementary information added.

3. General Approaches to Assessment

A major problem of predicting potential for job performance is that most jobs require a variety of behaviour patterns, resulting in a diversity of psychological characteristics to be measured and combined on an overall assessment of the individual. This leads to the controversy between those advocating the *Composite Criterion Approach* and others who recommend a *Multiple Criteria Approach,* a debate reviewed by Schmidt and Kaplan.[14] A composite criterion implies that different behavioural measures can be combined in a single measure of performance, either by a subjective judgement or a system of weighting individual dimensions, whilst the multiple-criteria approach suggests that performance is better measured in terms of a profile on different dimensions of performance. Neither approach can be recommended for general application, as both are useful for different purposes. For incentive payment systems a composite measure is ultimately needed, whilst training or performance needs will be better identified with multiple criteria. In general, however, we recommend the use of multiple criteria because of advantages in understanding and evaluating psychological and behavioural processes involved.

For a comprehensive analysis of the use of psychological measurement for personnel decisions, the text by Cronbach and Gleser[15] is recommended. Similarly texts in industrial psychology provide useful reviews, with Howell[16], Landy and Trumbo[17] or McCormick and Tiffin[18] providing useful overviews.

In assessing the potential of an individual for future job performance, four general approaches can be identified. These are illustrated diagrammatically in Figure 28.5.

The *Actuarial Approach* is a strategy for selection based on an empirically determined relationship between a composite index of performance, identified and measured from a behaviour sample (the predictor), and a composite performance criterion measure. Starting with a large number of predictive items (i.e. specific items of data about the individual) these are refined by identifying items which in practice distinguish between people who are successful and those who are poor in the job concerned. This can produce effective prediction measures based on application form, questionnaire, interview schedule, or other data collection methods, but the empirical development can be a costly and time-consuming process. Whilst such an approach has produced effective selection decisions it has many technical and practical problems. Apart from the cost it may well obscure unfair or illegal discriminatory practices based upon sex, race, sub-cultural or other differences which are not actually related to performance. If job requirements or type of applicant

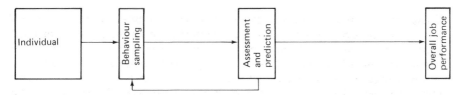

(a) Actuarial approaches

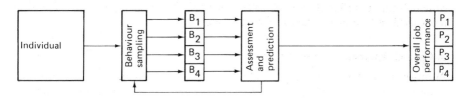

(b) Behaviour assessment approach

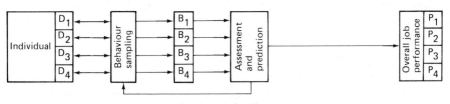

(c) Individual differences approaches ⟨ Psychological testing
                                        Attribute classification

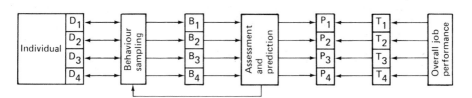

(d) Diagnostic approaches

| D | Specific psychological characteristic or trait (hypothetical construct) | | B | Specific behavioural attribute or potential demonstrated |

| P | Performance criterion measurement | | T | Important component task of job |

Figure 28.5. Different approaches to the assessment of individual potential for job performance

change over time the predictive capability may be seriously affected, resulting in poor decisions and a need to develop a revised procedure. Underlying these and other problems is the fact that predictions are based on trial and error development, without producing an understanding of why items are predictive.

The *Behaviour Assessment Approach* identifies specific factors of behaviour considered essential to effective job performance. Information about current and previous behaviour is collected by interview and other methods with different factors measured, usually upon a rating scale method (see section 7). These behaviour factors are related to similar factors of performance, either utilising composite measures or comparing profiles of multiple criteria. The identification of factors is based upon subjective judgements by assessors, so the selection of appropriate factors and their assessment (as predictors or criteria) are potentially subject to bias. Relationships may be established actuarially or judgementally, but this approach represents a movement towards analysis and understanding of the basis of assessment.

The *Individual Differences Approach* has already been discussed, the behaviour samples being used to identify individual differences in psychological characteristics which are indicators of specific behaviour. These characteristics are related to performance factors, again using composite measures or comparison of multiple criteria profiles. One form of this approach involves a *Psychological Test Orientation,* using standardised and relatively objective measures which are general predictors of specific elements of performance. An alternative is the *Attribute Classification Orientation* which is similar to the behaviour assessment approach, except that psychological characteristics and behavioural qualities are assessed. Again there is a distinct move towards improved analysis and understanding, but overall performance is usually based on an assessor's subjective judgement of necessary factors.

The *Diagnostic Approach* may be based on a *Psychological Test Orientation,* or on *Attribute Classification Orientation,* but more usually it involves an *Integration Orientation.* That is to say that where satisfactory tests can provide useful information these are used, but as part of a process in which other methods provide additional data about characteristics by attribute classification judgements. The major distinction of this approach is systematic job analysis to identify specific job requirements and the related performance evaluation criteria. Predictor-criterion relationships may be empirically or judgementally developed, but selection of these factors is based on detailed analysis and the actual assessment is usually based on comparison of a profile using multiple-criteria measures.

We recommend the Diagnostic Approach for any realistic attempt to assess future potential of individuals.

4. Job-Related Information

Regardless of the purpose or the general approach adopted, the assessor(s) obviously need job-related information as the basis of their activities. Current practice emphasises a systematic *Job Analysis* process to develop a detailed *Job Description* and *Performance Evaluation* criteria, using this data to produce the *Personnel Specification,* all as discussed in detail in Chapter 27. The personnel specification is an assessment of a hypothetical person, described in verbal terms, who can be predicted to meet the job performance requirements. This provides a basis for comparison with a similar specification developed from a systematic diagnosis and assessment of the individual, the *Candidate Specification* for a prospective employee or an *Employee Specification* for the existing employee.

5. Classification Frameworks

The emphasis on specific psychological characteristics and behaviour factors leads to the real danger that important aspects of the person's current capabilities or future potential may be overlooked. Similarly there are problems of describing the individual in a form which is meaningful, especially when the assessment is prepared to assist decision-making by people other than the assessor. Both problems are magnified by the point made earlier that over 18,000 trait names can be identified in common use. To help overcome these problems, several frameworks have been developed to classify data and/or characteristics under broad headings.

The left-hand side of Figure 28.1 above shows a basic set of categories within which a variety of sub-divisions or separate dimensions could be identified. Similarly any set of categories can be developed and standardised for use by the organisation. However a number of general frameworks have been developed, many having the additional advantage of a detailed manual to guide practitioners.

A review of the categories advocated in particular frameworks, which are widely used, is provided in Figure 28.6. An early framework published in the USA in 1943 by Fear[19] is a highly structured interview procedure, with lists of questions or instructions under general headings, to plan and guide the interview assessment. Another early framework, but still popular and widely used in the UK, was developed at the National Institute for Industrial Psychology by Rodger[20] as a means for summarising individual potential. The 'seven-point plan' provides a useful plan for a patterned interview (see Chapter 7), to ensure that the data collected covers most important features of the person. More importantly it enables specific subsidiary dimensions to be described verbally, as 'attribute classification' ratings, as psychological test scores, or all measures in combination. Consequently it is particularly appropriate for the general Diagnostic Approach to assessment.

The Sidney and Brown[21] plan is a modified version of this framework, representative of several such adaptions, which is similarly suitable for many purposes. Fraser,[22] formerly at the NIIP, conceived his plan for selection purposes and Attribute Classification in particular, as a guide to interview assessments. The five general categories of individual difference are composites of appropriate subsidiary dimensions, all derived from detailed job description, and a method for providing judgements as ratings or in numerical form is provided.

Schein[23] identifies five general categories of individual variables, emphasising the value of different methods of collecting data. The ROGBY scheme presented by Isbister,[24] formerly of the NIIP, is a highly structured and mechanistic system of prepared forms for collecting data and producing an assessment of individual potential for job performance. This system is particularly designed to guide the 'non-expert' management assessors in making judgements about people.

Ideally an organisation will use trained assessors, all using a common framework for different purposes. Standardisation of categories will aid development of shared understanding, terminology and interpretation, whilst permitting the use of different subsidiary factors for specific applications. As it is useful for all assessment purposes we suggest the *seven-point plan* as a basis for standardisation.

6. Data Collection Methods

Whilst a diverse array of data collection methods is available, the selection and combination of techniques depend on a number of considerations. Plumbley[25] regards

The Interview Guide (R.A. Fear)	Seven Point Plan (A. Rodger at N.I.I.P)	Nine Point Plan (E. Sidney and M.Brown)	Five Fold Framework (J.Munro-Fraser)	General Classes of Variable (E.H. Schein)	R.O.G.B.Y. (W.L.T. Isbister)
Early Home Background	Physical Make-up	Personal Data	Impact on Others	Biographical Information and Work History	Early Background
Work History	Attainments	Physique	Qualifications or Acquired Knowledge	Intellectual Level and Aptitudes	Educational Record
Education and Training	General Intelligence	Educational and Technical Qualifications and Experience	Innate Abilities	Specific Areas of Knowledge or Specific Skills	Part-Time Studies
Present Social Adjustment	Special Aptitudes	Work or Other Experience	Motivation	Attitudes and Interests	Working Record
Assessment Ratings for Specific aspects of individual's:	Interests	Mental Abilities	Adjustment or Emotional Balance	Motivation, Personality and Temperament	Present Background
· Aptitudes	Disposition	Social Roles			Non-Working Life
· Personality	Circumstances	Initiative			Evaluation of:
· Motivation		Emotional Stability			· Sense Data
· Character		Motivation			· What Aptitudes?
					· How effective?
					· What Sort?
					· How able?

Figure 28.6. General categories of information as adopted in different frameworks for assessment of personnel

these as being the attributes to be assessed and the degree of accuracy required, the type and level of appointment concerned, the age distribution of assessees, the probable acceptability of different methods, the time available and comparative costs. To these we would add *Current Employment Status* and the *Information Type* required.

If an existing employee is being assessed there will be ready access to many sources of data within the organisation, such as colleagues and personnel records; and current job performance can be directly observed. The selection and combination of techniques can be decided by cost-benefit considerations. For prospective employees, however, there will be additional constraints. Direct observation of current job activities will rarely be possible, and access to current colleagues will be severely limited, so the emphasis is on investigation of current activities using less direct methods. The variety of techniques used will be constrained by the time available and perhaps by the assessee refusing to co-operate with particular methods.

For assessing current job performance the emphasis of this information type will be on observation and appraisal data within the working environment. In assessing potential there is a need for wider information, not only about current job activities but also to identify capability or potential not necessarily demonstrated in the current job. Previous employment positions, education and training, social activities, etc. may all provide data abilities and skills the person has developed. Similarly the examination of both current and past behaviour enables the nature and type of psychological development to be assessed by identifying regular *Behaviour Patterns* that show specific psychological characteristics or trends which can be extrapolated for prediction.

In terms of our earlier discussion, data collection methods represent *Behaviour Sampling Techniques*, obtaining data representative of the individual's typical behaviour for relation to relevant performance criteria. Some methods, such as psychological tests, produce highly specific data whilst others, such as interviews, obtain diverse data. A problem is the capacity of people to adjust their behaviour according to their self-interest, in order to produce a favourable but misleading assessment — a problem shared by psychologists, work study practitioners and personnel specialists. For example Wesman[26] demonstrated the effectiveness of subjects at influencing personality test measures, whilst Green[27] showed that people do attempt to provide biassed data in selection assessments.

Methods commonly used for assessment include:

(a) JOB PERFORMANCE OBSERVATIONS
Existing employees can be directly observed under working conditions. Chapter 27 focused on the analysis of jobs but the methods discussed are especially applicable to analysis of individual performance at work, so the methods and sources identified in Figure 27.3 may be appropraite for assessment.

Reports from *Appraisal* systems may be sufficient for assessing current job performance, but assessment of potential involves additional sources and methods for fuller analysis of capabilities.

(b) SELF REPORT METHODS
For biographical data, or details of psychological characteristics, the individual is potentially the most comprehensive data source, but the data may not be accurate

or complete. Typically assessment begins with a *Written Narrative,* a letter of application, and a standardised *Application Form* (see Chapter 6). More specific data can also be collected using a checklist, an inventory, or a questionnaire and a useful guide to design is provided by Oppenheim.[28] Bass and Barrett[29] identify several advantages of standardised biographical questions, including a tendency to provide honest responses. Such data is factual and checkable, so written answers are rarely dishonest, but they may omit unfavourable information. In effect these methods are akin to a highly structured interview administered by the assessee himself, providing useful data for screening decisions (in the employment process) and for planning more detailed information needs to be met by other methods.

(c) REFERENCES (OR VERIFICATION)

A common practice is to obtain references before the assessment, or afterwards for verification purposes. These can take the form of a *Factual Check* or a *Character Reference* and, as discussed in Chapter 6, we consider the latter should be used with extreme caution (if at all). On the other hand the factual check for verification of data provided is essential, particularly of qualifications and previous positions of responsibility, and can encourage honest self-report data if the practice is made known early.

(d) PHYSICAL EXAMINATION

Although our main emphasis is upon psychological factors, specific physical characteristics or general health data may be needed for assessment. The former reflects a concern for physical demands or capabilities, so observation at the interview will often provide sufficient data. Concern for health is usually focused upon general considerations such as minimising costs and other problems of illness and accidents. In such cases, or for specific jobs such as airline pilot or professional sportsman, an examination by a medical practitioner will provide necessary data.

(e) SPECIAL EXERCISES

The assessee may participate in exercises designed to identify behaviour under special circumstances. The Written Exercise poses a problem for individual solution, while the Leaderless Group Discussion of problems can provide useful indicators of comparative behaviour — particularly leadership and social skills — on a group of assessees. Military organisations commonly utilise Initiative Tests or Leadership Exercises in assessing potential for officer training. The *Stress Interview,* developed by OSS research[30] for selecting potential spies, has been advocated (mainly in the USA) as a test of ability to cope with stress — but the realism and validity is highly questionable. Too often such exercises are adopted as a current fashion, and applied by ill-informed assessors. When designed to yield specific data they can be useful.

(f) WORK SAMPLING

Whilst job performance observation is not feasible for prospective employees, it is often practicable to observe performance of sample work activities. A common method is Task Observation, where the assessee undertakes a typical job-related activity. For example a prospective lecturer might be asked to demonstrate his capability in an impromptu lecturette, whilst a secretary normally expects to take dictation and to produce a sample of typing to show the level of competence. Greater complexity is possible in some cases when a simulator is available, such as the pilot training representation of an aeroplane cockpit and controls. Observation of the assessee in Simulator Operation provides a performance under imitation working conditions, as well as the ability to test reaction to rare but important problems which have to be dealt with in practice.

(g) STANDARDISED PSYCHOLOGICAL TESTS
Many tests are available for Special Aptitudes, Specific Abilities and General Intelligence. A comprehensive compilation of available tests is provided by Buros,[31] whilst most psychology journals review new tests as they are introduced.

Most tests are controlled by the publishers, restricting availability to qualified examiners. One reason is to prevent general familiarity with test content, which will normally invalidate most tests. The other principal reason is that the administration and interpretation of tests requires specific training and skills. We share the view expressed in a recent IPM survey:

> . . .tests, properly applied and validated, can play a useful part . . . Use of tests, in conjunction with personal interview by trained interviewers and well constructed application forms, can provide a better basis for decisions than the interview alone.[32]

(h) INTERVIEW
Despite criticism the interview continues as the common method used in almost all assessment. Ideally this will involve an individual interviewee interacting with a trained interviewer, as discussed in Chapter 7. Group interviews or panel interviews have less to commend them, except as exercises for demonstrating particular abilities in such circumstances. The popularity of the interview is due to the fact that a variety of information can be obtained, together with more perceptual data for interpretation. It also provides an opportunity to assess social skills, motivation and certain other characteristics not successfully measurable by other methods. The main problem is the interviewer, who needs specialised knowledge and training to minimise errors, and to recognise the extent to which personal bias may influence his conduct and interpretation of the data.

Figure 28.7 summarises these general methods for data collection. A combination of appropriate techniques will probably be necessary. Despite different titles, these methods are essentially behaviour sampling under test conditions determined by the practices adopted. As such, any test only provides data about the individual's behaviour in particular circumstances and at a particular point in time — any interpretation of the data can only be as accurate as the behaviour is representative and typical for that person.

7. Measurement Methods

Raw data in the form of items of information shows differences between people, but has to be recorded in order to be used for comparisons. At one extreme we have subjective measures, or unstructured judgements, where the assessor evaluates the available data in an idiosyncratic and probably biassed manner. The opposite extreme, represented by physical dimensions or weights, are objective measures where criteria are unambiguous, clearly understood, reproduceable by different assessors, and so relatively unaffected by human prejudice. As psychological measures are concerned with inference of hypothetical constructs, or attributions of be-

General Methods	Principle Variations Available
Job Peformance Observations	Analysis: Various methods as indicated in separate typology (Chapter 27, Figure 27.3) Appraisal: Various methods as indicated in separate typology (Sections 7 and 9, Figure 28.8)
Self-Reports of Behaviour	Written Narrative Application Form Checklist Inventory Questionnaire
Reference (or Verification)	Factual check Character reference
Physical Examination	Physical check General Health
Special Exercises	Written exercise Leaderless group discussion Initiative test Leadership exercise Stress interview Other specific designs
Work Sampling	Task observation Simulator operation
Standardised Psychological tests	Special aptitudes Specific abilities (achievement) General intelligence Specific attitudes Personal interests Personal values Personality dimensions Other psychological traits
Interview	Individual interviewee Group interviewees Panel interview

Figure 28.7. Data collection methods for the assessment of human capability and potential

havioural qualities, they are essentially subjective. Various methods have been developed to structure assessor judgements, reducing idiosyncracy, minimising bias and so moving closer to objectivity.

Figure 28.8 provides a general review of the measurement methods commonly used. For more detailed discussion our references to texts on psychological testing are recommended, whilst McCormick and Tiffin,[33] and Anastasi[34] provide useful summaries.

Order of Merit Comparisons avoid the common bias of central tendency, avoiding the high/low extremes of rating scales, but produce relatively unstructured subjective judgements. Rating Scales enable people or items to be classified, and a

Measurement Methods		Brief Description of Method	Potential for Scaling
Approach	Specific Techniques		
ORDER OF MERIT COMPARISON	Ranking	Items placed in order of merit (or similar) in relation to each other (i.e. best to worst)	Ordinal
	Paired Comparisons	Ranking based upon comparing merits of all items paired with each other, final ranking being derived from cumulative totals for each item.	
	Forced Distribution	Items are assigned to categories of comparative merit according to specified percentage totals which correspond to a 'Normal Distribution' of items compared.	
RATING SCALES	Numerical Rating	Scale of categories from high to low (or similar) identified in numerical terms (i.e. 1 to 7)	Classification, Indices and Cardinal
	Alphabetical Rating	Scale of categories from high to low (or similar) identified alphabetically (i.e. A to E)	
	Adjectival Rating	Categories, identified by adjectives (i.e. excellent, good, average, weak and poor) describing item	
	Graphic Rating	Pictorial scale from very high to very low (or similar) and intermediate descriptions generally indicated, for checkmark judgement of item	
	Descriptive Rating	Categories identified by brief verbal description of judgement relating to item	
STRUCTURED JUDGEMENT SCALES	Checklist	Descriptive items are listed for judgement (i.e. Yes or No) of their applicability	Aid to Judgement
	Scaled Checklist	Descriptive statements ranging from favourable to unfavourable, assigned predetermined weightings of importance, randomly listed for judgement of applicability	Cardinal
	Forced Choice Judgement	Two or more statements are clustered for choice of which is most applicable for the item considered	
	Behaviour Description Scale	Series of descriptive statements about item are presented for rating judgement, but assigned pre-determined weightings of importance	
SPECIALISED MEASUREMENT METHODS	Critical Incidents	Behavioural activities, satisfactory and unsatisfactory, are listed under classification categories	Primary Aids to Informed Judgement (But capable of use for Scaling purposes)
	Sociometric Nomination	Group or 'Role Set' positive and negative ratings upon specific items analysed and totals compared	
	Semantic Differential	Seven point bi-polar adjectival rating scales for description of objects or concepts	
	Repertory Grid Techniques	Investigatory technique for examining individual descriptions of similarity and difference between objects which can be adapted for comparative analysis	
	Protective Techniques	Variety of psychological techniques for indirect measurement of psychological characteristics	

Figure 28.8. General review of alternative measurement methods

numerical value applied, to provide a profile. For assessing people the use of independent dimensions is to minimise 'halo' or 'horns' effect, where an impression of one aspect of a person colours judgement of all other factors in a consistently positive or negative way. Numerical or alphabetical ratings minimise the evaluative nature of judgements, whilst adjectival and descriptive ratings emphasise comparability between raters, and graphic ratings permit more precise judgement.

Structured Judgement Scales increase standardisation for comparability of judgements. A checklist identifies items which distinguish between people, whilst a scaled checklist converts responses into specific numerical scale values. The forced choice method is intended to eliminate faking by concealing the derivation of final ratings or scores. Behavioural description scales provide meaningful descriptions, to improve accuracy and comparability of judgements, producing standardised scores upon a scale which is clearly defined — also permitting evaluation of 'typical' behaviour of the individual and differences when 'trying hard'. The other Specialised Measurement Methods are mainly aids to informed judgement in a particular structure, but can be adapted for scaling in specifically designed testing procedures.

The essential feature of measurement is to record differences and provide a basis for comparison. An *Ordinal Scale* identifies relative positions in a series, so individuals are compared on a relative basis, such as relative strength or quantity of the factor measured. A *Cardinal Scale* identifies this relative position, but also measures specific differences in numerical terms — as, for example, the heights of different people. The order of merit comparisons provide an ordinal scale for a specific group of people, whilst rating scales can be similarly used for ordinal classification or by producing a Numerical Index — essentially a cardinal scale for the particular population.

Ideally, however, measurement provides a cardinal scale based on an absolute standard criterion as for physical measures of size and weight. Standard cardinal scales are related to an average measure for a specified population under several assumptions, notably that the factor measured is normally distributed. The rating scales and structured judgement scales can all be used in the development of standardised cardinal scales and are commonly associated with psychological measurement procedures. All the methods are potentially usable for performance appraisal, although rating methods are more common.

8. Candidate Specification

The assessment of future potential necessitates collation and assembly of data in an overall assessment of the person concerned. At the simplest level this may consist of an overall judgement and brief note by the responsible assessor. More generally there is a need to provide a systematic written assessment to aid decision-making. This is particularly true for the Diagnostic Approach to assessment which we have generally advocated.

The Candidate Specification, for a prospective employee, re-titled Employee Specification for an existing employee, is a written summary of the assessment. All data will be collected and collated on a general basis as indicated by the Classification Framework which describes the capabilities and potential of the person. Information is recorded using the general categories. Specific items correspond to job-related information in many cases, as presented in the Personnel Specification prepared using the same framework, but with additions covering currently underused capabilities. Where specific factors have been measured, the appropriate comparison data, ratings, indices or numerical score will be recorded under the particular characteristic or attribute.

The resulting specification provides all the requisite information necessary to understand and interpret the individual assessment. This may be converted into an overall assessment rating and provides a detailed profile of the person for purposes of comparison. The comparison may be with similar assessments of other people, or with the requirements of a particular job, and with previous assessments of the same person, as a guide to organisational decision-making.

9. Performance Appraisal Reports

All employing organisations carry out some form of performance appraisal of their employees. At one extreme this may be an unsystematic informal judgement by a manager about his subordinates, whilst the opposite extreme can be a highly formal system with specified procedures and standardised forms. The IPM survey by Gill[35] provides a useful indication of current British practices, showing that 82 per cent of respondents had a formal appraisal scheme.

In the literature about appraisal systems Randell *et al.*[36] identify three general types (*performance, reward,* and *potential* reviews), each with different implications for design and conduct of appraisal schemes, and emphasise appropriate training of staff involved. An early discussion of appraisal interviewing by Maier[37] specifically warned against using a single method for multiple objectives. Anstey *et al.*[38] review objectives and methods of different schemes, indicating main strengths and weaknesses, whilst Fleishman and Bass[39] provide a collection of classic papers upon different aspects of appraisal.

The design of a suitable scheme depends on many factors, including the following:

(a) PURPOSE
We can identify three general categories of application: Distribution of Rewards (such as payments, power and status), Performance Improvement (needs for training, development or increased motivation) and Potential for Future Work (prediction for promotion, transfer, placement, etc.). Randell *et al.* observe:

> Organisations attempting to develop their staff appraisal and development procedures are strongly advised to keep the three activities of performance, reward and potential reviews not only separate in time but also in paper work, procedure and responsibility.[40]

We would add two further general points, the first being that the scheme should aim to improve the 'fit' between organisation and individual needs. The second point, rarely recognised in texts or surveys of practice, is that the system can provide useful data (e.g. criterion data and evaluative feedback) for general assessment and employment decision-making.

(b) PRACTICES
Specific practices should be appropriate to the purpose, circumstances and personnel involved. In all cases systematic analysis is likely to improve the design of the process, whilst managerial training should improve the conduct of assessment. An effective system will, at least, leave the employee feeling that he has been fairly

treated – this requires openness, exchange of information, considerate treatment and participatory practices.

(c) ASSESSORS

In most cases the assessee's immediate superior conducts the appraisal. The IPM survey[41] found this in 86 per cent of cases whilst the superior's superior was responsible in 7 per cent of cases. Some writers have advocated 'third party' involvement (e.g. superior's superior, superior's peer, assessee's peers or subordinates), to improve assessment and fairness, or a committee approach; but these are not widely adopted practices.

As every manager normally assesses his own subordinates, there is a diversity in the personal characteristics of assessors, which presents the major problem for the design and conduct of schemes. The problems of bias are magnified when different assessors are involved – the halo/horns effect, central tendency, lenient/harsh judgements, different understanding of terminology, etc. all impair comparability between reports of different assessors.

(d) MEASUREMENT METHODS

Arising from these problems of different assessors the methods, potentially as indicated in Figure 28.8, need to be carefully designed. Rating scales are commonly used, with other methods occasionally contributing to the overall assessment. Simple systems produce overall ratings, but many others involve a profile of rating upon subsidiary factors – behaviour attributes, psychological characteristics, or both. The introduction of *Management by Objectives*, as advocated by McGregor[42] and Odiorne,[43] has provided a different approach to appraisal – but it has been critically examined by Koontz[44] and others. Other Results-Oriented measures may be based on productivity, work study or cost accountancy criteria.

(e) DOCUMENTATION

Any formal system usually includes standard documentation, ranging from a simple rating form to a comprehensive questionnaire and multiple ratings of factors.

(f) FACTORS TO BE ASSESSED

The factors to be assessed must be pre-planned on a basis of job analysis, as discussed earlier, with typical psychological factors including inference of psychological characteristics and attribution of behavioural qualities. Performance indicators emphasise demonstrable results in terms of productivity criteria, work study data, or achievement of agreed objectives.

Good general overviews and detailed information upon the design and conduct of performance appraisal systems are provided by Cummings and Schwab,[45] Randell *et al*[46] and Stewart and Stewart.[47] Having designed and conducted the appraisal system, the end product is the regular periodic production of appraisal reports by the assessors. Such reports are typically provided upon standard forms including any information specifically required, an overall assessment and/or a profile of measurements of ratings of specific factors.

10. Relevant Decision-Making

So far we have described series of inter-related and inter-dependent phases of

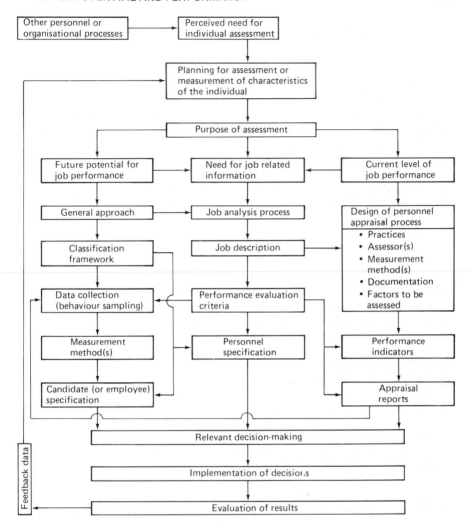

Figure 28.9. General overview of the process of assessing human potential and performance

activity, as set out in Figure 28.9. Depending on the purpose of the assessment, certain decisions will be made — by management, assessee or both — based on data from assessment activities.

For example the employment decision will be based on comparison of the Personnel Specification and the Candidate Specification to determine suitability for the job, then relative preference for different candidates. Similarly the Employee Specification, possibly together with appraisal reports for current up-dating, enables decisions to be made about promotion, placement or training. The Appraisal Report may provide a basis for payment decisions, or allocation of increased responsibility and status. Together the various reports can be used for counselling the employee — in performance improvement, vocational guidance or career programming — for him to make his own decisions.

11. Implementation of Decisions

When the decision has been made, the method of implementation will be important for the results actually achieved. This is particularly true for existing employees who may be more or less motivated by assessment decisions, or may develop more or less favourable attitudes to their superiors, and can decide to satisfy their needs and objectives by changing their employment. So the decision needs to be fair and based upon reliable and valid data, whilst the method of implementation should be appropriate to the personnel involved and the results desired.

12. Evaluation of Results

As with other processes identified elsewhere in this book we conclude with the necessary, but often ignored or neglected, final phase of evaluation of results, which indicate how effectively the objectives have been achieved by the process. In this case the results are modified by the previous two phases, referred to as Decision-Making and Implementation, which in practice will often be separate processes.

The main concern is to evaluate the quality and impact of the data provided by the assessment. Whether satisfactory or not this provides feedback for future assessments but, when unsatisfactory for some reason, specific changes may be necessary to reduce errors. Figure 28.10 lists the main errors which can occur, together with typical ways of avoiding such errors.

Broad categories of error types	Typical means of identifying and reducing errors in category	Design and planning considerations contributing generally to error avoidance
Constant errors	Validity: Checks upon predictor - criterion relationships, job representativeness of behaviour samples (i.e. job analysis) and weighting of items or factors	• Careful theoretical analysis • Identification of systematic process • Application of empirical research findings • Application of practical experience • Plan data collection to suit circumstances
Random or variable errors	Reliability: Checks upon population samples, personal representativeness of behaviour samples, consistency of measures over time and between different assessors	• Clear specification of measurement methods • Clear specification of interpretation methodology • Minimize (unnecessary) complexity • Minimise unsuitable sophistication • Maximise standardisation of techniques
Personal errors	Objectivity: Training and specific techniques to minimise human bias of assessor(s)	• Pilot testing of measuring instruments • Careful matching of samples to population • Utilise adequate size of samples
Interpretation errors	Standardisation: of procedures for administration, scoring and interpretation of measures	• Develop normative data for instruments when practical to do so

Figure 28.10. General approaches to error identification and reduction in procedures for testing or measuring psychological factors

Analysis of the type of error which has occurred enables action to be taken to identify the cause, and hence reduce the possibility of repetition. Feedback of evaluative data provides both specific and general information to improve subsequent design and conduct of the activities involved in the process.

REFERENCES

1. Howell W.C., *Essentials of Industrial and Organisational Psychology* (Dorsey) 1976.
2. Miner J.B., *Personnel Psychology* (Macmillan) 1969.
3. Fleishman E.A. and Bass A.R., *Studies in Personnel and Industrial Psychology* 3rd ed. (Dorsey) 1974.
4. Eiser J.R., 'Interpersonal Attributions' in H. Tajfel and C. Fraser (eds.), *Introducing Social Psychology* (Penguin) 1978, p. 235.
5. Eysenck H.J., *The Structure of Human Personality* (Methuen) 1960.
6. Cattell R.B., *The Scientific Analysis of Personality* (Penguin) 1965.
7. Allport G.W. and Odbert H.S., *Trait-Names: A Psycho-Lexical Study* (Psychological Monographs, No. 47) 1936.
8. Landy F.J. and Trumbo D.A., *Psychology of Work Behaviour* (Dorsey) 1976, pp. 87–130.
9. Anastasi A., *Psychological Testing* (Macmillan) 4th ed., 1976.
10. Cronbach L.J., *Essentials of Psychological Testing* (Harper and Row) 3rd ed., 1970.
11. Guion R.M., *Psychological Testing* (McGraw-Hill) 1965.
12. Tyler L.E., *Tests and Measurements* (Prentice-Hall) 2nd ed., 1971.
13. Gill D., *Appraising Performance* (IPM Information Report No. 25) 1977, p. 45.
14. Schmidt F.L. and Kaplan L.B., 'Composite Vs. Multiple Criteria: A Review and Resolution of the Controversy' *Personnel Psychology*, Vol. 24, 1971, pp. 419–34. (Adapted Version in Ref. No. 3, pp. 25–37.)
15. Cronbach L.J. and Gleser G.C., *Psychological Tests and Personnel Decisions* (University of Illinois Press) 2nd ed., 1965.
16. Howell, *op. cit.* 1976 (Chapters 5 and 6, pp. 106–180.)
17. Landy and Trumbo, *op. cit.* (Chapters 3–6, pp. 15–220)
18. McCormick E.J. and Tiffin J., *Industrial Psychology*, (Allen & Unwin) 1975, Chapters 2–8, pp. 20–222.
19. Fear R.A., *The Evaluation Interview: Predictions of Job Performance* (McGraw-Hill) 1958.
20. Rodger A., *The Seven-Point Plan* (National Institute for Industrial Psychology, Paper No. 1) 1952.
21. Sidney E. and Brown M., *The Skills of Interviewing* (Tavistock) 1961.
22. Fraser J.M., *Employment Interviewing* (McDonald & Evans) 1950, 4th ed. 1966.
23. Schein E.H., *Organisational Psychology* (Prentice-Hall) 3rd ed., 1979.
24. Isbister W.L.T., *Performance and Progress in Working Life* (Pergamon) 1968.
25. Plumbley P.R., *Recruitment and Selection* (Institute of Personnel Management) 1968.
26. Wesman A.G., 'Faking Personality Test Scores in a Simulated Employment Situation' *Journal of Applied Psychology*, Vol. 36, 1952, pp. 112–113.
27. Green R.F., 'Does a Selection Situation Induce Testees to Bias Their Answers On Interest and Temperament Tests?' *Education and Psychological Measurement*, Vol. 11, 1951, pp. 503–515.
28. Oppenheim A.N., *Questionnaire Design and Attitude Measurement* (Heinemann) 1966.
29. Bass B.M. and Barrett G.V., *Man, Work and Organisation* (Allyn & Bacon) 1972.
30. O.S.S. Assessment Staff, *Assessment of Men* (Rinehart) 1948.
31. Buros O.K. (ed.), *The Seventh Mental Measurements Yearbook* (Gryphon) 1972.
32. Sneath F., Thakur M. and Medjuck B., *Testing People at Work* (IPM Information Report No. 24) 1976, p. 49.
33. McCormick and Tiffin, *op. cit.* 1975 (Chapters 5, 6, 7 and 8, but particularly pp. 194–216).
34. Anastasi A., *Fields of Applied Psychology* (McGraw-Hill) 2nd ed., 1979, Chapters 2 and 3, pp. 23–91.
35. Gill, *op. cit.* 1977, p. 7.

36. Randell G., Shaw R., Packard P. and Slater J., *Staff Appraisal* (Institute of Personnel Management) 1972.
37. Maier N.R.F., *The Appraisal Interview: Objectives, Methods and Skills* (Wiley) 1958.
38. Anstey E., Fletcher C.A. and Walker J., *Staff Appraisal and Development* (Allen and Unwin) 1976.
39. Fleishman and Bass, *op. cit.*, Section 1, pp. 1—72.
40. Randell *et al., op. cit.*, p. 19.
41. Gill, *op. cit.*, 1977, p. 20.
42. McGregor D., *The Human Side of Enterprise* (McGraw-Hill) 1960.
43. Odiorne G.S., *Management by Objectives: A System of Managerial Leadership* (Pitman) 1965.
44. Koontz H., 'Shortcomings and Pitfalls in Managing by Objectives' *Management by Objectives* 1972, Vol. 1, No. 3, January.
45. Cummings O.L. and Schwab D.P., *Performance in Organisations: Determinants and Appraisal* (Scott, Foresman and Co.) 1973.
46. Randell *et al, op. cit.*, 1972.
47. Stewart V. and Stewart A., *Performance Appraisal* (Gower) 1978.

Section F
THE 'SMALL PRINT' OF THE CONTRACTS

29

Interaction IV — Method in Interpersonal Communication

This chapter is intended as a resource for the interactive episodes described in Chapters 7, 14 and 19. The significance of interpersonal communication cannot be doubted in managerial life. In her study of how managers spent their time, Rosemary Stewart found that the mean for discussion with one other person was 32 per cent of working hours and for discussion with two or more people it was 34 per cent.[1] Later Mintzberg[2] showed a mean of 78 per cent of working hours and 67 per cent of working activities being devoted to interpersonal communication.

Such interactions provide conundrums for those who participate because each participant is *performing* rather than being his true self. He is presenting a self to the observer and the listener which is an idealisation: how he wishes to be seen and evaluated; not what he is. Constantly people will display understanding to disguise unacceptable incomprehension, will conceal dislike by appearing friendly and will agree with what they inwardly reject.

Clarion calls to people to be 'open' and 'honest' will have only marginal effect. Man is a dissembler, particularly when social mobility is involved.

> Commonly we find that upward mobility involves the presentation of proper performances and that efforts to move upwards and efforts to keep from moving downward are expressed in terms of sacrifices made for the maintenance of front. Once the proper sign equipment has been obtained and familiarity gained in the management of it, then this equipment can be used to embellish and illumine one's daily performances with a favourable social style.[3]

In describing the way in which people express themselves, Goffman draws a distinction between the expression that a person *gives* and the expression that he *gives off*. The first involves what the person says or other direct attempts to communicate and to inform. The expression that the individual gives off is more involuntary and covers a range of actions and signs by which the individual gives clues to his real feelings about the situation as he attempts to sustain the performance he is presenting. We appear generally to be more able to learn how to interpret the involuntary impression given off by those with whom we are conferring than we are able to manipulate and control our own expressions that are given off. Although the human in communication is a dissembler, there are two types of such dissembling.

To some extent we express an artificial self to others quite deliberately and we are aware of the truth at the same time as we express the image. There is also, however, an extent to which we delude ourselves about the reality. In presenting a performance, we come to believe that the performance *is* the reality.

Therefore the interactive performer is by no means being cynical. He will delude himself as often as he misleads his interlocutor.

The Telecommunications Analogy

A convenient, and well established, method of approaching and understanding a communication is to draw the analogy with telecommunications. Here one examines the human process by comparing it with the electronic process. Figure 29.1 shows how the communication process begins with some abstract idea or thought in the mind of the person seeking to convey information. The first step in the communication process is for the central nervous system of that person to translate the abstractions into speech patterns. Then a signal is transmitted through the vocal organs (transmitter), and the patterns of speech travel through the atmosphere as sound waves.

Those waves are received by the ears and nervous impulses convey them from the ears to the brain. The message is unscrambled in the central nervous system of the receiver, which then instructs the listener to understand; the final stage comes when there is registration and the receiver understands.

Through these various stages of translation from the mind of one to the mind of the other there are a number of points at which error is possible, even likely. It is almost impossible to know whether the abstract idea in the mind of one person has transferred itself accurately to the mind of the other. One essential element in the whole process is feedback. This completes the circuit so that there is some indication from the listener that he has received and understood. It is probable that the feedback response will give some indication to the transmitter of the quality of the message that has been received. If the transmitter expects a reaction of pleasure and the feedback he receives is a frown, then he immediately knows that there is an inaccuracy in the picture that has been planted in the mind of the receiver, so that he has the opportunity to identify the inaccuracy and correct it.

A further element in the communication process is that of 'noise'. This is used as a generic term to describe anything which interferes in the transmission process: inaudibility, inattention, physical noise and so forth. The degree to which some noise element is present will impair the quality of both transmission and feedback.

A further development of this simple idea is enshrined in the so-called Ten Commandments of good communication that were set out as guide-lines by the American Management Association in 1955:[4]

1. Seek to clarify your ideas before communicating.
2. Examine the true purpose of each communication.
3. Consider the total physical and human setting whenever you communicate.
4. Consult with others, wherever appropriate in planning communications.
5. Be mindful, while you communicate, of the overtones as well as the basic content of your message.
6. Take the opportunity, when it arises, to convey something of help or value to the receiver.
7. Follow up your communication.

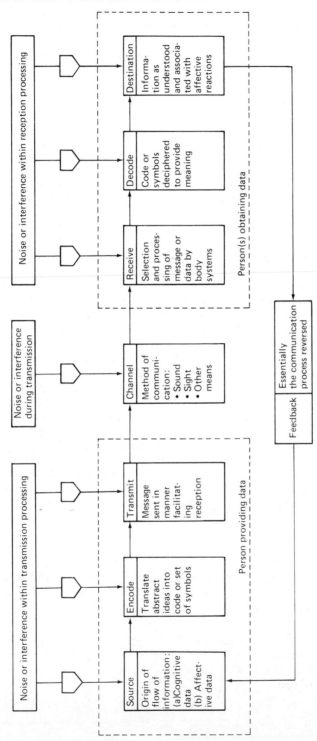

Figure 29.1. Analytical model of interpersonal communication based upon the telecommunications analogy

8. Communicate for tomorrow as well as for today.
9. Be sure your actions support your communications.
10. Last, but by no means least: seek not only to be understood but to understand — be a good listener.

It is unlikely that a body like the AMA would produce commandments to managers of quite that flavour today, because they are essentially unitary in the way in which the communication activity is perceived. Since that time we have come to realise that communication cannot be much improved by the process of managers thinking carefully about what they are doing and concentrating on doing it better. More recent analysis of the communication process has led to a greater understanding of the setting in which communication takes place, so that now perhaps we focus more on understanding the process and the activity of receiving and interpreting information than we do on the activities involved in transmitting information.

Peter Drucker[5] has described the four fundamentals of communication as:

perception

expectation

involvement

not information

Here Drucker is emphasising that it is the recipient who communicates. The traditional communicator only 'utters'. Unless somebody hears there is no communication there is only noise. It is not the utterer who can communicate; he can only make it possible or difficult for the recipient to perceive.

Barriers to Communication

It is the listener who will determine the extent to which the message is understood and what we hear or understand when someone speaks to us is shaped very largely by our own experience and background, so that instead of hearing what people tell us, we hear what our minds tell us they have said — the two may be different. There are various ways in which expectation determines communication content and a number of these ways of determination can impair the accuracy of message transmission. They act as 'noise' interfering both with transmission and feedback. We will look at some of the principal difficulties.

(a) THE FRAME OF REFERENCE

Few of us change our opinions alone. We are likely to be influenced by the opinions developed within the group with which we identify ourselves: the reference group. If a particular group of people hold certain values in common, individual members of that group will not easily modify their values unless and until there is a value shift through the group as a whole. This is perhaps most apparent in the relative intractability of opinions relating to political party allegiance. There are certain clearly identifiable social class groupings who tend to affiliate to particular political parties and a change in that affiliation by an individual is rare and difficult. Managers frequently direct to an individual a message, a request, instruction or rebuke which would find a more likely response if it were mediated through a representative of the group of employees rather than being directed at an individual. An interesting example of this is the way in which Safety Campaigns[6] are mounted, where the attempt is usually by the use of slogans and posters in order to persuade individual employees about the importance of safe working practices and similar aspects of behaviour rather than negotiating a change of behaviour through group representatives.

Whenever a matter is being discussed the people among whom it is being con-considered will view it from their particular personal frame of reference. Where the frames of reference of transmitter and receiver differ widely, there may be substantial difficulties in accurate transmission of messages and even greater difficulties in ensuring that the response of the receiver is that which the transmitter intended.

(b) THE STEREOTYPE

An extreme form of letting expectation determine communication content is stereotyping, where we expect a particular type of statement or particular type of attitude from a stereotype of person. It is for instance quite common for the English to expect certain types of behaviour and intention from the Irish ('Never stop talking and always ready for a fight'). Equally there is a stereotype expectation about the Scots, that they will be mean or at least extremely careful with money. People also have stereotypes that they put around certain office holders. There is a widespread stereotype of the shop steward which shows him as being militant, politically extreme in one, and only one direction, unreasonable, unintelligent and obstructive. Equally there are widespread stereotypes of different types of managers and for some people there is a stereotype of managers as a whole.

The effect of these stereotypes in communication matters is that the person who encounters someone for whom he has a stereotype will begin hearing what the person says in the light of the stereotype that he holds. If somebody has stereotype pictures in his mind of Irishmen and shop stewards, and if he then meets a shop steward with an Irish accent he will begin hearing what that person says and evaluating it in the context of his expectations. It will be some time before his listening, understanding and evaluation will adjust to the actual performance he is witnessing in contrast to that which he expected.

(c) COGNITIVE DISSONANCE

Another area of difficulty which has been explored so extensively by Festinger[7] and others is the extent to which people will cope successfully with information inputs that they find irreconcilable in some particular way. If someone receives information which is *consistent with what he already believes,* he is likely to understand it, believe it, remember it and take action upon it. If however he receives information which is *inconsistent with his established beliefs,* then he will have genuine difficulty in understanding, remembering and taking action.

A middle-aged married man was spending a night in a hotel and about nine in the evening there was a knock on the door. When he opened the door he found standing in the corridor the sort of vision that peoples the erotic fantasies of middle-aged men. When the vision spoke and indicated that her idea of an appropriate way to spend the next few hours was to join him inside his bedroom with the door firmly closed behind her, the middle-aged man had a cognitive dissonance difficulty! Hard experience for the previous thirty years had convinced him that young women looking like the vision in the corridor never ever expressed that sort of intention as far as he was concerned. He found it difficult to understand and impossible to take action appropriate to the situation! That type of problem is one that can be found in less beguiling form time and time again in working situations. It has an additional dimension to it. Not only do recipients of information find it difficult to understand, remember and take action, they will also grapple with the dissonance that the problematical new information presents. One of the ways in which they do this is to distort the message so that what they hear is what they want to hear, what they expect to hear and can easily understand rather than the difficult challenging information that is being put to them.

(d) THE HALO OR HORNS EFFECT

A slightly different aspect of expectation determining communication content is the halo or horns effect, which causes the reaction of receivers of information to move to extremes of either acceptance or rejection. When we are listening to somebody in whom we have confidence and who has earned our trust we may be predisposed to agree with what he says because we have placed an imaginary halo around his head. Because of our experience of his trustworthiness and reliability we have an expectation that what he says will be trustworthy and reliable. On the other hand if we have learned to distrust someone, then what we hear him say will be either ignored or treated with considerable caution. Perhaps the most common example of this is the reaction that people have to the leaders of political parties appearing on television.

(e) SEMANTICS AND JARGON

One difficulty about transferring ideas from one person to another is that ideas cannot be transferred because meaning cannot be transferred – all the communicators can use as their vehicle is words or symbols, but unfortunately the same symbols may suggest different meanings to different people. The meanings are in the hearers rather than the speakers and certainly not in the words themselves. A simple example of this is 'quite ill' which could have a variety of weightings according to how it was heard and the circumstances in which the comment was made.

The problem of jargon is where a word or a phrase has a specialised meaning that is immediately understandable by the *cognoscenti*, but meaningless or misleading to those who do not share the specialised knowledge. The Maslovian hierarchy of human needs is by now quite well known in management circles. On one occasion a lecturer was describing the ideas that were implicit in this notion and was rather surprised some months later in an examination paper to see that one of the students had heard not 'hierarchy' but 'high Iraqui'. The unfamiliarity of the word 'hierarchy' had been completely misinterpreted by that particular receiver, who had imposed his own meaning on what he heard because of the need to make sense of what it was that he received.

Another interesting example was in a School of Motoring, where for many years trainee drivers were given the instruction 'clutch out' or 'clutch in', which nearly always confused the trainee. Later the standard instruction was altered to 'clutch down' or 'clutch up'.

(f) NOT LISTENING AND FORGETTING

The final combination of problems to consider here is first the extent to which people do not listen to what is being said. Quite apart from the millions of wives who constantly complain that their husbands do not pay attention, there is a human predilection to be selective in listening. There are many examples of this, perhaps the most common being the way in which a listener can focus his attention on a

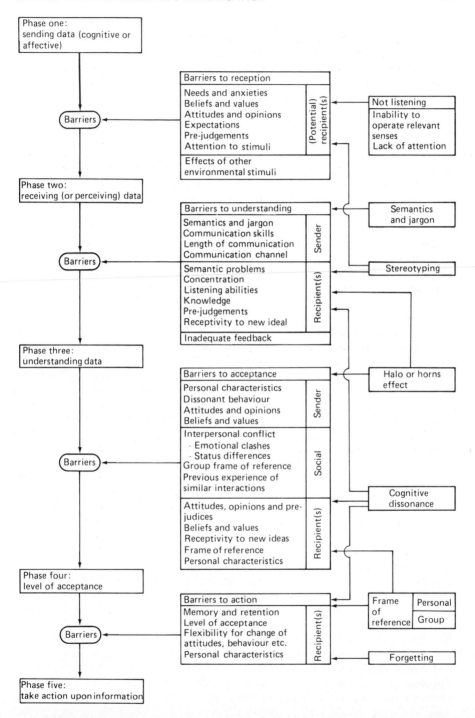

Figure 29.2. A summary of the major phases and barriers to effective communication

comment being made by one person in a general babble of sound by a group of people. This is complicated by the problem of noise that we have already considered, but it has the effect of the listener trying very hard to suppress all other signals other than the particular one that he is trying to pick up. However the rate of speech is something like 120 words per minute and the human brain can cope with the arrival of information at a higher rate. It is for instance quite common for people to achieve reading speeds of 500 words and more after appropriate training. This means that the rate of input of information might not be fast enough to engage the attention of the listener, whose attention may wander.

The rate at which we forget what we hear is considerable. We have probably forgotten half the substance of what we hear within a few hours of hearing it and no more than 10 per cent will remain after two or three days. Figure 29.2 provides a summary of the main phases in communication and the barriers to effectiveness.

Non-verbal Communication

In recent years there has been great interest in the extent to which communication takes place in addition to communication through articulated language. This has been particularly due to the work of Argyle[8,9] in the United Kingdom and Berne[10] in the United States, with the area becoming popular following the writings of Julius Fast.[11] A somewhat different approach is in the writings of Desmond Morris,[12] who has brought the eye of zoologist to this type of study.

The significance of non-verbal communication was demonstrated in the notorious affair of the Watergate Tapes. The transcription of those tapes demonstrated how much time in conversation was spent not speaking and the analysis of the transcription of what was *not* said as well as what *was* said in determining people's subsequent behaviour.

While communication is taking place there are various other things going on as well as speech. We can usually see the person with whom we are interacting and this itself adds a major dimension. Even if interaction is solely by letter or telex, where the exchanges appear to depend almost exclusively on language, there are still influential factors such as delay in answering, length of message and other subtleties to consider.

(a) BODILY CONTACT

It is relatively uncommon for people to communicate via bodily contact in working situations in Great Britain. Such communication is much more common in Mediterranean and African Countries, where the embrace is more familiar and there is more widespread use of kissing on both cheeks at welcome and parting.

In Britain bodily contact as communication is limited almost exclusively to the handshake. There is a mysterious folklore attached to the handshake which decrees that somebody shaking hands with a palm that is dry and a grip which is firm indicates that he has a strong and a reliable personality, whilst somebody whose handshake is relatively limp and moist is indicating a personality of low quality and generally not to be trusted. Despite the ease with which a handshake can be manipulated in the direction of firm dryness, the folklore continues and is powerful.

There are a number of variations about the handshake. First of all there is the duration; some people seek to sustain the grip on the other party for a relatively long period, whilst with other conjunctions it is quite brief. One variation is what is sometimes known as the 'Methodist' handshake where the left hand is added to the right in order to indicate a greater degree of warmth and feeling and to convey a sense of comfort and security. A further variation is 'jollying', which is usually used to encourage or to demonstrate friendship or sympathy, either to the person at the other end of the handshake or to an audience watching. The technique is to place the left hand on the forearm or elbow of the other person. More extravagant forms have the left hand on the shoulder of the other person or even between the shoulder blades.

(b) PROXIMITY AND CRITICAL SPACE

We take up a position in relation to the other person which will enable us to feel comfortable. This of course only applies when the two or more parties to an encounter have freedom of control over their relative positioning, and the lack of such freedom is one of the many contributors to the feeling of uncertainty and discomfort which is experienced by candidates for formal interview.

We tend to get slightly closer to those people whom we like and in whom we have confidence and to move slightly away from those people whom we suspect or distrust. If our suspicions are allayed, then we might move nearer again. There are many situations in which people experience an acutely uncomfortable degree of proximity. The most familiar is travelling in a lift, which produces proximity so unnatural as to cause discomfort to most people making the journey.

(c) GESTURE

Gesture can be looked at in two ways. First of all it can be used to emphasise and underline speech, so that the speaker who can control his gestures can use them directly as a manipulator. Alternatively and frequently, gestures derive from an emotional state and may involuntarily indicate that emotional state to a keen observer.

Examples of the first aspect of gesture would be for instance the stabbing forefinger of the orator who is seeking to compel the attention of his audience or the melodramatic banging of his shoe on the table, which Khrushchev produced at a meeting of the United Nations Organisation. It is interesting that many people will recall the incident when he banged on the table, although perhaps very few will recall the reason for his behaviour. Very common examples of gesture to emphasise speech are beckoning, waving, nodding, and shaking the head.

Krout[13] conducted some experiments in America which suggested a link between certain types of involuntary gesture and specific attitudes:

Steepled fingers indicated suspicion;
Hand to nose indicated fear;
Fingers to lips indicated shame;
Clenched fists indicated aggression;
Open hand dangling between the legs indicated frustration.

(d) POSTURE

Tallness tends to make one person dominate another, due to childhood conditioning when parents are always taller than their children during the formative years. Frequently tallness is emphasised by artificial devices such as the rostrum for the public speaker, or high-heeled shoes. Relative shortness is seen as an interpersonal disadvantage and frequently short people try to compensate by emphasising other dominating characteristics such as aggressiveness. Some short people feel they interact more effectively when sitting, which reduces the height differential. Conversely tall people deliberately seek dominance by standing.

Furthermore posture can be an indicator of emotional state, somewhere between the very tense and completely relaxed. At one extreme there is the 'open' posture. The person leans back comfortably, perhaps with hands behind the head, legs apart and muscles slack. At the opposite extreme there is the 'closed' posture, where the legs are crossed or pressed tightly together, feet sometimes off the floor or looped around the cross-bar on the chair, hands clenched leaning forward, shoulders hunched coiled like a spring. The closed posture stems from ancient behaviour in preparing to be attacked and can be compared with the stance of a boxer.

We cannot, however, take these extremes simply on their face value, as it is necessary to interpret the degree of tenseness for each individual. The naturally tense person may be perhaps very thin, and will exhibit an open posture less often than the normally more tranquil person, who may be pleasantly plump. Foot wagging may indicate nervousness, but some people wag their feet, like cats purring, as an indication of pleasure.

(e) GAZE

The influence of gaze and its direction has been investigated principally by Argyle.[14] One person influences his interaction with another in an important way by looking at him. In the main we look at other people to obtain information and also to obtain feedback and we look at the other approximately twice as much while *listening* as while *talking.*

Another aspect of gaze is that long periods of looking can be interpreted as a desire to be friendly and we tend to look at the other more when we are further apart, to compensate for the separation, whilst looking is almost taboo when people are very close. This is something which the public speaker will be familiar with. It is relatively easy to maintain eye contact with one member of a large audience for a sustained period, whilst such eye contact would not be sustained so comfortably if the person were closer.

Shifts of gaze can also be used to synchronize speech between people, so that a speaker will almost always give a prolonged look at the other before ending a statement as a way of indicating that it is becoming time for the other person to speak.

Looking too long or too intently, can disconcert and there are many instances of people expressing concern or discomfort about the basilisk stare of another person.

Interactive Incidents and Communication Ploys

Running through the majority of interviews and other types of discussion with which managers are concerned are certain standard aspects of behaviour, and in this section we consider these.

(a) RAPPORT

> *Definition: The situation in which effective social interaction*
> *between the interviewer and the respondent takes place.*

Every encounter has to begin and the opening is likely to be characterised by a degree of skirmishing as each party assesses the other. While this is going on both interviewer and respondent are tuning into each other and establishing some sort of relationship which will enable the subsequent interview to be effective. This is one of the most common types of human behaviour, which most people undertake quite instinctively dozens of times a day. In the working situation interview, however, there is a greater degree of formality and ritual about this stage of the encounter because the interview is of greater significance potentially than most casual encounters.

The standard methods which are likely to be used in establishing rapport by both parties, but particularly by the interviewer, who will be seen as appropriately controlling the encounter, are the following:

(i) *A friendly, easy manner.* This of course is easier to advocate than to produce. Many people aspire to have an open manner with others which is friendly and easy, but the experience of every individual is that not many of those encountered are successful at it.

(ii) *Attentiveness.* The interviewer needs to pay careful attention to what the respondent is saying, and to *demonstrate* that he is paying this attention. This focuses the thinking and the responsiveness on the respondent.

(iii) *Easy and non-controversial opening topic.* It has long been a music-hall joke that the British discuss the weather when they meet. What is happening in that discussion is that the participants are using an innocuous topic like the weather as a vehicle for their preliminary exchanges while they adjust to the other's tone and volume and assess the opposing personality. This of course is only a matter of seconds or minutes of ritual exchange rather than laborious drawn-out preliminaries to the conversation.

(iv) *Calmness.* The interviewer who is able to project a feeling of peacefulness and quiet will elicit a response from the other party more quickly and more constructively than the interviewer who consciously or unconsciously conveys a great air of business and preoccupation — the 'I have managed to fit you in but we only have ten minutes' syndrome. The busy and preoccupied atmosphere will defer the start of frank discussion and may in fact prevent it altogether.

(v) *Smile and eye contact.* We all respond when someone smiles at us, even though in some circumstances our response will be circumscribed by suspicion. The interviewer who smiles will warm the atmosphere between himself and the respondent and if he is able to maintain a degree of eye contact which will focus the attention of the two parties without being overbearing and relentless, then there is a speeding up of the process of establishing rapport.

All this presupposes that the interviewer begins in a situation of social advantage and that the respondent begins in a disadvantage situation and that the opening shots, as it were, from the interviewer are to equalise the social position between them.

(b) REWARD

Definition: Sustaining the interaction with the respondent.

The establishment of rapport is something which essentially takes place at the opening of an interview. After a very short period of such exchanges the interview will move round to the substance that the two people have come together to discuss. It is important that the interviewer does not leave behind the warm and affiliative behaviour that was displayed at the beginning. If he does this then his good behaviour appears to the respondent overtly manipulative in a calculating and worrying way. The interviewer is trying at the beginning not to establish a false sense of relaxation and security but an accurate and constructive sense of such security.

This therefore needs to be maintained while the interview proceeds. There are various ways in which it is conventionally done.

(i) *Interest.* The interviewer continues to display interest in what it is that the respondent is saying. If he can also indicate *agreement* with what the respondent is saying he will reinforce the other's responses.

(ii) *Eye behaviour.* Individually we influence the behaviour of other people, or seek to influence the behaviour, extensively by the use of our eyes. Gaze has already been referred to and there are other ways in which each individual develops a repertoire of signals which his eyes convey, such as encouragement, surprise, understanding etc. If the interviewer deploys these in an interactive situation he is able to sustain the interaction of the other without actually speaking while the other is seeking to speak.

(iii) *Noises.* Conversation contains a variety of noises that are ways of rewarding the other party. Unfortunately they are almost impossible to reproduce on paper for the sake of explanation, but they form that part of conversation that is inarticulate yet meaningful. In conjunction with eye behaviour, nods etc. they serve the purpose of keeping things going by encouraging the other without interrupting him.

(c) CLOSED QUESTIONS

Definition: Questions seeking precise, terse information.

Basic, factual information is usually elicited from a respondent in small packages and the method of eliciting is the closed question that does not invite anything more than a terse response:

'What time is it?'
'How much holiday do I get each year?'
'Who is in charge?'

An interview which proceeds along the lines of many closed questions from the interviewer is more of an interrogation than a conversation, and the information offered by the respondent is closely prescribed and strictly *factual*. But facts are of limited value in interactions. People come face to face because of a need to share or exchange opinions, attitudes and ideas. That type of exchange is dependent on a contrasting type of question . . .

(d) OPEN-ENDED QUESTIONS

*Definition: Questions avoiding terse replies, and
inviting the respondent to open up on a topic.*

Evidence of opinions, attitudes and ideas is elicited by enabling the respondent to speak rather than prescribing his answers. The open-ended question does little more than mention a topic or area and invite comment:

'How are you getting on?'
'Could you give me an outline of what is involved in your present post?'
'What about staff development in the department?'

This style of questioning is almost an extension of rapport in that it makes things easy for the respondent, who has latitude to decide what to talk about and is helped to relax and get going by beginning to talk, hearing himself talk and developing his poise. To ensure direction of the interview the interviewer will need to focus replies.

(e) FOLLOW-UP QUESTIONS

*Definition: Methods of developing and focusing
the answer to an open-ended question.*

Once the interviewer begins to get response, he builds on those responses. In this way he is developing what the respondent has been able to start. The interviewer in fact becomes the respondent, steadily enlarging the picture in his mind. To illustrate follow-up method, let us assume that a school-leaver, applying for a first job, has been posed the following conventional open-ended question:

'Can you tell me something of what you did at school, and your examination achievements?'

Depending on the response the interviewer might follow-up in one of three ways:

(i)   The respondent has replied to only part of the question and has not said anything about examinations, so there is a *reminder follow-up:*
      'And what about your examinations . . .?'

(ii) The respondent has replied with evidence that would have additional weight if further evaluated. This calls for the *forced-choice follow-up:*
      'Which was your stronger subject — French or Maths?'

(iii) The reply has given a cue to a potentially useful additional area of discussion, requiring the very common *second-step follow-up:*
      'So what was the main benefit from being captain of cricket?'

(f) DIRECT QUESTIONS

Definition: Questions demanding both a reply and precision.

With the direct question the interviewer is asserting his authority in the interactive situation and his 'right to know'. He is using the prescriptive *style* of the closed question, yet seeking the more informative response that the open-ended question is designed to obtain. It is most likely to be used where it is anticipated that the reply will be evasive:

'Why did you leave that job?'
'Did you take the money?'
'When will you let me know?'

(g) SUMMARY AND RE-RUN

Definition: Drawing together in summary various points
from the respondent and obtaining his confirmation.

As the interview progresses the respondent will produce lots of information, from which the interviewer will be selecting that which it is important to retain and understand. Periodically he will interject a summary sentence or two with an interrogative inflection:

'So the new M.D. did not see eye-to-eye with you and you felt the time had come to widen your experience with a move, but in retrospect you regret your decision?'

'You did take his wallet out of his locker, then. But this was because he had asked you to fetch it for him on your way back from the canteen because he owed Charlie a fiver?'

This tactic serves several useful purposes. It indicates that the interviewer is listening and gives the respondent the chance to correct a false impression. Also it can be a useful control device by drawing a phase of the interview to a close. After the respondent has assented to the summary and re-run, it is natural and easy to move on to a fresh topic.

(h) PROBES

Definition: Questioning to obtain information
that the respondent is reluctant to divulge.

The tactics described so far rest on the comfortable assumption that the interviewer is always and necessarily encouraging, supportive and permissive in his style, with the implication that this is what is required to conduct an effective interview. For most phases of most interviews we would argue that this is the appropriate mode, and that the most usual overall strategy will be to build a sympathetic, trusting relationship.

Any interview may still have phases in which the interviewer realises that information is being deliberately withheld by the respondent. When this happens the interviewer has to make an important decision that may be a difficult one: does he respect the respondent's unwillingness and let the matter rest, or does he persist with his inquiry? He will persist if he feels it important that he finds out what he was seeking.

Reluctance by respondents is quite common in disciplinary interviews for obvious reasons and in grievance interviews because the employee grievance usually implies a criticism of some other employee, like a supervisor. In selection interviews there is often some aspect of the applicant's employment history that he feels would be best glossed over.

If the interviewer decides to probe, this sequence may help:

(i) *Direct questions.* Open-ended questions are quite inappropriate as they give too much latitude to the respondent. The phrasing needs to be careful so as to avoid a defensive reply if possible.

(ii) *Supplementaries.* The first direct question may produce the required information. If it produces only an opaque or evasive response, then a supplementary question will be needed, re-phrasing or reiterating the first.

If this is not likely to produce what is required there is a rather nasty alternative, a device sometimes used by television policemen, that is:

(iii) *Overstatement.* If a question is put to the respondent which implies a reason for the respondent's reluctance which is more grave than the real reason, then the respondent will rush to correct the false impression; now being happy to replace the appalling with the disquieting as being the lesser of two evils.

> Q. 'There appears to be a gap in the record at the beginning of last year. You weren't in prison or anything were you?'

> A. 'Oh no, I was having treatment for ... er ... well, for alcoholism, actually.'

Crude and rather nasty, but effective. The probe stands the best chance of working if it is used at the point in the interview when the rapport between the parties is at its peak. Also a probe needs to be closed with care. If the respondent finally declares something he has been trying to conceal it is not the time for a pregnant silence or a gleeful 'Ah-ha'. Either of these would destroy rapport and demoralise the respondent, putting him one-down beyond redemption. There is a need for:

(iv) *Face-saving close.* The interviewer makes the disclosed information seem much less worrying than the respondent had feared, so that the interview can proceed with reasonable confidence.

> 'Yes, well you must be glad to have that behind you.'

(i) BRAKING

Definition: Slowing the rate of response from the respondent.

The encouraging and permissive interviewer may nod and smile his way to a situation in which the respondent is talking too much, having been relaxed to the point where he talks on and on ... and on. To re-establish control the interviewer may be tempted to become peevish and shut up the respondent in a curt irritable manner. We are, however, naturally inhibited from such candour and the following hierarchy of less drastic techniques could achieve the same objective. Probably no more than one or two will be needed in sequence, but a longer list is provided for the really tough cases.

(i) *Closed questions.* We have already seen that the closed question invites a terse response. One or two closed, specific data-seeking questions may stem the tide.

(ii) *The furrowed brow.* In contrast to the bland, reassuring behaviours of *reward,* the interviewer furrows his brow to indicate mild disagreement, lack of understanding or professional anxiety.

(iii) *Glazed abstraction.* We are all familiar with the look about the eyes of a person who has stopped listening. It is in two stages. First he maintains his other signals, like the nods and the smiles, but has altered his eyes and the other components of his expression from 'yes, that's interesting' to 'now let me have a turn'. The second stage is when he gives up and just waits for the diatribe to end, while his eyes speak of last night's film on television or the trip to the caravan planned for the forthcoming week-end. This is a pretty severe signal and can be particularly effective in decelerating a respondent because the behaviour is in such stark contrast to that which came earlier.

(iv) *Looking away.* If two people are conversing and one of them looks at his watch he is implying that the other had better stop talking as he is over-running his time. In interviews there is a very strong constraint on this signal. Others not quite so punitive are looking for matches, looking at the aircraft making rather a noise outside the window or looking (again) at the application form.

(v) *Interruption.* The simplest method of all, but the one which most people avoid at all costs.

(j) DISENGAGEMENT

Definition: Closing the interview without 'losing' the respondent.

Books about interviewing are replete with advice about starting interviews but seldom mention how to finish them. Closing an interview is as difficult a social task as beginning. Interviewers seem to have problems about how to close and get rid of the respondent and many respondents become agitated about over-running their time and look for a signal that will release them. A significant minority of interviews end with the respondent feeling aggrieved or put down, usually because it was clumsily closed by the interviewer. Yet the close is important because it is the phase where future action is clarified or confirmed. The difficulty is surprising when one considers that there is a simple, short sequence that can hardly fail.

(i) *First signal – verbal plus papers.* The interviewer indicates that he believes the interview to be approaching its conclusion. In case the respondent has stopped listening to him he adds to his speech an underlying action by gathering his papers together and tapping them square on the table top before putting them down in a neat pile.

'Well now, I think we have covered the ground, don't you?'

'I don't think there is anything else I need to ask you. Is there anything further you want from me?'

He is not only giving his closing signal; he is obtaining the respondent's *confirmation* of the impending closure.

(ii) *Explain next step.* The interviewer says, or repeats, what happens next.

> 'My colleagues and I will have a chat and I'll be writing to you about the beginning of next week.'

> 'Can we meet again next Wednesday, to see how things are proceeding?'

(iii) *Closing signal.* The interviewer stands up. The ground has been prepared so that all remains is the decisive act which closes the interview. It will probably be accompanied by a handshake, smiles and mumbled inanities about how nice it has been, but the decisive action is for the interviewer to stand, after which the interview will close itself.

(k) PITFALLS

Having reviewed some of the stages in an interview and the methods that may be used, we offer a word of warning about three common behaviours that are not productive.

(i) *Leading questions.* Questions which suggest a 'right' answer will receive that answer which is not necessarily informative; merely sycophantic.

> 'You do understand the plans for reorganisation, don't you?'

> 'Would you agree with me that . . .'

(ii) *Multiple questions.* Inputs from the interviewer that require the respondent to decide which to answer first at the same time as remembering the others are very difficult to handle, as well as curtailing the opportunities for development.

> 'Perhaps you could tell me something of your schooling and national service — assuming that you did national service — and then I would like to know why you are applying for this post.'

(iii) *Unreasonable exhortation.* In counselling, disciplinary and similar interviews it is common for the interviewer to exhort the respondent in some way. He should consider whether he is intending just to make noises or whether he expects the respondent to comply. Here are a few common exhortations that very few people can actually obey:

> 'Cheer up.'
> 'Relax!'
> 'Be your age.'
> 'Stop worrying.'

Effectiveness in Interviewing

Skill in interviewing varies between individuals and can only be partly improved by learning technique. Sidney, Brown and Argyle[15] suggest four key components of social skill:

(i) *Rewardingness.* Being helpful, kind, thoughtful and easy to deal with. The rewarding person can influence because he is able to withdraw the rewards as well as provide them.

(ii) *Perceptual sensitivity.* Accurately perceiving and interpreting the visual signals from the respondent.

(iii) *Synchronising skill.* The ability to create a smooth pattern of interaction with a variety of styles from respondents, without interruptions, awkward pauses or misunderstanding.

(iv) *Poise.* Enjoying and being at ease in social situations, not worrying about what others think of you.

The widespread wish to be socially skilful is reflected in the range of methods that have been evolved to enhance such skills. The best-known is sensitivity training, of which the most widespread device is the T-group.[16] A small number are brought together without any agenda or procedures, and without any nominated leader. They are invited to discuss what is happening, to understand the process and then develop their interpersonal relations. This has the effect of stripping away the conventions with which people are familiar and behind which they hide their true feelings. As a result the participants are more revealing in their behaviours and acquire an understanding of their effect on other people at the same time as coming to understand the behavioural cues they receive from the others.

Other techniques, like 3-D management, management grid and Coverdale training are other ways in which the same basic idea is applied.

Transactional Analysis (TA)[17] is a method of developing new attitudes and behaviour patterns that is based on a framework of three ego states: parent, adult and child, in which a person may be at any time. The manager who shakes his finger at an employee is in the parent state, the one who listens attentively to problems is an 'adult' and the one who reacts with woebegone helplessness is a child. The method then proceeds to analyse the nature of the transactions between people in these differing states with a view to developing healthier and more productive transactions.

Quite different, and virtually unique, is the work of Stephen Potter[18] who produced a series of urbane and penetrating analyses of how people try to score off each other in games and in all departments of life, but mainly in conversation. The remarkable thing about Potter's writing was that he shocked his readers by actually describing frankly, if extravagantly, the behaviours used, but never, ever *acknowledged* by people in trying to be 'one-up' on others. Not content with this he even went so far as to offer a primer for his readers in these anti-social behaviours, with detailed descriptions of, for instance, how to win at games without actually cheating, the art of criticising without actually listening, and Committeeship — the art of coming into a discussion without actually understanding a word of what anybody is talking about.

Essentially Potter was commenting on *manners* and his work is probably too sophisticated to be taken as other than agreeable humour in the context of interviewing in working situations, but it still provides a unique perspective on interpersonal behaviour.

REFERENCES

1. Stewart R., *Managers and their Jobs* (Pan Piper) 1970, p. 55.
2. Mintzberg H., *The Nature of Managerial Work* (Harper & Row) 1973.
3. Goffman E., *The Presentation of Self in Everyday Life* (Pelican) 1972, p. 45.
4. Quoted in Megginson L.C., *Personnel: A Behavioural Approach to Administration* (Irwin) 1972, p. 609.
5. Drucker P.F., 'What Communication Means' in *Management Today*, March 1970.
6. Strauss G. and Sayles L.R., *Personnel: The Human Problems of Management* (Prentice-Hall) 1972, p. 209.
7. Festinger L., *A Theory of Cognitive Dissonance* (Row Peterson) 1957.
8. Argyle M., *Social Interaction* (Tavistock) 1973.
9. Argyle M., *The Psychology of Interpersonal Behaviour* (Penguin Books) 1972.
10. Berne E., *Games People Play* (Deutsch) 1966.
11. Fast J., *Body Language* (Pan) 1971.
12. The most popular version in Morris D., *Manwatching* (Johnathan Cape) 1977.
13. Krout M.H., 'An Experimental Attempt to Determine the Significance of Unconscious Manual Symbolic Movements', *Journal of General Psychology*, 1954.
14. *Social Interaction, op. cit.*, pp. 105–110.
15. Sidney E., Brown M. and Argyle M., *Skills with People* (Hutchinson) 1973, pp. 35–36.
16. Smith P.B., 'Improving Skills in Working With People: the T Group', *Training Information Paper No. 4*, D.E.P. (HMSO) 1969.
17. Harris T.A., *I'm OK – Your're OK; A Practical Guide to Transactional Analysis* (Harper & Row) 1967.
18. Potter S., *The Complete Upmanship* (Rupert Hart-Davis) 1970.

30

Information for Employees and their Representatives

The material in this chapter relates to that in various other parts of the work. Mainly it relates to what we have called the contract for collective consent and the collective bargaining activities that are included under that general heading, but there is also some bearing on a number of areas in the individual contracts.

The question of information for employees and their representatives only becomes an issue when there is a move towards a greater degree of information *disclosure* rather than information provision. Disclosure implies a reluctance on the part of the holder of the information to let anyone else see it, and discussion moves away from *how* to get the information across and moves towards *whether* the attempt should be made at all because it is more important to preserve the sanctity of its concealment. For this reason we begin this chapter by reviewing the arguments for and against greater disclosure of information by managements to employees and their representatives, then review the present legal position and finally consider methods.

1. Arguments for Greater Information Disclosure

(a) INCREASES IN EFFICIENCY

When the National Board for Prices and Incomes examined over 650 productivity agreements in the late 1960s, it decided that most of them had improved the productive efficiency of the organisations within which they were negotiated and that one of the main reasons for the success of such agreements had been the policy of the managements to be open with union negotiators about the facts of the situation facing the company.

(b) IMPROVED INDUSTRIAL RELATIONS

Although 'improved industrial relations' is a mysterious state that is difficult to define, there is a commonsense argument that industrial relationships are improved when there is knowledge replacing ignorance. Misunderstanding and mistrust that stem from a suspicion of the motives of the other party give way to a better-informed attitude. Mistrust may harden to industrial action or withdrawn co-operation, but only if it is justified by the facts of the situation. The Bullock committee delivered the opinion that 'availability of information to employees and their representatives can increase mutual understanding and involvement',[1] and broad endorsement of such practices can be found in authoritative statements from the British Institute of Management[2] and the Ministry of Labour[3] nearly twenty years earlier. Some interesting empirical evidence comes from a survey of employee attitudes commissioned by the Confederation of British Industry in 1976.[4] This indicated that employees who felt that management kept them well informed and who believed the information they received also expressed attitudes such as:

> 'Management are well in touch with what is really going on in the company . . .'

> 'Management tells the reasons for what it asks employees to do.'

> 'Management is just as interested in listening to what employees have to say as in giving them its own point of view.'

In contrast, those employees who were dissatisfied with the amount and reliability of information provided typically feel that information is:

> 'frequently unfairly slanted . . .'

> 'provides insufficient opportunity for feedback from employees.'

> 'Management only start telling you about the company's economic situation when the news is bad.'

A year before the publication of this survey the CBI had already adopted as official policy the principle that greater disclosure was seen in itself as leading to more satisfactory working relationships between employers and employees.[5]

(c) EMPLOYEE PARTICIPATION IN MANAGEMENT DECISION-MAKING

If employees are to participate more directly in those decision-making processes traditionally reserved for the management, then greater information *and understanding of that information* is an essential pre-requisite:

> The Employment Protection Act will also have the effect of benefitting convenors and shop stewards, who alone in the industrial relations system have the time and capacity to increase their expertise in the affairs of their company. Whether they can increase their control over managerial decision-making remains to be seen. But none can doubt that company information for trade unionists is a condition *sine qua non* for any extension of participation by employee representatives in management, and that lies at the heart of the debate on disclosure.[6]

Without this element the argument in favour of greater disclosure is weaker and narrower: there is less need for employee representatives to be so well-informed, and they need information on a narrower range of topics, so the answer to this question is crucial to management policy on disclosure: is there a will to extend the degree of employee participation in decision-making or not? Professor Robertson believes that the provision of information is becoming attractive for this reason not only to those who seek radical changes in the capitalist system, but also to those who seek to strengthen the system:

> The disclosure of information . . . seems to lie at the heart of the great debate between capital and labour; both those who wish to destroy the capitalist system and those who are distressed by the conflicts apparent in the collective bargaining process, and wish to minimise them, see in the provision of information by employers to trades unions and their representatives a technique to help accomplish their differing objectives.[7]

(d) REASONABLENESS AND THE SPIRIT OF THE AGE

A final justification lies perhaps in the simple fact of fashion. It is becoming more common for information on all manner of topics to be more generally available than in the past. The much-maligned communications media — to say nothing of the predatory researchers from higher education — investigate and produce inform- ation on almost anything that has the remotest connection with the 'public interest'. Government departments constantly require returns from employers on a growing number of issues, and legislation seeks increasing openness. In a developing situation of that type it becomes reasonable to managers that employees should be given more information about their employing organisation. Furthermore the advent of the computer makes the compilation of such information easier than it used to be.

Gradually the reaction from managers of 'Why should this information be given to shop stewards?' is being replaced by the question 'Is there any reason why this information should not be given . . .?'

2. Arguments Against Greater Information Disclosure

Although the arguments in favour seem to be gaining in strength and general acceptance, what are the remaining reasons for reluctance?

(a) CONFIDENTIALITY

Some information could be damaging to the organisation if disclosed to a com- petitor or to the stock markets. Discussions about whether or not to invest large sums in a research and development programme would normally be kept as con- fidential as possible for as long as possible in order to gain what headstart over the competition can be achieved. Marketing and sales promotion campaigns are similarly customarily cloaked in secrecy until the last minute. Information that could affect share dealings leads to a range of obvious problems. The Commission on Industrial Relations surveyed attitudes in nearly a hundred companies in 1972 and found majority 'unwillingness' to disclose the following information:

> any breakdown of total costs; indirect costs; production costs; sales costs; details of pricing policy; criteria for investment decisions; value added by company activities; income from overseas earnings; actual or budgeted unit costs; labour cost per unit of output; information concerning sub-contractors and their con- tracts; periodic profit and loss statements; research and development; mergers/ take-overs; future pricing policy; diversification plans and marketing forecasts.[8]

Frequent reference was made to Stock Exchange rules, on which the CIR made interesting comment:

> It is wrong to suggest that the requirements of the Companies Acts and the Stock Exchange rules inhibit employers from disclosing financial information to employees. These requirements are not restrictive in what should be disclosed but are designed to safeguard the interests of shareholders by seeing that inform- ation likely to influence share values is not disclosed in a way which might create privileged interests. The principle is not that companies should be secretive but that they should be impartial . . . a restrictive policy finds no support in the Companies Acts or Stock Exchange Rules.[9]

In contrast to this attitude is the recent experience of Chrysler:

> The release of highly confidential information by Chrysler, under the provisions of the Industry Act, took place without dire consequences. This is a sign that

confidences released to trade unions during negotiations can be kept. As a result, Chrysler has extended its provisions of information to make it one of the leaders in the field of disclosure.[10]

The issue of confidentiality has been the most discussed manifest problem about disclosure and is one of the reasons why the legal requirements in successive pieces of legislation have tended to disappoint the trade union interests.

(b) THE PROBLEM OF UNCERTAINTY

Most senior managers cope with a range of uncertainty and indecisiveness that typically amazes the uninitiated when it is discovered and many people feel that this uncertainty is best concealed until the uncertainty has been resolved. Either it will make employees believe that the management is incompetent or it will create needless anxiety.

A typical situation has been the run up to a redundancy declaration. At first this is like a cloud no bigger than a man's hand on the horizon — something that could happen if . . . That possibility is then likely to come nearer and then recede again as alternatives are discussed, some orders that were unlikely are actually placed and others on which the Sales Director was counting are inexplicably diverted to the competition. Those who advocate concealing management uncertainty will argue that there is no need to alarm employees about a situation which may never happen, and the type of redundancy that was originally thought possible will usually turn out to be different from that which eventually transpires. As soon as the possibility is first broached employees and their representatives will quite naturally clamour for confirmation or denial and will rarely believe the simple answer 'we don't know'. The management is supposed to know. Are they in charge or aren't they? How could they be so incompetent as to let such a situation arise? If the calamity is averted, then the management will be accused of crying wolf and rumour-mongering.

The particular issue of advance warning about redundancy has been covered in the Employment Protection Act but much of the information that is so sensitive in disclosure discussions is the sort that could be a preliminary to that or some similar employee anxiety. Nevertheless the precedent of the requirement for employers to consult in advance of redundancy may help many managers over this particular psychological barrier.

(c) KNOWLEDGE IS POWER

Although it is seldom expressed in such uncompromising terms, much management resistance to the idea of information disclosure is at least partly a feeling that managers depend on an area of restricted knowledge to justify their elite position. If employees — particularly trade union officials — get hold of more of that specialised knowledge, then they get above themselves, just like Adam in the Garden of Eden. Aspiring professionals like accountants and personnel managers have assiduously cultivated the image of specialised knowledge (to which only they are privy) to justify their organisational position and increasing salary level.

These we regard as the main reasons for resisting disclosure, but there are many more detailed problems that are discussed by Arthur Marsh and Roger Rosewall[10] and in the published proceedings of a conference sponsored by the British Universities Industrial Relations Association.[11]

3. Legal Requirements for Information Disclosure

We now consider what the law currently requires that an employer shall disclose.

(a) THE BACKGROUND

The legislators have been very inhibited about disclosure, tending towards exhortation rather than guidance. The comments of the 'Donovan' Royal Commission in 1968 were perfunctory despite a recommendation for legislation on disclosure by a Labour Party working party in 1967. The first official declaration of intent was in the 1969 White Paper of the Labour Government:

> The government proposes to go beyond the recommendations of the Royal Commission by including in the Industrial Relations Bill a provision to enable trade unions to obtain from employers certain sorts of information that are needed for negotiations.[12]

The parliamentary Bill based on that White Paper never reached the statute book, but the Industrial Relations Act of the incoming Conservative government had similar requirements. These passed through Parliament but were not made operative before the Act was repealed. Also a long-awaited report from the Commission on Industrial Relations[13] did not produce the degree of prescription that most observers had anticipated. This did not begin to emerge until the Employment Protection Act 1975 and Industry Act 1975, with the Code of Practice on disclosure finally becoming operative in 1977, eight years after the 1969 White Paper.

This lengthy period of gestation shows that it has been a difficult subject on which to achieve a constructive consensus.

(b) THE INDUSTRY ACT 1975

The Industry Act makes provision for disclosure by *some* companies, as the powers in the Act are linked with planning agreements. There has not been great employer enthusiasm for these agreements which involve a close working relationship with, and dependence on, government. The information to be disclosed is to be given first to the appropriate government Minister and only later to trade unions.

Section 27 of the Act says that companies *may* be required to disclose information if they are wholly or mainly engaged in managing industry in the United Kingdom and making a significant contribution to an important industrial sector. This will be used either for the development of planning agreements or discussions at the National Economic Development Committee.

The subjects on which information or forecasts can be sought are:

   (i)   Persons normally employed (not individuals)
   (ii)   Capital expenditure
   (iii)   Fixed capital assets
   (iv)   Disposal, or intended disposal, of such assets
   (v)   Acquisition, or intended acquisition, of fixed capital assets
   (vi)   Productive capacity and utilisation
   (vii)   Output and productivity
 (viii)   Sales
   (ix)   Exports
   (x)   Sales of industrial or intellectual property (no details or know-how)
   (xi)   Expenditure on research and development (not details of the programme)

This information cannot be sought for a period earlier than the most recently completed financial year, but forecasts may be asked for over any period.

If a company regards some of the information requested as confidential or in some other way sensitive, it must still be given to the appropriate government minister, that is, the Secretary of State for Industry or for Agriculture. The minister will then judge its confidentiality and *can* decide that it should be withheld from other organs of government and from trade unions. He is not obliged so to decide and can only make such a decision on specific grounds set out in Section 30 of the Act:

(i) Against the national interest
(ii) Breach of statute
(iii) The information was given to the company in confidence
(iv) Disclosure would cause substantial injury to the company
(v) Disclosure would cause substantial injury to a substantial number of employees.

If the minister decides that the information should not be withheld from trade unions but the company managers wish to dispute his decision, they can require him to refer it to a special advisory committee. Equally, if a union is refused information by ministerial decision, it too can appeal to the same committee.

Although these procedures have so far been little used, they indicate the range of information that can potentially be disclosed, but they also show how sensitive the issue of confidentiality is.

(c) THE EMPLOYMENT PROTECTION ACT 1975

The Employment Protection Act makes provision for disclosure by *all* employers who negotiate with independent trade unions. If they ask for it, the representatives of those trade unions must be given all the information they need for collective bargaining purposes. In examining the provisions of this Act for trade union recognition (Chapter 11) we have already seen the definition of collective bargaining that is used, so that the disclosure imposed by this enactment upon reluctant employers is limited to matters concerned with the employment relationship, and general information about plans for investment and marketing is not included. The precise wording of the Act on the information to be disclosed is: [14]

a. information without which the trade union representatives would be to a material extent impeded in carrying on with him such collective bargaining, and
b. information which it would be in accordance with good industrial relations practice that he should disclose to them for the purposes of collective bargaining.

The next section of the Act sets down the categories of information that no employer shall be required to disclose: [15]

a. any information the disclosure of which would be against the interests of national security, or
b. any information which he could not disclose without contravening a prohibition imposed by or under an enactment, or
c. any information which has been communicated to the employer in confidence,

or which the employer has otherwise obtained in consequence of the confidence reposed in him by another person, or

d. any information relating specifically to an individual, unless he has consented
   to its being disclosed, or

e. any information the disclosure of which would cause substantial injury to the
   employer's undertaking for reasons other than its effect on collective bargaining, or

f. any information obtained by the employer for the purpose of bringing,
   prosecuting or defending any legal proceedings.

The information requested must be in the possession of the employer or an associated employer and must relate to his undertaking. Furthermore he is not required
to provide information the compilation of which would require work or expenditure
out of reasonable proportion to the value of the information in collective bargaining.

The enforcement procedure is bizarre. Non-compliance with the requirements of
the Industry Act is a criminal offence, but non-compliance with the disclosure
requirements of the Employment Protection Act can only result — after persuasion
— in compulsory arbitration on terms and conditions. Sections 19 and 20 of the
Act spell out the procedure, in which conciliation is followed by a hearing before
the Central Arbitration Committee if conciliation fails. If the CAC find the claim
well-founded they will make a declaration about what shall be disclosed and by
when. If the employer still refuses to comply, the CAC can make an award of terms
and conditions which become a term of the contract of employment for each
employee involved; so that the employer is not compelled to disclose the information
that the employee representatives have sought.

(d) THE CODE OF PRACTICE

Although lacking strict legal force, the Code of Practice[16] on disclosure is drafted
by ACAS and approved by Parliament as a basis of clarifying the call for 'information
which it would be in accordance with good industrial relations practice to disclose'.
Although the authors of the Code fight shy of producing a standard list of items to
disclose, they provide examples of information which 'could be relevant in certain
collective bargaining situations':[17]

i. Pay and benefits: principles and structure of payment systems; job evaluation
systems and grading criteria; earnings and hours analysed according to work
group, grade, plant, sex, out-workers and homeworkers, department or division,
giving, where appropriate, distributions and make-up of pay, showing any
additions to basic rate or salary; total pay bill; details of fringe benefits and non-
wage labour costs.

ii. Conditions of service: policies on recruitment, redeployment, redundancy,
training, equal opportunity and promotion; appraisal systems; health, welfare
and safety matters.

iii. Manpower: numbers employed analysed according to grade, department,
location, age and sex; labour turnover; absenteeism, overtime and short-time;
manning standards; planned changes in work methods, materials, equipment or
organisation; available manpower plans; investment plans.

iv. Performance: productivity and efficiency data; savings from increased productivity and output; return on capital invested; sales and state of order book.

v. Financial: cost structures; gross and net profits; sources of earnings; assets;
liabilities; allocation of profits; details of government financial assistance;
transfer prices; loans to parent or subsidiary companies and interest charged.

This list is neither a checklist of what is needed in every negotiating situation nor an exhaustive list of everything that might be appropriate.

The Code also provides some comment on the sort of information that might be withheld on the grounds that it might cause substantial injury to the undertaking:

> cost information on individual products; detailed analysis of proposed investment, marketing or pricing policies; and price quotas or the make-up of tender prices.[18]

All the *legal* requirements on disclosure that the Code seeks to elaborate apply only to disclosure of information to recognised trade unions. Other bodies, like staff associations, do not have a right to it, even though the employer may readily supply it.

Since the implementation of this section of the Act and the publication of the Code few unions have sought information under the terms of the Employment Protection Act, and fewer have been successful. One of the significant judgements was one which the CAC reached reluctantly on the grounds that the employer — BL Cars — could not be required to divulge information if the information required related to a matter on which the employer was not prepared to bargain. BL were planning to discontinue production at their MG plant and were willing to *consult* but not *bargain* about the decision. As the Act only requires the disclosure of information *for the purposes of collective bargaining*, an unwillingness to bargain eliminates a need to provide information.[19] Unions have had some limited success in obtaining more information from companies about payment arrangements by using these procedures.[20]

(e) HEALTH AND SAFETY AT WORK ACT 1974

A slightly different form of information disclosure is required by this Act, which directs that all employers with five or more employees should publish a written safety policy including an explanation of the principles informing that policy. The statement must also include the method whereby the policy will be put in to effect and the names of those within the organisation who are responsible for it.

4. Employer Practice on Employee Information

A survey of management practice in the provision of information to employees is that of Robin Smith on behalf of the British Institute of Management.[21] Among the most interesting conclusions he makes are the following:

> Many firms with unions prefer to use joint consultation machinery as the medium for disclosure of general performance indicators, particularly for 'good news' items. 'Bad news' items are however released to unions . . .

> Information is provided regularly to all employees by 56% of firms. House journals, notice boards, written communications direct to the individual and briefing groups are the most common methods . . .

> Over half the firms give middle managers more information than shareholders receive . . . A quarter now give manual workers more information than shareholders . . .

> The very largest firms, particularly multi-plant ones, have the greatest incidence of problems in operating disclosure and information policies.[22]

These results are based on replies to a postal questionnaire from 391 companies and indicate that disclosure is extensively practised. It also shows that there can be especial problems in larger organisations. Elsewhere the survey comments that those receiving the information frequently need training in how to handle it. Here we come to one of the persistent problems with disclosure that has already been referred to: the mystique of professionalism.

In the summer of 1979 Linda Dickens obtained information about disclosure practice in 48 companies and concluded that there had been little effect from the Employment Protection Act provisions. Half the respondents provided as much or more information to employees as was received by shareholders but one third of the unionised companies did not provide this type of data. She also found very few of the information agreements suggested by the Code of Practice. Employers are generally most willing to give details of manpower information — such as numbers of employees, hours worked, level of turnover, sickness absence and training — and least willing to provide particulars of future planning — such as mergers and acquisitions, diversification and research.[23]

Until recently trade unions ran courses for negotiators that were largely intended to enable shop stewards to penetrate the techniques and jargon of the work study officer, who had assiduously developed his own language and associated paraphernalia of expertise. With greater knowledge the steward was able to question work study assumptions. As we have already seen in this book, personnel officers have been carefully collecting their own group of mysteries to justify their elite position in the management hierarchy. Disclosure of information calls into question the mysteries of another profession: accountancy. Much of the information referred to in the Code of Practice is financial information that is traditionally garnered and protected by accountants who present it in inscrutable form to others in order to ensure that only other accountants can understand it.

The Employment Protection Act may start the process of de-mythologising the accountancy profession, since shop stewards and others want to know what the figures mean, and why they have been put together in such a way as to provide that particular meaning. The approaches that are needed are either to train employee representatives in the 'language' of accountants or to make the specialised language redundant by presenting the same information in non-specialised terms.

The Institute of Chartered Accountants has attempted to re-evaluate the scope and aims of published financial reports, but did not succeed in establishing criteria for testing the validity of the information needs it was assumed employees had.[24] By contrast the Sandilands Committee advocated separate reports to employees on some matters like the plans and prospects of the company, while other information could be adequately supplied by the same published accounts that were prepared for shareholders.[25]

Company annual statements to shareholders have become steadily more comprehensible to the lay reader, especially since the Companies Act 1967, and have to include much of the information of interest to employees, such as the average number and pay of employees, numbers receiving high salaries, changes in fixed assets and details of shares in other companies. It is proposed to require further information in a forthcoming extension to the existing Act which will oblige companies to reveal such data as employee costs and net earnings and company policy statements on industrial relations and industrial democracy.

There is a widespread management conviction that employees and their representatives have difficulty in understanding complex financial information:

Two of the biggest problem areas . . . are employees' lack of education or their inability to assimilate information, and the danger of misinterpretation.[26]

The general move towards comprehensibility of company accounts suggests that this conviction may sometimes result more from prejudice than fact. Alternatively it may be that employee representatives understand the information and interpret it in the light of a different set of values.

Smith ascertained the methods most popular with employers for communicating to employees:[27]

	% companies (N = 391)		
	regularly	*occasionally*	*never*
House journals free of charge	52	8	41
House journals on sale	2	–	98
Notice boards	66	20	14
Written communications direct to individuals	52	17	31
Briefing groups	51	16	33
General meetings of employees	30	6	64
Special reports	22	4	75

5. Various Methods of Communicating with Employees

Using Smith's table as a starting point, we move now to consider various aspects of methods whereby information is communicated to employees.

(a) HOUSE JOURNALS AND NEWSLETTERS

Monthly or quarterly publications by companies are a common practice in large and medium-sized companies, and provide an obvious medium for communication of 'hard' information — like the progress of wage negotiations — as well as the 'soft' gossip and chat. They also have the benefit in the eyes of most managers that they go to all employees and not just to representatives, so providing a safeguard against the resilient belief that the rank and file are more amenable to the management line than are their representatives. This was diplomatically expressed in the CBI statement of policy that trade union representatives should be no better or worse treated that their constituents in the amount and type of information provided, except in very special circumstances.[28]

The house journal presents a number of problems. It has to compete with an abundance of slick, professionally produced newspapers and magazines that are likely to come into the employee's household every week. It has to compete to be read, and it has to compete in sounding and seeming authoritative. This need to compete usually means that it will be expensive to produce in both editorial skill and attractive presentation. Typically it will cost nearly as much as some commerical publications to produce, yet will have a relatively minute circulation so that the cost per copy seems prohibitive. Another difficulty is the inevitable association of editorial policy with the management of the company, so that employees will properly regard it as a channel for selling them ideas. As a result the content may be viewed with the same reservations as the brochure of a travel agent. One way to reduce this difficulty is either to vest editorial policy control in a joint body, or to have a section of the journal devoted to 'vetted statements'; either statements on

sensitive issues that the management are making after getting employee representatives' consent, or *vice versa.*

As with so many aspects of employment matters the position of the journal
editor in the management hierarchy can be of crucial importance, as he will need
not only access to senior managers to obtain his material, he will also need to know
sufficient of developments and policy — and employee interests — to create each
issue of the journal as a vital and topical piece of communication in tune with the
current needs of both parties. He cannot simply be told what to say.

Perhaps the biggest drawback of the glossier type of house journal is the production time. If some material on industrial relations policy is carefully drafted and
cleared before going to the printer it will seldom still be news if it returns from the
printer four weeks later. Smith found that it was much more common for house
journals to carry material on financial matters than on manpower and industrial
relations issues.[29]

(b) NOTICE BOARDS

In some ways notice boards provide an extreme contrast to house journals, as they
are cheap and information can be revealed quickly, but the outreach of the information is less assured and it may not be retained by employees as they have
only their recollection on which to rely. It is not, therefore, a good medium for
statements of policy that have to be thought over and re-read, but is ideal for the
terse statement of facts that have to be announced widely and quickly: holiday
dates, new appointments, job vacancies, shift changes, short-time working, redundancy, visits by customers and so on.

The difficulties with notice boards are usually irritatingly trivial. First the tendancy
to over-crowding, mostly with notices that are out of date. This is best overcome by
putting two dates on each notice: the date it is going up and the date it is to come
down. Another difficulty is illegibility. Even though photo-copying is more expensive
than carbon, it is infinitely more likely to be read, especially when the reader is
standing several feet further away from the announcement than is usual with type-
written material. Various ploys, like different coloured headings for notices of
different types, cartoon characters in the corners etc., can help to arrest attention,
but the main thing is a simple administrative drill to ensure that the notice boards
remain 'live', so that important notices do not appear half buried by various pieces
of recent history due to the fact that there were no drawing pins available at the
time the vital statement was to be put up.

(c) WRITTEN COMMUNICATIONS DIRECT TO INDIVIDUALS

Sending duplicated messages direct to the individual employees may seem to overcome the disadvantages of house journals and notice boards as the coverage is
guaranteed, distribution can be quick and the communication can be retained for
further reflection. It is not usually appropriate to include it in a wage packet, as the
employee expects nothing in that which does not relate to his income and may
reject any other information for that reason.

(d) BRIEFING GROUPS

Briefing groups are a simple idea in communications that have been advocated
enthusiastically by the Industrial Society. The principle is that each manager has
regular short meetings with the members of the working group for which he is

responsible to brief them on management policies or recent decisions. It is custom-arily a consecutive process, with senior managers briefing middle managers, who then brief junior managers, who brief foremen and supervisors, who brief everyone else. The CIR suggest the following advantages of briefing groups:[30]

(i) it requires a company to identify individual managers' responsibilities for communicating and explaining information to employees;

(ii) it can be a means of disseminating information accurately and rapidly using normal operational channels, e.g. senior manager to managers, managers to supervisors, supervisors to work groups;

(iii) because it makes use of the face-to-face method questions can be asked by employees and answered by a manager who is fully briefed;

(iv) it provides the opportunity for the manager to regard himself and be regarded by his work groups as someone who has access to and communicates reliable information.

This is the first of the methods considered so far that provides for some degree of response from the employee, but it is still limited to asking questions about what the management thinks is important and which the particular management communi-cator is able to answer.

(e) GENERAL MEETINGS OF EMPLOYEES

On special occasions it can be useful to hold general meetings with all the employees, usually in the canteen. The cost in lost production may be considerable, but there is the opportunity for face-to-face contact with a top manager, so that employees can have the satisfaction of feeling that they are getting to the fountainhead and can raise more fundamental questions than are possible with someone who is simply passing on messages. However, coping with a mass meeting is a most difficult task at which few people have either skill or experience. Briefing groups are much easier.

(f) SPECIAL REPORTS

When there is a special development falling outside the normal cycle of company affairs, there will be an unusual need for communication, explanation and the anticipation of questions in order to win the appropriate response from employees. Such incidents include the attitude of the directors to a proposed takeover, the introduction of fundamentally new methods or models, palace revolutions and the like. In such a situation the special report can be a useful addition to the normal communications battery. The *special* nature of the incident calls for *special* treat-ment in the report as the employees will not have evolved sufficient familiarity with the topic to be able to take in new information without detailed exposition. Little can be taken for granted and the special report is likely to invoke clever visual presentation of financial information, like pie charts and notional allocations of the one hundred pence in every pound of sales income, as well as descriptive statements to give a perspective to figures ('last year our gas bill was the same as the combined gas bill for all the private households in Solihull'). Often special reports are the basis of a general meeting of employees.

(g) JOINT CONSULTATION

While bargaining is a way of reaching agreement and making decisions, joint consultation is a means of communicating prior to decisions being made or explaining the reasons for certain decisions after they have been made. In essence it is a regular meeting of a joint committee at which matters of common interest are discussed. It has lost favour as a practice because employee representatives feel that it is a poor substitute for negotiation as it is not a process of making decisions, merely representations. Managers tend to grow weary of it as they feel they are constantly fending off complaints about the lack of toilet paper or the cost of tea in the canteen.

Whilst joint consultation may be no substitute for negotiation, it can be a useful addition to it in a communications system. It provides the benefit of relatively small numbers like those in briefing groups as well as the usual attendance of key executives and employee representatives who can engage in authoritative discussion. Joint consultative procedures do, however, need constant attention and commitment by those involved to ensure that the agenda is always live, the discussion meaningful and the results visible.

(g) THE COMMUNICATIONS STRUCTURE ITSELF

With all the range of *methods* that are available for consideration, we must not overlook the crucial importance of *structure*. The above account of briefing groups took for granted that the organisation structure would require no more than three consecutive steps in communication for everybody to be reached. Long attenuated lines of communication are as disastrous for managers and shop stewards as they were for Napoleon trying to reach Moscow.

For most management/employee communications the centralised type of system is clearly the best as it enables accuracy and speed to be optimised; it defines roles and strengthens leadership. To many managers the criticism offered by Leavitt may be seen as a further benefit:

> Highly centralised groups may often be used for their consistency with general organisational designs, their speed, and their controllability; but they are also used as psychological defence devices to protect superiors' weaknesses from being exposed to subordinates and vice versa.[31]

Only the most naive still believe that information only passes through the formal overt structure of the organisation; there is a complex sub-structure of informal communications networks that will be of varying importance in supplementing that which is heard officially. In some situations – like national government – it appears that there is extensive use of informal communications, 'leaks', hypothetical questions, whispers, nods and winks as a process almost of consultation prior to making an *ex cathedra* statement. In other situations such preliminary disclosure is viewed with the gravest concern. If the management of an organisation provides little information members of that organisation will seek more assiduously the opinion of those *savants* whose organisational position often makes them privy to reliable information without the burden of having to keep it to themselves: chauffeurs, tea ladies and commissionaires being typical sources of news *from* the management, while work study engineers, personnel officers and quality assurance staff are among the better sources of information *for* the management.

6. Communication in General

Although we have centred our discussion in this chapter on disclosure of information and the methods of information, we would ask the reader to take note of the section in Chapter 29 that deals with barriers to communications and the tele-communications analogy. Those principles are just as important in written communications as in face-to-face situations.

We would also remind readers of the important place of face-to-face communication as compared with the written word. The 1972 Code of Practice described it as 'the most important' form of communication.

We have already referred to the problem of house journals having to compete with other writings for the attention of the reader. All management attempts to communicate with employees have to compete with other material for their attention. During the working day there will be a plethora of communications inputs to the employee — instructions, routine advices on pay etc., interaction with his colleagues, and many more — so that there is a narrow bandwidth available for the management to use for material that is persuasive, placatory or exhortative. Not only do the management need to present their material with the maximum of skill and judgement, they also need to consider carefully *what* it communicates. If the words from the senior management are all about darts matches, pension schemes, canteen organisation and the iniquity of the government, then the employee will conclude that that is what the management are interested in, rather than in jobs and work and work organisation, because they hear about that from the foreman, who is organisationally so inferior to (in Tom Lupton's phrase) 'that disorganised mess up there' which is the top management and the location of real power.

SUMMARY PROPOSITIONS

30.1. Industrial relations, and employee attitudes and behaviour generally, will benefit from the provision of information and the development of understanding of such information.

30.2. Information provision will be valued when subject to a minimum of restriction, with reasons for any restriction carefully considered and explained by management.

30.3. The method of transmitting information should be selected and designed according to the message, knowledge of problems of communication, and the particular context.

REFERENCES

1. *Report of the Committee of Inquiry on Industrial Democracy* (HMSO) 1977, p. 42.
2. *The Disclosure of Financial Information to Employees* (British Institute of Management) 1957.
3. *Positive Employment Policies* (Ministry of Labour) 1958.
4. *Employee Attitudes and Understanding* (Confederation of British Industry), 1976, p. 8.
5. *The Provision of Information to Employees: Guidelines for Action* (Confederation of British Industry), 1975, p. 6.

6. Smith R., 'Disclosure of Information: Can Britain Learn from Belgium' in *Personnel Management,* July 1977, p. 24.
7. Robertson E.J., 'Disclosure of Information — A Management View' in Kessler S. and Weekes B., *Conflict at Work* (BBC) 1971, p. 105.
8. Commission on Industrial Relations, *Disclosure of Information,* Report No. 31 (HMSO) 1972, pp. 31—33.
9. *Ibid.,* p. 25.
10. Marsh A. and Rosewall R., 'A Question of Disclosure' in *Industrial Relations Journal,* Summer 1976, pp. 10—15.
11. Marsh A. and Hussey R. (eds.), *Employees, Trade Unions and Company Information* (Touche Ross & Co.) 1981.
12. Department of Employment, *In Place of Strife: a Policy of Industrial Relations,* (HMSO) 1969, p. 48.
13. *Disclosure of Information, op. cit.*
14. Employment Protection Act 1975, section 17, p. 14.
15. *Ibid.* section 18 (1), p. 15.
16. Advisory Conciliation and Arbitration Service, Code of Practice 2, *Disclosure of Information to Trade Unions for Collective Bargaining Purposes* (HMSO) 1977.
17. *Ibid.,* pp. 3 and 4.
18. *Ibid.,* p. 4.
19. *National Union of General and Municipal Workers, Amalgamated Union of Engineering Workers, and Transport and General Workers Union v. BL Cars,* 1980.
20. For instance, *British Aerospace Dynamics Group v. APEX,* 1980; and *BTP Tioxide Ltd v. ASTMS,* 1980.
21. Smith R., *Keeping Employees Informed: Current U.K. Practice on Disclosure,* BIM Management Survey Report No. 31 (British Institute of Management) 1975.
22. *Ibid.,* p. 7.
23. Dickens L., 'What are Companies Disclosing for the 1980s?' in *Personnel Management,* April 1980.
24. Accounting Standards Steering Committee, *The Corporate Report* (Institute of Chartered Accountants in England and Wales) 1975, p. 1.
25. Department of Trade, *Inflation Accounting,* Report of the Inflation Accounting Committee, (HMSO) 1975, pp. 51—52.
26. Smith R., *Keeping Employees Informed, op. cit.,* p. 16.
27. *Ibid.,* p. 13.
28. *The Provision of Information to Employees, op. cit.*
29. Smith R., *Keeping Employees Informed, op. cit.* p. 28.
30. Commission on Industrial Relations, *Communications and Collective Bargaining,* Report No. 39 (HMSO) 1973, p. 13.
31. Leavitt H.J., *Managerial Psychology,* 2nd ed. (University of Chicago) 1964, p. 241.

31

Hours of Work

In earlier sections of this book we have argued that attitudes to work are changing partly because of the decline in the proportion of their lives that people spend at work. The Hudson Institute predicted that we could look forward shortly to a thirty-hour week in a forty-week year. John Hughes has argued[1] the need to reduce the working week for manual workers to thirty-seven or thirty-eight hours in order to ease the serious unemployment among manual employees and the young.

In 1979 the TUC became part of an international trade union campaign seeking to reduce the amount of time people spent at work by ten per cent. This was to be achieved by moving to a 35 hour week, longer holidays and retirement at 60.

The first Lord Leverhulme began to campaign for the six-hour working day in 1917, having discovered that an earlier reduction from ten hours to eight had increased output by over forty per cent. Sixty years later nearly all manual men had a basic working week approaching forty hours, with up to ten hours a week overtime. 1979, however, was the time when the psychological barrier of the forty-hour week was broken and over six million manual workers had had their hours reduced below forty per week by 1982.

The 1970s have seen, for the first time in nearly fifty years, a sustained and serious increase in unemployment. This has been universally condemned and worried about, yet the only tangible result has been the creation of work by government subsidy of job creation schemes, temporary employment subsidies and some earlier retirement. The most obvious strategy of sharing the work out more evenly between the employed and the unemployed has been ignored.

The manifold reasons for this include the basic conservatism of manual employees and employers, the general sluggishness of the economy which makes dramatic change more difficult even though making it more necessary, the growing feeling among employers that the employment of manual workers, organised in trade unions and with growing legal rights, is more trouble than it is worth, increasing labour costs, and a declining interest in manufacturing. But whatever the reasons, one is led to question whether major reduction in the working week is likely to come at all, if it has not even begun during a time when it would appear so timely. Whether the working hours become shorter or not, we need to consider some of the issues that such a possible reduction would raise.

(a) CENTRALITY OF WORK

Most fundamental may be the extent to which the centrality of work as a life interest could be affected. Work can become a central life interest for a variety of reasons, but principally because of the financial dependence of the job holder on his employment, the intrinsic qualities of the job in providing the means towards self-fulfilment, and the proportion of waking hours that are spent doing it.

The move from the six-day week to the five-and-a-half and five-day week greatly increased the scope people had to extend and vary their interests. A four-day week could provide still greater opportunities and would have an effect on attitudes to employment as the job is just one among a growing number of activities.

(b) OVERTIME

The greatest immediate practical problem is the large proportion of costly overtime that is already extending the working week. The two standard investigations of overtime working have been those of the Royal Commission[2] in 1968 and the National Board for Prices and Incomes[3] in 1970. Both agreed that it was a firmly entrenched feature of the British industrial relations scene and had resisted all attempts to reduce it. We consider overtime working in more detail later in the chapter, but we note here that it presents a major problem to the reduction of the normal working week; employees will be apprehensive that their earnings may be impaired through losing some overtime and employers will be apprehensive that the cost of overtime will become even greater as a larger proportion of hours worked will be at premium rates.

(c) NON-MANUAL RESISTANCE

Another peculiarity of the British scene is the almost universal practice of non-manual employees working shorter standard weeks than manual employees. This does not happen in other countries, but there is a clear advantage for the British non-manual employee when compared to his manual counterpart. As this has represented a differential in their favour they may seek to maintain that gap.

(d) UNSOCIAL HOURS

If the length of the working week is to be shortened, where will the reduction be made? Between 1959 and 1966 standard working hours for manual workers came down in two steps from 44 to 40. In nearly every case the reduction was made by finishing work earlier on each of the five days, although some groups at that time, and a few more since, altered the pattern by concentrating all the gains into one time by finishing, for instance, at mid-day on Friday. If a further reduction were to be made on the same scale it is doubtful whether an earlier finishing time on each of five days would be generally acceptable, since this would be time that employees would feel to be little value to them.

Roberts and his colleagues have carried out an interesting survey of attitudes to the length of the working week among 474 economically active males in the area of Liverpool and found very little enthusiasm for shorter hours, but rather more interest in a pattern of working hours that is more convenient to the individual.[4] They suggest that manual employees in particular are much more likely to find the quality of their lives enhanced by better pay and more satisfying work than by a reduction of hours. They conclude with the comment:

> ... industry should think in terms of tidying up hours of work around the present norm by introducing greater flexibility and mitigating the long hours

expected of some white-collar workers, rather than preparing for a general slide towards a much shorter working week.[5]

(e) SHIFTS

One great attraction of the eight-hour day is its adaptability to shift-working situations, as three eight-hour shifts fit neatly into a twenty-four hour day. For those processes where continuous manning is required, the implications of a shorter normal week are considerable. On the other hand double-day shift working might become a much more attractive proposition if the shifts were 6 till 1 and 1 till 8, instead of the present 6 till 2 and 2 till 10, as the employee would still have the majority of the evening left for social activities and television watching. Shift working also provides opportunities for part-time workers, like the 6 till 10 shifts that are sometimes offered for part-time workers.

VARIATIONS IN THE WORKING WEEK

In the remainder of this chapter we look further at the variations in the working week that have been mentioned so far: shifts, flexible working hours, overtime and part-time working.

1. Shift Working

In the article by John Hughes already cited in this chapter, he argues for an extension of shiftworking as well as a reduced number of weekly hours:

> ... increased shift working can offer an early and sizeable increase in employment in relation to the existing capital stock ... The potential improvement in utilisation of the capital stock through shift work, as an almost immediate resource gain, contrasts with the lead time associated with meeting demand solely through increased fixed capital investment ...[6]

This neatly summarises the argument for introducing shiftwork where it has not previously been used. There are, however, situations where there is no alternative to working shifts or at least abnormal hours. In the continuous process industries like steel-making and glass manufacture, the need for employees to be in attendance at all hours is dictated by the impracticality of interrupting the manufacturing cycle. In other circumstances there is the overwhelming imperative of customer demand, so that commuter trains are used more out of normal working hours than within them, and morning newspapers have to be prepared in the middle of the night.

The operation of shifts carries an implicit assumption that it is unattractive to the individual employee: it carries a premium payment all of its own and recently the drafters of incomes policies have introduced the notion of special treatment for those who work 'unsocial hours'. Such a generalisation may make sound industrial relations sense, but is no more accurate a statement about individuals than the statement that gentlemen prefer blondes. Wedderburn gives examples of the range of reactions he discovered in interviewing 500 shiftworkers:

> One young couple work the same shift so that they can use their spare time together working on their old house; another couple work opposing shifts, so

that they can manage a handicapped child between them. One young father loves shiftwork because he sees more of his infant children; another feels he is losing contact with his time-locked school children. One can fish all day in uncrowded waters; another gave up fishing because weekend shiftwork meant that he missed crucial competitions. One foreman enjoys the total responsibility that shiftwork gives him; another fears that he has missed his chances of promotion, isolated on shiftwork.[7]

For most people the prospect of working shifts may well be appalling, but for a substantial minority it provides a welcome element of flexibility in the employment contract at a time in their lives when it is perhaps very conveneient for them to spend a period working unusual hours − for a higher rate of pay. A survey by the Labour Research Department found an upward trend in shiftworking and suggested that two and a half million British workers work shifts regularly.[8]

There are various patterns of working shifts, each of which brings with it a slightly different set of problems and opportunities.

(a) THE PART-TIMER SHIFT

Here a group of people are employed for a few hours daily at the beginning or end of normal working hours. The most common group are the office cleaners, who may work from 6.00 a.m. until 9.00 a.m. or for a similar period in the evening. Also there are some shifts for four or five hours in the evening to provide a small amount of extra output. Usually these shift-workers are married women, who welcome the hours because they fit in with their domestic routine. For this reason they are often known as 'housewives' shifts', even though this must be no more than a sobriquet.

The advantages to the employer are that he is making use of relatively small units of time that would be insufficient for a full-time employee, but he is getting more use out of his plant, whether it be manufacturing plant or the computer, and there is a reliable labour market as it is a very convenient working arrangement for a fairly large number of people. The snags are that the employees are permanently operating outside normal hours so they are never integrated into the main working community. Also those working such shifts are usually looking upon it as a temporary pattern of work, out of which they will move as soon as their circumstances change. Where the employer is seeking a short spell of additional work from people who require little training (either because the work is straightforward or because the skills − like computer card-punching − are generally available) the part-timer shift may be an ideal arrangement. It is less satisfactory as a permanent feature.

(b) THE PERMANENT NIGHT SHIFT

This is another arrangement which creates a special category of employee who is set apart (or cut off) from everyone else. He is working full-time, but has no contact with the rest of the organisation's members, who leave before he arrives and return after he has left. Apart from the specialised applications like national newspapers, this form is usually used either to undertake cleaning and maintenance of plant while it is idle or to increase output on a rather more permanent basis than can be achieved through part-timer shifts. A further development is to run a permanent night shift as a means of increasing output without disturbing the normal day pattern of the bulk of the employees.

The attraction of this arrangement is that it makes use of plant at times when it would otherwise be idle and, if it is used for maintenance, it avoids maintenance interrupting production. It also avoids the upheaval of the existing work force that would be involved by introducing double-day shifts.

The drawbacks can be considerable. As with part-timer shifts, employees are operating permanently outside normal working hours, and as they are full-time employees that may be even more serious than it is with part-timers. There is an inevitable 'apartheid' for the regular night worker, who is out of touch with the mainstream of union and company activities. A further problem is the provision of services, like catering, medical and routine personnel services. For the evening worker these are either unnecessary or can be provided relatively cheaply by a few daily employees working occasional overtime. For night workers the services are both more difficult to provide and more costly. Night working is the form that is likely to be most difficult for employees to sustain as most human beings are diurnal rather than nocturnal creatures. A small minority of employees seem genuinely to prefer working regular nights and to maintain this rhythm for their working lives over many years, but for most it will be undertaken either reluctantly or for relatively short periods. Sergean indicates some of the reasons why both employer and employee may shun regular nights:

> One sense in which night work can be regarded as less efficient is in terms of the increased demand which it makes upon the human organism. To speak of efficiency in this way does not mean that output will necessarily be lower at night, or that errors will be more frequent. But though night-time performance may be maintained at its day-time level, studies which have made use of various psycho-physiological tests and measures in shift situations — reaction time, oxygen consumption, energy expenditure, and so on — have shown that this is only achieved at the cost of increased fatigue among the shiftworkers concerned.[9]

(c) ALTERNATING DAY AND NIGHT SHIFTS

If night working is being used to increase output rather than for cleaning and maintenance, then alternation is another possibility. It mitigates many of the difficulties of regular night working, but does present the employee with the problem of regular, drastic changes in his daily rhythms. The surveys of both the NBPI[10] and the BIM[11] found that alternating day and night shifts were more widespread than permanent nights. In the NBPI survey shiftworkers on alternating days and nights outnumbered regular nightworkers by 6 to 1.

(d) DOUBLE-DAY SHIFT

This variant is surprisingly unpopular. In a Ministry of Labour survey in 1965 only 16.7 per cent of shiftworkers were working in this way.[12] In 1970 only 6.3 per cent of the shiftworkers questioned by NBPI were working double-day shifts.[13] This initially seems surprising as it is a pattern of working which involves the least disruption. Instead of working a normal day shift, employees work either 6 till 2 or 2 till 10. This means that plant is in use for sixteen hours, all employees are present for a large part of the 'normal' day, there is no night working and the rotation between the early and late shift enables a variety of leisure activities to be followed.

One of the reasons for resisting the method is that overtime is usually no longer possible, so that employees do not have that additional flexibility in their hours and earnings under their own control. Another problem is the fact that it may be the first experience of shifts for the bulk of employees, if it is introduced in place of a system of regular days or regular days and nights. There may also be difficulties about transport in the early morning and all the inconvenience of eating at unfamiliar times.

(e) THREE-SHIFT WORKING

This represents a further development and the most widespread pattern: 6 till 2, 2 till 10 and 10 till 6. The twenty-four-hour cycle is covered so that there is continuous operation. There is a further subdivision: *discontinuous* three-shift working is where the plant is running but stops for the week-end, and *continuous* shift-working is an extension into the week-end whereby the plant never stops. NBPI found slightly more people on continuous than discontinuous systems. Here we have the inescapable night shift and, with continuous working, the final loss of overtime and the sacrosanct week-end. If shifts are run on the traditional pattern of changing every week the shift workers have the unattractive feature of the 'dead fortnight' of two weeks when normal evening social activities are not possible because of late return home after a 2 till 10 shift or early departure for a 10 till 6 shift. The most common solution to this is to accelerate the rotation with a 'continental' shift pattern. Below is a typical arrangement for a four-week cycle of four shifts:[14]

Week 1	Week 2	Week 3	Week 4		
M T W T F S S	*M T W T F S S*	*M T W T F S S*	*M T W T F S S*		
A A B B C C C	D D A A B B B	C C D D A A A	B B C C D D D	6 a.m.	— 2 p.m.
D D A A B B B	C C D D A A A	B B C C D D D	A A B B C C C	2 p.m.	— 10 p.m.
C C D D A A A	B B C C D D D	D D A A B B B	C C D D A A A	10 p.m.	— 6 a.m.

Reductions in the number of hours in the basic working week have induced a range of variations in shiftworking pattern that were not necessary until the forty-hour barrier was broken. Useful examples of such variations have been described by IDS.[15]

2. Flexible Working Hours

The most recent aspect of working hours we consider is one that is very simple and so obvious that it is surprising that it was not thought of earlier and that it has not been adopted even more widely. Flexible working hours can be defined as:

> ... an arrangement whereby, within set limits, employees may begin and end work at times of their own choice, provided that they are all present at certain 'core-time' periods of the day and that, within a 'settlement period' — usually a week or a month — they work the total number of hours agreed. Not surprisingly, there are wide variations in the degree of flexibility different schemes allow.[16]

The first formal scheme of this type was introduced in Western Germany in 1967 and the practice has grown rapidly there and in other European countries, especially Switzerland. The idea was first tried in Britain in 1971 and is widely used, but still only by a minority of organisations. By the beginning of 1974 Sloane estimated that 100,000 employees in 500 organisations were affected.[17]

A typical arrangement is where the organisation abandons a fixed starting and finishing time for the working day. Instead employees start work at a predetermined time in the period between 8.00 a.m. and 10.00 a.m. and finish between 4.00 p.m. and 6.00 p.m. They are obliged to be present during the *core time* of 10 till 4, but can use the *flexible time* at the beginning and end of the working day to produce a pattern of working hours that fits in with their personal needs and preferences. The main advantage of this scheme is that it enables people to avoid peak travel times and the awkward rigidity of the inflexible starting time. From the organisation's point of view it can eliminate the tendency towards a frozen period at the beginning and end of the day when nothing happens — for the first twenty minutes everyone is looking at the paper or putting on make-up and for the last twenty minutes everyone is preparing to go home. If the process of individual start-up and slow-down is spread over a longer period the organisation is operational for longer.

The scheme described above assumes that the necessary number of hours will be worked each day. The variations on the theme increase flexibility by allowing a longer *settlement period*, so that the employee can work varying lengths of time on different days, provided that he completes the quota appropriate for the week or month or whatever other settlement period is agreed. This means that someone can take a half day off for shopping or a full day off for a long week-end in the country as long as the quota is made up within a prescribed period.

As most organisations depend on a high degree on interaction between individual staff members for their operations to be viable, people are required all to be in attendance for the core time period of the day when the organisation is fully manned, although this is waived in schemes where people are allowed to take half or whole days off. A further control is on the *bandwidth*, which is the time between the earliest feasible starting time and the latest possible finishing time. If this becomes too great the working day attenuates in a rather costly way.

Reactions to the schemes from employers and employees have generally been favourable. Employers feel that the arrangement creates a more satisfactory working atmosphere with heightened morale:

> Flexible working hours raise morale and job satisfaction, create a better working climate, all but eliminate time lost through lateness and the need for petty discipline this can entail, and lead to a greater degree of self-regulation and responsibility on the part of employees, with work started more quickly on arrival and jobs in hand more often finished before departure.[18]

Many, but not all, employers believe that flexible working hours increase productivity. The studies of employee reaction to flexible working hours show a widespread feeling that working conditions significantly improved with the introduction of the scheme, with hardly any respondents being willing to return to inflexible hours.[19] One feature of flexible hours which is often resented by employees is the way in which their *attendance is registered,* as there has been a tendency to reintroduce time clocks or the more sophisticated elapsed time recorders as a way of controlling the attendance of the individual. Whilst it is conventional for employees to 'fight' mechanical time recording because of its rigidity, there is also the feeling that it is at least fair. There can be no suspicion that some people are not putting in their full complement of hours, nor that some have bluer eyes than others.

In many areas of white-collar employment time-keeping is a matter of mutual trust rather than control. In this type of situation there might be strong resistance to mechanical time recording, largely because the motives for its introduction would be suspect. Management will also have reservations about installing expensive time-recording equipment that has not previously been necessary.

Trade union response to flexibility of working hours has been guarded. It has been cautiously welcomed where no disadvantage can be perceived, but there has been some concern about the possibility that earnings could drop in some establish-ments due to a loss of overtime and feeling that the collective sense of the employees is weakened because they are making their own individual arrangement with the employer.

The most detailed and extensive evaluation has been carried out in various parts of the public sector of employment,[20] and one of the studies found the following results from a questionnaire asking the employees to state the main advantage of flexible hours:

		Percentage of staff
a)	The ability to adjust lunch breaks	73
b)	The ability to finish earlier	69
c)	A better balance between work and domestic commitments	62
d)	The ability to build up a half-day off	55
e)	Better travel	45

There is little doubt that the number of employees working flexible hours is now substantially greater than the 100,000 estimated in 1974.

3. Overtime

Working overtime has proved to be a resilient practice, with over half male manual employees working overtime regularly and, in 1980, receiving an average of 10.1 hours a week. Including those who do not work overtime we find that the average actual hours worked by full-time manual working males was 45.4 in 1980, compared with 45.7 in 1977 and 47.9 in 1953. The basic hours in each year were 39.7, 39.9 and 44.4.[21]

When the Prices and Incomes Board examined the reasons for overtime being worked in 1970 they found the following spread of reasons given in the returns from establishments:[22]

	Percentage
To meet normal level of demand	51.0
Occasional peaks in demand or emergencies	45.8
Shortage of labour	32.3
Less costly than recruiting extra labour	11.4
Technological process or type of service to customer	13.6
To increase pay	23.8
Others	8.9

The three most popular of those reasons are much more difficult to justify at a time when relatively high unemployment has replaced full employment and there is a world-wide trade recession. The next most popular reason, of needing to increase pay, might well be more significant at a time of general incomes restraint. It seems likely, however, that by far the most important reason is not mentioned, and that is the attempt by the employee to exercise greater control over his own work.

Working overtime is nearly always a decision which the employee is free to make or not make each time the overtime possibility occurs. Seldom can the employer decree. If the total time spent working in a week includes an element that the em-ployee provides or withholds at will, he then acquires an actual degree of control of how much time he works and how much he earns that is variable according to his own decision. He also acquires a degree of influence over what happens in normal hours as well, as he has something to bargain with in dealings with his employer.

The day-by-day mediation of overtime working is yet another of those means towards mutual control between the individual and the representative of the organisation that we have considered throughout this volume. Because of the uncertainty about labour costs that uncontrolled voluntary overtime involves, employers frequently seek to reduce or control it. Rarely is it possible to do this by the means that is, *prima facie,* the most obvious, namely by not asking people to work overtime. There is then a strong employee reaction, normal-hours productivity slumps, manifold problems occur and the only solution is to re-introduce overtime.

Overtime can be more effectively reduced or eliminated through negotiation. One way is to negotiate the introduction of continuous shift-working, which virtually eliminates most overtime possibilities, since one man's overtime becomes another man's normal time. The other method is to 'buy out' overtime by negotiating a higher rate for normal hours and banning overtime in exchange. This method became quite popular in the productivity bargaining era of 1966 onwards, but any employer contemplating such an initiative needs to remember that he is not simply providing *compensation* for lost overtime earnings: he is also removing the element of control in the hands of the employee that overtime represents. Furthermore he may find it difficult to have his cake and eat it. If overtime is eliminated, the potential flexibility in manning that it represents for the employer is eliminated as well.

In these last few pages we have been considering overtime as a problem. This is not the only view. It may be a useful element in the local industrial relations climate to reinforce the degree of employee autonomy that it provides, and in many situations overtime is not the difficulty that we have implied; it remains a useful way of overcoming short-time bottlenecks and crises of demand.

It was the view of the Prices and Incomes Board that consistent high overtime was in itself a warning that resources might be being wasted, making remedial action appropriate. They suggested a series of check questions on which it is difficult to improve:[23]

1. Does management collect regular data about how much overtime is worked, by what sections, occupational groups or departments, and for what purposes?
2. Is substantial overtime regularly worked by any section, occupational group or department and if so why?
3. Does management have relevant indices of performance of work or work standards which enable it to tell whether manpower and other resources are being used effectively?
4. How much scope is there for raising productivity by means of improved methods, changes in working practices, better manpower planning, the provision of better incentives and so on?
5. Do the answers to the previous questions reveal that there is substantial regular overtime combined with considerable scope for improving efficiency?
6. If so, what should be done? In particular:
   a) to what extent is it possible to secure higher efficiency simply by exercising greater care in the use of overtime?
   b) can hourly productivity be raised to satisfactory levels by negotiating the introduction (or revision) of work-studied incentive payment schemes?

c) is an appraisal of the possibility of shiftwork desirable?

d) is it desirable to negotiate a comprehensive agreement embracing hours, pay and improved methods of working practices?

7. What new controls, including arrangements for joint scrutiny of hours of work, will be desirable to ensure that satisfactory levels of efficiency once achieved are maintained?

4. Part-time Working

The fourth variant on the hours of work theme is part-time working. More than four million members of the working population are employed on this basis and working for less than thirty hours a week:

| | Males (June 1976) | | Females (June 1976) | |
	number	percentage	number	percentage
Full-time	12,673,000	94.6	5,506,000	60.2
Part-time	714,000	5.4	3,646,000	39.8

With one worker out of every five being part-time it is obviously a mode of employment that is of importance to consider, and it is tending to become more important as in 1971 only one worker out of seven was part-time.

One difficult question is 'what is part-time?'. The figures quoted above relate to those working less than *thirty* hours a week, yet an important feature of the Employment Protection Act was to confer the legal status of full-time work on all those who work more than *sixteen* hours a week. For many practical purposes the answer to our question is that anyone who works less than the normal hours is a part-timer, but for legal purposes it is only the person working less than sixteen hours a week who does not have the same employment *rights* as his full-time counterpart. For this reason it is unrealistic to regard part-time employees as second-class citizens in comparison with full-time employees. They cannot necessarily be used (some would use the word 'exploited') simply as a convenience to deal with short-term problems or jobs that others will not tackle, if such use means regarding them as having no entitlement to those other benefits of employment apart from salary that full-time workers enjoy. Part-time workers acquire entitlement to holidays and holiday pay, sickness pay, maternity rights, pension contributions and so forth if they are employed for more than sixteen hours a week.

Part-timing is predominantly a female occupation, because so many women either wish to work only part-time or because their share of domestic responsibilities only allows them to work in this way. Many of them will be working short shifts, as we have described already, and sometimes two will share a full working day between them. Others will be in positions for which only a few hours within the normal day are required or a few hours at particular times of the week. Retailing is an occupation that has considerable scope for the part-timer, as there is obviously a greater need for counter personnel on Saturday mornings than on Monday mornings. Also many shops are now open for longer periods than would be normal hours for a full-time employee, so that the part-timer helps to fill the gaps and provide the extra manning at peak periods. Catering is another example, as are market research interviewing, office cleaning, typing, and some posts in education.

A specialised form of part-time work is that which is a form of overtime, in which a person works extra time for a second employer in order to increase his earnings. Known as *moonlighting*, this is perhaps more common among men than women and includes such jobs as taxi-driving and bartending as well as the more specialised tasks like dealing with other people's income tax claims. The second employer gains considerable benefit, as he is obtaining the services of perhaps a skilled and experienced employee without having to invest in that person's training or future career. The man who drives a fire engine during the week and a coach at the week-end is an example.

REFERENCES

1. Hughes J., 'Shiftwork and the Shorter Working Week: Two Ways to Make Jobs', *Personnel Management*, May 1977, pp. 18–20.
2. Whybrew E.G., *Overtime Working in Britain*, Royal Commission on Trade Unions and Employers' Associations, Research Paper No. 9 (HMSO) 1968.
3. National Board for Prices and Incomes, *Hours of Work, Overtime and Shiftworking*, Report No. 161 (HMSO) 1970.
4. Roberts K., Clark S., Cook F.G. and Semeonoff E., 'How Many Hours in a Week?' *Personnel Management*, June 1974, pp. 33–41.
5. *Ibid.*, p. 41.
6. Hughes J., *op. cit.*, p. 19.
7. Wedderburn A., 'Waking up to Shiftwork', *Personnel Management*, February 1975, p. 32.
8. *Bargaining Report 19* (Labour Research Dept.) 1982.
9. Sergean R., 'Shiftwork', chapter in Torrington D. (ed.) *Handbook of Industrial Relations* (Gower Press) 1972, p. 187.
10. National Board for Prices and Incomes, *op. cit.*, p. 201.
11. British Institute of Management, *Shift Work*, Information Summary 119, (BIM) 1969, p. 2.
12. *Ministry of Labour Gazette*, April 1965.
13. National Board for Prices and Incomes, *op. cit.*, p. 201.
14. *Ibid.*, p. 3.
15. IDS Study 244, *Implementing a Shorter Working Week* (Incomes Data Services), June 1981.
16. Sloane P.J., *Changing Patterns of Working Hours*, Department of Employment Manpower Paper No. 13, (HMSO) 1975, p. 3.
17. *Ibid.*, p. 9.
18. *Ibid.*, p. 11.
19. *Ibid.*, p. 13.
20. Drye E.S., 'Flexible Hours in DHSS Local Offices' in *Management Services in Government*, February 1975. This article is summarised in IDS Brief No. 119, *Flexible Working Hours* (Incomes Data Services Ltd) April 1976.
21. Details from Kinchin Smith M. and Palmer S. 'Getting to the Bottom of Overtime' in *Personnel Management*, February 1981.
22. Department of Employment, *Employment Gazette* (HMSO) December 1977.
23. National Board for Prices and Incomes, *op. cit.*, (Supplement) p. 155.
    Ibid., pp. 52–3.

32

Manpower Planning and Personnel Records

For many years the question of personnel records has suffered from the clerical chore syndrome. Following the most famous of all the many criticisms of personnel by Peter Drucker, '. . . partly a file clerk's job, partly a housekeeping job . . .', personnel people have tried to play down their record-keeping function and emphasise other aspects. In 1968 Mumford and Ward included the comment about personnel management in Britain:

> In too many firms it is still restricted, to record-keeping and personnel procedures such as recruitment, plus odd jobs which line management finds it convenient to hand over to someone else.[1]

What seemed to be missing was any imaginative appreciation of the use to which records could be put, particularly with the development of the sophisticated methods of information storage and analysis presented by the computer. Mumford and Ward paid close attention to the role of the personnel manager in firms introducing their first computers:

> The picture proved to be a depressing one. In many firms the personnel manager played no part whatsoever in the change process, other than recruiting new specialist staff on the instructions of the computer group. Often he sat within the four walls of his office apparently quite oblivious to the stresses and difficulties that were occurring outside. He did not seem to perceive that he had any part to play in the new developments. Even more depressing was the fact that other management did not think he had any role either. They did not expect him to involve himself in the human relations problems of change . . .[2]

Although the general status of the personnel function has risen so much in the period since those words were written, it is not so certain that personnel specialists are making full use of the information systems and the computer facilities that are offered by this new technology. There is still a resistance to what appears mechanical and anti-human.

There is, however, a growing need for *manpower information* as the cost of employment increases and the demands on employees become more varied, and this information has to begin with personnel records. The age profile of the organisation, the supply of people with degrees in chemistry or qualified to train in first aid, the numbers in different categories, and countless other pieces of information that will be needed by the management of the organisation to decide future possibilities and constraints, all start from the records of individuals.

Stemming from this is a need for *personnel information*. That is the data about individual members of the organisation that is needed by members of management in developing the available human resources for the future. Here we have to find the answers to questions about the career development of individuals, recurring appraisal of performance and potential, discipline, management succession, pension entitlement, redundancy liability and so on.

It is not only the management of the organisation that require data about employees. Employees themselves require access to *personal information*. A reference to be written for a building society or a prospective employer will be based on the record of the individual held in the organisation, and he will frequently seek information about his sick leave entitlement, days of holiday remaining and much more.

Wille has lamented the small extent to which data is regarded as a fundamental corporate resource:

> Knowledge is power; information is the first step to knowledge; data is the raw material out of which a computer system can provide information.[3]

Much of the knowledge necessary for personnel specialists is derived from their records, which must be relevant, up-to-date, and — perhaps sadly — ever more detailed. This raises a problem that has only recently begun to cause interest: *privacy*. After the initial concern of individuals about the way in which their ability to enter into commercial contracts was threatened by the data banks held by credit companies, there has come a concern about the potential threat to employees of the information held about them in company files which might be inaccurate, might be seen by people who should not see it, or might be used in a context for which it was not collected.

In this chapter we set out to provide the framework of a record system that will meet the needs of manpower, personnel and personal information as described above, and we also consider the question of how such information can be stored and used without threatening the privacy of those about whom the information has been collected.

There are at least three publications which suggest possible headings under which information might be recorded. ACAS[4] suggest a range of typical forms that could be used, and this is probably the most helpful reading for those concerned with a record system that is to be manually maintained. Wille[5] and Pettman and Tavernier[6] provide very detailed lists which would be more appropriate where records are computerised, and some of which — like 'Date of death of disabled child, day, month, year' — may seem to be taking record-keeping to an extreme.

Having examined a number of information systems we feel that there are basically two types of information to be kept. The *personnel record* of the individual is the general account of the man. Largely compiled during the process of his selecting, and being selected for, employment in the organisation, it is periodically up-dated to make the account more comprehensive and is a permanent record. Alongside is the *current employment register* of the employee. This is a day-by-day register of incidents, like changes in rate of pay, holiday entitlement and others, which do not form a part of the permanent record, but which are needed for short periods, either for monitoring working performance — like disciplinary warnings — or as a preliminary to the aggregation of manpower information — like the number of hours overtime worked.

It is not easy to make a clear distinction between the two, but we would regard it as important to maintain permanently a record of an employee's education through school and university, because this helps to understand the pattern of experiences that make him what he is at forty or sixty. In contrast the record of holiday entitlement in one year is valueless the year after. The separation into personnel record and current employment register helps to avoid the accumulation of excessive, irrelevant data.

The Personnel Record

The initial personnel dossier is put together in three stages of the mutual selection process. First there is the pre-employment phase during which a job description and personnel specification are prepared and an advertisement placed. Although used for selection this is also information for the record in order to help with later decisions. If an employee is being considered for a new post after a period of service it can be helpful to have available an account of what has been involved in the job he currently holds as well as the qualities that were deemed necessary for the appointment. The content and placing of the advertisement can be used to analyse the effectiveness of various recruitment methods.

The second stage is where the employee writes his own information in answer to the standard questions provided by the application form and thereby provides the core of his permanent record — the information about him to which reference will most frequently be made. This consists of personal details, educational record and working experience. The term 'personal details' is the one that provides the problems. This is where applicants feel they are being discriminated against because they are being asked to provide information that will damn them in the eyes of the selectors, or they feel that the information being sought is unreasonably inquisitive. Relatively straightforward are:

> Surname and initials
> First names
> Address and telephone number
> Nationality
> Date of birth
> Sex
> Bank

More doubtful are:

> Marital status
> Number of children
> Place of birth
> Whether a registered disabled person
> Trade union membership
> Next of kin
> Religion

Thirdly come those additional pieces of information that stem from the selection process and would be added within the personnel function when the appointment was confirmed. The results of any tests that formed part of the selection procedure can be included for future reference, as can the reasoning that led to the employee being offered employment. There would also be his contract of employment or its salient points for reference in any case of dispute over its terms. A note of trade union membership could now be added, when there is less likelihood of such inquiry being seen as threatening, and the necessary details of doctor, next of kin and national insurance number can be incorporated, as they will no longer seem irrelevant.

Much of this information will not alter through the individual's employment and will remain relevant, even though the significance of some of it will wane. The remainder will require regular amendment during what we can call the career development phase. As the career develops we need to record first changes in the personal details, like address, and secondly the changes in the person's capacity and potential. Any decisions that have to be made about the individual's employment can then be made in the light of up-to-date information about him. Much of this will simply be recording changes, as in the terms of the contract and the nature of jobs undertaken, but the educational record is also extended by recording additional skills or qualifications obtained during the employment, and the selection decision has a broadening by the addition of the results from performance appraisal.

The Current Employment Register

The more transitory part of the dossier has two sections. The first is employment incidents, where a note would be kept of all those features of the individual's employment that are *important for the time being* for routine administrative reasons or to provide manpower information. The main categories are notes of sickness and absence, possibly with the addition of lateness and accidents. This will be needed to determine entitlements and for management control of individual reliability. Disciplinary incidents, especially warnings, have to be recorded very carefully and some organisations record grievances as well. Days of holiday remaining is another category and there is often a brief note made under the heading 'medical'. Care is needed here to avoid the risk of recording confidential medical information about an employee in a set of records to which non-medical people have access. This verges on the problem of duplication which is mentioned later in this chapter, but there is a proper and necessary place for simple medical facts like recording the ailment that caused six weeks' absence. For some personnel there will be a note of what sort of entitlement there is to a company car or what arrangement is made for defraying the cost of private telephone bills, and finally a note of the reason for leaving is a useful fragment for analysis as manpower information. If the organisation is one in which it is common for ex-employees to be re-engaged, then the reason for leaving would be better located in the personnel record which will be kept and reopened when the person rejoins.

The second section of the current employment register contains all the particulars relating to payment. As with medical information — although for different reasons — there is the likelihood of duplication. Almost invariably there is a salaries and wages department, separate from personnel, which will keep considerable payroll detail, like tax codes and deductions, that would be superfluous to all but the most obsessive personnel specialists. Also some of the information, like an attachment of earnings order, might be such that the employee wishes it to be concealed

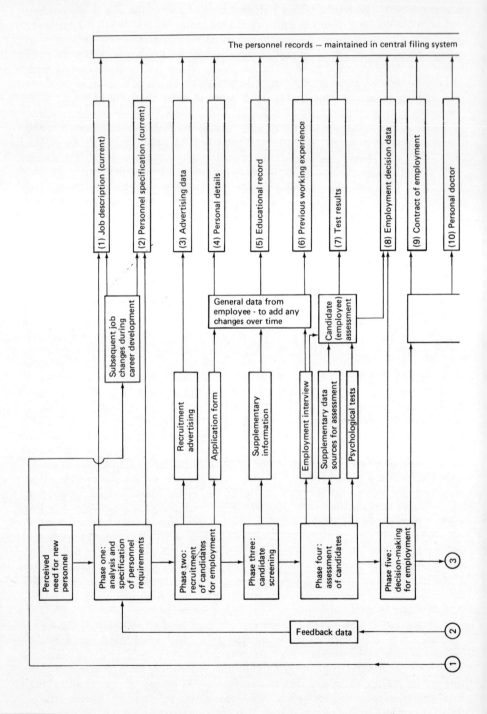

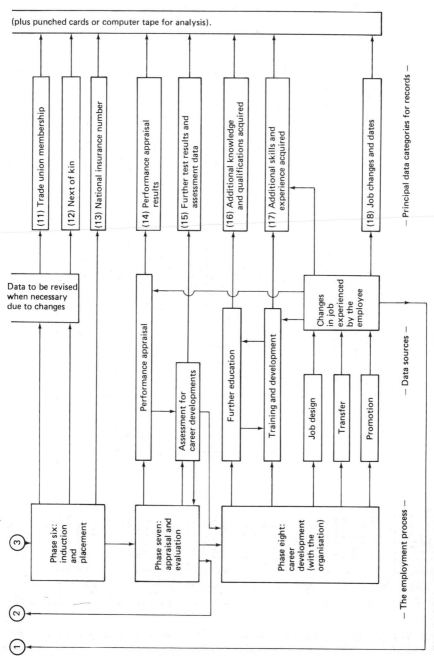

Figure 32.1. A systematic approach to compilation of personnel records

from career-influencing people in personnel. The necessary details seem to be job evaluated grade, salary scale, current rate of pay, any incentive or bonus entitlement, overtime and shift premia, pension status and a copy of the itemised pay statement. All this could have a bearing on considerations about possible promotion, grievances and some manpower information, although most manpower information is likely to be derived from the salaries and wages department direct.

Personnel and personal information would be taken directly from the personnel record or the current employment register, and various items in each document would be used for the collection of manpower information that is always collective rather than individual. Figures 32.1 and 32.2 represent the two types of document.

Maintaining the Records

Just as the personnel record is largely compiled during the mutual selection process, the information can mostly be recorded on the application form, with some of it — like items 1, 2 and 3 — being notes referring the inquirer to a reference source of the information needed. Although much of the data may be transferred later to punched cards or computer tape, it has to exist as a primary source on paper in plain language. The expansion of the record during career development can be either alteration of the information on the application form or the attachment of additional documents, like contracts of employment. In some circumstances the additional documents will not be appended, but noted as a reference to another file or department.

As the current employment register is of information that soon becomes expendable, it is impracticable for it to be recorded on an appendix to the application form, and loose-leaf ledger sheets, index cards or punched cards are more common.

In many organisations all the information will be recorded manually only, but for any organisation with more than a few hundred employees such methods become laborious to maintain and slow to analyse, and even for smaller companies the cost of manual record-keeping may be prohibitive.

The first step towards mechanising the procedure is to use punched cards, which make it possible to analyse information stored on cards very much quicker than by simple manual systems. Each record card in a bank has a series of holes punched at the edge at differing points according to the information recorded. If, for instance, an employee is male hole number one might be punched and, if female, hole number two would be punched. Other punches could be for day-worker, shift-worker, skilled, unskilled and so forth. The deck of cards can then be sorted in to a large number of categories. A rod or bodkin is pushed through the unskilled hole and extracts the cards for all those in that category, so one can quickly sort a number of different categories. A drawback is that once a hole becomes obsolete, as when an unskilled employee becomes semi-skilled, it cannot be crossed out, so that a new card is required even though only one piece of information has altered.

The further step in mechanising record-keeping is to computerise. Pettman and Tavernier describe some of the advantages:

> ... the principal immediate benefit of the computer is its ability to process vast quantities of data quickly. Tabulation speeds are currently in excess of ten lines a second; this means that lengthy lists of personnel with a wide range of relevant data can be printed out in minutes. The sequence in which the data is printed

			Manpower information				
Individual personnel record and current employment register \\ Collective personnel data and records			Absence / Sickness / Turnover	Recruitment effectiveness / Reasons for leaving / Redundancy & retirement provision	Age distribution / Safety and health / Numbers in grades	Skills & experience stock / Qualifications stock / Succession planning / Training needs	Labour cost analysis / Salary review / Grade drift
The personnel record	Job	(1) Job description (current)					
		(2) Personnel specification (current)					
		(3) Advertising data		•			
	General	(4) Personal details		•	• •	•	
		(5) Educational records				• •	
		(6) Previous working experience				•	
		(7) Test results				•	
		(8) Employment decision data		•		•	
		(9) Contract of employment					•
		(10) Personal doctor			•		
		(11) Trade union membership					
		(12) Next of kin					
		(13) National insurance number					
	Progress	(14) Performance appraisal results				• •	•
		(15) Further test results & assessment data				•	
		(16) Additional knowledge & qualifications				• • •	•
		(17) Additional skills & experience acquired				• •	•
		(18) Job changes and dates	•	•	•	• •	•
The current employment register	Employment incidents section — Attendance factors	(a) Sickness	•		•		•
		(b) Absence	•		•		•
		(c) Lateness					•
	Specific incidents	(d) Accidents			•		•
		(e) Discipline					
		(f) Grievances					
	General records	(g) Holidays					•
		(h) Medical			•		•
		(i) Car					•
		(j) Telephone					•
		(k) Hours - for part timers					•
		(l) Day release arrangements					•
		(m) Reason for leaving		•			
	Payment section — Standard payments	(n) Job evaluated grade				•	• •
		(o) Salary scale				•	• •
		(p) Current rate of pay					• • •
	Additions	(q) Incentive					•
		(r) Bonus					•
		(s) Overtime premium					•
		(t) Shift premium					•
	Other items	(u) Pension status					• •
		(v) Itemised pay statement					

Figure 32.2. The two types of information record and typical manpower information

can be varied according to the purpose. Names can be printed alphabetically, by code number, by clock number, by department, by job classification, by level of wages, by date of birth, by date of entry etc. However, the use of computers cannot be justified merely to give head counts or for producing sheafs of paper faster and with fewer clerks. It is more important that the computer can provide more detailed data and enables the personnel department to carry out a wider variety of analysis which would otherwise be impossible and it can handle a series of variables and apply statistical tests.[7]

Although the computer can do so much, there are still widespread reservations about its 'inhumanity' and problems of access to the information stored. In the early systems it was quite common for information to be available at certain times of the day only, but the newer and more sophisticated systems are gradually overcoming that problem, as well as the other of language. Today many programmes allow the layman to communicate with the computer in ordinary language.

It is worth extracting two basic points that Rosemary Stewart identified in her study:

The most common impact on those managers involved in the development of the applications studied was substantial extra work.[8]

The provision of better information makes some decisions harder, as the decisions may be complicated by knowing more about the different factors involved.[9]

Like so many other aspects of personnel work we have considered in this book, the more sophisticated technique may make for better management, but that does not mean an easy time for the manager. Also it may bring about a great divide in the ranks of personnel workers, some of whom will have more creative jobs while many of their colleagues find their work becomes less original and more structured. This ties in with the comments made at the beginning of this book about the likelihood of future organisations having a greater centralisation of decision-making and responsibility. This assumption is based on the type of prediction made by Leavitt and Whisler.[10] Their view was that middle-management jobs would move into two broad classifications. A minority would move into the upper echelons of planners and thinkers, while the majority would find themselves in positions of lower status concentrating on simple implementation of decisions made by others after studying the entrails of the computer output.

There is no serious reason to argue with the accuracy of Leavitt and Whisler's prediction except the understandable resistance of middle managers to such developments. The story of computer technology is rich with stories of the middle managers who do not believe that the computer can do what is claimed for it and who resist its application in new areas. The survey by Hunt and Newell in the United States[11] tended to confirm that the Leavitt and Whisler predictions were right, although the situation had been confused by the general recession in business of the 1970s. This has reduced the number of middle managerial personnel and has thus obscured the effect of computers on manning levels.

Another factor in the application of computers specifically in the personnel field is the availability of appropriate programmes and information systems designed for personnel applications. Predictably the Americans have developed these for commercial applications[12] but in the United Kingdom most of the work that has been done has been in tailor-making systems for large, specialised applications like the various armed services, nationalised industries and the PRISM system for non-industrial civil servants.

The advent of the microcomputer has widened the interest in computerised record and the ease of using the BASIC language has produced many more programs for personnel applications, developed within organisations for their own use. There is not yet, however, a widespread availability of personnel programs for sale.

Duplication

A feature of records that makes for unnecessary expense and problems of both confidentiality and privacy is the tendency to duplication. In addition to the main personnel records in the personnel department, there will nearly always be duplication of most of these in the salaries and wages department for the payroll, as well as others in the medical department and perhaps an independent training section, the general manager's office and the company secretary's as well. The reasons for the duplication are usually a mixture of specialised need, access, and control. The way in which records are organised may suit the salaries and wages department but not the company secretary, as their use of those records will be different. Because of this they will tend to develop their own system. Records are of little use unless they are accessible, but access to personnel records has to be limited for reasons of confidentiality and the elaborate process of signing documents in and out, or consulting them only in certain places or at specific times is another stimulus for executives to establish their own. Those in charge of records usually see in their proprietorship an element of their own status within the organisation, and if two or three people of similar rank are vying with each other for status, the one of them who controls access to the records on which all of them depend will have a clear advantage.

The only way to avoid duplication is either to have a very strict administrative diktat to prevent record proliferation, or to have an extremely efficient centralised system that is neutral and has well developed means of access and retrieval. The possibility of a computerised personnel information system is the most likely way of achieving this.

Privacy and Confidentiality

Confidentiality relates to information sought, obtained or held by an organisation, the disclosure of which might be detrimental to that organisation or to a third party who supplied it. The guarantee to the reference writer that everything he says 'will be treated in the strictest confidence' is to protect the reference writer rather than the person about whom the reference is written. *Privacy* relates to information sought, obtained or held by an organisation about a past, present or prospective employee the use of which might be to the detriment of that employee.

A Home Office document on computers and privacy suggests that there are three areas of potential danger to privacy: [13]

1. Inaccurate, incomplete or irrelevant information;

2. The possibility of access to information by people who should not or need not have it;

3. The use of information in a context or for a purpose other than that for which it was obtained.

This raises various questions. At the selection stage an applicant may doubt the relevance of interviewer inquiries about such matters as marital status and whether or not the applicant's spouse is working, but he might be much more concerned about the storage of that information for future, unspecified usage. The newer computers provide easy access to all types of programme, not only by printing it but also by showing it on visual display units. This requires safeguards to be built into the design of the computer software. If Mr A fills in an application form when seeking a particular post he will expect that form to be read by one or two people. Is the employer entitled to send it for consideration elsewhere without Mr A's permission? A well-meaning personnel officer may decide he is not suitable for the post, but would stand a better chance of another position coming vacant in a different department. Is he justified in having it considered without obtaining Mr A's permission first?

The problems of privacy are fully discussed in the Younger Report,[14] which includes ten basic principles for handling personal information in computer systems. At a more general level we suggest the following guidelines:

(i) The best protection for the individual against inaccurate or incomplete information is for him to check it. This is implicit in providing formal warnings prior to dismissal. The possibility of extending this personal checking facility could be explored.

(ii) Application forms should seek information that is relevant to an application for employment. If further information is to be recorded on the same form after the employment has begun, it should be located separately and completion of that section should not be requested initially.

(iii) Personal information about employees – past, present or prospective – should be divulged only to those who need to know it and where the employee has given permission, or his permission can reasonably be presumed.

(iv) Information should not be kept when it is no longer needed, and at that time it should be destroyed rather than thrown away.

(v) Where manpower information is to be derived from personnel records and current employment registers, the identity of the individual should be separated from the rest of the data.

We await British legislation on computer privacy as the British government has now endorsed OECD guidelines on privacy protection and transborder data flows as well as signing the Council of Europe's *Convention for the Protection of Individuals with Regard to Automatic Processing of Personal Data*. When this convention comes into effect it will confirm the right of countries with legislation on data protection to refuse to allow personal information to be sent to other countries which do not have comparable safeguards.

Current proposals for legislation[15] are for a Registrar and small staff to require the registration of

. . . all users of data systems which process automatically information relating to identifiable individuals.[16]

The Registrar will have the power to inspect and require modifications to the system.

Planning for the Future

Although information will be recorded to deal with day-to-day matters and the career development of individuals, it is also the source for data which can be used to plan the future of the organisation. A recent statement of the aims and objectives of manpower planning was:[17]

The aims of manpower planning are to ensure that the organisation:

obtains and retains the quantity and quality of manpower it needs;
makes the best use of its manpower resources;
is able to anticipate the problems arising from potential surpluses or deficits of manpower.

To reach these objectives, the manpower planner forecasts demand and supply and then sets up operations to ensure there is a supply to meet the demand.

There are many variations in approach to this sort of planning. In most cases it is deliberately imprecise, avoiding any attempt to predict and control exactly what will happen in the future and seeking to develop clear ideas of where the organisation needs to go in manpower terms, recognising the practical choices that are available and putting into practice policies that will best move the organisation towards the identified goals. This involves rough and ready calculations after trying to identify all the necessary variables.

There is then a range of more disciplined approaches, with the calculations becoming more sophisticated. This has led to the growth of a small number of specialist manpower planners, mainly in large organisations, developing a range of advanced techniques. Those working in this area include Bartholomew,[18] Bryant[19] and Forbes et al.[20]

The less numerate manpower planner would be helped by the excellent introduction produced by the Department of Employment[21] and the more recent text by Bramham.[22] Further texts that give a slightly different review of the field are those of Gray[23] and Stainer.[24]

Manpower Planning Methods

Some of the simpler methods used in manpower planning include the following:

(a) AGE STRUCTURE

The importance of age distribution of employees is frequently overlooked. Seldom is it even, and if it is skewed it can have a marked effect on wastage and promotion. The employment, for instance, of many young people may produce high wastage levels, as they are the group most likely to move on for experience or because they see promotion channels blocked. On the other hand a relatively old workforce will certainly produce high wastage. If the age distribution is known, manpower difficulties can be anticipated. Simple bar charts for the organisation as a whole, or for specific departments or occupations, quickly show imbalances in the age distribution.

(b) WORKLOAD ANALYSIS

Expectations of expected workload by extrapolation from the present can be used as one of the bases of determining future manpower needs. The method described by Bramham[25] has four stages. First the different types of work are classified and the average number of hours for each type noted. Secondly comes a forecast of

		Year 1	Year 2	Year 3	Year 4	Year 5	Total Years 1—5
S U P P L Y	1. Numbers available at start of year	300	350	360	375	375	
	2. Intake from apprenticeship during year	20	30	35	50	50	185
	3. Losses through wastage						
	i Retirements	10	8	12	20	25	75
	ii Early retirement (1% p.a.)	3	4	4	4	4	19
	iii Dismissals (2% p.a.)	6	7	8	8	8	37
	iv Deaths (2% p.a.)	6	7	8	8	8	37
	v Promotions etc. (5% p.a.)	15	17	20	21	21	94
	vi Resignations	30	35	25	30	20	140
	Total i—vi	70	78	77	91	86	402
	4. Total available at end of year (1 + 2 − 4)	250	302	318	334	339	
D E M A N D	5. Numbers required at start of year	300	350	360	375	375	
	6. Additional requirements during year	50	10	15	0	0	75
	7. Total requirement at end of year (5 + 6)	350	360	375	375	375	
	8. Additional number of fitters required during year	100	58	57	41	36	292

(Based on 'Company Manpower Planning', Department of Employment Manpower Paper No. 1 (HMSO) 1968, page 34, figure 1.)

Figure 32.3. Forecast of recruitment needs of engineering fitters

what future requirements for each type of work will be. This is converted into man hours by reference to the first stage and finally into manpower. If it takes half an hour to install a gas meter and 12,000 are to be installed next year, that will require 6,000 man hours, which is equivalent to 150 men, assuming 1,800 hours per man year.

(c) RECRUITMENT NEEDS

Another absolutely straightforward and invaluable method is for predicting future recruitment needs. Figure 32.3 is a chart based on the model of the Department of Employment Manpower Paper,[26] which not only demonstrates the method, but also points clearly to the nature of the recruitment problem. One hundred extra fitters are needed in Year 1, which is a very high target, so that alternative strategies may have to be considered, like sub-contracting, shiftworking, recruitment overseas, new plant or (perhaps) moderating the sales targets that have produced this extra demand.

REFERENCES

1. Mumford E. and Ward T.B., *Computers: Planning for People* (Batsford) 1968, p. 79.
2. *Ibid.,* p. 80.
3. Wille E., 'Training to Make the Most of the Computer', in *Personal Management,* October 1974, p. 36.
4. *Personnel Records,* Advisory Booklet No. 3 (ACAS) 1981.
5. Wille E., *The Computer in Personnel Work* (IPM) 1966, pp. 29–35.
6. Pettman B.O. and Tavernier G., *Manpower Planning Workbook* (Gower) 1976, pp. 7–10.
7. *Ibid.,* p. 12.
8. Stewart R., *How Computers Affect Management* (Macmillan) 1971, p. 235.
9. *Ibid.,* p. 236.
10. Leavitt H.J. and Whisler T.L., 'Management in the 1980's', in *Harvard Business Review,* November/December 1958, pp. 41–48.
11. Hunt J.G. and Newell P.F., 'Management in the 1980's Revisited', *Personnel Journal,* January 1971, pp. 35–45.
12. See, for example, Rogers R.E., 'An Integrated Personnel System', *Personnel Administration,* March/April 1970, pp. 22–28.
13. Home Office, *Computers and Privacy,* Cmnd 6353 (HMSO) 1975, p. 4.
14. Home Office, *Report of the Committee on Privacy,* Chairman: Rt Hon. Kenneth Younger, Cmnd 5012 (HMSO) 1972.
15. Home Office, *Data Protection,* Cmnd 8539 (HMSO) 1982.
16. *Ibid.,* p. 4.
17. Armstrong M., *Handbook of Personnel Management Practice* (Kogan Page) 1977, p. 61.
18. Bartholomew D.J., *Manpower Planning, Selected Readings* (Penguin) 1976.
19. Bryant D., 'Recent Developments in Manpower Research', in *Personnel Review,* Summer 1972, pp. 14–31.
20. Forbes A.F., Morgan R.W., Rowntree J.A., 'Manpower Models in Use in the Civil Service Department', in *Personnel Review,* Summer 1975, pp. 23–36.
21. Department of Employment, *Company Manpower Planning, Manpower Paper No. 1* (HMSO) 1967.
22. Bramham J., *Practical Manpower Planning* (IPM) 1975.
23. Gray D.H., *Manpower Planning – An Approach to the Problem* (IPM) 1966.
24. Stainer G., *Manpower Planning* (Heinemann) 1971.
25. Bramham, *op. cit.,* p. 48.
26. Department of Employment, *op. cit.,* p. 34.

APPENDICES

I — 'ARCADIA' : A systematic approach to the employment process

    Phase one   : Analysis and specification of personnel requirements
    Phase two   : Recruitment of candidates for employment
    Phase three : Candidate screening
    Phase four : Assessment of candidates
    Phase five : Decision-making for employment
    Phase six   : Induction and placement
    Phase seven : Appraisal and evaluation

II — 'ASDICE' : A systematic approach to training programme development

    Phase one   : Assessment of training needs
    Phase two   : Specification of training objectives
    Phase three : Design of the training programme
    Phase four : Instruction methods selection
    Phase five : Conduct of training
    Phase six   : Evaluation of training programme

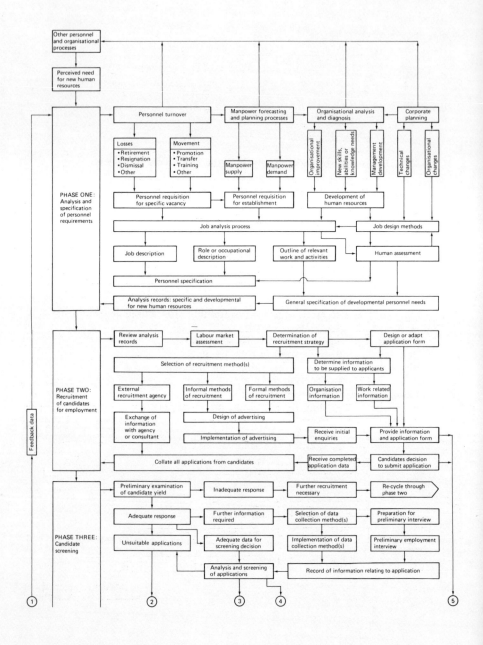

Appendix I 'ARCADIA' : A systematic approach to the employment process

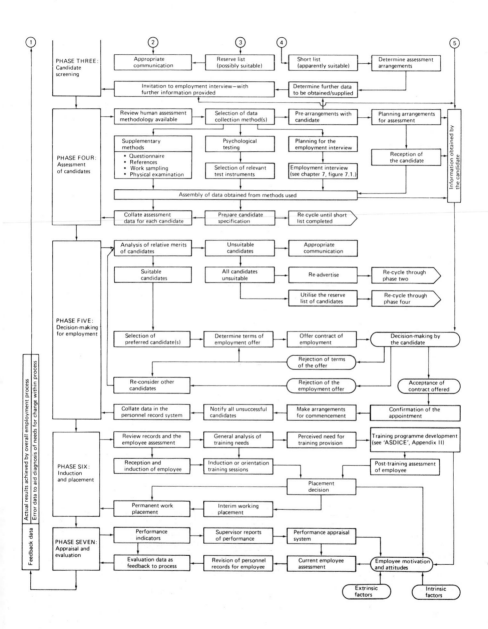

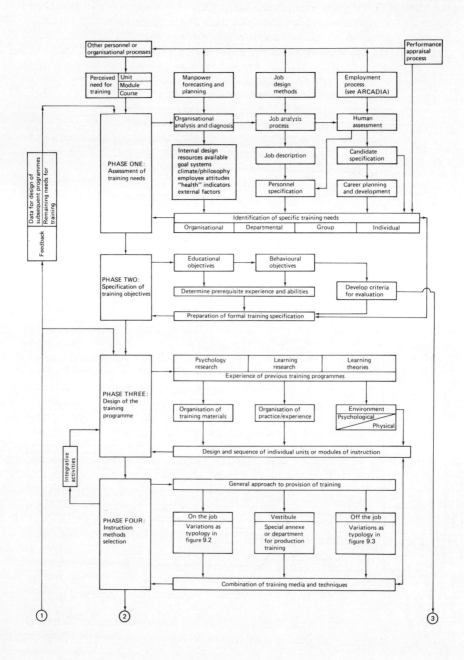

Appendix II 'ASDICE' : A systematic approach to training programme development

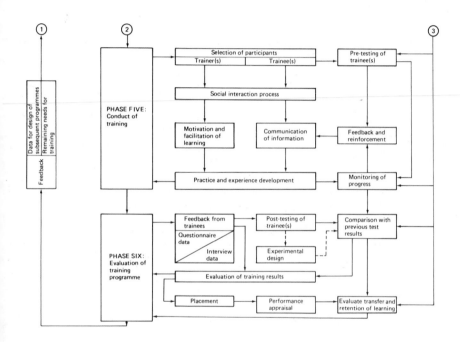

Name Index

Subject Index